Worth Series in Outstanding Contributions

Labor Economics

EDITED BY

Orley Ashenfelter

PRINCETON UNIVERSITY

WORTH PUBLISHERS

Labor Economics

Copyright © 1999 by Worth Publishers
All rights reserved
Manufactured in the United States of America
Library of Congress Catalog Card Number: 98-88437
ISBN: 1-57259-684-8
Printing: 2 3 4 5   02

Executive Editor: Stephen Dietrich

Design: Barbara Rusin

Design Director: Jennie R. Nichols

Production Editor: Margaret Comaskey

Production Manager: Barbara Anne Seixas

Composition: Stratford Publishing Services, Inc.

Printing and Binding: R. R. Donnelley & Sons, Inc.

Worth Publishers
33 Irving Place
New York, NY 10003
http://www.worthpublishers.com

Labor Economics

Series Editor

Orley Ashenfelter

CONTENTS

Economics of Immigration

Wage Inequality

Economics of Discrimination

Series Preface

In the fall of 1997 Stephen Dietrich, of Worth Publishers, approached me with a question: "What," he asked, "can we at Worth do to offer a useful product to assist with the graduate training of academic economists?" "There is only one catch," he added. "We would like this book or books to appear within the next year."

I responded with a proposal that I felt certain no publisher would agree to: "Create a beautifully typeset and designed set of readings for graduate courses in economics where up-to-date textbooks do not exist; make sure the readings are selected because they are the articles most widely used in graduate courses; and, most important, put a low enough price on the book so graduate students might actually want to buy it!"

My proposal was a reaction to my own experience in graduate teaching and advising. First, since the scale of operation is so small, graduate-level textbooks in most fields simply do not exist. Even in the larger fields, where texts do exist, it is usually necessary to supplement them with additional readings. Second, although there are many books of collected essays or articles, they are rarely designed to represent the revealed preferences of graduate instructors. The essays are often selected by topic or author, rather than by the demand for them as supplementary reading in a graduate course. Finally, the pricing of textbooks and collections of essays, at both the graduate and undergraduate level, has reached such dizzying heights that many students simply refuse to purchase them.

The set of books in this series is a direct response to these concerns and to Stephen Dietrich's original question. The editors have tried to create volumes that will be useful to a wide range of economists, and especially useful for graduate instruction. In return, Worth Publishers has prepared attractive books that should be affordable for virtually anyone.

An additional benefit of typesetting these articles rather than replicating them is that many authors have taken the opportunity to correct typesetting errors in the original publications and to update references. In this sense, the reprinted articles in these volumes are actually superior to the originals. It is my hope that this series of books will continue to grow and provide a valuable service to the economics profession.

Orley Ashenfelter
Princeton University
1998

Preface

My goal in selecting the articles to appear in this volume was to create a book that would be an aid to the teaching of graduate courses in labor economics. The articles selected were those most popular on graduate reading lists. The brief biographies of the authors that accompany the articles will, I hope, provide a little feeling for the characters and personalities that inhabit the very vibrant and active field of labor economics

Some readers may be interested in precisely how the articles were selected for inclusion in this volume. I began by obtaining the graduate reading lists from seventeen institutions.[1] I tabulated the frequency with which articles appeared on these lists, and I then selected the top twenty for inclusion in this volume. Articles were selected for inclusion only if they had appeared in journals; that is, I did not include chapters from books, articles that appeared only in books, or unpublished papers in the volume.

These articles might well be called the "greatest recent hits" of labor economics. For some, it may be interesting to speculate about what it is that characterizes these articles. I will leave this to others, but it may be useful to provide a few additional facts for those who choose to speculate. First, I have placed the articles in the volume by topic, not by the frequency with which they appear on the graduate reading lists. Second, no article appeared on more than 60% of the reading lists, so it appears that, although there is considerable overlap, graduate reading lists differ considerably from place to place.

Finally, a number of the biographies of the authors that accompany the articles were written by the authors of *other* papers selected for inclusion, as indicated with a byline. I am therefore indebted to these authors of the papers in this volume not only for writing their papers, but for their help with the preparation of biographies that display the range of personalities that inhabit the field of labor economics.

Orley Ashenfelter
Princeton University
1998

---

[1] *These institutions were, in alphabetical order, Boston University, Brown University, Harvard University, Massachusetts Institute of Technology, Michigan State University, Northwestern University, Princeton University, Rutgers University, Temple University, University of California—Berkeley, University of Iowa, University of Maryland, University of Pennsylvania, University of Texas—Austin, University of Wisconsin, Vanderbilt University, and Yale University. I would like to thank all the instructors in these institutions for their cooperation.*

Labor Economics

Labor Economics

RETURNS TO HUMAN CAPITAL

Robert J. Willis and Sherwin Rosen

Robert J. LaLonde

Joshua D. Angrist and Alan B. Krueger

Orley Ashenfelter and Alan Krueger

Education and Self-Selection

ROBERT J. WILLIS
State University of New York at Stony Brook and National Bureau of Economic Research

SHERWIN ROSEN
University of Chicago and National Bureau of Economic Research

A structural model of the demand for college attendance is derived from the theory of comparative advantage and recent statistical models of self-selection and unobserved components. Estimates from NBER-Thorndike data strongly support the theory. First, expected lifetime earnings gains influence the decision to attend college. Second, those who did not attend college would have earned less than measurably similar people who did attend, while those who attended college would have earned less as high school graduates than measurably similar people who stopped after high school. Positive selection in both groups implies no "ability bias" in these data.

I. INTRODUCTION

In this paper we specify and estimate a model of the demand for college education derived from its effect on expected lifetime earnings compared with its cost. Attention is focused on specifying the role of earnings expectations in the derived demand for schooling; these are found to be empirically important determinants of the decision to attend college. In addition to including financial incentives, the model allows for a host of selectivity or sorting effects in the data that are related to "ability bias," family effects, and tastes that have occupied other researchers. Background and motivation are presented in Section II. The structure of the model, a variant of a simultaneous-equations problem involving discrete choices, is presented in Section III. The estimates, based on data from the NBER-Thorndike sample, appear in Section IV. Some implications and conclusions are found in Section V.

Thanks are due to Sean Becketti for excellent research assistance, to Lung Fei Lee for advice on statistical issues, and to Richard Layard and W. M. Gorman for criticism of an initial draft. This research was supported by NSF and the National Bureau of Economic Research, but this is not an official NBER publication. The order of the authors' names was selected by a random device.

Reprinted with permission from Robert J. Willis and Sherwin Rosen, "Education and Self-Selection," Journal of Political Economy: (1979), vol. 87, no. 5, pt. 2, pp. S7–36. © 1979 by The University of Chicago.

II. NATURE OF THE PROBLEM

Estimates of rates of return to education have been controversial because they are based on ex post realizations and need not reflect structural parameters necessary for correct predictions. For example, it is well understood that college and high school graduates may have different abilities so that income forgone during college by the former is not necessarily equal to observed earnings of the latter. Our objective here is twofold. One is to estimate life earnings conditioned on actual school choices that are purged of selection bias. The other is to determine the extent to which alternative earnings prospects, as distinct from family background and financial constraints, influence the decision to attend college.

One would need to go no further than straightforward comparisons of earnings outcomes among school classes for structural rate of return estimates if educational wage differentials were everywhere equalizing on the direct, opportunity, and interest costs of schooling. For then the supplies of graduates (or "demands" for each level of education) would be nearly elastic at the qualifying wage differentials, and the distribution of human wealth would be approximately independent of the distribution of schooling.[1] However, recent evidence on the structure of life earnings based on panel data strongly rejects this as a serious possibility. Total variance of earnings among people of the same sex, race, education, and market experience is very large, and more than two-thirds of it is attributable to unobserved components or person-specific effects that probably persist over much of the life cycle.[2] The panel evidence therefore suggests that supply elasticities are substantially less than completely elastic at unique wage differentials and that there are inframarginal "ability rents." Put in another way, observed rates of return are not wholly supply determined and depend on interactions with relative demands for graduates as well.

A natural approach has been to incorporate measures of ability into the statistical analysis, either directly or as indicators of unobserved factors, in order to, in effect, impute ability rent. But merely partitioning observed earnings into schooling and ability components does not use any of the restrictions imposed on the data by a school-stopping rule, and that decision embodies all the economic content of the problem. Some of that additional structure is incorporated here.

Economic theories of education, be they of the human-capital or signaling varieties, are based on the principle of maximum capital value: schooling is pursued to the point where its marginal (private) internal rate of return equals the rate of interest. It is easy to show that this leads to a recursive econometric model in which (i) schooling is related to

---

[1] *The equalizing difference model originates with Friedman and Kuznets (1945). Jacob Mincer (1974) has developed it most completely in recent years.*

[2] *See Lillard and Willis (1978) for additional detail and confirmation of these remarks. Related studies have reached similar conclusions, e.g., Weiss and Lillard (1978). Of course, it is conceivable, but unlikely, that educational wage differentials are exactly equalizing for each individual, although considerable lifetime income inequality exists among individuals. This possibility is rejected in the empirical findings presented below.*

a person's ability and family background, and (ii) earnings are related to "prior" school decisions and ability. Earnings gains attributable to education do not appear explicitly in the schooling equation. Instead, the cost-benefit basis of the decision is embedded in cross-equation restrictions on the overall model, because the earnings equation is a constraint for the maximum problem that determines education attainment.[3] There are many estimates of recursive models in the literature, but very few have tested the economic (wealth-maximizing) hypothesis.[4]

We begin with the assumption of marked heterogeneity and diversity in the population, as in the unobserved-component approach to panel data. Costs and benefits of alternative school-completion levels are assumed to be randomly distributed among people according to their capacities to finance education, tastes, perceptions, expectations, and an array of talents that affect performance in work activities associated with differing levels of schooling. Some of these things are observed, while others are unobserved. Individuals are sorted into educational classes according to the interaction of a selection criterion (such as maximum present value) and the underlying joint distribution of tastes, talents, expectations, and parental wealth. The selection rule partitions the underlying joint density into a corresponding realized educational distribution. The supply function of graduates at any level of school is "swept out" of the joint taste, talent, parental wealth distribution as increased wage differentials enlarge the subset of the partition relevant for that class.

Let Y_{ij} represent the potential lifetime earnings of person i if schooling level j is chosen, X_i a vector of observed talent or ability indicators of person i, and τ_i an unobserved talent component relevant for person i. Similarly, split family background and taste effects into an observed vector Z_i and an unobserved component ω_i. Let V_{ij} denote the value of choosing school level j for person i. Then a general school-selection model is:

$$Y_{ij} = y_j(X_i, \tau_i), \qquad j = 1, \ldots, n; \tag{1}$$

$$V_{ij} = g(y_j, Z_i, \omega_i); \tag{2}$$

$$i \text{ belongs to } j \text{ if } V_{ij} = \max(V_{j1}, \ldots, V_{in}); \tag{3}$$

---

[3] The basic model is discussed in Becker (1975). See Rosen (1977) for an elaboration of this argument and a survey of the relevant literature. Blaug (1976) also stresses the need for estimating structural demand for schooling relationships, and Griliches (1977) discusses the difficulty of doing so in conventional models. Part of Griliches's discussion is pursued in Griliches, Hall, and Hausman (1977). The model elaborated here is conceptually distinct from that work, though some of the statistical techniques are similar. A similar remark applies to the work of Kenny, Lee, Maddala, and Trost (in press).

[4] There is aggregate-time-series evidence that earnings are important determinants of professional school enrollment (see Freeman [1971]) and numerous subsequent studies by the same author); but there is virtually no micro evidence even though such data have been most often studied in the human-capital and signaling frameworks.

and

$$(\tau, \omega) \sim F(\tau, \omega) \tag{4}$$

Equation (1) shows how potential earnings in any given classification vary with talent and ability.[5] The earnings function differs among school classes because work activities associated with alternative levels of education make use of different combinations of talent. Equation (2) translates the earnings stream from choice j into a scaler such as present value and is conditioned on family background to reflect tastes and financial barriers to extending schooling. Equation (3) is the selection rule: the person chooses the classification that maximizes value and is observed in one and only one of the n possibilities open to him. Equation (4) closes the model with a specification of the distribution of unobservables. Since observed assignments of individuals to schooling classes are selected on (X, Z, τ, ω), earnings observed in each class may be nonrandom samples of population potential earnings, because those with larger net benefits in the class have a higher probability of being observed in it.

This formulation is suggested by the theory of comparative advantage.[6] It allows for a rather eclectic view of the role of talent in determining observed outcomes, since the X's may affect earning capacity differently at different levels of schooling (see eq. [1]) and covariances among the unobservables are unrestricted. Indeed, there may be negative covariance among talent components. For example, plumbers (high school graduates) may have very limited potential as highly schooled lawyers, but by the same token lawyers may have much lower potential as plumbers than those who actually end up choosing that kind of work. This contrasts with the one-factor ability-as-IQ specifications in the literature which assume that the best lawyers would also be the best plumbers and would imply strictly hierarchical sorting in the absence of financial constraints. In effect an IQ-ability model constrains the unobserved ability components to have large positive covariances—an assumption that is probably erroneous and is not necessary for our methods. Note also that population mean "rates of return" among alternative schooling levels have no significance as guides to the social or private profitability of investments in schooling. For example, a random member of the population might achieve a negative return from an engineering degree, yet those with appropriate talents who choose engineering will obtain a return on the time and money costs of their training which is at least equal to the rate of interest.

---

[5] *Actually, expository convenience dictates a more restrictive formulation than is necessary. The X and Z need not be orthogonal. They may have some elements in common, but identification requires that they not have all elements in common (see below).*

[6] *Roy (1951) gives a surprisingly modern and rigorous treatment of a selection problem based on the theory of comparative advantage. See Rosen (1978) for extensions and elaboration on this class of problems. Heckman (1976), Lee (1976), and Maddala (1977) develop the appropriate estimation theory.*

There are difficult estimation problems associated with selectivity models. In brief, the unobservables impose distinct limits on the amount of structural information that can be inferred from realized assignments in the data. For example, it would be very desirable to know the marginal distribution of talents in (4), since it would then be possible to construct the socially efficient assignment of individuals to school classes, defined as the one that maximizes overall human wealth. Then the deadweight losses due to capital market imperfections could be computed by comparing optimal with observed assignments. However, the marginal density is not itself identified, since unobserved financial constraints and talent jointly determine observed outcomes. These issues will be made precise shortly, but, roughly speaking, we do not necessarily know if a person chose college education because he had talent for it or because he was wealthy. What can and will be done is to map out the joint effects of the unobservables embedded in the actual demand curve for college attendance, which embodies all constraints inherent in the actual market but which nevertheless is a valid structural basis for prediction. Selectivity or ability bias in unadjusted rate of return computations that do not take account of the sorting by talent inherent in observed assignments can also be computed.

A few limitations to these methods must be noted at the outset. It is crucial to the spirit of the model, based as it is on human diversity, that few covariance restrictions be placed on the distribution of unobservables. This practically mandates the assumption of joint normality, since no other nonindependent multivariate distribution offers anything close to similar computational advantages. While the general selection rule specified below is likely to emerge from a broad class of economic models of school choice, it is not known how sensitive the results are to the normality assumptions. In addition, nonindependence forces some aggregation in the number of choices considered for computational feasibility, even though the statistical theory can be worked out for any finite number.[7] This rules out of consideration other selection aspects of the problem that should be considered, such as choice of school quality.[8] All people in our sample have at least a high school education, and we have chosen a dichotomous split between choice of high school and more than high school (college attendance). Some internal diagnostic tests help check on the validity of this aggregation. Experiments with a college completion or more classification, compared with a high school graduation or some college classification, yielded results very similar to those reported below.

---

[7] *The problem is that the aggregates are sums of distributions that are themselves truncated and selected. Therefore the distributions underlying the aggregate assignments are not necessarily normal. We are unaware of any systematic analysis of this kind of aggregation problem.*

[8] *Methods such as conditional logit have been designed to handle high-dimensional classifications (McFadden 1973) but require independence and other (homogeneity) restrictions that are not tenable for this problem. Hausman and Wise (1978) have worked out computational methods on general normal assumptions for three choices. Note also that maximum-likelihood methods are available, but are extremely expensive because multiple integrals must be evaluated. Hence we follow the literature in using consistent estimators.*

III. THE MODEL

Specification of the econometric model is tailored to the data at our disposal. More details will be given below, but at this point the important feature is that earnings are observed at two points in the life cycle for each person, one point soon after entrance into the labor market and another point some 20 years later. The earnings stream is parameterized into a simple geometric growth process to motivate the decision rule. This is a reasonable approximation to actual life earnings patterns for the period spanned by the data. Two levels of schooling are considered, labeled level A (for more than high school) and level B (for high school).

If person i chooses A, the expected earnings stream is

$$y_{ai}(t) = 0 \qquad\qquad 0 < t \leq S,$$

$$y_{ai}(t) = \bar{y}_{ai} \exp\left[g_{ai}(t-S)\right], \qquad S \leq t < \infty,$$

(5)

where S is the incremental schooling period associated with A compared to B and $t - S$ is market experience. If alternative B is chosen, the expected earnings stream is

$$y_{bi}(t) = \bar{y}_{bi} \exp\left(g_{bi}t\right), \qquad 0 \leq t < \infty.$$

(6)

Thus earnings prospects of each person in the sample are characterized by four parameters: initial earnings and rates of growth in each of the two alternatives. Diversity is represented by a random distribution of the vector $(\bar{y}_a, g_a, \bar{y}_b, g_b)$ among the population.[9]

Equations (5) and (6) yield convenient expressions for present value. Assume an infinite horizon, a constant rate of discount for each person, r_i, with $r_i > g_{ai}, g_{bi}$, and ignore direct costs of school. Then the present value of earnings is

$$V_{ai} = \int_g^\infty y_{ai}(t) \exp\left(-r_i t\right) dt = \left[\bar{y}_{ai} / (r_i - g_{ai})\right] \exp(-r_i S)$$

(7)

if A is chosen and

$$V_{bi} = \int_0^\infty y_{bi}(t) \exp(-r_i t) dt = \bar{y}_{bi} / (r_i - g_{bi})$$

(8)

---

[9] *Wise (1975), Lazear (1976), and Zabalza (1977) have used initial earnings and growth of earnings to study life earnings patterns. The distribution of potential earnings and growth is not constrained in our model, thus, e.g., allowing the possibility that $\bar{y}_a$ and g_a are negatively correlated (and similarly for $\bar{y}_b$ and g_b), as in Mincer (1974). On this see Hause (1977).*

if B is chosen. These are likely to be good approximations, since the consequences of ignoring finite life discount corrections and nonlinearities in earnings paths toward the end of the life cycle are lightly weighted for nonnegligible values of r.

SELECTION RULE

Assume that person i chooses A if $V_{ai} > V_{bi}$ and chooses B if $V_{ai} \leq V_{bi}$. Define $I_i = \ln(V_{ai}/V_{bi})$. Substitution from (5) to (8) yields $I_i = \ln \bar{y}_{ai} - \ln \bar{y}_{bi} - r_i S - \ln(r_i - g_{ai}) + \ln(r_i - g_{bi})$. A Taylor series approximation to the nonlinear terms around their population mean values $(\bar{g}_a, \bar{g}_b, \bar{r})$ yields

$$I_i = \alpha_0 + \alpha_1 (\ln \bar{y}_{ai} - \ln \bar{y}_{bi}) + \alpha_2 g_{ai} + \alpha_3 g_{bi} + \alpha_4 r_i, \tag{9}$$

with

$$\begin{aligned}
\alpha_1 &= I, \\
\alpha_2 &= \partial I / \partial g_a = 1/(\bar{r} - g_a) > 0, \\
\alpha_3 &= \partial I / \partial g_b = -1/(\bar{r} - \bar{g}_b) < 0, \\
\alpha_4 &= -[S + (\bar{g}_a - \bar{g}_b)/(\bar{r} - \bar{g}_a)(\bar{r} - \bar{g}_b)].
\end{aligned} \tag{10}$$

Hence the selection criteria are

$$\begin{aligned}
\Pr(\text{choose A}) &= \Pr(V_a > V_b) = \Pr(I > 0), \\
\Pr(\text{choose B}) &= \Pr(V_a \leq V_b) = \Pr(I \leq 0).
\end{aligned} \tag{11}$$

EARNINGS AND DISCOUNT FUNCTIONS

Let X_i represent a set of measured characteristics that influence a person's lifetime earnings potential, and let $u_{1i}, \ldots, u_{4i}$ denote permanent person-specific unobserved components reflecting unmeasured factors influencing earnings potential.[10] Specify structural (in the sense of population) earnings equations of the form

$$\begin{aligned}
\ln \bar{y}_{ai} &= X_i \beta_a + u_{1i}, \\
g_{ai} &= X_i \gamma_a + u_{2i}
\end{aligned} \tag{12}$$

if A is chosen and

---

[10] The τ's of Section II are related to $(u_1 \ldots, u_4)$ by a set of implicit prices that vary across school classifications, as in Mandelbrot (1960). See Rosen (1978) for the logic of why these differences in valuation can be sustained indefinitely and cannot be arbitraged.

$$\ln \bar{y}_{bi} = X_i \beta_b + u_{3i},$$

$$g_{bi} = X_i \gamma_b + u_{4i} \tag{13}$$

if B is chosen. The variables on the left-hand sides of (12) and (13) are to be interpreted as the individual's expectation of initial earnings and growth rates at the time the choice is made. In order to obtain consistent estimates of $(\beta_a, \gamma_a, \beta_b, \gamma_b)$ from data on realizations it is assumed that expectations were unbiased. Hence forecast errors are assumed to be independently normally distributed, with zero means.

Let Z_i denote another vector of observed variables that influence the schooling decision through their effect on the discount rate. Then

$$r_i = Z_i \delta + u_{5i}, \tag{14}$$

where u_5 is a permanent unobserved component influencing financial barriers to school choice. The vector (u_j) is assumed to be jointly normal, with zero means and variance-covariance matrix $\Sigma = [\sigma_{ij}]$. The Σ is unrestricted.

REDUCED FORM

The structural model is (9), (12), (13), and (14). A reduced form of the selection rule is obtained by substituting (12)–(14) into (9):

$$\begin{aligned}
I = \alpha_0 &+ X \left[\alpha_1 (\beta_a - \beta_b) + \alpha_2 \gamma_a + \alpha_3 \gamma_b \right] + \alpha_4 Z \delta + \alpha_1 (u_1 - u_3) \\
&+ \alpha_2 u_2 + \alpha_3 u_3 + \alpha_5 u_5 \\
&\equiv W \pi - \epsilon,
\end{aligned} \tag{15}$$

with $W = [X, Z]$ and $-\epsilon = \alpha_1 (u_1 - u_3) + \alpha_2 u_2 + \alpha_3 u_4 + \alpha_5 u_5$. Thus, an observationally equivalent statement to (9) and (11) is

$$\Pr (A \text{ is observed}) = \Pr(W\pi > \epsilon) = F\left(\frac{W\pi}{\sigma_\epsilon} \right), \tag{16}$$

where $F(\cdot)$ is the standard normal c.d.f. Equation (16) is a probit function determining sample selection into categories A or B, to be estimated from observed data.[11]

---

[11] For completeness, $-\epsilon$ should be redefined to take account of deviations between realizations and expectations at the time school decisions were made. Thus, let $\ln \bar{Y}_{ai} = \ln \bar{y}_{ai} + v_{1i}$, where $\bar{Y}_{ai}$ is realized initial earnings, $\bar{y}_{ai}$ is expected initial earnings, and v_{1i} is normally distributed forecast error. Similarly, forecast errors v_{2i}, v_{3i}, and v_{4i} are defined for g_{ai}, $\ln \bar{y}_{bi}$, and g_{bi}. Then the complete definition of $-\epsilon$ is obtained from replacing u_{ji} with $(u_{ji} + v_{ji})$, $j = 1, \ldots, 4$, in (15). Clearly this has no operational significance for the model, given the assumption of unbiased expectations.

SELECTION BIAS AND EARNINGS FUNCTION

The decision rule selects people into observed classes according to largest expected present value. Hence the earnings actually observed in each group are not random samples of the population, but are truncated nonrandom samples instead. The resulting bias in observed means may be calculated as follows. Note that Pr [observing $y_a(t)$] = Pr $(I > 0)$ = Pr $(W\pi > \epsilon)$. Therefore, from (12), $E(\ln \bar{y}_a | I > 0) = X\beta_a + E(u_1 | W\pi > \epsilon)$. Define $\rho_1 = \rho(u_1/\sigma_1, \epsilon/\sigma_\epsilon) = \sigma_{1\epsilon}/\sigma_1\sigma_\epsilon$. Then $E(\ln \bar{y}_a | I > 0) = X\beta_a + \sigma_1\rho_1 E(\epsilon/\sigma_\epsilon | \epsilon/\sigma_\epsilon < W\pi/\sigma_\epsilon) = X\beta_a + \sigma_1\rho_1 [-f(W\pi/\sigma_\epsilon)/F(W\pi/\sigma_\epsilon)]$, where F is the cumulative normal density and f is its p.d.f. Define

$$\lambda_a \equiv -f(W\pi/\sigma_\epsilon)/F(W\pi/\sigma_\epsilon) \tag{17}$$

as the truncated mean (with truncation point $W\pi/\sigma_\epsilon$) of the normal density due to selection. Making use of the definition of ρ_1 and λ_a yields

$$E\left(\ln \bar{y}_a \middle| I > 0\right) = X\beta_a + \frac{\sigma_{1\epsilon}}{\sigma_\epsilon}\lambda_a. \tag{18}$$

A parallel argument for g_a, $\bar{y}_b$, and g_b yields

$$E\left(g_a \middle| I > 0\right) = X\gamma_a + \frac{\sigma_{2\epsilon}}{\sigma_\epsilon}\lambda_a, \tag{19}$$

$$E\left(\ln \bar{y}_b \middle| I \leq 0\right) = X\beta_b + \frac{\sigma_{3\epsilon}}{\sigma_\epsilon}\lambda_b, \tag{20}$$

and

$$E\left(g_b \middle| I \leq 0\right) = X\gamma_b + \frac{\sigma_{4\epsilon}}{\sigma_\epsilon}\lambda_b, \tag{21}$$

with

$$\lambda_b = E\left(\epsilon/\sigma_\epsilon \middle| \frac{\epsilon}{\sigma_\epsilon} > \frac{W\pi}{\sigma_\epsilon}\right) = f(W\pi/\sigma_\epsilon)/[1 - F(W\pi/\sigma_\epsilon)] \tag{22}$$

and

$$\sigma_{k\epsilon} = -[\alpha_1(\sigma_{1k} - \sigma_{3k}) + \alpha_2\sigma_{2k} + \alpha_3\sigma_{4k} + \alpha_5\sigma_{5k}], \qquad k = 1, \ldots, 4. \qquad (23)$$

Note from (17) that $\lambda_a \le 0$. Therefore the observed (conditional) means of initial earnings and rates of growth among persons in A are greater or less than their population means as $\sigma_{1\epsilon}$ and $\sigma_{2\epsilon} \lessgtr 0$, from (18) and (19). Conversely, $\lambda_b \ge 0$ (see [22]), and there is positive or negative selection bias in initial earnings and growth rates for people observed in class B according to $\sigma_{3\epsilon}$ (and $\sigma_{4\epsilon}$) $\gtrless 0$. Since σ_{ij} is unrestricted, $\sigma_{k\epsilon}$ is also unrestricted, and selection bias can go in either way. In particular, it is possible that the bias is positive in both groups, consistent with the comparative-advantage argument sketched above. Positive bias in A and negative bias in B would be consistent with a single-factor (hierarchical) interpretation of ability. Of course, neither finding yields a definitive "ability" interpretation because of the presence of expectational errors and financial factors (σ_{5k}) in (23): the assignments are based on talent, expectations, and wealth, not on talent alone.

ESTIMATION

Consider the following regressions applied to observed data:

$$\ln \bar{y}_a = X\beta_a + \beta_a^*\lambda_a + \eta_1,$$

$$g_a = X\gamma_a + \gamma_a^*\lambda_a + \eta_2,$$

$$\ln \bar{y}_b = X\beta_b + \beta_b^*\lambda_b + \eta_3, \qquad (24)$$

$$g_b = X\gamma_b + \gamma_b^*\lambda_b + \eta_4.$$

Equations (18)–(21) suggest that β_a^* estimates $\sigma_{1\epsilon}/\sigma_\epsilon$, γ_a^* estimates $\sigma_{2\epsilon}/\sigma_\epsilon$, and so on. Including λ_a or λ_b in the regressions along with X corrects for truncation and selectivity bias, and $E(\eta_{ij}) = 0$ for $j = 1, \ldots, 4$. In addition, $E(\eta_{ij}^2)$ is heteroskedastic (see below), because the observations are truncated and at different points for different people. Equation (24) cannot be implemented directly because λ_a and λ_b are not known. However, it can be shown[12] that consistent estimates of (24) are obtained by replacing λ_a and λ_b with their values predicted from the reduced-form probit equation (16). These values are

$$\hat{\lambda}_{ai} = -f(W_i\pi\hat{/}\sigma_\epsilon / F(W_i\pi\hat{/}\sigma_\epsilon),$$

$$\hat{\lambda}_{bi} = f(W_i\pi\hat{/}\sigma_\epsilon / [1 - F(W_i\pi\hat{/}\sigma_\epsilon)] \qquad (25)$$

and are entered as least-squares regressors along with X_i. Estimation of (24) with λ_i replaced by $\hat{\lambda}_i$ corrects for selectivity bias in the observations. What is more interesting for

---

[12] See Heckman (1976) and Lee (1976).

the economic theory of educational choice is that these estimates provide a basis for estimating the structural selection rule or structural probit function (9) and (11). The structural probit is

$$\Pr (\text{choose A}) = \Pr \{[\alpha_0 + \alpha_1 (\ln \bar{y}_a - \ln \bar{y}_b) + \alpha_2 g_a$$
$$+ \alpha_3 g_b + \alpha_4 Z\delta]/\sigma_\epsilon > \epsilon/\sigma_\epsilon\}, \tag{26}$$

from (9), (11), and (14). Use the consistent estimates of structural earnings and growth described above to predict earnings gains for each person in the sample according to

$$\ln (\widehat{\bar{y}_{ai} / \bar{y}_{bi}}) = X_i(\hat{\beta}_a - \hat{\beta}_b),$$
$$\hat{g}_{ai} = X_i \hat{\gamma}_a, \tag{27}$$
$$\hat{g}_{bi} = X_i \hat{\gamma}_b,$$

where $\hat{\beta}$ and $\hat{\gamma}$ are estimated by the method above.[13] These predicted values are inserted into (26) and estimated by the usual probit method to test the economic restrictions (10).[14]

OTHER TESTS

Alternative estimates are available to serve as an internal consistency check on the model. In particular, the model can be specified using the observed level of earnings at time $\bar{t}$ and earnings growth instead of initial earnings. From (5) and (6) it follows that

$$\ln y_a(\bar{t}) = X_i(\beta_a + \gamma_a \bar{t}) + u_1 + \bar{t}u_2,$$
$$\ln y_b(\bar{t}) = X_i(\beta_b + \gamma_b \bar{t}) + u_3 + \bar{t}u_4. \tag{28}$$

Substitute for the level equations in (12) and (13) and this model also can be estimated as described above. However, now the structural probit is of the form

$$\Pr (\text{A is chosen}) = \Pr (\{\theta_0 + \theta_1 [\ln y_a(t) - \ln y_b(t)]$$
$$+ \theta_2 g_a + \theta_3 g_b\} + \theta_4 r/\sigma_\epsilon > \epsilon/\sigma_\epsilon). \tag{29}$$

---

[13] This method is due to Lee (1978), who used it to study unionization status. Our model differs somewhat in that there is more than one structural equation in each classification.

[14] Heckman (1976) and Lee (1977) show that OLS estimates of the standard errors of β_a, γ_a, β_b, and γ_b in (24) are biased if $\sigma_{k\epsilon}/\sigma_\epsilon \neq 0$ when estimated values of λ_b are used in place of their true values. Lee also shows that the usual estimates of standard errors for the structural probit (26) are biased when estimated values of $\ln (\bar{y}_a/\bar{y}_b)$, g_a and g_b are used in place of their true values and derives exact asymptotic distributions for these parameters. We use Lee's (1977) results to compute consistent estimates of standard errors below.

Since $\ln y_a(\bar{t}) - \ln y_b(\bar{t}) = \ln \bar{y}_a - \ln \bar{y}_b + (g_a - g_b)\bar{t} - g_a S$, the following restrictions are implied:

$$
\begin{aligned}
\theta_1 &= \alpha_1, \\
(\bar{t} - S)\theta_1 + \theta_2 &= \alpha_2, \\
-\bar{t}\theta_1 + \theta_3 &= \alpha_3.
\end{aligned}
\tag{30}
$$

Hence we have a check on the validity of the model. Of course, its main validation is the power to predict behavior and assignments on independent data.

IDENTIFICATION

Two natural questions regarding identification arise in this model.

1. Estimation of the selection rule or structural probit equation are possible only if the vectors X and Z have elements that are not in common. If X and Z are identical, the predicted values of $\ln \bar{y}_a - \ln \bar{y}_b$, g_a, and g_b are colinear with the other explanatory variables in (26), and its estimation is precluded. Note, however, that even if X and Z are identical, the reduced-form probit (16) is estimable, and it still may be possible to estimate initial earnings and growth-rate equations and selection bias. The reason is that, although the $\hat{\lambda}$ corrections in (24) are functions of the same variables that enter the $X\beta$ or $X\gamma$ parts of these equations, they are nonlinear functions of the measured variables. Structural earnings equations might be identified off the nonlinearity, though in any particular application there may be insufficient nonlinearity if the range of variation in $W\pi$ (see [15]) is not large enough.[15]

In the general discussion of Section II, X was tentatively associated with measured abilities and Z with measured financial constraints (and tastes), corresponding to the Beckerian distinction between factors that shift the marginal rate of return to investment schedule and those that shift the marginal supply of funds schedule. Evidently, if one

---

[15] *Heckman (1979) raises some subtle issues regarding specification error in selection models. Elements of Z may be incorrectly specified in X and can be statistically significant in least-squares regressions because of truncation. Conversely, coefficients on selection-bias variables λ_a and λ_b can be significant because variables are incorrectly attributed to selection when they more properly belong directly in X. E.g., some might argue that family background belongs in structural earnings equations and our selectivity effects work (see below) because family background comes in the back door through its indirect effect on $\hat{\lambda}$. However, a reversal of the argument suggests that family-background variables might have significant estimated direct effects on earnings merely because they work through selection and resulting truncation. There is no statistically satisfactory way of resolving this problem. In any event, we cannot be "agnostic" about specification because both the economic and statistical theories require certain nontestable zero identifying restrictions. The problem is even more complicated in the present context because the theory is based on unobserved talent and financial constraint shifters and must have observable counterparts to be operational. Evidently choice among alternative specifications ultimately must rest on predictive performance outside the sample.*

takes a sufficiently broad view of human investment and in particular of the role of child care in the new home economics, easy distinctions between the content of X and of Z become increasingly difficult, if not impossible, to make. If X and Z are indistinguishable, the economic theory of school choice has no empirical content. In the empirical work below a very strong dichotomy with no commonalities is maintained: X is specified as a vector of ability indicators and Z as a vector of family-background variables. This hypothesis is maintained for two reasons. First, it provides a test of the theory in its strongest form. Certainly, if the theory is rejected in this form there is little hope for it. Second, there have been no systematic attempts to find empirical counterparts for the things that shift marginal rate of return and marginal cost of fund schedules that cause different people to choose different amounts of schooling. The validity of the theory rests on the possibility of actually being able to find an operational set of indicators, and this distinction is the most straightforward possibility.

2. Given resolution of problem 1, not all parameters in the model can be estimated. Some are overidentified and some are underidentified. The selectivity-bias-corrected structural earnings equations (24) directly estimate β_a, β_b, γ_a, γ_b, and the structural probit (26) provides estimates of $(\alpha_1/\sigma_\epsilon, \alpha_2/\sigma_\epsilon, \alpha_3/\sigma_\epsilon, \alpha_4/\sigma_\epsilon)$. Furthermore, from the approximations in (10), the coefficient on $\ln(\bar{y}_a/\bar{y}_b)$ in (26) estimates $1/\sigma_\epsilon$ (given that $\alpha_1 = 1$), so that it is also possible to estimate population average real rates of interest. In addition, there are 15 parameters in the unobserved-component variance-covariance matrix Σ. Following a development similar to the one leading to (18)–(21), it can be shown that the variances of residuals in (24) are

$$\mathrm{var}\left(\eta_{ij}\right) = \sigma_{jj} + \frac{\sigma_{je}}{\sigma_\epsilon}\left(\frac{W_i\pi}{\sigma_\epsilon}\lambda_{ai} - \lambda_{ai}^2\right), \qquad j = 1,2;$$

$$\mathrm{var}\left(\eta_{ij}\right) = \sigma_{jj} + \frac{\sigma_{je}}{\sigma_\epsilon}\left(\frac{W_i\pi}{\sigma_\epsilon}\lambda_{bi} - \lambda_{bi}^2\right), \qquad j = 3,4.$$

(31)

Similar expressions hold for covariances between η_{i1} and η_{i2} and between η_{i3} and η_{i4}. Hence it is possible to estimate the own-population variances σ_{jj} for $j = 1, \ldots, 4$, two within-group covariances, and four covariances σ_{je} for $j = 1, \ldots, 4$. These, along with the estimate of σ_ϵ, provide only 11 statistics to estimate 15 parameters. Evidently all the covariance terms in Σ cannot be estimated without additional zero or other restrictions because we never observe the path not taken. This is the basis for the statement above that deadweight losses from assignments based jointly on wealth and talent rather than on talent alone cannot be imputed. The demand function for college attendance implicit in (26) reflects the joint density of talent, wealth, tastes, and expectations, and their separate effects cannot be disentangled.

IV. ESTIMATION

The model has been estimated on a sample of 3,611 respondents to the NBER-Thorndike-Hagen survey of 1968–71.[16] These data refer to male World War II veterans who applied for the army air corps. They do not come from a random sample of the population, since the military screening criteria were based on certain aspects of ability and physical fitness. Therefore it is not possible to extrapolate these results to the population at large. However, the sample's advantages more than compensate for this. First, it covers more than 20 years of labor-market experience, far longer than any other panel of comparable size and most appropriate for measuring lifetime earnings effects of educational choice as the theory requires. Second, it contains extensive information on family background and talent. While several other panels are as good on family background, virtually none compare in their range of talent and ability indicators most appropriate to the theory of comparative advantage.

The sample actually used is a subset of 5,085 total respondents. Forty-two observations were dropped for not responding to the age question, another 480 persons were deleted because they were pilots, had extended military service, or did not report a job in 1969, and 952 were dropped because they did not report both initial ($\bar{y}$) and latest ($y[\bar{t}]$) earnings required for structural estimation. Definitions of variables are given in Appendix A. Individuals were put into two categories: group A represents those who entered college and group B those who stopped school after high school graduation. Not all members of group A completed college, and a substantial fraction completed more than a college education. They are labeled "college attendees" hereafter. Descriptive statistics appear in table 1. Notice that more than 75 percent of the sample chose to attend college for some period, reflecting the unusual ability distribution in the sample and eligibility for a liberal school subsidy (the GI Bill). However, the presence of the GI Bill is common to both college attendees and high school graduates.

There are some obvious differences between the two groups. Both mean and relative variance of earnings in both years are smaller for high school graduates, as tends to be true in other samples. In addition, high school graduates had smaller earnings growth over the period, had more siblings and were lower in birth order than college attendees, and were more likely to have taken vocational training in high school. Their fathers had less schooling and were more likely to be blue-collar workers as well. Four ability measures have been chosen for analysis, out of some 16 indicators available in the data. Math and reading scores are related to IQ type of ability (in fact, it is known that math score is highly correlated with IQ score in these data), while the other two are more associated with manual skills. The four together seem well suited to the comparative-advantage logic underlying the formulation of the model. High school graduates tend to score lower in the math and reading-comprehension tests, about the same in manual dexterity, and

---

[16] *These data have been extensively analyzed by other investigators, especially Taubman (1975), who also discovered them. For complete documentation see NBER (1973).*

TABLE 1

DESCRIPTIVE STATISTICS

Variable	High School (Group B)		More than High School (Group A)	
	Mean	SD	Mean	SD
Father's ED	8.671	2.966	10.26	3.623
Father's ED^2	83.99	55.53	118.4	78.09
DK ED	.0999	...	.0464	...
Manager	.3628	...	.4954	...
Clerk	.1239	...	.1450	...
Foreman	.2238	...	.1695	...
Unskilled	.1492	...	.0819	...
Farmer	.1062	...	.0720	...
DK job	.0177	...	.0124	...
Catholic	.2933	...	.2138	...
Jew	.0405	...	.0617	...
Old sibs	1.143	1.634	.9035	1.383
Young sibs	.9381	1.486	.8138	1.266
Mother works:				
Full 5	.0468	...	.0486	...
Part 5	.0392	...	.0504	...
None 5	.7168	...	.7507	...
Full 14	.0822	...	.0936	...
Part 14	.0708	...	.0851	...
None 14	.6384	...	.6713	...
H.S. shop	.2592	...	.0908	...
Read	20.57	10.17	24.06	11.63
NR read	.0291	...	.0128	...
Mech	59.24	18.27	58.88	18.96
NR mech	.0025	...	0	...
Math	18.13	11.82	28.94	17.17
NR math	.0683	...	.0188	...
Dext	50.04	9.359	50.68	9.811
NR dext	0	...	.0071	...
Exp	29.33	2.439	24.54	2.907

TABLE 1 (CONTINUED)

DESCRIPTIVE STATISTICS

Variable	High School (Group B)		More than High School (Group A)	
	Mean	SD	Mean	SD
Exp^2	866.1	147.1	610.4	147.4
S13–15	...	...	.3106	...
S16	...	...	.3993	...
S20	...	...	.0823	...
Year 48	46.62	1.584	48.05	1.869
Year 69	69.11	.3691	69.08	.3437
$\ln \bar{y}$	8.635	.4107	8.526	.3871
$\ln y(\bar{t})$	9.326	.4573	9.639	.4904
g	.0309	.0251	.0535	.0283
λ_a	−1.2870	.2873	−.3193	.2256
λ_b	.4666	.3763	1.605	.5212
No. observations	791		2820	

Note: Variables are defined in Appendix A.

somewhat better on mechanical ability. In line with the previous discussion, all ability measures in table 1 are assigned to *X,* while the family-background measures—reflecting financial constraints, tastes, and perceptions—are assigned to Z. Experience, school-completion dummies (for group A), and year of reported earnings are used exclusively as controls in structural earnings equations.

The first columns in table 2 present estimated coefficients and asymptotic *t*-statistics of the reduced-form probit selection into group A—equation (16). These effects more or less parallel the summary of table 1 given above. Math score has a particularly strong positive effect and mechanical score a strong negative effect on the college attendance decision. The effect of mother's working is somewhat unexpected. Mother's home time when the respondent was 5 years old or younger has virtually no effect on college attendance, whereas the respondent was more likely to go to college if his mother worked when he was 6–14 years of age. This is more supportive of market investment through relaxation of financial constraints than of home investment in kind.[17]

---

[17] *Recall that female labor-force participation during the war increased. The normalized category for mother's work classifications is nonresponse. We do not know how many did not respond because no mother was in the home.*

Structural estimates of earning and growth equations corrected for selection are found in table 3. These are somewhat different from the typical earnings equations found in the literature, because they include a much sparser set of regressors. For example, we know respondents' unemployment experience, weeks worked, weeks ill, marital status, and so forth but have not included them in the regressions. The logic of this lies in the model itself: at the time the college attendance decision was made, there is no reason to expect that respondents knew the outcomes of such variables. It is more in the spirit of the choice framework of the model to allow these "current" events to be captured indirectly via their correlations with included variables in order to estimate expected or anticipated values relevant to the structural probit.[18] The problem is more difficult in the case of school-completion differences among members of group A in table 3 and, in truth, raises an unresolvable aggregation problem. The anticipations argument above suggests that school-completion differences within group A may not enter the earnings equations, so that included variables pick up average completion experience in the sample. Alternatively, it can be argued that the level of schooling achieved within group A should be controlled by including school-completion dummies. This latter specification is reported in table 3 and is the one used to estimate the structural probit in table 2. Of course we do not switch on the school-completion dummies to estimate the earnings advantages of college attendance, since that would clearly stack the deck in favor of finding strong financial effects. Earnings and structural probit equations were also estimated with school dummies deleted, and the results were very similar to those reported here. However, it is clear that this issue only can be resolved by going into a more disaggregated model with multiple classifications.

With the exception of experience, most of the variables have little effect on initial earnings in either A or B (see cols. 1 and 2 of table 3).[19] Experience effects are the strongest and are known to be most important at early and late stages of career patterns, facts borne out in these data since experience has little effect on later (surveyed around 1969) earnings. The ability measure that has the largest effect on initial earnings is math score for college attendees. Ability indicators are more important for earnings growth (cols. 3 and 4) and later earnings (cols. 4 and 5). Dexterity and reading scores have positive effects on g_b and $y_b(\bar{t})$, while math and reading scores have positive effects on $\ln y_a(\bar{t})$ but

---

[18] A related and thorough discussion of this issue appears in Hanoch (1967), to which the reader is referred. It has not escaped our attention that current variables such as hours of work and unemployment experience might serve as indicators of an unobserved "taste for leisure" component, but we have not experimented with that possibility.

[19] Initial earnings is recall data from the 1955 Thorndike survey and refers to a period as much as 9 years prior to that survey date. Late earnings is closer to the NBER survey date and probably has less recall error in it. The low R^2 statistics in table 3 are due to the fact that we are looking at within-group variation, whereas most results in the literature get a lot of mileage out of current variables and explanation of between-group mean variation. It is also worth noting that the standard errors in the earnings and growth equations computed from the exact asymptotic distribution reported in the table are virtually identical with those estimated by OLS.

TABLE 2

COLLEGE SELECTION RULES: PROBIT ANALYSIS

Variable	Reduced Form (16)		Structure (26)		Structure (29)	
	Coefficient	t	Coefficient	t	Coefficient	t
Constant	.0485	.20	.1512	.22	.1030	.17
Background:						
Father's ED	−.0145	−.41	−.0168	−.54	−.0152	−.49
Father's ED^2	.0037	2.05	.0038	2.26	.0037	2.26
DK ED	−.4059	−3.96	−.3924	−2.79	−.4001	−2.91
Manager	.1897	2.17	.1825	2.13	.1871	2.21
Clerk	.0556	.54	.0561	.59	.0554	.59
Foreman	.0182	.19	.0210	.23	.0200	.22
Unskilled	−.0910	−.85	−.0948	−.89	−.0928	−.87
Farmer	−.2039	−2.12	−.2256	−2.27	−.2094	−2.14
DK job	−.0413	−.19	−.0629	−.29	−.0609	−.28
Catholic	−.1144	−1.91	−.0982	−1.51	−.1083	−1.66
Jew	−.0293	−.23	.0143	.12	−.0158	−.14
Old sibs	−.0162	−.93	−.0162	−.93	−.0161	−.93
Young sibs	.0122	.63	.0096	.49	.0112	.57
Mother works:						
Full 5	.1039	.66	.1168	.81	.1104	.76
Part 5	.2179	1.42	.2106	1.52	.2156	1.56
None 5	.0655	.63	.0677	.65	.0661	.64
Full 14	.2898	2.29	.2884	2.30	.2888	2.33
Part 14	.2709	2.20	.2768	2.02	.2693	2.03
None 14	.1980	1.91	.1990	1.92	.1966	1.92
H.S. shop	−.4411	−6.14	−.4397	−3.74	−.4379	−3.90
Ability:						
Read:	.0047	1.67	...	...	...	...
NR read	−.2575	−1.41	...	...	...	...
Mech	−.0070	−4.29	...	...	...	...
NR mech	−3.0236	−1.04	...	...	...	...
Math	.0244	12.34	...	...	...	...
NR math	−.7539	−5.75	...	...	...	...
Dext	.0019	.72	...	...	...	...

TABLE 2 (CONTINUED)

COLLEGE SELECTION RULES: PROBIT ANALYSIS

Variable	Reduced Form (16) Coefficient	t	Structure (26) Coefficient	t	Structure (29) Coefficient	t
NR dext	2.2797	.47	...	...	...	...
Earnings:						
$\ln(\bar{y}_a/\bar{y}_b)$	...	...	5.1486	2.25	...	...
g_a	...	...	138.3850	1.83	7.6632	.11
g_b	...	...	−44.2697	−1.28	71.8981	2.34
$\ln y_a(t)/y_b(t)$	...	...	...	...	5.1501	2.57
Observations	3611		3611		3611	
Limit observations	791		791		791	
Nonlimit observations	2820		2820		2820	
−2 ln (likelihood ratio)	579.5		568.8		576.6	
χ^2 degree freedom	28		23		23	

Note: t is asymptotic t-statistic; DK: Don't know, dummy variable; NR: No response, dummy variable; other variables are defined in Appendix A.

exhibit much weaker effects on earnings growth. Interestingly enough, the effect on mechanical score is negative in all cases, raising obvious questions about what it is that this test supposedly measures (recall, however, the sample truncation on high-ability military personnel). Even so, it seems to have a more important negative effect for members of group A. This, along with the results for dexterity and math scores, lends support to the comparative-advantage hypothesis.

Selectivity biases are particularly interesting in that regard. The coefficients of λ_b show no selectivity bias for initial earnings of high school graduates, but positive bias for growth rates. Therefore, observed earnings patterns of high school graduates show higher rates of growth compared with the pattern that would have been observed for the average member of this sample had he chosen not to continue school. On the other hand, the coefficients of λ_a show positive selection bias for initial earnings of college attendees and negative bias for earnings growth. The latter is due to the fact that there are no selection effects for late earnings. Thus, the observed earnings pattern among members of group A is everywhere higher than the population mean pattern would have been and converges toward the population mean late earnings level. *Positive selection among both A and B also lends support to comparative advantage.*

TABLE 3

STRUCTURAL EARNINGS ESTIMATES: EQUATIONS (24) AND (28), OLS

	Dependent Variable					
Regressor	$\ln \bar{y}_a$ (1)	$\ln \bar{y}_b$ (2)	g_a (3)	g_b (4)	$\ln y_a(\bar{t})$ (5)	$\ln y_b(\bar{t})$ (6)
Constant	8.7124	2.8901	.1261	.2517	10.3370	7.5328
	(16.51)	(1.37)	(3.90)	(2.11)	(5.52)	(2.08)
Read	.0009	−.0019	.0001	.0003	.0027	.0057
	(1.21)	(−1.17)	(1.11)	(3.20)	(2.80)	(3.28)
NR read	.0791	.0506	−.0034	−.0046	.0033	−.0402
	(1.24)	(.58)	(−.76)	(−.89)	(.04)	(−.42)
Mech	−.0002	−.0005	−.0001	−.0001	−.0021	−.0017
	(−.48)	(−.54)	(−2.16)	(−1.13)	(−3.59)	(−1.73)
NR mech	...	.1969	...	.0002	...	.2196
		(.69)		(.01)		(.68)
Math	.0015	−.0013	.0001	−.0000	.0030	−.0019
	(2.02)	(.74)	(1.18)	(−.20)	(3.31)	(−1.00)
NR math	−.1087	.0562	.0015	.0006	−.0877	.0712
	(−1.94)	(.83)	(.38)	(.15)	(−1.24)	(.96)
Dext	.0008	−.0019	−.0000	.0003	.0002	.0036
	(1.03)	(−1.21)	(−.78)	(2.77)	(.16)	(2.19)
NR dext	.0751	...	−.0004	...	.1466	...
	(.28)		(−.02)		(.43)	
Exp	−.0523	.4260	−.0028	−.0154	−.0129	.0776
	(−1.49)	(3.10)	(−1.11)	(−1.93)	(−.29)	(.53)
Exp^2	.0015	−.0067	.0000	.0002	−.0000	−.0012
	(2.22)	(−2.95)	(.21)	(1.82)	(−.01)	(−.49)
Year 48	−.0020	−.0156	...	...	...	...
	(−.48)	(−1.72)				
Year 69	...	...	...	...	−.0067	.0039
					(−.26)	(.09)
S13–15	.1288	...	−.0062	...	.0168	...
	(5.15)		(−3.49)		(.52)	
S16	.0760	...	.0026	...	.1095	...
	(3.82)		(1.79)		(4.26)	
S20	.1318	...	.0049	...	.2560	...
	(4.10)		(2.13)		(6.15)	

TABLE 3 (CONTINUED)

STRUCTURAL EARNINGS ESTIMATES: EQUATIONS (24) AND (28), OLS

	Dependent Variable					
Regressor	$\ln \bar{y}_a$ (1)	$\ln \bar{y}_b$ (2)	g_a (3)	g_b (4)	$\ln y_a(\bar{t})$ (5)	$\ln y_b(\bar{t})$ (6)
λ_a	−.1069	. . .	.0058	. . .	.0206	. . .
	(−3.21)		(2.45)		(.49)	
λ_b	. . .	−.0558	. . .	.0118	. . .	.2267
		(−.66)		(2.39)		(2.48)
R^2	.0750	.0439	.1578	.0513	.0740	.0358

Note: NR: No response, dummy variable; other variables are defined in Appendix A; t-values are shown in parentheses.

The most novel empirical results are the structural probit estimates in table 2, which show how anticipated earnings gains affect the decision to attend college. The predicted earnings variables are statistically significant except for g_b in (26) and g_a in (29).[20] More striking, however, is the agreement of the sign patterns predicted by the theory (see eq. [10] and recall that the structural probit coefficients are normalized by σ_e, from [26] and [29]). The model passes two internal consistency checks. The first is restriction (30). Working backward to normalized α estimates from directly estimated θ's in column 5 of table 2 yields[21] a predicted (α/σ_e) vector of (5.15, 155.90, −52.68), which is similar to the direct estimates in column 3 of (5.15, 138.39, −44.27). Working forward from actual estimates of normalized α to predicted estimates of θ gives prediction (5.15, 37.04, 80.31), compared with actual (5.15, 7.66, 71.90). These comparisons probably would not be so close if the two-parameter approximation to earnings patterns in (5) and (6) was not reasonably good. Second, equations (15) and (26) indicate that estimated coefficients on the Z variables in structural and reduced-form probits should be the same. Direct comparison of

---

[20] Recall (n. 14) that the t-statistics for the structural probit in table 2 are based on consistent estimates of the standard errors, as suggested by Lee (1977). The t-statistics on background variables are not very different from the biased values computed by a standard probit algorithm. However, the t-statistics on the predicted earnings and growth variables are substantially reduced when corrected for bias; e.g., the standard probit estimates of t-values for ln $(\bar{y}_a/\bar{y}_b)$, g_a, and g_b in (26) are (10.8, 8.15, −4.81), compared with the unbiased values of (2.25, 1.83, −1.28) in table 2.

[21] There are two ways of estimating $\bar{t}$ and $(\bar{t}-S)$ for these computations. First, a direct estimate of $t-S$ is obtained as the difference between average year of 1969 job and average year of initial job for members of group A in table 1. A direct estimate of $\bar{t}$ is the average difference between 1969 job and initial job for members of group B. However, an independent estimate of S is the average years of schooling among members of group A minus 12.0. Hence another estimate of $(\bar{t}-S)$ is the direct estimate of $(\bar{t}-S)$ minus the direct estimate of S; and another estimate of $(\bar{t}-S)$ is the direct estimate of $\bar{t}$ minus the direct estimate of S. The two estimates for each parameter were averaged for purposes of these checks. They are 24.19 for $\bar{t}$ and 19.68 for $(\bar{t}-S)$.

coefficients of Z in table 2 shows extremely close similarity of $\alpha_4\delta$ in all three equations. In sum, the results give direct, internally consistent evidence on the validity of the economic theory of the demand for schooling derived from its (private) investment value. The economic hypothesis cannot be rejected.

V. CONCLUSIONS

The structural probit estimates of table 2 support the economic hypothesis that expected gains in life earnings influence the decision to attend college. They also show important effects of financial constraints and tastes working through family-background indicators, a finding in common with most other studies of school choice.[22] Availability of the GI Bill might well be expected to dull the observed monetary effects, but they remain strong enough to persist for a significant fraction of the sample.

The estimates also show positive sorting or positive selection bias in observed earnings of both high school graduates and college attendees. To be clear about the implications of these results it is necessary to distinguish between the effects of measured abilities and unmeasured components on earnings prospects in A or B. The selection results refer to unmeasured components of variance. If we examine a subpopulation of persons with given measured abilities (i.e., with the same values of X in [12] and [13]), the empirical results on selectivity imply that those persons who stopped schooling after high school had better prospects as high school graduates than the average member of that subpopulation and that those who continued on to college also had better prospects there than the average member of the subpopulation. That is, the average earnings at most points in the life cycle of persons with given measured characteristics who actually chose B exceeded what earnings would have been for those persons (with the same characteristics) who chose A instead. Conversely, average earnings for those who actually chose A were greater than what earnings would have been for measurably similar people who actually chose B had they continued their schooling instead. This is a much different picture than emerges from the usual discussions of ability bias in the literature, based on hierarchical or one-factor ability considerations. The one-factor model implies that persons who would do better than average in A would also do better than average in B. That is, positive selectivity bias in B cannot occur in the strict hierarchical model.[23]

---

[22] See Radner and Miller (1970) and Kohn, Manski, and Mundel (1976) for logit models of college choice. These models contain more detail in personal and college attributes but do not make any attempt to assess the effects of anticipated earnings on college attendance decisions. See Abowd (1977) for another approach to the selection problem focusing on school quality.

[23] It should be emphasized that the special nature of this sample makes it impossible to extrapolate this result to the entire population. The reason is that the selection criteria for sample eligibility were established by entrance requirements into the army and our sample is a subset of those who volunteered for the air corps. It is possible to conceive of systematic truncation and selection rules by the military that would support the comparative-advantage argument in this subset, even though roughly hierarchical talents and positive correlations among alternative income prospects might well characterize the population at large.

The most attractive and simplest interpretation is the theory of comparative advantage, because hierarchical assignments are not observed. While the results are consistent with comparative advantage, they do not prove the case because life-persistent luck and random extraneous opportunities could have played just as important roles in the observed assignments as differential talents did. For all we know, those who decided to stop school after high school may have married the boss's daughter instead, or made better career connections in the military, and so forth. The important point is that their prospects in B were higher than average.

As noted above, the population average rate of discount, $\bar{r}$, is an identifiable statistic in the model. Estimates are obtained by applying restriction (10) to the estimates in table 2. Maintain the hypothesis that $\alpha_1 = 1$. Then the estimated coefficient of $\ln(\bar{y}_a/\bar{y}_b)$ in table 2 estimates $(1/\sigma_e)$, from equation (26). Since all the equations of the structural probit are normed by σ_e this estimate provides a basis for estimating the population parameters in (10).

Straightforward computations using the structural probit estimates (26) in table 2 yield

$$\left(\bar{r} - \bar{g}_a\right) = .0372,$$
$$\left(\bar{r} - \bar{g}_b\right) = .1163. \tag{32}$$

Estimates of $\bar{g}_a$ and $\bar{g}_b$ are necessary to impute values of $\bar{r}$, and a slight ambiguity arises because the growth rates are functions of measured characteristics (see [12] and [13]). For illustrative purposes we use the overall sample mean values of characteristics (the X's) to impute $\bar{g}_a$ and $\bar{g}_b$ from the structural earnings estimates in table 3, purged of selectivity bias. The average person in the sample would have obtained growth rates $\bar{g}_a = .0591$ and $\bar{g}_b = .0262$ in A and B, respectively. The population mean discount rate, $\bar{r}$, is overidentified. The first equation of (32) yields an estimate of $\bar{r} = .0963$, while the second gives $\bar{r} = .1425$. Two more estimates of $\bar{r}$ are implied by the structural probit that uses the late earnings difference rather than the initial earnings differences. These are $\bar{r} = .0981$ and $\bar{r} = .1240$. Even if the precise derivation and specification of the model in Section III strain the reader's credulity, it is nonetheless clear that the structural specification is consistent with more casual derivations, and the estimated sign patterns in the structural probit, if not the precise restrictions among coefficients, would be predicted by virtually any economic model.

The positivity of earnings selection effects in both groups also implies that selection bias in simple rate of return estimates could go in either direction. The following procedure gives a rough and ready indication in this sample. First the two-parameterization of earnings in (5) and (6) implies that the average internal rate of return, i, is estimated by $\ln(y_a/y_b)$ $+ \ln(i - g_b) - \ln(i - g_a) - iS = 0$, where i is the rate of discount that equates average present values. Using sample mean values of $\bar{y}_a$, $\bar{y}_b$, g_a, and g_b in table 1 and a schooling increment of 4.11 years yields a simple unadjusted rate of return of $i = 9.0$ percent. This is comparable to the statistic usually presented in rate of return studies that make no allowance for differential ability between high school and college graduates. Several adjustments must be made to this number, however. First, correcting for selectivity alone yields an adjusted mean rate of return of $i = 9.8$ percent, which is actually larger, not smaller, than the observed mean rate of return. The 9.8 percent figure is obtained by subtracting the selectivity bias corrections from the observed sample means of $\bar{y}_a$, $\bar{y}_b$, g_a, and g_b and in principle could be larger or smaller than the unadjusted figure due to positive selection in both A and B. It does not make any allowance for differential measured ability effects between the two groups. A more meaningful computation in the context of the model is to use measured abilities and the parameters of the corrected earnings and growth-rate functions to answer the following question: What is the expected rate of return to college of the typical person who chose A as compared to the expected rate of return of the typical person who chose B? This is a "standardized" comparison: the rates of return differ between the typical A person and the typical B person because their measured abilities differ and because the values of these abilities (the regression coefficients in table 3) differ in A or B. Assuming that persons with the average characteristics of those who chose B would have exhibited the same values of experience and initial year of earnings as those who actually chose A and vice versa, the average rate of return for persons of type A is 9.9 percent, while the average is 9.3 percent for persons of type B. Thus, those who actually chose A had measured abilities that were more valuable in A than did those who actually chose B.

PREDICTIONS

The model passes the test of empirical verification of its structural restrictions. How well does it do in predicting assignments on independent data? The sample used is not a random drawing of the U.S. population and for this reason cannot be extrapolated to the population at large. However, only a subset of the NBER-Thorndike-Hagen sample was used to estimate it, and the remaining remnant is more likely to be a suitable group for prediction purposes. The remnant refers to those who did not report initial earnings. For this reason it may not be a random sample of the relevant population either. And while there is no reason to suppose that the censoring of initial earnings was systematically related to the selection mechanism of the model, it should be noted that a somewhat smaller proportion of these individuals (66 percent of them) chose to attend college than in the sample used for structural estimation.

One indirect test of the model's predictive content has been calculated. First, the reduced-form probit was reestimated for the remnant, which does not involve extrapolations, since the sample selection between A and B and the content of $W = [X,Z]$ is known for these people. Results appear in Appendix B. While there is some conformity with table 2, there are also many differences between reduced-form estimates in the two samples. In short, family-background coefficients are not too stable.

The second experiment involves an extrapolation. Both initial earnings differences and growth rates were predicted for members of the remnant sample from the structural earnings estimates of table 3 and then used to reestimate the structural probit of this group (no *t*-statistics are reported for structural probit coefficients because of the large expense of doing so). The results also appear in Appendix B. The sign reversals on family-background indicators carry over to these estimates too, though the coefficients and signs of the Z variables in the structural estimates are very close to those found in the reduced-form estimates in Appendix B. However, the coefficients on the earnings differences and growth rates for the remnant sample are very close to those estimated for the original sample of table 2.

ENROLLMENT FUNCTIONS

Perhaps the simplest and most useful summary of the results is obtained from the demand function for college attendance implicit in the structural probit estimates. Recalling the definition of the index function in (9), the probability of attending college is given by Pr (A is chosen) $= F(I/\sigma_\epsilon)$, where F is the standard normal c.d.f. Let m denote the size of the relevant population, and let N represent the number choosing to attend college. Then the number enrolled in college is given by

$$N = mF(I/\sigma_\epsilon). \tag{33}$$

This would be equivalent to a supply function of graduates were it not for the aggregation involved in group A. The supply of graduates is somewhat different since we do not know how long people outside the sample would stay in school. The normality assumptions imply that the enrollment function (33) follows the cumulative normal curve. It therefore has zero elasticity at its extremes and positive elasticities in between. The major point of interest here is responsiveness of enrollments to earnings opportunities near the sample mean. From the definitions of present value in Section III, note that dln (V_a/V_b)/dln $(\bar{y}_a/\bar{y}_b) = 1$. A 1 percent change in relative initial earnings changes relative capital values by 1 percent. To clarify a possible point of confusion on this conceptual experiment, dln $(\bar{y}_a/\bar{y}_b)$ represents a permanent—not a transitory—change in lifetime prospects, because it increases relative differences between potential earnings in A compared with B not only initially but forevermore (see [5] and [6]). Differentiating (33) yields an elasticity formula

$$\text{dln } N/\text{dln } \left(\bar{y}_a/\bar{y}_b\right) = \left[F'\left(I/\sigma_\epsilon\right)\left(\alpha_1/\sigma_\epsilon\right)\right]/F\left(I/\sigma_\epsilon\right),$$

where I/σ_ϵ is evaluated at the desired sample proportion. For example, the elasticity evaluated at a sample proportion of .5 (half in A and half in B) is 4.1. On the other hand, the initial earnings elasticity at the observed sample proportion is 1.94, still a substantial response given the presence of marked diversity in the population. By way of comparison, an increment of father's education of 1.59 years (the difference in means of father's schooling between groups in table 1) elicits a relative response of .0337.

APPENDIX A

DEFINITIONS OF VARIABLES FOR TABLES

Father's ED	Father's years of school. Nonresponse assigned mean.
Father's ED^2	Square of Father's ED.
DK ED	Dummy variable: 1 if respondent did not know father's education.
Manager	Dummy variable: 1 if father was a businessman, manager, or professional.
Clerk	Dummy variable: 1 if father had white-collar occupation other than those in management.
Foreman	Dummy variable: 1 if father was a foreman, supervisor, or skilled craftsman
Unskilled	Dummy variable: 1 if father was semiskilled operative or unskilled laborer
Farmer	Dummy variable: 1 if father was a farmer.
DK job	Dummy variable: 1 if respondent did not know father's occupation.
Catholic	Dummy variable: 1 if respondent is Catholic.
Jew	Dummy variable: 1 if respondent is Jewish.
Old sibs	Number of older siblings.
Young sibs	Number of younger siblings.
Mother works:	
Full 5	Dummy variable: 1 if mother worked full time when respondent was less than 6 years of age.
Part 5	Dummy variable: 1 if mother worked part time when respondent was less than 6 years of age.
None 5	Dummy variable: 1 if mother did not work when respondent was less than 6 years of age.
Full 14	Dummy variable: 1 if mother worked full time when respondent was 6–14 years of age.
Part 14	Dummy variable: 1 if mother worked part time when respondent was 6–14 years of age.
None 14	Dummy variable: 1 if mother did not work when respondent was 6–14 years of age.
H.S. shop	Dummy variable: 1 if respondent majored in vocational courses in high school.
Read	Raw score on college undergraduate level reading comprehension test. Continuous variable, nonrespondents assigned mean.
NR read	Dummy variable: 1 if reading score not reported.
Mech	Raw score on pictorial representation of mechanical problem test. Continuous variable, nonrespondents assigned mean.
NR mech	Dummy variable: 1 if mechanical score not reported.
Math	Raw score on mathematics test (performance in advanced arithmetic, algebra, and trigonometry). Continuous variable with nonrespondents assigned mean.
NR math	Dummy variable: 1 if math score unreported.
Dext	Score on test of finger dexterity. Continuous variable, nonrespondents assigned mean.

NR dext	Dummy variable: 1 if dexterity score not reported.
Exp	Continuous variable: Age − Schooling − 6.
Exp^2	Square of Exp.
S13–15	Dummy variable: 1 if respondent received 13–15 years of school.
S16	Dummy variable: 1 if respondent received 16 years of school.
S20	Dummy variable: 1 if respondent received 20 or more years of school.
Year 48	Year in which initial postwar earnings are reported. Continuous variable.
Year 69	Year in which earnings at time of NBER survey are reported. Continuous variable.
ln $\bar{y}$	Log of earnings on first job after finishing school, in 1967 prices.
ln $y(t)$	Log of earnings at time of NBER survey in 1967 prices.
g	(ln earn 69 − ln earn 48) ÷ (Year 69 − Year 48) percentage rate of growth between the two observations.
λ_a	See equation (17), based on estimates in table 2, column 1.
λ_b	See equation (22), based on estimates in table 2, column 1.

APPENDIX B

COLLEGE SELECTION RULES: PROBIT ANALYSIS
(INDEPENDENT SUBSAMPLE OF INDIVIDUALS WITH NO REPORT ON INITIAL EARNINGS)

Variable	Reduced Form (16)		Structure (26)	Structure (29)
	Coefficient	t	Coefficient	Coefficient
Constant	−.4424	−.986	−.1170	−.1514
Background:				
Father's ED	−.0183	.27	.0131	.0123
Father's ED^2	.0020	.61	.0023	.0023
DK ED	−.2645	−1.69	−.2548	−.2608
Manager	.2009	1.50	.1689	.1768
Clerk	.1664	.92	.1523	.1490
Foreman	−.1276	−.83	−.1359	−.1369
Unskilled	−.3118	−1.79	−.3298	.3260
Farmer	.1353	.75	.1174	−.1332
DK job	−.3515	−1.04	−.3133	−.3426
Catholic	−.0887	−.80	−.0847	−.1024
Jew	−.2169	−.95	−.1879	−.2159
Old sibs	.0335	1.02	.0343	.0336
Young sibs	.0191	.56	.0170	.0176

APPENDIX B (CONTINUED)

COLLEGE SELECTION RULES: PROBIT ANALYSIS
(INDEPENDENT SUBSAMPLE OF INDIVIDUALS WITH NO REPORT ON INITIAL EARNINGS)

Variable	Reduced Form (16) Coefficient	t	Structure (26) Coefficient	Structure (29) Coefficient
Mother works:				
Full 5	−.6039	−2.06	−.6080	−.6080
Part 5	−.0470	−.18	−.0409	−.0351
None 5	−.0200	−.11	−.0345	−.0248
Full 14	.1656	.67	.1747	.1764
Part 14	−.1248	−.58	−.1258	−.1310
None 14	−.0581	−.31	−.0360	.0448
H.S. shop	−.5387	−3.95	−.5436	−.5395
Ability:				
Read	.0056	1.07	. . .	. . .
NR read	.2393	.74	. . .	. . .
Mech	−.0480	−1.64	. . .	. . .
NR mech	. . .	. . .	. . .	. . .
Math	.0251	6.80	. . .	. . .
NR math	−.4775	−2.15	. . .	. . .
Dext	.0050	1.03	. . .	. . .
NR dext	. . .	. . .	. . .	. . .
Earnings:				
$\ln (\bar{y}_a/\bar{y}_b)$	. . .	. . .	4.9674	. . .
g_a	. . .	. . .	122.1460	−1.8761
g_b	. . .	. . .	−34.8393	76.4555
$\ln [y_a(t)/y_b(t)]$	. . .	. . .	. . .	4.8837
Observations	952		952	952
Limit observations	321		321	321
Nonlimit observations	631		631	631
−2 ln (likelihood ratio)	184.446		179.419	184.446
χ^2 degree freedom	. . .		. . .	. . .

Note: t is asymptotic t-statistic; DK: Don't know, dummy variable; NR: No response, dummy variable; other variables are defined in Appendix A.

REFERENCES

Abowd, John M. "An Econometric Model of the U.S. Market for Higher Education." Ph.D. dissertation. Univ. Chicago, 1977.

Becker, Gary S. *Human Capital,* 2d ed. New York: Nat. Bur. Econ. Res., 1975.

Blaug, Mark. "The Empirical Status of Human Capital Theory: A Slightly Jaundiced Survey." *J. Econ. Literature* 14 (September 1976): 827–55.

Freeman, Richard, *The Market for College Trained Manpower: A Study in the Economics of Career Choice.* Cambridge, Mass.: Harvard Univ. Press, 1971.

Friedman, Milton, and Kuznets, Simon. *Income from Independent Professional Practice.* New York: Nat. Bur. Econ. Res., 1945.

Griliches, Zvi. "Estimating the Returns to Schooling: Some Econometric Problems." *Econometrica* 45 (January 1977): 1–22.

Griliches, Zvi; Hall, B.; and Hausman, Jerry. "Missing Data and Self-Selection in Large Panels." Discussion Paper no. 573. Harvard Inst. Econ. Res., 1977.

Hanoch, Giora. "An Economic Analysis of Earnings and Schooling." *J. Human Resources* 2, no. 3 (1967): 310–29.

Hause, J. "The Fine Structure of Earnings and the On-the-Job-Training Hypothesis." Mimeographed. Univ. Minnesota, 1977.

Hausman, Jerry, and Wise, D. "A Conditional Probit Model for Qualitative Choice." *Econometrica* 46 (March 1978): 403–26.

Heckman, James J. "The Common Structure of Statistical Models of Truncation. Sample Selection and Limited Dependent Variables and a Simple Estimator for Such Models." *Ann. Econ. and Soc. Measurement* 5 (Fall 1976): 475–92.

———. "Sample Selection Bias as a Specification Error." In *Female Labor Supply: Theory and Estimation,* edited by J. P. Smith. Princeton, N.J.: Princeton Univ. Press, 1979.

Kenny, L.; Lee, L.; Maddala, G. S.; and Trost, R. "Returns to College Education: An Investigation of Self-Selection Bias in Project Talent Data." *Internat. Econ. Rev.* (in press).

Kohn, M. G.; Manski, C. F.; and Mundel, D. S. "An Empirical Investigation of Factors Which Influence College-going Behavior." *Ann. Econ. and Soc. Measurement* 5 (Fall 1976): 391–420.

Lazear, Edward. "Age, Experience and Wage Growth." *A.E.R.* 66 (September 1976): 548–58.

Lee, Lung Fei. "Estimation of Limited Dependent Variables Models by Two-Stage Methods." Ph.D. dissertation. Univ. Rochester, 1976.

———. "On the Asymptotic Distributions of Some Two-Stage Consistent Estimators: Unionism and Wage Rates Revisited." Mimeographed. Univ. Minnesota, 1977.

———. "Unionism and Wage Rates: A Simultaneous Equations Model with Qualitative and Limited Dependent Variables." *Internat. Econ. Rev.* 19 (June 1978): 415–33.

Lillard, L., and Willis, Robert. "Dynamic Aspects of Earnings Mobility." *Econometrica* 46, no. 5 (1978): 985–1012.

McFadden, D. "Conditional Logit Analysis of Qualitative Choice Behavior." In *Frontiers in Econometrics,* edited by P. Zarembka. New York: Academic Press, 1973.

Maddala, G. S. "Self-Selectivity Problems in Econometric Models." In *Applications in Statistics,* edited by P. R. Krishnaia. Amsterdam: North-Holland, 1977.

Mandelbrot, Benoit. "Paretian Distributions and Income Maximization." *Q.J.E.* 76 (February 1960): 57–85.

Mincer, Jacob. *Schooling, Experience and Earnings.* New York: Nat. Bur. Econ. Res., 1974.

National Bureau of Economic Research. "The Comprehensive NBER-TH Tape Documentation," Mimeographed. March 1973.

Radner, Roy, and Miller, L. S. "Demand and Supply in U.S. Higher Education." *A.E.R.* 60 (May 1970): 326–34.

Rosen, Sherwin. "Human Capital: Relations between Education and Earnings." In *Frontiers of Quantitative Economics,* edited by Michael D. Intriligator. Vol. *3B.* Amsterdam: North-Holland, 1977.

———. "Substitution and Division of Labor," *Economica* 45 (August 1978): 235–50.

Roy, Andrew D. "Some Thoughts on the Distribution of Earnings." *Oxford Econ. Papers,* n.s. 3 (June 1951): 135–46.

Taubman, Paul. *Sources of Inequality of Earnings.* Amsterdam: North-Holland, 1975.

Weiss, Yoram, and Lillard, Lee A. "Experience, Vintage, and Time Effects in the Growth of Earnings: American Scientists, 1960–1970." *J.P.E.* 86, no. 3 (June 1978): 427–47.

Wise, D. "Academic Achievement and Job Performance." *A.E.R.* 65 (June 1975): 350–66.

Zabalza, A. "The Determinants of Teacher Supply." Mimeographed. London School Econ., 1977.

ABOUT THE AUTHORS

Robert J. Willis

Robert J. Willis is currently a professor of economics at the University of Michigan, having received his Ph.D. from the University of Washington in 1971. He joined the University of Michigan in 1995 and holds joint appointments with the Survey Research Center at the Institute for Social Research and the Population Studies Center. Before coming to Michigan, Professor Willis held appointments at the University of Chicago, SUNY at Stony Brook, Stanford University, and the Graduate Center of City University of New York. He has been elected to the Board of Directors of the Population Association of America, has served on advisory boards for a number of surveys including the Panel Study of Income Dynamics, the High School and Beyond Survey, and the Health and Retirement Survey, and was recently appointed as representative to the Census Advisory Board by the American Economics Association. Bob Willis' main research interests include labor economics, economic demography, and economic development.

An important contribution in Willis' early work involved a new economic model of fertility (see "A New Approach to the Economic Theory of Fertility Behavior," *Journal of Political Economy,* March/April 1973). In this and a series of subsequent papers, Professor Willis outlined a new approach to an economic analysis of fertility. The role of women received special emphasis in his approach, particularly those women who were not working in the market sector. Willis' model demonstrated that, even for women who were not working, there exists a "shadow cost" of bearing children analogous to the role wages play for working women. The "shadow price" will increase with the husband's income, which offers one explanation for the often observed low income elasticity for children.

Another important contribution involved joint work with Sherwin Rosen on selection mechanisms involving schooling choice (the paper reprinted here). Until this paper, economists had typically compared the incomes of college and high school graduates in order to compute the "rate of return" to schooling. Willis and Rosen pointed out that individuals self-select themselves into schooling groups, and that unless one simultaneously estimated the selection mechanism alongside a schooling income equation, rates of return calculations were not interpretable. This paper had a significant methodological impact in a wide variety of applications where individuals choose the group to which they belong.

Willis' more recent work concerned the motivations for money and time transfers between the generations. This work was originally macro in character, attempting to explain long-term swings in fertility. In his models, expected transfers across generations became a central motive for having children, especially when modern capital markets were weak or government-mandated intergenerational transfers to the aged were empirically insignificant. More recently, this line of research has examined microdata from countries undergoing significant demographic transitions, such as Taiwan, Malaysia, and Indonesia.

Beginning in 1996, Willis became principal investigator of the Health and Retirement Survey (HRS), a longitudinal study of Americans in the years immediately before, during, and after their retirement from the labor force.

Sherwin Rosen

The Chicago School began with Frank Knight and Henry Simons, who were followed by Milton Friedman, H. Gregg Lewis, George Stigler, and Gary Becker. Sherwin Rosen was born in Chicago. After graduating from Purdue University, he earned his Ph.D. degree from the University of Chicago in 1966. The first fifteen years of his professional career were spent at the University of Rochester. When Chicago invited him to return in 1977, he did so to carry on the tradition of the Chicago School.

His early research reflects, in part, the influence of his teacher, H. Gregg Lewis. A solid theoretical model is developed to guide the empirical analysis. The paper reprinted here exemplifies an outstanding empirical study describing how income depends on both schooling and ability. Adam Smith's theory of compensating differences prompted Sherwin to write his now classic article, "Hedonic Prices and Implicit Markets" J.P.E. (1974). In addition to his publications in labor economics (value of saving a life, super stars, executive compensation), he has made some truly original contributions in pure economic theory, the most notable being "Monopoly and Product Quality" [with M. Mussa, J.E.T. (1978)]. There are not many whose writings are cited by both theorists and applied economists.

According to Melvin W. Reder, "The two main characteristics of Chicago School economists are (1) belief in the power of neoclassical price theory to explain observed economic behavior and (2) belief in the efficacy of free markets to allocate resources and distribute incomes" [The New Palgrave (1987, p. 413)]. Add to this the ability to contribute to economic theory and to do empirical work, and you have Sherwin Rosen. He is a Fellow of the Econometrics Society, the American Academy of Arts and Science, and the National Academy of Sciences. He is married to Sharon Ginsberg (June 11, 1961) and resides in—where else?—Chicago.

Evaluating the Econometric Evaluations of Training Programs with Experimental Data

ROBERT J. LaLONDE

This paper compares the effect on trainee earnings of an employment program that was run as a field experiment where participants were randomly assigned to treatment and control groups with the estimates that would have been produced by an econometrician. This comparison shows that many of the econometric procedures do not replicate the experimentally determined results, and it suggests that researchers should be aware of the potential for specification errors in other non-experimental evaluations.

Econometricians intend their empirical studies to reproduce the results of experiments that use random assignment without incurring their costs. One way, then, to evaluate econometric methods is to compare them against experimentally determined results.

This paper undertakes such a comparison and suggests the means by which econometric analyses of employment and training programs may be evaluated. The paper compares the results from a field experiment, where individuals were randomly assigned to participate in a training program, against the array of estimates that an econometrician without experimental data might have produced. It examines the results likely to be reported by an econometrician using nonexperimental data and the most modern techniques, and following the recent prescriptions of Edward Leamer (1983) and David Hendry (1980), tests the extent to which the results are sensitive to alternative econometric specifications.[1] The

Graduate School of Business, University of Chicago, 1101 East 58th Street, Chicago, IL 60637. This paper uses public data files from the National Supported Work Demonstration. These data were provided by the Inter-University Consortium for political and Social Research. I have bene-fited from discussions with Mariam Akin, Orley Ashenfelter, James Brown, David Card, Judith Gueron, Nick Papandreou, Robert Willig, and the participants of workshops at the universities of Chicago, Cornell, Iowa, Princeton, and MIT.

Reprinted with permission from Robert J. LaLonde, "Evaluating the Econometric Evaluations of Training Programs with Experimental Data," American Economic Review, Vol. 76 No. 4 (September 1986), pp. 604–620.

[1] *These papers depict a more general crisis of confidence in empirical research. Leamer (1983) argues that any solution to this crisis must divert applied econometricians from "the traditional task of iden-tifying unique inferences implied by a specific model to the task of determining the range of inferences generated by a range of models." Other examples of this literature are Leamer (1985), Leamer and Herman Leonard (1983), and Michael McAleer, Adrian Pagan, and Paul Volker (1985).*

goal is to appraise the likely ability of several econometric methods to accurately assess the economic benefits of employment and training programs.[2]

Section I describes the field experiment and presents simple estimates of the program effect using the experimental data. Sections II and III describe how econometricians evaluate employment and training programs, and compares the nonexperimental estimates using these methods to the experimental results presented in Section I. Section II presents one-step econometric estimates of the program's impact, while more complex two-step econometric estimates are presented in Section III. The results of this study are summarized in the final section.

I. THE EXPERIMENTAL ESTIMATES

The National Supported Work Demonstration (NSW) was a temporary employment program designed to help disadvantaged workers lacking basic job skills move into the labor market by giving them work experience and counseling in a sheltered environment. Unlike other federally sponsored employment and training programs, the NSW program assigned qualified applicants to training positions randomly. Those assigned to the treatment group received all the benefits of the NSW program, while those assigned to the control group were left to fend for themselves.[3]

During the mid-1970s, the Manpower Demonstration Research Corporation (MDRC) operated the NSW program in ten sites across the United States. The MDRC admitted into the program AFDC women, ex-drug addicts, ex-criminal offenders, and high school dropouts of both sexes.[4] For those assigned to the treatment group, the program guaranteed a job for 9 to 18 months, depending on the target group and site. The treatment group was divided into crews of three to five participants who worked together and met frequently with an NSW counselor to discuss grievances and performance. The NSW

---

[2] Examples of nonexperimental program evaluations are Orley Ashenfelter (1978), Ashenfelter and David Card (1985), Laurie Bassi (1983a,b; 1984), Thomas Cooley, Thomas McGuire, and Edward Prescott (1979), Katherine Dickinson, Terry Johnson, and Richard West (1984), Nicholas Kiefer (1979a,b), and Charles Mallar (1978).

[3] Findings from the NSW are summarized in several reports and publications. For a quick summary of the program design and results, see Manpower Demonstration Research Corporation (1983). For more detailed discussions see Dickinson and Rebecca Maynard (1981); Peter Kemper, David Long, and Craig Thornton (1981); Stanley Masters and Maynard (1981); Maynard (1980); and Irving Piliavin and Rosemary Gartner (1981).

[4] The experimental sample included 6,616 treatment and control group members from Atlanta, Chicago, Hartford, Jersey City, Newark, New York, Oakland, Philadelphia, San Francisco, and Wisconsin. Qualified AFDC applicants were women who (i) had to be currently unemployed, (ii) had spent no more than 3 months in a job in the previous 6 months, (iii) had no children less than six years old, and (iv) had received AFDC payments for 30 of the previous 36 months. The admission requirements for the other participants differed slightly from those of the AFDC applicants. For a more detailed discussion of these prerequisites, see MDRC (1983).

program paid the treatment group members for their work. The wage schedule offered the trainees lower wage rates than they would have received on a regular job, but allowed their earnings to increase for satisfactory performance and attendance. The trainees could stay on their supported work jobs until their terms in the program expired and they were forced to find regular employment.

Although these general guidelines were followed at each site, the agencies that operated the experiment at the local level provided the treatment group members with different work experiences. The type of work even varied within sites. For example, some of the trainees in Hartford worked at a gas station, while others worked at a printing shop.[5] In particular, male and female participants frequently performed different sorts of work. The female participants usually worked in service occupations, whereas the male participants tended to work in construction occupations. Consequently, the program costs varied across the sites and target groups. The program cost $9,100 per AFDC participant and approximately $6,800 for the other target groups' trainees.[6]

The MDRC collected earnings and demographic data from both the treatment and the control group members at the baseline (when MDRC randomly assigned the participants) and every nine months thereafter, conducting up to four post-baseline interviews. Many participants failed to complete these interviews, and this sample attrition potentially biases the experimental results. Fortunately the largest source of attrition does not affect the integrity of the experimental design. Largely due to limited resources, the NSW administrators scheduled a 27th-month interview for only 65 percent of the participants and a 36th-month interview for only 24 percent of the non-AFDC participants. None of the AFDC participants were scheduled for a 36th-month interview, but the AFDC re-survey during the fall of 1979 interviewed 75 percent of these women anywhere from 27 to 44 months after the baseline. Since the trainee and control group members were randomly scheduled for all of these interviews, this source of attrition did not bias the experimental evaluation of the NSW program.

Naturally, the program administrators did not locate all of the participants scheduled for these interviews. The proportion of participants who failed to complete scheduled interviews varied across experimental group, time, and target group. While the response rates were statistically significantly higher for the treatment as opposed to the control group members, the differences in response rates were usually only a few percentage

---

[5] Kemper and Long present a list of NSW projects and customers (1981, Table IV.4, pp. 65–66). The trainees produced goods and services for organizations in the public (42 percent of program hours), nonprofit (29 percent of program hours), and private sectors.

[6] The cost per training participant is the sum of program input costs, site overhead costs, central administrative costs, and child care costs minus the value of the program's output. These costs are in 1982 dollars. If the trainees' subsidized wages and fringe benefits are viewed as a transfer instead of a cost, the program costs per participant are $3,100 for the AFDC trainees and $2,700 for the other trainees. For a more detailed discussion of program costs and benefits, see Kemper, Long, and Thornton.

TABLE 1

THE SAMPLE MEANS AND STANDARD DEVIATIONS OF PRE-TRAINING EARNINGS AND
OTHER CHARACTERISTICS FOR THE NSW AFDC AND MALE PARTICIPANTS

| Variable | Full National Supported Work Sample | | | |
| | AFDC Participants | | Male Participants | |
	Treatments	Controls	Treatments	Controls
Age	33.37	33.63	24.49	23.99
	(7.43)	(7.18)	(6.58)	(6.54)
Years of School	10.30	10.27	10.17	10.17
	(1.92)	(2.00)	(1.75)	(1.76)
Proportion High School Dropouts	.70	.69	.79	.80
	(.46)	(.46)	(.41)	(.40)
Proportion Married	.02	.04	.14	.13
	(.15)	(.20)	(.35)	(.35)
Proportion Black	.84	.82	.76	.75
	(.37)	(.39)	(.43)	(.43)
Proportion Hispanic	.12	.13	.12	.14
	(.32)	(.33)	(.33)	(.35)
Real Earnings	$393	$395	$1,472	$1,558
1 year Before	(1,203)	(1,149)	(2,656)	(2,961)
Training	[43]	[41]	[58]	[63]
Real Earnings	$854	$894	$2,860	$3,030
2 years Before	(2,087)	(2,240)	(4,729)	(5,293)
Training	[74]	[79]	[104]	[113]
Hours Worked	90	92	278	274
1 year Before	(251)	(253)	(466)	(458)
Training	[9]	[9]	[10]	[10]
Hours Worked	186	188	458	469
2 years Before	(434)	(450)	(654)	(689)
Training	[15]	[16]	[14]	[15]
Month of Assignment	−12.26	−12.30	−16.08	−15.91
(Jan. 78–0)	(4.30)	(4.23)	(5.97)	(5.89)
Number of Observations	800	802	2,083	2,193

Note: The numbers shown in parentheses are the standard deviations and those in the square brackets are the standard errors.

points. For the 27th-month interview, 72 percent of the treatments and 68 percent of the control group members completed interviews. The differences in response rates were larger across time and target group. For example, 79 percent of the scheduled participants completed the 9th-month interview, while 70 percent completed the 27th-month interview. The AFDC participants responded at consistently higher rates than the other target groups; 89 percent of the AFDC participants completed the 9th-month interview as opposed to 76 percent of the other participants. While these response rates indicate that the experimental results may be biased, especially for the non-AFDC participants, comparisons between the baseline characteristics of participants who did and did not complete a 27th-month interview suggests that whatever bias exists may be small.[7]

Table 1 presents some sample statistics describing the baseline characteristics of the AFDC treatment and control groups as well as those of the male NSW participants in the other three target groups.[8] As would be expected from random assignment, the means of the characteristics and pretraining hours and earnings of the experimental groups are nearly the same. For example, the mean earnings of the AFDC treatments and the AFDC controls in the year before training differ by $2, the mean age of the two groups differ by 3 months, and the mean years of schooling are identical. None of the differences between the treatment's and control's characteristics, hours, and earnings are statistically significant.

The first two columns of Tables 2 and 3 present the annual earnings of the treatment and control group members.[9] The earnings of the experimental groups were the same in the pre-training year 1975, diverged during the employment program, and converged to some extent after the program ended. The post-training year was 1979 for the AFDC females and 1978 for the males.[10]

---

[7] This study evaluates the AFDC females separately from the non-AFDC males. This distinction is common in the literature, but it is also motivated by the differences between the response rates for the two groups. The Supported Work Evaluation Study (Public Use Files User's Guide, Documentation Series No. 1, pp. 18–27) presents a more detailed discussion of sample attrition. My working paper (1984, tables 1.1 and 2.3), compares the characteristics and employment history of the full NSW sample to the sample with pre- and postprogram earnings data. Randall Brown (1979) reports that there is no evidence that the response rates affect the experimental estimates for the AFDC women or ex-addicts, while the evidence for the ex-offenders and high school dropouts is less conclusive.

[8] The female participants from the non-AFDC target groups were not surveyed during the AFDC resurvey in the fall of 1979 and consequently do not report 1979 earnings and are not included with the AFDC sample. Excluding these women from the analysis does not affect the integrity of the experimental design.

[9] All earnings presented in this paper are in 1982 dollars. The NSW Public Use Files report earnings in experimental time, months from the baseline, and not calendar time. However, my working paper describes how to convert the experimental earnings data to the annual data reported in Tables 2 and 3.

[10] The number of NSW male treatment group members with complete pre- and postprogram earnings is much smaller than the full sample of treatments or the partial sample of control group members. This difference is largely explained by the two forms of sample attrition discussed earlier. In addition, however, (i) this paper excludes all males who were in Supported Work in January 1978, or entered the program before January 1976; (ii) in one of the sites, the administrators randomly assigned .4 instead of one-half of the qualified high school dropouts into the treatment group.

TABLE 2

ANNUAL EARNINGS OF NSW TREATMENTS, CONTROLS, AND EIGHT CANDIDATE COMPARISON GROUPS FROM THE *PSID* AND THE *CPS-SSA*

Year	Treatments	Controls	Comparison Group[a,b]							
			PSID-1	PSID-2	PSID-3	PSID-4	CPS-SSA-1	CPS-SSA-2	CPS-SSA-3	CPS-SSA-4
1975	$895	$877	$7,303	$2,327	$937	$6,654	$7,788	$3,748	$4,575	$2,049
	(81)	(90)	(317)	(286)	(189)	(428)	(63)	(250)	(135)	(333)
1976	1,794	646	7,442	2,697	665	6,770	8,547	4,774	3,800	2,036
	(99)	(63)	(327)	(317)	(157)	(463)	(65)	(302)	(128)	(337)
1977	6,143	1,518	7,983	3,219	891	7,213	8,562	4,851	5,277	2,844
	(140)	(112)	(335)	(376)	(229)	(484)	(68)	(317)	(153)	(450)
1978	4,526	2,885	8,146	3,636	1,631	7,564	8,518	5,343	5,665	3,700
	(270)	(244)	(339)	(421)	(381)	(480)	(72)	(365)	(166)	(593)
1979	4,670	3,819	8,016	3,569	1,602	7,482	8,023	5,343	5,782	3,733
	(226)	(208)	(334)	(381)	(334)	(462)	(73)	(371)	(170)	(543)
Number of Observations	600	585	595	173	118	255	11,132	241	1,594	87

[a] The Comparison Groups are defined as follows: *PSID*-1: All females who were household heads continuously from 1975 through 1979, who were between 20 and 55-years-old and did not classify themselves as retired in 1975; *PSID*-2: Selects from the *PSID*-1 group all women who received AFDC in 1975; *PSID*-3: Selects from the *PSID*-2 all women who were not working when surveyed in 1976; *PSID*-4: Selects from the *PSID*-1 group all women with children, none of whom are less than 5-years-old; *CPS-SSA*-1: All females from Westat *CPS-SSA* sample; *CPS-SSA*-2: Selects from *CPS-SSA*-1 all females who received AFDC in 1975; *CPS-SSA*-3: Selects from *CPS-SSA*-1 all females who were not working in the spring of 1976; *CPS-SSA*-4: Selects from *CPS-SSA*-2 all females who were not working in the spring of 1976.

[b] All earnings are expressed in 1982 dollars. The numbers in parentheses are the standard errors. For the NSW treatments and controls, the number of observations refer only to 1975 and 1979. In the other years there are fewer observations, especially in 1978. At the time of the resurvey in 1979, treatments had been out of Supported Work for an average of 20 months.

TABLE 3

ANNUAL EARNINGS OF NSW MALE TREATMENTS, CONTROLS, AND SIX CANDIDATE
COMPARISON GROUPS FROM THE *PSID* AND *CPS-SSA*

| Year | Treatments | Controls | Comparison Group[a,b] | | | | | |
			PSID-1	*PSID*-2	*PSID*-3	*CPS-SSA*-1	*CPS-SSA*-2	*CPS-SSA*-3
1975	$3,066	$3,027	$19,056[a]	$7,569	$2,611	$13,650	$7,387	$2,729
	(283)	(252)	(272)	(568)	(492)	(73)	(206)	(197)
1976	4,035	2,121	20,267	6,152	3,191	14,579	6,390	3,863
	(215)	(163)	(296)	(601)	(609)	(75)	(187)	(267)
1977	6,335	3,403	20,898	7,985	3,981	15,046	9,305	6,399
	(376)	(228)	(296)	(621)	(594)	(76)	(225)	(398)
1978	5,976	5,090	21,542	9,996	5,279	14,846	10,071	7,277
	(402)	(227)	(311)	(703)	(686)	(76)	(241)	(431)
Number of Observations	297	425	2,493	253	128	15,992	1,283	305

[a] The Comparison Groups are defined as follows: *PSID*-1: All males who were household heads continuously from 1975 through 1978, who were less than 55-years-old and did not classify themselves as retired in 1975; *PSID*-2: Selects from the *PSID*-1 group all men who were not working when surveyed in the spring of 1976; *PSID*-3: selects from the *PSID*-1 group all men who were not working when surveyed in either spring of 1975 or 1976; *CPS-SSA*-1: All males based on Westat's criteria, except those over 55-years-old; *CPS-SSA*-2: Selects from *CPS-SSA*-1 all males who were not working when surveyed in March 1976; *CPS-SSA*-3: Selects from the *CPS-SSA*-1 unemployed males in 1976 whose income in 1975 was below the poverty level.
[b] All earnings are expressed in 1982 dollars. The numbers in parentheses are the standard errors. The number of observations refer only to 1975 and 1978. In the other years there are fewer observations. The sample of treatments is smaller than the sample of controls because treatments still in Supported Work as of January 1978 are excluded from the sample, and in the young high school target group there were by design more controls than treatments.

Columns 2 and 3 in the first row of Tables 4 and 5 show that both the unadjusted and regression-adjusted pre-training earnings of the two sets of treatment and control group members are essentially identical. Therefore, because of the NSW program's experimental design, the difference between the post-training earnings of the experimental groups is an unbiased estimator of the training effect, and the other estimators described in columns 5–10(11) are unbiased estimators as well. The estimates in column 4 indicate that the earnings of the AFDC females were $851 higher than they would have been without the NSW program, while the earnings of the male participants were $886 higher.[11] Moreover, the other columns show that the econometric procedure does not affect these estimates.

---

[11] *It is commonly believed that the NSW program had little impact on the earnings of the male participants (see MDRC; A. P. Bernstein et al., 1985). My working paper discusses why this estimated impact differs from the results discussed elsewhere. The 1978 earnings data were largely collected during the 36th-month interview, where the difference between the male treatment and control group members' earnings averaged $175 per quarter.*

TABLE 4

EARNINGS COMPARISONS AND ESTIMATED TRAINING EFFECTS FOR THE NSW AFDC PARTICIPANTS USING COMPARISON GROUPS FROM THE *PSID* AND THE *CPS-SSA*[a,b]

| Name of Comparison Group[d] | Comparison Group Earnings Growth 1975–79 (1) | NSW Treatment Earnings Less Comparison Group Earnings | | | | Difference in Differences: Difference in Earnings Growth 1975–79 Treatments Less Comparisons | | Unrestricted Difference in Differences: Quasi Difference in Earnings Growth 1975–79 | | Controlling for All Observed Variables and Pre-Training Earnings | |
| | | Pre-Training Year, 1975 | | Post-Training Year, 1979 | | | | | | | |
		Unadjusted (2)	Adjusted[c] (3)	Unadjusted (4)	Adjusted[c] (5)	Without Age (6)	With Age (7)	Unadjusted (8)	Adjusted[c] (9)	Without AFDC (10)	With AFDC (11)
Controls	$2,942	$−17	$−22	$851	$861	$833	$883	$843	$864	$854	—
	(220)	(122)	(122)	(307)	(306)	(323)	(323)	(308)	(306)	(312)	
PSID-1	713	−6,443	−4,882	−3,357	−2,143	3,097	2,657	1,746	1,354	1,664	$2,097
	(210)	(326)	(336)	(403)	(425)	(317)	(333)	(357)	(380)	(409)	(491)
PSID-2	1,242	−1,467	−1,515	1,090	870	2,568	2,392	1,764	1,535	1,826	—
	(314)	(216)	(224)	(468)	(484)	(473)	(481)	(472)	(487)	(537)	
PSID-3	665	−77	−100	3,057	2,915	3,145	3,020	3,070	2,930	2,919	—
	(351)	(202)	(208)	(532)	(543)	(557)	(563)	(531)	(543)	(592)	
PSID-4	928	−5,694	−4,976	−2,822	−2,268	2,883	2,655	1,184	950	1,406	2,146
	(311)	(306)	(323)	(460)	(491)	(417)	(434)	(483)	(503)	(542)	(652)
CPS-SSA-1	233	−6,928	−5,813	−3,363	−2,650	3,578	3,501	1,214	1,127	536	1,041
	(64)	(272)	(309)	(320)	(365)	(280)	(282)	(272)	(309)	(349)	(503)
CPS-SSA-2	1,595	−2,888	−2,332	−683	−240	2,215	2,068	447	620	665	—
	(360)	(204)	(256)	(428)	(536)	(438)	(446)	(468)	(554)	(651)	
CPS-SSA-3	1,207	−3,715	−3,150	−1,122	−812	2,603	2,615	814	784	−99	1,246
	(166)	(226)	(325)	(311)	(452)	(307)	(328)	(305)	(429)	(481)	(720)
CPS-SSA-4	1,684	−1,189	−780	926	756	2,126	1,833	1,222	952	827	—
	(524)	(249)	(283)	(630)	(716)	(654)	(663)	(637)	(717)	(814)	

[a] The columns above present the estimated training effect for each econometric model and comparison group. The dependent variable is earnings in 1979. Based on the experimental data, an unbiased estimate of the impact of training presented in col. 4 is $851. The first three columns present the difference between each comparison group's 1975 and 1979 earnings and the difference between the pre-training earnings of each comparison group and the NSW treatments.

[b] Estimates are in 1982 dollars. The numbers in parentheses are the standard errors.

[c] The exogenous variables used in the regression adjusted equations are age, age squared, years of schooling, high school dropout status, and race.

[d] See Table 2 for definitions of the comparison groups.

EARNINGS COMPARISONS AND ESTIMATED TRAINING EFFECTS FOR THE NSW MALE PARTICIPANTS USING COMPARISON GROUPS FROM THE *PSID* AND THE *CPS-SSA*[a,b]

| Name of Comparison Group[d] | Comparison Group Earnings Growth 1975–78 (1) | NSW Treatment Earnings Less Comparison Group Earnings | | | | Difference in Differences: Difference in Earnings Growth 1975–78 Treatments Less Comparisons | | Unrestricted Difference in Differences: Quasi Difference in Earnings Growth 1975–78 | | Controlling for All Observed Variables and Pre-Training Earnings (10) |
| | | Pre-Training Year, 1975 | | Post-Training Year, 1978 | | | | | | |
		Unadjusted (2)	Adjusted[c] (3)	Unadjusted (4)	Adjusted[c] (5)	Without Age (6)	With Age (7)	Unadjusted (8)	Adjusted[c] (9)	
Controls	$2,063	$39	–$21	$886	$798	$847	$856	$897	$802	$662
	(325)	(383)	(378)	(476)	(472)	(560)	(558)	(467)	(467)	(506)
PSID-1	2,043	–15,997	–7,624	–15,578	–8,067	425	–749	–2,380	–2,119	–1,228
	(237)	(795)	(851)	(913)	(990)	(650)	(692)	(680)	(746)	(896)
PSID-2	6,071	–4,503	–3,669	–4,020	–3,482	484	–650	–1,364	–1,694	–792
	(637)	(608)	(757)	(781)	(935)	(733)	(850)	(729)	(878)	(1024)
PSID-3	3,322	455	455	697	–509	242	–1,325	629	–552	397
	(780)	(539)	(704)	(760)	(967)	(884)	(1078)	(757)	(967)	(1103)
CPS-SSA-1	1,196	–10,585	–4,654	–8,870	–4,416	1,714	195	–1,543	–1,102	–805
	(61)	(539)	(509)	(562)	(557)	(452)	(441)	(426)	(450)	(484)
CPS-SSA-2	2,684	–4,321	–1,824	–4,095	–1,675	226	–488	–1,850	–782	–319
	(229)	(450)	(535)	(537)	(672)	(539)	(530)	(497)	(621)	(761)
CPS-SSA-3	4,548	337	878	–1,300	224	–1,637	–1,388	–1,396	17	1,466
	(409)	(343)	(447)	(590)	(766)	(631)	(555)	(582)	(761)	(984)

[a] The columns above present the estimated training effect for each econometric model and comparison group. The dependent variable is earnings in 1978. Based on the experimental data an unbiased estimate of the impact of training presented in col. 4 is $886. The first three columns present the difference between each comparison group's 1975 and 1978 earnings, and the difference between the pre-training earnings of each comparison group and the NSW treatments.
[b] Estimates are in 1982 dollars. The numbers in parentheses are the standard errors.
[c] The exogenous variables used in the regression adjusted equations are age, age squared, years of schooling, high school dropout status, and race.
[d] See Table 3 for definitions of the comparison groups.

II. NONEXPERIMENTAL ESTIMATES

In addition to providing researchers with a simple estimate of the impact of an employment program, MDRC's experimental data can also be used to evaluate several nonexperimental methods of program evaluation. This section puts aside the NSW control group and evaluates the NSW program using some of the econometric procedures found in studies of the employment and training programs administered under the MDTA, CETA, and JTPA.[12]

The researchers who evaluated these federally sponsored programs devised both experimental and nonexperimental procedures to estimate the training effect, because they recognized that the difference between the trainees' pre- and post-training earnings was a poor estimate of the training effect. In dynamic economy, the trainees' earnings may grow even without an effective program. The goal of these program evaluations is to estimate the earnings of the trainees had they not participated in the program. Researchers using experimental data take the earnings of the control group members to be an estimate of the trainees' earnings without the program. Without experimental data, researchers estimate the earnings of the trainees by using the regression-adjusted earnings of a comparison group drawn from the population. This adjustment takes into account that the observable characteristics of the trainees and the comparison group members differ, and their unobservable characteristics may differ as well.

Any nonexperimental evaluation of a training program must explicitly account for these differences in a model describing the observable determinants of earnings and the process by which the trainees are selected into the program. However, unlike in an experimental evaluation, the nonexperimental estimates of the training effect depend crucially on the way that the earnings and participation equations are specified. If the econometric model is specified correctly, the nonexperimental estimates should be the same (within sampling error) as the training effect generated from the experimental data, but if there is a significant difference between the nonexperimental and the experimental estimates, the econometric model is misspecified.[13]

The first step in a nonexperimental evaluation is to select a comparison group whose earnings can be compared to the earnings of the trainees. Tables 2 and 3 present the mean annual earnings of female and male comparison groups drawn from the *Panel Study of Income Dynamics (PSID)* and Westat's Matched *Current Population Survey—Social Security Administration File (CPS-SSA)*. These groups are characteristic of two types of comparison groups frequently used in the program evaluation literature. The *PSID*-1 and the

---

[12] *These acronyms refer to the Manpower Development and Training Act–1962, the Comprehensive Employment and Training Act–1973, and the Job Training Partnership Act–1982.*

[13] *Thomas Fraker, Maynard, and Lyle Nelson (1984) describe a similar study using the NSW AFDC and Young High School Dropouts. Instead of focusing the study on models of earnings and program participation, their study evaluates several strategies for choosing matched comparison groups. They use grouped Social Security earnings data when comparing the annual earnings of the NSW treatments to the earnings of each of the comparison groups.*

CPS-SSA-1 groups are large, stratified random samples from populations of household heads and households, respectively.[14] The other, smaller, comparison groups are composed of individuals whose characteristics are consistent with some of the eligibility criteria used to admit applicants into the NSW program. For example, the *PSID*-3 and *CPS-SSA*-4 comparison groups in Table 2 include females from the *PSID* and the *CPS-SSA* who received AFDC payments in 1975, and were not employed in the spring of 1976. Tables 2 and 3 show that the NSW trainees and controls have earnings histories that are more similar to those of the smaller comparison groups, whose characteristics are similar to theirs, than those of the larger comparison groups.[15]

The second step in a nonexperimental evaluation is to specify a model of earnings and program participation to adjust for differences between the trainees and comparison group members. Equations (1) through (4) describe a conventional model of earnings and program participation that is typical of the kind econometric researchers use for this problem:

$$(1) \qquad y_{it} = \delta D_i + \alpha X_{it} + b_i + n_t + \epsilon_{it}$$

$$(2) \qquad \epsilon_{it} - \rho \epsilon_{it-1} = \nu_{it}$$

$$(3) \qquad d_{is} = y_{is} + \gamma Z_{is} + \eta_{is}$$

$$(4) \qquad D_i = 1 \quad \text{if } d_{is} > 0; \qquad D_i = 0 \quad \text{if } d_{is} < 0.$$

In equation (1), earnings in each period are a function of a vector of individual characteristics, X_{it}, such as age, schooling, and race for individual i in time t; a dummy variable indicating whether the individual participated in training in period $s + 1$, D_i; and an error

---

[14] *The PSID file including the poverty subsample selects only women and men who were household heads continuously from 1975 to 1979, and 1978, respectively. The CPS-SSA file matches the March 1976 Current Population Survey with Social Security earnings. Only individuals in the labor force in March 1976 with nominal income less than $20,000 and household income less than $30,000 are in this sample. In 1976, 2 percent of the females and 21 percent of the males had earnings at the Social Security maximum. In this paper, females younger than 20 or older than 55 and males older than 55 are excluded from the comparison groups.*

[15] *Not only are the pre-training earnings of the PSID-3 comparison group in Table 2 similar to the earnings of the NSW experimental groups, but the characteristics of these groups are similar as well. The mean age for the PSID-3 women is 40.95; the mean years of schooling is 10.31; the proportion of high school dropouts is 0.63; the proportion married is 0.01; the proportion black is 0.85; and the proportion Hispanic is 0.03. I experimented with matching the comparison groups even more closely to the pre-training characteristics of the experimental sample. However, these closely matched comparison groups are extremely small. For example there were 57 women from the PSID who received welfare payments in 1975, were not employed at the time of the survey in 1976, resided in a metropolitan area, and had only school-age children. The mean earnings of this group were $1,137 in 1975; $673 in 1976; $743 in 1977; $1,222 in 1978; and $1,697 in 1979.*

with individual- and time-specific components and a serially correlated transitory disturbance. The transitory disturbance follows the first-order serial correlation process described in equation (2). Equations (3) and (4) specify the participation decision: an individual participates in training and is admitted into the program in period $s + 1$ if the latent variable d_{is} rises above zero. The participation equation is typically rationalized by the notion that the supply of individuals who decide to participate in training depends on the net benefit they expect to receive from participation and on the demand of the program administrators for training participants. The participation latent variable is typically a function of a vector of characteristics Z_{is}, current earnings y_{is}, and an error.

The estimators described in the column headings in Tables 4 and 5 (as well as many others in the literature) are based on econometric specifications that place different restrictions on the training model represented by equations (1)–(4) (although one common restriction assumes that the unobservables in the earnings and participation equations are uncorrelated). These estimates are consistent only insofar as their restrictions are consistent with the data. The restrictions can be tested provided the nonexperimental data base has sufficient information on the pre-training earnings and demographic characteristics of the trainees and comparison group members. An econometrician is unlikely to take seriously an estimate based on a model that failed one of these specification tests. Therefore, the results of such tests can often aid the researcher in choosing among alternative estimates. It follows, then, that simply checking whether the nonexperimental estimates replicate the experimental results and whether these estimates vary across different econometric procedures is not the only motivation for comparing experimental to nonexperimental methods. By making this comparison, we can also discover whether the nonexperimental data alone reliably indicate when an econometric model is misspecified and whether specification tests, which are supposed to ensure that the econometric model is consistent with the data, lead researchers to choose the "right" estimator.

In practice, the available data affect the composition of the comparison groups and the flexibility of the econometric specifications. For example, since there is only one year of pre-training earnings data, we cannot evaluate all of the econometric procedures that have been used in the literature, nor can we test all of the econometric specifications analyzed in this paper with the nonexperimental data alone.[16]

Nevertheless, several one-step estimators are evaluated in Tables 4 and 5, starting with the simple difference between the treatment and comparison group members' post-training

---

[16] *One limitation of the NSW Public Use File is that there is only one year of pre-experimental data available in calendar time as opposed to experimental time. Consequently, there are several nonexperimental procedures which require more than a year of pre-training earnings data that are not evaluated in this paper. If additional data were available, it is possible that these procedures would adequately control for differences between the NSW treatments and comparison group members and that the results of the specification tests would correctly guide an econometrician away from some of the estimates presented in this paper to the estimates based on these other procedures. See John Abowd (1983), Ashenfelter, Ashenfelter and Card, Bassi (1983b; 1984); and James Heckman and Richard Robb (1985).*

earnings in column 4. Column 5 presents this earnings difference controlling for age, schooling, and race. This cross-sectional estimator is based on a model where these demographic variables are assumed to adequately control for differences between the earnings of the trainees and comparison group members. Column 6 presents the difference between the two nonexperimental groups' pre- and post-training earnings growth. This estimator allows for an unobserved individual fixed effect in the earnings equation and for the possibility that individuals with low values of this unobservable are more likely to participate in training. The cross-sectional estimator described in column 5 is now biased since the training dummy variable is correlated with the error in the earnings equation. Differencing the earnings equation removes the fixed effect, leaving[17]

$$(5) \qquad y_{it} - y_{is} = \delta D_i + \beta \cdot AGE_i + (\eta_i - \eta_s) + \epsilon_{is} - \epsilon_{is}.$$

The comparison group's earnings growth represents the earnings growth that the trainees would have experienced without the program. However, since the trainees may experience larger earnings growth than the comparison group members simply because they are usually younger, column 7 presents the difference between the earnings growth of the two groups controlling for age.

Column 8 presents the difference between the post-training earnings of the treatment and comparison group members, holding constant the level of pre-training earnings, while the estimator in column 9 controls both for pre-training earnings and the demographic variables. These estimators are consistent when the model of program participation stipulates that the trainees' pre-program earnings fell (see Table 1) because some of the training participants experienced some bad luck in the years prior to training. In this case, we would expect the trainees' earnings to grow even without the program.[18] The difference in differences estimator in columns 6 and 7 is now biased, since the training dummy variable is correlated with the transitory component of pre-training earnings in equation (5).[19] Finally, columns 10 and 11 report the estimates of the training effects controlling for all observed variables. Besides the variables described earlier, the additional regressors are employment status in 1976, AFDC status in 1975, marital status, residency in a metropolitan area with more than 100,000 persons, and number of children.

---

[17] *The other demographic variables, schooling and race, are constant over time.*

[18] *Researchers have observed this dip in pre-training earnings for successive MDTA and CETA cohorts since 1964. See Ashenfelter (Table 1); Ashenfelter and Card (Table 1); Bassi (1983a, Table 4.1); and Kiefer (1979a, Table 4-1).*

[19] *This estimator is similar to one devised by Arthur Goldberger (1972) (or see G. S. Maddala, 1983) to evaluate the Head Start Program where participation in the program depended on a child's test score plus a random error. Similarly, participation in a training program can be thought of as a function of pre-training earnings and a random error. My working paper shows that this estimator is consistent as long as the unobservables in the earnings and participation equations are uncorrelated, and all of the observable variables in the model are used as regressors in the earnings equation.*

Unlike the experimental estimates, the nonexperimental estimates are sensitive both to the composition of the comparison group and to the econometric procedure. For example, many of the estimates in column 9 of Table 4 replicate the experimental results, while other estimates are more than $1,000 larger than the experimental results. More specifically, the results for the female participants (Table 4) tend to be positive and larger than the experimental estimate, while for the male participants (Table 5), the estimates tend to be negative and smaller than the experimental impact.[20] Additionally, the nonexperimental procedures replicate the experimental results more closely when the nonexperimental data include pre-training earnings rather than cross-sectional data alone or when evaluating female rather than male participants.

The sensitivity of the nonexperimental estimates to different specifications of the econometric model is not in itself a cause for alarm. After all, few econometricians expect estimators based on misspecified models to replicate the results of experiments. Hence the considerable range of estimates is understandable given that inconsistent estimators are likely to yield inaccurate estimates. Before taking some of these estimates too seriously, many econometricians at a minimum would require that their estimators be based on econometric models that are consistent with the pre-training earnings data. Thus, if the regression-adjusted difference between the post-training earnings of the two groups is going to be a consistent estimator of the training effect, the regression-adjusted pre-training earnings of the two groups should be the same.

Based on this specification test, econometricians might reject the nonexperimental estimates in columns 4–7 of Table 4 in favor of the ones in columns 8–11. Few econometricians would report the training effect of $870 in column 5, even though this estimate differs from the experimental result by only $19. If the cross-sectional estimator properly controlled for differences between the trainees and comparison group members, we would not expect the difference between the regression adjusted pre-training earnings of the two groups to be $1,550, as reported in column 3. Likewise, econometricians might refrain from reporting the difference in differences estimates in columns 6 and 7, even though all these estimates are within two standard errors of $3,000. As noted earlier, this estimator is not consistent with the decline in the trainees' pre-training earnings.

This point can also be made with the estimates for the NSW male participants (Table 5). For example, all but one of the difference in differences estimates in column 6 are within one standard error of the experimental estimate. Yet for two reasons it is unlikely econometricians would report these estimates. First, as the results in column 7 suggest, since the trainees are younger their earnings might be expected to grow faster than the earnings of the comparison group members even without training. Second, as shown in

---

[20] *The magnitude of these training effects is similar to the estimates reported in studies of the 1964 MDTA cohort, the 1969–70 MDTA cohort, and the 1976–77 CETA cohort. (See my working paper, Table I.1.)*

Table 1, the pre-training earnings of the male participants fell in the period before training, suggesting that the trainees' earnings will grow even if the program is ineffective. Here again, econometricians might turn to the considerable range of estimates in columns 8–10.

The results of these specification tests suggest that an econometrician might report one of the estimates in columns 8–11. However, even without the experimental data, a researcher would find that the estimated training effect is still sensitive to the set of variables included in the earnings equation and to the composition of the comparison group. In Table 4, the estimates using the female household heads with school-age children (*PSID*-4) as a comparison group differ by more than $1,000. The largest estimate overstates the experimental result by $1,300, while the smallest estimate is within $100 of the experimental estimate. Likewise in column 11, we find that the same estimator with different comparison groups yields a set of estimates that vary by more than $1,000. The estimates for the male participants exhibit the same sensitivity to the choice of a comparison group and to the set of variables used as regressors in the earnings equation. However, the estimated standard errors associated with these training effects are larger than for the female estimates, making it more difficult to draw many conclusions from these results.

Without additional data it is difficult to see how a researcher would choose a training effect from among estimates. Moreover, the nonexperimental data base alone does not allow the econometrician to test whether these estimates are based on econometric models that adequately control for differences between the earnings of the trainees and comparison group members. In this case, comparisons between the experimental and nonexperimental estimates is the best specification test available.[21]

Specification tests that use pre-training earnings data are an appealing means to choose between alternative estimates, but these tests are not themselves always sufficient to identify unreliable estimators. This point becomes clear when we compare the estimates using the *PSID*-3 comparison group (as defined in Table 2) and those using the NSW control group. The characteristics of these two groups are nearly the same, as are their unadjusted and adjusted pre-training earnings. In each case the cross-sectional estimator in column 5 appears to be an unbiased estimate of the training effect. Moreover, both sets of estimates are unaffected by alternative econometric procedures. Thus both the experimental and nonexperimental estimates pass the same specification tests; nevertheless the nonexperimental estimate is approximately $2,100 larger than the experimental result. If a researcher did not know that one set of estimates was based on an experimental data set, it is hard to see how she or he would choose between two estimates where one training effect is roughly 3.5 times larger than the other.

---

[21] *Ashenfelter, Ashenfelter and Card, and Bassi (1984) have noted in their studies using nonexperimental data that their results are sensitive to alternative econometric specifications and that there is evidence for male training participants that the econometric models are misspecified.*

III. TWO-STEP ESTIMATES

The unobservables in the earnings equation were uncorrelated with those in the participation equation in all of the econometric models analyzed in the previous section. If, instead, the unobservables are correlated, none of the one-step least squares procedures are consistent estimators of the training effect. Individuals with high unobservables in their participation equation are more likely to participate in training. Yet if the unobservables in the earnings and participation equations are negatively correlated, these individuals are likely to have relatively low earnings, even after controlling for the observable variables in the model. Consequently, least squares underestimates the impact of training.

James Heckman (1978) proposes a two-step estimator that controls for the correlation between the unobservables by using the estimated conditional expectation of the earnings error as a regressor in the earnings equation. If the errors in the earnings and participation equations are jointly normally distributed, this conditional expectation is proportional to the conditional expectation of the error in the participation equation. Using the notation introduced in the last section, this relationship is expressed formally as

$$(6) \qquad E\left(b_i + \epsilon_{it} \mid Z_i, D_i\right) = \rho\sigma_\epsilon\left[D_i \frac{\phi(\gamma Z_i)}{1 - \Phi(\gamma Z_i)} - \left(1 - D_i\right)\frac{\phi(\gamma Z_i)}{\Phi(\gamma Z_i)}\right] = rH_i,$$

where Z_i is a vector of observed variables, ρ is the correlation between the unobservables in the model, σ_ϵ^2 is the variance of the unobservables in the earnings equation, and $\phi(\cdot)$ and $\Phi(\cdot)$ are the normal density and distribution functions. Therefore the earnings equation can be rewritten as

$$(7) \qquad Y_{it} = \delta D_i + \beta X_{it} + rH_i + \nu_i^*,$$

where ν_i^* is the orthogonal error by construction. To estimate the training effect, δ, the researcher first uses the coefficients from a probit estimate of the reduced-from participation equation to calculate the conditional expectation, H_i, for both the trainees and comparison group members,[22] and, second, uses this estimate, $\hat{H}_i$, as a regressor in the earnings equation. The training effect is then estimated by least squares.[23]

---

[22] *This is a choice-based sampling problem, since the probability of being in the nonexperimental data set is high for the NSW treatment group members and low for the comparison group members. The estimated probability of participation depends not only on the observed variables but on the numbers of trainees and comparison group members. Heckman and Richard Robb (1985) show that this procedure is robust to choice-based sampling. For an example of an application of this estimator in the evaluation literature, see Mallar.*

[23] *Since the estimated value of this conditional expectation is used as a regressor instead of the true value, the estimated standard errors associated with the least squares estimates are inconsistent and must be corrected. See Heckman (1978; 1979); William Greene (1981); John Ham (1982); and Ham and Cheng Hsiao (1984).*

Table 6 presents estimates for the female and male training participants using the NSW controls, the *PSID*-1 and *CPS-SSA*-1 as comparison groups.[24] Unless some variables are excluded from the earnings equation, the training effect in this procedure is identified by the nonlinearity of the probit function. Hence, the rows of Table 6 allow us to evaluate the sensitivity of these estimates to different exclusion restrictions. The second column associated with each set of training effects presents the estimated participation coefficient. If the unobservables are uncorrelated, this estimate should not be significantly different from zero. Therefore, these estimates allow us to test whether this restriction on the correlation between the unobservables is consistent with the nonexperimental data, and to examine whether this specification test leads econometricians to choose the "right" estimator.

The experimental estimates in Table 6 are consistent with MDRC's experimental design. All of these estimates are nearly identical to the experimental results presented in Tables 4 and 5. And furthermore, since the unobservables are uncorrelated by design, the estimated participation coefficients are never significantly different from zero.

Turning to the nonexperimental estimates we find that although the instruments used to identify the earnings equation have some effect on the results, generally these estimates are closer to the experimental estimates than are the one-step estimates (in column 11 of Tables 4 and 5). For the females, the difference between the two-step and one-step estimates are small relative to the estimated standard errors, and the estimates of the participation coefficient are only marginally significantly different from zero. Interestingly, in one case when the *PSID*-1 sample is used as a comparison group, the estimated participation coefficient is significant (the *t*-statistic is 2.25) and the training effect of $1,129 is $968 closer to the experimental result than the one-step estimate. Additionally, this estimate is identical to the estimate using the *CPS-SSA*-1 comparison group, whereas the one-step estimates differed by $1,056. However, if an econometrician reported this training effect, she or he would have to argue that variables such as place of residence and prior AFDC status do not belong in the earnings equation. Otherwise, the econometrician is left to choose between a set of estimates that vary by as much as $1,308.

The two-step estimates are usually closer than the one-step estimates to the experimental results for the male trainees as well. One estimate, which used the *CPS-SSA*-1 sample as a comparison group, is within $600 of the experimental result, while the one-step estimate falls short by $1,695. The estimates of the participation coefficients are negative, although unlike these estimates for the females, they are always significantly different from zero. This finding is consistent with the example cited earlier in which individuals with high participation unobservables and low earnings unobservables were more likely to be in training. As predicted, the unrestricted estimates are larger than the one-step estimates. However, as with the results for the females, this procedure may leave

---

[24] *The two-step estimates using the smaller comparison groups were associated with large estimated standard errors.*

TABLE 6

ESTIMATED TRAINING EFFECTS USING TWO-STAGE ESTIMATOR

Variables Excluded from the Earnings Equation, but Included in the Participation Equation	Comparison Group	NSW AFDC Females		NSW Males	
		Heckman Correction for Program Participation Bias, Using Estimate of Conditional Expectation of Earnings Error as Regressor in Earnings Equation			
		Estimate of Coefficient for			
		Training Dummy	Estimate of Expectation	Training Dummy	Estimate of Expectation
Marital Status, Residency in an SMSA, Employment Status in 1976.	PSID-1	$1,129 (385)	−$894 (396)	−$1,333 (820)	−$2,357 (781)
AFDC Status in 1975, Number of Children	CPS-SSA-1	1,102 (323)	−606 (480)	−22 (584)	−1,437 (449)
	NSW Controls	837 (317)	−18 (2376)	899 (840)	−835 (2601)
Employment Status in 1976, AFDC Status in 1975, Number of Children	PSID-1	1,256 (405)	−823 (410)	—	—
	CPS-SSA-1	439 (333)	−979 (481)	—	—
	NSW Controls	—	—	—	—
Employment Status in 1976, Number of Children	PSID-1	1,564 (604)	−552 (569)	−1,161 (864)	−2,655 (799)
	CPS-SSA-1	552 (514)	−902 (551)	13 (584)	−1,484 (450)
	NSW Controls	851 (318)	147 (2385)	889 (841)	−808 (2603)
No Exclusion Restrictions	PSID-1	1,747 (620)	−526 (568)	−667 (905)	−2,446 (806)
	CPS-SSA-1	805 (523)	−908 (548)	213 (588)	−1,364 (452)
	NSW Controls	861 (318)	284 (2385)	889 (840)	−876 (2601)

Notes: The estimated training effects are in 1982 dollars. For the females, the experimental estimate of impact of the supported work program was $851 with a standard error of $317. The one-step estimates from col. 11 of Table 4 were $2,097 with a standard error of $491 using the PSID-1 as a comparison group, $1,041 with a standard error of $503 using the CPS-SSA-1 as a comparison group, and $854 with a standard error of $312 using the NSW controls as a comparison group. Estimates are missing for the case of three exclusions using the NSW controls since AFDC status in 1975 cannot be used as an instrument of the NSW females. For the males, the experimental estimate of impact of the supported work program was $886 with a standard error of $476. The one-step estimates from col. 10 of Table 5 were −$1,228 with a standard error of $896 using the PSID-1 as a comparison group, −$805 with a standard error of $484 using the CPS-SSA-1 as a comparison group, and $662 with a standard error of $506 using the NSW controls as a comparison group. Estimates are missing for the case of three exclusions for the NSW males as AFDC status is not used as an instrument in the analysis of the male trainees.

econometricians with a considerable range ($1,546) of imprecise estimates; although, like the results for the females, there is no evidence that the results of the specification tests would lead econometricians to choose the "wrong" estimator.

IV. CONCLUSION

This study shows that many of the econometric procedures and comparison groups used to evaluate employment and training programs would not have yielded accurate or precise estimates of the impact of the National Supported Work Program. The econometric estimates often differ significantly from the experimental results. Moreover, even when the econometric estimates pass conventional specification tests, they still fail to replicate the experimentally determined results. Even though I was unable to evaluate all nonexperimental methods, this evidence suggests that policymakers should be aware that the available nonexperimental evaluations of employment and training programs may contain large and unknown biases resulting from specification errors.[25]

This study also yields several other findings that may help researchers evaluate other employment and training programs. First, the nonexperimental procedures produce estimates that are usually positive and larger than the experimental results for the female participants, and are negative and smaller than the experimental estimates for the male participants. Second, these econometric procedures are more likely to replicate the experimental results in the case of female rather than male participants. Third, longitudinal data reduces the potential for specification errors relative to the cross-sectional data. Finally, the two step procedure certainly does no worse than, and may reduce the potential for specification errors relative to, the one-step procedures discussed in Section II.

More generally, this paper presents an alternative approach to the sensitivity analyses proposed by Leamer (1983, 1985) and others for bounding the specification errors associated with the evaluation of economic hypotheses. This objective is accomplished by comparing econometric estimates with experimentally determined results. The data from an experiment yield simple estimates of the impact of economic treatments that are independent of any model specification. Successful econometric methods are intended to reproduce these estimates. The only way we will know whether these econometric methods are successful is by making the comparison. This paper takes the first step along this path, but there are other experimental data bases available to econometricians and much work remains to be done. For example, there have been several other employment and training experiments testing the effect of training on earnings, four Negative Income Tax Experiments testing hypotheses about insurance and medical demand, a housing experiment testing hypotheses about housing labor supply, a medical insurance experiment

---

[25] *There is some evidence that this message has been passed on to the appropriate policymakers. See Recommendations of the Job Training Longitudinal Survey Research Advisory Panel to Office of Strategic Planning and Policy Development, U.S. Department of Labor, November 1985. This has led to at least a tentative decision to operate some part of the Job Training Partnership Act program sites using random assignment. (See Ernst Stromsdorfer et al., 1985.)*

testing hypotheses about demand and supply, and a time-of-day electricity pricing experiment testing hypotheses about electricity demand.[26] There clearly remain many opportunities to use the experimental method to assess the potential for specification bias in the evaluation of social programs, and in other areas of econometric research as well.

REFERENCES

Abowd, John, "Program Evaluation," Working Paper, University of Chicago, 1983.

Aiken, Linda and Kehrer, Barbara, *Evaluation Studies Review Annual,* Vol. 10, Beverly Hills: Sage Publications, 1985.

Ashenfelter, Orley, "Estimating the Effect of Training Programs on Earnings," *Review of Economics and Statistics,* February 1978, *60,* 47–57.

———— and Card, David, "Using the Longitudinal Structure of Earnings to Estimate the Effect of Training Programs," *Review of Economics and Statistics,* November 1985, *67,* 648–60.

Bernstein, A. P. et al., "The Forgotten Americans," *Business Week,* September 2, 1985, 50–55.

Bassi, Laurie, (1983a) "Estimating the Effect of Training Programs With Non-Random Selection," Princeton University, 1983.

————, (1983b) "The Effect of CETA on the Post-Program Earnings of Participants," *Journal of Human Resources,* Fall 1983, *18,* 539–556.

————, "Estimating the Effects of Training Programs with Nonrandom Selection," *Review of Economics and Statistics,* February 1984, *66,* 36–43.

Brown, Randall, "Assessing the Effects of Interview Nonresponse on Estimates of the Impact of Supported Work," Mathematica Policy Research Inc., Princeton, 1979.

Burtless, Gary, "Are Targeted Wage Subsidies Harmful? Evidence from a Wage Voucher Experiment," *Industrial and Labor Relations Review,* October 1985, *39,* 105–114.

Cooley, Thomas, McGuire, Thomas and Prescott, Edward, "Earnings and Employment Dynamics of Manpower Trainees: An Exploratory Econometric Analysis," in Ronald Ehrenberg, ed., *Research in Labor Economics,* Vol. 4, Suppl. 2, 1979, 119–47.

Dickinson, Katherine and Maynard, Rebecca, *The Impact of Supported Work on Ex-Addicts,* New York: Manpower Demonstration Research Corporation, 1981.

————, Johnson, Terry and West, Richard, *An Analysis of the Impact of CETA Programs on Participants' Earnings,* Washington: Department of Labor, Employment and Training Administration, 1984.

Fraker, Thomas, Maynard, Rebecca and Nelson, Lyle, *An Assessment of Alternative Comparison Group Methodologies for Evaluating Employment and Training Programs,* Princeton: Mathematica Policy Research Inc., 1984.

Goldberger, Arthur, "Selection Bias in Evaluating Treatment Effects," Discussion Paper No. 123–72, Institute for Research on Poverty, University of Wisconsin, 1972.

Goldman, Barbara, "The Impacts of the Immediate Job Search Assistance Experiment," Manpower Demonstration Research Corporation, New York, 1981.

---

[26] *See Linda Aiken and Barbara Kehrer (1985), Abt Associates (1984), Gary Burtless (1985), Barbara Goldman (1981), Goldman et al. (1985), Jerry Hausman and David Wise (1985), J. Ohls and G. Carcagno (1978), and SRI International (1983).*

———— et al., "Findings From the San Diego Job Search and Work Experience Demonstration," New York: Manpower Demonstration Research Corporation, 1985.

Greene, William, "Sample Selection Bias as a Specification Error: Comment," *Econometrica,* May 1981, *49,* 795–98.

Ham, John, "Estimation of a Labor Supply Model with Censoring Due to Unemployment and Underemployment," *Review of Economic Studies,* July 1982, *49,* 335–54.

———— and Hsiao, Cheng, "Two-Stage Estimation of Structural Labor Supply Parameters Using Interval Data From the 1971 Canadian Census," *Journal of Econometrics,* January/February 1984, *24,* 133–58.

Hausman, Jerry A. and Wise, David A., *Social Experimentation,* NBER, Chicago: University of Chicago Press, 1985.

Heckman, James, "Dummy Endogenous Variables in a Simultaneous Equations System," *Econometrica,* July 1978, *46,* 931–59.

————, "Sample Selection Bias as a Specification Error," *Econometrica,* January 1979, *47,* 153–61.

———— and Robb, Richard, "Alternative Methods for Evaluating the Impact of Interventions: An Overview," Working Paper, University of Chicago, 1985.

Hendry, David, "Econometrices: Alchemy or Science?" *Economica,* November 1980, *47,* 387–406.

Kemper, Peter and Long, David, "The Supported Work Evaluation: Technical Report on the Value of In-Program Output Costs," Manpower Demonstration Research Corporation, New York, 1981.

————, ————, and Thornton, Craig, "The Supported Work Evaluation: Final Benefit-Cost Analysis," Manpower Demonstration Research Corporation, New York, 1981.

Kiefer, Nicholas, (1979a) *The Economic Benefits of Four Employment and Training Programs,* New York: Garland Publishing, 1979.

————, (1979b) "Population Heterogeneity and Inference from Panel Data on the Effects of Vocational Training," *Journal of Political Economy* October 1979, *87,* S213–26.

LaLonde, Robert, "Evaluating the Econometric Evaluations of Training Programs With Experimental Data," Industrial Relations Section, Working Paper No. 183, Princeton University, 1984.

Leamer, Edward, "Let's Take the Con Out of Econometrics," *American Economic Review,* March 1983, *73,* 31–43.

————, "Sensitivity Analysis Would Help," *American Economic Review,* June 1985, *75,* 308–13.

———— and Leonard, Herman, "Reporting the Fragility of Regression Estimates," *Review of Economics and Statistics,* May 1983, *65,* 306–12.

McAleer, Michael, Pagan, Adrian and Volker, Paul, "What Will Take the Con Out of Econometrics?," *American Economic Review,* June 1985, *75,* 293–306.

Maddala, G. S., *Limited Dependent and Qualitative Variables in Econometrics,* Cambridge: Cambridge University Press, 1983.

Mallar, Charles, "Alternative Econometric Procedures for Program Evaluations: Illustrations From an Evaluation of Job Corps," *Proceedings of the American Statistical Association,* 1978, 317–21.

————, Kerachsky, Stuart and Thornton, Craig, *The Short-Term Economic Impact of the Jobs-Corps Program,* Princeton: Mathematica Policy Research Inc., 1978.

Masters, Stanley and Maynard, Rebecca, "The Impact of Supported Work on Long-Term Recipients of AFDC Benefits," Manpower Demonstration Research Corporation, New York, 1981.

Maynard, Rebecca, "The Impact of Supported Work on Young School Dropouts," Manpower Demonstration Research Corporation, New York, 1980.

Ohls, J. and Carcagno, G., *Second Evaluation of the Private Employment Agency Job Counsellor Project,* Princeton: Mathematica Policy Research Inc., 1978.

Piliavin, Irving and Gartner, Rosemary, "The Impact of Supported Work on Ex-Offenders," Manpower Demonstration Research Corporation, New York, 1981.

Stromsdorfer, Ernst et al., "Recommendations of the Job Training Longitudinal Survey Research Advisory Panel to the Office of Strategic Planning and Policy Development, U.S. Department of Labor," unpublished report, Washington, November 1985.

Abt Associates, "AFDC Homemaker-Home Health Aid Demonstration Evaluation," 2nd Annual Report, Washington, 1984.

Manpower Demonstration Research Corporation, *Summary and Findings of the National Supported Work Demonstration,* Cambridge: Ballinger, 1983.

SRI International, *Final Report of the Seattle-Denver Income Maintenance Experiment: Design and Results,* Washington: Department of Health and Human Services, 1983.

ABOUT THE AUTHOR

Robert J. LaLonde

Bob LaLonde is professor of public policy in the Harris Graduate School of Public Policy Studies at the University of Chicago. LaLonde's use of field experiments in the evaluation of the impact of employment programs is widely regarded as a key innovation in the way economists study public policy issues.

After a B.A. at the University of Chicago in 1980, LaLonde received a Ph.D. in economics from Princeton University in 1985. He was assistant and then associate professor of industrial relations in the Graduate School of Business of the University of Chicago from 1985 to 1994, at which time he moved to the Department of Economics at Michigan State University. In 1999 LaLonde returned to the University of Chicago to his current appointment in the Harris School. From 1987 to 1988 he served as Senior Staff Economist for the President's Council of Economic Advisors.

LaLonde spends part of his time every year predicting the quality of the Bordeaux vintage in his role as Chicago correspondent for a small wine publication. Despite his fine palate, LaLonde uses only the weather data for his controversial predictions!

Does Compulsory School Attendance Affect Schooling and Earnings?

JOSHUA D. ANGRIST

ALAN B. KRUEGER

We establish that season of birth is related to educational attainment because of school start age policy and compulsory school attendance laws. Individuals born in the beginning of the year start school at an older age, and can therefore drop out after completing less schooling than individuals born near the end of the year. Roughly 25 percent of potential dropouts remain in school because of compulsory schooling laws. We estimate the impact of compulsory schooling on earnings by using quarter of birth as an instrument for education. The instrumental variables estimate of the return to education is close to the ordinary least squares estimate, suggesting that there is little bias in conventional estimates.

Every developed country in the world has a compulsory schooling requirement, yet little is known about the effect these laws have on educational attainment and earnings.[1] This paper exploits an unusual natural experiment to estimate the impact of compulsory schooling laws in the United States. The experiment stems from the fact that children born in different months of the year start school at different ages, while compulsory schooling laws generally require students to remain in school until their sixteenth or seventeenth birthday. In effect, the interaction of school-entry requirements and compulsory schooling laws compels students born in certain months to attend school longer than students born in other months. Because one's birthday is unlikely to be correlated with personal attributes other than age at school entry, season of birth generates exogenous

We thank Michael Boozer and Lisa Krueger for outstanding research assistance. Financial support was provided by the Princeton Industrial Relations Section, an NBER Olin Fellowship in Economics, and the National Science Foundation (SES-9012149). We are also grateful to Lawrence Katz, John Pencavel, an anonymous referee, and many seminar participants for helpful comments. The data and computer programs used in the preparation of this paper are available on request.

[1] *See OECD [1983] for a comparison of compulsory schooling laws in different countries.*

variation in education that can be used to estimate the impact of compulsory schooling on education and earnings.

In the next section we present an analysis of data from three decennial Censuses that establishes that season of birth is indeed related to educational attainment. Remarkably, in virtually all of the birth cohorts that we have examined, children born in the first quarter of the year have a slightly *lower* average level of education than children born later in the year. School districts typically require a student to have turned age six by January 1 of the year in which he or she enters school (see HEW [1959]). Therefore, students born earlier in the year enter school at an older age and attain the legal dropout age at an earlier point in their educational careers than students born later in the year. If the fraction of students who want to drop out prior to the legal dropout age is independent of season of birth, then the observed seasonal pattern in education is consistent with the view that compulsory schooling constrains some students born later in the year to stay in school longer.

Two additional pieces of evidence link the seasonal pattern in education to the combined effect of age at school entry and compulsory schooling laws. First, the seasonal pattern in education is *not* evident in college graduation rates, nor is it evident in graduate school completion rates. Because compulsory schooling laws do not compel individuals to attend school beyond high school, this evidence supports our hypothesis that the relationship between years of schooling and date of birth is entirely due to compulsory schooling laws. Second, in comparing enrollment rates of fifteen- and sixteen-year olds in states that have an age sixteen schooling requirement with enrollment rates in states that have an age seventeen schooling requirement, we find a greater decline in the enrollment of sixteen-year olds in states that permit sixteen-year olds to leave school than in states that compel sixteen-year olds to attend school.

The variety of evidence presented in Section I establishes that compulsory schooling laws increase educational attainment for those covered by the laws. In Section II we consider whether students who attend school longer because of compulsory schooling receive higher earnings as a result of their increased schooling. Two-stage least squares (TSLS) estimates are used in which the source of identification is variation in education that results solely from differences in season of birth—which, in turn, results from the effect of compulsory schooling laws. The results suggest that men who are forced to attend school by compulsory schooling laws earn higher wages as a result of their increased schooling. The estimated monetary return to an additional year of schooling for those who are compelled to attend school by compulsory schooling laws is about 7.5 percent, which is hardly different from the ordinary-least-squares (OLS) estimate of the return to education for all male workers.

To check further whether the estimated schooling-earnings relationship is truly a result of compulsory schooling, we explore the relationship between earnings and season of birth for the subsample of college graduates. Because these individuals were not constrained by compulsory schooling requirements, they form a natural control group to test whether season of birth affects earnings for reasons other than compulsory schooling. The results of this exploration suggest that there is no relationship between earnings and season of birth for men who are not constrained by compulsory schooling. This strengthens our interpretation that the TSLS estimate of the return to education reflects the effect of compulsory school attendance.

Our findings have important implications for the literature on omitted variables bias in estimates of the return to education (see Griliches [1977] and Willis [1986] for surveys). Economists have devoted a great deal of attention to correcting for bias in the return to education due to omitted ability and other factors that are positively correlated with both education and earnings. This type of a bias would occur, for example, in Spence's [1973] signaling model, where workers with high innate ability are assumed to find school less difficult and to obtain more schooling to signal their high ability. In contrast to this prediction, estimates based on season of birth indicate that, if anything, conventional OLS estimates are biased slightly downward.

I. Season of Birth, Compulsory Schooling, and Years of Education

If the fraction of students who desire to leave school before they reach the legal dropout age is constant across birthdays, a student's birthday should be expected to influence his or her ultimate educational attainment.[2] This relationship would be expected because, in the absence of rolling admissions to school, students born in different months of the year start school at different ages. This fact, in conjunction with compulsory schooling laws, which require students to attend school until they reach a specified birthday, produces a correlation between date of birth and years of schooling.[3]

Students who are born early in the calendar year are typically older when they enter school than children born late in the year. For example, our tabulation of the 1960 Census (the earliest census that contains quarter of birth), shows that, on average, boys born in the first quarter of the year enter first grade when they are 6.45 years old, whereas boys born in the fourth quarter of the year enter first grade when they are 6.07 years old.[4] This

---

[2] Beginning with Huntington [1938], researchers in many fields have investigated the effect of season of birth on a variety of biological and behavioral variables, ranging from fertility to schizophrenia. We consider the impact of other possible season of birth effects below.

[3] Angrist and Krueger [1990] formally model the link between age at school entry and compulsory schooling. A testable implication of this model is that age at school entry should be linearly related to years of education. Data on men born 1946 to 1952 are generally consistent with this prediction.

[4] Figures in the text are for boys born in 1952. The average entry age to first grade for those born in the second quarter is 6.28, and the average age of first graders born in the third quarter is 6.08. Other years show a similar pattern (see Angrist and Krueger [1990]). These averages are affected by holding back or advancing students beyond the normal start age, and by differences in start age policy across schools. Nonetheless, the results show that students born in the beginning of the year tend to enter school at an older age than those born near the end of the year.

pattern arises because most school districts do not admit students to first grade unless they will attain age six by January 1 of the academic year in which they enter school. Consequently, students who were born in the beginning of the year are older when they start school than students who were born near the end of the year. Because children born in the first quarter of the year enter school at an older age, they attain the legal dropout age after having attended school for a shorter period of time than those born near the end of the year. Hence, if a fixed fraction of students is constrained by the compulsory attendance law, those born in the beginning of the year will have less schooling, on average, than those born near the end of the year.

Figures I, II, and III document the relationship between education and season of birth for men born 1930–1959. Each figure depicts the average years of completed schooling by quarter and year of birth, based on the sample of men in the 1980 Census, 5 percent Public Use Sample. (The data set used in the figures is described in greater detail in Appendix 1.) The graphs show a generally increasing trend in average education for cohorts born in the 1930s and 1940s. For men born in the late 1950s, average education is trending down, in part because by 1980 the younger men in the cohort had not completed all of their schooling, and in part because college attendance fell in the aftermath of the Vietnam War.

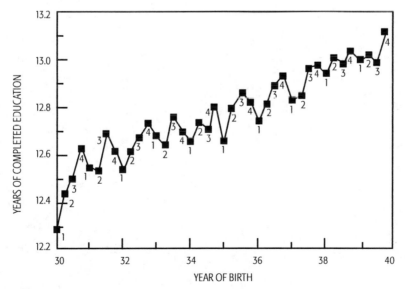

FIGURE I

Years of Education and Season of Birth; 1980 Census

Note. Quarter of birth is listed below each observation.

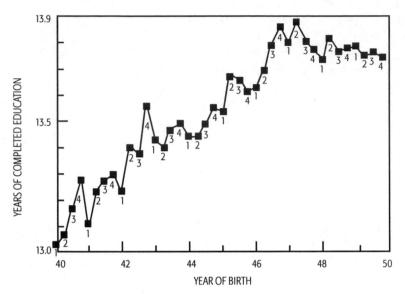

Figure II

Years of Education and Season of Birth; 1980 Census

Note. Quarter of birth is listed below each observation.

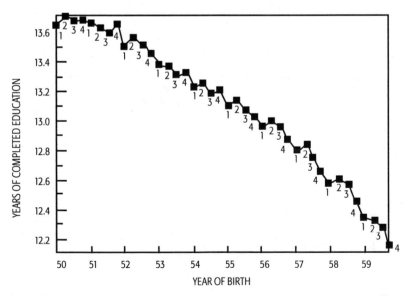

Figure III

Years of Education and Season of Birth; 1980 Census

Note. Quarter of birth is listed below each observation.

A close examination of the plots indicates that there is a small but persistent pattern in the average number of years of completed education by quarter of birth. Average education is generally higher for individuals born near the end of the year than for individuals born early in the year. Furthermore, men born in the fourth quarter of the year tend to have even more education than men born in the beginning of the *following* year. The third quarter births also often have a higher average number of years of education than the following year's first quarter births. Moreover, this seasonal pattern in years of education is exhibited by the cohorts of men that experienced a secular decline in educational levels, as well as by the cohorts that experienced a secular increase in educational levels.

To further examine the seasonal pattern in education, it is useful to remove the trend in years of education across cohorts. A flexible way to detrend the series is by subtracting off a moving average of the surrounding birth cohort's average education. For each quarter we define a two-period, two-sided moving average, $MA(+2,-2)$, as the average education of men born in the two preceding and two succeeding quarters.[5] Specifically, for the cohort of men born in year c and quarter j, the $MA(+2,-2)$, denoted MA_{cj}, is

$$MA_{cj} = (E_{-2} + E_{-1} + E_{+1} + E_{+2})/4,$$

where E_q is the average years of education attained by the cohort born q quarters before or after cohort c,j. The "detrended" education series is simply $E_{cj} - MA_{cj}$.

The relationship between season of birth and years of education for the detrended education series is depicted in Figure IV for each ten-year-age group. The figures clearly show that season of birth is related to years of completed education. For example, in 27 of the 29 birth years, the average education of men born in the first quarter of the year (January–March) is less than that predicted by the surrounding quarters based on the $MA(+2,-2)$.

To quantify the effect of season of birth on a variety of educational outcome variables, we estimated regressions of the form,

$$\left(E_{icj} - MA_{cj}\right) = \alpha + \sum_{j}^{3} \beta_j \, Q_{icj} + \epsilon_{icj}$$

$$\text{for } i = 1,\ldots,N_c; \quad c = 1,\ldots,10; \quad j = 1,2,3.$$

where E_{icj} is the educational outcome variable for individual i in cohort c (i.e., years of education, graduated high school, graduated college, or years of post-high school education), MA_{cj} is the $MA(+2,-2)$ trend for the education variable, and Q_{icj} is a dummy variable indicating whether person i was born in the jth quarter of the year. Because the

---

[5] *We note that none of our conclusions is qualitatively changed when we use a linear age trend (with age measured to the quarter of the year), a quadratic age trend, or unrestricted year-of-birth dummies.*

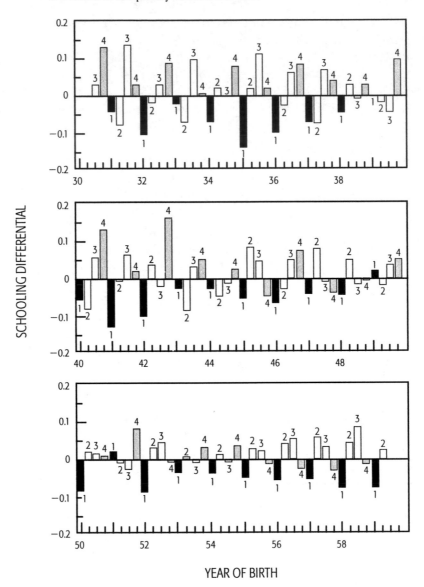

FIGURE IV

Season of Birth and Years of Schooling; Deviations from *MA* (+2,−2)

dependent variable in these regressions is purged of *MA*(+2,−2) effects, it is necessary to delete observations born in the first two quarters and last two quarters of the sample.

Table I reports estimates of each quarter of birth (main) effect (β_j) relative to the fourth quarter, for men in the 1980 Census who were born in the 1930s and 1940s.[6] The

---

[6] *We focus on men born in the 1930s and 1940s because many individuals in the 1950s birth cohorts had not yet completed their education by 1980.*

TABLE I

THE EFFECT OF QUARTER OF BIRTH ON VARIOUS EDUCATIONAL OUTCOME VARIABLES

Outcome variable	Birth cohort	Mean	Quarter-of-birth effect[a]			F-test[b] [P-value]
			I	*II*	*III*	
Total years of education	1930–1939	12.79	−0.124 (0.017)	−0.086 (0.017)	−0.015 (0.016)	24.9 [0.0001]
	1940–1949	13.56	−0.085 (0.012)	−0.035 (0.012)	−0.017 (0.011)	18.6 [0.0001]
High school graduate	1930–1939	0.77	−0.019 (0.002)	−0.020 (0.002)	−0.004 (0.002)	46.4 [0.0001]
	1940–1949	0.86	−0.015 (0.001)	−0.012 (0.001)	−0.002 (0.001)	54.4 [0.0001]
Years of educ. for high school graduates	1930–1939	13.99	−0.004 (0.014)	0.051 (0.014)	0.012 (0.014)	5.9 [0.0006]
	1940–1949	14.28	0.005 (0.011)	0.043 (0.011)	-0.003 (0.010)	7.8 [0.0017]
College graduate	1930–1939	0.24	−0.005 (0.002)	0.003 (0.002)	0.002 (0.002)	5.0 [0.0021]
	1940–1949	0.30	−0.003 (0.002)	0.004 (0.002)	0.000 (0.002)	5.0 [0.0018]
Completed master's degree	1930–1939	0.09	−0.001 (0.001)	0.002 (0.001)	-0.001 (0.001)	1.7 [0.1599]
	1940–1949	0.11	0.000 (0.001)	0.004 (0.001)	0.001 (0.001)	3.9 [0.0091]
Completed doctoral degree	1930–1939	0.03	0.002 (0.001)	0.003 (0.001)	0.000 (0.001)	2.9 [0.0332]
	1940–1949	0.04	−0.002 (0.001)	0.001 (0.001)	−0.001 (0.001)	4.3 [0.0050]

[a] Standard errors are in parentheses. An $MA(+2,-2)$ trend term was subtracted from each dependent variable. The data set contains men from the 1980 Census, 5 percent Public Use Sample. Sample size is 312,718 for 1930–1939 cohort and is 457,181 for 1940–1949 cohort.
[b] F-statistic is for a test of the hypothesis that the quarter-of-birth dummies jointly have no effect.

F-tests reported in the last column of the table indicate that, after removing trend, the small within-year-of-birth differences in average years of education are highly statistically significant. For both cohorts the average number of completed years of schooling is about one tenth of a year lower for men born in the first quarter of the year than for men born in the last quarter of the year. Similarly, the table shows that, for the 1930s cohort, men born in the first quarter of the year are 1.9 percentage points less likely to graduate from high school than men born in the last quarter of the year.[7] For the 1940s cohort the gap in the high school graduation rate between first and fourth quarter births is 1.5 percentage points. Because the high school dropout rate is 23 percent for men born in the 1930s and 14 percent for men born in the 1940s, first quarter births are roughly 10 percent more likely to drop out of high school than fourth quarter births.

The seasonal differences in years of education and in high school graduation rates are smaller for men born in the 1940s than for men born in the 1930s, but the quarter-of-birth effects are still statistically significant. As discussed below, one explanation for the attenuation of the seasonal pattern in education over time is that compulsory attendance laws are less likely to be a binding constraint on more recent cohorts.

The evidence that children born in the first quarter of the year tend to enter school at a slightly older age than other children, and that children born in the first quarter of the year also tend to obtain less education, is at least superficially consistent with the simple age at entry/compulsory schooling model.

To further explore whether the differences in education by season of birth are caused by compulsory schooling laws, the bottom part of Table I estimates the same set of equations for measures of post-secondary educational achievement. This sample provides a test of whether season of birth influences education even for those who are not constrained by compulsory schooling laws (because compulsory schooling laws exempt students who have graduated from high school). Consequently, if compulsory schooling is responsible for the seasonal pattern in education, one would not expect to find such a pattern for individuals who have some post-secondary education.

The seasonal pattern in years of education is much less pronounced and quite different for the subsample of individuals who have at least a high school education. In this sample, second quarter births tend to have higher average education, while those born in other quarters have about equal levels of education. The difference in average years of education between first and fourth quarter births is statistically insignificant for high school graduates. On the other hand, first quarter births are slightly less likely to graduate from college, and the gap is statistically significant. In view of the enormous sample sizes (in excess of 300,000 observations), however, the F-tests are close to classical critical values for the null hypothesis that season of birth is unrelated to post-high school educational outcomes.

Table I also shows the effect of quarter of birth on the proportion of men who have a master's degree and on the proportion of men who have a doctoral degree.[8] These results show no discernible pattern in educational achievement by season of birth. Because individuals with higher degrees did not discontinue their education as soon as they were

---

[7] *Notice that because the quarter-of-birth dummies are mutually exclusive, the linear probability model is appropriate in this situation.*

[8] *For purposes of Table I we assumed that individuals with a college degree completed sixteen or more years of education, individuals with a master's degree completed eighteen or more years of education, and individuals with a doctoral degree completed twenty or more years of education.*

legally permitted, these findings provide further support for the view that compulsory schooling is responsible for the seasonal pattern in education. Moreover, because season of birth is correlated with age at school entry, the lack of a seasonal pattern in postsecondary education suggests that differences in school entry age alone do not have a significant effect on educational attainment. In the absence of compulsory schooling, therefore, we would not expect to find differences in education by season of birth.

A. DIRECT EVIDENCE ON THE EFFECT OF COMPULSORY SCHOOLING LAWS

For the combined effects of compulsory schooling and school start age to adequately explain the seasonal pattern in education, it must be the case that compulsory attendance laws effectively force some students to stay in school longer than they desire. Table II provides evidence that compulsory schooling laws are effective in compelling a small proportion of students to remain in school until they attain the legal dropout age. This evidence makes use of the fact that some states allow students to drop out of school upon attaining their sixteenth birthday, while others compel students to attend school until their seventeenth or eighteenth birthday.[9] A summary of the compulsory schooling requirement in effect in each state in 1960, 1970, and 1980 is provided in Appendix 2.

The first three rows of Table II focus on individuals who were born in 1944 using data from the 1960 Census.[10] Students who were born between January and March of 1944 were age sixteen when the 1960 Census was conducted (Census Day is April 1), while those who were born between April and December of 1944 were not yet age sixteen. Consequently, students born in January–March were able to drop out of school in the states that had an age sixteen compulsory attendance law, but were not able to legally drop out of school in states that had an age seventeen or age eighteen compulsory attendance law. On the other hand, students born in April–December of 1944 were not able to legally withdraw from school under either regime.

This institutional framework allows for a difference-in-differences analysis. The figures in columns (1) and (2) of Table II are the percentage of students enrolled in school on April 1, broken down by the compulsory schooling age in the state and by the age of the student. The results for 1960 are striking. In states where sixteen-year olds are permitted to drop out of school, the percent of students enrolled is 4.5 points lower for students

---

[9] There are three exceptions: Mississippi and South Carolina eliminated their compulsory schooling laws in response to Brown v. Board of Education in 1954. South Carolina reenacted compulsory schooling in 1967, and Mississippi in 1983. In 1960 Maine had an age fifteen compulsory schooling law. Ehrenberg and Marcus [1982] and Edwards [1978] also provide evidence on the impact of compulsory schooling legislation on school enrollment.

[10] The sample underlying this table includes both boys and girls. Wisconsin and Texas require students to complete the school term in which they reach the legal dropout age, and therefore were dropped from the sample. In addition, school districts in metropolitan sections of New York were excluded from the sample because they are allowed to alter the compulsory schooling requirement.

TABLE II

PERCENTAGE OF AGE GROUP ENROLLED IN SCHOOL BY BIRTHDAY
AND LEGAL DROPOUT AGE[a]

| Date of birth | Type of state law[b] | | Column |
	School-leaving age: 16 (1)	School-leaving age: 17 or 18 (2)	(1) − (2)
Percent enrolled April 1, 1960			
1. Jan 1–Mar 31, 1944	87.6	91.0	−3.4
(age 16)	(0.6)	(0.9)	(1.1)
2. Apr 1–Dec 31, 1944	92.1	91.6	0.5
(age 15)	(0.3)	(0.5)	(0.6)
3. Within-state diff.	−4.5	−0.6	−4.0
(row 1 − row 2)	(0.7)	(1.0)	(1.2)
Percent enrolled April 1, 1970			
4. Jan 1–Mar 31, 1954	94.2	95.8	−1.6
(age 16)	(0.3)	(0.5)	(0.6)
5. Apr 1–Dec 31, 1954	96.1	95.7	0.4
(age 15)	(0.1)	(0.3)	(0.3)
6. Within-state diff.	−1.9	0.1	−2.0
(row 1 − row 2)	(0.3)	(0.6)	(0.6)
Percent enrolled April 1, 1980			
7. Jan 1–Mar 31, 1964	95.0	96.2	−1.2
(age 16)	(0.1)	(0.2)	(0.2)
8. Apr 1–Dec 31, 1964	97.0	97.7	−0.7
(age 15)	(0.1)	(0.1)	(0.1)
9. Within-state diff.	−2.0	−1.5	0.5
(row 1 − row 2)	(0.1)	(0.2)	(0.3)

[a] Standard errors are in parentheses.
[b] Data set used to compute rows 1–3 is the 1960 Census, 1 percent Public Use Sample; data set used to compute rows 4–6 is 1970 Census, 1 percent State Public Use Sample (15 percent form); data set used to compute rows 7–9 is the 1980 Census, 5 percent Public Use Sample. Each sample contains both boys and girls. Sample sizes are 4,153 for row 1; 12,512 for row 2; 7,758 for row 4; 24,636 for row 5; 42,740 for row 7; and 131,020 for row 8.

who have turned age sixteen than for those who are almost age sixteen (see row 3). In contrast, there is only a statistically insignificant 0.6 percentage point decline in the enrollment rate between age fifteen and sixteen in states where students must wait until age seventeen or eighteen to drop out.

Column 3 of Table II reports the difference in the enrollment rate for children of a given age between states with different compulsory schooling laws. For example, sixteen year olds are 3.4 percent less likely to be enrolled in states with a school-leaving age of sixteen, whereas fifteen year olds have a similar enrollment rate in both sets of states. The contrast between the within-state and within-age-group comparisons is a difference-in-differences estimator of the effect of compulsory school attendance that controls for both additive age and state effects. For the 1944 cohort the difference-in-differences estimate indicates that compulsory school attendance laws increased the enrollment rate by four percentage points in states with an age seventeen or age eighteen minimum schooling requirement.

Rows 4–6 of Table II report the corresponding statistics for individuals born in 1954 using data from the 1970 Census, and rows 7–9 report the corresponding statistics for individuals born in 1964 using data from the 1980 Census. These results lead to a similar conclusion: the dropout rate is increased for students when they become legally eligible to leave school. The difference-in-differences estimates of the enrollment effect of compulsory schooling for the 1954 and 1964 cohorts are 2 and 0.5 percentage points. A significant number of students leave school around the time of their birthday, although the effect of compulsory attendance laws is smaller in 1970 than in 1960, and smaller still in 1980 than in 1970.

Although the fraction of students kept in school by compulsory education laws may seem small relative to the total population of students, the estimate represents a nontrivial fraction of the pool of students who eventually drop out of high school. In 1960 about 12 percent of sixteen-year-old students had dropped out of school in states where they were permitted to do so. Therefore, our estimates imply that in 1960 compulsory attendance laws kept approximately one third of potential dropouts in school. By 1980 only 5 percent of sixteen-year olds had dropped out of school, so our estimates imply that compulsory schooling laws kept roughly 10 percent of potential dropouts in school in that year.

The waning effect of compulsory schooling may result from an increase in desired levels of education for more recent cohorts, which makes compulsory schooling less of a constraint, or from increasingly lax enforcement of compulsory schooling laws. In either case the declining effect of compulsory schooling laws is consistent with the smaller seasonal pattern in education for recent cohorts.

B. WHY DO COMPULSORY SCHOOLING LAWS WORK?

The evidence presented so far suggests that compulsory schooling laws are effective at increasing the enrollment and education of at least some students. What explains the efficacy of this legislation? Although we do not have any direct evidence on why compulsory schooling laws are effective, in principle, there are two main enforcement mechanisms for the laws.[11] First, the Fair Labor Standards Act prohibits the employment of children

---

[11] This subsection draws heavily from information presented in Kotin and Aikman [1980], to which the reader is referred for further information on the enforcement and requirements of state compulsory schooling laws.

under age fourteen, and every state in the United States has a child labor law that further restricts employment of youths. In most states children are prohibited from working during school hours unless they have reached the compulsory schooling age in that state. Moreover, in all states young workers must obtain a work certificate (or work permit) to be eligible for employment. These work certificates are often administered and granted by the schools themselves, which provides an opportunity to monitor whether students below the compulsory school age are seeking employment. Consequently, child labor laws restrict or prohibit children of compulsory school age from participating in the work force, the principal alternative to attending school.

Second, compulsory school attendance laws provide for direct enforcement and policing of school attendance. Every state compulsory schooling law provides for truant officers to administer the law, and for other enforcement mechanisms. Truant officers typically have broad powers, such as the right to take children into custody without a warrant. However, the principal responsibility for school attendance rests with the child's parents. A parent who fails to send his or her child to school could face criminal penalties, such as misdemeanor-level fines or imprisonment.

Although we have outlined the ways in which compulsory schooling laws are enforced, it should also be noted that there are several exemptions to compulsory schooling laws in many states. As mentioned previously, students are exempt from compulsory school attendance if they have a high school or equivalent degree. Furthermore, in many states children are exempt from the schooling requirement if they suffer from certain physical, mental, or emotional disabilities; if they live far from a school; or if they are disruptive to other students. Additionally, all states are constitutionally bound to allow students to attend private schools in lieu of public schools, and 26 states permit "home schooling" as an alternative to public schools.

Finally, we note that compulsory schooling laws are believed to effectively increase schooling in other countries as well (see OECD [1983]). Moreover, the fact that age at school entry is correlated with educational attainment because of compulsory schooling is well-known in countries where the impact of compulsory schooling laws is more prominent. For example, a federal government document from Australia contains the following caution: "There are differences between states in the ages of students at similar levels of schooling. This is largely due to the time students may commence school [which differs by as much as one year across states]. Such factors should be borne in mind when utilizing school leaver data" [Department of Employment, Education, and Training, 1987].

II. ESTIMATING THE RETURN TO EDUCATION

Do the small differences in education for men born in different months of the year translate into differences in earnings? This question is first addressed in Figure V, which presents a graph of the mean log weekly wage of men age 30–49 (born 1930–1949), by quarter of birth. The data used to create the figure are drawn from the 1980 Census, and are described in detail in Appendix 1.

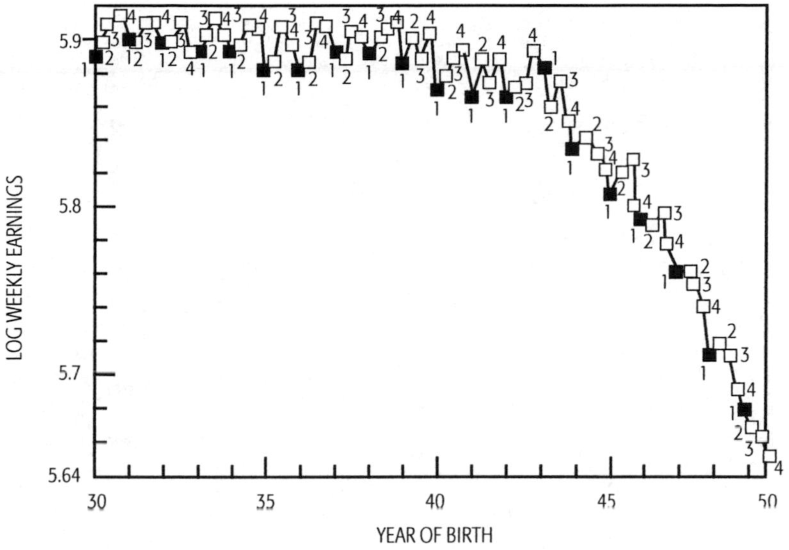

FIGURE V
Mean Log Weekly Wage, by Quarter of Birth, All Men Born 1930–1949; 1980 Census

Two important features of the data can be observed in Figure V. First, men born in the first quarter of the year—who, on average, have lower education—also tend to earn slightly less per week than men born in surrounding months. Second, the age-earnings profile is positively sloped for men between ages 30 and 39 (born 1940–1949), but fairly flat for men between ages 40 and 49 (born 1930–1939).[12] The latter observation is important because quarter of birth is naturally correlated with age: men born in the beginning of the year are older than those born at the end of the year, and will have higher earnings if they are on the upward sloping portion of the age-earnings profile. Therefore, we mainly focus on 40–49 year-old men, whose wages are hardly related to age. Analyzing this sample enables us to avoid the effects of life-cycle changes in earnings that are correlated with quarter of birth.

In Table III we use the seasonal pattern in education to calculate the rate of return to a year of education based on an application of Wald's [1940] method of fitting straight lines. This estimator simply computes the return to education as the ratio of the difference in earnings by quarter of birth to the difference in years of education by quarter of birth. We present estimates that compare earnings and education between men born in

[12] Longitudinal estimates of the age-earnings profile, which follow the same cohorts over time, also typically show a relatively flat relationship between age and earnings for 40–49 year-old men.

the first quarter of the year and men born in the last three quarters of the year.[13] This comparison is selected because the first quarter showed the largest blip in education in Figure IV. Panel A of Table III provides estimates for the sample of 40–49 year-old men (born 1920–1929) in the 1970 Census, and Panel 4B provides estimates for 40–49 year-old men (born 1930–1939) in the 1980 Census.[14]

The results of the Wald estimates are very similar to typical OLS estimates of the return to education for this population. In 1970, for example, men born in the first quarter of the year earned a 0.7 percent lower weekly wage and had completed 0.126 fewer years of education than men born in the last three quarters of the year. The ratio of these two numbers, 0.072, is a consistent estimate of the return to education provided that season of birth is uncorrelated with earnings determinants other than education. Intuitively, the Wald estimator is likely to provide a consistent estimate in this case because unobserved earnings determinants (e.g., ability) are likely to be uniformly distributed across people born on different dates of the year.[15]

The last row of each panel in Table III provides the OLS estimate of the return to education. The OLS estimate is the coefficient on education from a bivariate regression of the log weekly wage on years of education. The Wald estimate of the return to education (0.072) is slightly less than the OLS estimate (0.080) for middle-aged men in the 1970 Census, but the difference between the two estimates is not statistically significant.

Panel B of Table III presents the corresponding set of estimates for 40–49 year-old men (born 1930–1939) using the 1980 Census. For this sample the Wald estimate of the return to education, 0.102, is greater than the estimate from an OLS regression. But again, the difference between the Wald and OLS estimates of the return to education is not statistically significant.

We have also computed Wald estimates of the return to education for 30–39 year-old men using the 1970 and 1980 Censuses. In contrast to the estimates for 40–49 year-old men, estimates for younger men yield a trivial and statistically insignificant return to education. However, unless the effect of age on earnings is taken into account, simple Wald

---

[13] *The Wald estimate is a special case of instrumental variables [Durbin, 1954]. In this case the Wald estimate is equivalent to instrumental variables where a dummy variable indicating whether an individual is born in the first quarter of the year is used as an instrument for education, and there are no covariates.*

[14] *Elsewhere, we have shown that World War II veteran status is related to quarter of birth for men born between 1925 and 1928. This is not an issue for men born after 1930, however, because they were not covered by the World War II draft. Furthermore, the veterans' earnings premium for men born 1925–1928 is negative but very close to zero (see Angrist and Krueger [1989]).*

[15] *We note that our procedure will slightly understate the return to education because first-quarter births, whose birthdays occur midterm, are more likely to attend some schooling beyond their last year completed. Consequently, the difference in years of school attended between first and later quarters of birth is less than the difference in years of school completed. Since the difference in completed education rather than the difference in years of school attended appears in the denominator of the Wald estimator, our estimate is biased downward. In practice, however, this is a small bias because the difference in completion rates is small.*

TABLE III

PANEL A: WALD ESTIMATES FOR 1970 CENSUS—MEN BORN 1920-1929[a]

	(1) Born in 1st quarter of year	(2) Born in 2nd, 3rd, or 4th quarter of year	(3) Difference (std. error) (1) − (2)
ln (wkly. wage)	5.1484	5.1574	−0.00898
			(0.00301)
Education	11.3996	11.5252	−0.1256
			(0.0155)
Wald est. of return to education			0.0715
			(0.0219)
OLS return to education[b]			0.0801
			(0.0004)

PANEL B: WALD ESTIMATES FOR 1980 CENSUS—MEN BORN 1930-1939

	(1) Born in 1st quarter of year	(2) Born in 2nd, 3rd, or 4th quarter of year	(3) Difference (std. error) (1) − (2)
ln (wkly. wage)	5.8916	5.9027	−0.01110
			(0.00274)
Education	12.6881	12.7969	−0.1088
			(0.0132)
Wald est. of return to education			0.1020
			(0.0239)
OLS return to education			0.0709
			(0.0003)

[a] The sample size is 247,199 in Panel A, and 327,509 in Panel B. Each sample consists of males born in the United States who had positive earnings in the year preceding the survey. The 1980 Census sample is drawn from the 5 percent sample, and the 1970 Census sample is from the State, County, and Neighborhoods 1 percent samples.
[b] The OLS return to education was estimated from a bivariate regression of log weekly earnings on years of education.

estimates for men this age will be biased downward because they are on the upward sloping portion of the age-earnings profile.

A. TSLS ESTIMATES

To improve efficiency of the estimates and control for age-related trends in earnings, we estimated the following TSLS model:

(1)
$$E_i = X_i \pi + \sum_c Y_{ic} \delta_c + \sum_c \sum_j Y_{ic} Q_{ij} \theta_{jc} + \epsilon_i$$

(2)
$$\ln W_i = X_i \beta + \sum_c Y_{ic} \xi_c + \rho E_i + \mu_i,$$

where E_i is the education of the ith individual, X_i is a vector of covariates, Q_{ij} is a dummy variable indicating whether the individual was born in quarter j ($j = 1, 2, 3$), and Y_{ic} is a dummy variable indicating whether the individual was born in year c ($c = 1, \ldots, 10$), and W_i is the weekly wage. The coefficient ρ is the return to education. If the residual in the wage equation, μ, is correlated with years of education due to, say, omitted variables, OLS estimates of the return to education will be biased.

The excluded instruments from the wage equation in the TSLS estimates are three quarter-of-birth dummies interacted with nine year-of-birth dummies. Because year-of-birth dummies are also included in the wage equations, the effect of education is identified by variation in education across quarters of birth within each birth year.[16] Quarter of birth (Q_j) is a legitimate instrument if it is uncorrelated with μ and correlated with education.

Tables IV, V, and VI present a series of TSLS estimates of equation (2) for the 1920–1929 cohort, 1930–1939 cohort, and 1940–1949 cohort, respectively. For comparison, the OLS and TSLS estimates of each specification are presented. For example, column (1) of Table IV shows that the OLS estimate of the return to education for 40–49 year-old men in the 1970 Census is 0.080 (with a t-ratio of 200.5), holding year-of-birth effects constant. Column (2) shows that when the same model is estimated by TSLS using quarter-of-birth dummies as instruments for years of education, the return to education is 0.077 (with a t-ratio of 5.1). In columns (3) and (4) we add a quadratic age term to the OLS and TSLS equations. This variable, which is measured up to the quarter of a year, is included to control for within-year-of-birth age effects on earnings.

The remaining columns repeat the first four columns, but also include race dummies, a dummy for residence in an SMSA, a marital status dummy, and eight region-of-residence dummies. Regardless of the set of included regressors, the TSLS and OLS estimates of the return to education for this sample are close in magnitude, and the difference between them is never statistically significant.[17]

In Table V we present estimates of the same set of models using 40–49 year-old men from the 1980 Census. Again, the similarity between the various OLS and TSLS estimates

---

[16] *The TSLS estimates differ from the Wald estimates in two important respects. First, the TSLS estimates include covariates. Second, the TSLS models are identified by the variation in education across each quarter of birth in each year, whereas the Wald estimate is identified by the overall difference in education between the first quarter and the rest of the year.*

[17] *Because the OLS estimates of the return to education are extremely precise with these large samples, the standard error of the TSLS estimates is approximately equal to the standard error of the difference between the OLS and TSLS estimates. The TSLS standard error can thus be used to perform an approximate Hausman [1978] specification test.*

TABLE IV

OLS AND TSLS ESTIMATES OF THE RETURN TO EDUCATION FOR MEN BORN 1920–1929: 1970 CENSUS[a]

Independent variable	(1) OLS	(2) TSLS	(3) OLS	(4) TSLS	(5) OLS	(6) TSLS	(7) OLS	(8) TSLS
Years of education	0.0802	0.0769	0.0802	0.1310	0.0701	0.0669	0.0701	0.1007
	(0.0004)	(0.0150)	(0.0004)	(0.0334)	(0.0004)	(0.0151)	(0.0004)	(0.0334)
Race (1 = black)	—	—	—	—	-0.2980	-0.3055	-0.2980	-0.2271
					(0.0043)	(0.0353)	(0.0043)	(0.0776)
SMSA (1 = center city)	—	—	—	—	0.1343	0.1362	0.1343	0.1163
					(0.0026)	(0.0092)	(0.0026)	(0.0198)
Married (1 = married)	—	—	—	—	0.2928	0.2941	0.2928	0.2804
					(0.0037)	(0.0072)	(0.0037)	(0.0141)
9 Year-of-birth dummies	Yes	Yes	Yes	Yes	Yes	Yes	Yes	Yes
8 Region of residence dummies	No	No	No	No	Yes	Yes	Yes	Yes
Age	—	—	0.1446	0.1409	—	—	0.1162	0.1170
			(0.0676)	(0.0704)			(0.0652)	(0.0662)
Age-squared	—	—	-0.0015	-0.0014	—	—	-0.0013	-0.0012
			(0.0007)	(0.0008)			(0.0007)	(0.0007)
χ^2 [dof]	—	36.0 [29]	—	25.6 [27]	—	34.2 [29]	—	28.8 [27]

[a] Standard errors are in parentheses. Sample size is 247,199. Instruments are a full set of quarter-of-birth times year-of-birth interactions. The sample consists of males born in the United States. The sample is drawn from the State, County, and Neighborhoods 1 percent samples of the 1970 Census (15 percent form). The dependent variable is the log of weekly earnings. Age and age-squared are measured in quarters of years. Each equation also includes an intercept.

TABLE V

OLS AND TSLS ESTIMATES OF THE RETURN TO EDUCATION FOR MEN BORN 1930–1939: 1980 CENSUS[a]

Independent variable	(1) OLS	(2) TSLS	(3) OLS	(4) TSLS	(5) OLS	(6) TSLS	(7) OLS	(8) TSLS
Years of education	0.0711	0.0891	0.0711	0.0760	0.0632	0.0806	0.0632	0.0600
	(0.0003)	(0.0161)	(0.0003)	(0.0290)	(0.0003)	(0.0164)	(0.0003)	(0.0299)
Race (1 = black)	—	—	—	—	−0.2575	−0.2302	−0.2575	−0.2626
					(0.0040)	(0.0261)	(0.0040)	(0.0458)
SMSA (1 = center city)	—	—	—	—	0.1763	0.1581	0.1763	0.1797
					(0.0029)	(0.0174)	(0.0029)	(0.0305)
Married (1 = married)	—	—	—	—	0.2479	0.2440	0.2479	0.2486
					(0.0032)	(0.0049)	(0.0032)	(0.0073)
9 Year-of-birth dummies	Yes	Yes	Yes	Yes	Yes	Yes	Yes	Yes
8 Region-of-residence dummies	No	No	No	No	Yes	Yes	Yes	Yes
Age	—	—	−0.0772	−0.0801	—	—	−0.0760	−0.0741
			(0.0621)	(0.0645)			(0.0604)	(0.0626)
Age-squared	—	—	0.0008	0.0008	—	—	0.0008	0.0007
			(0.0007)	(0.0007)			(0.0007)	(0.0007)
χ^2 [dof]	—	25.4 [29]	—	23.1 [27]	—	22.5 [29]	—	19.6 [27]

[a] Standard errors are in parentheses. Sample size is 329,509. Instruments are a full set of quarter-of-birth times year-of-birth interactions. The sample consists of males born in the United States. The sample is drawn from the 5 percent sample of the 1980 Census. The dependent variable is the log of weekly earnings. Age and age-squared are measured in quarters of years. Each equation also includes an intercept.

TABLE VI

OLS AND TSLS ESTIMATES OF THE RETURN TO EDUCATION FOR MEN BORN 1940-1949: 1980 CENSUS[a]

Independent variable	(1) OLS	(2) TSLS	(3) OLS	(4) TSLS	(5) OLS	(6) TSLS	(7) OLS	(8) TSLS
Years of education	0.0573	0.0553	0.0573	0.0948	0.0520	0.0393	0.0521	0.0779
	(0.0003)	(0.0138)	(0.0003)	(0.0223)	(0.0003)	(0.0145)	(0.0003)	(0.0239)
Race (1 = black)	—	—	—	—	-0.2107	-0.2266	-0.2108	-0.1786
					(0.0032)	(0.0183)	(0.0032)	(0.0296)
SMSA (1 = center city)	—	—	—	—	0.1418	0.1535	0.1419	0.1182
					(0.0023)	(0.0135)	(0.0023)	(0.0220)
Married (1 = married)	—	—	—	—	0.2445	0.2442	0.2444	0.2450
					(0.0022)	(0.0022)	(0.0022)	(0.0023)
9 Year-of-birth dummies	Yes	Yes	Yes	Yes	Yes	Yes	Yes	Yes
8 Region-of-residence dummies	No	No	No	No	Yes	Yes	Yes	Yes
Age	—	—	0.1800	0.1325	—	—	0.1518	0.1215
			(0.0389)	(0.0486)			(0.0379)	(0.0474)
Age-squared	—	—	0.0023	0.0016	—	—	0.0019	0.0015
			(0.0006)	(0.0007)			(0.0005)	(0.0007)
χ^2 [dof]	—	101.6 [29]	—	49.1 [27]	—	93.6 [29]	—	50.6 [27]

[a] Standard errors are in parentheses. Sample size is 486,926. Instruments are a full set of quarter-of-birth times year-of-birth interactions. Sample consists of males born in the United States. The sample is drawn from the 5 percent samples of the 1980 Census. The dependent variable is the log of weekly earnings. Age and age-squared are measured in quarters of years. Each equation also includes an intercept.

of the return to education is striking. For example, comparing the OLS and TSLS models in columns (7) and (8)—which include quadratic age and several covariates—the OLS estimate of the return to education is 0.063 (with a t-ratio of 210.7), and the TSLS estimate of the return to education is 0.060 (with a t-ratio of 2).

Table VI presents estimates for 30–39-year-old men (born 1940–1949) using data from the 1980 Census. This sample has a slightly negative and insignificant Wald estimate of the return to education. However, the TSLS estimate of the return to education is positive and statistically significant. Furthermore, in each of the four specifications the return to education estimated by TSLS is statistically indistinguishable from the return estimated by OLS. Including age and age-squared to control for within-year-of-birth earnings trends leads to an even higher TSLS estimate of the return to education.

All of the TSLS estimates we have presented so far are overidentified because several estimates of the return to education could be constructed from subsets of the instruments. For example, one could compare the return to education using variation in education between first and fourth quarter births in 1940, between second and third quarter births in 1940, between second and third quarter births in 1941, etc. The χ^2 statistics presented at the bottom of Tables IV, V, and VI test the hypothesis that the various combinations of instruments yield the same estimate of the return to education. This statistic is calculated as the sample size times the R^2 from a regression of the residuals from the TSLS equation on the exogenous variables and instruments [Newey, 1985]. In spite of the huge sample sizes, the overidentifying restrictions are not rejected in the models in Tables IV and V. The models in Table VI lead to a rejection of the overidentifying restrictions, but the models that include a quadratic age trend are close to not rejecting at the 0.01 level.

In addition to the log weekly wage, we have also examined the impact of compulsory schooling on the log of annual salary and on weeks worked. This exercise suggests that the main impact of compulsory schooling is on the log weekly wage, and not on weeks worked. For example, when the log of weeks worked is used as the dependent variable in column (6) of Table VII instead of the log weekly wage, the TSLS estimate is 0.016 with a standard error of 0.008. This is within sampling variance of the OLS estimate, which is 0.008 with a standard error of 0.0002.

B. ALLOWING THE SEASONAL PATTERN IN EDUCATION TO VARY BY STATE OF BIRTH

Although most schools admit students born in the beginning of the year at an older age, school start age policy varies across states and across school districts within many states. Therefore, because compulsory schooling constrains some students to remain in school until their birthday, the relationship between education and season of birth is expected to vary among states that have different start age policies. This additional variability can be used to improve the precision of the TSLS estimates.

To incorporate the cross-state seasonal variation in education, we computed TSLS estimates that use as instruments for education a set of three quarter-of-birth dummies interacted with fifty state-of-birth dummies, in addition to three quarter-of-birth dummies interacted with nine year-of-birth dummies.[18] The estimates also include fifty state-of-birth dummies in the wage equation, so the variability in education used to identify the return to education in the TSLS estimates is solely due to differences by season of birth. Unlike the previous TSLS estimates, the seasonal differences are now allowed to vary by state as well as by birth year.

Table VII presents the TSLS and OLS estimates of the new specification for the sample of 40–49 year-old men in the 1980 Census. This is the same sample used in the estimates in Table V. Freeing up the instruments by state of birth and including 50 state-of-birth dummies in the wage equation results in approximately a 40 percent reduction in the standard errors of the TSLS estimates. Furthermore, in the specifications in each of the columns in Table VII, the estimated return to education in the TSLS model is slightly greater than the corresponding TSLS estimate in Table V, whereas in each of the OLS models the return is slightly smaller in Table VII than in Table V. As a consequence, the difference between the TSLS and OLS estimates is of greater significance. For example, the TSLS estimate in column (6) of Table VII is 0.083 with a standard error of 0.010, and the OLS estimate is 0.063 with a standard error of 0.0003: the TSLS estimate is nearly 30 percent greater than the OLS estimate.

One possible explanation for the higher TSLS estimate of the return to education may be that compulsory schooling pushes some students to graduate high school, so that part of the TSLS estimate reflects a high school "completion" effect. On the other hand, using 1980 Census data, Card and Krueger [1992a] find little evidence of nonlinearity in the return to education for middle-aged men with three to fifteen years of education. If the earnings function is log-linear, then our estimates may be representative of the average return to education in our sample.[19]

To further explore this issue, we computed OLS estimates of the return to education for men with nine to twelve years of schooling, and found little difference between estimates for this subsample and the full sample. For example, the OLS estimate of the return to education for men born 1930–1939 with nine to twelve years of education is 0.059, compared with 0.063 for the full sample in column (5) of Table V. We also note that we obtained similar TSLS estimates of the return to education when our extracts were restricted to men with a high school degree or less.

---

[18] In the context of the model, we added a set of state-of-birth dummy variables interacted with quarter-of-birth dummy variables to equation (1), and a set of 50 state-of-birth dummies to equation (2). Although in principle we could also interact the state-of-birth-by-quarter-of-birth effects with year of birth, to have a total of 1,500 exclusion restrictions, estimation of such a model is computationally burdensome.

[19] Heckman and Polachek [1974] provide some additional evidence that the earnings function is approximately log-linear.

TABLE VII

OLS AND TSLS ESTIMATES OF THE RETURN TO EDUCATION FOR MEN BORN 1930–1939: 1980 CENSUS[a]

Independent variable	(1) OLS	(2) TSLS	(3) OLS	(4) TSLS	(5) OLS	(6) TSLS	(7) OLS	(8) TSLS
Years of education	0.0673	0.0928	0.0673	0.0907	0.0628	0.0831	0.0628	0.0811
	(0.0003)	(0.0093)	(0.0003)	(0.0107)	(0.0003)	(0.0095)	(0.0003)	(0.0109)
Race (1 = black)	—	—	—	—	−0.2547	−0.2333	−0.2547	−0.2354
					(0.0043)	(0.0109)	(0.0043)	(0.0122)
SMSA (1 = center city)	—	—	—	—	0.1705	0.1511	0.1705	0.1531
					(0.0029)	(0.0095)	(0.0029)	(0.0107)
Married (1 = married)	—	—	—	—	0.2487	0.2435	0.2487	0.2441
					(0.0032)	(0.0040)	(0.0032)	(0.0042)
9 Year-of-birth dummies	Yes	Yes	Yes	Yes	Yes	Yes	Yes	Yes
8 Region-of-residence dummies	No	No	No	No	Yes	Yes	Yes	Yes
50 State-of-birth dummies	Yes	Yes	Yes	Yes	Yes	Yes	Yes	Yes
Age	—	—	−0.0757	−0.0880	—	—	−0.0778	−0.0876
			(0.0617)	(0.0624)			(0.0603)	(0.0609)
Age-squared	—	—	0.0008	0.0009	—	—	0.0008	0.0009
			(0.0007)	(0.0007)			(0.0007)	(0.0007)
χ^2 [dof]	—	163 [179]	—	161 [177]	—	164 [179]	—	162 [177]

[a] Standard errors are in parentheses. Excluded instruments are 30 quarter-of-birth times year-of-birth dummies and 150 quarter-of-birth times state-of-birth interactions. Age and age-squared are measured in quarters of years. Each equation also includes an intercept term. The sample is the same as in Table VI. Sample size is 329,509.

C. Estimates for Black Men

Using data on men born in the first half of the twentieth century, many researchers find that OLS estimates of the return to education are lower for black men than for white men (e.g., Welch [1973]). At least part of the lower return to education for black men appears to be due to the lower quality schools that were provided for black students in these cohorts (see Card and Krueger [1992b]). If schools attended by black students were of inferior quality, then we would expect to find a lower return to compulsory schooling for black workers than for white workers.

In Table VIII we provide estimates of the return to education for the sample of black men born 1930–1939. As in Table VII the excluded instruments for education are interactions between quarter-of-birth and year-of-birth dummies, and interactions between quarter-of-birth and state-of-birth dummies. Both the OLS and TSLS estimates indicate that the return to education is lower for black men than for the entire male population. In view of the lower quality of schools attended by black students, this finding provides some additional support for the plausibility of the TSLS estimates. Moreover, the TSLS estimates for this subsample are within sampling variance of the OLS estimates. Unlike the estimates for the entire sample, however, the TSLS estimates are slightly less than the OLS estimates.

III. Other Possible Effects of Season of Birth

The validity of the identification strategy used in Section II rests on the assumption that season of birth is a legitimate instrument for education in an earnings equation. From Section I it would seem that season of birth is related to education because of compulsory schooling requirements. However, for the TSLS estimates to be consistent, it must also be the case that season of birth is uncorrelated with the residual in the earnings equation (μ). In other words, if season of birth influences earnings for reasons other than compulsory schooling, our approach is called into question. Although we believe the evidence in Section I establishes that season of birth influences education exclusively because of compulsory schooling, it is useful to consider the impact of other possible effects of season of birth.

First, several educational psychologists have examined the effect of age at school entry on educational achievement.[20] Most of this literature, however, analyzes extremely small samples, focuses on test scores rather than graduation rates, and takes age at entry to school as exogenous. Furthermore, much of the past literature fails to adequately control for the effects of age.[21] Nevertheless, the previous research indicates that there might be a relationship between age at school entry and academic performance. The consensus in

---

[20] See Halliwell [1966] for a survey of the literature on early school entry and school success; see DiPasquale, Moule, and Flewelling [1980] for a survey of the "birthday effect" on educational achievement.

[21] This point is also made by Lewis and Griffin [1981] in the context of season-of-birth effects in diagnoses of schizophrenia.

TABLE VIII

OLS AND TSLS ESTIMATES OF THE RETURN TO EDUCATION FOR BLACK MEN BORN 1930-1939: 1980 CENSUS[a]

Independent variable	(1) OLS	(2) TSLS	(3) OLS	(4) TSLS	(5) OLS	(6) TSLS	(7) OLS	(8) TSLS
Years of education	0.0672	0.0635	0.0671	0.0555	0.0576	0.0461	0.0576	0.0391
	(0.0013)	(0.0185)	(0.0003)	(0.0199)	(0.0013)	(0.0187)	(0.0013)	(0.0199)
SMSA (1 = center city)	—	—	—	—	0.1885	0.2053	0.1884	0.2155
					(0.0142)	(0.0308)	(0.0142)	(0.0324)
Married (1 = married)	—	—	—	—	0.2216	0.2272	0.2216	0.2307
					(0.0193)	(0.0136)	(0.0100)	(0.0140)
9 Year-of-birth dummies	Yes	Yes	Yes	Yes	Yes	Yes	Yes	Yes
8 Region-of-residence dummies	No	No	No	No	Yes	Yes	Yes	Yes
49 State-of-birth dummies	Yes	Yes	Yes	Yes	Yes	Yes	Yes	Yes
Age	—	—	-0.0309	-0.3274	—	—	-0.2978	-0.3237
			(0.2538)	(0.2560)			(0.0032)	(0.2497)
Age-squared	—	—	0.0033	0.0035	—	—	0.0032	0.0035
			(0.0028)	(0.0028)			(0.0027)	(0.0028)
χ^2 [dof]	—	184 [176]	—	181 [173]	—	178 [176]	—	175 [173]

[a] Standard errors are in parentheses. Excluded instruments are 30 quarter-of-birth times year-of-birth dummies and 147 quarter-of-birth times state-of-birth interactions. (There are no black men in the sample born in Hawaii.) Age and age-squared are measured in quarters of years. Each equation also includes an intercept term. The sample is drawn from the 1980 Census. Sample size is 26,913.

this literature is that, if anything, students who start school at an older age are more mature and perform better in school.

Although we do not find this evidence convincing, it is worth noting what bias the prevailing interpretation of the psychological season of birth effect might have on our estimates. Assume, for the moment, that children born in the beginning of the year are better students because they are older than their classmates. Men born in the first quarter of the year would therefore have greater unobserved ability for a given level of schooling. However, men born in the first quarter also have less education, probably due to the dominant effect of compulsory education laws. Assuming that this unobserved ability is rewarded in the labor market, any estimator of the return to education that is identified by variations in education due to season of birth would be biased downward.

Second, we note that if season of birth were related to the socioeconomic status of children's parents, one might expect to find a connection between season of birth and education. If this were the case, season of birth would be an unsatisfactory instrumental variable for our purposes. Lam and Miron [1987], however, present a variety of evidence suggesting that season of birth is unrelated to the socioeconomic status (and other characteristics) of parents. For example, they find that the seasonal pattern in births is virtually identical for illegitimate births and legitimate births. In addition, they find that the seasonal pattern of birth is similar across urban and rural families, across regions of the United States that have diverse economic and cultural conditions, and within countries before and after dramatic economic transitions.

Furthermore, both of these alternative explanations are hard pressed to explain why the effect of season of birth on education is smaller for more recent cohorts, as is clear from Table I. There is no obvious reason why the psychological or socioeconomic explanations for the seasonal pattern of education would have less force for the 1940s cohort than for the 1920s cohort. On the other hand, if season of birth influences education because of compulsory schooling, one would expect to find a smaller effect for individuals in more recent cohorts, who are likely to be less constrained by the compulsory schooling requirement.

Third, assuming that the earnings function is consistently estimated by OLS (e.g., no correlation between education and the error) and that the only impact of quarter of birth on earnings is through education, then quarter-of-birth dummies should be insignificant in an earnings equation that also includes education. We tested this proposition by adding three quarter-of-birth dummies to the OLS models for the sample of prime-age men in column 5 of Tables IV and V. The prob-value for an F-test of the null hypothesis that the quarter-of-birth dummies jointly equal zero is 0.73 in the 1970 Census and 0.13 in the 1980 Census.

Finally, and perhaps most convincing, we have estimated the effect of season of birth on the earnings of college graduates, a sample whose schooling was not prolonged by compulsory attendance. If season of birth affects education for a reason other than compulsory schooling (e.g., psychological effects of school start age), we would expect season of birth to be related to earnings for this sample. On the other hand, if season of birth only affects education and earnings because of compulsory schooling, we would not expect any relationship in this sample. The estimates suggest that quarter of birth has no effect on earnings for college graduates, a finding which supports the estimation framework employed throughout the paper. For example, using the sample of 40–49-year-old college graduates in the 1970 Census, an F-test of the joint significance of quarter-of-birth dummies in an earnings regression that includes year-of-birth dummies is not rejected at the 25 percent level. Similar results hold for 40–49-year-old men in 1980. We take this as strong evidence that, in the absence of compulsory schooling, season of birth would have no effect on earnings.

IV. CONCLUSION

Differences in season of birth create a natural experiment that we use to study the effect of compulsory school attendance on schooling and earnings. Because individuals born in the beginning of the year usually start school at an older age than that of their classmates, they are allowed to drop out of school after attaining less education. Our exploration of the relationship between quarter of birth and educational attainment suggests that season of birth has a small effect on the level of education men ultimately attain. To support the contention that this is a consequence of compulsory schooling laws, we have assembled evidence showing that some students leave school as soon as they attain the legal dropout age, and that season of birth has no effect on postsecondary years of schooling.

Variation in education that is related to season of birth arises because some individuals, by accident of date of birth, are *forced* to attend school longer than others because of compulsory schooling. Using season of birth as an instrument for education in an earnings equation, we find a remarkable similarity between the OLS and the TSLS estimates of the monetary return to education. Differences between the OLS and the TSLS estimates are typically not statistically significant, and whatever differences that do exist tend to suggest that omitted variables, or measurement error in education, may induce a downward bias in the OLS estimate of the return to education.[22] This evidence casts doubt on the importance of omitted variables bias in OLS estimates of the return to education, at least for years of schooling around the compulsory schooling level.

Our results provide support for the view that students who are compelled to attend school longer by compulsory schooling laws earn higher wages as a result of their extra schooling. Moreover, we find that compulsory schooling laws are effective in compelling

---

[22] *Siegel and Hodge [1968] find that the correlation between individuals' education reported in the 1960 Census and in a Post Enumeration Survey is 0.933. This correlation gives an upper bound estimate of the ratio of the variance of true education to the variance of reported education because individuals may consistently misreport their education in both surveys. Moreover, the downward bias in the OLS estimate of the return to education due to measurement error will be exacerbated because the included covariates are likely to explain some of the true variation in education, and because of variability in the quality of education.*

some students to attend school. Do these results mean that compulsory schooling laws are necessarily beneficial? A complete answer to this question would require additional research on the social and private costs of compulsory school attendance. For example, compulsory attendance may have the benefit of reducing crime rates. And they may impose a social cost because students who are compelled to attend school may interfere with the learning of other students.

Appendix 1: Data

The empirical analysis draws on a variety of data sets, each constructed from Public Use Census Data. The sample used in Table I to compute quarter-of-birth main effects on educational outcomes consists of all men born 1930–1949 in the 1980 Census 5 percent sample. The sample used to compute the difference-in-differences estimates of the effect of compulsory schooling laws on enrollment in Table II consists of all sixteen-year olds in each of the following Census samples: the 1960 Census 1 percent sample, the two 1 percent State samples from the 1970 Census, and the 1980 Census 5 percent sample. The two samples used to compute the estimates in Tables III–VI consist of men with positive earnings born between 1920–1929 in the three 1970 Census 1 percent samples drawn from the 15 percent long-form, and the sample of men with positive earnings born between 1930–1949 in the 1980 Census 5 percent sample. Information on date of birth in the Censuses is limited to quarter of birth. A more detailed description of the data sets used in the tables and figures is provided below.

A. Samples used in Table I, Tables III–VII, and Figures I–V

1. 1970 Census. The 1970 Census micro data are documented in *Public Use Samples of Basic Records from the 1970 Census* [Washington, DC: U. S. Department of Commerce, 1972]. Our extract combines data from three separate public-use files: the State, County group, and Neighborhood files. Each file contains a self-weighting, mutually exclusive sample of 1 percent of the population (as of April 1, 1970), yielding a total sample of 3 percent of the population. The data sets we use are based on the questionnaire that was administered to 15 percent of the population.

The sample consists of white and black men born between 1920–1929 in the United States. Birth year was derived from reported age and quarter of birth. In addition, we excluded any man whose age, sex, race, veteran status, weeks worked, highest grade completed or salary was allocated by the Census Bureau. Finally, the sample is limited to men with positive wage and salary earnings and positive weeks worked in 1969.

Weekly earnings is computed by dividing annual earnings by annual weeks worked. Annual earnings is reported in intervals of $100. This variable was converted to a continuous variable by taking the average of the interval endpoints. Weeks worked is reported as a categorical variable in six intervals, and was also converted to a continuous variable by taking the mean of interval endpoints.

Nine region dummies were coded directly from the Census Regions variable in the Neighborhoods 1 percent sample, from state of residence in the State 1 percent sample, and from county locations in the County Group file. If county groups straddled two states, the counties were allocated to the region containing the greatest land-mass of the county group. The education variable is years of schooling completed. The marital status variable equals one if the respondent is currently married with his spouse present. The SMSA variable equals one if the respondent works in an SMSA.

2. 1980 Census. The 1980 Census micro data are documented in *Census of Population and Housing, 1980: Public Use Microdata Samples* [Washington, DC: U. S. Department of Commerce, 1983]. Our extract is drawn from the 5 percent Public Use Sample (the A Sample). This file contains a self-weighting sample of 5 percent of the population as of April 1, 1980.

The extract we created consists of white and black men born in the United States between 1930–1959. Birth year was derived from reported age and quarter of birth. We excluded respondents whose age, sex, race, quarter of birth, weeks worked, years of schooling, or salary was allocated by the Census Bureau. For the estimates in Tables IV–VII and Figure V, the sample is limited to men with positive wage and salary earnings and positive weeks worked in 1979; for the estimates in Table I, the sample includes all men, regardless of whether they worked in 1979.

Weekly earnings in 1979 is computed by dividing annual earnings by weeks worked. Dummies for nine Census regions are coded from state of residence. The education variable is years of completed schooling. The marital status dummy equals one if the respondent is currently married with his spouse present. The SMSA variable equals one if the respondent lives in an SMSA.

B. Samples Used to Compute the Enrollment Estimates in Table II

Table II uses data from the 1960, 1970, and 1980 Censuses. The 1960 Census data are documented in *A Public Use Sample of Basic Records from the 1960 Census* [Washington, DC: U. S. Department of Commerce, 1975]. Our extract for 1960 is drawn from the 1 percent Public Use Sample. The sample used consists of boys and girls born in 1944. The extract of the 1970 Census used in Table II is drawn from the two 1 percent State files (the State samples of the 5 percent Form and of the 15 percent Form) because these files identify state of residence. The sample consists of boys and girls born in 1954. Finally, the sample of boys and girls born in 1964 in the 1980 Census, 5 percent sample are used as well. In each of the three samples, individuals with allocated age or enrollment were excluded.

APPENDIX 2: COMPULSORY SCHOOL ATTENDANCE AGE BY STATE

State	1960	1970	1980	Notes
1 Alabama	16	16	16	
2 Alaska	16	16	16	
4 Arizona	16	16	16	
5 Arkansas	16	16	15	
6 California	16	16	16	
8 Colorado	16	16	16	
9 Connecticut	16	16	16	
10 Delaware	16	16	16	
11 D.C.	16	16	16	
12 Florida	16	16	16	
13 Georgia	16	16	16	
15 Hawaii	16	18	18	Increased to 18 midyear, 1970
16 Idaho	16	16	16	
17 Illinois	16	16	16	
18 Indiana	16	16	16	
19 Iowa	16	16	16	
20 Kansas	16	16	16	
21 Kentucky	16	16	16	
22 Louisiana	16	16	16	
23 Maine	15	17	17	
24 Maryland	16	16	16	
25 Massachusetts	16	16	16	
26 Michigan	16	16	16	
27 Minnesota	16	16	16	
28 Mississippi	—	—	—	Age 14 starting 1983
29 Missouri	16	16	16	
30 Montana	16	16	16	
31 Nebraska	16	16	16	
32 Nevada	17	17	17	
33 New Hampshire	16	16	16	
34 New Jersey	16	16	16	
35 New Mexico	16	17	17	
36 New York	16	16	16	May be changed by city districts

APPENDIX 2: (CONTINUED)

State	1960	1970	1980	Notes
37 North Carolina	16	16	16	
38 North Dakota	17	16	16	
39 Ohio	18	18	18	
40 Oklahoma	18	18	18	
41 Oregon	18	18	18	
42 Pennsylvania	17	17	17	
44 Rhode Island	16	16	16	
45 South Carolina	—	16	16	Reinstated in 1967
46 South Dakota	16	16	16	
47 Tennessee	17	17	16	Increased to age 17 in 1983
48 Texas	16	17	17	Must finish school term
49 Utah	18	18	18	
50 Vermont	16	16	16	
51 Virginia	16	17	17	
53 Washington	16	16	18	
54 West Virginia	16	16	16	
55 Wisconsin	16	16	16	Must finish school term
54 Wyoming	17	17	16	

Source: U.S. Office of Education, *Digest of Education Statistics* (Washington, DC: GPO, various years).

REFERENCES

Angrist, Joshua D., and Alan Krueger, "Why Do World War Two Veterans Earn More than Nonveterans?" NBER Working Paper No. 2991, May 1989. [Published in *Journal of Labor Economics,* 12 (January 1994), 74–97.]

———, and ———, "The Effect of Age at School Entry on Educational Attainment: An Application of Instrumental Variables with Moments from Two Samples," NBER Working Paper No. 3571, December 1990.[Published in *Journal of the American Statistical Association,* 87 (October 1992), 412–37.]

Card, David, and Alan Krueger, "Does School Quality Matter? Returns to Education and the Characteristics of Public Schools in the United States," *Journal of Political Economy,* 100 (February 1992a), 1–40.

———, and ———, "School Quality and Black/White Earnings: A Direct Assessment," *Quarterly Journal of Economics,* CVII (February 1992b), 151–200.

Department of Health, Education and Welfare, *State Legislation on School Attendance* (Washington, DC: Circular No. 573, January 1959).

Department of Employment, Education and Training, *School Leavers* (Canberra, Australia: Edition 8,1987), p. 35.

DiPasquale, Glenn, Allan Moule, and Robert Flewelling, "The Birthdate Effect," *Journal of Learning Disabilities,* XIII (May 1980) 234–37.

Durbin, J. "Errors in Variables," *Review of the International Statistical Institute,* XXII (1954), 23–32.

Edwards, Linda, "An Empirical Analysis of Compulsory Schooling Legislation, 1940–1960," *Journal of Law and Economics,* XXI (April 1978), 203–22.

Ehrenberg, Ronald, and Alan Marcus, "Minimum Wages and Teenagers' Enrollment-Employment Outcomes: A Multinomial Logit Model," *Journal of Human Resources,* XXVII (1982), 39–58.

Griliches, Zvi, "Estimating the Returns to Schooling—Some Econometric Problems," *Econometrica,* XLV (January 1977), 1–22.

Halliwell, Joseph, "Reviewing the Reviews on Entrance Age and School Success," *Journal of Educational Research,* LIX (May–June 1966), 395–401.

Hausman, Jerry, "Specification Tests in Econometrics," *Econometrica,* XLVI (November 1978), 1251–71.

Heckman, James, and Solomon Polachek, "Empirical Evidence on the Functional Form of the Earnings-Schooling Relationship," *Journal of the American Statistical Association,* LXIX (1974), 350–54.

Huntington, Ellsworth, *Season of Birth: Its Relation to Human Abilities* (New York, NY: Wiley, 1938).

Kotin, Lawrence, and William F. Aikman, *Legal Foundations of Compulsory School Attendance* (Port Washington, NY: Kennikat Press, 1980).

Lam, David, and Jeffrey Miron, "The Seasonality of Births in Human Populations," unpublished paper, *Population Studies Center Research Report* No. 87-114, University of Michigan, 1987.

Lewis, Marc, and Patricia Griffin, "An Explanation for the Season of Birth Effect in Schizophrenia and Certain Other Diseases," *Psychological Bulletin,* LXXXIX (1981), 589–96.

Newey, Whitney, "Generalized Method of Moments Specification Testing," *Journal of Econometrics,* XXIX (1985), 229–56.

Organization for Economic Cooperation and Development, *Compulsory Schooling in a Changing World* (Paris: OECD, 1983).

Siegel, Paul, and Robert Hodge, "A Causal Approach to the Study of Measurement Error," *Methodology in Social Research,* Hubert Blalock and Ann Blalock, eds. (New York, NY: McGraw Hill Book Co., 1968), Chapter 2, pp. 29–59.

Spence, Michael, "Job Market Signaling," *Quarterly Journal of Economics,* LXXXVII (1973), 355–75.

Wald, Abraham, "The Fitting of Straight Lines if Both Variables Are Subject to Error," *Annals of Mathematical Statistics,* XI (1940), 284–300.

Welch, Finis, "Education and Racial Discrimination," in *Discrimination in Labor Market,* O. Ashenfelter and A. Rees, eds. (Princeton, NJ: Princeton University Press, 1973), pp. 43–81.

Willis, Robert J., "Wage Determinants: A Survey and Reinterpretation of Human Capital Earnings Functions," *Handbook of Labor Economics,* I, O. Ashenfelter and R. Layard, eds. (Amsterdam: Elsevier Science Publishers BV, 1986), Chapter 10.

ABOUT THE AUTHORS

Joshua Angrist: Mr. IV

Bob Solow once famously remarked that everything reminds Milton Friedman of the money supply, while everything reminds him of sex. I think it is fair to say that everything reminds Joshua Angrist of identification issues. Indeed, the screen saver on Angrist's computer flashes "ALWAYS USE IV!" after a period of dormancy.

Identification issues concern the sources of variability in key variables that are used to estimate economic relationships. In many studies, the ideal source of variability would stem from an experiment in which the X variable is randomly assigned to ensure that it is independent of omitted variables. Actual experiments are rare in economics, but Angrist has ingeniously used instrumental variables (IV) models to exploit "natural experiments" that approximate the experimental design. Perhaps the best example of this type of work is Angrist's 1990 *American Economic Review* article, which uses the Vietnam-era draft lottery to estimate the effect of past military service on men's earnings.

Using IV and the natural experiments approach, Angrist has made important contributions in three substantive areas of economics: (1) the effect of military service on civilian outcomes, such as employment and earnings; (2) the economics of education; and (3) the Israeli labor market. Together with Guido Imbens and Donald Rubin, he has also contributed to the interpretation of instrumental variables estimates. A common thread runs through all Angrist's work: he has developed several novel and persuasive ways of estimating and interpreting economic relationships.

Angrist's interest in labor economics started when he was an undergraduate economics major at Oberlin College. He wrote a senior thesis on labor supply that attracted the attention of my colleague Orley Ashenfelter, who was brought in as an outside reader of Oberlin senior theses. Ashenfelter recruited Angrist to attend graduate school at Princeton, but Angrist first made a detour to Israel, where he studied at Hebrew University, married, and served in the Israeli army (which perhaps sparked his interest in the effect of military service on life outcomes).

After completing his Ph.D. at Princeton in 1989, Angrist taught at Harvard University and then Hebrew University before moving to his present post in the MIT economics department.

Alan B. Krueger

Alan B. Krueger

Alan Krueger is the Bendheim Professor of Economics and Public Affairs at Princeton University. He has held a joint appointment in the Economics Department and the Woodrow Wilson School at Princeton University since 1987. He currently is the editor of the *Journal of Economic Perspectives* and is a research associate of the National Bureau of Economic Research. In 1994–1995, he served as the Chief Economist of the U.S. Department of Labor. He earned his B.S. degree with honors from Cornell University's School of Industrial and Labor Relations and his Ph.D. in economics from Harvard University.

Alan Krueger is a prolific scholar who has done pathbreaking work on a wide range of core substantive issues in labor economics, including the impacts of school quality and years of schooling on earnings, the determinants of interindustry wage differentials, the impact of technological change on the wage structure, and the labor market effects of social insurance policies. Krueger has also been a leader in the development of new and more credible approaches to identifying the effects of policy interventions on labor market and educational outcomes. For example, Krueger's work with Joshua Angrist that is reprinted here provides a remarkably novel and lucid approach to estimating the returns to schooling. He has similarly contributed to the development of convincing new quasi-experimental, empirical strategies for examining the effects of school inputs on earnings and the impact of the minimum wage on employment.

Krueger's formidable research contributions and public policy work have earned him multiple honors. He was awarded the Kershaw Prize for the best public policy researcher under the age of 40 by the Association of Public Policy and Management in 1997. He was also elected a fellow of the Econometric Society in 1996 and elected a member of the National Academy of Social Insurance in 1992.

Lawrence Katz

Estimates of the Economic Return to Schooling from a New Sample of Twins

ORLEY ASHENFELTER

ALAN KRUEGER

This paper uses a new survey to contrast the wages of genetically identical twins with different schooling levels. Multiple measurements of schooling levels were also collected to assess the effect of reporting error on the estimated economic returns to schooling. The data indicate that omitted ability variables do not bias the estimated return to schooling upward, but that measurement error does bias it downward. Adjustment for measurement error indicates that an additional year of schooling increases wages by 12–16 percent, a higher estimate of the economic returns to schooling than has been previously found. (JEL J31)

This paper uses a new survey of identical twins to study the economic returns to schooling. We estimate the returns to schooling by contrasting the wage rates of identical twins with different schooling levels. Our goal is to ensure that the correlation we observe between schooling and wage rates is not due to a correlation between schooling and a worker's ability or other characteristics. We do this by taking advantage of the fact that monozygotic (from the same egg) twins are genetically identical and have similar family backgrounds. In our survey we also took some unusual steps to measure a worker's schooling level accurately. We obtained independent estimates of each sibling's schooling level by asking the twins to report on both their own and their twin's schooling. These new data provide a simple and powerful method for assessing the role of measurement error in estimates of the economic returns to schooling.

Industrial Relations Section, Princeton University, Princeton, NJ 08544. This research was supported by the Industrial Relations Section, Princeton University, and the National Science Foundation (SES-9012149). We are indebted to Graham Burge, Greg Fisher, Kevin Hallock, and Michael Quinn for excellent assistance with data collection and processing, and to Michael Boozer for assistance with econometric computations. We are also indebted to Andy Miller of the Twins Days Festival, Twinsburg, Ohio, for help in arranging our interview survey of twins. We have received helpful comments on an earlier draft from James Heckman, David Neumark, and the referees.

Reprinted with permission from Orley Ashenfelter and Alan Krueger, "Estimates of the Economic Return to Schooling from a New Sample of Twins," American Economic Review, Vol. 84 No. 5 (December 1994), pp. 1157–1173.

[1] Jacob Mincer (1974) shows that if the return to schooling is independent of schooling level, and if the only costs of schooling are forgone earnings, then the proportional increase in earnings per year of

The results of our study indicate that the economic returns to schooling may have been underestimated in the past.[1] We estimate that each year of school completed increases a worker's wage rate by 12–16 percent. This estimate is nearly double previous estimates, and it is much greater than the estimate we would have obtained from these data had we been unable to adjust for omitted ability variables and measurement error. Surprisingly, we find no evidence that unobserved ability is positively related to the schooling level completed; instead, we find some weak evidence that unobserved ability may be negatively related to schooling level. We also find significant evidence of measurement error in schooling levels. Our results indicate that measurement error may lead to considerable underestimation of the returns to schooling in studies based on siblings.

We begin the paper with a discussion of the data we have collected. We compare our sample with more conventional data and with other surveys of twins, and we report on the extent of the measurement error we have found. We next report the detailed results of our study of the earnings of twins using conventional econometric methods to adjust for measurement error. In a final section of the paper we provide estimates and tests of the restrictions from a simple model of the earnings process that incorporates errors in the measurement of schooling.

I. DATA COLLECTION AND APPRAISAL

Our goal was to obtain a sample of data on twins in which we could obtain independent measures of each sibling's schooling level. We realized at the outset that this would be a simple task if both twins could be interviewed simultaneously. Both twins could then be asked questions about themselves and their siblings. A natural place to interview twins for this purpose is one of the many "twins festivals" held throughout the United States. In fact, we chose to attend the 16th Annual Twins Days Festival in Twinsburg, Ohio, in August of 1991. The Twinsburg Festival is the largest gathering of twins in the world, and in 1991, it attracted over 3,000 sets of twins, triplets, and quadruplets, many of whom were children. We managed to interview over 495 separate individuals over the age of 18 during the three days of the festival.

A. DATA COLLECTION

Our data-collection instrument was patterned after the questionnaire used by the Bureau of the Census for the Current Population Survey (CPS). (A copy of the questionnaire we used is available from the authors upon request.) Many of the questions on the survey are identical to those administered in the CPS, but some were written by us and are relevant only for a study of twins. Monozygotic (commonly called "identical") twins result from the splitting of a fertilized egg and are considered to be genetically identical. Dizygotic (commonly called

---

schooling is the rate of return on schooling investments. We follow conventional practice and simply call the proportional earnings increase per year of schooling the rate of return.

"fraternal") twins result from the fertilization of separate eggs and lead only to siblings that are genetically similar, as are non-twin brothers and sisters. One goal of our survey instrument was to determine whether the twins we interviewed were identical or fraternal. Much of our analysis below is restricted to a sample of identical twins.[2]

Our interviewing technique employed a team of five interviewers. The Twinsburg Festival maintains a research pavilion, which consists of a tent near the main entrance to the festival where researchers are located. To carry out our survey we placed an advertisement in the festival program inviting all adult twins to come to our booth to be interviewed. As an incentive we offered to make a contribution to the Twins Festival Scholarship Fund for every pair of adult twins who completed an interview. Our interviewers also roved throughout the festival grounds and approached every adult twin pair they encountered with a request for an interview. We were pleasantly surprised to find that virtually every pair of twins that we approached agreed to participate in our interviews. (Only four pairs of twins refused to be interviewed.) At the outset we were concerned that our questions about earnings, when asked in a face-to-face interview, might lead to some nonresponse. As it turned out, our concerns were misplaced, and virtually every twin provided the requested data (leading to a response rate for this question that is far higher than in the CPS). We asked each twin about his or her wage rate on the most recent job, but we have included twins in our sample only if they held jobs within the previous two years. In every case we separated the twins for the purposes of our interview, so that no twin heard his or her sibling's response to the questionnaire.

Although we report on a detailed comparison of our survey with data from the CPS below, we have some casual impressions about our sample of twins that should be kept in mind. Much of the purpose of a twins festival is to celebrate the similarity of the twins who are present. For the participants, these festivals provide an environment where twins are not so unusual as they ordinarily seem. The participants therefore tend to dress alike and to celebrate their similarity. As a result, we suspect that twins in our sample may bear stronger similarities than would be the case in a random sample of twins. For example, our sample contains a far greater representation of identical twins relative to fraternal twins than would exist in a random sample. These similarities will cause no problem for estimating the returns to schooling, but they may make a comparison of our study with other studies of twins more difficult.

On the other hand, the twins in our study do vary in dimensions that the twins in other studies do not. For example, the Jere Behrman et al. (1980) study is based on a sample of male veterans of World War II. Our study has a representation considerably broader than this, and it includes women as well as men.

---

[2] *We determined whether twins were identical by their answers to the question "Is your twin brother/sister an identical twin? That is, are you monozygotic twins?" In a study of questionnaire responses by pairs who claimed to be monozygotic twins Seymour Jablon et al. (1967) found that fewer than 3 percent were incorrect as measured by serological tests.*

TABLE 1

DESCRIPTIVE STATISTICS

	Means (standard deviations in parentheses)		
Variable	Identical twins[a]	Fraternal twins[a]	Population[b]
Self-reported education	14.11 (2.16)	13.72 (2.01)	13.14 (2.73)
Sibling-reported education	14.02 (2.14)	13.41 (2.07)	—
Hourly wage	$13.31 (11.19)	$12.07 (5.40)	$11.10 (7.41)
Age	36.56 (10.36)	35.59 (8.29)	38.91 (12.53)
White	0.94 (0.24)	0.93 (0.25)	0.87 (0.34)
Female	0.54 (0.50)	0.48 (0.50)	0.45 (0.50)
Self-employed	0.15 (0.36)	0.10 (0.30)	0.12 (0.32)
Covered by union	0.24 (0.43)	0.30 (0.46)	—
Married	0.45 (0.50)	0.54 (0.50)	0.62 (0.48)
Age of mother at birth	28.27 (6.37)	29.38 (7.05)	—
Twins report same education	0.49 (0.50)	0.43 (0.50)	—
Twins studied together	0.74 (0.44)	0.38 (0.49)	—
Helped sibling find job	0.43 (0.50)	0.24 (0.43)	—
Sibling helped find job	0.35 (0.48)	0.22 (0.41)	—
Sample size	298	92	164,085

[a] *Source:* Twinsburg Twins Survey, August 1991.
[b] *Source:* 1990 Current Population Survey (Outgoing Rotation Groups File). Sample includes workers aged 18–65 with an hourly wage greater than $1.00 per hour.

B. REPRESENTATIVENESS OF THE SAMPLE

Table 1 provides sample means and standard deviations for the variables we study below and for a few additional variables designed to measure the extent to which the twins shared a common environment. The table also contains similar data from the Current Population Survey for comparison purposes. Two things are clear from this table. First, although similar to the CPS sample, our sample of twins is better educated and more highly paid than the CPS sample. Likewise, our sample of twins is younger and contains more women and whites than the CPS sample. Second, it is clear that the identical twins in our sample tend to have similar education levels, and that identical twins bear a closer similarity than fraternal twins. For example, 49 percent of identical twins (but 43 percent of fraternal twins) report attaining exactly the same level of education, while 74 percent of identical twins (but 38 percent of fraternal twins) report having studied together during high school.

Table 2 reports the correlations among the (logarithmic) wages, (self-reported and sibling-reported) education levels, and father's and mother's education levels for our sample of twins. In all our analyses we have randomly selected one twin as the first in each pair. We write S_1^1 for the self-reported education level of the first twin, S_1^2 for the sibling-reported education level of the first twin, S_2^2 for the self-reported education level of the second twin, and S_2^1 for the sibling-reported education level of the second twin. (That is, S_n^m, $m, n = 1, 2$, refers to the education level of the nth twin as reported by the mth twin.) All six of the possible correlations are reported in the table. It is apparent that the independent measures of education levels are highly correlated. There are, of course, two measures of the father's and mother's education levels, and we have reported the correlations across both of these also. It is apparent from the table that the wage rates and education levels of identical twins are highly correlated and that they are more highly correlated than the wage rates and education levels of fraternal twins.

It is possible to compare some of the correlations in Table 2 with other reports of sibling correlations. For identical twins, Behrman et al. (1980) report intrapair correlations of 0.76 for years of schooling and 0.55 for (the logarithm of) earnings. These may be contrasted with our estimates of intrapair correlations for identical twins of 0.66 for self-reported schooling and 0.56 for (the logarithm of) wages rates. For fraternal twins Behrman et al. report intrapair correlations of 0.55 for schooling (compared to our estimate of 0.54) and 0.30 for earnings (compared to our estimate of 0.36). Although they are not identical, the correlation coefficients from the Behrman et al. data differ only a little from those in our survey.

C. The Extent of Measurement Error

The correlations in Table 2 provide a comprehensive set of estimates of the measurement error in these data. In the classical model of measurement error we may write $S_n^m = S_n + \nu_n^m$ where S_n is the true schooling level and ν_n^m ($m = 1, 2$) are measurement errors that are uncorrelated with S_n ($n = 1, 2$) and with each other.[3] In this model the correlation between the two measures of schooling, S_n^1 and S_n^2, is just

$$\text{Var}(S_n) / \left[\text{Var}(S_n^1) \cdot \text{Var}(S_n^2)\right]^{1/2}$$

---

[3] *We call this the "classical measurement error model." The assumption that the measurement errors are uncorrelated with each other may be relaxed by allowing a family fixed effect in the measurement error, or a correlation between the two reports by a single twin, and we do so in Section III.*

TABLE 2

CORRELATION MATRICES

A. Identical Twins

Variable	Y_1	Y_2	S_1^1	S_1^2	S_2^2	S_2^1	E_F^1	E_F^2	E_M^1	E_M^2
Y_1	1.000									
Y_2	0.563	1.000								
S_1^1	0.382	0.168	1.000							
S_1^2	0.375	0.140	0.920	1.000						
S_2^2	0.267	0.272	0.658	0.697	1.000					
S_2^1	0.248	0.247	0.700	0.643	0.877	1.000				
Father's education (E_F^1)	0.155	0.088	0.345	0.266	0.361	0.416	1.000			
Father's education (E_F^2)	0.159	0.091	0.357	0.278	0.320	0.389	0.857	1.000		
Mother's education (E_M^1)	0.102	0.088	0.348	0.343	0.392	0.410	0.614	0.644	1.000	
Mother's education (E_M^2)	0.126	0.087	0.316	0.321	0.322	0.337	0.503	0.579	0.837	1.000

B. Fraternal Twins

Variable	Y_1	Y_2	S_1^1	S_1^2	S_2^2	S_2^1	E_F^1	E_F^2	E_M^1	E_M^2
Y_1	1.000									
Y_2	0.364	1.000								
S_1^1	0.142	0.233	1.000							
S_1^2	0.128	0.256	0.869	1.000						
S_2^2	0.140	0.367	0.543	0.535	1.000					
S_2^1	0.136	0.387	0.621	0.565	0.951	1.000				
Father's education (E_F^1)	0.109	0.028	0.332	0.408	0.353	0.407	1.000			
Father's education (E_F^2)	0.025	-0.107	0.259	0.392	0.230	0.253	0.803	1.000		
Mother's education (E_M^1)	0.147	-0.117	0.025	0.127	0.244	0.244	0.547	0.458	1.000	
Mother's education (E_M^2)	-0.065	-0.178	0.180	0.216	0.109	0.180	0.587	0.600	0.742	1.000

Note: Y_1 and Y_2 represent sibling 1's and sibling 2's log hourly wage rate, respectively.

This correlation is the fraction of the variance in the reported measures of schooling that is due to true variation in schooling. This ratio is sometimes called the "reliability ratio" of the schooling measure.

The two estimates of the reliability ratio for the twins schooling levels in Table 2 are 0.92 and 0.88. These estimates indicate that between 8 percent and 12 percent of the measured variance in schooling levels is error. Previous estimates of the reliability ratio in schooling levels (derived by resurveying) by Paul Siegel and Robert Hodge (1968) and William Bielby et al. (1977) have ranged between 0.80 and 0.93 and are very similar to our estimates from the survey of twins.

Since both twins were asked about the schooling levels of their parents, it is also possible to estimate the measurement error in parental schooling levels. These estimates of the reliability ratio in the schooling levels of the twins' parents are lower than the estimates of the reliability ratios for the twins themselves. The reliability ratios are around 0.86 for the father's schooling and 0.84 for the mother's schooling.

II. CONCEPTUAL FRAMEWORK AND BASIC EMPIRICAL RESULTS

A. CONCEPTUAL FRAMEWORK

We denote by y_{1i} and y_{2i} the logarithms of the wage rates of the first and second twins in the ith pair. We let X_i represent the set of variables that vary by family, but not across twins. In our study the variables in X_i include age, race, and any measures of family background. We let Z_{1i} and Z_{2i} represent the sets of variables that may vary across the twins. In our study these variables include the education levels, union status, job tenure, and marital status of each twin.

A general setup (see e.g., Gary Chamberlain, 1982) specifies wage rates as consisting of an unobservable component that varies by family μ_i, observable components that vary by family, X_i, observable components that vary across individuals, Z_{1i} and Z_{2i}, and unobservable individual components (ϵ_{1i} and ϵ_{2i}). This implies

$$(1) \qquad y_{1i} = \alpha X_i + \beta Z_{1i} + \mu_i + \epsilon_{1i}$$

and

$$(2) \qquad y_{2i} = \alpha X_i + \beta Z_{2i} + \mu_i + \epsilon_{2i}$$

where we assume that the equations are identical for the two twins. A general representation for the correlation between the family effect and the observables is

$$(3) \qquad \mu_i = \gamma Z_{1i} + \gamma Z_{2i} + \delta X_i + \omega_i$$

where we have assumed that the correlations between the family effect and the observables for each twin are the same, and where ω_i is uncorrelated with Z_{1i}, Z_{2i}, and X_i. The coefficients γ measure the "selection effect" relating earnings and the observables, while the coefficients β measure the structural (or selection-corrected) effect of the observables on earnings.[4] The data on twins make it possible to measure the selection effect and therefore to identify the rate of return to schooling. The reduced form for this model is obtained by substituting (3) into (2) and (1) and collecting terms:

---

[4] *These selection effects are precisely "omitted-variable bias."*

(4)
$$y_{1i} = [\alpha + \delta]X_i + [\beta + \gamma]Z_{1i} + \gamma Z_{2i} + \epsilon'_{1i}$$

(5)
$$y_{2i} = [\alpha + \delta]X_i + \gamma Z_{1i} + [\beta + \gamma]Z_{2i} + \epsilon'_{2i}$$

where $\epsilon'_{1i} = \omega_i + \epsilon_{1i}$ and $\epsilon'_{2i} = \omega_i + \epsilon_{2i}$. Although equations (4) and (5) may be fitted by ordinary least squares (OLS), generalized least squares (GLS) is the optimal estimator for these equations because of the cross-equation restrictions on the coefficients. (Generalized least squares also provides the appropriate estimates of standard errors for the estimated coefficients.)

In this framework Z_{2i} may influence y_{1i} and Z_{1i} may influence y_{2i} in the reduced form. That is, both siblings' education levels (or any other variable that varies across twins) may enter into both siblings' wage equations because of the correlation between the family effect and schooling levels. These correlations are entirely a result of selection effects. If, for example, families that would otherwise have high wage rates are more likely to educate their children, then the component of γ for the schooling variable should be positive. Finally, it is clear that the coefficients β of the variables that differ across twins are identified. They may be estimated because the selection effects γ may be estimated. On the other hand, the coefficients α of the variables that vary only across families are not identified.

The difference between (1) and (2) [or (4) and (5)] is

(6)
$$y_{1i} - y_{2i} = \beta(Z_{1i} - Z_{2i}) + \epsilon_{1i} - \epsilon_{2i}.$$

In (6) the individual effect μ_i has been removed. The least-squares estimator for this equation is called the "fixed-effects" estimator. In equations (4) and (5) the selection effect is estimated explicitly and then subtracted to obtain the structural estimate of the return to schooling. In (6) the selection effect is eliminated by differencing. We report estimates of all these equations below in order to provide direct evidence on the size of the selection effect.

B. The Effect of Measurement Error

Classical measurement error in schooling will lead to bias in the estimators of the effect of schooling on wage rates. In a bivariate regression, the least-squares regression coefficient in the presence of measurement error in schooling is attenuated by an amount equal to the reliability ratio; that is,

$$\operatorname{plim} \hat{\beta}_{OLS} = \beta_{OLS}\left(1 - \operatorname{Var}(\nu) \, / \, \left[\operatorname{Var}(\nu) + \operatorname{Var}(S)\right]\right)$$

where β_{OLS} is the population regression coefficient if schooling were perfectly measured, $\operatorname{Var}(S)$ is the variance in true schooling levels, and $\operatorname{Var}(\nu_j^1) = \operatorname{Var}(\nu_j^2) = \operatorname{Var}(\nu)$ is the assumed common variance of measurement error. Our estimates of the reliability ratio in the level of schooling are about 0.90, indicating that the ordinary least-squares regression estimator would be biased downward by about 10 percent relative to its value in the absence of measurement error.

In the presence of selection effects, however, the ordinary least-squares estimator will be biased even in the absence of measurement error (because of the omitted sibling's schooling variable). The fixed-effects estimator eliminates this selection (or "omitted variable") bias, but it does so at the expense of introducing far greater measurement-error bias. In the presence of classical measurement error (see Zvi Griliches, 1979), the probability limit of the fixed-effects estimator, $\hat{\beta}_{FE}$, is

$$\beta_{FE}\left(1 - \frac{\mathrm{Var}(\nu)}{\left[\mathrm{Var}(\nu) + \mathrm{Var}(s)\right]\left(1 - \rho_s\right)}\right)$$

where ρ_s is the correlation between the measured schooling levels of the twins and β_{FE} is the population fixed-effects estimator that would be obtained in the absence of measurement error. For the fixed-effects estimator, the attenuation caused by measurement error is increased because of the correlation between the schooling level of the twins. For example, with a reliability ratio of 0.9 and a correlation between the twins' self-reported schooling of 0.66, the fixed-effects estimator would be biased downward by $0.1/(1 - 0.66) = 0.294$, or about 30 percent relative to its value in the absence of measurement error.

One simple procedure for reducing the effect of measurement error on either estimator is to average the multiple reports on schooling and to use this average as the independent variable in equation (6). Assuming classical measurement error and using $(S_1^1 - S_2^2)/2 + (S_1^2 - S_2^1)/2$ as the independent variable in equation (6) leads to a modified fixed-effects estimator with the following property:

$$\mathrm{plim}\,\hat{\beta}_{avg} = \beta\left[1 - \left(\frac{\mathrm{Var}(\nu)}{\left[\mathrm{Var}(s) + \mathrm{Var}(\nu)\right]\left(1 - \rho_s\right)} + \frac{2\mathrm{Var}(S_1 - S_2)}{2}\right)\right].$$

Measurement error causes a smaller asymptotic bias here than in the standard fixed-effects estimator because the averaging decreases the measurement error as a fraction of the total variance in the independent variable. We report the results of estimates based on averages of the schooling data below to appraise further the importance of measurement error in estimation of the returns to schooling.

A straightforward consistent estimator for equation (4), (5), or (6), assuming classical measurement error, may be obtained by the method of instrumental variables using the independent measures of the schooling variables as instruments. For example, we may fit

(7)
$$y_{1i} - y_{2i} = \beta(S_1^1 - S_2^2) + \epsilon_{1i} - \epsilon_{2i} = \beta \Delta S' + \Delta \epsilon$$

using $\Delta S'' = (S_1^2 - S_2^1)$ as an instrument for $\Delta S'$. We also report these estimates below.

Finally, since we have multiple measures of schooling for each twin it is possible to relax the classical assumption that the measurement errors ν_1^1 and ν_2^1 (or ν_1^2 and ν_2^2) are uncorrelated. For example, if a twin who reports an upward-biased measure of her own schooling is more likely to report an upward-biased measure of her sibling's schooling, then the correlation, ρ_ν, between the measurement errors ν_1^1 and ν_2^1 (and ν_1^2 and ν_2^2) will be positive. A positive correlation in the measurement error in each sibling's report will lead to a higher correlation between S_1^1 and S_2^1 than between S_1^1 and S_2^2 (and a higher correlation between S_1^2 and S_2^2 than between S_1^1 and S_2^2), because the own-reports contain a common measurement-error component that the cross-sibling reports do not contain. In contrast, in the presence of classical measurement error these correlations would be identical. In fact, the correlations in Table 2 are consistent with the hypothesis of positively correlated measurement error in the siblings' reports.

In the presence of correlated measurement errors the instrumental-variables estimators of equation (4), (5), or (6) will be inconsistent. For example, instrumental variables used to obtain the fixed-effects estimator in (6) leads to

$$\text{plim } \hat{\beta}_{\text{FEIV}} = \beta / \{1 - 2\rho_\nu[\text{Var}(\nu)/\text{Var}(\Delta S)]\}.$$

A straightforward consistent estimator of equation (6) may be obtained by instrumental-variables estimation of

(8)
$$y_{1i} - y_{2i} = \beta(S_1^1 - S_2^1) + \epsilon_{1i} - \epsilon_{2i} = \beta \Delta S^* + \Delta \epsilon$$

in which $\Delta S^{**} = S_1^2 - S_2^2$ is used as an instrument for ΔS^*, and we report this estimate below.[5]

C. THE BASIC EMPIRICAL RESULTS

Table 3 contains simple estimates of the effect of schooling on earnings that control only for demographic variables (that may be considered strictly exogenous). In columns (i) and (ii) we report the results of stacking equations (1) and (2) and fitting them by least squares and generalized least squares (the seemingly-unrelated-regression method due to Arnold Zellner [1962]). The results in columns (i) and (ii) are comparable to most of the estimates that have appeared in the literature which ignore the potential correlation between schooling level and family background. For example, a regression fitted to data

---

[5] Note that the estimates using averages of the schooling differences will be inconsistent in the presence of correlated measurement errors, but as in the classical case, the inconsistency will be reduced by averaging.

TABLE 3

ORDINARY LEAST-SQUARES (OLS), GENERALIZED LEAST-SQUARES (GLS), INSTRUMENTAL-VARIABLES (IV), AND FIXED-EFFECTS ESTIMATES OF LOG WAGE EQUATIONS FOR IDENTICAL TWINS[a]

Variable	OLS (i)	GLS (ii)	GLS (iii)	IV[a] (iv)	First difference (v)	First difference by IV (vi)
Own education	0.084 (0.014)	0.087 (0.015)	0.088 (0.015)	0.116 (0.030)	0.092 (0.024)	0.167 (0.043)
Sibling's education	—	—	−0.007 (0.015)	−0.037 (0.029)	—	—
Age	0.088 (0.019)	0.090 (0.023)	0.090 (0.023)	0.088 (0.019)	—	—
Age squared (÷100)	−0.087 (0.023)	−0.089 (0.028)	−0.090 (0.029)	−0.087 (0.024)	—	—
Male	0.204 (0.063)	0.204 (0.077)	0.206 (0.077)	0.206 (0.064)	—	—
White	−0.410 (0.127)	−0.417 (0.143)	−0.424 (0.144)	−0.428 (0.128)	—	—
Sample size:	298	298	298	298	149	149
R^2:	0.260	0.219	0.219	—	0.092	—

Notes: Each equation also includes an intercept term. Numbers in parentheses are estimated standard errors.
[a] Own education and sibling's education are instrumented for using each sibling's report of the other sibling's education as instruments.

from the 1990 CPS with an identical specification as that in column (i) of Table 3 gives an estimate of the effect of schooling on the wage of 8.3 percent per year completed (compared to 8.7 percent in the data for twins). Estimates of the effect of age and gender on wage rates are also similar in the CPS, but estimates of the effect of race on wage rates are very different (9 percent vs. −40 percent).

The results in column (iii) of Table 3 correspond to stacking equations (4) and (5) and fitting them by generalized least squares. These are the results that include the sibling's education level in each twin's wage equation. The coefficient of this variable is a measure of the selection effect, γ, in equation (3). As the table indicates, this effect is small and negative, indicating that the selection effect in these data is negative. In this sample the better-educated families are not those who would otherwise be the most highly compensated in the labor market. This result also implies that a regression estimator of the returns to schooling that does not adjust for the selection effect will be downward-biased.

A regression of the intrapair difference in wage rates on the intrapair difference in schooling levels (which is the fixed-effects estimate) is reported in column (v) of Table 3. This result confirms that the OLS regression result is smaller, not larger, than the intrapair regression estimate. This result is dramatically different from the result reported by Behrman et al. (1980). Behrman et al. report a simple regression estimate of the return to schooling similar to what we report in column (i), but their intrapair regressions [comparable to those in our column (v)] indicate schooling returns that are only around 40 percent as large.[6]

Figure 1 contains the scatter diagram of the intrapair (logarithmic) wage difference against the intrapair schooling difference. This diagram displays much of what the basic data contain. First, it is clear that many twins report identical education levels, so that many intrapair education differences are zero. Second, there is still a large amount of variability in the reported wage differences of identical twins with the same education levels. The standard deviation of the difference in the log wages is 0.56 for identical twins with identically reported education levels. This may be compared with a standard deviation in the difference in log wages in the overall sample of 0.58. Finally, and despite the variability in wage rates, there is a clear tendency for better-educated twins to report higher wage rates.

Columns (iv) and (vi) in Table 3 report the instrumental-variables estimates which are intended to correct for measurement error in the education data. Here we use each sibling's report of his (or her) sibling's education level as an instrumental variable for his (or her) sibling's education level. These instrumental-variables estimates are much larger

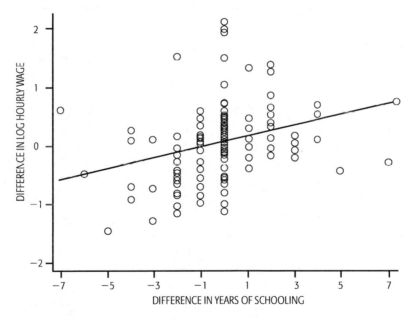

FIGURE 1

Intrapair Returns to Schooling, Identical Twins

---

[6] *We are comparing the regression coefficient in line Y-1 in Behrman et al.'s (1980) table 6.1, which is for identical and fraternal twins, with the regression coefficient in line Y-4 in their table 6.2, which is for identical twins only. The result in line Y-4 in table 6.2 of Behrman et al. is a typographical error and should read 0.03, not 0.003.*

than the least-squares estimates, and they are consistent with our finding above that a considerable fraction of the variability in reported differences in twins' education levels is due to measurement error. If we accept the sibling reports as valid instruments, it seems likely that conventional methods are producing serious underestimates of the economic returns to schooling. A conventional test of the difference between the least-squares estimate (0.09) and the instrumental-variables estimate (0.17) rejects the hypothesis that these are equal with a t ratio of 1.97 (see Jerry Hausman, 1978). A table containing estimates similar to those in Table 3 for the pooled sample of fraternal and identical twins is available from the authors upon request.

Table 4 contains some further tests of the effect of measurement error on estimates of the returns to schooling. In this table we report the results of reestimating the least-squares and generalized least-squares results of Table 3 using simple averages of the multiple indicators of education levels as independent variables. As expected, all of the estimates in Table 4 are larger than the corresponding estimates in Table 3. These results provide further evidence that measurement error is producing a downward bias in conventional estimates of the returns to schooling.

Table 5 contains an analysis that parallels the analysis in Table 3 except that variables measuring union status, marital status, years of tenure on the current job, and the education of the worker's parents have been added to the regressions. The estimated returns to schooling here are even larger than in Table 4. In addition, worker job tenure has a strong positive and precisely determined effect on wage rates. Marital status and union status have positive effects on wages, but neither effect is measured precisely. It is also worth noting that when we control for a standard list of variables, as we do in Table 5, the fixed-effect estimate of the return to schooling is attenuated compared to the GLS estimate.

Many of the results in Tables 3, 4, and 5 are similar to those that have been reported elsewhere in the study of the determination of wage rates. Wage rates are concave in age, males earn more than females, and parental education seems to have very little independent effect on wage rates. One anomaly in Tables 3, 4, and 5 is the estimated effect of race on wage rates, which indicates that white workers earn less than nonwhite workers. It seems possible that this result is due to selection in the relatively small sample of nonwhites who attended the twins festival and turned up in our sample. We have, therefore, computed the results in Tables 4 and 5 deleting the sample of nonwhite workers. The results of these regressions for white workers do not differ in any material way from those already reported. (The effect of schooling on wage rates is slightly higher for white twin pairs than for the group as a whole, but this difference is not statistically significant.)

Finally, we implement an instrumental-variables approach that is consistent in the presence of measurement errors that are correlated between the twins' reports of their own schooling and of their siblings' schooling. Specifically, we include $\Delta S^* = S_1^1 - S_2^1$ in the first-differenced wage equations, and use $\Delta S^{**} = S_1^2 - S_2^2$ as an instrument for ΔS^*. These instrumental-variables first-difference estimates, along with least-squares first-difference estimates, are reported in Table 6. When no other covariates are included, the

TABLE 4

ESTIMATES USING AVERAGE OF SCHOOLING REPORTS,
LOG WAGE EQUATIONS FOR IDENTICAL TWINS

Variable	OLS (i)	GLS (ii)	GLS (iii)	First difference (iv)
Average own education[a]	0.087 (0.015)	0.094 (0.016)	0.098 (0.016)	0.117 (0.026)
Average sibling's education[b]	—	—	−0.017 (0.016)	
Age	0.089 (0.019)	0.091 (0.023)	0.091 (0.023)	—
Age squared (÷ 100)	−0.088 (0.023)	−0.091 (0.029)	−0.091 (0.029)	—
Male	0.203 (0.063)	0.202 (0.077)	0.208 (0.077)	—
White	−0.406 (0.127)	−0.382 (0.144)	−0.385 (0.144)	—
Sample size:	298	298	298	149
R^2:	0.272	0.223	0.225	0.122

Notes: Each equation also includes an intercept term. Numbers in parentheses are estimated standard errors.
[a] Average own education is equal to $(S_1^1 + S_1^2)/2$.
[b] Average sibling's education is equal to $(S_2^2 + S_2^1)/2$.

instrumental-variable estimate that is robust to correlated measurement errors is 0.129, which is 20 percent greater than the OLS estimate of 0.107. Similar results hold when other variables are added to the regression [see columns (iii) and (iv)]. In each case, however, the new instrumental-variables estimates yield returns to education that are 3 percentage points smaller than specifications that use differences in sibling reports of education as the instrument for differences in own-reported education. Apparently, the classical model of measurement error is too restrictive for these data.

III. A SIMPLE MODEL OF WAGE RATES, SCHOOLING, AND MEASUREMENT ERROR

A. CLASSICAL MEASUREMENT ERRORS

A simplified version of equation (6), which represents the intrapair difference in wage rates, is

$$(9) \qquad \Delta y_i = \beta \Delta s_i + \Delta \epsilon_i$$

TABLE 5

GLS, IV, AND FIXED-EFFECTS ESTIMATES OF AUGMENTED
LOG-WAGE EQUATIONS FOR IDENTICAL TWINS

Variable	GLS (i)	GLS (ii)	IV[a] (iii)	First difference (iv)	First difference by IV (v)
Own education	0.105 (0.016)	0.105 (0.016)	0.147 (0.034)	0.091 (0.022)	0.179 (0.041)
Sibling's education	—	−0.008 (0.016)	−0.062 (0.035)	—	—
Age	0.082 (0.023)	0.082 (0.023)	0.082 (0.019)	—	—
Age squared (÷ 100)	−0.094 (0.029)	−0.094 (0.029)	−0.092 (0.024)	—	—
Male	0.147 (0.080)	0.149 (0.081)	0.139 (0.066)	—	—
White	−0.472 (0.143)	−0.482 (0.144)	−0.506 (0.130)	—	—
Covered by union	0.115 (0.072)	0.118 (0.072)	0.153 (0.081)	0.063 (0.090)	0.095 (0.095)
Married	0.089 (0.065)	0.086 (0.065)	0.051 (0.073)	0.142 (0.081)	0.140 (0.086)
Years of tenure	0.025 (0.005)	0.024 (0.005)	0.020 (0.005)	0.028 (0.006)	0.028 (0.006)
Father's education	0.001 (0.014)	0.001 (0.014)	0.006 (0.013)	—	—
Mother's education	0.013 (0.017)	0.015 (0.018)	0.019 (0.017)	—	—
Sample size:	284	284	284	147	147
R^2:	0.320	0.320	—	0.257	—

Notes: Each equation also includes an intercept term. Numbers in parentheses are estimated standard errors.
[a] Own education and sibling's education are instrumented using sibling's report of the other sibling's education as instruments.

where β represents the return to schooling, Δy_i represents the intrapair difference in log wages, Δs_i represents the *true* intrapair difference in schooling, and $\Delta \epsilon_i$ is an error that is independent of schooling levels. Letting $\Delta s'_i$ and $\Delta s''_i$ represent the self-reported schooling difference $(S_1^1 - S_2^2)$ and the sibling-reported schooling difference $(S_1^2 - S_2^1)$, we may also write

$$(10) \qquad \Delta s'_i = \Delta s_i + \Delta v'_i$$

$$(11) \qquad \Delta s''_i = \Delta s_i + \Delta v''_i$$

TABLE 6

OLS AND IV FIRST-DIFFERENCE ESTIMATES OF LOG-WAGE EQUATIONS FOR IDENTICAL TWINS, ASSUMING CORRELATED MEASUREMENT ERRORS

Variable	OLS (i)	IV (ii)	OLS (iii)	IV (iv)
ΔS^*	0.107 (0.025)	0.129 (0.030)	0.112 (0.023)	0.132 (0.028)
Δ Covered by union	—	—	0.089 (0.088)	0.099 (0.089)
Δ Married	—	—	0.157 (0.080)	0.160 (0.080)
Δ Years of tenure	—	—	0.028 (0.006)	0.028 (0.006)
Sample size:	149	149	147	147
R^2:	0.105	—	0.286	—

Notes: ΔS^* is the difference between sibling 1's report of her (his) own education and her (his) report of sibling 2's education. The instrument used for ΔS^* is ΔS^{**}, the difference between sibling 2's report of sibling 1's education and sibling 2's report of sibling 2's own education. Numbers in parentheses are estimated standard errors.

where we assume that $\Delta v'_i$ and $\Delta v''_i$ are classical measurement errors in schooling that are uncorrelated with the true schooling levels, with each other, and with $\Delta\epsilon$. Notice that any fixed tendency for some families to misreport their schooling levels has been eliminated by differencing. This setup leads to a very simple method-of-moments estimation scheme.

The theoretical covariance matrix of the three variables Δy, $\Delta S'$, and $\Delta S''$ is contained in Table 7, where $\sigma^2_{\Delta S}$, $\sigma^2_{\Delta\epsilon}$, $\sigma^2_{\Delta v'}$, and $\sigma^2_{\Delta v''}$ are the variances of ΔS, $\Delta\epsilon$, $\Delta v'$, and $\Delta v''$. This may be contrasted with the empirical covariance matrix for our data on identical twins in Table 8. The simple model in equations (7)–(9) has several implications for this empirical covariance matrix. First, and most important, there is the restriction that the covariance between the wage difference and the education difference should be the same for each measure of the education difference. Remarkably, Table 8 indicates that this equality holds almost precisely in the data. Second, if self-reported measures of education are more accurate than sibling-reported measures of education, then the variance of self-reported education differences (3.69) should be less than the variance of sibling-reported education differences (3.90). The empirical covariance matrix is also consistent with this hypothesis.

TABLE 7

THEORETICAL COVARIANCE MATRIX ASSUMING FULL INDEPENDENCE

Variable	Δy	$\Delta s'$	$\Delta s''$
Δy	$\beta^2\sigma^2_{\Delta s} + \sigma^2_{\Delta\epsilon}$	$\beta\sigma^2_{\Delta s}$	$\beta\sigma^2_{\Delta s}$
$\Delta s'$		$\sigma^2_{\Delta s} + \sigma^2_{\Delta v'}$	$\sigma^2_{\Delta s}$
$\Delta s''$			$\sigma^2_{\Delta s} + \sigma^2_{\Delta v''}$

TABLE 8

EMPIRICAL COVARIANCE MATRIX

Variable	Δy	$\Delta S'$	$\Delta S''$	ΔS^*	ΔS^{**}
Δy	0.336	0.338	0.360	0.349	0.350
$\Delta S'$		3.691	2.158	3.059	2.790
$\Delta S''$			3.902	2.911	3.149
ΔS^*				3.257	2.714
ΔS^{**}					3.225

Table 9 contains the maximum-likelihood estimates of the basic parameters set out in Table 7. Since equations (7)–(9) are over-identified, there are two estimates of the rate of return to schooling in the unrestricted model. This implies that there are also two estimates of the variance in the difference in wage rates that is explained by schooling differences. The first estimate of the return to schooling is simply the ordinary instrumental-variables estimate (reported earlier in Table 4) of $\text{Cov}(\Delta y, \Delta S'') / (\text{Cov}(\Delta S', \Delta S'') = 0.167$. The second estimate, which corresponds to the instrumental-variables estimate we would obtain if we used the own reports of schooling as instruments for the sibling reports, is nearly identical at

$$\text{Cov}(\Delta y, \Delta S'')/\text{Cov}(\Delta S', \Delta S'') = 0.157.$$

The restricted maximum-likelihood estimate of the return to schooling is in between these two estimates at 0.161.[7]

B. CORRELATED MEASUREMENT ERRORS

The theoretical moments displayed in Table 7 are derived under the assumption that the measurement errors in equations (10) and (11) are independent. When the measurement errors in (10) and (11) are not independent of each other, the covariance between $\Delta S'$ and $\Delta S''$ is no longer a straightforward measure of $\sigma_{\Delta S}^2$ as indicated in Table 7. Instead, $\text{Cov}(\Delta S', \Delta S'') = \sigma_{\Delta S}^2 + \text{Cov}(\Delta \nu', \Delta \nu'')$. Writing $\text{Var}(\nu_1^1 = \text{Var}(\nu_2^2) = \sigma_{\nu'}^2$, and $\text{Var}(\nu_2^1) = \text{Var}(\nu_1^2) = \sigma_{\nu''}^2$, it follows that $\text{Cov}(\Delta S', \Delta S'') = \sigma_{\Delta S}^2 - \rho_\nu \sigma_{\nu'} \sigma_{\nu''}$, where ρ_ν represents the correlation between ν_1^1 and ν_2^1 (and also between ν_1^2 and ν_2^2). This implies that the instrumental-variables estimator of the model (9)–(11) will be inconsistent. A positive correlation in the person-specific measurement errors will lead to an upward bias in the estimated return to schooling.

---

[7] *The model in equations (9)–(11), assuming normality of $\Delta \epsilon$, $\Delta \nu'$, and $\Delta \nu''$, has a likelihood function familiar in factor analysis. See D. N. Lawley and A. E. Maxwell (1963) and K. G. Jöreskog (1969). Arthur Goldberger (1972) shows that maximum-likelihood estimation in this model is similar to generalized least-squares (or optimum minimum-distance) estimation. Computations were made using the software LISREL.*

TABLE 9

MAXIMUM-LIKELIHOOD ESTIMATES

| Parameter | Independent errors | | | Correlated errors |
| | Unrestricted estimates | | Restricted estimates | Restricted estimates |
	(i)	(ii)	(iii)	(iv)
β	0.167 (0.043)	0.157 (0.041)	0.162 (0.037)	0.129 (0.029)
$\sigma^2_{\Delta s}$	2.158 (0.359)	2.158 (0.359)	2.157 (0.359)	2.712 (0.347)
$\sigma^2_{\Delta \epsilon}$	0.276 (0.038)	0.283 (0.038)	0.280 (0.035)	0.291 (0.034)
$\sigma^2_{\Delta \nu'}$	1.533 (0.312)	1.533 (0.312)	1.556 (0.301)	—
$\sigma^2_{\Delta \nu''}$	1.744 (0.327)	1.744 (0.327)	1.721 (0.313)	—
$\sigma^2_{\nu'}$	—	—	—	0.500 (0.129)
$\sigma^2_{\nu''}$	—	—	—	0.583 (0.132)
ρ_ν	—	—	—	0.515 (0.136)

Note: Estimated asymptotic standard errors are in parentheses.

To explore this issue we write the schooling differences as reported by each twin as

$$(12) \qquad \Delta S^* = \Delta S + \Delta \nu^*$$

$$(13) \qquad \Delta S^{**} = \Delta S + \Delta \nu^{**}$$

where $\Delta S^* = S^1_1 - S^1_2$, $\Delta S^{**} = S^2_1 - S^2_2$, and the measurement errors are indexed accordingly. Notice that any fixed tendency for one twin to misreport schooling levels has been eliminated by differencing in (12) and (13). Augmenting (9)–(11) with (12)–(13) also leads to a simple method-of-moments estimation scheme.

The theoretical covariance matrix of the five variables Δy, $\Delta S'$, $\Delta S''$, ΔS^*, and ΔS^{**} is contained in Table 10. This augmented theoretical covariance matrix may be contrasted with the full empirical covariance matrix in Table 8. The model in equations (10)–(13) has many implications for this empirical covariance matrix. As before, the covariance between the wage difference and the schooling difference should be identical for all four measures of the schooling difference. Inspection of Table 8 indicates that this restriction is remarkably consistent with the data. Most important, however, the presence of correlated measurement

TABLE 10

THEORETICAL MOMENT MATRIX ASSUMING CORRELATED MEASUREMENT ERRORS

Parameter	Δy	$\Delta S'$	$\Delta S''$	ΔS^*	ΔS^{**}
Δy	$\beta^2\sigma^2_{\Delta S}+\sigma^2_{\Delta S}$	$\beta\sigma^2_{\Delta S}$	$\beta\sigma^2_{\Delta S}$	$\beta\sigma^2_{\Delta S}$	$\beta\sigma^2_{\Delta S}$
$\Delta S'$		$\sigma^2_{\Delta S}+2\sigma^2_{\nu'}$	$\sigma^2_{\Delta S}-2\rho_\nu\sigma_{\nu'}\sigma_{\nu''}$	$\sigma^2_{\Delta S}+\sigma^2_{\nu'}-\rho_\nu\sigma_{\nu'}\sigma_{\nu''}$	$\sigma^2_{\Delta S}+\sigma^2_{\nu'}-\rho_\nu\sigma_{\nu'}\sigma_{\nu''}$
$\Delta S''$			$\sigma^2_{\Delta S}+2\sigma^2_{\nu''}$	$\sigma^2_{\Delta S}+\sigma^2_{\nu''}-\rho_\nu\sigma_{\nu'}\sigma_{\nu''}$	$\sigma^2_{\Delta S}+\sigma^2_{\nu''}-\rho_\nu\sigma_{\nu'}\sigma_{\nu''}$
ΔS^*				$\sigma^2_{\Delta S}+\sigma^2_{\nu'}+\sigma^2_{\nu''}-2\rho_\nu\sigma_{\nu'}\sigma_{\nu''}$	$\sigma^2_{\Delta S}$
ΔS^{**}					$\sigma^2_{\Delta S}+\sigma^2_{\nu'}+\sigma^2_{\nu''}-2\rho_\nu\sigma_{\nu'}\sigma_{\nu''}$

errors implies that the covariance between $\Delta S'$ and $\Delta S''$ will differ from the covariance between ΔS^* and ΔS^{**}. In fact, the data in Table 8 indicate that these covariances do differ. A straightforward calculation leads to an estimate of $\rho_\nu = 0.52$ from the data in Table 8. This implies that an instrumental-variables estimate of the return to schooling that ignores the presence of correlated measurement errors will be biased upward.

Column (iv) of Table 9 provides the maximum-likelihood estimates of the parameters set out in Table 8. As the table indicates, there are, in principle, four different estimates of the return to schooling. One of these, Cov(Δy, ΔS^{**})/Cov(ΔS^*, ΔS^{**}) is the instrumental-variables estimate where the second twin's report of the twins' schooling difference is used as an instrument for the first twin's report of their schooling difference. This estimate, which is also contained in column (ii) of Table 6, is 0.13 (= 0.350/2.714) and is essentially identical to the fully restricted estimate in Table 9.

The estimates of the parameters in Table 9 imply that measurement error is a sizable fraction of the variance in the difference in the reported measures of schooling, ranging from 17 percent of the variance in a twin's report of the difference in schooling [Var(ΔS^*)] to 26 percent of the variance of the self-reported difference in schooling [Var($\Delta S'$)]. The result is that our least-squares estimates of the return to schooling are biased downward. For example, a test of the significance of the difference between the least-squares estimate (0.09) and the restricted maximum-likelihood estimate (0.13) of the return to schooling leads to rejection of the hypothesis that they are equal ($t = 2.3$). Measurement error is a serious problem in the estimation of intrapair schooling differences because of the high correlation between the schooling levels of twins, as Griliches (1979) indicated some time ago.

IV. CONCLUSION

We went into the field to collect a new sample of data on twins in order to address specifically some important questions about the returns to schooling that have remained unresolved for over a decade. In 1980, Behrman et al. reported dramatic and widely publicized results from a study of identical twins that indicated that the economic returns to schooling were only about 3 percent per year completed, or about 40 percent of the size of the conventional estimates. Our results are very different. First, we find no evidence that conventional estimates of the returns to schooling are biased upward by imperfect controls for other family-related factors that may affect earnings. Second, we find that measurement errors in self-reported schooling differences result in a substantial downward bias in conventional estimates of the returns to schooling.

If our procedures for adjusting the estimated returns to schooling for measurement error are accepted, then our best estimate is that increased schooling increases average wage rates by about 12–16 percent per year completed. This is larger than most estimates in the prior literature. Even if our procedures of adjustment for measurement error are not accepted, within-pair estimates of the returns to schooling in our data are never less than 9 percent per year completed. Only additional data collection is likely to lead to better estimates of the returns to schooling.

How are we to interpret the 12–16 percent difference in average earnings associated with a one-year difference in the education of identical twins? Is it not possible that, within twin pairs, those who obtain more education would earn more (or less) even if they had not obtained the additional education? As with all empirical studies in economics, the ideal way to answer this question would require the random assignment of subjects to schooling levels so that all other differences were controlled. To the extent that schooling differences between twins are not random, it is possible that our estimates of the economic return to schooling are biased. If, for example, a family is more likely to send a twin further in school when that twin shows exceptional promise, our estimates of the return to schooling will be biased upward. If, on the other hand, a family is more likely to try to equalize the subsequent incomes of twins by sending the less promising child for further schooling, our estimates of the return to schooling will be biased downward. There are now many examples in the literature of attempts to control for unobserved factors that may be correlated with schooling levels. The results of our study, like the results of many of these other studies, suggest that unobserved factors do not cause an upward bias in simple estimates of the economic returns to schooling.[8]

---

[8] In one of the earliest studies, Gary Becker (1993) concludes there is little evidence that the estimated monetary returns to schooling are biased by omitted ability variables. Griliches (1977) also characterizes most of the available literature as providing little evidence of upward bias in estimated schooling effects due to omitted variables. Ashenfelter and David Zimmerman (1993), in their study of brothers and father-son pairs, find an upward bias in returns to schooling due to omitted variables that is about the same size as the downward bias due to measurement error. Joshua Angrist and Krueger (1991), in their study of the effect of compulsory schooling on the returns to schooling, also find that instrumental-variables estimates are greater than least-squares estimates. Additional evidence that the returns to schooling may have been badly underestimated has also been found by Hausman and William Taylor (1981), Kristin Butcher and Anne Case (1992), Thomas Kane and Cecilia Rouse (1993), and David Card (1993).

REFERENCES

Angrist, Joshua and Krueger, Alan. "Does Compulsory Schooling Affect Schooling and Earnings?" *Quarterly Journal of Economics,* November 1991, *106*(4), pp. 979–1014.

Ashenfelter, Orley and Zimmerman, David. "Estimates of the Return to Schooling with Data on Fathers, Sons, and Brothers." Mimeo, Princeton University, August 1993. [Published in *Review of Economics and Statistics,* 79, February 1997, pp. 1–9.]

Becker, Gary. *Human capital,* 3rd Ed. Chicago: University of Chicago Press, 1993.

Behrman, Jere; Hrubec, Zdenek; Taubman, Paul and Wales, Terence. *Socioeconomic success: A study of the effects of genetic endowments, family environment, and schooling.* Amsterdam: North-Holland, 1980.

Bielby, William; Hauser, Robert and Featherman, David. "Response Errors of Non-Black Males in Models of the Stratification Process," in D. J. Aigner and A. S. Goldberger, eds., *Latent variables in socioeconomic models.* Amsterdam: North-Holland, 1977, pp. 227–51.

Butcher, Kristin and Case, Anne. "The Effect of Sibling Sex Composition on Women's Educational Attainment." Mimeo, Princeton University, June 1992. [Published in *Quarterly Journal of Economics, 109,* August 1994, pp. 531–63.]

Card, David. "Using Geographic Variation in College Proximity to Estimate the Return to Schooling." Mimeo, Princeton University, July 1993. [Published in "Aspects of Labor Market Behaviour: Essays in Honour of John Vanderkamp," L. Christofides et al., eds. Toronto: University of Toronto Press, 1995.

Chamberlain, Gary. "Multivariate Regression Models for Panel Data." *Journal of Econometrics,* January 1982, *18*(1), pp. 5–46.

Goldberger, Arthur. "Maximum-Likelihood Estimation of Regressions Containing Unobservable Independent Variables." *International Economic Review,* February 1972, *13*(1), pp. 1–15.

Griliches, Zvi. "Estimating the Returns to Schooling: Some Econometric Problems." *Econometrica,* January 1977, *45*(1), pp. 1–22.

––––––. "Sibling Models and Data in Economics: Beginnings of a Survey." *Journal of Political Economy,* October 1979, *87*(5), Part 2, pp. S37–S64.

Hausman, Jerry. "Specification Tests in Econometrics." *Econometrica,* November 1978, *46*(6), pp. 1251–71.

Hausman, Jerry and Taylor, William. "Panel Data and Unobservable Individual Effects." *Econometrica,* November 1981, *49*(6), pp. 1377–98.

Jablon, Seymour; Neel, James; Gershowitz, Henry and Atkinson, Glenn. "The NASNRC Panel: Methods of Construction of the Panel, Zygosity Diagnosis, and Proposed Use." *American Journal of Human Genetics,* March 1967, *19*(2), pp. 133–61.

Jöreskog, K. G. "A General Approach to Confirmatory Maximum Likelihood Factor Analysis." *Psychometrika,* June 1969, *34*(2), pp. 183–202.

Kane, Thomas and Rouse, Cecilia. "Labor Market Returns to Two- and Four-Year Colleges: Is a Credit a Credit and Do Degrees Matter?" Industrial Relations Section Working Paper No. 311, Princeton University, January 1993.

Lawley, D. N. and Maxwell, A. E. *Factor analysis as a statistical method.* London: Butterworks, 1963.

Mincer, Jacob. *Schooling, experience and earnings.* New York: National Bureau of Economic Research, 1974.

Siegel, Paul and Hodge, Robert. "A Causal Approach to the Study of Measurement Error," in Hubert Blalock and Ann Blalock, eds., *Methodology in social research.* New York: McGraw-Hill, 1968, pp. 28–59.

Zellner, Arnold. "An Efficient Method of Estimating Seemingly Unrelated Regressions and Tests for Aggregation Bias." *Journal of the American Statistical Association,* June 1962, *57*(298), pp. 348–68.

ABOUT THE AUTHORS

Orley Ashenfelter

Orley Ashenfelter has been with the Department of Economics and the Industrial Relations Section at Princeton since 1968. He was, in fact, both awarded his Ph.D. and promoted to associate professor (with tenure) at the same meeting of the board of trustees in 1970.

His research over the past thirty years has covered a wide range of issues in applied labor economics. Indeed, this body of research has been reprinted en masse in *The Collected Essays of Orley C. Ashenfelter,* Volumes I–III, Elgar, 1997. Orley has served as the editor of the *American Economic Review* since 1985, a fellow of the National Academy of Sciences since 1993, and on numerous advisory boards. In addition, Orley has produced a steady flow of first-class graduate students, and these now compose a significant fraction of the stock of major labor economists.

No summary of Orley's career, however, would be complete without mentioning his contributions to oenological economics. From the reislings of the Czech Republic to the cabernets of South Australia, no nontrivial wine varieties have escaped the scrutiny of his hedonic regressions. Indeed, when the *Encyclopaedia Britannica* first writes up Ashenfelter, O.C. (1942–) in the mid-twenty-first century, the scholarly contribution they will stress is "Qualite des Millesimes et Conditions Meteorologiques: Les Cas Bordelais."

Alan B. Krueger

Alan Krueger is the Bendheim Professor of Economics and Public Affairs at Princeton University. He has held a joint appointment in the Economics Department and the Woodrow Wilson School at Princeton University since 1987. He currently is the editor of the *Journal of Economic Perspectives* and is a research associate of the National Bureau of Economic Research. In 1994–1995, he served as the Chief Economist of the U.S. Department of Labor. He earned his B.S. degree with honors from Cornell University's School of Industrial and Labor Relations and his Ph.D. in economics from Harvard University.

Alan Krueger is a prolific scholar who has done pathbreaking work on a wide range of core substantive issues in labor economics, including the impacts of school quality and years of schooling on earnings, the determinants of inter-industry wage differentials, the impact of technological change on the wage structure, and the labor market effects of social insurance policies. Krueger has also been a leader in the development of new and more credible approaches to identifying the effects of policy interventions on labor market and educational outcomes. For example, Krueger's work with Joshua Angrist that is reprinted here provides a remarkably novel and lucid approach to estimating the returns to schooling. He has similarly contributed to the development of convincing new quasi-experimental, empirical strategies for examining the effects of school inputs on earnings and the impact of the minimum wage on employment.

Krueger's formidable research contributions and public policy work have earned him multiple honors. He was awarded the Kershaw Prize for the best public policy researcher under the age of 40 by the Association of Public Policy and Management in 1997. He was also elected a fellow of the Econometric Society in 1996 and elected a member of the National Academy of Social Insurance in 1992.

RETURNS TO EXPERIENCE AND JOB MATCHING

Boyan Jovanovic

Katharine G. Abraham and Henry S. Farber

Robert Topel

Job Matching and the Theory of Turnover

BOYAN JOVANOVIC

Bell Laboratories, Inc., and Columbia University

A long-run equilibrium theory of turnover is presented and is shown to explain the important regularities that have been observed by empirical investigators. A worker's productivity in a particular job is not known ex ante and becomes known more precisely as the worker's job tenure increases. Turnover is generated by the existence of a nondegenerate distribution of the worker's productivity across different jobs. The nondegeneracy is caused by the assumed variation in the quality of the worker-employer match.

The objective of this paper is to construct and to interpret a model of permanent job separations. A permanent job separation involves a change of employers for the worker. Temporary separations (consisting mainly of temporary layoffs) have been the subject of recent theoretical work by Baily (1974), Azariadis (1975), and Feldstein (1976), and are not considered here.

Recent evidence on labor turnover falls into two categories: the cross-sectional industry studies (Stoikov and Ramon 1968; Burton and Parker 1969; Pencavel 1970; Parsons 1972; Telser 1972), and the more recent studies using longitudinal data on individuals (Bartel 1975; Bartel and Borjas 1976; Freeman 1976; Jovanovic and Mincer 1978). The strongest and most consistent finding of all these studies is a negative relationship between quits and layoffs on the one hand, and job tenure on the other. This finding is equally strong for quits as it is for layoffs. Jovanovic and Mincer (1978) find that roughly one-half of this negative relationship is explained by the negative structural dependence of the separation probability on job tenure. The rest of the observed dependence is only apparent and is caused by the fact that within any nonhomogeneous group a negative correlation between job tenure and the separation probability will exist, simply because those people with a lower propensity to change jobs will tend to have longer job tenure and vice versa. Other observed relationships are as follows: women, young workers, production workers, those with less schooling, and those in the private sector tend to turn over more, as do those

This is a shortened version of my Ph.D. thesis. I would like to thank R. E. Lucas for suggesting this problem to me and for his constant encouragement and advice throughout the preparation of this work. I would also like to thank Gary Becker and Lester Telser for their help at various stages of the preparation of the thesis.

workers not covered by a pension plan and those who work in industries with lower concentration ratios or with smaller average firm size. None of these relationships is nearly as strong as that between job tenure and separation probabilities.

Existing models of turnover (that is the "permanent separations" component of turnover) all involve imperfect information. New information arrives either about one's current match or about a possible alternative match that leads to a job change. In fact, a natural distinction among the models can be made along these lines. In one category are models in which turnover occurs as a result of the arrival of information about the current job match, and the present model falls into this category, as do the models of Viscusi (1976), Wilde (1977), and Johnson (1978).[1] These are models in which a job is an "experience good" in the terminology of Nelson (1970); that is, the only way to determine the quality of a particular match is to form the match and "experience it." In the second category are "pure search-good" models of job change (Kuratani 1973; Lucas and Prescott 1974; Burdett 1977; Jovanovic 1978b; Mortensen 1978; Wilde 1978). In those models, jobs are pure search goods and matches dissolve because of the arrival of new information about an alternative prospective match. Hirshleifer (1973) introduces the more appropriate designation "inspection goods." *Inspection* is evaluation that can take place prior to purchase, *experience* only after purchase.

In this paper, a job match is treated as a pure experience good. The paper makes two separate contributions. First, it is the only explicitly equilibrium treatment of turnover in its category. An equilibrium wage contract is proved to exist and a particular wage contract is demonstrated to be an equilibrium one. This particular wage contract has the property that at each moment in time the worker is paid his marginal product conditional upon all the available information at that time.

Second, the characterization of the model's implications regarding the tenure-turnover relationship and the tenure-wage relationship is more explicit than that of earlier models, and the predictions are largely consistent with the evidence. The model predicts that workers remain on jobs in which their productivity is revealed to be relatively high and that they select themselves out of jobs in which their productivity is revealed to be low. Since wages always equal expected marginal products for all workers, the model generates (on average) wage growth as tenure increases. Since job tenure and labor market experience are correlated across workers, this also implies wage growth over the life cycle. The model also predicts that each worker's separation probability is a decreasing function of his job tenure. Loosely speaking, this is because a mismatch between a worker and his employer is likely to be detected early on rather than late. The learning mechanism is such that longer job tenure has a negative structural effect on the worker's separation probability. After correcting for the regression bias that arises because of the spurious correlation between job tenure and the separation probability in a heterogeneous group of workers, Jovanovic and Mincer (1978) find that this structural dependence is very strong.

---

[1] *I became aware of the work of these three authors after the present work was largely finished.*

Before developing the model we summarize the major assumptions of the job-matching approach to turnover. First it is assumed that for each worker a nondegenerate distribution of productivities exists across different jobs. The same is true for the employer—workers differ in their productivities in a given task that the employer needs to have performed. The problem is one of optimally assigning workers to jobs.

The second assumption is that employers can contract with workers on an individual basis. The employer is then able to reward a worker with whom he matches well by paying the worker relatively more. Individual contracting creates a structure of rewards that provides proper signals for the attainment of optimal matches. An extreme example of individual contracting is a piece-rate wage scale. A less extreme and a widely prevalent example is a system of promotion or delayed pay increases based on the quality of the worker's performance on the job over a past period of time of some given length. These are examples where workers' pay is contingent on their performance.

The third major assumption of the job-matching approach is that imperfect information exists on both sides of the market about the exact location of one's optimal assignment. Following an initial assignment, new information becomes available, and reassignment becomes optimal in certain cases. The job-matching model generates turnover as the phenomenon of optimal reassignment caused by the accumulation of better information with the passage of time.

THE MODEL

Assume that firms' production functions exhibit constant returns to scale and that labor is the only factor of production. Under competitive conditions, the size of firm is then indeterminate. Each worker's output is assumed to be observed instantaneously by the worker and by the employer so that informational asymmetries do not arise. Let $X(t)$ be the contribution by a worker to the total output of the firm over a period of length t, and let

$$X(t) = \mu t + \sigma z(t) \qquad \text{(for each } t > 0) \tag{1}$$

where μ and σ are constants and $\sigma > 0$, and where $z(t)$ is a standard normal variable with mean zero and variance t (a standard Wiener process with independent increments so that cov $[z(t), z(t')] = \min [t, t']$). Then $X(t)$ is normally distributed with mean μt and with variance $\sigma^2 t$. Assume that σ is the same for each firm-worker match while in general μ differs across matches. The interpretation of μ is not one of worker ability but a measure of the quality of the match. When the match is formed, μ is unknown. As the match continues, further information (in the form of output as given by eq. [1]) is generated. A "good match" is one possessing a large μ. Let μ be normally distributed across matches, with mean m and with variance s, and assume that job changing involves drawing a new value of μ from this distribution and the successive drawings are independent. The latter assumption guarantees that the worker's prior history is of no relevance in assessing his μ

on a newly formed match. The only way to learn about μ is to observe the worker on the job for a period of time. This independence assumption also means that the informational capital thus generated is completely match specific and is analogous to the concept of firm-specific human capital.[2]

For a worker with job tenure t and cumulative output $X(t) = x$ the above assumptions imply that the available information on μ on his current job can be characterized by a posterior distribution that is normal (see Chernoff 1968, p. 266) with

$$\text{posterior mean} \equiv E_{xt}(\mu) = (ms^{-1} + x\sigma^{-2})(s^{-1} + t\sigma^{-2})^{-1}$$
$$\text{posterior variance} \equiv S(t) = (s^{-1} + t\sigma^{-2})^{-1}$$

(2)

The pair $[X(t), t]$ is therefore a sufficient statistic for the information contained in the entire posterior distribution. (This property is essentially due to the independent increments property of the Wiener process.) Furthermore, $E_{X(t)t}(\mu)$ is normally distributed with mean m and variance $s - S(t)$ (Chernoff 1968).

Firms are assumed to be risk neutral and to maximize the mathematical expectation of revenues discounted by the rate of interest, r. They compete for workers by offering wage contracts. In a long-run equilibrium the payments practices of each firm would be well understood and would not need to be explicitly written. An implicit contract equilibrium is studied here. The present model abstracts entirely from the consideration of shocks stemming from the product market. All firms face the same product price, normalized at unity, so that a maintained hypothesis of the model is that demand conditions are stationary. Assume that the firm's wage policy can be characterized by a wage function $w[X(t), t]$. This is the wage paid to the worker with tenure t if his cumulative output contribution is equal to $X(t)$. If the firm wishes to fire a certain worker, rather than doing so directly the firm is assumed to lower his wage by an amount sufficient to induce him to quit. All the job separations are therefore at the worker's initiative, but since some of the separations are disguised layoffs their empirical counterpart is really total separations (quits plus layoffs).

Workers are assumed to live forever,[3] and this assumption justifies the exclusion of age as an explicit argument from the wage function. As long as he remains with the firm, the worker receives payment according to the wage function $w(\cdot)$. He has the option of quitting at any time. Let Q be the present value of quitting a job and then pursuing the

[2] To elaborate: When dealing with random variables the concept of information specificity is associated with the concept of independence while perfect informational generality is associated with perfect correlation.

[3] More generally, one could assume that workers' lifetimes are exponentially distributed implying the absence of aging—one would not make a different prediction about the length of the remaining life of a worker who has already lived a long time than for a worker who has only lived a short time.

best alternative. The infinite horizon, constant discount rate, and the independence of the successive drawings of μ imply that Q is a constant.[4] Let $\alpha(Q,[w])$ be the present value to the worker of obtaining a job with a firm which offers $w(\cdot)$ as its wage contract and when the value of quitting is Q. Then if c represents the direct and the foregone earnings costs of job changing,

$$Q = \alpha(Q,[w]) - c. \tag{3}$$

The constant c is assumed to be parametrically given for each worker, although it may vary across workers. Let T be the quitting time and let $H(x, t \mid [w], Q) = \text{prob } (X[t] \leq x$ and $T > t$ given $[w]$ and $Q)$ and $F(t \mid [w], Q) = \text{prob } (T \leq t$ given $[w]$ and $Q)$. Then F is the probability that the worker quits before tenure t, while H is the probability that he does not quit before tenure t, and that by that time his cumulative output does not exceed x. Then define the appropriate densities $h(x, t \mid [w], Q)$ and $f(t \mid [w], Q)$ by $h = \partial H/\partial x$ and $f = \partial F/\partial t$. Both f and h are chosen by the worker in response to a wage function $w(\cdot)$ and a present value of quitting Q. Then

$$\alpha\big(Q, [w]\big) = \int_0^\infty e^{-rt} \int_{-\infty}^\infty wh\, dx\, dt + Q \int_0^\infty e^{-rt} f\, dt. \tag{4}$$

Equation (4) holds at the optimally chosen functions h and f. Since f integrates to a number not exceeding unity, $\partial\alpha/\partial Q = \int_0^\infty e^{-rt} f\, dt < 1$. Then it is easily seen that for given functions h, f, and w, equations (3) and (4) possess exactly one solution for the pair of scalars (α, Q).

All new workers look alike to the firm, and each worker is offered the same wage contract.[5] In differential form, equation (1) reads $dX(t) = \mu dt + \sigma dz(t)$. Letting E_{xt} be the mathematical expectation operation conditional on $X(t) = x$ at t, the discounted revenue from the output of a single worker is $E\int_0^\infty e^{-rt} dX(t) = E\int_0^\infty e^{-rt} E_{X(t)t} dX(t) = E\int_0^\infty e^{-rt} E_{X(t)t}(\mu) dt + E\int_0^\infty e^{-rt} \sigma E_{X(t)t} dz(t)$. The stochastic integrals are Itô integrals (see Kushner [1971] for their definition) and the last integral is therefore zero, by the independent increments property of the Wiener process, so that

$$E\int_0^\infty e^{-rt} dX(t) = E\int_0^\infty e^{-rt} E_{X(t)t}(\mu) dt = \int_0^\infty e^{-rt} \int_{-\infty}^\infty E_{xt}(\mu) h(x, t \mid [w], Q) dx\, dt \equiv \beta(Q, [w]).$$

---

[4] *The constancy of Q over time means that the worker never returns to a job from which he once separated. In other words, if it existed, the option of recall would never be exercised by the worker.*

[5] *Similarly, all firms look alike to the worker ex ante. Straightforward extensions of the model to the case where there are observable differences in characteristics among workers are outlined at the end of the paper. Salop (1973) takes up the search problem when the worker is able to distinguish among firms ex ante and has partial information not only about the wage offered by the firm but also about the likelihood that he will receive an employment offer from the firm in the event that he samples it. In Salop's analysis the most attractive opportunities are sampled first, and the job seeker lowers his acceptance wage with his duration of unemployment as his remaining opportunities worsen.*

Firms are aware of the worker's optimal quitting response to the wage contract {w}, and this is reflected in the above equation. Now let $\pi(Q, \{w\})$ be the discounted expected net revenue from the employment of a given worker who is offered the contract {w} and who has a present value of quitting equal to Q. Then

$$\pi(Q, [w]) = \beta(Q, [w]) - \alpha(Q, [w]) + \gamma(Q, [w]) \tag{5}$$

where $\gamma = Q\int_0^\infty e^{-rt}f(t \mid [w], Q)dt$.

In maximizing $\pi(Q, [w])$ over functions $[w]$, the firm treats Q as given, since Q is determined by the wage policies of other firms.

EQUILIBRIUM

Let B be the set of competitive equilibrium wage contracts, and for any $w(\cdot)$ let $Q([w])$ denote the unique solution for Q from equation (3). Then, if $w(\cdot) \in B$, (E1) each worker follows his optimal quitting policy in response to $w(\cdot)$ and to $Q([w])$; (E2) $\pi\{Q([w]), [w]\} \geq \pi\{Q([w]), [\hat{w}]\}$ for all $\hat{w}(\cdot) \neq w(\cdot)$, so that $w(\cdot)$ maximizes expected profits; (E3) $\pi\{Q([w]), [w]\} = 0$ (zero expected profit constraint). Let $w^*(x, t) = E_{xt}(\mu)$ for all (x, t). This wage contract states that the worker will be paid his expected (marginal) product at each moment in time. Let $Q^* = Q([w^*])$.

THEOREM 1. $w^* \in B$.

Proof. E3 is clearly satisfied by w^*. To prove E1 and E2, suppose by contradiction that E2 is not satisfied by w^* so that there exists some $w \in B$ such that if a deviant firm offers it

$$\pi(Q^*, [w^*]) < \pi(Q^*, [w]), \tag{6}$$

while the worker must be doing at least as well as under w^*:

$$\alpha(Q^*, [w^*]) \leq \alpha(Q^*, [w]). \tag{7}$$

(The value of quitting the deviant firm is unchanged at Q^*.) From (5),

$$\begin{aligned}\pi(Q^*, [w]) &- \pi(Q^*, [w^*]) + \alpha(Q^*, [w]) - \alpha(Q^*, [w^*]) \\ &= \beta(Q^*, [w]) - \beta(Q^*, [w^*]) + \gamma(Q^*, [w]) - \gamma(Q^*, [w^*]).\end{aligned} \tag{8}$$

Then equations (6) and (7) imply that the left-hand side of (8) is strictly positive. But the right-hand side of (8) is equal to $\int_0^\infty e^{-rt}\int_{-\infty}^\infty w^*(x, t)\{h(x, t \mid [w], Q^*) - h(x, t \mid [w^*], Q^*)\}dxdt +$

$Q^* \int_0^\infty e^{-rt}\{f(t \mid [w], Q^*) - f(t \mid [w^*], Q^*)\}dt$, and this expression cannot be positive since the quitting policy implied by $\{h(x, t \mid [w^*], Q^*), f(t \mid [w^*], Q^*)\}$ is optimal for the workers when faced with the wage contract $w^*(x, t)$ and the present value of quitting Q^*. Q.E.D.

Since workers and firms are risk neutral, $w^*(x, t)$ is not a unique equilibrium contract, any random variable ξ possessing the property $E_{xt}(\xi) = w^*(x, t)$ would also qualify. A pure piece-rate wage involving a payment of $X(t + \Delta t) - X(t)$ over the interval $(t, t + \Delta t)$ therefore also qualifies as equilibrium since $E_{xt}dX(t) = w^*(x, t)dt + \sigma E_{xt}dz(t) = w^*(x, t)dt$. Any such contract leads to identical turnover behavior as under $w^*(x, t)$. Even within the class of functions of x and t alone, $w^*(x, t)$ may not be unique. The following theorem guarantees, however, that turnover behavior is unique.

THEOREM 2. If $w \in B$ then $h\{x, t \mid [w], Q([w])\} = h\{x, t \mid [w^*], Q([w^*])\}$, and $f\{t \mid [w], Q([w])\} = f\{t \mid [w^*], Q([w^*])\}$.

Proof. See Jovanovic 1978a. The proof is lengthy and not particularly instructive. Theorem 2 states that the separation policy of the worker is unique even though the wage contract leading to it is not. This turnover behavior is identical with that which results in a situation in which each firm offers a wage contract $w^*(x, t) = E_{xt}(\mu)$.

Pareto Optimality of Turnover. Since all the agents are risk neutral, the correct optimality criterion is the maximization of the discounted expectation of aggregate output. Theorem 2 implies that whatever the prevailing equilibrium wage contract, the worker behaves so as to maximize his own expected discounted output. He collects all of the rent associated with the match, and the decision about whether or not to terminate the match rests with him (although the firm is equally involved in the separation decision since it lowers the worker's wage to the point where it knows the worker will quit). Therefore, a separation occurs if and only if the rent associated with the match falls to zero. A central planner could improve on this situation only if he knew *which* workers and *which* firms would make good matches.

Assume that the worker is faced with the wage contract $w^*(x, t) = E_{xt}(\mu)$ and a present value of quitting Q. The sufficient statistics (state variables) are $X(t)$ and t. It is more convenient to use instead $w(t)$ and t as the two state variables, where $w(t) = E_{x(t)t}(\mu)$. Since $w(t)$ is normally distributed with mean m and variance $s - S(t)$ for all t, it satisfies the stochastic differential equation

$$dw(t) = S(t)\sigma^{-1}dz(t) \qquad w(0) = m \tag{9}$$

so that the worker's wage follows a driftless random process with ever-decreasing incremental variance that tends to zero as tenure tends to infinity. Let $V(w, t)$ be the ("current") value of the game to the worker who has tenure t and wage $w(t) = w$. Then letting E_{wt} denote the mathematical expectation operator conditioned upon w and t,[6]

$$V(w,\ t) = w\Delta t + e^{-r\Delta t}E_{wt}V(w[t + \Delta t],\ t) + o(\Delta t). \qquad (10)$$

Subtracting $V(w,\ t)$ from both sides, dividing through by Δt, taking the limit as Δt tends to zero, and applying Itô's Lemma (see Kushner 1971) yields

$$w - rV\big(w,\ t\big) + \frac{S(t)^2}{2\sigma^2}V_{ww}\big(w,\ t\big) + V_t\big(w,\ t\big) = 0. \qquad (11)$$

As with most optimal stopping problems involving Markov processes, the space of points $(w,\ t)$ can be divided into a continuation region and a stopping region (see Shiryaev 1973). The continuation region consists of those wage-tenure combinations at which it is optimal for the worker to remain with the firm. Equations (10) and (11) hold for all wage-tenure combinations that belong to the continuation region. Let $[\theta(t),\ t]$ be the boundary of the continuation region so that along the boundary $V[\theta(t),\ t] = Q$, and $\theta(t)$ may be thought of as the reservation wage at which the worker quits the firm. Evaluating equation (11) at $w = \theta(t)$, $\theta(t) = rQ - [S(t)^2/2\sigma^2]V_{ww}[\theta(t),\ t] - V_t[\theta(t),\ t]$. A well-known "smooth-fit" condition of optimal stopping (see Shiryaev 1973) states that along the boundary,[7] $V_t[\theta(t),\ t] = \partial Q/\partial t = 0$, implying that

$$\theta\big(t\big) = rQ - \frac{S(t)^2}{2\sigma^2}V_{ww}\big[\theta(t),t\big]. \qquad (12)$$

---

[6] $o(\Delta t)$ *represents terms tending to zero faster than Δt does. Note that the option of stopping on $(t,\ t + \Delta t)$ (in which case a reward Q is collected) is exercised with a probability that behaves essentially as does*

$$\left\{1 - N\left[\frac{\hat{x}}{(\Delta t)^{1/2}}\right]\right\} < \frac{(\Delta t)^{1/2}}{\sqrt{2\pi}\hat{x}}\exp\left[-\frac{\hat{x}^2}{2(\Delta t)^{1/2}}\right] = o(\Delta t)$$

(see Feller 1966, p 171), where the inequality follows by a well-known result on the Mill's ratio and where $\hat{x}$ is equal to $w - \theta(t)$.

[7] *An informal proof is as follows: $V(w,\ t) = Q + \int_{\theta(f)}^{w}V_w(y,\ t)dy$ is maximized with respect to $\theta(t)$ (the reservation wage at t). Therefore differentiating both sides with respect to $\theta(t)$, setting the result equal to zero, and taking the limit as w tends to $\theta(t)$, one obtains that $V_w[\theta(t),\ t] = 0$, which in turn implies $V_t[\theta(t),\ t] = 0$ since $V[\theta(t),\ t] = Q = constant$.*

In the interior of the continuation region $V(w, t) > Q$. Since at the reservation wage $V[\theta(t), t] = Q$,[8] and since $V_w[\theta(t), t] = 0$, this implies that $V_{ww}[\theta(t), t] \geq 0$. Note that $S(t)$ declines monotonically to zero which suggests that $\theta(t)$ should be monotonically increasing up to rQ. It is possible to prove (see the Appendix) that $\theta(t) < rQ$ for all t, that $d\theta/dt \geq 0$, and that $\lim_{t \to \infty} \theta(t) = rQ$ so that the reservation wage increases up to its limit from below. The reason for the increase in the reservation wage is the decrease of the incremental variance of the wage process as tenure increases. A large incremental variance implies a large dispersion in possible future wages. If wages turn out to be very high the worker does not quit. If they become very low, the worker partially avoids this adverse outcome by quitting and collecting Q. In the absence of the opportunity to quit, the risk-neutral worker's welfare would be unaffected by changes in the incremental variance. The limit of the reservation wage is rQ. This is because the wage tends to a constant as t tends to infinity. There is nothing further to be learned, and at the point of indifference between staying and quitting the capitalized value of this constant wage must be equal to the present value of quitting, Q.

To obtain an approximation to the probability of job separation by tenure, set $\theta(t) = rQ$ for all t. Then for this approximation to the reservation wage,[9]

$$F(t\,|\,[w], Q) = 2\left\{1 - N\left[\frac{m - rQ}{p(t)^{1/2}}\right]\right\} = 2N\left[\frac{-m + rQ}{p(t)^{1/2}}\right]$$

with density

$$f(t\,|\,[w], Q) = \frac{(2\pi)^{-1/2}(m - rQ)}{p(t)^{3/2}}\exp\left[\frac{-(m - rQ)^2}{2p(t)}\right]$$

where $N(x) = (2\pi)^{-1/2}\int_{-\infty}^{x} e^{z^2/2}\,dz$, and where $p(t) = s - S(t)$ is the precision. The unique mode of this distribution is $(m - rQ)^2$. After the mode, the probability of turnover declines rapidly to zero. Some workers never change jobs, since $\lim_{t \to \infty} F(t\,|\,\cdot) < 1$.

To determine the predicted behavior of the separation probability by tenure, consider the hazard rate, $\phi(t) = f/(1 - F)$. Then $\phi(t)$ is the density of separation conditional upon an attained level of tenure, t. The model predicts a nonmonotonic relationship: first

---

[8] *In the Appendix it is shown that $\theta(t) < rQ$ for all t, implying that $V_{ww} > 0$ along the boundary, where it is also true that $V_w = 0$. So, if it was true that the continuation region was bounded from above, this would imply that $V < Q$ for some point in the interior of the continuation region sufficiently close to the boundary, which cannot be true. Therefore, $\theta(t)$ is single valued and it bounds the continuation region from below so that the optimal policy does have the reservation wage property. This is not surprising since it is known (Rothchild 1974, p. 709) that optimal search rules from normal distributions with unknown means and known variance have the reservation price property when the prior distribution is also normal.*

[9] *The wage is a standard Wiener process in the $s - S(t)$ scale (see the discussion preceding eq. [9]). Therefore the formula represents the first passage probability for a Wiener process through a linear boundary (Cox and Miller 1965, p. 221).*

$[\phi'(t)] > 0$ and then $\phi'(t) < 0$ as t gets relatively large. That $\phi(t)$ must eventually decline follows since $\lim_{t \to \infty} f(t) = 0$, while $1 - F(t)$ is bounded away from zero. The precise mathematical expression for the tenure level t^* at which $\phi'(t)$ changes sign and finally becomes negative cannot be obtained in closed form, but since $f' > 0$ implies $\phi' > 0$ clearly $t^* \geq m - rQ =$ the mode of f. If the mode of f is close to zero, $\phi'(t)$ is likely to become negative early on, as appears to be the case empirically (see Jovanovic and Mincer 1978).

The tenure-wage profile (defined as the conditional expectation of the wage given that the worker has attained tenure t) may also be calculated[10] and is equal to $\hat{w}(t) = (m + (m - rQ)2N\{-a[s - S(t)]^{1/2}\}/[1 - 2N\{ - a[s - S(t)]^{1/2}\}])$. Note that $\hat{w}(t)$ increases monotonically from m when tenure is zero up to $[m + (m - rQ)2N(-as^{-1/2})/\{1 - 2N(-as^{-1/2})\}]$ when tenure tends to infinity. Therefore, as low-wage workers quit and high-wage workers stay, the model implies that the average wage of a cohort of workers increases with tenure, eventually at a decreasing rate. In the limit, as tenure becomes indefinitely large, the average wage of those members of the cohort who have not quit approaches a constant as the wage of each worker becomes constant and equal to his true productivity. This then is an alternative explanation for wage growth on the job.

A mismatch leads to a lower wage and an early separation. Thus, holding constant market experience, average past earnings are likely to be lower for a worker who has experienced many job separations.[11] This prediction appears to be consistent with evidence from the National Longitudinal Study (NLS) mature men's sample (see Bartel and Borjas 1976).

Job durations over the life cycle are identically and independently distributed random variables. The turnover generated by the model therefore forms a pure renewal process (see Feller 1966, chap. 11). Let y denote the worker's labor market experience and $R(y) + o(\Delta y)$ denote the probability that the worker experiences a job separation on the market experience interval $(y, y + \Delta y)$. Then $R(y)$ is the renewal density which satisfies the equation

$$R(y) = f(y) + \int_0^y f(t)R(y - t)dt. \tag{13}$$

Jovanovic and Mincer (1978) prove that a monotonically declining $\phi(t)$ implies a monotonically declining $R(y)$. In other words, a monotonically declining separation probability

---

[10] *The probability that a Wiener process will not cross a linear boundary by a particular time and that it will end up at a particular value at that time is also available in closed form (see Cox and Miller 1965, p. 221, eq. 71). After appropriate adjustment the conditional density of wages (by tenure level) is obtained, and $\hat{w}(t)$ is the mathematical expectation of this distribution.*

[11] *Holding everything else constant. This statement should not be interpreted as saying that within a group of observationally equivalent people those that have changed jobs often in the past have had lower average past earnings than those that have not changed jobs often. In other words, the model does not imply that "movers" should do worse than "stayers" even though empirically this appears to be true.*

by tenure is *by itself* sufficient to cause turnover to decline monotonically over the life cycle.[12]

Last, the model generalizes straightforwardly to incorporate permanent differences in workers' characteristics such as level of schooling, ability, race, sex, and so on. The parameters of the model (S, m, σ^2, r) can then be regarded as functions of these variables, with each distinct group of workers treated as though they belonged to a distinct market of workers of that type. The entire analysis remains valid so long as informational symmetry between workers and employers is maintained, so that issues of signaling and self-selection are sidestepped. The nature of the assumed functional dependence between σ, r, m, and s on the one hand, and the workers' personal characteristics on the other, will determine the predicted relationships between turnover and these personal characteristics. This is not pursued here, but is an interesting problem for future research.

APPENDIX

We now prove the assertions made in the text following equation (12) about $\theta(t)$, the boundary of the optimal continuation region. We prove that $\theta(t) < rQ$ for all t, that $\theta(t)$ is nondecreasing, and that it approaches rQ as t tends to infinity. Some transformations of the original problem were necessary before these assertions could be proved, and since these transformations move one away from the economics of the problem, it seemed preferable to include these proofs in the Appendix.

Suppose that a probability space (Ω, F, P) is given, with ω being the elementary events ($\omega \in \Omega$). For any real-valued F-measurable function $f(\omega)$, the mathematical expectation operator E is defined as $E[f(\omega)] = \int f(\omega)dP$. Let $X(t) \in R^1$ be a Markov process defined on the above space. A particular sample path of the process is written as $[X(t, \omega)]_{t=0}^{\infty}$. Let E_{xt} be the expectation operator conditional upon $X(t) = x$.

Consider the following problem of optimally stopping $X(t)$: Let a utility function $u(x)$ be given, when $u(x)$ denotes the instantaneous payoff to the player at time t if the game is still in progress at t and if $X(t) = x$. Let $G(x)$ be the terminal payoff function denoting the utility to the player if the game is stopped exactly at t and $X(t) = x$. The player's objective is to maximize his expected discounted utility from playing the game (with r = the discount rate)

$$E\left(\int_0^{T(\omega)} e^{-rt} u\big[X(t, \omega)\big]dt + e^{-rT(\omega)} G\Big\{X\big[T(\omega), \omega\big]\Big\}\right) \tag{A1}$$

over F-measurable stopping time functions $T(\omega)$. A further restriction on $T(\omega)$ is that it must not anticipate the future. A rigorous discussion of this requirement appears in Shiryaev (1973). For most stopping problems, and certainly for the problems discussed below, this requirement means that the solution to the optimal stopping problem can be characterized by a continuation region for the process $X(t)$ so that

---

[12] *A similar relationship holds for wages: Let $L(y)$ be the mathematical expectation of the wage at a given level of labor market experience y. Then $L(y)$ satisfies the equation $L(y) = \hat{w}(y)[1 - F(y)] + \int_0^y f(t)L(y - t)dt$. Eq. (13) is known as the renewal equation which, for any given continuous density $f(t)$, possesses a unique solution $R(y)$ (Feller 1966) such that $R(0) = f(0)$ and $\lim_{y \to \infty} R(y) = [\int_0^\infty tf(t)dt]^{-1}$.*

the first exit time from the region is the optimal stopping time for $X(t)$. Let $C(x, t)$ be the value of the game to the player at t, conditional upon $X(t) = x$. Then

$$C(x, t) = E_{xt}\left(\int_t^{T^*(\omega)} e^{-r(s-t)} u[X(s, \omega)] ds + e^{-r[T^*(\omega)-t]} G\{X[T^*(\omega), \omega]\} \right) \tag{A2}$$

where $T^*(\omega)$ is the optimal stopping policy and $C(x, t)$ is the current value function. Let

$$U(x, t) = E_{xt} \int_t^\infty e^{-r(s-t)} u[X(s, \omega)] ds. \tag{A3}$$

Let $g(x, t) = G(x) - U(x, t)$, for all (x, t), and let

$$\psi(x, t) = E_{xt} e^{-r[T^*(\omega)-t]} g\{X[T^*(\omega), \omega], T^*(\omega)\}, \tag{A4}$$

and consider the problem of maximizing

$$E\, e^{-rT(\omega)} g\{X[T(\omega), \omega], T(\omega)\} \equiv E\, g^*\{X[T(\omega), \omega], T(\omega)\}, \tag{A5}$$

over stopping-time functions $T(\omega)$. Let $\hat{T}(\omega)$ be the optimal policy for this problem. Then the following theorem holds.

THEOREM 3. If $E \int_0^\infty e^{-rt} \mid u[X(t, \omega), t] \mid dt < \infty$, then $\hat{T}(\omega) = T^*(\omega)$, and

$$C(x, t) = U(x, t) + \psi(x, t). \tag{A6}$$

Proof. Shiryaev 1973, p. 101. Theorem 3 asserts that stopping problems such as (A1) which involve an instantaneous utility obtainable while the game is played can be transformed into problems such as (A5) which involve only a terminal payoff function $g(x, t)$. Note that $U(x, t)$ is the current value of the policy "never stop the game no matter what happens to $X(t)$."

Let $X(t)$ satisfy the stochastic Itô equation

$$X(t) = X(0) + \int_0^t a[X(s), s] ds + \int_0^t b[X(s), s] dv(s) \tag{A7}$$

(or $dX(t) = a[X(t), t] dt + b[X(t), t] dv(t)$ in differential form). Here $v(t)$ is the standard Wiener process and $X(t)$ is a Markov process with instantaneous mean $a(\cdot)$ and instantaneous variance $[b(\cdot)]^2$.

The following theorem contains the basic results associated with the problem of optimally stopping $X(t)$ when $X(t)$ is defined by equation (A7).

THEOREM 4. Let $X(t)$ be defined by equation (A7), and let the stopping problem be given by equation (A5). Let $T_0 < \infty$ be given, and in addition to the other requirements on $T(\omega)$, let $T(\omega) \in [0, T_0]$ for all $\omega \in \Omega$. Let $J = \{(t, x): t \in [0, T_0], x \in R^1\}$, and let $V(x,t) = \sup E_{xt} \xi\{X[T(\omega), \omega], T(\omega)\}$, where the sup is taken over the admissable functions $T(\omega)$. Assume that the functions $a(\cdot)$, $b(\cdot)$ and $\xi(\cdot)$ are all twice continuously differentiable in x and once in t, and that for all $(x, t) \in J$, $|\xi| + |\xi_t| + |\xi_x| + |\xi_{xx}| \le \hat{k}(1 + |x|)^k$, $|a_{xx}| + |b_{xx}| + |a_x| + |b_x| \le \hat{k}(1 + |x|)^k$, and that $|a_x| + |b_x| \le \hat{k}$ where $\hat{k}$ and k are positive constants. Let $D = [(t, x): V > \xi]$ and $A = \{(t, x): \xi_t(\cdot) + a(\cdot)\xi_x(\cdot) + (1/2)[b(\cdot)]^2 \xi_{xx}(\cdot) > 0\}$. Then the following propositions hold: (1) $V \ge \xi$ on J. (2) If V is differentiable, then $V_t(\cdot) + a(\cdot)V_x(\cdot) + (1/2)[b(\cdot)]^2 V_{xx}(\cdot) = 0$ for $(t, x) \in J$. (3) The first exit time of the process $[t, X(t)]$ from D is an optimal stopping time. Therefore D is the region of the continued observations, and along its boundary, $V = \xi$. (4) $A \subset D$. (5) If A is connected, so is D.

Proof. Miroshnichenko 1975, p. 387. Consider now the worker's problem. Let $w^*[X(t), t] = E_{X(t)t}(\mu) \equiv W^*(t)$ be the basic Markov process defined on (Ω, F, P). The worker maximizes discounted expected earnings. His instantaneous utility is $W^*(t)$, while the terminal payoff function is a constant, Q. Therefore the counterpart of equation (A1) is

$$E\left[\int_0^{T(\omega)} e^{-rt} W^*(t, \omega)dt + e^{-rT(\omega)}Q\right]. \tag{A8}$$

The process $W^*(t)$ has zero drift. Therefore the counterpart of $U(x, t)$ is $E_{W^*t} \int_t^\infty e^{-r(s-t)}W^*(s, \omega)ds = r^{-1}W^*$. Therefore, $g(x, t) = Q - r^{-1}W^*$. Since $E\int_0^\infty e^{-rt}|W^*(t, \omega)|dt < \infty$, theorem 3 may be applied to the problem to conclude that the solution to the worker's problem of maximizing the expression in (A8) is identical to the solution to the problem of maximizing

$$Ee^{-rT(\omega)}\{Q - r^{-1}W^*[T(\omega), \omega]\}. \tag{A9}$$

If $T^*(\omega)$ is the optimal solution, then equation (A6) yields

$$C(W^*, t) = r^{-1}W^* + Ee^{-r[T^*(\omega)-t]}\{Q - r^{-1}W^*[T^*(\omega), \omega]\} \tag{A10}$$

where $C(W^*, t)$ is the worker's current value function. Now let $W(y)$ be the standard Wiener process, with $W(0) = m$; $W^*(t)$ is a standard Wiener process in the $s - S(t)$ scale (Chernoff 1968, p. 226). Letting $y \equiv s - S(t) \Rightarrow t = \sigma^2[(s - y)^{-1} - s^{-1}]$, and $Y^*(\omega) \equiv s - S[T^*(\omega)]$,

$$Ee^{-r[T^*(\omega)-t]}\{Q - r^{-1}W^*[T^*(\omega), \omega]\} = Ee^{-r[T^*(\omega)-t]}(Q - r^{-1}W\{s - S[T^*(\omega), \omega]\})$$
$$= \{Q - r^{-1}W[Y^*(\omega), \omega]\}\exp(-r\sigma^2\{[s - Y^*(\omega)]^{-1} - (s - y)^{-1}\}) \tag{A11}$$

where $T^*(\omega) \in [0,\infty) \Rightarrow Y^*(\omega) \in [0, s)$. The problem has therefore been transformed into one of stopping a standard Wiener process, $W(y)$, on the interval $[0, s)$, with only a terminal payoff function

$$\xi(W, y) \equiv (Q - r^{-1}W)\exp\{-r\sigma^2[(s - y)^{-1} - s^{-1}]\}. \tag{A12}$$

Theorem 4 may now be applied to this problem with $a(\cdot) = 0$, $b(\cdot) = 1$. Let $V(W, y)$ be the present value function for this problem defined by

$$V(W, y) = E_{Wy} \, \xi\{W[Y^*(\omega), \omega], Y^*(\omega)\}. \qquad (A13)$$

Since $\xi_{ww} = 0$,

$$A = [(W, y):\xi_y > 0] = [(W, y):y \in [0, s), W > rQ]. \qquad (A14)$$

Proposition 4 of the theorem asserts that $A \subset D$ where D is the continuation region for the process $[W(y), y]$. Let $[\theta(y), y]$ be the boundary of the continuation region. Then $[\theta(y), y] \notin A \Rightarrow$

$$\theta(y) \leq rQ \qquad \text{for } y \in [0, s). \qquad (A15)$$

Then $\theta(y)$ is the reservation wage in the (W, y) space. Let $\hat{\theta}(t)$ be the reservation wage in the (W, t) space. Then $\hat{\theta}(t) = \theta[s - S(t)]$.

THEOREM 5. $\theta(y) < rQ$ for $y \in [0, s)$.

Proof. Along the boundary,

$$V[\theta(y), y] = \xi[\theta(y), y]. \qquad (A16)$$

In view of (A15), it is sufficient to prove that $\theta(y) \neq rQ$ for any $y \in [0, s)$. By contradiction, suppose that for some $y° \in [0, s)$, $\theta(y°) = rQ$. Equation (A16) then implies that $V[\theta(y°), y°] = \xi(rQ, y°) = 0$. Consider now the value of the following policy at $(rQ, y°)$: For some δ such that $y° + \delta < s$, continue the game until $y° + \delta$. Then if $v(y° + \delta) < rQ$, stop the game at $y° + \delta$, and collect $\xi[v(y° + \delta), y° + \delta] > 0$. If $v(y° + \delta) > rQ$, continue the game until $y = s$, and collect a payoff equal to zero. But prob $[v(y° + \delta) < rQ$ given that $v(y°) = rQ] = 1/2$, and so there is a positive expected payoff under this policy. Since this policy is feasible, $V[\theta(y°), y°]$ must also be positive. This completes the proof of the theorem.

Let $F(y)$ be the probability that the worker's optimal policy will lead him to quit before y. Then $F(y°) = \text{prob}\{\inf_{0 \leq y \leq y°} [W(y) - \theta(y)] \leq 0\}$. Let $f(y)$ be the density. Then

$$E\xi\left\{W\left[Y*(\omega), \omega\right], Y*(\omega)\right\} = \int_0^s \xi\left[\theta(y), y\right] f(y) dy. \qquad (A17)$$

The Envelope Theorem

Let α and β be two parameters. Assume that the evolution of $X(t)$ is not affected by α and β. Let $u(x, t, \alpha)$ be the instantaneous utility function in present value terms, and let $G(x, t, \beta)$ be the terminal payoff function also in present value terms. Let $[\theta(t; \alpha, \beta), t]$ be the optimally determined boundary of the continuation region for the process $[X(t), t]$. The function $\theta(t, \alpha, \beta)$ is assumed to be single valued.

Let $h(x, t, \alpha, \beta)$ be the probability (density) that the game will not have been stopped before t, and that $X(t) = x$, and let $f(t, \alpha, \beta)$ be the probability (density) that the game will be stopped exactly at t. It is clear that $\theta(\cdot)$, $h(\cdot)$, and $f(\cdot)$ are in one-to-one correspondence with one another and should be thought of as decision variables. Let T be the horizon, $0 < T \leq \infty$. Let $V(\alpha, \beta)$ be the value of the game at time zero. Then,

$$V(\alpha, \beta) = \int_0^T \int_{-\infty}^{\infty} u(x, t, \alpha) h(x, t, \alpha, \beta) dx dt + \int_0^T G\big[\theta(t, \alpha, \beta), t, \beta\big] f(t, \alpha, \beta) dt. \tag{A18}$$

THEOREM 6 (ENVELOPE THEOREM). *If α and β do not affect the evolution of $X(t)$, and if $u(\cdot)$, $G(\cdot)$, $h(\cdot)$, $f(\cdot)$, and $\theta(\cdot)$ are differentiable with respect to α and β, then $dV/d\alpha = \partial V/\partial \alpha = \int_0^T \int_{-\infty}^{\infty} u_\alpha(x, t, \alpha) h(x, t, \alpha, \beta) dx dt$ and $dV/d\beta = \partial V/\partial \beta = \int_0^T G_\beta[\theta(t, \alpha, \beta), t, \beta] f(t, \alpha, \beta) dt.$*

Proof. Unless stated otherwise, $u(\cdot)$, $G(\cdot)$, $h(\cdot)$, $f(\cdot)$, and $\theta(\cdot)$ are all evaluated at (x, t, α, β). Furthermore, since the proof for α is almost identical with the proof for β, only the latter is given:

$$\frac{dV}{d\beta} = \int\int uh_\beta dx dt + \int \big(G_x \theta_\beta + G f_\beta\big) dt + \int G_\beta f dt. \tag{A19}$$

Therefore if it can be shown that

$$\int\int uh_\beta dx dt + \int (G_x \theta_\beta + G f_\beta) dt = 0 \tag{A20}$$

the theorem will have been proved. Since the worker's policy in response to α and β is optimal,

$$V(\alpha, \beta) \geq \int\int uh(x, t, \alpha, \beta + d\beta) dx dt + \int G[\theta(t, \alpha, \beta + d\beta), t, \beta] f(t, \alpha, \beta + d\beta) dt \tag{A21}$$

for all $d\beta \neq 0$. Subtracting $V(\alpha, \beta)$ from both sides of (A21), dividing through by $d\beta$, and taking the limit as $d\beta \to 0$, the result is

$$\int\int uh_\beta dx dt + \int (G_x \theta_\beta + G f_\beta) dt \leq 0. \tag{A22}$$

A change in β implies, in general, a change in the optimal stopping policy. But the policy which was optimal prior to the shift in β remains a feasible policy. Therefore

$$\frac{dV}{d\beta} \geq \frac{\partial V}{\partial \beta} = \int G_\beta f dt. \tag{A23}$$

Equations (A23) and (A19) imply that

$$\int\int uh_\beta dx dt + \int (G_x \theta_\beta + G f_\beta) dt \geq 0, \tag{A24}$$

and (A24) and (A19) imply that (A20) holds $\Rightarrow dV/d\beta = \partial V/\partial \beta$ and the theorem is proved.

The results of Theorem 6 are now used to obtain qualitative information about the derivatives of the worker's current value function $C(W^*, t)$. Since $W^*(0) = m$,

$$
\begin{aligned}
C(m,0) &= r^{-1}m + \int_0^s \xi[\theta(y), y] f(y) dy \\
&= r^{-1}m + \int_0^s [Q - r^{-1}\theta(y)] \exp\left\{ -r\sigma^2 \left[(s-y)^{-1} - s^{-1}\right]\right\} f(y) dy \\
&= \alpha[Q,(w^*)].
\end{aligned}
\tag{A25}
$$

By the envelope theorem, since $\xi[\theta(s), s] = 0$,

$$
\begin{aligned}
\frac{\partial C}{\partial s} &= \int_0^s \frac{\partial \xi}{\partial s}[\theta(y), y] f(y) dy + \xi[\theta(s), s] f(s) \\
&= r\sigma^2 \int_0^s \left[(s-y)^{-2} - s^{-2}\right] \xi[\theta(y), y] f(y) dy.
\end{aligned}
\tag{A26}
$$

Since $f(y)$ is a density, it is nonnegative, while theorem 5 implies that $\xi[\theta(y), y] > 0$ for $y \in [0, s)$. Therefore $(\partial C/\partial s)(m, 0) > 0$. But the state $(m, 0)$ is arbitrary. If the state is (W, y), where $y = s - S(t)$, the analogue of the right-hand side of equation (A25) would hold, with s replaced by $S(t)$. The only way in which the worker's welfare is affected by the mere passage of time is through the decrease in $S(t)$. Since $\partial C(W^*, t)/\partial S(t) > 0$,

$$
\frac{\partial C(W^*,t)}{\partial t} = \frac{\partial C}{\partial S(t)} \frac{dS(t)}{dt} = \frac{-\partial C}{\partial S(t)} \sigma^{-2}[S(t)]^2 < 0.
\tag{A27}
$$

The envelope theorem cannot be directly applied in (A25) to calculate $\partial C/\partial m$ because m is the starting point of the standard Wiener process $W(y)$, and if it is changed it changes the probabilities of reaching a given boundary $\theta(y)$. However, $f(y^\circ)$ is the derivative of $F(y^\circ)$ which in turn is defined by

$$
\begin{aligned}
F(y^\circ) &= \text{prob}\left\{ \inf_{0 \le y \le y^\circ} [W(y) - \theta(y)] \le 0 \,\middle|\, W(0) = m \right\} \\
&= \text{prob}\left(\inf_{0 \le y \le y^\circ} \{W(y) - [\theta(y) + dm]\} \le 0 \,\middle|\, W(0) = m + dm \right)
\end{aligned}
\tag{A28}
$$

This means that if $[\theta(y), f(y)]$ was a feasible policy pair prior to the change in m, then the new feasible policy pair is $[\theta(y) + dm, f(y)]$. In other words, after the change in m, the boundary $[\theta(y) + dm]$ induces the same first-passage density $f(y)$ as did the boundary $\theta(y)$ prior to the change in m, and this holds for all boundaries $\theta(y)$. Therefore, the change from m to $m + dm$ can be considered as having no effect on the feasibility of reaching a boundary, but simply as changing the form of the payoff function from

$\xi(W, y)$ to $\xi(W + dm, y)$. Application of theorem 6 then yields

$$\frac{\partial}{\partial m}\left\{\int_0^s \xi\big[\theta(y), y\big]f(y)dy\right\} = -r^{-1}\int_0^s \exp\left\{-r\sigma^2\left[(s-y)^{-1} - s^{-1}\right]\right\}f(y)dy \tag{A29}$$

and

$$\frac{\partial C}{\partial m}(m, 0) = r^{-1}\left(1 - \int_0^s \exp\left\{-r\sigma^2\left[(s-y)^{-1} - s^{-1}\right]\right\}f(y)dy\right),$$

and since $f(y)$ is a density, $\partial C/\partial m > 0$. Again, the state $(m, 0)$ is arbitrary, and a similar result holds for $(\partial C/\partial W)(W, y)$. Letting $\hat{f}(t) \equiv f(y)(dy/dt)$ be the first-passage probability in the original time scale,

$$\frac{\partial C}{\partial m} = r^{-1}\left[1 - \int_0^\infty e^{-rt}\hat{f}(t)dt\right]. \tag{A30}$$

THEOREM 7. $\hat{\theta}(t)$ is nondecreasing in t.

Proof. By contradiction, suppose that at t^*, $\theta(t)$ is decreasing. Then there exists an $\epsilon > 0$ sufficiently small such that the points $[\theta(t^*), t^* + \tau]$ for $\tau \in [0, \epsilon]$ all lie in the continuation region. Therefore, since $C > Q$ in the continuation region,

$$C[\theta(t^*), t^* + \epsilon] > C[\theta(t^*), t^*] = Q. \tag{A31}$$

But

$$C\big[\theta(t^*), t^* + \epsilon\big] = C\big[\theta(t^*), t^*\big] + \int_0^\epsilon \frac{\partial C}{\partial t}\big[\theta(t^*), t^* + \tau\big]d\tau < C\big[\theta(t^*), t^*\big] \tag{A32}$$

in view of (A27). Since (A32) is a contradiction to (A31), the theorem is proved.

THEOREM 8. $\lim_{t\to\infty} \hat{\theta}(t) = rQ$.

Proof. Since $\hat{\theta}(t) = \theta[s - S(t)] = \theta(y)$, it is sufficient to prove that

$$\lim_{y\to s} \theta(y) = rQ. \tag{A33}$$

By contradiction, suppose that $\lim_{y\to s} \theta(y) = \eta$ and that $\eta < rQ$. Now choose $\delta > 0$ such that $\eta + \delta < rQ$. By theorem 7, $\theta(y)$ is nondecreasing in y. Therefore the point $(\eta + \delta, s - \epsilon)$ must lie in the continuation region for any $\epsilon > 0$. In terms of the present value function $V(W, y)$ and the present value of the payoff function $\xi(W, y)$, this means that

$$V(\eta+\delta, s-\epsilon) = \int_{s-\epsilon}^{s} \xi[\theta(y), y] f(\eta+\delta, s-\epsilon, y) dy > \xi(\eta+\delta, s-\epsilon) \qquad \text{(A34)}$$

where $f(\eta + \delta, s - \epsilon, y)$ is the probability (density) that the game will end at $y \in [s - \epsilon, s)$ given that $W(s - \epsilon) = \eta + \delta$. Since ξ is decreasing in W and decreasing in y, and since $\theta(y)$ is nondecreasing, $\xi[\theta(s - \epsilon), s - \epsilon] > \xi[\theta(y), y]$ for $y \in (s - \epsilon, s)$. Therefore

$$V(\eta+\delta, s-\epsilon) < \xi[\theta(s-\epsilon), s-\epsilon] \int_{s-\epsilon}^{s} f(\eta+\delta, s-\epsilon, y) dy. \qquad \text{(A35)}$$

Furthermore, $f(\eta + \delta, s - \epsilon, y)$ is the first-passage density of the standard Wiener process (originating at $\eta + \delta$ at $s - \epsilon$) through the boundary $\theta(y)$ on the interval $[s - \epsilon, s)$. Then the integral on the right-hand side of (A35) is smaller than the probability that the same standard Wiener process will cross the threshold $\sup_{y \in (s-\epsilon, s)} \theta(y) = \eta$. From Feller (1966, p. 171) this latter probability is equal to $2[1 - N(\epsilon^{-1/2}\delta)]$ where $N(x) = \int_{-\infty}^{x} (2\pi)^{-1/2} \exp[-(1/2)u^2] du$. Therefore

$$V(\eta+\delta, s-\epsilon) < \xi[\theta(s-\epsilon), s-\epsilon] 2[1 - N(\epsilon^{-1/2}\delta)]. \qquad \text{(A36)}$$

Equations (A36), (A34), and (A12) then imply that

$$[Q - r^{-1}\theta(s-\epsilon)] 2[1 - N(\epsilon^{-1/2}\delta)] > [Q - r^{-1}(\eta+\delta)] > 0. \qquad \text{(A37)}$$

But since $\theta(y)$ is nondecreasing, and since by assumption $\lim_{y\to s} \theta(y) = \eta < rQ$,

$$(Q - r\eta) 2[1 - N(\epsilon^{-1/2}\delta)] > [Q - r^{-1}(\eta+\delta)]. \qquad \text{(A38)}$$

The right-hand side of (A38) is positive and does not depend on ϵ. Therefore ϵ may be chosen sufficiently small such that the inequality in (A38) does not hold. The theorem is proved.

REFERENCES

Azariadis, Costas. "Implicit Contracts and Underemployment Equilibria." *J.P.E.* 83, no. 6 (December 1975): 1183–1202.

Baily, Martin N. "Wages and Employment under Uncertain Demand." *Rev. Econ. Studies* 41, no. 1 (January 1974): 37–50.

Bartel, A. P. "Job Mobility and Earnings Growth." Working Paper, Nat. Bur. Econ. Res., 1975.

Bartel, A. P., and Borjas, G. J. "Middle-Age Job Mobility." Working Paper, Nat. Bur. Econ. Res., 1976.

Burdett, Kenneth. "Theory of Employee Search: Quit Rates." *A.E.R.* 68 (March 1978): 212–20.

Burton, John F., and Parker, John E. "Interindustry Variations in Voluntary Labor Mobility." *Indus. and Labor Relations Rev.* 22, no. 1 (January 1969): 199–216.

Chernoff, H. "Optimal Stochastic Control." *Sankhya,* Ser. A, 43, no. 2 (June 1968): 111–42.

Cox, David R., and Miller, H. D. *The Theory of Stochastic Processes.* New York: Wiley, 1965.

Feldstein, Martin S. "Temporary Layoffs in the Theory of Unemployment." *J.P.E.* 84, no. 5 (October 1976): 937–57.

Feller, William. *An Introduction to Probability Theory and Its Applications.* Vol. 2. 2d ed. New York: Wiley, 1966.

Freeman, R. B. "Exit Voice Tradeoff in the Labor Market: Unionism, Quits, and Job Tenure." Unpublished paper, Harvard Univ., 1976.

Hirshleifer, Jack. "Where Are We in the Theory of Information?" *A.E.R.* 87 (May 1973): 31–39.

Johnson, W. "A Theory of Job Shopping." *Q.J.E.* 92 (May 1978): 261–77.

Jovanovic, Boyan. "Job Matching and the Theory of Turnover." Ph.D. dissertation, Univ. Chicago, June 1978. (*a*)

———. "Labor Turnover Where Jobs Are Pure Search Goods." Unpublished paper, Columbia Univ., February 1978. (*b*)

Jovanovic, Boyan, and Mincer, Jacob. "Labor Mobility and Wages." Unpublished paper, Columbia Univ., June 1978.

Kuratani, M. "Theory of Training, Earnings, and Employment: An Application to Japan." Ph.D. dissertation, Columbia Univ., 1973.

Kushner, Harold. *Introduction to Stochastic Control.* New York: Holt, Rinehart & Winston, 1971.

Lucas, Robert E., Jr., and Prescott, Edward C. "Equilibrium Search and Unemployment." *J. Econ. Theory* 7, no. 2 (February 1974): 188–209.

Miroshnichenko, T. P. "Optimal Stopping of an Integral of a Wiener Process." *Theory of Probability and Its Appl.* 9, no. 4 (July 1975): 355–62.

Mortensen, Dale T. "Specific Human Capital Bargaining and Labor Turnover." Discussion Paper, Northwestern Univ., March 1978.

Nelson, Phillip. "Information and Consumer Behavior." *J.P.E.* 78, no. 2 (March/April 1970): 311–29.

Parsons, Donald O. "Specific Human Capital: An Application to Quit Rates and Layoff Rates." *J.P.E.* 80, no. 6 (November/December 1972): 1120–43.

Pencavel, John H. *An Analysis of the Quit Rate in American Manufacturing Industry.* Princeton, N.J.: Princeton Univ. Press, 1970.

Rothschild, Michael. "Searching for the Lowest Price When the Distribution of Prices Is Unknown." *J.P.E.* 82, no. 4 (July/August 1974): 689–711.

Salop, Steven. "Systematic Job Search and Unemployment." *Rev. Econ. Studies* 40 (April 1973): 191–202.

Shiryaev, Al'Bert N. *Statistical Sequential Analysis: Optimal Stopping Rules.* Providence, R.I.: American Mathematical Society, 1973.

Stoikov, Vladimir, and Ramon, R. L. "Determinants of the Differences in the Quit Rate among Industries." *A.E.R.* 58, no. 5 (December 1968): 1283–98.

Telser, Lester G. *Competition, Collusion and Game Theory.* Chicago: Aldine Atherton, 1972.

Viscusi, K. "Job Hazards and Worker Quit Rates: An Analysis of Adaptive Worker Behavior." Unpublished paper, Northwestern Univ., 1976.

Wilde, L. "An Information-theoretic Approach to Job Quits." Social Science Working Paper no. 150, California Inst. Technol., 1977.

ABOUT THE AUTHOR

Boyan Jovanovic

Boyan Jovanovic is professor of economics at New York University. Known in the field of labor economics for his influential work on theories of worker–firm job matching, Jovanovic is also well known for his theoretical work in the economics of market structure and in the theory of economic growth.

Born in Yugoslavia, Jovanovic obtained B.Sc. and M.Sc. degrees in 1972 and 1973 at the London School of Economics and completed a Ph.D. in economics at the University of Chicago in 1978. After several years as a research scientist at Bell Labs, Jovanovic joined New York University in 1983.

Although Jovanovic works as an economist on his day job, he is a musician at night. Well known in Greenwich Village for his skill on the piano, guitar, and drums (in that order), Jovanovic works under a stage name when playing a gig.

Job Duration, Seniority, and Earnings

KATHARINE G. ABRAHAM

HENRY S. FARBER

An important stylized fact about labor markets is that workers with longer seniority with their current employer have higher earnings than other workers with the same total labor market experience. This study shows that the measured positive cross-sectional return to seniority is largely a statistical artifact due to the correlation of seniority with an omitted variable representing the quality of the worker, job, or worker-employer match. The implication is that earnings do not, in fact, rise very much with seniority.

It is a commonly accepted empirical finding that workers with more seniority on their current job earn more than other workers with the same total labor market experience. The standard explanations for a positive correlation between seniority and earnings are based on the existence of implicit employment contracts under which earnings grow with time on the job in order to provide workers with appropriate incentives regarding turnover and/or effort. For example, if a job involves investment in firm-specific training, then it may be optimal for workers and employers to structure implicit employment agreements such that compensation is deferred until late in the job so that workers will not quit (taking their specific capital with them).[1] Another possible motivation for such a deferral arrangement exists where effort is important. The promise of eventual compensation in excess of the opportunity value of time provides the worker with an incentive to exert the appropriate level of effort on the job. A worker who left or whose performance

The Brookings Institution, 1775 Massachusetts Avenue, NW, Washington, DC 20036, and Department of Economics, E52-252f, MIT, Cambridge MA 02139, respectively. We thank Joe Altonji for providing us with the data, Jim Powell for providing valuable econometric advice, and Leslie Sundt for able research assistance in preparing the data for analysis. Useful comments on an earlier version of this paper were received from Altonji, Jerry Hausman, Steve Nickell, Bob Topel, and participants in numerous workshops. Farber received support from the National Science Foundation. The views expressed here are our own and should not be attributed to the trustees, officers, or staff members of the institutions with which we are affiliated.

Reprinted with permission from Katherine G. Abraham and Henry S. Farber, "Job Duration, Seniority, and Earnings," American Economic Review, Vol. 77 No. 3 (June 1987), pp. 278–297.

[1] *See Gary Becker (1964), Jacob Mincer (1974), and Dale Mortensen (1978) for discussions of investment in firm-specific training. Mincer and Boyan Jovanovic (1981) present an analysis of the relationships among seniority, mobility, and earnings that relies on investment in specific human capital.*

fell below agreed-upon standards and in consequence was fired would lose the opportunity to enjoy the benefits of the high deferred wages.[2]

The firm-specific human capital explanation and effort-incentive wage deferral explanations differ in their implications regarding the relationship between earnings and productivity growth over the work life.[3] However, they share the implication not only that the seniority-earnings profile will be upward sloping, but also that there will be a positive return to seniority even after controlling for total labor market experience.

The empirical support for these views of the labor market rests entirely on the positive cross-sectional association between seniority and earnings, but this is not sufficient evidence to establish that earnings rise with seniority. An alternative interpretation of the cross-sectional evidence is based on the idea that workers who are 1) better workers, 2) in better jobs, or 3) in better worker-employer matches earn more throughout their jobs and also stay on their jobs longer. It is straightforward to show that the distribution of seniority in a cross section has a higher mean for workers on longer jobs. Thus, as long as those workers who earn more from the start have longer average completed job durations, the ordinary least squares estimate of the return to seniority in a cross-section earnings function is biased upward.

The key testable link in this argument is that workers in long jobs earn more from the start than observationally equivalent workers in short jobs. Why might this be true? First, some workers may be more stable and more productive than others. To the extent that there are turnover and training costs, stability per se can raise an employee's value to the firm. Second, some employers may choose to pay higher wages than others (some jobs are "better" than others), so that workers are unlikely either to shirk or to quit.[4] Finally, some worker/job matches may be better than others, in the sense that the worker is more productive in those matches than in other possible matches, so that the specific value of the match is shared between the employer and the worker, and the match is much less likely to be broken off.[5] To the extent that worker, job, and/or match quality are unmeasured, they represent omitted variables in a cross-section earnings regression.

---

[2] *See W. Kip Viscusi (1980), Becker and George Stigler (1974), and Edward Lazear (1979) for models in which wage deferral provides this sort of incentive for workers. George Akerlof and Lawrence Katz (1986) argue that such deferral arrangements cannot, in fact, yield efficient effort levels unless the present value of promised earnings at the start of the job exceeds the present value of earnings on the next-best alternative job.*

[3] *James Medoff and Abraham (1980, 1981) and Abraham and Medoff (1982) offer evidence on the relationship between seniority-related earnings growth and seniority-related productivity growth.*

[4] *The efficiency wage literature suggests various possible reasons why some employers might pay higher wages than others to workers of equal quality. These include differences in the costs of turnover, differences in the costs of monitoring worker shirking, and differences in the value of worker loyalty. Carl Shapiro and Joseph Stiglitz (1984) and Jeremy Bulow and Lawrence Summers (1986) present formal efficiency wage models. Janet Yellen (1984), Stiglitz (1984), and Katz (1986) survey the literature.*

[5] *Mortensen and Jovanovic (1979) both present theoretical analyses of the effects of heterogeneous match quality that have these implications.*

Here we develop a simple stochastic model of earnings determination that illustrates the upward bias in the estimated return to seniority just described and provides the basis for two related approaches to correcting this bias. These approaches are implemented using data from the *Panel Study of Income Dynamics*. The results of this empirical analysis reveal 1) that workers on longer jobs earn more in every year on the job, and 2) that much of the apparent cross-section return to seniority reflects omitted variable bias.

I. COMPLETED JOB DURATION IN THE EARNINGS FUNCTION

Suppose that the earnings of a particular worker i on job j in year t can be written

$$(1) \qquad \ln W_{ijt} = \beta_1 S_{ijt} + \beta_2 EXP_{ij} + \mu_{ij} + \eta_{ijt},$$

where W = hourly earnings, S = current seniority (tenure), β_1 = return to seniority, EXP = pre-job experience, β_2 = return to pre-job experience, μ = a person/job-specific error term representing the excess of earnings enjoyed by this person on this job over and above the earnings that could be expected by a randomly selected person / job combination, and η = a person/job/time-period-specific error term.

For simplicity of exposition, other factors that might influence earnings are omitted from the theoretical discussion and all variables are assumed to be measured as deviations from their means. In this formulation, μ_{ij} captures the net influence of three unobservables on hourly earnings: unobserved person quality, unobserved job quality, and unobserved match quality. The error μ_{ij} is assumed to be fixed over the course of a job and may be correlated with S and EXP. The error η_{ijt} is assumed to be orthogonal to S, EXP, and μ.

In equation (1), β_2 represents the returns to experience per se, including the returns to general human capital and any other growth in earnings that occurs automatically with time in the labor market. Additionally, earnings are likely to grow with experience because more experienced workers typically end up in better jobs and/or better matches.[6] This will be reflected in higher values of μ_{ij} as EXP_{ij} increases. Let the relationship between pre-job experience and μ be approximated by

$$(2) \qquad \mu_{ij} = \alpha EXP_{ij} + \phi_{ij},$$

where α captures the growth in μ_{ij} with experience and ϕ_{ij} is the component of μ_{ij} that is uncorrelated with EXP_{ij}. Substituting into equation (1) yields

$$(3) \qquad \ln W_{ijt} = \beta_1 S_{ijt} + (\beta_2 + \alpha)EXP_{ij} + \phi_{ij} + \eta_{ijt},$$

---

[6] *See Kenneth Burdett (1978), Jovanovic, and Robert Topel (1986).*

where β_1 is the total return to seniority and $\beta_2 + \alpha$ is the total return to pre-job experience including both the return to experience per se and systematic returns to search. The net return to seniority is appropriately defined as the excess of the growth in earnings on a given job over and above the total returns to general labor market experience, or $\beta_1 - (\beta_2 + \alpha)$.

In practice, earnings functions are generally estimated using cross-section data and ϕ_{ij} is not observable. The standard cross-section earnings equation is

$$(4) \qquad \ln W_{ijt} = b_1 S_{ijt} + b_2 EXP_{ij} + v_{ijt},$$

where v is the estimating equation error. Omission of ϕ_{ij} from equation (4) means that b_1 and b_2 may be biased estimators of the return to seniority, β_1, and the return to experience, $\beta_2 + \alpha$. Deriving the expected values of b_1 and b_2 requires knowing more about the relationship between ϕ_{ij} and S_{ijt}. In particular, we need to know the partial relationship between ϕ_{ij} and S_{ijt}, holding EXP_{ij} constant.[7]

It was argued above that good workers and workers in good jobs or good matches are likely to stay on their jobs longer. Formally, this implies that the completed duration of jobs is positively related to μ_{ij}. Let this relationship be expressed as

$$(5) \qquad D_{ij} = \gamma\mu_{ij} + \epsilon_{ij},$$

where D_{ij} is the completed length of the current job, γ is a parameter that summarizes the relationship between D and μ, and ϵ_{ij} captures the variation in completed job duration that cannot be linked to the earnings advantage associated with worker, job, and/or match quality.[8] Substituting from equation (2),

$$(6) \qquad D_{ij} = \alpha\gamma EXP_{ij} + \gamma\phi_{ij} + \epsilon_{ij}.$$

Holding initial experience constant, completed job duration is positively related to ϕ_{ij}.

What does this tell us about the relationship between ϕ_{ij} and S_{ijt}? In a cross section of individuals, those with longer current seniority are likely to be on longer-lasting jobs. More formally, if each year of any given job is equally likely to be represented in the

---

[7] By construction, ϕ_{ij} is uncorrelated with EXP_{ij}. However, if S_{ijt} and EXP_{ij} are correlated, omitting ϕ_{ij} may bias both b_1 and b_2.

[8] There is a large literature that estimates turnover probabilities as a function of wage rates. Donald Parsons (1977) and Richard Freeman and Medoff (1984) present surveys of some of this work. Job duration can be viewed as an inverse turnover measure. The prediction that job duration should be positively related to μ is consistent with evidence that, ceteris paribus, turnover rates are negatively related to wages.

cross-section sample of observations used to estimate the earnings function, then on average the observed seniority on the job will be halfway through the job so that

(7)
$$S_{ijt} = 1/2 \times D_{ij} + \xi_{ijt}$$
$$= 1/2 \times \alpha\gamma EXP_{ij} + 1/2 \times \gamma\phi_{ij} + 1/2 \times \epsilon_{ij} + \xi_{ijt},$$

where ξ_{ijt} is a random variable with zero mean. Thus, the existence of a positive relationship between ϕ and D, holding pre-job experience constant, implies the existence of a positive relationship between ϕ and S, holding pre-job experience constant. The distribution of ξ_{ijt} will vary depending upon the completed length of the job. However, its mean is always zero, as are its covariances with μ_{ij}, ϕ_{ij}, D_{ij}, and EXP_{ij}.

Using the relationships in equations (4) to (7), it can be shown that the expected value of the seniority coefficient, b_1, in equation (3) is

(8)
$$E(b_1) = \beta_1 + \frac{\left[\gamma \times \mathrm{var}\left(EXP_{ij}\right) \times \mathrm{var}\left(\phi_{ij}\right)\right]}{\left[2 \times \left[\mathrm{var}\left(S_{ijt}\right) \times \mathrm{var}\left(EXP_{ij}\right) - \mathrm{cov}^2\left(S_{ijt}, EXP_{ij}\right)\right]\right]}.$$

$E(b_2)$ is larger than β_1 provided γ (the coefficient summarizing the relationship between D and μ) is positive. The expected value of the pre-job experience coefficient, b_2, in equation (4) is

(9)
$$E(b_2) = \beta_2 + \alpha K_1,$$

where the multiplicand of α is

(10)
$$K_1 = \frac{\left[\mathrm{var}\left(EXP_{ij}\right) \times \left\{\mathrm{var}\left(S_{ijt}\right) - 1/4 \times \mathrm{var}\left(D_{ij}\right) + 1/4 \times \mathrm{var}\left(\epsilon_{ij}\right)\right\}\right]}{\left[\mathrm{var}\left(S_{ijt}\right) \times \mathrm{var}\left(EXP_{ij}\right) - \mathrm{cov}^2\left(S_{ijt}, EXP_{ij}\right)\right]}.$$

It is straightforward to show that K_1 is positive but less than one so that the experience coefficient (b_2) is a downward-biased estimate of $\beta_2 + \alpha$. Therefore, $b_1 - b_2$ has an expected value greater than the true net return to seniority, $\beta_1 - (\beta_2 + \alpha)$, both because b_1 is an upward-biased estimate of β_1 and, secondarily, because b_2 is a downward-biased estimate of $\beta_2 + \alpha$.

One approach to correcting the estimates of b_1 and b_2 from equation (4) is to find an instrument for the seniority variable.[9] Equation (7) suggests a suitable instrument: ξ_{ijt},

---

[9] *Joseph Altonji and Robert Shatotko's (1987) analysis of the return to seniority uses this approach, though with a somewhat different instrument than ours.*

which equals $S_{ijt} - 1/2 \times D_{ij}$. By construction, this instrument is correlated with seniority but orthogonal to everything else in the equation. The vector of parameters estimated using ξ as an instrument for S equals

$$(11) \qquad \bar{b} = \left(Z'X\right)^{-1} Z'W,$$

where $\bar{b}$ is a 2×1 vector containing $\bar{b}_1$ and $\bar{b}_2$, X is the $n \times 2$ matrix containing values of S_{ijt} and EXP_{ij}, Z is the $n \times 2$ matrix containing values of ξ_{ijt} and EXP_{ij}, and W is the $n \times 1$ matrix of observations on the log wage. The instrumental variables estimator of the seniority coefficient, $\bar{b}_1$, has expected value β_1. In addition, the instrumental variables estimator of the experience coefficient, $\bar{b}_2$, has expected value $\beta_2 + \alpha$. Finally, $\bar{b}_1 - \bar{b}_2$ is an unbiased estimate of the net return to seniority.

The key assumption underlying the proposed instrumental variables estimator is that observed seniority in a cross section is, on average, half completed job duration. This assumption may not hold exactly. For example, a sample might include a disproportionate number of workers near the start of their work lives who are, on average, closer to the start of their jobs than they are to the end. In this case, the deviation of seniority from one-half completed duration may be correlated with duration and thus not be a valid instrument for seniority. However, if some more general relationship between seniority and completed job duration holds, such as

$$(12) \qquad S_{ijt} = \omega_0 + \omega_1 D_{ij} + \xi_{ijt},$$

then, regardless of the values of ω_0 and ω_1, the residual from this regression is an appropriate instrument for seniority. Using estimates of these residuals to calculate the instrument yields consistent estimates of the returns to experience and seniority.

An alternative approach to removing the upward bias in the estimated total return to seniority is to control explicitly for completed job duration in the earnings equation. Intuitively, the tenure coefficient is biased only because S_{ijt} is associated with D_{ij}, which in turn is correlated with ϕ_{ij}. This suggests that controlling for D_{ij} should eliminate the upward bias in the estimated tenure coefficient. Augmenting the standard cross-section earnings equation by adding D_{ij} as an explanatory variable yields

$$(13) \qquad \ln W_{ijt} = \hat{b}_1 S_{ijt} + \hat{b}_2 EXP_{ij} + \hat{b}_3 D_{ij} + \pi_{ijt},$$

where π is the estimating equation error.

It can readily be shown that $E(\hat{b}_1)$ equals β_1 so that $\hat{b}_1$ is an unbiased estimator of the gross return to seniority. The experience coefficient in equation (13) has expected value:

(14) $$E\left(\hat{b}_2\right) = \beta_2 + \alpha K_2,$$

where

(15) $$K_2 = \frac{\left[\text{var}\left(EXP_{ij}\right) \times \text{var}\left(\epsilon_{ij}\right)\right]}{\left[\text{var}\left(D_{ij}\right) \times \text{var}\left(EXP_{ij}\right) - \text{cov}^2\left(D_{ij}, EXP_{ij}\right)\right]}.$$

The value of K_2 is positive but less than one, which means that $\hat{b}_2$ is an underestimate of $\beta_2 + \alpha$. Thus, so long as α is positive, $\hat{b}_1 - \hat{b}_2$ is an upward-biased estimate of the net return to seniority ($\beta_1 - [\beta_2 + \alpha]$). None of these results are sensitive to the precise form of the linear relationship between seniority and completed duration, and this approach can be used to bound the true return to seniority.

A major attraction of the augmented OLS approach is that it provides a direct estimate of the relationship between completed job duration and earnings, $\hat{b}_3$. This is an indicator of the importance of the relationship of individual, job, and/or match heterogeneity with earnings through job duration. In addition, it serves as a useful device for investigating the underlying hypothesis that better workers, jobs, or matches are associated with higher earnings *throughout* the job. In terms of the earlier analysis, it can be shown that

(16) $$E(b_3) = (1 - K_2)/\gamma,$$

where K_2 is as just defined. Thus, $\hat{b}_3$ is a downward-biased estimate of $1/\gamma$, the coefficient of the regression of μ_{ij} on D_{ij}.

The preceding discussion assumes that individual-, job-, and match-specific earnings components all have the same incremental association with job duration. A more general specification would allow for separate earnings increments associated with unobserved individual characteristics and job/match characteristics. Given that any bias in the estimated return to seniority attributable to omitted earnings components is mediated through the relationship of those omitted earnings components with completed job duration, all of the results just described for the simple model are unaffected by a generalization to multiple unobserved earnings components.

Using the identity that links total experience with pre-job experience and seniority ($EXP_{ijt} = EXP_{ij} + S_{ijt}$) and ignoring second-order terms, valid inferences regarding the net return to seniority can be drawn from an earnings function specification that includes either pre-job experience or total experience along with seniority. Where pre-job experience is used, the net return to seniority ($\beta_1 - [\beta_2 + \alpha]$) is calculated as the difference between the coefficient on seniority and the coefficient on pre-job experience. Where total experience is used, the net return to seniority is simply the coefficient on seniority.

To facilitate discussion regarding the net return to seniority, the empirical analysis proceeds using total experience.[10]

II. Estimating Completed Job Duration

The first step in implementing the analysis described in the preceding section is to derive a measure of completed job duration. The *Panel Study of Income Dynamics (PSID)* is used in the empirical analysis. Unfortunately, there is a general problem with virtually all longitudinal data sets, including the *PSID*, when information is required on the completed duration of a spell of any kind. This is that the individuals are followed for only a limited period of time so that there are likely to be many jobs which do not end by the date at which the individual is last observed. Some procedure must be used to impute completed durations to these jobs.

We take the approach of estimating a parametric model of job duration that accounts for the censoring of duration in those jobs for which the end is not observed. This model is then used to compute an estimate of expected completed job duration *conditional* on the job lasting at least as long as the last observed seniority level. This estimate is used as the measure of completed job duration for the censored spells. The actual completed job duration is used for jobs for which the end is observed. This procedure has the advantage of using all available information on duration.

A. The Jobs Sample

All of the subsequent analysis is performed using data for male household heads aged 18–60 who participated in the *PSID*.[11] We used only observations from the random national sample portion of the *PSID* (the so-called Survey Research Center or SRC subsample). Persons who were retired, permanently disabled, self-employed, employed by

---

[10] *For the instrumental variables estimator, this requires the minor modification that total experience (and its square, if included) must be instrumented for along with seniority. The natural additional instruments are pre-job experience (and its square). In a model without squared terms, the IV estimator of the specification using pre-job experience and the IV estimator using total experience with pre-job experience as an additional instrument yield identical estimates of the underlying parameters.*

[11] *Altonji kindly provided us with an extract containing the variables which we used in performing our analyses. The procedures followed in creating this extract are described in detail in an appendix to Altonji and Shakotko. In order to delete non-SRC subsample observations, we added information on whether a given individual was part of the SRC subsample or the nonrandom continuation subsample from the Survey of Economic Opportunity. We also smoothed the tenure variable in instances where a given individual had been assigned the midpoint value of a tenure interval. If the individual on a given job changed tenure intervals in succeeding years, we computed a smooth tenure variable forward and backward from the change point. If all observations for the individual on a given job were in the same tenure interval, we computed a smooth tenure variable forward and backward from the middle observed year on the job assuming that tenure in that year was equal to the midpoint of the interval.*

the government, or residents of Alaska or Hawaii were excluded from the sample. Because we were concerned that different processes might govern tenure attainment and earnings in the union sector than in the nonunion sector, we also excluded observations on unionized jobs.[12] We were also concerned about differences across occupations in the processes determining job duration and earnings. In what follows, we therefore focus our discussion on results for two occupational subgroups. The first is a subset of white-collar occupations including nonunion professional, technical, and managerial employees.[13] The second subsample is comprised of nonunion blue-collar employees. In each year from 1968 through 1981 in which those individuals satisfying our selection criteria were household heads, information was available on number of years they had held their current job, number of years they had worked prior to taking the current job, years of education, race, marital status, disability status, occupation, industry, region, and earnings.

There are 985 jobs held by 706 individuals represented in the nonunion white-collar subsample, and 1417 jobs held by 831 individuals represented in the nonunion blue-collar sample. Our concern at this point is with ascertaining how long each of these jobs ultimately lasted.

Various characteristics of the jobs in each of the samples are reported in Table 1. Variables that can change over time in an unpredictable fashion (for example, marital status, occupation) are assumed constant and measured at the first point the job is observed in the sample. Any jobs for which there are some blue-collar years and some white-collar years appear in both occupational subsamples. The last observed seniority on a job is always considered to be the seniority at the last date the person is observed with an employer, whether or not there has been a change of occupation during the course of the job. There were 87 cases in which an individual reported moving from blue-collar status to white-collar status, and 83 cases in which an individual reported moving from white-collar status to blue-collar status while a job was in progress.[14]

We observe the actual completed duration for 391 of 985 jobs in the white-collar sample and for 775 of 1417 jobs in the blue-collar sample. Not surprisingly, a large proportion of

---

[12] In some years, unionization refers to union membership, and in other years, to working on a job covered by a collective bargaining agreement. Where both measures were available, collective bargaining coverage was used. Observations on jobs for which the worker changed union status during the course of the job do not appear in the sample. In 371 jobs, workers were coded nonunion in some years and union in others. If 1) at least two-thirds of the observed years on one of these jobs were coded nonunion, 2) there were no runs of three or more years coded union, and 3) the first and last years observed on the job were coded nonunion, then the entire job was considered a nonunion job and was included in our sample.

[13] Excluded from the analysis were the approximately 16 percent of all nonunion jobs that were clerical and sales jobs. This is too few to support separate job duration models for these groups. At the same time, these jobs seemed likely to differ significantly from other white-collar jobs.

[14] It is likely that these numbers overstate the true number of changes since there are undoubtedly some errors in classification that produce spurious movements between the two broad occupational groups.

TABLE 1

SELECTED CHARACTERISTICS OF JOBS SAMPLES FOR OCCUPATIONAL SUBGROUPS[a]

	Managerial and Professional Nonunion			Blue Collar Nonunion		
	All	Complete	Censored	All	Complete	Censored
Proportion with Years of Tenure at Last Date Job Observed in Range:						
$T \leq 1$	.280	.483	.147	.483	.639	.294
$1 < T \leq 3$	.235	.251	.224	.215	.216	.213
$3 < T \leq 10$	.257	.205	.291	.109	.115	.268
$T > 10$	.228	.0614	.338	.119	.0310	.224
Mean of:[b]						
Years of Tenure at Last Date Job Observed	6.76 [8.05]	2.96 [4.03]	9.25 [9.00]	4.07 [6.43]	1.9 [3.2]	6.7 [8.1]
Years of Pre-Job Experience	9.76 [8.09]	10.00 [7.76]	9.61 [8.30]	10.68 [9.49]	9.8 [9.0]	11.8 [10]
(Years Pre-Job Experience)^2	160.8 [253.7]	160.2 [230.1]	161.1 [268.1]	204.2 [348.6]	175.7 [325.1]	238.5 [372.0]
Years of Education	14.6 [2.09]	14.5 [2.1]	14.7 [2.1]	11.3 [2.43]	11.4 [2.3]	11.3 [2.6]
Proportion:						
Nonwhite	.0416	.0537	.0337	.138	.139	.137
Married	.862	.854	.867	.845	.823	.872
Disabled	.0528	.0563	.0505	.0932	.0761	.114
Managerial	.483	.517	.461	—	—	—
Prof., Tech.	.517	.483	.539	—	—	—
Foreman, Craft	—	—	—	.439	.421	.461
Oper., Labor	—	—	—	.561	.579	.539
No. of Observations	985	391	594	1417	775	642

[a] Except for tenure and years of previous experience, all variables are reported as of the first year the job was observed. Previous experience was computed as the difference between reported experience in the first year the job was observed and seniority at that point.
[b] Standard deviations are shown in brackets.

the completed jobs are relatively short. However, in both samples, there are a sizable number of completed jobs lasting 3 to 10 years and over 10 years. Longer jobs are more common among the still-in-progress jobs.

B. SPECIFICATION AND ESTIMATION OF THE JOB DURATION MODEL

The proportional hazard Weibull specification serves as the basis of the estimation reported here. In that specification, the probability that a job has completed duration (*D*) greater than or equal to *T* is

(17)
$$Pr(D \geq T) = \exp[-\lambda T^\tau],$$

where τ is a positive parameter. The proportional hazard assumption implies that

(18)
$$\lambda = e^{-Z\Gamma},$$

where Z is a vector of observable individual characteristics hypothesized to affect job duration and Γ is a vector of parameters.

If the parameters of this distribution are estimated, there is some ambiguity in the interpretation of the estimate of τ. The obvious interpretation is that the estimated value of τ indicates "true" duration dependence in the hazard of a job ending. An alternative interpretation is that the estimate of τ is biased downward by unmeasured heterogeneity in match quality. For the purposes of this study, we are interested only in an accurate estimate of completed duration, and we proceed with the simple Weibull specification.[15]

The contribution to the likelihood function made by a completed job is the probability-density that the job lasted *exactly* S_f years given that the job lasted at least S_0 years.[16] Given a Weibull distribution for duration, this is

(19)
$$Pr\left(D = S_f \mid D > S_0\right) = \lambda \tau S_f^{\tau-1} \exp\left[-\lambda\left(S_f^\tau - S_0^\tau\right)\right].$$

Similarly, the contribution to the likelihood function made by a job with a censored duration is the probability that the job lasted *more than* S_f years given that the job lasted at least S_0 years. This is

(20)
$$Pr\left(D > S_f \mid D > S_0\right) = \exp\left[-\lambda\left(S_f^\tau - S_0^\tau\right)\right].$$

The log-likelihood function is formed from these probabilities as

(21)
$$\ln(L) = \sum_j \left\{ C_j \ln Pr\left(D_j > S_{fj} \mid D_j > S_{0j}\right) + \left(1 - C_f\right) \ln Pr\left(D_j = S_{fj} \mid D_j > S_{0j}\right) \right\},$$

---

[15] *See Tony Lancaster (1979) for a parametric approach to the problem of estimating unmeasured heterogeneity in a Weibull model of unemployment duration. James Heckman and Burton Singer (1984) present a nonparametric approach to estimating duration models with unmeasured heterogeneity.*

[16] *It is important to condition on the length of the job as of the date it is first observed because the sampling scheme is such that jobs will not be observed unless they last long enough to make it to the start of the sample period.*

where j indexes jobs and C_j is an indicator variable that equals one if the completed job duration is censored (i.e., the job does not end during the sample period) and equals zero otherwise (i.e., the completed job duration is observed).[17]

Table 2 contains estimates of the Weibull job duration model estimated over the subsamples of 985 white-collar jobs and 1417 blue-collar jobs, respectively. These estimates were derived by maximizing the likelihood function defined above with respect to the parameters Γ and τ.[18] In interpreting the estimates of the determinants of the baseline hazard (λ), recall that the hazard rate was specified such that $\lambda = e^{-Z\Gamma}$. Thus, an increase in a variable with a positive coefficient reduces λ and increases the expected duration of the job. The hypothesis that the models of completed job duration for the two occupational groups are the same is strongly rejected.[19] The marginal effect of pre-job experience on job duration for white-collar workers is never statistically significant at the .05 level, while among blue-collar workers, having more pre-job experience has a significant positive association with completed job duration. The estimates also suggest that education has a stronger positive relationship with job duration in white-collar occupations than in blue-collar occupations.

C. PREDICTION OF JOB DURATION FOR INCOMPLETE JOBS

We used the parameter estimates from the appropriate column of Table 2 to predict the expected completed job duration of each of the incomplete jobs in each sample. This expectation is computed conditionally on the job lasting longer than the last observed seniority. Note that the job duration model we have estimated is based on data for the preretirement period. It will capture the net effects of quit and layoff processes on job duration, but it will not capture the effect of the competing retirement process which comes into play for older workers. If we predicted job durations without taking retirement into account, some would be implausibly long. We therefore assume that all jobs that are in progress when the worker reaches age 65 end at that point. For an individual/job match with observable characteristics Z that has lasted S_f years as of the last date we observe it, the conditional expected completed job duration is

$$(22) \qquad \hat{E}\left(D \mid D > S_f\right) = \frac{1}{Pr\left(D > S_f\right)} \int_{S_f}^{S_{65}} \lambda \tau t^\tau e^{-\lambda t^\tau} dt + \frac{Pr\left(D > S_{65}\right)}{Pr\left(D > S_f\right)} * S_{65},$$

---

[17] Note that this specification of the likelihood function assumes that unmeasured factors affecting completed job durations are independent across spells. However, within each sample, there are multiple observations on job durations for some individuals. Given the nonlinear nature of the model, an appropriate tractable procedure for accounting for the induced correlation is not obvious.

[18] The algorithm described by Ernst Berndt et al. (1974) was used to find the maximum.

[19] The hypothesis that the parameters of the models for the two subgroups are identical except for a constant shift and the occupation dummies in $Z\Gamma$ can be rejected at any reasonable level of significance. The test statistic, distributed as χ^2 with 22 degrees of freedom, is 52.3 (p-value < .001). The independence assumption of this test is not strictly satisfied, since the two samples contain some jobs in common.

TABLE 2

SELECTED COEFFICIENTS FROM FINAL TENURE MODELS[a]

	Managerial and Prof. Nonunion (1)	Blue Collar Nonunion (2)
Γ **(Inverse Baseline Hazard, $\lambda = e^{-z\Gamma}$)**		
Years of Experience	−.0288 (.0204)	.0611 (.0010)
(Years of Experience)^2	.00123 (.00071)	−.00113 (.00027)
Years of Education	.0699 (.0244)	.0243 (.0136)
Nonwhite (yes = 1)	−.412 (.224)	−.0387 (.0878)
Married (yes = 1)	.270 (.135)	.464 (.073)
Disabled (yes = 1)	.0768 (.218)	.180 (.113)
Manager (yes = 1)	−.0764 (.1121)	—
Foreman, Craftworker (yes = 1)	—	.0656 (.0623)
"Duration" Parameter		
τ	.380 (.028)	.394 (.017)
Log-Likelihood	−900.4	−1097.9
Sample Size	985	1417

[a] These coefficient estimates are from a Weibull proportional hazards model implemented using the jobs samples described in Table 1. All explanatory variables are reported as of the start of the job. Professional/technical employees are the omitted occupational group in the col. 1 model and operatives/laborers are the omitted occupational group in the col. 2 model. The numbers shown in parentheses are asymptotic standard errors.

where S_{65} represents the seniority attained if a match lasts until the worker turns 65,

$$(23) \quad \begin{aligned} Pr\big(D > S_f\big) &= \exp\big[-\lambda S_f^\tau\big], \\ Pr\big(D \geq S_{65}\big) &= \exp\big[-\lambda S_{65}^\tau\big], \end{aligned}$$

and

$$\lambda = e^{-z\Gamma}.$$

TABLE 3

DISTRIBUTION OF COMPLETED JOB DURATIONS[a]

Proportion with Completed Job Duration in Range:	Managerial and Professional Nonunion			Blue Collar Nonunion		
	All	Complete	Censored	All	Complete	Censored
$D \leq 1$	.193	.483	.00168	.354	.639	.0109
$1 < D \leq 3$	.105	.251	.00842	.155	.216	.0826
$3 < D \leq 10$	.182	.205	.167	.253	.115	.419
$D > 10$	.521	.0614	.823	.238	.0310	.488
No. of Observations	985	391	594	1417	775	642

[a] For the completed job subsample, the distribution of actual completed job duration is shown. For the censored job subsample, the distribution of predicted completed job duration is reported.

With an appropriate change of variables, this expected duration can be computed numerically using incomplete *gamma* functions. We also use the square of completed job duration in the earnings function estimation. For incomplete jobs, this is estimated analogously to completed job duration.

As noted earlier, actual job duration was observed for a substantial fraction of the jobs in both samples, and this measure was used in these cases. For the jobs with censored duration, the predicted values were used. Table 3 contains the breakdown of the completed durations of the jobs in the two occupational samples. As expected, the censored jobs are generally longer than the completed jobs.

III. IS SENIORITY HALF COMPLETED JOB DURATION?

Samples of individual-year observations from the two *PSID* jobs samples just discussed are used to estimate the earnings functions which constitute the core of our analysis. Recall that the samples consist only of nonunion male heads of households. There are 3493 individual-year observations on the 706 workers in the 985 white-collar jobs, and 3554 individual-year observations on the 831 workers in the 1417 blue-collar jobs. The means and standard deviations of the central variables for each of the samples are contained in the first column of Tables 4A and 4B.

Two alternative approaches to removing the bias in the estimated return to seniority have been suggested: 1) using the residual from a regression of seniority on completed duration as an instrument for seniority, and 2) including completed duration as a regressor in the earnings function. Both approaches started from the recognition that a true random sample of years from jobs would have the property that, on average, seniority equals one-half completed duration. This is equivalent to the hypothesis that in a regression of seniority on completed duration the constant term is zero and the coefficient on completed duration is .5.

TABLE 4A

SELECTED COEFFICIENTS FROM ln (AVERAGE HOURLY EARNINGS) MODELS
MANAGERIAL AND PROFESSIONAL NONUNION SAMPLE[a]

	Mean [s.d.]	OLS (1)	IV (2)	OLS (3)	OLS (4)
Years of Experience	18.14 [10.08]	.0349 (.0027)	.0392 (.0058)	.0288 (.0027)	.0263 (.0031)
(Years of Experience)^2	430.77 [407.84]	−.00062 (.00006)	−.00077 (.00014)	−.00048 (.00007)	−.00043 (.00007)
Years of Current Seniority	8.88 [8.34]	.0106 (.0011)	.00585 (.00128)	.00548 (.00178)	.00520 (.00256)
E (Completed Job Duration)	20.83 [12.18]	—	—	.0198 (.0024)	.0265 (.0050)
{E (Completed Job Duration)}^{2}	631.55 [505.56]	—	—	−.00035 (.00006)	−.00059 (.00016)
E (Job Duration) ×[=1 if 3 < Seniority ≤ 10]	6.02 [10.46]	—	—	—	−.00094 (.00432)
{E (Job Duration)}^{2} ×[=1 if 3 < Seniority ≤ 10]	165.4 [325.3]	—	—	—	.00009 (.00015)
E(Job Duration) ×[=1 if Seniority > 10]	11.09 [15.78]	—	—	—	−.00798 (.00455)
{E(Job Duration)}^{2} ×[=1 if Seniority > 10]	380.1 [572.9]	—	—	—	.00030 (.00015)
R^2	—	.3696	.3575	.3871	.3883

[a] All models also include controls for education, race, marital status, disability, occupation, industry, region, and year. E (Completed Job Duration) is computed using the estimates in col. 1 of Table 2. The numbers shown in parentheses are standard errors. Sample size = 3493.

In order to investigate this directly, we regressed seniority on the completed duration for the two occupational subsamples. The results are

$$S_{ijt} = -2.24 + \underset{(.18)}{.534} \cdot \underset{(.007)}{D_{ij}}, \quad R^2 = .61 \text{ (white collar)}$$

(24)

$$S_{ijt} = -1.31 + \underset{(.097)}{.550} \cdot \underset{(.005)}{D_{ij}}, \quad R^2 = .75 \text{ (blue collar)},$$

and the numbers in parentheses are OLS standard errors.[20] Clearly, the hypothesis that the coefficient on completed duration is .5 can be rejected in both samples at conventional

---

[20] *Given that D_{ij} is a predicted value for the observations from censored jobs, the OLS standard errors are not appropriate. However, the inferences are unchanged by use of (computationally tedious) standard errors that account for the fact that D_{ij} is predicted as well as general heteroskedasticity of the form analyzed by Halbert White (1980). See Whitney Newey (1984) for computational details on the correct standard errors.*

TABLE 4B

SELECTED COEFFICIENTS FROM ln (AVERAGE HOURLY EARNINGS) MODELS
BLUE-COLLAR NONUNION SAMPLE[a]

	Mean [s.d.]	OLS (1)	IV (2)	OLS (3)	OLS (4)
Years of Experience	17.34 [11.14]	.0205 (.0024)	.0173 (.0040)	.0117 (.0026)	.0120 (.0026)
(Years of Experience)^2	424.70 [470.81]	−.00045 (.00006)	−.00042 (.00009)	−.00026 (.00006)	−.00028 (.00006)
Years of Current Seniority	6.31 [7.46]	.0142 (.0011)	.00290 (.00172)	.00241 (.00213)	−.00054 (.00302)
E (Completed Job Duration)	13.86 [11.75]	—	—	.0154 (.0021)	.0381 (.0057)
{E (Completed Job Duration)}^{2}	362.44 [444.45]	—	—	−.00014 (.00006)	−.00104 (.00024)
E (Job Duration) ×[=1 if 3 < Seniority ≤ 10]	4.57 [8.27]	—	—	—	−.00592 (.00538)
{E (Job Duration)}^{2} ×[=1 if 3 < Seniority ≤ 10]	102.13 [211.7]	—	—	—	.00031 (.00024)
E(Job Duration) ×[=1 if Seniority > 10]	6.45 [12.90]	—	—	—	−.0241 (.0055)
{E(Job Duration)}^{2} ×[=1 if Seniority > 10]	215.1 [461.9]	—	—	—	.00103 (.00024)
R^2	—	.3878	.3513	.4041	.4098

[a] All models also include the controls listed in Table 4A. fn. a. E (Completed Job Duration) is computed using col. 2, Table 2. Standard errors are shown in parentheses. Sample size = 3554.

levels of significance. This means that completed duration is not orthogonal to the deviation of seniority from one-half completed duration so that this deviation is not a valid instrument for seniority. However, the coefficient of completed duration is not far from one-half, which suggests that the general approach is valid.

On the basis of these results, the IV estimation of the earnings function proceeds using the residuals from the regression of seniority on completed duration to instrument seniority. We also present OLS estimates of earnings functions augmented with our measure of completed duration.

IV. EARNINGS FUNCTION ESTIMATES

Consider an earnings function for individual i in job j in year t of the form:

$$(25) \qquad \ln(W_{ijt}) = \theta_0 + \theta_1 S_{ijt} + \theta_2 E_{ijt} + \theta_3 E_{ijt}^2 + X_{ijt}\Omega + \epsilon_{ijt},$$

where $\ln(W_{ijt})$ is the logarithm of real average hourly earnings, S_{ijt} is seniority, E_{ijt} is total experience, X_{ijt} is a vector of other individual characteristics, and ϵ_{ijt} represents unmeasured factors affecting earnings.[21] The coefficient θ_1 is the net return to seniority and corresponds to $\beta_1 - (\beta_2 + \alpha)$ in the model of Section I. The coefficient θ_2 is the return to general labor market experience and corresponds to $\beta_2 + \alpha$ in the model of Section I.

Tables 4A and 4B contain estimates of earnings functions for the samples of professional, technical, and managerial workers and of blue-collar workers, respectively. In addition to the regressors shown, all models include controls for education, race, marital status, disability, occupation, industry, region, and year. The standard errors presented are the "simple" standard errors computed from $\hat{\sigma}^2(X'X)^{-1}$ for the OLS models and from $\hat{\sigma}^2(Z'X)^{-1}$ for the IV models.[22]

In both tables, column 1 contains a standard OLS earnings equation that neither instruments for seniority nor includes completed job duration as a regressor. These estimates suggest that there are sizable returns both to general labor market experience and to seniority with a particular employer for workers in both occupational groups. The estimated net return to seniority is on the order of 1 to 1.5 percentage points per year.

The column 2 models were estimated by IV using pre-job experience, the square of pre-job experience, and the residual from the regression of seniority on completed job duration as instruments for total experience, the square of total experience, and seniority. The IV coefficient estimates provide consistent estimates of the return to general labor market experience and the net return to seniority. While instrumenting has relatively little effect on the estimated return to experience, the estimated net return to seniority falls substantially. The return for white-collar workers falls from 1.1 to 0.6 percent per year. The return for blue-collar workers falls from 1.4 to 0.3 percent per year; moreover, the corrected estimate is not significantly different from zero at conventional levels. This suggests that most of the cross-sectional correlation between earnings and seniority controlling for experience reflects the influence of omitted variables.

The coefficients in column 3 were estimated using ordinary least squares, but with completed job duration and its square added to the list of explanatory variables. The first thing to note about these augmented OLS models is that the estimated returns to seniority are virtually identical to those obtained using the IV approach. This confirms that a substantial portion of the usual cross-sectional return to seniority is due to an omitted worker, job, and/or match quality measure. The virtual equality of the results using the

---

[21] We have estimated all of the models in this section with pre-job experience and its square in place of total experience and its square, and the qualitative conclusions emerging from the analysis do not change.

[22] These standard errors are not strictly appropriate for the estimation here because they do not account for the fact that the measure of completed job duration is predicted for the observations on censored jobs. Standard errors that are corrected both for this fact and for general heteroskedasticity (see Newey and White) were computed for a number of specifications. These were uniformly very close to the simple standard errors, and in no case was any inference resulting from a statistical test changed.

augmented OLS approach and the IV approach also suggests that the bias in the augmented OLS estimates that we discussed in Section I is not a problem in practice.[23]

Perhaps the most interesting aspect of the augmented OLS estimates is that there is a *very* strong positive association between completed duration and earnings in both occupational groups. Consider two otherwise equivalent workers, one of whom holds a job that will eventually last 20 years and the other of whom holds a sequence of two 10-year jobs. In a white-collar occupation, the worker in the single 20-year job is estimated to earn 9.3 percent (standard error = 0.8 percent) more *in each year* than the worker in the sequence of 10-year jobs. In a blue-collar occupation, the worker in the single 20-year job is estimated to earn 11.2 percent (standard error = 1.0 percent) more *in each year* than the worker in the sequence of 10-year jobs.

The finding that workers in longer jobs earn more in every year on the job than workers in shorter jobs is verified by the results in column 4. These results are based on specifications that allow the effect of completed duration on earnings to differ by seniority level. Specifically, completed duration and its square are included in the regression along with interactions of these two variables with two dummy variables indicating seniority of 3 to 10 years and seniority greater than 10 years. The hypothesis that these additional four variables have zero coefficients cannot be rejected for the white-collar sample, but can be rejected for the blue-collar sample.[24] Closer examination of the estimated parameters reveals that, consistent with the results of the formal test, the four interaction terms have inconsequential coefficients in the white-collar sample. For blue-collar workers, the wage advantage of long jobs falls with seniority after starting at a much higher level than suggested by the results in column 3 of Table 4B. Thus, there is still a positive wage advantage to being in longer blue-collar jobs at all levels of seniority. It simply is not uniform in magnitude.

Overall, the results in this section strongly confirm our expectations. Rather small estimates of the return to seniority are found using either the IV or the augmented OLS approach relative to the standard cross-sectional OLS regression. The corrected estimate of the net return to seniority is 0.5 to 0.6 percent per year for white-collar workers and a statistically insignificant 0.2 to 0.3 percent per year for blue-collar workers. In addition, our results provide direct evidence that workers in longer jobs earn substantially more throughout the job than workers in shorter jobs.

---

[23] *Recall that the theoretical discussion implied that the IV estimate of the net return to seniority is a consistent estimate of $\beta_1 - |\beta_2 - \alpha|$ while the augmented OLS approach yields an upward biased estimate. In fact, we find that the augmented OLS estimate of the net return to seniority is slightly, though not significantly, smaller than the IV estimate.*

[24] *The test statistics for the white-collar sample is 1.69 and that for the blue-collar sample is 8.48, both distributed as F with 4 and approximately 3500 degrees of freedom. The critical value of this distribution is 2.37 at the 5 percent level and 3.32 at the 1 percent level.*

V. SOME ISSUES OF SPECIFICATION AND ESTIMATION

Probably the most significant potential problem with the analysis just described is that the key job duration variable had to be estimated for jobs whose end was not observed. This introduces three conceptually distinct sources of measurement error that could affect our estimates.

The first source of measurement error is that the expected value is used in place of the actual realization of completed job duration. This is not a problem so long as the correct parameters and the correct model have been used in computing expected job duration. In this case, the measurement error is exactly the deviation between expected and actual job duration. This is uncorrelated with expected job duration (the included regressor) by construction. Thus, there is no bias from this source in our estimated earnings function coefficients.

The second source of measurement error is that the parameters of the job duration model are only estimates, so that the predictions of expected job duration are themselves subject to error. However, it can be shown that in large samples, the estimation error in the parameters of the job duration model is of small enough order that coefficient estimates in equations which use the derived measure of duration as an explanatory variable are consistent.

The third source of measurement error is that the job duration model may be misspecified. If misspecification results in random errors in expected completed duration then classical measurement error is introduced. In the context of the augmented OLS estimates, this measurement error will tend to 1) bias the coefficient on completed duration toward zero, and 2) result in an estimated return to seniority that is higher than it would be in the absence of measurement error. The estimated return to seniority would, however, still be useful as an upper bound. If misspecification results in systematic measurement error, the coefficient on completed duration and the estimated return to seniority will be biased in an unknown way.

Given the finding of a large positive return to completed duration and the sharp reduction in the return to seniority using the augmented OLS estimates, it is unlikely that random measurement error is a serious problem. In any case, since the effects of random measurement error are predictable, our findings provide bounds on the "true" effects. We can do nothing about the potential of systematic measurement error except to note that our results are conditional on the Weibull specification of completed job duration.[25]

The appropriateness of the method used to impute completed durations for the censored jobs clearly merits careful investigation. One obvious question is whether the particular function of the explanatory variables and last-observed seniority that we use in

---

[25] *While the first two sources of measurement error do not induce inconsistency in the earnings function parameter estimates, they do affect the estimates of the standard errors of the coefficients. As discussed in fn. 22, appropriate standard errors that are corrected for the effects of these errors and for general heteroskedasticity are almost identical to the usual standard errors.*

creating our measure of completed duration is appropriate or whether it is contributing to the fit of the model simply because it incorporates the information on last-observed seniority. One way to investigate this is to reestimate the augmented OLS model including last-observed seniority and its square directly as regressors. If our measure of completed job duration has a significant effect on earnings even after controlling for last-observed seniority, then we have added support for our measure.

The first columns of Tables 5A and 5B contain estimates of earnings functions that include measures of completed job duration and its square, but not last-observed seniority (repeated here for comparison purposes). The second columns of these tables contain estimates of earnings functions that include last-observed seniority and its square, but no completed duration measure. When entered separately, both completed job duration and last-observed seniority contribute significantly to the fit of the model. Do these relationships hold up if we control for both simultaneously? The third column of Tables 5A and 5B contain estimates of earnings functions for the two occupational groups that include measures of both completed duration and last observed seniority. After controlling for completed duration, last-observed seniority is not a significant determinant of earnings. However, even after controlling for last observed seniority, completed duration adds significantly to the models' explanatory power.[26] Thus, our measure of completed duration contains information on earnings well beyond the information contained directly in the variables that are used in its computation, including the last-observed seniority.

Perhaps the most important question concerning our completed job duration variable is whether the relationship between completed job duration and earnings differs between the observations that come from jobs where actual completed durations are observed and from jobs where completed durations are predicted. To answer this question, we reestimated the augmented OLS earnings functions with two additional variables: 1) the interaction between completed job duration and a dummy variable that equals one if the job duration is uncensored and equals zero otherwise; and 2) the interaction between the square of completed job duration and the same dummy variable. This allows completed duration and its square to have different effects where they are actually observed (uncensored jobs) and where they are predicted (censored jobs). These estimates are contained in column 4 of Tables 5A and 5B.

For white-collar workers, the hypothesis that the effects are the same (that the two new variables have zero coefficients) can be rejected at the 5 percent level, but not at the 1 percent level. However, the interaction terms have rather small coefficients relative to

---

[26] *This is verified by F-tests of the general specification in col. 3 against the restricted specification in cols. 1 and 2. The test statistics for the hypothesis that last-observed seniority adds explanatory power to the model are 0.845 for white-collar workers and 0.295 for blue-collar workers. The test statistics for the hypothesis that completed job duration adds explanatory power are 9.30 for white-collar workers and 12.1 for blue-collar workers. All the test statistics are distributed as F with 2 and approximately 3500 degrees of freedom. The critical value of this distribution is 4.61 at the 1 percent level of significance.*

TABLE 5A

SELECTED COEFFICIENTS FROM ALTERNATIVE ln (AVERAGE HOURLY EARNINGS) MODELS
MANAGERIAL AND PROFESSIONAL NONUNION SAMPLE[a]

	Mean [s.d.]	OLS (1)	OLS (2)	OLS (3)	OLS (4)
Years of Experience	18.14 [10.08]	.0288 (.0027)	.0272 (.00280)	.0280 (.0028)	.0288 (.0027)
(Years of Experience)^2	430.77 [407.84]	−.00048 (.00007)	−.00042 (.00007)	−.00046 (.00007)	−.00051 (.00007)
Years of Current Seniority	8.88 [8.34]	.00548 (.00178)	−.00472 (.00311)	.00186 (.00345)	.00865 (.00244)
E (Completed Job Duration)	20.83 [12.18]	.0198 (.0024)	—	.0167 (.0041)	.0220 (.0025)
{E (Completed Job Duration)}^{2}	631.55 [505.56]	−.00035 (.00006)	—	−.00030 (.00009)	−.00044 (.00007)
Years Last Observed Seniority	12.08 [9.52]	—	.0275 (.0031)	.00682 (.00567)	—
(Years Last Observed Seniority)^2	236.8 [304.9]	—	−.00043 (.00008)	−.00007 (.00012)	—
E(Job Duration) × [=1 if Uncensored]	12.15 [34.45]	—	—	—	−.00067 (.00592)
{E(Job Duration)}^{2} × [=1 if Uncensored]	133.41 [629.26]	—	—	—	.00030 (.00028)
R^2	—	.3871	.3841	.3874	.3885

[a] See Table 4A, fn. a. Sample size = 3493.

the coefficients on the basic variables. For blue-collar workers, the hypothesis that the effects are the same cannot be rejected at either the 5 or 1 percent level, and the point estimates of the interaction terms' coefficients are insubstantial.[27] In sum, observed completed duration in uncensored jobs and our estimate of completed duration in censored jobs have almost identical relationships with earnings.

The last potential issue we consider here is related to the fact that, because we use pooled time-series cross-section data to estimate our earnings functions, there are repeated observations on particular individuals. If the earnings function residuals are correlated across observations within individuals, our standard errors are likely to be understated. We are reluctant to present estimates of a fixed-effect model because all of the variation in

---

[27] *The test statistics are 3.95 for the white-collar sample and 2.95 for the blue-collar sample, both distributed as F with 2 and approximately 3500 degrees of freedom. The critical value of this distribution is 3.00 at the 5 percent level and 4.61 at the 1 percent level.*

TABLE 5B

SELECTED COEFFICIENTS FROM ALTERNATIVE ln (AVERAGE HOURLY EARNINGS) MODELS
BLUE-COLLAR NONUNION SAMPLE[a]

	Mean [s.d.]	OLS (1)	OLS (2)	OLS (3)	OLS (4)
Years of Experience	17.34 [11.14]	.0117 (.0026)	.0135 (.00256)	.0118 (.00259)	.0119 (.0027)
(Years of Experience)^2	424.70 [470.81]	−.00026 (.00006)	−.00028 (.00006)	−.00026 (.00006)	−.00027 (.00006)
Years of Current Seniority	6.31 [7.46]	.0241 (.00213)	−.00304 (.00322)	.00375 (.00352)	.00412 (.00307)
E (Completed Job Duration)	13.86 [11.75]	.0154 (.0021)	—	.0175 (.0052)	.0167 (.0022)
{E (Completed Job Duration)}^{2}	362.44 [444.45]	−.00014 (.00006)	—	−.00017 (.00012)	−.00020 (.00008)
Years Last Observed Seniority	8.80 [8.82]	—	.0255 (.0031)	−.00377 (.00730)	—
{Years Last Observed Seniority}^{2}	155.2 [263.8]	—	−.0031 (.00008)	.00005 (.00017)	—
E (Job Duration) × [=1 if Uncensored]	12.92 [33.92]	—	—	—	.00556 (.00627)
{E (Job Duration)}^{2} × [=1 if Uncensored]	13.77 [60.21]	—	—	—	−.00053 (.00030)
R^2	—	.4041	.4001	.4042	.4051

[a] See Table 4B, fn. a. Sample size = 3554.

the measure of completed duration in such a model comes from those workers who change jobs within the sample period. These job changes will be dominated by short jobs which are not representative of the sample of jobs as a whole.[28] A *very* conservative alternate approach to this problem is to reestimate the key specifications of the model on a single-year cross section. If the inferences from such a specification are similar to those from the pooled model, then we can have more confidence in the overall validity of the results. The estimation of a single-year cross section also has the advantage that it provides results directly comparable to much of the existing literature on earnings functions.

In order to carry out this analysis, 1973 was selected as a representative year, and the analyses of Tables 4A and 4B were repeated on 1973 cross sections of 244 white-collar workers and 240 blue-collar workers. The single-year estimates are contained in Tables 6Aa and 6B, and two things are clear from a comparison of these results with the results

---

[28] *Note that year effects are removed in all specifications through the use of a complete set of year dummies.*

TABLE 6A

SELECTED COEFFICIENTS FROM 1973 CROSS SECTION ln (AVERAGE HOURLY EARNINGS) MODELS—MANAGERIAL AND PROFESSIONAL NONUNION SAMPLE[a]

	Mean [s.d.]	OLS (1)	IV (2)	OLS (3)	OLS (4)
Years of Experience	18.38 [10.12]	.0349 (.0104)	.0514 (.0199)	.0273 (.0106)	.0278 (.0126)
(Years of Experience)^2	440.06 [402.58]	−.00066 (.00025)	−.00111 (.00049)	−.00049 (.00025)	−.00050 (.00029)
Years of Current Seniority	9.00 [7.97]	.0135 (.0043)	.00653 (.00524)	.00721 (.00684)	.0109 (.0104)
E (Completed Job Duration)	20.99 [13.00]	—	—	.0230 (.0090)	.0432 (.0181)
{E (Completed Job Duration)}^{2}	642.94 [534.27]	—	—	−.00041 (.00023)	−.00095 (.00054)
E (Job Duration) × [=1 if 3 < Seniority ≤ 10]	6.40 [10.92]	—	—	—	−.0180 (.00159)
{E (Job Duration)}^{2} × [=1 if 3 < Seniority ≤ 10]	174.22 [341.65]	—	—	—	.00044 (.00051)
E(Job Duration) × [=1 if Seniority > 10]	11.19 [16.01]	—	—	—	−.0231 (.0173)
{E(Job Duration)}^{2} × [=1 if Seniority > 10]	385.70 [585.00]	—	—	—	.00060 (.00054)
R^2	—	.4318	.4105	.4566	.4640

[a] See Table 4A, fn. a. Sample size = 244.

in Tables 4A and 4B. First, as we expected, the results are less precisely estimated due to the much smaller sample sizes. Second, the results are very similar in character to those derived using the pooled samples. The "standard" OLS results in column 1 of Tables 6A and 6B show statistically significant net returns to seniority. The IV estimates of the return to seniority are much smaller than the OLS estimates, and they are *not* significantly different from zero in either occupational group. The augmented OLS estimates of the return to seniority, contained in column 3 of Tables 6A and 6B, are quite similar to those derived with the IV estimator. In addition, the augmented OLS estimates imply that workers in longer jobs earn significantly more throughout the job than workers in shorter jobs. We conclude that the general findings of the previous section are not simply due to an exaggerated precision that comes from ignoring the error component structure in a pooled sample.

TABLE 6B

Selected Coefficients from 1973 Cross Section ln (average hourly earnings) Models—Blue-Collar Nonunion Sample[a]

	Mean [s.d.]	OLS (1)	IV (2)	OLS (3)	OLS (4)
Years of Experience	18.47 [11.32]	.0340 (.0100)	.0133 (.0149)	.0205 (.0099)	.0188 (.0099)
(Years of Experience)^2	468.83 [484.73]	−.00075 (.00020)	−.00036 (.00033)	−.00046 (.00022)	−.00046 (.00022)
Years of Current Seniority	6.50 [7.60]	.0102 (.0038)	−.00453 (.00646)	.00063 (.00840)	−.00781 (.0122)
E (Completed Job Duration)	14.57 [12.88]	—	—	.0194 (.0075)	.0502 (.0208)
{E (Completed Job Duration)}^{2}	402.81 [491.00]	—	—	−.00028 (.00024)	−.00161 (.00088)
E (Job Duration) × [=1 if 3 < Seniority ≤ 10]	4.86 [8.95]	—	—	—	−.00108 (.0199)
{E (Job Duration)}^{2} × [=1 if 3 < Seniority ≤ 10]	114.07 [237.2]	—	—	—	.00031 (.00086)
E(Job Duration) × [=1 if Seniority > 10]	7.05 [13.81]	—	—	—	−.0381 (.0203)
{E(Job Duration)}^{2} × [=1 if Seniority > 10]	245.9 [508.6]	—	—	—	.00171 (.00089)
R^2	—	.4958	.4048	.5182	.5344

[a] See Table 4B, fn. a. Sample size = 240.

VI. Concluding Comments

The basis for considering implicit contracts under which compensation is deferred from early until late in workers' time with their employers to be an important feature of the labor market has been the simple cross-sectional evidence that long seniority workers have higher wages, even taking their total labor-market experience into account. The evidence presented in this study seriously undermines the empirical foundations of this sort of implicit contract. Contrary both to the conventional wisdom and to our own prior expectations, there seems to be only a small average return to seniority in excess of the average return to general labor market experience. For the nonunion professional, technical, and managerial sample, the corrected estimates of the seniority coefficient suggest that the true return to seniority is approximately half a percent per year, rather than the approximately 1 percent per year suggested by the standard cross-section model. For the nonunion blue-collar sample, the corrected estimates yield a statistically insignificant return to seniority of approximately one-quarter of 1 percent per year, rather than the statistically significant 1.5 percent per year suggested by the standard model.[29]

This evidence does not imply that implicit contracts entailing the posting of a bond by workers through a deferral of compensation are never important. Indeed, they could be very important for some subgroups of workers and even a small return to seniority could translate into a substantial cumulative contribution to annual earnings over a period of time. It is also possible that parts of the total compensation package other than earnings, such as fringe benefits or other perquisites, are structured so as to reward longevity with a particular employer.[30] However, earnings deferral under implicit contracts appears to be a much less important factor in both white- and blue-collar labor markets than has generally been believed.

The other result of our study that is potentially very important for the understanding of the nature of the long-term employment relationship is that workers in long jobs earn substantially more throughout their jobs than do workers in short jobs. Whether this is due to individual differences, inter-job differences, or match-specific differences, this finding has important implications for the decisions of workers and employers as they affect investment in match-specific capital and the dynamics of the employment relationship. Note that our finding of a correlation between completed duration and earnings does *not* imply that it is the length of the job that *causes* earnings. It is likely that, at least to some extent, the higher earnings throughout the job provide an incentive for workers to remain on their job. Viewed in this light, our results are consistent with the currently popular efficiency wage models.

The finding of a strong positive relationship between job duration and earnings in both of the occupational subsamples provides strong evidence against another view of long-term employment relationships based on models of incomplete information where firms offer workers insurance regarding their unknown abilities. In particular, Milton Harris and Bengt Holmstrom (1982) argue that the positive return to experience found in most data sets could reflect such insurance contracts. A simple version of this model considers the case where a worker and all firms are initially uncertain about the worker's productivity, and where that uncertainty is reduced over time as the worker and all firms learn about the worker's productivity from the worker's stream of output. The optimal contract for the firm to offer the worker specifies an initial wage equal to the expected value of the worker's productivity minus an insurance premium, and the employer guarantees not to reduce the initial wage if the worker is revealed to be relatively unproductive. Since all new information about productivity is common knowledge, workers

---

[29] *Our findings regarding the returns to seniority are consistent with those obtained by Altonji and Shakotko.*

[30] *Freeman and Medoff provide evidence that the value of nonwage benefits such as vacations and pension plans rise with seniority. There may also be less tangible advantages that accrue with seniority.*

revealed to be relatively productive receive wage increases either from their original employer or by taking a new job with another employer. Workers revealed to have low productivity cannot duplicate their original wage elsewhere and for that reason are more likely to stay with their original employer. Thus, this simple insurance model predicts a *negative* correlation between job duration and earnings. Our results indicate that this correlation is strongly positive.

The recognition that the direction of causality between earnings and job duration is ambiguous highlights the difficulty of using our results to make definitive statements on the existence of particular types of labor contracts. Observed job durations are generated as the result of mobility decisions that are poorly understood. While we conclude tentatively that the evidence from earnings functions is not consistent with simple earnings deferral models of incentive contracts or with the simple model of insurance contracts, it is clear that further analysis of the joint determination of job duration and earnings is necessary for a full understanding of long-run employment relationships.

REFERENCES

Abraham, Katharine G. and Medoff, James L., "Length of Service and the Operation of Internal Labor Markets," *Proceedings of the Thirty-Fifth Annual Meeting of the Industrial Relations Research Association,* December 1982, 308–18.

Akerlof, George A. and Katz, Lawrence F., "Do Deferred Wages Dominate Involuntary Unemployment as a Worker Discipline Device?," NBER Working Paper No. 2025, September 1986.

Altonji, Joseph and Shakotko, Robert, "Do Wages Rise with Job Seniority?," *Review of Economic Studies,* June 1987, *54,* 437–59.

Becker, Gary S., *Human Capital,* NBER, Ann Arbor: University Microfilms, 1964.

———— and Stigler, George J., "Law Enforcement, Malfeasance and Compensation of Enforcers," *Journal of Legal Studies,* January 1974, *3,* 1–18.

Berndt, Ernst K. et al., "Estimation and Inference in Nonlinear Structural Models," *Annals of Economic and Social Measurement,* 1974, *3/4,* 653–65.

Bulow, Jeremy and Summers, Lawrence. "A Theory of Dual Labor Markets with Application to Industrial Policy, Discrimination, and Keynsian Unemployment," *Journal of Labor Economics,* July 1986, *4,* 376–415.

Burdett, Kenneth, "A Theory of Employee Job Search and Quit Rates," *American Economic Review,* March 1978, *68,* 212–20.

Freeman, Richard B. and Medoff, James L., *What Do Unions Do?,* New York: Basic Books, 1984.

Harris, Milton and Holmstrom, Bengt, "Ability Performance and Wage Differentials," *Review of Economic Studies,* July 1982, *49,* 315–33.

Heckman, James and Singer, Burton, "A Method for Minimizing the Impact of Distributional Assumptions in Econometric Models for Duration Data," *Econometrica,* March 1984, *52,* 271–320.

Jovanovic, Boyan, "Job Matching and the Theory of Turnover," *Journal of Political Economy,* October 1979, *87,* 972–90.

Katz, Lawrence F., "Efficiency Wage Theories: A Partial Evaluation," in Stanley Fischer, ed., *NBER Macroeconomics Annual 1986,* Cambridge: MIT Press, 235–76.

Lancaster, Tony, "Econometric Methods for the Duration of Unemployment," *Econometrica,* July 1979, *47,* 939–56.

Lazear, Edward, "Why Is There Mandatory Retirement?," *Journal of Political Economy,* December 1979, *87,* 1261–84.

Medoff, James L. and Abraham, Katharine G., "Experience, Performance and Earnings," *Quarterly Journal of Economics,* December 1980, *95,* 703–36.

——— and ———, "Are Those Paid More Really More Productive: The Case of Experience," *Journal of Human Resources,* Spring 1981, *16,* 186–216.

Mincer, Jacob, *Schooling, Experience and Earnings,* NBER *Studies in Human Behavior and Social Institutions,* No. 2, New York: Columbia University Press, 1974.

——— and Jovanovic, Boyan, "Labor Mobility and Wages," in Sherwin Rosen, ed., *Studies in Labor Markets,* NBER Universities-National Bureau Conference Series, No. 31, Chicago: University of Chicago Press, 1981, 21–64.

Mortensen, Dale T., "Specific Capital and Labor Turnover," *Bell Journal of Economics,* Autumn 1978, *9,* 572–86.

Newey, Whitney K., "A Method of Moments Interpretation of Sequential Estimators," *Economics Letters,* 1984, *14,* 201–06.

Parsons, Donald O., "Models of Labor Market Turnover: A Theoretical and Empirical Survey," in Ronald G. Ehrenberg, ed., *Research in Labor Economics,* Vol. 1, Greenwich: JAI Press, 1977, 185–223.

Shapiro, Carl and Stiglitz, Joseph, "Involuntary Unemployment as a Worker Discipline Device," *American Economic Review,* June 1984, *74,* 433–44.

Stiglitz, Joseph, "Theories of Wage Rigidity," mimeo., Princeton University, 1984.

Topel, Robert, "Job Mobility, Search, and Earnings Growth: A Reinterpretation of Human Capital Earnings Functions," in Ronald G. Ehrenberg, ed., *Research in Labor Economics,* Vol. 8, 1986, 199–223.

Viscusi, W. Kip, "Self-Selection, Learning-Induced Quits and the Optimal Wage Structure," *International Economic Review,* October 1980, *21,* 529–46.

White, Halbert, "A Heteroskedasticity-Consistent Covariance Matrix Estimator and a Direct Test for Heteroskedasticity," *Econometrica,* May 1980, *48,* 817–38.

Yellen, Janet, "Efficiency Wage Models of Unemployment," *American Economic Review Proceedings,* May 1984, *74,* 200–08.

ABOUT THE AUTHORS

Katharine Abraham

Katharine Abraham is Commissioner of the Bureau of Labor Statistics. From the moment she was appointed in 1993 she was thrust into one of the most controversial debates in U.S. statistical policy—that on the consumer price index—and has guided the B.L.S. through a turbulent period with diplomacy, composure, and integrity. She has held positions at the Sloan School of Management, M.I.T., the Brookings Institution, the University of Maryland, College Park, and at the National Bureau of Economic Research, and she received her B.S. from Iowa State University and her Ph.D. from Harvard University.

Most of Katharine Abraham's research is deeply informed empirical work on the labor market. She is an expert on the core issues in both personnel economics (e.g., internal labor markets, compensation, and the organization of work) and the "outside" labor market, such as how unemployment affects the labor market. She was therefore an obvious choice to head the principal fact-finding agency of the federal government in the field of labor economics and statistics, an agency that has charge of both the household surveys and those concerning firms.

Katharine Abraham has researched many of the important topics in the field of empirical labor economics, such as unemployment and wage growth in the post-war United States, the operation of internal labor markets, union and nonunion promotions and layoffs, and real wages over the business cycle. She has used international comparisons to understand the contribution of different regimes to labor market adjustment, as in her work on job security in the United States and Germany and between the United States and Japan. She is perhaps best known for her work (with J. Medoff) on the relationships among earnings, productivity, and job tenure. Her findings have been interpreted by many as demonstrating that earnings rise more with job tenure than does productivity. The work therefore set off a wave of theoretical explanations for the notion, demonstrating the close link in labor economics between empirical findings and theoretical breakthroughs. Her Ph.D. dissertation established her as the authority on measuring vacancy rates—the employer-side measure of labor market tightness. Katharine Abraham is the author of *Job Security in America: Lessons from Germany* (with S. Houseman) and the editor of *New Developments in the Labor Market: Toward a New Institutional Paradigm* (with R. McKersle).

Henry S. Farber

Henry S. Farber—known by one and all as Hank—was born in 1951 in Linden, New Jersey. He holds an undergraduate degree in economics from Rensselaer Polytechnic Institute, a master's degree in industrial and labor relations from Cornell University, and a Ph.D. in economics from Princeton University.

Hank isn't someone who makes major life changes lightly. He's been married to the same woman since 1972. He is the most loyal of friends. His first faculty job was in the department of economics at the Massachusetts Institute of Technology; he stayed there for fourteen years, and left only to return to Princeton. Despite the fact that he rides a motorcycle and is an active member of the BMW Car Club of America, I have to say that Hank isn't a California kind of guy. I am reminded, however, that some of his most productive periods have been spent at the Center for Advanced Study in the Behavioral Sciences at Stanford University.

Hank's early work focused on union behavior, bringing modern econometric tools to bear on questions that hitherto had been the province of more traditional industrial relations scholars. These elegant and illuminating papers look at such things as why workers join unions, the tradeoffs that unions are willing to make in collective bargaining over wages, and the effects of arbitration on the collective bargaining process. Over time, of course, the union sector has accounted for a shrinking share of total employment. Hank has written on that subject, too.

The paper by Hank and myself reprinted here, which addresses the question of why longer-seniority workers earn higher wages, was Hank's first major departure from his union research agenda. Over the last ten years Hank's research portfolio has become considerably more diverse. He has done work that lies well outside the mainstream of labor economics research, including a variety of empirical analyses of the litigation process. He has written definitive papers on changes in workers' attachment to their jobs and on the phenomenon of worker displacement. When I talk to reporters about the latter subjects, I invariably refer them to Hank's work. In contrast to his early research, which was most notable for its econometric sophistication, these papers are most notable for the care and thoroughness with which the underlying data are treated.

Hank's contributions to the economics profession extend well beyond his own research and writing. Over his years as a practicing economist he has been exceptionally generous of his time and energy, to the lasting benefit of his many coauthors and other colleagues and, especially, his students, a good number of whom are now well-regarded scholars in their own right.

Katharine G. Abraham

Specific Capital, Mobility, and Wages: Wages Rise with Job Seniority

ROBERT TOPEL

University of Chicago and National Bureau of Economic Research

The idea that wages rise relative to alternatives as job seniority accumulates is the foundation of the theory of specific human capital, as well as other widely accepted theories of compensation. The fact that persons with longer job tenures typically earn higher wages tends to support these views, yet this evidence ignores the decisions that have brought individuals to the combination of wages, job tenure, and experience that are observed in survey data. Allowing for sources of bias generated by these decisions, this paper uses longitudinal data to estimate a lower bound on the average return to job seniority among adult men. I find that 10 years of current job seniority raise the wage of the typical male worker in the United States by over 25 percent. This is an estimate of what the typical worker would lose if his job were to end exogenously. Overall, the evidence implies that accumulation of specific capital is an important ingredient of the typical employment relationship and of life cycle earnings and productivity as well. Continuation of these relationships has substantial specific value for workers.

I. INTRODUCTION

The idea that wages rise relative to alternatives over the duration of a job is the foundation for several important theories of productivity and compensation. Most prominently, a key prediction of Becker's (1964) model of investment in specific human capital is that wages rise with job tenure (seniority), leaving workers with a stake in the specific value of the employment relationship. Related theories of agency in durable employment relations

Financial support from the National Science Foundation and the William Ladany Research Fund at the University of Chicago is gratefully acknowledged. I have benefited from the comments of Kevin M. Murphy, Joe Altonji, George Borjas, Charles Brown, David Card, Henry Farber, Richard Freeman, Larry Katz, Sherwin Rosen, Nachum Sicherman, and an anonymous referee. I also thank workshop participants at Arizona State, California at Los Angeles, Chicago, Columbia, Harvard, Illinois, Ohio State, Princeton, Santa Barbara, Stony Brook, Texas A&M, and the Center for Naval Analyses. Will Carrington provided able assistance. I am responsible for any errors.

(Becker and Stigler 1974; Lazear 1981) also generate deferred compensation that encourages workers' effort and improves performance (see also Lazear and Rosen 1981; Rosen 1986). Deferred compensation in the form of rising wages can also induce profitable self-selection of heterogeneous workers that enhances productivity (Salop and Salop 1976). Other contracting models (Freeman 1977; Harris and Holmstrom 1982) produce qualitatively similar predictions for the shape of job-specific wage profiles. These ideas are sufficiently established that the assumption of rising wage profiles has become an accepted point of departure for subsequent work (e.g., Shleifer and Summers 1988).

In all these models, a major component of earning capacity is both unique to a particular employment relationship and increasing in importance as the relationship ages. Senior workers would suffer substantial wage losses if their jobs were to end. Thus a common theme is specialization and, from a worker's perspective, the *accumulation* of job-specific capital. The credibility of this view is enhanced by the common finding from survey data that workers with longer job tenures typically earn more. This has been interpreted to mean that seniority raises earnings for the typical worker and, by related evidence, that turnover rates (quits and layoffs) are strongly and negatively related to job tenure.[1] These relationships are the empirical foundation for the view that specific capital is an important ingredient of life cycle earnings and productivity in modern labor markets.

This interpretation of the evidence is open to criticism because it ignores the job-changing decisions that have brought workers to the combinations of wages, job tenure, and market experience that are observed in survey data. These decisions can affect the relationship of job tenure to wages in two ways. First, recent evidence indicates that many job-changing decisions are the outcome of a career process by which workers are sorted into more durable and productive jobs (Hall 1982; Topel and Ward 1992). High-wage jobs tend to survive, which can mean that persons with long job tenures earn higher wages. The second possibility is that more productive or able persons change jobs less often, for which there is also empirical support. Again, persons with long job tenures will earn high wages. In either case, the wage earned by the representative worker need not *rise* as tenure accumulates, yet in a cross section of workers those with greater tenure earn more because tenure is correlated with unobserved characteristics of workers or their jobs. Recent empirical research tends to support this view: adjusting for unobserved factors in various ways, at least four recent studies have concluded that the true returns to job-specific experience are minor (Topel 1986; Abraham and Farber 1987; Altonji and Shakotko 1987; Marshall and Zarkin 1987).[2] This reinterpretation of the evidence has found widespread acceptance in subsequent literature (Mortensen 1988a, 1988b; Rosen 1988).

This conclusion has important implications for the way that economists view labor markets. In Becker's (1964) terminology, it means that human capital investments are

---

[1] Mincer and Jovanovic (1981) provide evidence on both points. Others include Borjas and Rosen (1980) and Mincer (1986, 1988).

[2] Mincer (1988) and Brown (1989) provide direct evidence that job training enhances wage growth.

mainly general rather than firm specific, so that the main component of workers' embodied skills is portable among firms. Thus investment in human capital does not account for the prevalence of "lifetime jobs" in the United States and other labor markets (Hall 1982) or for the sharply lower turnover rates of more senior workers. Further, in the absence of specific capital, the costs of worker displacement and unemployment are likely to be small: even for relatively senior workers these events should not have important effects on workers' wealth because previously accumulated skills are portable. Finally, the independence of wages and job tenure undermines the entire compensation literature that treats the timing of wages as a strategic device for affecting worker productivity. Either the problems of moral hazard and asymmetric information that underlie this literature are unimportant or they are solved by other means.

As the title suggests, this paper provides strong evidence that wages do rise with job seniority. I analyze longitudinal data on earnings and job histories for 1,540 men drawn from the first 16 waves (1968–83) of the Panel Study of Income Dynamics (PSID). The main finding is that the average returns to seniority are substantial. The estimates imply that 10 years of job seniority raise the wage of the typical male worker in the United States by over 25 percent relative to what he could earn elsewhere. Both theory and related evidence imply that this estimate is a lower bound; the true returns are probably larger. This estimate does not vary across broad occupational categories; professionals and nonunion blue-collar workers receive roughly similar returns, though the presumed rationing of union jobs alters this conclusion for workers covered by collective bargaining. For them, a job displacement that forces a move to a nonunion sector would reduce earnings of a worker with 10 years of seniority by nearly 40 percent. This effect is much larger than traditional estimates of union wage premiums (Lewis 1986) because it reflects the full cost of leaving the union sector, including forgone specific capital, and may account for the much greater average durations of union jobs.

All this evidence is based on a two-stage estimation procedure. The basic idea is that within-job wage growth combines the returns to general and job-specific experience. Thus the first stage estimates the determinants of wage growth but is unable to distinguish separate returns to general market experience and job-specific seniority. The second stage is a cross-sectional comparison of the wages of workers who started new jobs at different points in their careers. This stage yields an upper bound on the returns to general experience alone. In combination with estimates from the first stage, this translates to a lower bound on the returns to seniority in the typical employment relationship. In all cases that I have examined, the estimated returns to seniority are substantial. Along the way, additional sources of bias are examined and are found to have very minor effects on the results.

The paper is organized as follows. Section II provides preliminary evidence of important effects of job seniority on wages, based on the observed wage changes of workers who were displaced from their former jobs. Workers with longer prior job tenures suffer substantially greater losses from displacement, as would occur if wages rise with the duration of employment. The basic econometric framework is then developed and potential sources of bias in estimating the returns to job seniority and experience are explicitly modeled. Section III describes the PSID data and methods of selecting the sample. The main empirical results follow in Section IV.

Because these results and conclusions are substantially different from those reported in important recent studies, Section V of the paper compares my procedures and findings with those of Abraham and Farber (1987) and Altonji and Shakotko (1987), who also analyzed the PSID data. I find that earlier efforts understate within-job wage growth because of both significant problems of measurement error and methodological biases. Section VI concludes the paper.

II. Modeling the Returns to Experience and Job Tenure

A. Some Preliminary Evidence

Do wages depend on job seniority? The methods I develop below rely on panel data that follow the evolution of wages within jobs, but suggestive evidence is provided by tabulating the wage changes of workers whose jobs end exogenously. If job tenure raises wages relative to alternatives, then more senior workers will suffer larger wage reductions when employment is terminated. The estimates in table 1 are based on the Displaced Workers Survey that was administered with the January Current Population Survey (CPS) in 1984 and 1986. The sample consists of 4,367 men who report that they have been displaced from a job for economic reasons (layoffs or plant closings) in the past 5 years and who are currently employed. The table reports the mean change in log weekly earnings for these workers, as well as the average number of weeks unemployed since displacement and the reason for termination. There is little doubt that displacement is costly: the average worker who has found new employment suffers a 14 percent reduction in earnings. More important for present purposes, this reduction in average earning capacity is strongly related to prior job

TABLE 1

Wage Changes of Displaced Workers by Years of Prior Job Seniority, January CPS, 1984 and 1986

	Years of Seniority on Prior Job				
	0–5	6–10	11–20	21+	Total
Average change in log weekly wage	−.095 (.010)	−.223 (.021)	−.282 (.026)	−.439 (.071)	−.135 (.009)
Percentage displaced by plant closing	.352 (.008)	.463 (.021)	.528 (.026)	.750 (.043)	.390 (.007)
Weeks unemployed since displacement	18.69 (.413)	24.54 (1.202)	26.66 (1.536)	31.79 (3.288)	20.41 (.385)

Note: Estimates refer to male respondents between the ages of 20 and 60. Sample size is 4,367. Nominal data are deflated by the GNP price deflator for consumption expenditure. Figures in parentheses are standard errors.

tenure: those with longer jobs lose more, and they experience more unemployment after displacement. Thus the "costs" of displacement are strongly related to prior job tenure.

There are two possible explanations for this finding. One is that wages rise with seniority, so workers with longer job tenures are truly more specialized than their junior counterparts. The other is that long jobs paid higher wages throughout, and so tenure acts as a proxy for the relative "quality" of the terminated job. Distinguishing these hypotheses requires panel data on individuals' job histories, as below. A third hypothesis—that workers with long former jobs are more able—is not supported by these estimates. This finding is consistent with evidence developed below, which shows that biases due to unobserved personal characteristics are a minor concern.

B. A Prototype Model

A prototype model of wage determination is

$$y_{ijt} = X_{ijt}\beta_1 + T_{ijt}\beta_2 + \epsilon_{ijt}, \tag{1}$$

where y_{ijt} denotes the (log) wage for individual i on job j at time t, X_{ijt} is total labor market experience, and T_{ijt} is current job tenure (seniority). Parameters β_1 and β_2 represent average returns to an additional year of either experience or tenure, respectively, and are the parameters of interest for the remainder of the paper. Other observables that may enter (1) are ignored for ease of exposition. No generality is lost by also ignoring higher-order terms in X and T; they will be introduced in the empirical analysis.

The most popular interpretation of (1) is that β_1 represents the return on general human capital (training and the like) that accumulates with experience, while β_2 represents the return on accumulated job-specific capital that would be lost if a job were to end. Biases in estimating these returns are generated by covariance between the regressors and the unobservables, ϵ. In what follows my main concern will be with covariance that is the outcome of optimizing behavior, as workers seek to locate and maintain a productive (high-wage) employment relationship. Thus one can decompose the unobservables as

$$\epsilon_{ijt} = \phi_{ijt} + \mu_i + \nu_{ijt}, \tag{2}$$

where ϕ_{ijt} represents the stochastic component of wages that may be specific to a worker-firm pair, and μ_i is a person-specific effect that accounts for unobserved differences in earning capacity across individuals (e.g., "ability"). The ν_{ijt} account for marketwide random shocks as well as measurement error that is known to plague survey data. I assume that the components of (2) are mutually orthogonal and (for now) that μ_i and ν_{ijt} are orthogonal to the regressors in (1). Notice that fixed "job effects" ($\phi_{ijt} = \phi_{ij}$) are a special case of (2) in which the specific value of a job does not evolve over time. This component captures the notion of a "good match" in the sense of wages that are higher than what a worker could obtain elsewhere. It will generate bias in estimating (1) if ϕ is correlated with experience or job tenure. Thus let the auxiliary regression of ϕ on the observables be

$$\phi_{ijt} = X_{ijt}b_1 + T_{ijt}b_2 + u_{ijt}. \qquad (3)$$

In light of (3), least squares applied to (1) will yield biased estimates of β_1 and β_2 since $E\hat{\beta}_1 = \beta_1 + b_1$ and $E\hat{\beta}_2 = \beta_2 + b_2$. In much of what follows, I seek evidence on the importance of the parameters b_1 and b_2.

Theory offers some guidance on the signs of these effects. In light of job matching or search theories of job mobility (e.g., Burdett 1978; Jovanovic 1979a, 1979b, 1984), it is plausible that a productive (high-wage) match, once found, is unlikely to end. Given this, it is tempting to argue that job quality, ϕ, and tenure are positively related ($b_2 > 0$) in survey data.[3] This argument ignores the fact that persons who change jobs gain, on average, from their move, and they are included in the data at low job tenures.[4] In fact, the basic theory of search and matching implies that $b_2 < 0$—a comparison of wages for workers with different job tenures will *understate* the returns to seniority—as the following argument demonstrates.

Consider identical individuals who sample new job offers from a stable offer distribution $G(y)$. Offers arrive randomly at an exogenous rate. If the true values of β_1 and β_2 are zero, an optimal job-changing policy is to accept any offer that exceeds the wage on the current job. Thus high-wage jobs survive because they are less likely to be dominated by an alternative offer. Under these conditions, the current wage of any individual is the maximum offer received since entering the market. The expected value of this maximum clearly rises with experience since the number of offers sampled increases. Thus $b_1 > 0$. In contrast, current job tenure indicates only the order in which the maximum offer was received: persons with high tenure received their best offer earlier. But the distribution of the maximum offer (the first order statistic) depends only on the number of offers (experience) and not on their order (tenure).[5] This means that $E(y \mid X, T) = E(y \mid X)$ and there is no sample selection on tenure ($b_2 = 0$).[6] In this case experience is a sufficient statistic for

---

[3] *Most matching models generate wage dispersion from the assumption that individuals' productivities vary among tasks. A contrasting "segmented markets" view is that wage differentials merely reflect the existence of "good" and "bad" jobs, for unspecified reasons (e.g., Doeringer and Piore 1971). Which of these is true does not affect the following analysis.*

[4] *Lang (1987) makes a related point.*

[5] *For n offers received, the density of the maximum offer is $f(y) = G(y)^{n-1}g(y)$, which depends only on n. With random (Poisson) arrival of offers, the expected number of offers is proportional to time in the market (experience).*

[6] *Formally, the absence of a tenure effect in this case requires that experience effects be represented by a sequence of dummy variables for each level of experience.*

the distribution of wages and there is no bias in estimating β_2. But things are different if $\beta_2 > 0$.

If $\beta_2 > 0$, acceptable new job offers must compensate workers for the forgone returns to tenure on the current job, so there is less mobility than when $\beta_2 = 0$. Since a regression compares conditional means, the issue is whether $E(y \mid X, T + 1) = E(y \mid X, T) + \beta_2$. That is, do persons with one extra year of job tenure earn a wage that is higher, on average, by β_2? With $\beta_2 > 0$, some otherwise acceptable offers have been rejected. Inclusion of these marginal workers reduces the average wage of "stayers." Further, persons who change jobs require higher average wage offers to induce their move. This raises the average wage of movers. Both of these selection effects imply $E(y \mid X, T + 1) - E(y \mid X, T) < \beta_2$, so *least squares applied to (1) must underestimate the return to seniority.*[7] Thus a basic matching technology with rising within-job wage profiles implies $b_1 > 0$ but $b_2 < 0$. Yet the notion that "good jobs survive" still holds. Let X_0 denote experience at the start of a job, so $X = X_0 + T$. Then (3) is equivalent to $\phi = X_0 b_1 + T(b_1 + b_2)$. Thus the durability of high-wage jobs means that $b_1 + b_2 > 0$,[8] so the *sum* of the returns to experience and tenure will be biased up in a wage regression on survey data.

In light of this analysis, there can be no presumption that standard regression techniques applied to cross-sectional data will overestimate the returns to tenure. Optimizing search behavior generally implies the opposite, though there are other sources of selection that may reinforce or offset these effects. For example, mobility costs tend to reinforce $b_2 < 0$ by reducing the set of acceptable wage offers, while costly search may cause $b_2 > 0$ because only persons with relatively poor employment matches are actively searching. Panel data on individuals' careers provide leverage for isolating these effects. I turn to this subject next.

III. A Two-Stage Estimation Procedure

Panel data from sources such as the PSID provide information on wages at different stages of a single job, as well as on different jobs for a single individual. Given this, within-job wage growth can be studied from the first differences of (1) for persons who do not change jobs, which eliminates fixed job and individual effects:

$$y_{ijt} - y_{ijt-1} = \beta_1 + \beta_2 + \epsilon_{ijt} - \epsilon_{ijt-1} \tag{4}$$

---

[7] *The selection is easiest to see in a two-period case. If workers receive one offer per period, then exchangeability implies that $E(y_2 \mid y_2 > y_1) = E(y_1 \mid y_1 > y_2)$. If wages grow by β among stayers, then $E(y_2 \mid y_1 + \beta > y_2) < E(y_2 \mid y_1 + \beta < y_2)$. Thus, $E(y_1 + \beta \mid y_1 + \beta > y_2) - E(y_2 \mid y_2 > y_1 + \beta) < \beta$. Other factors may increase or decrease the bias. For example, mobility costs strengthen the bias.*

[8] *Topel and Ward (1992) find direct evidence for both $b_1 > 0$ and $b_1 + b_2 > 0$. They estimate that approximately one-third of wage growth during the first 10 years in the labor market is due to job-changing activity. Controlling directly for unobserved personal heterogeneity, they also find that wage increases and transitions to higher-paying jobs sharply reduce job mobility because acceptable offers must be better to induce a move. Endogenous search intensity weakens the bias because persons with high wages are less likely to sample.*

since $\Delta X = \Delta T = 1$ between periods of a single job. If $\epsilon_{ijt} - \epsilon_{ijt-1}$ has mean zero, then least squares applied to (4) will yield a consistent estimate of average within-job wage growth, $\beta_1 + \beta_2$.[9] Given (4), an estimate of β_1 can be obtained from initial wages on new jobs:

$$y_{0ijt} = X_{0ijt}\beta_1 + \phi_{ij} + \mu_i + \nu_{ijt},\qquad(5)$$

where X_0 is initial experience on the job. The error term in (5) is nonrandom because only *acceptable* new job offers are observed. For example, ϕ and X_0 are positively correlated if expected match quality rises with time in the market. One approach to this problem is to explicitly model the mobility decisions that underlie this selection bias, in which case standard sample selection corrections (e.g., Heckman 1976) might be applied. With this strategy, identification relies crucially on distributional assumptions (wage offers must be normally distributed), as well as on other strong restrictions (Topel 1986).

A more robust alternative is simply to note the selection bias implicit in (5) and to treat $(\beta_1 + \beta_2) - \hat{\beta}_1$ as an estimate of the return to seniority. If β_1 is biased up, this two-step procedure yields a lower bound on the return to seniority. More generally, since $X = X_0 + T$, model (1) may be rewritten as

$$y = X_0\beta_1 + TB + \epsilon,\qquad(6)$$

where $B \equiv \beta_1 + \beta_2$. With (6), a two-step model is given by the first differences of within-job wage growth (4) and

$$y - T\hat{B} = X_0\beta_1 + e,\qquad(7)$$

where $\hat{B} = \widehat{\beta_1 + \beta_2}$ is the consistent first step estimator of the sum of the returns to experience and tenure, derived from (4), and $e = \epsilon + T(B - \hat{B})$. As a second-step model, equation (7) is preferable to (5) because it makes use of data from all periods of all jobs.

The two-step model given by (4) and (7) yields unbiased estimators of β_1 and β_2 only if $EX_0'\epsilon = 0$. This condition will not hold if job matching is important. Nevertheless, we may calculate the expected values of the two-step estimators of β_1 and β_2 up to the unknown parameters b_1 and b_2. When least squares is applied to (4) and (7), some algebra establishes that these are

$$E\hat{\beta}_1 = \beta_1 + b_1 + \gamma_{X_0T}(b_1 + b_2)\qquad(8a)$$

---

[9] *This is assumed for now, though mobility decisions may also generate selection in (5), because only acceptable values of $\Delta\epsilon$ are observed. This point is examined in Sec. IVD.*

and

$$E\hat{\beta}_2 = \beta_2 - b_1 - \gamma_{X_0 T}\left(b_1 + b_2\right),$$ (8b)

where $\gamma_{X_0 T}$ is the least-squares coefficient from a regression of tenure on initial experience, X_0.

Equations (8a) and (8b) indicate that the two-step procedure yields biased estimators of the returns to market experience and job tenure. The biases are equivalent, but of opposite signs, because the sum $\beta_1 + \beta_2$ is consistently estimated from the first-step model. If systematic job changing is important ($b_1 > 0$, $b_1 + b_2 > 0$), productive employment relationships are located later in the typical worker's career. Then (8a) implies that $E\hat{\beta}_1 > \beta_1$—the estimated returns to experience are biased up because they include the return to changing jobs—while (8b) implies $E\hat{\beta}_2 < \beta_2$ for the same reason. Thus the two-step model establishes a lower bound on the average return to seniority. Notice in particular the difference between the bias in (8b) and the least-squares bias, b_2, in estimating β_2. Though earlier discussion indicates that the sign of b_2 is not well established by theory, the bias in (8b) is negative as long as "better" jobs are located as time in the labor market accumulates. Virtually any model of optimal job changing has this property.

There are two possible caveats to this conclusion. First, if job changing is the outcome of optimizing behavior for workers, then jobs offering low wage *growth* may not survive. Since equation (4) applies to an employment relationship that survived from date $t - 1$ to t, average wage growth in this sample of "stayers" may exceed the rate of growth in the population of all jobs. In this case β_2 could be overestimated. Second, persons who change jobs frequently may be less productive, on average, than persons in stable employment relations. Then X_0 is lower for able persons—they started their current jobs earlier—and so $\hat{\beta}_1$ is biased down. Again, β_2 could be overestimated. I provide evidence on both of these effects below.

IV. ESTIMATION

A. THE DATA

The procedure described above is applied to panel data from the first 16 (1968–83) waves of the PSID.[10] Complete sample selection criteria are reported in the Appendix. For the estimates that follow, attention is restricted to white males between the ages of 18 and 60 (inclusive) who were not self-employed, employed in agriculture, or employed by the government. All individuals are from the random, nonpoverty sample of the PSID. The data analyzed here consist of 13,128 job-years on 1,540 individuals and 3,228 jobs. Summary statistics and definitions for all variables used in estimation are reported in Appendix table A1.

---

[10] *The data were kindly supplied by Joe Altonji and Nachum Sicherman.*

The wage data refer to (log) average hourly earnings in calendar years 1967–82. Since the parameters in (1) refer to relative earnings differences at a point in time, the usual regression strategy is to control for aggregate real wage growth and inflation by including year-specific intercepts. There are two problems with this in the current context. First, cross sections of the PSID data may not be representative of the underlying population at each point in time. The records available for analysis include households that participated in the survey at the last survey date (here 1983). Households that left the survey before 1983 are not in the data. Thus even if the 1983 sample is representative, past cross sections based on these households will reflect the sample selection rule that causes households to remain in the PSID. Second, in following any fixed population in panel data, time is not statistically exogenous for the same reason that experience is not: average match quality rises with time in the market. In this situation, treating time effects as exogenous may lead to an understatement of the return to seniority and an overstatement of temporal wage growth.[11] To avoid these problems, I deflated the wage data by a wage index for white males calculated from the annual demographic (March) files of the CPS (see Murphy and Welch 1992). This index nets out both real aggregate wage growth and changes in any aggregate price level (the gross national product price deflator for consumption was used), so that wage data from different time periods of the panel are expressed in comparable units. Values for the wage index are reported in the Appendix.

A key step in the analysis was the construction of a consistent measure of current job tenure. Because of a number of sources of measurement error, reported tenure in the PSID data is not reliable. It is often recorded in intervals of several years, and recorded values are often inconsistent between successive years of the same job. This measurement error is magnified in the first-step model, which uses changes in seniority between successive years to estimate parameters of wage growth. The problem is acute when higher-order terms (T^2, T^3) are added to the model. To correct for these problems, the measure of job tenure used here relies on the fact that tenure must rise by 1 year in each year of a job: For jobs that start within the panel, tenure is started at zero and incremented by one each year. For jobs that were in progress at the beginning of an individual's record, current tenure is measured relative to the maximum reported during the job, again imposing the restriction that tenure change by one each year. Within jobs, the resulting sequence of measured job tenures is perfectly correlated with labor market experience, as required.[12]

---

[11] In fact, average real wages rise slightly more rapidly in the PSID than in random samples of the CPS. A vector of year dummies was included in a standard log wage regression as specified below. The year effects indicated that PSID wages grew by about 7.0 percent relative to CPS cross sections during the 1970s. When the same regression was applied to the subsample of individuals who entered the data in 1968–69 (n = 6,929), the time effects were eliminated. Thus there is no evidence that wages of individual PSID cohorts grew more rapidly than the population.

[12] There are many cases of ambiguity about job endings. For example, reported tenure within a job may fall to zero and then rise smoothly. These cases suggest unrecorded changes of employer. These "jobs" were deleted, but doing so had no material effect on the results. See the Appendix for details.

B. Wage Growth within Jobs

If the evolution of wages within jobs follows a random walk, then the residuals of the wage growth model are serially independent and least squares applied to (4) is an efficient estimator of $\beta_1 + \beta_2$. As in Topel and Ward (1992), close examination of the time-series properties of within-job wage changes yields two important conclusions. First, there is no evidence of positive serial correlation in within-job wage innovations, $\epsilon_{ijt} - \epsilon_{ijt-1}$. This is a strong finding since one might expect that some types of jobs offer steeper wage profiles than others. The lack of serial correlation implies that heterogeneity in permanent rates of wage growth among jobs is empirically unimportant. Second, I find that the within-job evolution of the wage has a strong permanent component that closely approximates a random walk, so the residuals satisfy

$$\phi_{ijt} = \phi_{ijt-1} + \eta_{ijt}, \tag{9}$$

where η_{ijt} is serially independent with mean zero.[13] Because of (9), values of η_{ijt} reflect "permanent" changes in a worker's expected lifetime wealth. For example, these may reflect uncertain returns on investments in human capital or simply new information about a worker's productivity. If these changes are firm-specific rents, they will affect future job-changing decisions. In contrast, if they mainly represent changes in general human capital, then future job mobility will be unaffected by them. These possibilities have different implications for interpreting the estimated returns to seniority; I will return to this subject below.

Given these findings, table 2 reports various specifications for first-stage models of within-job wage growth. Generalizing the earlier discussion, these and all subsequent models allow for higher-order effects of experience and tenure on wages (e.g., X^2), the effects of which are identified from within-job wage changes (e.g., $\Delta X^2 = 2X - 1$). As above, the model is underidentified by one parameter because linear terms in experience and tenure are perfectly correlated within jobs. Thus the first coefficient in column 1 (.1242) is an estimate of $\beta_1 + \beta_2$ for new entrants to the labor force ($X = 0$). Wage profiles are concave in both experience and tenure, though the usual quadratic specification is insufficient to describe the data: after an initial period of rapid growth, wage profiles flatten out. This is captured in column 3 by quartics in both experience and tenure.[14] To illustrate the impact of job tenure on wage changes within a job, at the bottom of the table I report predicted wage growth for a worker with 10 years of market experience and varying job tenures. Wage growth clearly declines as tenure accumulates, with experi-

---

[13] Detailed evidence on these points appears in Topel (1990).

[14] As Welch (1979) points out, the usual quadratic underestimates wage growth for young workers. Murphy and Welch (1987) also advocate a quartic specification for the experience profile.

TABLE 2

MODELS OF ANNUAL WITHIN-JOB WAGE GROWTH, PSID WHITE MALES, 1968–83
(DEPENDENT VARIABLE IS CHANGE IN LOG REAL WAGE; MEAN = .026)

| | Model | | |
	(1)	(2)	(3)
Δ Tenure	.1242 (.0161)	.1265 (.0162)	.1258 (.0162)
Δ Tenure^2 ($\times 10^2$)	...	−.0518 (.0178)	−.4592 (.1080)
Δ Tenure^3 ($\times 10^3$)	...	...	.1846 (.0526)
Δ Tenure^4 ($\times 10^4$)	...	...	−.0245 (.0079)
Δ Experience^2 ($\times 10^2$)	−.6051 (.1430)	−.6144 (.1430)	−.4067 (.1546)
Δ Experience^3 ($\times 10^3$)	.1460 (.0482)	.1620 (.0485)	.0989 (.0517)
Δ Experience^4 ($\times 10^4$)	.0131 (.0054)	.0151 (.0055)	.0089 (.0058)
R^2	.022	.023	.025
Standard error	.218	.218	.218

PREDICTED WITHIN-JOB WAGE GROWTH BY YEARS OF JOB TENURE
(WORKERS WITH 10 YEARS OF LABOR MARKET EXPERIENCE)

| | Tenure | | | | | | | | | |
	1	2	3	4	5	6	7	8	9	10
Predicted wage growth (%)	.068	.060	.052	.046	.041	.037	.033	.030	.028	.026

Note: Estimate are based on within-job first differences of log average hourly earnings. Standard errors are in parentheses. Number of observations is 8,683.

ence held constant, a pattern that is difficult to reconcile with the idea that tenure has a negligible effect on wage *levels*.

The results that follow are based on the model in column 3 of table 2.

C. ESTIMATED RETURNS TO MARKET EXPERIENCE AND JOB TENURE

The main results for the separate returns to experience and tenure are reported in table 3. In implementation of the second-step model that underlies these results, consistent estimates of $\beta_1 + \beta_2$ and the parameters of higher-order terms in experience and tenure are taken from the within-job growth model in column 3 of table 2. Denote these terms by $\chi\hat{\Gamma}$. Subtracting $\chi\hat{\Gamma}$ from both sides of the wage equation and letting **F** denote the vector of other factors (education etc.) that affect wages yield the second-step model

Specific Capital, Mobility, and Wages

TABLE 3

SECOND-STEP ESTIMATED MAIN EFFECTS OF EXPERIENCE (β_1) AND TENURE (β_2) ON LOG
REAL WAGES, AND LEAST-SQUARES BIAS IN WAGE GROWTH (b_1 AND b_2)

	Experience Effect, β_1 (1)	Within-Job Wage Growth, $\beta_1 + \beta_2$ (2)	Tenure Effect, β_2 (3)	Wage Growth Bias, $b_1 + b_2$ (4)
Main effect	.0713	.1258	.0545	.0020
	(.0181)	(.0161)	(.0079)	(.0004)
ESTIMATED CUMULATIVE RETURN TO JOB TENURE				
	5 Years	10 Years	15 Years	20 Years
Two-step model	.1793	.2459	.2832	.3375
	(.0235)	(.0341)	(.0411)	(.0438)
OLS	.2313	.3002	.3203	.3563
	(.0098)	(.0105)	(.0110)	(.0116)

Note: Estimated within-job wage growth ($\beta_1 + \beta_2$) from table 2, col. 3. Dependent variable for other estimates is log real hourly earnings less the effects of variables that are consistently estimated from the within-job wage growth model. Other regressors in the second-step model (10) include years of completed schooling, marital status, residence in an SMSA, current disability, union membership, and eight indicators for census region of residence. Estimated cumulative returns are based on the main effect of job tenure ($\beta_2 = .0545$) plus the effects of higher-order terms in tenure shown in col. 3 of table 2. Standard errors (in parentheses) are corrected to reflect sampling error in the first-step estimates. Methods developed in Murphy and Topel (1985) are used for this. Number of observations is 10,685.

$$y - \chi \hat{\Gamma} = X_0 \beta_1 + F\gamma + e, \qquad (10)$$

which is in the form of equation (7). As shown in column 1 of the table, the estimated value of β_1 from implementing (10) is about 7 percent. This estimator is substantially smaller than the value of $\beta_1 + \beta_2$ estimated from within-job growth, which is reproduced in column 2. The remainder is the main effect of job tenure on wages, β_1. I estimate that in the first year of the typical new job, the real wage rises by over 5 percent ($\beta_2 = .0545$) because of the accumulation of job-specific experience alone.

Cumulative returns to various lengths of job tenure are reported in the bottom panel of the table. The estimates are based on the main effect of $\beta_2 = .0545$, together with the concavity of the wage profile implied by the effects of higher-order terms in table 2. The returns to seniority are large: I estimate that 10 years of job seniority increase the wage of the typical worker by 28 percent ($e^{.2459} - 1$), relative to alternatives. For comparison, I also report estimates of the wage profile generated by ordinary least squares (OLS) applied to (1). These effects are larger, though not dramatically so. Since I have argued that the two-step procedure generates a lower bound on the true returns, the OLS estimates may actually be close to the truth.

Are these results reasonable? An appropriate interpretation of the estimated returns to seniority in table 3 is that they represent the reduction in earning capacity that would be suffered by a person whose job ends for exogenous reasons. Accordingly, these results imply that a person with 15 years of current job tenure would suffer an immediate 33 percent ($e^{.2832} - 1$) wage loss if his job ended exogenously. This is the experiment underlying the estimated losses of displaced workers in table 1, which showed an average wage reduction for workers in this tenure category of about 32 percent. Despite obvious differences in the composition of the two samples, the similarity of these estimates is gratifying. The results here also indicate that workers may bounce back from these losses fairly rapidly: relative wage growth is most rapid at the beginning of new jobs, so initial wage losses would vastly overstate changes in lifetime wealth caused by a job termination.

A final point about these estimates is noteworthy. Though the two-step procedure cannot identify the bias terms b_1 and b_2 separately, their sum is clearly identified since $\beta_1 + \beta_2$ is consistently estimated. In fact, $b_1 + b_2$ is the component of wage *growth* that is caused by systematic job changing. And since $E\phi = X_0 b_1 + T(b_1 + b_2)$, the notion that "good jobs survive" is equivalent to $b_1 + b_2 > 0$. This sum can be estimated directly by reinserting the term $T(b_1 + b_2)$ on the right side of equation (10) and applying least squares. The resulting estimate, shown in column 4 of table 3, is a wage growth bias of about 0.2 percent per year. Finally, from (8) the bias in the two-step estimators of β_1 and β_2 is

$$b_1 + \gamma_{X_0 T}(b_1 + b_2). \tag{11}$$

A regression of current tenure on initial experience yields $\gamma_{X_0 T} = -.25$, so the second term in (11) is $-.25 \times .0020 = -.0005$, or one-twentieth of one percentage point per year. This means that the bias in the two-step estimator of β_2, the return to job tenure, is virtually independent of any covariance of job tenure with the unobservables, that is, of the unsigned value of b_2. Since $b_1 \geq 0$, the downward bias in the estimated return to seniority is solely due to improvement in match quality with total labor market experience.

D. OTHER SOURCES OF BIAS

Under the stated assumptions, the estimates in table 3 are a lower bound on the average returns to job seniority. Other sources of bias can weaken this conclusion, and at least two are worth investigating. One possibility is that the sample used to estimate $\beta_1 + \beta_2$ is weighted toward jobs with unusually high wage growth, which may affect the interpretation of the return to seniority. The second possibility is that more able or productive persons are also less mobile, so estimated returns reflect the longer average job durations of high-wage individuals. I treat these in turn.

Selection Bias in Wage Growth The cumulative returns shown in table 3 are estimates of job-specific wage premiums that would be earned by a typical worker as he accumulates seniority. The most popular interpretation of these returns is that workers anticipate rising compensation over the life of a job, as in contract models such as Becker (1964), Salop and Salop (1976), or Lazear (1981). A second interpretation is also possible, however, since jobs that yield high wage growth may be more likely to survive. In this case returns to seniority are realized period by period, though they may not be anticipated at the start of a job.

To illustrate this point, rewrite the wage growth model (4):

$$y_{ijt} - y_{ijt-1} = \beta_1 + \beta_2 + \eta_{ijt} + \nu_{ijt} - \nu_{ijt-1}, \tag{4'}$$

where η_{ijt} is the "permanent" increment to the wage defined in (9). For a job that ends between dates $t - 1$ and t, the wage y_{ijt} that *would* have been earned up to t is not recorded, but it may have been known by workers. If a substantial component of η_{ijt} is firm specific, then knowledge of η will affect mobility decisions, and so jobs with high values of $y_{ijt} - y_{ijt-1}$ will be more likely to survive. This means that average wage growth among workers who do not change jobs may overstate growth in the population, which is to say that $E\eta > 0$ in the sample. An estimate of $\beta_1 + \beta_2$ based on wage changes within jobs includes this selection effect, which would cause a corresponding overestimate of the *anticipated* returns to seniority, β_2, by the preceding methods.

As a practical matter, both $\beta_2 > 0$ and $E\eta > 0$ imply that wages rise with seniority. Senior workers earn more, relative to alternatives, than they did when they started their jobs. This means that previous conclusions are not materially affected if $E\eta > 0$, but also that it is difficult to distinguish these alternatives in the data. The difference in the interpretation of the returns to seniority is of some theoretical interest, however. Some headway in distinguishing these explanations is possible by examining the relationship between current wage growth and subsequent job changing.

The key condition for $E\eta > 0$ to be quantitatively important is that a substantial component of η_{ijt} must be *firm specific*.[15] Then a large value of η_{ijt} has a permanent effect on the value of a job, reducing mobility in period t and all subsequent periods.[16] For example, since the wage follows a random walk, job-changing decisions in period $t + 1$ are based on $\eta_{ijt} + \eta_{ijt+1}$, and the expected value of η_{ijt} must be smaller for jobs that end in $t + 1$ than for those that survive to later periods. More generally, when η is firm specific, the expected value of η_{ijt} is increasing in R_{ijt}, the remaining life of the job measured from date t. Thus

$$0 \leq E(\eta_t \mid R_t \geq 0) < E(\eta_t \mid R_t \geq 1) < E(\eta_t \mid R_t \geq 2) < \cdots . \tag{12}$$

---

[15] *The decision to change jobs depends on the job-specific component of an alternative offer, ϕ, relative to innovations to job-specific capital on the current job, η. Mobility occurs when $\phi - \eta$ is larger than some critical value, say k. If ϕ and η are independent normal random variables, the expected value of η in the sample of nonmovers is $E(\eta \mid \phi - \eta < k) = [\sigma_\eta^2 / (\sigma_\eta^2 + \sigma_\phi^2)^{1/2}] \times [f(k)/F(k)]$, where $F(k)$ is the standard normal distribution function. Thus the amount of selection depends on the relative magnitudes of σ_η^2 and σ_ϕ^2.*

[16] *Timing is also important. Even when η is firm specific, it may take time to locate an acceptable new job. Then η_{ijt} affects mobility only after period t, and estimates of $\beta_1 + \beta_2$ based on (4') are unbiased ($E\eta = 0$).*

TABLE 4

EFFECTS OF SELECTION BIAS IN WAGE GROWTH ON THE ESTIMATED
RETURNS TO JOB SENIORITY

A. RELATIONSHIP BETWEEN REMAINING JOB DURATION AND CURRENT WAGE GROWTH

Remaining Job Duration (Years)	Job Ends in Period:					
	$t+1$	$t+2$	$t+3$	$t+4$	$t+5$	$t+6$
1. .0006						
(.0010)						
2.	−.012	−.015	.013	.012	.020	.004
	(.012)	(.013)	(.013)	(.014)	(.015)	(.017)

B. RETURNS TO JOB SENIORITY BASED ON VARIOUS
REMAINING JOB DURATIONS IN FIRST-STEP MODEL

	Remaining Job Duration in Estimating Wage Growth (Years)			
	≥ 0	≥ 1	≥ 3	≥ 5
Main effects:				
Experience (β_1)	.0713	.0792	.0716	.0607
	(.0181)	(.0204)	(.0245)	(.0292)
Tenure β_2	.0545	.0546	.0559	.0584
	(.0079)	(.0089)	(.0109)	(.0132)
Estimated tenure profile:				
5 years	.1793	.1725	.1703	.1815
	(.0235)	(.0265)	(.0319)	(.0379)
10 years	.2459	.2235	.2181	.2330
	(.0341)	(.0376)	(.0437)	(.0514)
15 years	.2832	.2439	.2503	.2565
	(.0411)	(.0445)	(.0504)	(.0594)
20 years	.3375	.2865	.3232	.3066
	(.0438)	(.0469)	(.0531)	(.0647)

Note: In panel A, other regressors are as reported in table 3. Remaining job duration is the number of years from t to the last observed year of the job. An interaction of remaining duration with a dummy for jobs that censor at the end of the panel is also included, but it had no effect on the results. In row 2 the omitted category is jobs that lasted 6 or more years beyond the current date. In panel B, the first-step models use jobs with different remaining job durations. For example, the last column estimates wage growth at t from jobs that survive 5 or more years beyond t. Standard errors are in parentheses.

Evidence on the inequalities in (12) is presented in table 4. Panel A shows the relationship between the remaining life of a job and current wage growth, after observables are controlled for. The estimate in row 1 shows that there is no linear relationship between these variables. Row 2 is less restrictive, allowing separate effects for jobs that end in years $t + 1$, $t + 2$, and so on. Since the omitted category is jobs that survive 6 or more years, all these effects should be negative but decreasing in magnitude if (12) is satisfied. This pattern does not hold, though there is minor evidence that jobs that end in periods $t + 1$ and $t + 2$ have slightly lower growth.

Panel B of table 4 makes the test more stringent. If high-growth jobs tend to survive, then the inequalities (12) imply that estimates of the first-step model of wage growth based on more durable jobs will overstate $\beta_1 + \beta_2$, which will increase the estimated returns to job seniority. I find no evidence for this effect. In fact, tenure profiles estimated from jobs with longer remaining durations—5 or more years beyond the current date in the last column—are virtually the same as the full-sample estimates reproduced in the first column of the table. Overall, I have not been able to find any evidence that selection on η plays an important role in affecting estimates of wage growth or the returns to seniority. This evidence favors substantial, *anticipated* returns to seniority in the typical employment relationship.

Ability Bias in the Returns to Job Tenure To this point I have maintained the assumption that unobserved characteristics of individuals, μ_i, are unrelated to observed job tenure. Yet an alternative rationale for the positive relationship between job tenure and wages is that workers' unobserved productivities are negatively related to mobility. For example, more able (high-wage) persons may change jobs less often, so tenure and wages will be positively correlated in survey data even if $\beta_2 = 0$. Evidence suggestive of this is that education, an *observed* element of human capital, is negatively related to job changing. Alternatively, if turnover is costly to employers, then the net productivity of stable workers will be greater, and employers will pay more to obtain them. In either case, unobserved characteristics that raise wages (μ_i) are positively correlated with observed tenure, which raises the estimated returns to job seniority.

Because μ_i is a fixed effect, covariance of μ with the regressors in (1) will not bias estimators of $\beta_1 + \beta_2$, which is based on wage changes. Yet estimates of β_1 and β_2 from the second-step model (7) will be biased if μ_i and initial experience, X_0, are correlated. In this case, the bias in the estimated return to seniority from the second-step model is

$$E\hat{\beta}_2 - \beta_2 = -b_1 - \gamma_{X_0 T}(b_1 + b_2) - \gamma_{X_0 \mu}, \qquad (13)$$

where $\gamma_{X_0 \mu} = (X_0' X_0)^{-1} X_0' \mu$. If high-$\mu$ persons change jobs less often, then on average they started their current jobs earlier. This implies $\gamma_{X_0 \mu} < 0$, so the second-step estimator of β_2 may overstate the returns to seniority.

The importance of this bias can be evaluated if there is an instrumental variable that is uncorrelated with the fixed effects, μ_i, but correlated with X_0. A plausible candidate is *total* experience, X. Specifically, I assume that the distribution of μ_i is unrelated to experience (successive cohorts of workers are equally able and equally mobile) so that $E(X'\mu) = 0$. With this condition, X may be used as an instrumental variable for X_0 in estimating the second-step model (7). The resulting bias in the instrumental variables estimator of β_2 is

$$E\hat{\beta}_2^{IV} - \beta_2 = -b_1 - \frac{\gamma_{XT}}{1-\gamma_{XT}}(b_1 + b_2),$$ (14)

where γ_{XT} is the least-squares coefficient from a regression of tenure (T) on experience (X). This bias in the instrumental variables estimator is independent of the distribution of μ_i. Further, $\gamma_{XT} = .50$ in the data, and previous results imply $b_1 + b_2 > 0$ (see table 3). Thus the right-hand side of (14) is negative, so that β_2^{IV} provides a lower bound on β_2 even when μ_i and tenure are correlated. If μ_i and tenure are correlated, then the estimated return to seniority will be lower when X is used as an instrument for X_0 in the second-step model.[17]

Estimates of the returns to seniority when X is used as an instrument in (7) differ trivially from those reported above. The estimated main effect of seniority (β_2) falls from .055 per year, reported in table 3, to .052 under instrumental variables. Over a 10-year horizon, this implies a difference of only 3 percent in the cumulative return to seniority, relative to the 25 percent cumulative return shown above. This is fairly strong evidence that unobserved personal characteristics do not account for the substantial returns to seniority shown in table 3.

E. OCCUPATIONAL DIFFERENCES IN WAGE PROFILES

All the preceding results refer to workers in an array of occupations, ranging from laborers to highly paid professionals. It is not hard to imagine technological or other differences across occupations that would generate corresponding differences in wage profiles. For example, investments in specific skills may be more important among professionals, while collective bargaining agreements may limit the ability of employers to back-load wages in unionized environments. Thus the preceding results may be sensitive to aggregation across diverse groups. Because of sample size limitations in the PSID, it is not possible to examine these issues in fine detail. Instead, evidence is presented for three broad categories of workers. Among craftsmen, operatives, and laborers, I treat union and nonunion workers separately.[18] The third category consists of professional and service occupations. I finesse issues of promotion and the like by categorizing all periods of a job on the basis of the reported occupation in its first observed period.

Estimates of the time-series properties of wage changes showed only minor differences across groups. Briefly, the earlier finding that wages follow a random walk within jobs also holds for each of the occupational groups. The only difference worth noting is a substantially smaller variance in wage changes among unionized workers. Since collective bargaining arrangements normally set wages according to scale, this finding is plausible.

---

[17] *Comparison of eqq. (14) and (13) implies that $E\hat{\beta}_2^{IV} < E\hat{\beta}_2 < \beta_2$ when $\gamma_{X_0\mu} = 0$. Thus least squares is the preferred estimator in (7) if unobserved characteristics and tenure are uncorrelated.*

[18] *Jobs were categorized as "union" if the respondent indicated union membership in more than half of the years of the job. Other definitions were also tried, but the results were not sensitive to these changes.*

Table 5 shows estimated main effects of experience and job tenure, as well as cumulative returns to various levels of tenure, for each occupational group. The main finding is that estimated returns to tenure are quite similar across broad occupational categories. Differences in returns between white- and blue-collar professionals are trivial, as are differences in returns between union and nonunion workers within blue-collar professions. In fact, aggregation of the three wage profiles cannot be rejected.

Conceptually, the cumulative returns shown in table 5 measure the return to T years of job seniority in sector i as $y^i(X, T) - y^i(X, 0)$, the difference between the wage at tenure T and the wage in the typical alternative job in the same sector. This comparison may be inappropriate for union members. Since union jobs (u) are normally rationed, the relevant alternative may be employment in a nonunion job (n). In this case the correct estimate of the return to T years of seniority is $y^u(X, T) - y^n(X, 0)$. This estimate will differ from the return to seniority for unionized workers because (i) unionized workers earn a premium that is lost in moving to the nonunion sector, and (ii) the returns to total market experience differ between the union and nonunion sectors. This point is demonstrated by comparing the two columns of cumulative returns for union members. When measured relative to another union job, $y^u(X, 0)$, estimated returns are essentially identical to those in other sectors. But measured relative to the nonunion alternative, $y^n(X, 0)$, returns are both larger and rising.[19] According to the estimates in the last column, the typical union worker with 15 years of seniority would suffer a 50 percent ($e^{4111} - 1$) wage cut if his current job were to end and he was forced to seek employment in the nonunion sector. This estimate of what a union worker would lose if his job were to end combines the union seniority effect, $y^u(X, T) - y^u(X, 0)$, and the union wage premium for new workers, $y^u(X, 0) - y^n(X, 0)$.[20]

V. COMPARISONS WITH OTHER RESEARCH

My results and conclusions are substantially different from those reported in recent research. Specifically, the PSID data have also been analyzed by Altonji and Shakotko (1987) and by Abraham and Farber (1987), who conclude that the true returns to job seniority are minor. This difference in results cannot be attributed to the samples analyzed since they are virtually the same. An accounting of the reasons for our different findings is therefore warranted.

---

[19] *The typical union member in these data started his job at $X_0 = 10$ years of labor market experience. For these calculations, I assume $X_0 = 10$ and allow both experience and tenure to accumulate from that point. Thus a person with 5 years of job tenure also has 15 years of labor market experience, and so on. Effects of other regressors (education etc.) also differed between union and nonunion jobs. The calculations refer to a person with average characteristics, so these differences are reflected in the estimates.*

[20] *A referee has pointed out that an estimate of the union wage premium at various levels of tenure is the difference in the cost of displacement for union and nonunion workers, assuming that all find nonunion jobs. This is $[y^u(X, T) - y^n(X, 0)] - [y^u(X, T) - y^n(X, 0)] = y^u(X, T) - y^n(X, T)$. This is the difference between col. 4 and col. 2 of table 5. Notice that this measure of the union wage premium rises with tenure.*

TABLE 5

ESTIMATED RETURNS TO JOB SENIORITY BY OCCUPATIONAL CATEGORY
AND UNION STATUS, TWO-STEP ESTIMATOR

Main Effects	Professional and Service	Craftsmen, Operatives, and Laborers	
		Nonunion	Union
Experience (β_1)	.0707	.1066	.0592
	(.0288)	(.0342)	(.0338)
Tenure (β_2)	.0601	.0513	.0399
	(.0127)	(.0146)	(.0147)
$\beta_1 + \beta_2$	.1309	.1520	.0992
	(.0254)	(.0311)	(.0297)

Estimated Cumulative Returns to Tenure at:	Professional and Service (1)	Craftsmen, Operatives, and Laborers		
			Union Relative to:	
		Nonunion (2)	Union Sector (3)	Nonunion Sector (4)
5 years	.1887	.1577	.1401	.2299
	(.0388)	(.0428)	(.0437)	(.0931)
10 years	.2400	.2073	.2033	.3286
	(.0560)	(.0641)	(.0620)	(.0854)
15 years	.2527	.2480	.2384	.4111
	(.0656)	(.0802)	(.0739)	(.0855)
20 years	.2841	.3295	.2733	.4904
	(.0663)	(.0914)	(.0783)	(.0957)
Number of observations	4,946	2,642	2,741	

Note: The effects of higher-order terms in experience and tenure ($X^2, X^3, X^4, T^2, T^3, T^4$) are estimated from models of within-job wage growth in each occupation. These are not reported separately. Other second-step regressors are as listed in the note to table 4. For union workers, the column labeled "union sector" measures $y''(X, T) = y''(X, 0)$, so it is the wage premium relative to starting a new union job. The column labeled "nonunion sector" measures $y''(X, T) - y''(X, 0)$, so it is the premium relative to a new nonunion job.

Altonji and Shakotko apply an instrumental variables procedure to a model like (1). They note that the deviation of job tenure from its observed, job-specific average is orthogonal to factors that are fixed within a job. If job effects are not time varying ($\phi_{ijt} - \phi_{ij}$), then $\Sigma(T_{ijt} - \overline{T}_{ij})(\phi_{ij} + \mu_i) = 0$, and so $DT_{ijt} = T_{ijt} - \overline{T}_{ij}$ is a valid instrumental variable.[21] They

---

[21] The preceding evidence that the evolution of the wage within jobs follows a random walk is not consistent with fixed job effects unless the entire random walk component occurs in general human capital.

therefore estimate a version of (1) by instrumental variables, using $Z = (X, DT)$ as instruments. It turns out that this instrumental variables estimator is a variant of the two-step procedure outlined above, which facilitates comparison. Let $W = (X, T)$, so the instrumental variables estimator of (1) is $(\hat{\beta}_1^{IV}, \hat{\beta}_2^{IV})' = (Z'W)^{-1}Z'y$. When these moments are written out, some algebra establishes that

$$\hat{B}^{IV} = \left(T'D'DT\right)^{-1}T'D'Dy, \tag{15a}$$

$$\hat{\beta}_1^{IV} = \left(X'X_0\right)^{-1}X'\left(Y - T\hat{B}^{IV}\right). \tag{15b}$$

Notice that (15a) is simply the least-squares estimator of $B = \beta_1 + \beta_2$ using deviations from within-job means rather than wage changes as a first-step model. This estimator of B is consistent when there are fixed job effects. The estimator of β_1 in (15b) is equivalent to using $X \equiv X_0 + T$ as an instrument for X_0 in the second-step model (7). Given a consistent estimator $\hat{B}$ of B, this instrumental variables procedure is equivalent to the test used above for the importance of individual effects. Straightforward calculations yield

$$E\hat{\beta}_1^{IV} = E\hat{\beta}_1^{ts} + \left(\frac{\gamma_{XT}}{1 - \gamma_{XT}} - \gamma_{X_0T}\right)(b_1 + b_2), \tag{16}$$

where β_1^{ts} is the second-step estimator of β_1 found by applying least squares to (7), and γ_{XT} and γ_{X_0T} are the least-squares coefficients from regressions of tenure (T) on X and X_0, respectively. Empirically, $\gamma_{XT} = .50$ and $\gamma_{X_0T} = -.25$. Since $b_1 + b_2 > 0$, this means that the instrumental variables procedure produces a greater upward bias in the return to experience and, so, a greater downward bias in the return to tenure. This is one reason for the small tenure effects estimated by Altonji and Shakotko.

A second reason for our different results is measurement error in recorded job tenure. As I noted earlier, job tenure in the PSID contains a large number of inconsistencies. For individuals used here, within-job, year-to-year changes in recorded job tenure range from -31 years to 7.5 years, and 36 percent of all changes in tenure fall below the theoretical value of 1.0. Because tenure is recorded in intervals, many jobs last several years with no change in reported tenure. This measurement error is magnified when within-job changes in tenure are used to estimate parameters of wage growth, so that estimated values of $\beta_1 + \beta_2$ will be biased down. In fact, the measurement error problem is so serious that reasonable estimates of the parameters of wage growth cannot be derived from the uncorrected data.

A final reason for the difference in our findings is that I use different methods to control for aggregate changes in real wages. As noted earlier, my estimates are based on wage data that are deflated by a real wage index calculated from cross sections of the CPS. This means that wages in different years are expressed in comparable units. In contrast, Altonji and Shakotko control for changes in real wages by including a time trend in their regressions. If aggregate wage growth is truly linear and if cross sections of the panel are random samples of the population at each point in time, then this method is appropriate. Then because experience, tenure, and time change at the same rate during a job, within-job wage growth provides an estimate of $\beta_1 + \beta_2 + \beta_t$, where β_t is the trend rate of growth of aggregate wages. Comparison of average sample wage *levels* over time identifies β_t separately. Problems arise if the average "quality" of the sample improves through time; the data indicate that this is the case in the PSID. Then the average sample wage grows during the panel even if $\beta_t = 0$, causing β_t to be overestimated. This causes an additional downward bias in estimated returns to job tenure because $\hat{\beta}_2 = (\beta_1 + \beta_2 + \beta_t) - \hat{\beta}_1 - \hat{\beta}_t$.

Table 6 documents each of these points. Column 1 of the table reproduces the basic findings of Altonji and Shakotko, using the uncorrected PSID data on current job tenure, as well as their instrumental variables procedure and specification. For these estimates, all terms in job tenure, such as T^2, are instrumented by deviations from within-job means, for example, $T^2 - \bar{T}^2$, but the levels of all terms in experience, such as X and X^2, are treated as exogenous. The estimates confirm the small return to job tenure that was found by Altonji and Shakotko. Column 2 reproduces this specification in the corrected data, where tenure rises by one in each year of a job. In these data, estimated returns are more substantial: at 20 years of seniority the cumulative return from the corrected tenure data is roughly triple the estimate from the error-ridden data, though still smaller than in the two-step procedure set out above.

Column 3 takes the next step, replacing current experience with initial experience in the list of instrumental variables. Since higher-order terms in experience are also endogenous, they are also instrumented by deviations from job-specific means. For example, $X^2 - \bar{X}^2$ serves as an instrument for X^2. With fixed job effects, this means that the effects of higher-order terms in experience and tenure are consistently estimated. With this adjustment in the instrument list, estimated returns are larger still. Finally, column 4 drops the endogenous time trend from the list of instrumental variables, which results in estimated returns that are roughly equivalent to those produced by the two-step method employed above. This is not surprising since (18) indicates that the instrumental variables specification is essentially equivalent to a two-step procedure.

In contrast, the very small effects of seniority estimated by Abraham and Farber (1987) are caused solely by differences in methodology. They argue that completed tenure (the ultimate duration of the job) is a good proxy for unobserved dimensions of job or worker quality when either good jobs survive or able persons are less mobile. Since completed duration is unobserved for most observations in available panel data (the data end during each person's last observed job, which tends to be his longest), they fill in "expected" completed job tenure for censored observations based on the frequency of job endings in the data. Call the ultimate estimate of completed duration $T^* = T^L + R$, where T^L is the last observed job tenure for a particular job and R is the predicted residual life of the job (= 0 for uncensored spells).

TABLE 6

EFFECTS OF MEASUREMENT ERROR AND ALTERNATIVE INSTRUMENTAL VARIABLES
ON THE ESTIMATED RETURN TO JOB TENURE

Basic Instruments	Original Tenure Data: $(X, T - \bar{T}, \text{Time})$ (1)	Corrected Tenure Data		
		$(X, T - \bar{T}, \text{Time})$ (2)	$(X^0, T - \bar{T}, \text{Time})$ (3)	$(X^0, T - \bar{T})$ (4)
Main effect of job tenure (β_2)	.030 (.007)	.032 (.006)	.035 (.007)	.045 (.007)
Cumulative returns at tenure:				
5 years	.078 (.0206)	.098 (.017)	.121 (.019)	.155 (.021)
10 years	.074 (.025)	.122 (.024)	.177 (.022)	.223 (.025)
15 years	.052 (.031)	.131 (.028)	.211 (.020)	.264 (.024)
20 years	.052 (.039)	.161 (.035)	.252 (.018)	.316 (.024)

Note: The basic specification is identical to that in earlier tables. Other instruments are as follows. In all models: $T^2 - \bar{T}^2, T^3 - \bar{T}^3, T^4 - \bar{T}^4$, education, union membership, disability, residence in an SMSA, census region, and married. In cols. 1 and 2: X^2, X^3, and X^4. In cols. 3 and 4: $X^2 - \bar{X}^2, X^3 - \bar{X}^3, X^4 - \bar{X}^4$.

The procedure they propose for estimating β_2 is to include T^* as a regressor in an augmented version of (1):

$$y_{ijt} = X_{ijt}\beta_1 + T_{ijt}\beta_2 + T_{ij}^*\theta + \xi_{ijt}^1. \tag{17}$$

Intuitively, T^* is meant to capture the effects of unobservables, ϕ and μ, and so to reduce the bias in the least-squares estimate of β_2. Again if $\bar{T}_{ij}$ denotes the average observed value of tenure on job j, (17) is equivalent to

$$y = X_0\beta_1 + (T - \bar{T})(\beta_1 + \beta_2) + \bar{T}(\beta_1 + \beta_2) + T^*\theta + \xi^1. \tag{18}$$

Least squares applied to (17) is equivalent to estimating (18) and imposing the restriction that the coefficients on $T - \bar{T}$ and $\bar{T}$ be identical. Notice that $X_0 \equiv X - T$ and $\bar{T}$ are fixed within a job, so $T - \bar{T}$ is orthogonal to both of them by construction. Thus estimates of (18) *without* the implied parameter restriction will yield a consistent estimate of $\beta_1 + \beta_2$ in the case of fixed job effects. But the selection problem being addressed is that job-specific variables such as $\bar{T}$ will be correlated with the unobservables, so the least-squares estimate of $\beta_1 + \beta_2$ multiplying $\bar{T}$ will be biased. Thus imposing the cross-parameter restriction implicit in (17) yields an inconsistent estimator of $\beta_1 + \beta_2$.[22]

The evidence on these points is presented in table 7. For purposes of comparison, the models in table 7 include only a quadratic in experience and only a linear effect of tenure, which is the functional form used by Abraham and Farber.[23] Because the estimated residual life of a job is a (nonlinear) function of the observables,[24] I also report estimates that control for the *observed* completed duration of a job, T^L, plus the interaction of T^L with an indicator that is one for jobs that censor at the end of the panel. Column 1 reports least-squares estimates, while columns 2 and 4 report the restricted estimates that include measures of completed tenure in the regression. The unrestricted models that are not subject to the bias just described are in columns 3 and 5. These estimates are derived by applying (18) and solving for β_2 from estimates of $\beta_1 + \beta_2$ and β_1.

The estimates in columns 2 and 4 are qualitatively the same as those produced by Abraham and Farber, showing negligible effects of tenure in comparison to column 1. Columns 3 and 5 show that the implicit restrictions in columns 2 and 4 are decisively rejected, however, and that relaxing these restrictions changes the results. In these models, $\beta_1 + \beta_2$ is consistently estimated and the estimated return to seniority is of the same magnitude as the least-squares estimate in column 1. The effect of completed job tenure is larger than in columns 2 and 4 as well. Thus the estimates are consistent with the notion that good jobs last longer, in the sense that long jobs pay high wages throughout;

---

[22] This inconsistency is a short panel bias caused by the fact that the PSID (and other data sources) contains incomplete longitudinal histories. To see this, let T^0 be the first observed value of tenure on a job ($T^0 = 0$ for jobs that begin during the panel). Then $\bar{T} = (T^0 + T^L)/2$. Substitute this and $T^* = T^L + R$ into (18), yielding

$$y = X_0\beta_1 + (T - \bar{T})B + T^L(\theta + .5B) + R\theta + .5T^0B + \xi^1. \tag{19}$$

Again, T^L, R, and T^0 are fixed within jobs, and they are orthogonal to $T - \bar{T}$ by construction. According to the theory that motivates this approach, they will be correlated with the unobservables because of mobility decisions, so the restricted estimate of B will be inconsistent. With complete longitudinal histories, this source of bias vanishes because $T^0 = R = 0$ when the beginning and end of each job are observed. In this case, least-squares estimation of (19) is equivalent to a two-step procedure given by the deviations from means estimator of B and

$$y - T\hat{B} = X_0\beta_1 + T^L\theta + \xi^2. \tag{20}$$

Equation (20) is in the form of the second-step model (7), augmented by the proxy variable T^L. If T^L is a positive predictor of the unobservables ($\theta > 0$) and more durable jobs occur later in careers ($\text{cov}[X_0, T^L] > 0$), then inclusion of T^L in the model will reduce the upward bias in estimating β_1 and raise the estimated return to seniority.

[23] Basic conclusions are unchanged for less restrictive functional forms.

[24] To model job endings, I estimated a discrete time proportional hazards model in which the hazard rate is $\lambda = \exp(Z\gamma)$, and Z includes the full vector of regressors used in the wage models. The estimates are available on request.

TABLE 7

LEAST-SQUARES MODELS CONDITIONING ON (ESTIMATED) COMPLETED JOB TENURE, PSID WHITE MALES

	(1)	(2)	(3)	(4)	(5)
Experience	.0418	.0379	.0345	.0397	.0401
	(.0013)	(.0014)	(.0015)	(.0013)	(.0014)
Experience^2	−.00079	−.00069	−.00072	−.00074	−.00073
	(.00003)	(.000032)	(.000069)	(.000030)	(.000069)
Tenure	.0138	−.0015	.0137	.0060	.0163
	(.00052)	(.0015)	(.0038)	(.00073)	(.0038)
Imputed completed tenure	...	...	...	.0053	.0067
				(.00036)	(.00042)
Observed completed tenure	...	.0165	.0316	...	...
		(.0016)	(.0022)		
✕ censor	...	−.0025	−.0024	...	...
		(.00073)	(.00073)		
$\overline{\text{Experience}^2}$	...	...	−.00061	...	−.00075
			(.000036)		(.000033)
$\overline{\text{Tenure}}$	...	...	.0142	...	.0429
			(.0033)		(.0016)
R^2	.422	.428	.432	.433	.435

Note: See note to table 4 for other regressors. Dependent variable is log average hourly earnings. Standard errors are in parentheses. Cols. 2 and 4 implement versions of the restricted model given by eq. (17). Estimates in cols. 3 and 5 are based on the unrestricted model (18).

yet this fact does not reduce the estimated returns to seniority. As above, the returns to job seniority are substantial.

The main reason for this difference in results is a severe underestimate of within-job wage growth from the restricted model: evaluated at the sample mean level of experience (18.4 years), the restricted estimates in column 4 yield a predicted annual rate of wage growth of only 1.9 percent.[25] The corresponding estimate from column 5 is 3.0 percent. The reason for the bias is apparent from the estimated impact of $\overline{T}$, which is a biased estimate of $\beta_1 + \beta_2$. For example, in column 3, this estimate is .0142, compared to an unrestricted estimate of .0345 + .0137 = .0482. Thus the restricted estimates of $\beta_1 + \beta_2$ are biased down because they combine these two effects. This underestimate of within-job growth accounts for most of the lost value of β_2 in the restricted model.

---

[25] The corresponding estimate from Abraham and Farber (1987) is 1.7 percent.

VI. CONCLUSION

The idea that compensation rises with job tenure or seniority is the most fundamental prediction of the theory of specific human capital. It is also a key prediction of other contracting models in which the timing of compensation over the life of a job plays a strategic role in recruiting and motivating employees. Estimates of the return to seniority based on survey data have tended to support this class of theories, though these estimates have ignored potential biases generated by individuals' mobility decisions. Theory provides only limited guidance on the direction of these biases, and virtually none on their importance. When I correct for these biases in longitudinal data, my estimates imply a very strong connection between job seniority and wages in the typical employment relationship: other things constant, 10 years of job seniority raise the wage of the typical worker by over 25 percent. For the procedures that I have used, theory and related evidence suggest that this estimate is a lower bound on the true return to job seniority.

These results conform to several related facts about wages and the durability of jobs. For example, turnover rates are substantially lower among senior workers, even when individual and job-specific factors that affect mobility are controlled for (Topel and Ward 1992), and the typical employment relationship in the United States is remarkably durable (Hall 1982). These observations are difficult to explain in the absence of rising wages and accumulating specific capital. Further, estimates of the "costs" of displacement and unemployment indicate that the wage losses from these events are substantially larger for workers who had held their jobs longer (Carrington 1990; Topel 1990). Results in this paper imply this, but also the period of recovery from an initial wage loss may be fairly short.

These conclusions must be tempered by the fact that tenure measures time only in a particular job and may be only remotely related to the relevant concept of human capital. In one sense this measurement error implies that true returns may be even larger. Yet if human capital is specific to industries or sectors of the economy, and not to jobs, then job tenure may easily capture the returns to the broader concept of human capital, especially when job changes are infrequent. Nevertheless, the evidence presented here offers no support for the view that seniority has a negligible impact on wages.

APPENDIX

The Data

The data used in this study come from the first 16 waves of the Panel Study of Income Dynamics. The sample is restricted to white male heads of households who had positive earnings during the previous calendar year and who were between the ages of 18 and 60 at the survey date. Persons from Alaska and Hawaii were excluded. Jobs were excluded if the respondent reported that he was self-employed at any time during the job, if he worked for the government, if he reported agricultural employment, or if the observation came from the poverty subsample of the PSID. Finally, since wages refer to average hourly earnings in the year preceding the survey, observations for which current job tenure was less than 1 year were deleted. Other exclusions based on reported job tenure are described below.

Job tenure is the key variable in the analysis. Measured job tenure in the data is often recorded in wide intervals, and a large number of observations are lost because tenure is missing. Further, a large number of inconsistencies occur in the data. For example, reported tenure may fall by 10 years or more between years of a single job, and periods of missing tenure are followed by years in which a respondent reports more than 20 years of seniority for the remainder of the job. In the recorded tenure data, the year-to-year changes in job tenure range from −31 years to 7.5 years. In 324 cases (3.8 percent), measured tenure declines between years of a job, and in 51 cases the decline is greater than 5 years. Because tenure is recorded in intervals, 36 percent of all year-to-year changes in tenure fall below the theoretical value of 1.0.

In light of these errors, I reconstructed job tenure as follows. For jobs that begin in the panel, tenure is started at zero and incremented by one for each year in which a person works. Thus experience and tenure progress at the same rate. For jobs that were in progress at the beginning of a person's record, I gauged starting tenure relative to the period in which the person achieved his maximum reported tenure on a job. Again, tenure and experience increment by one for each year in which the person works.

Even with this procedure, there are many ambiguities about starting and ending dates of jobs. In many cases, the recorded sequence of job tenures seems to indicate a job change (e.g., tenure falls to zero and then rises smoothly for the remainder of the job, or the worker indicates unemployment due to a permanent layoff), though no change of employer is recorded in the data. I considered a large number of such circumstances generated by numerous cross-checks on the data. Basically, I deleted all jobs for which significant ambiguities occurred. In practice, these deletions had very minor effects on the results and none on the conclusions.

All the sample selection criteria are documented in the programs and output underlying this research. These are available at cost. Summary statistics are reported in table A1.

TABLE A1

VARIABLE DEFINITIONS AND SUMMARY STATISTICS, PSID WHITE MALES, 1968–83

Variable	Definition	Mean	Standard Deviation
Real wage	Log average hourly earnings deflated by CPS wage index and GNP price deflator	1.131	.497
Experience	Years in labor market	20.021	11.045
Tenure	Years of current job seniority	9.978	8.944
Education	Years of completed schooling	12.645	2.809
Married	1 if currently married, spouse present	.925	.263
Union	1 if union member	.344	.473
SMSA	1 if resides in SMSA	.644	.478
Disabled	1 if currently reporting disability	.074	.262

Survey Year	Percentage of Sample	CPS Real Wage Index
1968	.052	1.000
1969	.050	1.032
1970	.051	1.091
1971	.053	1.115
1972	.057	1.113

TABLE A1 (CONTINUED)

Survey Year	Percentage of Sample	CPS Real Wage Index
1973	.058	1.151
1974	.060	1.167
1975	.061	1.188
1976	.065	1.117
1977	.065	1.121
1978	.069	1.133
1979	.071	1.128
1980	.073	1.128
1981	.072	1.109
1982	.071	1.103
1983	.068	1.089

REFERENCES

Abraham, Katharine G., and Farber, Henry S. "Job Duration, Seniority, and Earnings." *A.E.R.* 77 (June 1987): 278–97.

Altonji, Joseph G., and Shakotko, Robert A. "Do Wages Rise with Job Seniority?" *Rev. Econ. Studies* 54 (July 1987): 437–59.

Becker, Gary S. *Human Capital: A Theoretical and Empirical Analysis, with Special Reference to Education.* New York: Columbia Univ. Press (for NBER), 1964.

Becker, Gary S., and Stigler, George J. "Law Enforcement, Malfeasance, and Compensation of Enforcers." *J. Legal Studies* 3 (January 1974): 1–18.

Borjas, George J., and Rosen, Sherwin. "Income Prospects and Job Mobility of Young Men." In *Research in Labor Economics,* vol. 3, edited by Ronald G. Ehrenberg. Greenwich, Conn.: JAI, 1980.

Brown, James N. "Why Do Wages Increase with Tenure? On-the-Job Training and Life-Cycle Wage Growth Observed within Firms." *A.E.R.* 79 (December 1989): 971–91.

Burdett, Kenneth. "A Theory of Employee Job Search and Quit Rates." *A.E.R.* 68 (March 1978): 212–20.

Carrington, William. "Specific Human Capital and Worker Displacement." Ph.D. dissertation, Univ. Chicago, 1990.

Doeringer, Peter B., and Piore, Michael J. *Internal Labor Markets and Manpower Analysis.* Lexington, Mass.: Heath, 1971.

Freeman, Smith. "Wage Trends as Performance Displays Productive Potential: A Model and Application to Academic Early Retirement." *Bell J. Econ.* 8 (Autumn 1977): 419–43.

Hall, Robert E. "The Importance of Lifetime Jobs in the U.S. Economy." *A.E.R.* 72 (September 1982): 716–24.

Harris, Milton, and Holmstrom, Bengt. "A Theory of Wage Dynamics." *Rev. Econ. Studies* 49 (July 1982): 315–33.

Heckman, James J. "The Common Structure of Statistical Models of Truncation, Sample Selection and Limited Dependent Variables and a Simple Estimator for Such Models." *Ann. Econ. and Soc. Measurement* 5 (Fall 1976): 475–92.

Jovanovic, Boyan. "Firm-specific Capital and Turnover." *J.P.E.* 87 (December 1979): 1246–60. (*a*)

———. "Job Matching and the Theory of Turnover." *J.P.E.* 87, no. 5, pt. 1 (October 1979): 972–90. (*b*)

———. "Matching, Turnover, and Unemployment." *J.P.E.* 92 (February 1984): 108–22.

Lang, Kevin. "Reinterpreting the Return to Seniority." Manuscript. Boston: Boston Univ., November 1987.

Lazear, Edward P. "Agency, Earnings Profiles, Productivity, and Hours Restrictions." *A.E.R.* 71 (September 1981): 606–20.

Lazear, Edward P., and Rosen, Sherwin. "Rank-Order Tournaments as Optimum Labor Contracts." *J.P.E.* 89 (October 1981): 841–64.

Lewis, H. Gregg. *Union Relative Wage Effects: A Survey.* Chicago: Univ. Chicago Press, 1986.

Marshall, Robert C., and Zarkin, Gary A. "The Effect of Job Tenure on Wage Offers." *J. Labor Econ.* 5 (July 1987): 301–24.

Mincer, Jacob. "Wage Changes in Job Changes." In *Research in Labor Economics,* vol. 8, pt. A, edited by Ronald G. Ehrenberg. Greenwich, Conn.: JAI, 1986.

———. "Job Training, Wage Growth and Labor Turnover." Manuscript. New York: Columbia Univ., 1988.

Mincer, Jacob, and Jovanovic, Boyan. "Labor Mobility and Wages." In *Studies in Labor Markets,* edited by Sherwin Rosen. Chicago: Univ. Chicago Press (for NBER), 1981.

Mortensen, Dale T. "Matching: Finding a Partner for Life or Otherwise." *American J. Sociology* 94 (suppl., 1988): S215–S240. (*a*)

———. "Wages, Separations, and Job Tenure: On-the-Job Specific Training or Matching?" *J. Labor Econ.* 6 (October 1988): 445–71. (*b*)

Murphy, Kevin M., and Topel, Robert H. "Estimation and Inference in Two-Step Econometric Models." *J. Bus. and Econ. Statis.* 3 (October 1985): 370–79.

Murphy, Kevin M., and Welch, Finis. "The Structure of Wages." Manuscript. Chicago: Univ. Chicago, 1987. [Published in *Q.J.E.* 107 (February 1992): 285–326.]

Rosen, Sherwin. "Prizes and Incentives in Elimination Tournaments." *A.E.R.* 76 (September 1986): 701–15.

———. "Transactions Costs and Internal Labor Markets." *J. Law, Econ., and Organization* 4 (Spring 1988): 49–64.

Salop, Joanne, and Salop, Steven. "Self-Selection and Turnover in the Labor Market." *Q.J.E.* 90 (November 1976): 619–27.

Shleifer, Andrei, and Summers, Lawrence H. "Breach of Trust in Hostile Takeovers." In *Corporate Takeovers: Causes and Consequences,* edited by Alan J. Auerbach. Chicago: Univ. Chicago Press (for NBER), 1988.

Topel, Robert H. "Job Mobility, Search, and Earnings Growth: A Reinterpretation of Human Capital Earnings Functions." In *Research in Labor Economics,* vol. 8, pt. A, edited by Ronald G. Ehrenberg. Greenwich, Conn.: JAI, 1986.

———. "Specific Capital, Mobility, and Wages: Wages Rise with Job Seniority." Working Paper no. 3294. Cambridge, Mass.: NBER, March 1990.

———. "Specific Capital and Unemployment: Measuring the Costs and Consequences of Worker Displacement." *Carnegie-Rochester Conf. Ser. Public Policy* (1990), vol. 33, 181–214.

Topel, Robert H., and Ward, Michael. "Job Mobility and the Careers of Young Men." *Q.J.E.* 107 (May 1992): 441–79.

Welch, Finis. "Effects of Cohort Size on Earnings: The Baby Boom Babies' Financial Bust." *J.P.E.* 87, no. 5, pt. 2 (October 1979): S65–S98.

ABOUT THE AUTHOR

Robert H. Topel

Bob Topel is one of a small number of economists to emerge in the early 1980s fully equipped with theoretical and empirical tools, along with substantive interests sufficient to advance the frontiers of modern labor economics. Following the burst of enthusiasm and intellectual interest that the human capital theme attracted with its introduction in the 1950s and early 1960s, labor economics steadily developed into a mature field where the majority of the intellectual interest was absorbed in dotting i's in theory and in econometric methodology. During this period, substance and originality gave ground to "rigor" and "elegance."

Then, along came Bob! The tools easily passed muster, but there was also a difference. Bob Topel was not a tool kit in search of an application; rather, he was and is an economist with a keen interest in the world about him and with the brains and energy necessary to learn and, in turn, to educate. His first and abiding interest is unemployment, and he, more than any other, has taught us that it is neither the worst thing that can happen nor as simple as the order statistics of sequential search. Rather, most of what we see is just part of the ordinary happenings of exploration and adjusting over business and life cycles.

Bob is not monothematic. In addition to his work on unemployment, there is excellent work concerning local labor markets. The work on the effects of immigration on wages and employment of native workers is as good as it gets, and there are a few simple "data" papers concerning the collection of survey information. His paper with Mike Ward on "Job Mobility and the Careers of Young Men" in the *Quarterly Journal of Economics,* 1992, is a must. Although his achievements are impressive, he is only at midcareer. We can expect to continue to read and to learn from Bob.

Bob Topel received his B.A. from the University of California, Santa Barbara, and his 1980 Ph.D. from UCLA. With the exception of a one-year sojourn to UCLA, he has spent his professional career at the University of Chicago. He currently holds the Isidore Brown and Gladys J. Brown Professorship in Urban and Labor Economics in the Graduate School of Business, University of Chicago.

Economics

Labor Economics

Labor Economics

Economics

LABOR DEMAND AND SUPPLY

Walter Y. Oi

James Heckman

Edward P. Lazear

Thomas E. MaCurdy

Orley Ashenfelter

Economics

Labor as a Quasi-Fixed Factor

WALTER Y. OI[1]
University of Washington

The cyclical behavior of labor markets reveals a number of puzzling features for which there are no truly satisfying explanations. Included among these are (1) occupational differences in the stability of employment and earnings, (2) the uneven incidence of unemployment, (3) the persistence of differential labor turnover rates, and (4) discriminatory hiring and firing policies. I believe that the major impediment to rational explanations for these phenomena lies in the classical treatment of labor as a purely variable factor.

In this paper I propose a short-run theory of employment which rests on the premise that labor is a quasi-fixed factor. The fixed employment costs arise from investments by firms in hiring and training activities. The theory of labor as a quasi-fixed factor is developed in Part I. In Part II, the implications of this theory are subjected to various empirical tests. Finally, Part III turns to an examination of alternative theories and an extension of my theory to a theory of occupational wage differentials.

The concept of labor as a quasi-fixed factor is, in my opinion, the relevant one for a short-run theory of employment. Its implications are amenable to empirical verification and are, in the main, borne out by the available evidence. Thus my theory provides a unified explanation for various aspects of the cyclical functioning of labor markets.

I. A SHORT-RUN THEORY OF EMPLOYMENT

According to the theory presented here cyclical changes in employment are explained by differential shifts in factor demands and supplies. The first two sections develop a theory of factor demands assuming rigid wage rates. In the next two sections this assumption is relaxed, allowing for variations in factor supplies.

[1]This paper is taken from my unpublished doctoral dissertation "Labor as a Quasi-fixed Factor of Production" (University of Chicago, 1961). I wish to express my indebtedness to Professors A. C. Harberger, H. G. Lewis, and A. E. Rees. A reading of two unpublished articles by Professor Gary S. Becker led me to revise the theory substantially. Financial and clerical assistance from the Social Science Research Council and the Transportation Center, Northwestern University are also gratefully acknowledged.

A. NATURE OF THE CLASSICAL SHORT-RUN ADJUSTMENT PROCESS

In the classical short-run model certain paths of adjustment are barred to the firm. These barriers usually postulate the presence of fixed factors, short-run changes in output being effected by varying only the remaining factors.

Changes in the amount demanded of any factor are composed of two parts: (*a*) response to changes in the rate of output—the scale effect—and (*b*) response to variations in relative factor prices—the substitution effect. With an assumption of rigid wage rates, the substitution effects may be neglected and attention focused on the scale effects.

Consider a firm faced by a decline in product demand. The adjustment process involves a reduction in output accompanied by a decline in the demand for each variable factor. There is no reason to expect that the demands for all variable factors will be decreased by the same proportion. The reduced demands for variable factors lead to an increase in the relative employment of fixed factors. In a sense, the firm now employs too much of the fixed factors and would, therefore, try to substitute fixed factors for variable factors. Consequently, those variable factors that tend to be most substitutable for, or least complementary with, the fixed factors will experience the greatest relative declines in demand due to any given decrease in product demand. The converse holds for an increase in product demand. Thus the variable factors that are most substitutable with the fixed factors will exhibit the greatest relative shifts in factor demands.

B. DEMAND FOR A QUASI-FIXED FACTOR OF PRODUCTION

A quasi-fixed factor is defined as one whose total employment cost is partially variable and partially fixed. In the classical short-run model all factors are classified as either variable or fixed. Each factor may, however, possess a different degree of fixity along some continuum rather than lie at one extreme or the other.

From a firm's viewpoint labor is surely a quasi-fixed factor. The largest part of total labor costs is the variable-wages bill representing payments for a flow of productive services. In addition the firm ordinarily incurs certain fixed employment costs in hiring a specific stock of workers. These fixed employment costs constitute an investment by the firm in its labor force. As such, they introduce an element of capital in the use of labor. Decisions regarding the labor input can no longer be based solely on the current relation between wages and marginal value products but must also take cognizance of the future course of these quantities. The theoretical implications of labor's fixity will be analyzed before turning to the empirical magnitude of these fixed costs.

For analytic purposes fixed employment costs can be separated into two categories called, for convenience, hiring and training costs. Hiring costs are defined as those costs that have no effect on a worker's productivity and include outlays for recruiting, for processing payroll records, and for supplements such as unemployment compensation. These costs are closely related to the number of new workers and only indirectly related to the flow of labor's services. Training expenses, on the other hand, are investments in the human agent, specifically designed to improve a worker's productivity. The effect of training on productivity could be summarized by a production function showing the increment to a worker's marginal value product in the tth period, ΔM_t, due to an investment in training of K dollars per worker.[2]

$$\Delta M_t = g(K). \tag{1}$$

The total discounted cost, C, of hiring an additional worker is the sum of the present value of expected wage payments, the hiring cost, H, and training expense, K.

$$C = \sum_{t=0}^{T} W_t(1+r)^{-t} + H + K, \tag{2}$$

where W_t is the expected wage in the tth period, r denotes the rate at which future costs are discounted, and T denotes the expected period of employment. The total discounted revenue, Y, generated by the additional worker is similarly defined as the present value of his expected marginal value products that, in each period, consist of his marginal product without training, M_t, and the increment due to his training, ΔM_t.

$$Y = \sum_{t=0}^{T} (M_t + \Delta M_t)(1+r)^{-t}. \tag{3}$$

Profits will be maximized when the total discounted cost of an additional worker is just equal to the total discounted revenue.

$$H + K = \sum_{t=0}^{T} (M_t + \Delta M_t - W_t)(1+r)^{-t}. \tag{4}$$

Equation (4) yields the first implication. In equilibrium a worker's total marginal product, $M_t + \Delta M_t$, must exceed the wage rate, W_t, so long as the firm incurs any fixed employment costs. Even under perfect competition wages would be equated to marginal value products if and only if labor is a completely variable factor.

At this point, a digression on the firm's investment in training is in order. The net value of training to the firm is simply the present value of the expected increment in marginal value product, ΔM_t, due to training.

---

[2] *The training activity typically entails direct money outlays as well as numerous implicit costs such as the allocation of old workers to teaching skills and rejection of unqualified workers during the training period.*

$$V = \sum_{t=0}^{T} \Delta M_t \left(1 + r\right)^{-t}. \tag{5}$$

An investment in training will prove profitable if the net value to the firm, V, exceeds the training expense, K. Conceptually training may be categorized as either general or specific. Specific training is defined as that which increases a worker's productivity to a particular firm without affecting his productivity in alternative employments. The time required to adapt workers to the firm's particular production processes, or to its accounting and marketing processes, exemplifies specific training. General training, on the other hand, is defined as that which increases a worker's productivity in several competing employments, as, for example, the training of workers to operate computers or to read railroad tariffs.

Rational behavior implies that the bulk of a firm's investment in training must be devoted to specific training. If training were completely general, all returns would accrue to the worker and none to the firm. Upon completion of general training, the worker would find that his marginal productivity to several firms has been increased. He could now demand a higher wage, either from a competing firm or from his present employer. In either case, the net value of the training to the firm would be reduced to zero. Indeed, a firm could capture these returns only if there were impediments to competition such as imperfect knowledge or binding labor contracts. Thus, no rational firm would underwrite completely general training.[3] If, however, training is specific to a firm, then the worker's alternative marginal product remains unaffected. In this latter case, the firm could weigh the expected returns from this investment against the training cost. To simplify the analysis, I shall assume that the firm bears all specific training costs. As will be shown in section D below, the implications of the theory are not seriously affected by relaxing this assumption.

Returning to the equilibrium condition, it is clear that some expectations model must be formulated since the variables refer to future quantities. Suppose that the firm formulates the following single-valued expectations:

$$W_t = W^*, \, M_t = M^*, \, \Delta M_t = \Delta M^* \qquad (\text{for all } t = 0, \, 1, \, 2, \, \ldots \, T). \tag{6}$$

Substituting these expected values into equation (4), the equilibrium condition reduces to

$$M^* + \Delta M^* = W^* + \frac{H + K}{\sum\limits_{t=0}^{T} \left(1 + r\right)^{-t}} \tag{7}$$

---

[3] *That a firm offers general training to its employees does not necessarily imply that the firm underwrites the general training expense. The worker may bear the training cost by accepting a lower wage than that which he could obtain in some alternative employment.*

The concept of a periodic rent, R, may be defined as

$$R = \frac{H+K}{\sum_{t=0}^{T}(1+r)^{-t}}.$$
(8)

The periodic rent represents the fixed employment costs during each period. It is the surplus that must be earned by each worker in order to amortize the initial fixed employment costs over the expected period of employment, realizing a rate of return of r per cent on this investment. Thus, the equilibrium condition may be rewritten as

$$M^* + \Delta M^* = W^* + R.$$
(9)

In equilibrium, the total expected marginal value product must exceed the expected wage rate by the amount of the periodic rent. The degree of fixity, f, of a factor will be defined as the ratio of the periodic rent, R, to the total employment cost, $W^* + R$. A value of zero corresponds to a completely variable factor while the degree of fixity, f, of a completely fixed factor is designated by a value of unity.

The periodic rent drives a wedge between the wage rate and the marginal value product, the relative magnitude of the wedge being measured by the degree of fixity. In the short run, any fixed employment costs associated with the acquisition of a labor force in prior periods are sunk costs; as such they should not affect a firm's short-run decisions.

Suppose that the firm is initially in a position of long-run equilibrium; that is, the equilibrium condition, equation (9), is satisfied by every factor or grade of labor. For a competitive firm, a decline in product demand is equivalent to a fall in product price, P^*.[4] The relevant comparison for short-run profit maximization is that between total expected marginal value product and the expected wage rate, representing the variable component of the total employment cost. Thus the short-run equilibrium condition applicable to cyclical declines in product demands becomes

$$M^* + \Delta M^* = W^*.$$
(10)

The employment of a quasi-fixed factor will only be reduced when $M^* + \Delta M^*$ falls below W^*.

For a completely variable factor, the long- and short-run equilibrium conditions, (9) and (10), are equivalent. Any decline in P^* will reduce the demand for a variable factor; with falling employment, the variable factor's marginal physical product will be increased

---

[4] The term, $M^* + \Delta M^*$, in eq. (9) denotes the expected marginal value product. For a competitive firm, this is simply the expected product price, P^*, times the expected marginal physical product, $X^* + \Delta X^*$.

until the equilibrium conditions are again satisfied. The decline in P^* may not be sufficient, however, to warrant a reduction in the demand for some other factor with a higher degree of fixity. In fact, there is, for each quasi-fixed factor, a critical price at which the firm will reduce its demand for that factor. Furthermore, the critical price, in relation to the long-run equilibrium price, will be lower for factors with higher degrees of fixity. Thus, a given decline in P^* may induce a reduction in demand for factors with low degrees of fixity without affecting the demand for factors with higher degrees of fixity.

Consider next, the case of an increase in P^*. Beginning at an initial position of long-run equilibrium, there is no reason to expect differential shifts in demand for factors with varying degrees of fixity. Alternatively, in the initial position, the firm may have adjusted to a prior decline in P^*. Specifically, assume that the short-run equilibrium condition, (10), is satisfied by each quasi-fixed factor. The demand for a factor will be increased if its total marginal product, $M^* + \Delta M^*$, exceeds its total expected employment cost, $W^* + R$. In this latter case, the argument is completely analogous to that for a decline in P^*. Each quasi-fixed factor again has its unique critical price at which the demand for it will be increased; these critical prices will be higher for factors with greater degrees of fixity. Thus, a given increase in P^* leads to greater relative shifts in demand for the factors with the lower degrees of fixity.

Up to now, changes in P^* have been treated as if they were known with certainty. The introduction of uncertainty about future product prices reinforces the argument. Suppose that a firm makes appropriate adjustments in factor employments in response to an increase in P^*. If the subsequent increase in actual product prices is less than the expected increase, the firm will be obliged to reduce employment. The readjustment due to an error in forecasting product demand necessarily shortens the expected period of employment, thereby increasing the magnitude of the ex post periodic rent.[5] The costs of these readjustments are greater for factors with higher degrees of fixity since the periodic rent comprises a larger share of the total employment costs for these factors. Conversely, consider the case where a reduction in the quantity employed of some factor is greater than that warranted by the subsequent decline in actual prices. The readjustment in this case involves the reemployment of that factor, with additional outlays for hiring and training. One might argue that the firm will simply recall those workers who were previously laid off, thereby avoiding the hiring and training expenses. The Bureau of Labor Statistics data on accessions for the period 1953–58 reveal that only 39 per cent of total accessions in the manufacturing sector were recalls. Even in this case, readjustments are costlier for factors with higher degrees of fixity since the firm cannot be assured that workers who were laid off will be available for recall. If a readjustment in factor employments is

---

[5] *A reduction in the expected period of employment, T, increases the periodic rent, R, since the initial fixed employment cost of H + K dollars must be amortized over a smaller number of periods. From equation (8), the elasticity of R with respect to T is found to be negative, independent of H + K, and less than one in absolute value.*

required by the subsequent course of actual prices, it will be preferable to make these readjustments in the employment of factors with low degrees of fixity. Such a policy will tend to minimize the costs of readjustments (reversals) in factor employments due to discrepancies between actual and expected product prices.[6]

In summary, certain fixed employment costs are associated with the employment of labor. Firms may invest in hiring—to acquire particular workers—or in specific training to improve labor's productivity. The periodic rent, representing the amortization of these fixed employment costs, drives a wedge between the marginal value product and the wage rate. The relative magnitude of this wedge, measured by the degree of fixity, differs among occupations or grades of labor. In a sense, the periodic rent forms a buffer absorbing short-run variations in a factor's marginal value product. Thus, short-run changes in product demands lead to differential shifts in factor demands, depending on the degree of fixity. Factors with lower degrees of fixity will experience relatively greater shifts in demand as the result of any given short-run change in product demand.

C. SHORT-RUN FACTOR SUPPLIES

In the preceding sections all factor supplies were assumed to be infinitely elastic at fixed market wage rates. This assumption is surely reasonable for a single competitive firm. The supply curve of labor as a whole or of certain skill categories may, however, be less than infinitely elastic or may shift over time. This section deals with the effect of variations in short-run factor supplies on relative factor employments.

Consider the extreme case in which all factor supplies have zero elasticity and markets adjust rapidly. In a downswing, the demand for labor shifts to the left, the percentage shift being smaller for factors with higher degrees of fixity. The downward shifts in demand lead to reductions in wage rates only; factor employments are determined exogenously by the assumed supply conditions. The relative decline in wage rates will be smaller for factors with higher degrees of fixity. This case is, however, inconsistent with the emergence of involuntary unemployment and may be dismissed as unrealistic.

Granted the existence of involuntary unemployment in cyclical downswings, the relevance of the concept of a market supply curve becomes highly questionable. If all factor demands have the same wage-rate elasticity, and if all wages fall by the same proportion, the ultimate decline in the employment of high fixity labor will still be less than the decline in the employment of labor with lower degrees of fixity. On the other hand, if the elasticity of demand and/or the relative fall in wages are greater for labor with lower degrees of fixity, there is a tendency in the opposite direction. This could offset or perhaps even reverse the differential shifts in employment predicted by the fixed-cost hypothesis.

---

[6] *The case where the readjustment involves no reversal in the direction of change in factor employments has not been discussed. This is the case where an increase (or decrease) in employment is less than that warranted by the actual price change. There is no a priori reason why this type of error should lead to differential costs for factors with different degrees of fixity.*

With the exception of the 1929–33 recession, the available evidence suggests a widening of occupational wage differentials in the downswing and a narrowing in the upswing.[7] Even in the 1929–33 recession, the data are consistent with a hypothesis that there was no change in the occupational wage structure. As will be shown in Part II, the wage rate of an occupation is highly correlated with its degree of fixity. Thus, over a cycle, the high-wage occupations with greater degrees of fixity exhibit smaller relative changes in wage rates. Finally, I suspect that the high-wage, skilled jobs tend to be most complementary with the fixed factor, capital. *Ceteris paribus,* greater complementarity with the fixed factor implies a lower elasticity of demand. The evidence thus indicates smaller relative changes in wage rates and lower elasticities of demand for factors with higher degrees of fixity. The observed short-run variations in factor supplies therefore predict differential shifts in employment contrary to those implied by the fixed-cost hypothesis.

D. SPECIFICITY OF LABOR TO A FIRM

The provision of specific training alters the labor input. Labor no longer represents an anonymous variable factor but rather a differentiated stream of services from certain workers who have received specific training. These workers are, in a sense, specific to the firm.

In section B, I tacitly assumed that each factor received a wage equal to its marginal productivity in alternative employments. Since a worker's alternative marginal product is unaffected by specific training, competitive wages should not affect the expected period of employment. Examination of equation (5), however, shows that the net value of specific training is increased by an extension of the expected period of employment. Consequently, it behooves a firm to initiate practices that tend to minimize the turnover of specifically trained workers.

Policies aimed at this goal are exemplified by pension and profit-sharing plans, provision of better working conditions, promotion from within, and payment of wage premiums. Under some profit-sharing plans, workers forfeit all benefits unless they remain with the firm for a specified period of time. Firms may also adopt discriminatory hiring policies, hiring only those workers who possess characteristics associated with long employment tenure.

A wage policy of paying premiums to specifically trained workers may prove mutually profitable for both workers and firm. Consider the analysis of section B where the incidence of all training expenses falls on the firm, with workers bearing none of the costs. In this case, a wage premium is clearly profitable for the worker and should encourage longer periods of employment. From the firm's viewpoint, the payment of a wage premium affects total employment costs in two opposing ways. First, the wage premium

---

[7] *Phillip W. Bell, "Cyclical Variations and Trends in Occupational Wage Differentials in American Industries Since 1914," Review of Economics and Statistics, XXXIII, No. 4 (November, 1954), 329–37.*

increases the present value of expected wage payments. Second, if the wage premium induces longer employment tenure, the initial fixed employment costs can be amortized over a larger number of periods, thereby reducing the periodic rent. Such a wage policy would be profitable for the firm if the following inequality holds:

$$
\frac{\Delta W}{W} \le \left(\frac{R}{W}\right) \frac{\sum_{t=T+1}^{T+k} (1+r)^{-t}}{\sum_{t=0}^{T+k} (1+r)^{-t}}. \tag{11}
$$

The equality in (11) indicates the maximum relative wage premium, $\Delta W/W$, consistent with an induced increase in the period of employment of k periods. For a given increment of k periods the maximum relative wage premium will be larger for factors with higher degrees of fixity or with lower initial expected periods of employment. If the equality in (11) applies, the added wage costs would just offset the savings to the firm from longer expected periods of employment. If, however, the inequality holds for some factor, that factor does not satisfy the full equilibrium condition given by (9). The expected total marginal product will exceed the expected total employment cost. Hence the firm has an incentive to invest further in specific training. The firm may also choose to pay even higher wage premiums if by doing so it induces an even greater extension in the expected period of employment.

Suppose that a share of the training cost is borne by the worker. During the training period a worker might accept a wage below his alternative marginal product; the difference represents his investment in specific training. The firm could compensate the worker for his investment by promising him a wage premium upon completion of the specific training. If the present value of his expected wage premiums exceeds his share of the training cost, the arrangement would be acceptable to a rational worker. Consider the extreme case in which all specific training costs are paid by the worker.[8] The worker clearly prefers to remain with the firm since his marginal product and wages in the specific firm are higher than his alternative marginal product. In this case, however, all labor costs become variable to the firm, and the firm has no motive for retaining these workers during a cyclical downswing.

A sensible policy is to have both parties share the specific training expense. If both workers and firm have made investments in specific training, both can gain from longer expected periods of employment. The specifically trained worker could receive a wage

---

[8] *Firms and workers may differ in their evaluation of expected periods of employment and pertinent discount rates. As a result, the optimum investment per worker in specific training may differ depending on the incidence of these training costs.*

above his alternative marginal product but below his total marginal product to the firm.[9] At the same time, the firm could lower its total employment cost by amortizing the fixed employment costs over a longer period of time. Short-run variations in factor supplies would tend to be smaller for workers who had invested in specific training. Thus the payment of wage premiums and the sharing of the specific training costs promote even greater stability of employment for specifically trained workers.

To sum up, the specificity of labor to a firm favors the establishment of policies to lengthen expected periods of employment. To achieve lower labor turnover, a firm might adopt a policy by which workers were required to share specific training expenses and were rewarded by subsequent wage premiums. Under such a policy, both workers and firm would benefit from lower labor turnover. Finally, the gains from lower labor turnover are greater for factors with higher degrees of fixity. Thus a higher degree of fixity leads not only to greater stability of employment in terms of numbers or man-hours employed but also to lower labor turnover rates.

II. TESTS OF THE THEORY

A. WAGE RATE AS INDEX OF DEGREE OF FIXITY

A direct test of the theory would require estimates of the degree of fixity for different grades of labor. Since such data are not readily available,[10] an auxiliary variable that is closely correlated with the degree of fixity must be employed as a proxy. The use of an occupation's wage rate as the proxy seems justifiable and derives support from the empirical evidence presented in this section.

A study undertaken by the International Harvester Company (hereinafter referred to as "IH") in 1951 estimated fixed employment costs for three job categories.[11] The total fixed cost associated with an annual labor turnover of 28,623 workers was $15.9 million, or roughly 5.4 per cent of total wage payments. The component cost items were placed in three categories. The IH estimates of the amount invested in each new worker are presented in the first four columns of Table 1; my revised estimates appear in the last column.

Hiring costs comprised less than 5 per cent of total fixed costs. They include the costs of terminating, laying off, and recalling since each worker has a positive probability of passing through each stage during his prospective tenure with the firm. The IH study weighted each cost by its relative frequency.

---

[9] *Where training is specific to a firm the situation closely resembles one of bilateral monopoly. From the firm's viewpoint, the specifically trained worker is differentiated from other workers. At the same time, the worker finds that his value to his present employer is higher than his value to some competing employer. I wish to thank Professor Rees for pointing out this analogue.*

[10] *The necessary data include (1) the initial fixed employment cost, H + K, (2) the discount rate, r, (3) the expected period of employment, T, and (4) the expected wage rate, W*.*

[11] *International Harvester Company, "The Costs of Labor Turnover" (mimeographed), 1951.*

TABLE 1

AMOUNT OF MONEY INVESTED PER NEW EMPLOYEE, INTERNATIONAL HARVESTER COMPANY, 1951

Costs	Common Labor	Two-Year Progressive Student	Four-Year Apprentice	IH Average	Revised IH Average
Hiring costs:					
Recruiting	$ 4.33	$ 86.38		$ 5.48	$ 5.48
Hiring	13.23	29.08	$ 28.89	13.23	13.19
Orientation	1.56	1.56	1.56	1.56	1.56
Terminating	3.77	3.77	3.77	3.77	3.77
Laying off	1.21	1.21	1.21	1.21	1.21
Recalling	1.30	1.30	1.30	1.30	1.30
Total	25.40	123.30	36.73	26.55	26.51
Training costs:					
Training	9.08	11,850.00	18,503.00	238.40	151.36
Tools and materials			164.76	41.19	41.19
Unfilled requisitions	14.92			83.12	24.66
Intrawork transfers	3.50			94.14	64.49
Total	27.50	11,850.00	18,667.76	456.85	281.70
Unemployment compensation	73.52	73.52	73.52	73.52	73.52
Total fixed employment cost	126.42	12,046.82	18,778.01	556.92	381.73

Source: International Harvester Company, *op. cit.*

Training cost is by far the major fixed employment cost. Two items under this heading require further explanation. "Unfilled requisitions" refers to the implicit cost of lost output, resulting from the lag between the separation and subsequent replacement of a worker.[12] In the IH study the hourly cost of lost productive time was the gross profits per man-hour of $1.84. I have revised the estimate by assuming that standby, overtime labor is used to recoup any lost productive time; the result is a substantial reduction in this cost item. "Intrawork transfers" represents additional training expenses due to transfers of old workers to new jobs within the plant.

Finally, the cost of unemployment compensation represents the difference between the firm's actual contributions and the minimum legal contributions for unemployment

---

[12] *Supplementary data in the IH study showed an average lag between separation and replacement of 39.1 hours. The lag was longer for jobs with higher skill requirements.*

compensation.[13] Higher labor turnover will, in general, increase a firm's actual contributions.[14] The difference between the actual and minimum legal contributions resembles hiring costs and is therefore included in fixed employment costs.

Each component of total fixed costs appears to rise either at the same rate as the wage rate of a job or faster. The data in Table 1 suggest that the ratio of total fixed employment costs to wage rate increases as one moves to higher wage jobs. If the IH estimates of Table 1 are coupled with some assumptions about wage rates and expected periods of employment, it is possible to estimate degrees of fixity for two overlapping groups of workers. Thus, degrees of fixity of 0.073 and 0.041 were obtained for "All employees" and "Common laborers."[15] The high-wage, highly skilled jobs appear to be associated with higher degrees of fixity. In the subsequent empirical tests I shall assume that an occupation's wage rate serves as an index of the degree of fixity.

B. Cyclical Behavior of Employment by Occupation

During cyclical changes in aggregate employment different rates of change in employment are observed for different occupations even within the same firm. This phenomenon is the subject of the first empirical test of the theory.

The basic proposition of Part I may be stated as follows: those factors with the highest degrees of fixity and the lowest degrees of substitutability with the fixed factor will experience the smallest relative changes in employment due to any given change in product demand. For the empirical test occupational wage differentials are assumed to reflect differences in the degree of fixity. The hypothesis submitted to a test is: "there is no relation between wage rates and the observed rates of change in employment." The alternative hypothesis is that the high-wage occupations will experience smaller rates of change in employment.

The contingency table was chosen as the experimental design for testing the hypothesis. The contingency table tests for the independence of two variables of classification. The χ^2 statistic is the criterion for the acceptance or rejection of the null hypothesis. The occupations in a firm are first divided into two equal groups according to the wage rate of the occupation. The same occupations are again separated, by reference to the observed rates

---

[13]Actual unemployment compensation tax rates differ widely among firms, across states, and over time. For a discussion of these differences the reader is referred to R. A. Lester, "Financing Unemployment Compensation," Industrial and Labor Relations Review, XIV, No. 1 (October, 1960), 52–67.

[14] An exception to this generalization arises if all separated workers immediately obtain new jobs. This is, however, rarely the case.

[15] In arriving at these estimates I assumed expected periods of employment of 24 and 12 months for "All employees" and "Common labor." The discount rate was fixed at 1 per cent per month; variations of ±0.5 per cent had very little effect on the degree of fixity. Finally, the IH study reported average hourly earnings for "All employees" of $1.952 in 1951. This figure was converted to a monthly wage and applied to "All employees." For "Common labor" I arbitrarily fixed an hourly wage of $1.50.

of change in employment over a fixed time interval, into equal groups. All occupations thus fall into the cells of a contingency table where the cells identify groups of occupations with different wages and percentage changes in employment. The marginal totals, which are fixed in advance, determine the number of occupations in each cell to be expected if in fact the null hypothesis is true. The major advantages of the contingency table over alternative test procedures[16] include the following:

1. No assumptions are required about the joint probability distribution of the two variables of classification.

2. The design is fairly insensitive to extreme values. Since the wage rate is an imperfect index, the possibility of a few extreme observations must be acknowledged.

Data for this test were taken from the BLS industry wage structure studies. Each study presents data on employment, hours, and earnings, classified by occupation, sex, state, and industry, for a single year. Since two adjacent studies are needed, attention was focused on the period 1928–31. For each of four industries a sample of states was selected. The states included in the sample reported roughly the same number of establishments covered in the two adjacent surveys. The states were also grouped by geographic region.[17] For each state, the occupations were classified as high wage or low wage, depending on whether an occupation's wage rate was above or below the median wage rate for all occupations. The occupations were then reclassified by the observed percentage change in employment into two equal groups. Employment, in this context, refers to the number of employees; the alternative concept of man hours yielded virtually identical results. The two-way divisions fix the marginal totals which, in turn, determine the expected numbers of occupations under the null hypothesis.

The contingency tables for four industries are presented in Tables 2 and 3, where the numbers in parentheses denote the expected numbers under the null hypothesis.[18] For furniture and men's clothing, the χ^2 statistic indicates that the null hypothesis can be rejected at a 5 per cent level of significance. The χ^2 statistic is significant at only a 10 per cent level for lumber mills. Finally, the data for foundries are consistent with the null

---

[16] Two alternative test procedures are (1) a least-squares regression between the wage rate and the percentage change in employment, and (2) a Student's "t" test for the difference in mean percentage changes in employment for two groups of occupations classified by wage rates. The contingency table design resembles a non-parametric correlation technique known as tetrachoric r. This latter technique is described in W. J. Dixon and F. J. Masey, Introduction to Statistical Analysis (New York: McGraw-Hill Book Co., 1951), p. 235.

[17] In these studies the BLS attempted wherever possible to cover the same establishments as those covered in the preceding study of the same industry. Hence, inclusion of only those states showing approximate equality in the number of establishments covered tends to minimize errors arising from a shifting establishment composition within states. Geographic grouping was incorporated to minimize differential shifts in product demands.

[18] The procedure was slightly altered for lumber mills. The larger number of occupations in this industry permitted a three-way division.

TABLE 2

No. of Occupations in Selected Industries, Classified by Wage Group and Per Cent Change in Employment*

Wage Group	Per Cent Change in Employment (No. of Employees)		Total	χ^2 Statistic†
	Below Median	**Above Median**		
Furniture:				
High wage	40 (29.26)	18 (28.74)	58	16.345 (3.841)
Low wage	17 (27.74)	38 (27.26)	55	
All wages	57	56	113	
Foundries:				
High wage	20 (18)	16 (18)	36	0.889 (3.841)
Low wage	16 (18)	20 (18)	36	
All wages	36	36	72	
Men's clothing:				
High wage	13 (9.76)	7 (10.24)	20	4.102 (3.841)
Low wage	7 (10.24)	14 (10.76)	21	
All wages	20	21	41	

* Source of the data and detailed breakdown by states are shown in my thesis, Appendix C, C-5, C-6, and C-7.
† Numbers in parentheses denote the 5 per cent critical values.

hypothesis. The discrepancies between actual and expected numbers of occupations in the cells of the contingency tables conform to the pattern anticipated by the fixed-cost hypothesis. Given these systematic discrepancies,[19] the additive nature of χ^2 permits a test for the aggregate of all four industries. For the four industries combined, the null hypothesis can be rejected at a 1 per cent level. Thus, the evidence from the BLS studies refutes the null hypothesis, and the alternative can be accepted. The wage rate of an occupation is associated with its percentage change in employment. Low-wage occupations, corresponding to low degrees of fixity, do experience relatively greater changes in employment.

---

[19] *The contingency table design can only uncover an association between two variables of classification. The direction of this association is only discernible from an examination of discrepancies between actual and expected numbers.*

TABLE 3

No. of Occupations in the Lumber Industry Classified by Wage Group and Per Cent Change in Employment, 1928–30*

Wage Group	Per Cent Change in Employment			Total	χ^2 Statistic†
	Lowest 3d	Middle 3d	Top 3d		
No. of employees (ΔE):					
High wage	14	17	11	42	6.999
	(13.57)	(14.86)	(13.57)		(9.488)
Middle wage	19	15	12	46	
	(14.86)	(16.28)	(14.86)		
Low wage	9	14	19	42	
	(13.57)	(14.86)	(13.57)		
All wages	42	46	42	130	

* Source of data and breakdown by states are shown in my thesis, Appendix C, Table C-8.
† Numbers in parentheses denote the 5 per cent critical values.

C. Employment of Non-Production Workers

Non-production workers in manufacturing industries are more highly paid[20] and tend to be more specific to the firm than their production worker counterparts. Thus, according to the fixed-cost hypothesis, non-production workers should exhibit greater employment stability.

Consider a simple model in which the desired rate of employment in the tth year, E_t^*, is a linear function of the rate of output, X_t. That is, the desired demand for some factor is solely a function of the scale effect, ignoring all substitution effects.

$$E_t^* = a + bX_t. \tag{12}$$

Suppose the actual change in employment from the preceding period is some proportion, k, of the desired change.

$$E_t - E_{t-1} = k(E_t^* - E_{t-1}). \tag{13}$$

Substitution in (13) by the expression for E_t^* in (12) yields the following reduced form, containing only observable quantities:

---

[20] *Data from the 1954 Census of Manufactures indicate that the average annual earnings of non-production workers always exceeded those of production workers. The ratio of the earnings of non-production to those of production workers ranged from a low of 1.47 in chemicals to a high of 2.11 in textile mill products.*

$$E_t = ak + bkX_t + (1 - k)E_{t-1}. \tag{14}$$

The parameter, k, may be interpreted as a short-run coefficient of adjustment. Higher values of k imply faster short-run adjustments. Indeed, a value of unity means that actual and desired rates of employment always coincide. If non-production workers are truly specific to the firm, they should exhibit a smaller k relative to production workers.

The slope parameters of the reduced form, equation (14), were estimated by least squares using annual data for the "All Manufacturing" sector. The analysis was confined to the prewar period, 1920–39, because of a strong secular trend in employment of non-production workers during the postwar period[21] that destroyed the validity of the demand relation. Output, X_t, was measured by the Federal Reserve Board's Index of Industrial Production. The least-squares estimates are given by equations (15) and (16), where N_t and P_t, respectively, designate non-production and production worker employment.

$$N_t = ak + .0132X_t + .5611N_{t-1} \qquad (R^2 = .7793). \tag{15}$$
$$ (.0024) \quad (.1100)$$

$$P_t = AK + .0722X_t + .3318P_{t-1} \qquad (R^2 = .7219). \tag{16}$$
$$ (.0146) \quad (.1340)$$

The short-run coefficient of adjustment for non-production workers is 0.44 while that for production workers is 0.67; the difference is statistically significant at the 10 per cent level. Furthermore, an examination of seasonally adjusted monthly employment data for the postwar period reveals lags in the turning points of non-production worker employment. The turning points in non-production worker employment for the "All Manufacturing" sector lagged from two to six months behind the turning points in production worker employment. The smaller short-run coefficient of adjustment and the lags in turning points are entirely consistent with the higher degree of fixity of non-production workers.

D.   Differential Unemployment and the Fixed-Cost Hypothesis

Involuntary unemployment is never uniformly distributed among all workers. The fixed-cost hypothesis may help to explain some of these differences. Fixed employment costs constitute an investment by the firm in its labor force. A firm faced by a cyclical decline in product demand could protect this investment by following a discriminatory layoff policy.

---

[21] In the prewar period, the ratio of non-production to production workers exhibited no secular trend. From 1947 to 1958, virtually all the increase in manufacturing employment is attributable to the growth in non-production worker employment. For a discussion of these trends the reader is referred to United States Bureau of Labor Statistics, "Non-production Workers in Factories, 1919-56," Monthly Labor Review, LXXX, No. 4 (April, 1957), 435–40.

To the extent that labor is a quasi-fixed factor, each new hire, whether an addition or a replacement, entails an investment outlay by the firm for hiring and training. Suppose that a firm is obliged to reduce the rate of employment of some factor. At any point in time each firm observes a distribution of its workers according to their expected periods of employment. The average employment tenure of the workers who remain employed can be lengthened by laying off the workers with the shortest expected periods of employment. Such a discriminatory layoff policy tends to reduce the voluntary quit rate facing the firm. The policy tends to lower total fixed employment costs by minimizing the number of future new hires that would be required to replace old workers who might voluntarily quit in subsequent periods. Thus, an implication of the fixed-cost hypothesis is that the incidence of unemployment should be highest for those workers with the shortest expected periods of employment. Since a worker's prospective employment tenure cannot be known with certainty and since labor contracts are rarely binding on employees, the firm can never exercise complete control over the expected period of employment. Furthermore, seniority rights or other union practices may prevent a firm from following a discriminatory layoff policy.

Certain personal characteristics such as age, sex, and marital status are allegedly associated with employment tenure. Middle-aged workers would, in general, be expected to have longer expected periods of employment than either very young or very old workers; this expectation has been corroborated by a study of labor turnover in Swedish factories.[22] At the same time, married males with spouse present tend to be less mobile and should exhibit longer employment tenures than either single males or males who are divorced, widowed, or separated.

Unemployment rates classified by race, age, sex, and marital status are presented in Table 4 for the census year 1950.[23] For both races, and in almost all age groups, married persons with spouse present revealed the lowest unemployment rates. The only exception for males was in the "14–17" age group, while single women had lower unemployment rates in two cases. The observed differentials in male unemployment rates thus conform to the pattern implied by differences in expected periods of employment.

The distribution by age of unemployment rates is roughly the same, except for level, for each race-marital status group of the male labor force; similar patterns are evident in data for other years. Unemployment rates fall over the range from fourteen to thirty-five years of age even when marital status is held constant. Beyond thirty-five years of age increasing age is associated with higher unemployment rates although the trend is reversed in the oldest age group ("65 and over"). The problems inherent in defining the

---

[22] Magnus Hedberg, "Labor Turnover, the Flow of Personnel through the Factory" (Stockholm: Swedish Council for Personnel Administration). (Mimeographed.)

[23] This table is reproduced from Phillip M. Hauser's article with his kind permission. The reader is referred to "Differential Unemployment and Characteristics of the Unemployed in the United States, 1940–1954," The Measurement and Behavior of Unemployment (Princeton, N.J.: Princeton University Press, 1957), pp. 243–80.

TABLE 4

UNEMPLOYMENT RATES BY COLOR, AGE, SEX, AND MARITAL STATUS, 1950

Sex and Age	White			Non-White		
	Single	Married, Spouse Present	Other Status	Single	Married, Spouse Present	Other Status
Male:						
14 and over	9.4	3.1	8.7	12.1	5.7	11.2
14–17	10.6	7.8	4.4	9.5	*	*
18–19	11.2	6.3	17.1	14.1	8.6	18.7
20–24	9.9	4.5	12.0	14.1	7.2	15.8
25–29	8.4	3.1	10.2	12.5	6.8	13.9
30–34	7.6	2.5	8.8	11.2	5.8	11.4
35–44	7.9	2.6	9.0	9.9	5.1	11.3
45–54	8.5	3.0	9.0	10.5	5.2	10.0
55–64	9.5	3.7	8.8	10.3	6.0	10.3
65–74	8.3	4.3	6.7	7.0	5.7	8.9
75 and over	3.1	2.8	3.8	*	2.7	6.5
Female:						
14 and over	4.7	3.2	5.6	10.7	6.6	8.1
14–17	12.6	13.9	16.1	13.8	18.7	*
18–19	6.9	6.6	17.5	15.8	12.0	22.8
20–24	4.3	4.0	9.5	12.3	10.1	15.0
25–29	3.5	3.5	7.1	8.8	7.8	11.8
30–34	3.4	3.3	6.5	6.0	6.5	9.5
35–44	2.8	2.7	5.6	6.5	5.7	6.6
45–54	2.3	2.8	5.0	5.5	5.0	6.4
55–64	3.0	2.8	5.0	4.7	4.6	5.5
65–74	3.1	2.3	3.9	6.9	7.8	4.9
75 and over	3.0	2.8	2.8	*	*	3.3

* Base less than 3,000.
Source: Hauser, *op. cit.,* pp. 256–57.

labor force for older workers make the interpretation of their unemployment rates particularly difficult. Hauser speculates that this reversal in the age pattern might be attributable to a withdrawal of older workers from the labor force when they become unemployed.[24] A logical implication of the withdrawal hypothesis is that the labor-force participation rate of older workers will be negatively correlated with cyclical changes in

[24] *Ibid., p. 251.*

employment. The latter implication is not supported by data presented in a study by Long.[25] I cannot explain this contradiction, but the data indicate, in the main, higher unemployment rates for younger and older workers than for middle-aged workers.

The sex differentials in unemployment rates cannot be explained by differences in expected periods of employment. The volatility of female labor-force participation rates suggests that unemployment rates are not the appropriate. variable. Furthermore, the evidence that there are differences in employment tenure by sex is not at all convincing.[26] Finally, the occupational differentials in unemployment rates are also consistent with the implications of the fixed cost hypothesis.

E. ADDITIONAL EVIDENCE

The analysis of subsection ID implies that labor of higher degrees of fixity should enjoy lower labor turnover rates. Manufacturing industries vary widely in the skill composition of their labor forces. The high-wage industries typically employ larger proportions of skilled workers with higher degrees of fixity. Low labor turnover rates should, therefore, be observed for high-wage industries. Other factors that affect labor turnover rates were held constant by a multivariate regression model that cannot be fully reported here.[27] Based on annual data for sixty-four manufacturing industries from 1951 to 1958, the regression model revealed a partial correlation between an industry's average quit rate and its wage rate of −0.497, a value that is significantly different from zero at the 1 per cent level. A turnover rate, defined as the lower of the total accessions and total separations rates, provides a measure of average replacement demand. Using this latter variable, the partial correlation drops to −0.195, which is significant at the 10 per cent level. Thus, an industry's wage rate, which presumably reflects the average degree of fixity of the labor force, is related to its labor turnover rate. The low-wage industries that employ workers with lower degrees of fixity do experience higher labor turnover rates.[28]

The differential shifts in factor demands over a cycle imply greater inequality of wage incomes during periods of low employment. In a recession the demand for labor with

---

[25] Clarence D. Long, The Labor Force under Changing Income and Employment (Princeton, N.J.: Princeton University Press, 1958), pp. 323–25, Table B-2.

[26] The BLS turnover data by sex for two-digit manufacturing industries reveal slightly higher turnover rates for females. Hauser finds (p. 244) that females in a previous state of employment are less vulnerable to unemployment than males. This same stability of employment of female workers was also found in the Philadelphia study; see United States Department of Labor, Bureau of Labor Statistics, The Social and Economic Character of Unemployment in Philadelphia (Bulletin No. 520, April, 1929).

[27] This portion of the study derived from a paper I read at the winter, 1960, meetings of the Econometrics Society. I wish to thank Stanley Lebergott and Jacob Mincer for their helpful comments.

[28] There is, of course, an identification problem. For example, high wage rates that result from union bargaining may reduce turnover rates. Although this difficulty is recognized, the results still appear to verify the implication of the fixed-cost hypothesis.

high wages and high degrees of fixity falls by a smaller percentage than that for labor in the low-wage occupations. The greater decline of employment in the low-wage occupations implies larger relative declines in wage incomes in these occupations than in the high-wage occupations. The changes in the distribution of wage incomes during the recession of 1929–33, discovered by Mendershausen,[29] indicated an increase in the dispersion of wage incomes as unemployment increased. The pattern held despite the fact that hourly wage differentials failed to widen in this recession.

III. ALTERNATIVE HYPOTHESES

In this paper certain aspects of the cyclical behavior of labor markets have been explained by the fixed-cost hypothesis. What are the alternative hypotheses that offer explanations for the same phenomena? The theory that changes in factor employments are due to variations in relative wage rates was considered in subsection IC. This theory was dismissed because it implied changes in factor employments that were contrary to the observed changes.

Another theory is contained in the Reder model.[30] Although Reder's theory is primarily addressed to occupational wage differentials, it implies systematic changes in factor employments. According to Reder, firms adjust to a downswing by raising hiring standards. As a result the average quality of workers in each skill category is improved. The higher standards displace some workers from each skill category. Some of the displaced workers in the higher skill categories are downgraded to lower skill jobs, creating even further displacement of workers in these lower skill categories. The successive bumping effect sifts down through the skill hierarchy of jobs and results in relatively greater unemployment in the low-skill categories. In the upswing, firms adjust by relaxing hiring standards and upgrading workers to higher skill jobs. It is never explicitly stated, but Reder seems to assume that all factor demands shift proportionally. If this interpretation of Reder is correct, there is nothing in his theory that implies differential shifts in employment. The theory is, however, consistent with the emergence of differential unemployment rates since unemployed workers would be classified by their previous occupational status.

There are two possible ways in which differential shifts in employment could be deduced from Reder's theory. First, workers in high-skill jobs could perform the tasks of low-skill jobs while retaining their old job titles. This would appear to be highly unlikely. A second possibility is that hiring standards for high-skill jobs are advanced less than those for low-skill jobs. The elusive nature of hiring standards makes it difficult to test the latter possibility.

---

[29] Horst Mendershausen, Changes in Income Distribution during the Great Depression ("Studies in Income and Wealth," Vol. VII [New York: National Bureau of Economic Research, 1946]), 69–70.

[30] M. W. Reder, "The Theory of Occupational Wage Differentials," American Economic Review, XLV, No. 5 (December, 1955), 833–52, see esp. pp. 833–40.

As a theory of the cyclical behavior of occupational wage differentials, Reder's theory has an intuitive appeal.[31] If the theory were stated formally, I believe that its basic behavioral relation could be put as follows: the relative rate of change in the wage rate of an occupation, $\Delta W/W$, is proportional to the relative excess demand for or supply of that grade of labor. Algebraically, it may be written:

$$\frac{\Delta W}{W} = k\left(\frac{D-S}{S}\right), \tag{17}$$

where k is a constant and D and S denote the amounts demanded and supplied of some grade of labor.

In the Reder model the cyclical adjustments involving the upgrading and downgrading of workers generate differential shifts in S for different occupations. In a downswing, the downgrading of workers creates larger excess supplies (in absolute values) in the lower skill jobs. If the same k applies for all occupations—and this must be assumed—the differences in excess supply imply relatively larger declines in the wage rates of low-skill jobs. The fixed-cost hypothesis would also predict a widening of occupational wage differentials in a downswing and a narrowing in the upswing if the behavioral relation (17) holds. Unlike the Reder model, the fixed-cost hypothesis involves differential shifts in D. The advantage of the latter explanation over Reder's theory is that it can simultaneously explain the cyclical behavior of occupational wage differentials and of relative factor employments.

IV. CONCLUDING REMARKS

The central theme of this paper has been the treatment of labor as a quasi-fixed factor. This concept of labor was suggested by J. M. Clark, who dealt primarily with the social cost of unemployment.[32] The theory of the demand for a quasi-fixed factor generated implications regarding the short-run behavior of labor markets. Differences in the degree of fixity for different occupations imply (1) differential short-run shifts in employment, (2) differences in labor turnover rates, (3) emergence of differential unemployment rates in the cycle, and (4) cyclical variations in relative wage rates. The implications of the fixed-cost hypothesis are, in the main, borne out by the data examined.

The theory of labor as a quasi-fixed factor may also help to explain other phenomena. It is sometimes argued that a firm will maintain its labor force even though the wage rate

[31] Reynolds agrees with Reder's explanation of the cyclical behavior of occupational wage differentials; see L. G. Reynolds and C. B. Taft, The Evolution of Wage Structure (New Haven, Conn.: Yale University Press, 1956), p. 364.

[32] Studies in the Economics of Overhead Costs (Chicago: University of Chicago Press, 1923), pp. 357–85.

exceeds the current marginal value product. If the labor has a high degree of fixity, it is to the firm's advantage to maintain its labor force rather than to risk high replacement demands in future periods. Fixed employment costs could also account for a range of indeterminacy in wages frequently mentioned in the literature.[33] In the short run, the specificity of labor to a firm places an upper limit on the wage rate equal to labor's total marginal product; the lower limit is determined by labor's alternative marginal product. Under collective bargaining a short-run wage rate could be set and maintained anywhere within this range.[34]

The classical treatment of labor as a completely variable factor may be adequate for a long-run analysis. To explain the short-run behavior of labor markets, I believe that labor should be viewed as a quasi-fixed factor of production.

---

[33] *Reynolds and Taft, op. cit., p. 1.*

[34] *The range of indeterminacy will be wider for factors (grades of labor) with higher degrees of fixity. This range is, however, a short-run phenomenon. The firm would not continue to invest in specific training unless it could recoup the benefits.*

ABOUT THE AUTHOR

Walter Y. Oi

It is rare when an economist can point to a major policy shift and, in a fundamentally important sense, say, "I did that." More than any other person, Walter Oi ended the U.S. military draft. Like most good ideas, this one was in the environment, particularly Milton Friedman's Chicago environment, but Walter's *American Economic Review* article "Cost of the Draft" (May 1967) and follow-on papers culminated in his co-chairing the 1970/71 White House Conference on Youth that laid the empirical framework for the all-voluntary force that replaced compulsory service (the draft).

Walter received his B.S. and M.A. from UCLA before moving to the University of Chicago, where he graduated in 1961. He has been on the faculty of several universities and visited others, but he is most closely associated with the University of Washington where he first rose to national prominence and with the University of Rochester where he currently holds the Elmer B. Milliman Professorship. He chaired the Rochester economics department from 1976 until 1982 and has been able to avoid doing so since that time.

Among many others, the paper reprinted here, the *American Economic Review* paper on the draft, and a pair of papers that resulted from a manuscript that had passed informally through the profession for several years, "Are Workers Overpaid in Big Firms?" *Australian Journal of Management,* 1988, and "Low Wages and Small Firms" in *Research in Labor Economics,* 1991, have been studied and admired by students and faculty alike.

Walter Oi is truly an economist's economist; he is one of a small number who, in an important sense, has trained one and perhaps two generations of economists. His work is too wide-ranging for easy classification, but the labor economics fraternity is honored to call him one of its own.

Shadow Prices, Market Wages, and Labor Supply

JAMES HECKMAN[1]

In recent research on married women in the labor market, a common set of variables is used to explain their wage rates, hours of work, and decision to work. Typically, these topics are treated separately, although Kalachek and Raines [14] and Boskin [7] estimate an expected hours of work equation for all women by separately estimating an hours of work relation for working women, and an equation determining the probability that a woman works. In other research, observations on non-working women are assumed to lie on the same hours of work function as observations for working women, with a particular value of zero for their hours of work (Leibowitz [15 and 16]). No theoretical justification is provided for this procedure. Moreover, a "missing variable" problem arises in regressing hours worked on wage rates since wages are not reported for non-working women. One solution to this problem is to estimate a wage function on a subsample of working women to predict missing wages. However, this procedure can lead to biased parameter estimates for wage functions and hence for labor supply functions (Aigner [1], Gronau [11]).

In this paper, we derive a common set of parameters which underlie the functions determining the probability that a woman works, her hours of work, her observed wage rate, and her asking wage or shadow price of time. We rely on two behavioral schedules: the function determining the wage a woman faces in the market (the "offered wage"), and the function determining the value a woman places on her time (the "asking wage"). If a woman works, her hours of work adjust to equate these wages if she has freedom to set her working hours. If a woman does not work, no offered wage matches her asking wage. If we estimate both wage schedules, we can use the estimated parameters to determine the probability that a woman works, her actual hours of work given that she works, the

[1] Reuben Gronau made valuable comments at an early stage of this research. I am indebted to Jacob Mincer, Marc Nerlove, Paul Schulz, members of the Columbia University Labor Workshop, members of the research staff of the Rand Corporation, Santa Monica, California, and members of the Labor Workshop of the University of Chicago for their comments on a previous version of this paper. Ralph Shnelvar was exceptionally skillful and patient in programming the function optimizations. I assume responsibility for all errors in the paper. This research was sponsored by National Science Foundation and Office of Economic Opportunity grants to the National Bureau of Economic Research.

potential market wage rates facing non-working women, and the implicit value of time for non-working women.

We develop a statistical procedure which yields estimates of this common parameter set. This procedure extends Tobit (Tobin [23]) to a simultaneous equations system, and differs from it by allowing different parameters to affect the probability that a woman works and her hours of work. The method allows us to utilize an entire sample of observations on women, whether or not they work, to estimate the functions determining their hours of work, wage rates, and probabilities of working. However, we utilize the sample information in a way distinct from previous studies.

In Section 1, we derive the shadow price or asking wage function, and present the general model. In Section 2, we discuss statistical issues, and in Section 3 we present parameter estimates derived from the procedure presented in Section 2.

1. SHADOW PRICES AND MARKET WAGES

We assume that households maximize a well behaved twice differentiable utility function subject to time, wealth, and other constraints. Proceeding in the usual fashion, we may derive the conventional demand relations for goods and leisure as functions of parametric prices and wages, non-labor income, and other constraints. However, as Hotelling [13], Samuelson [21], and Pollak [20] have shown, these are not the only functions associated with a constrained maximum, nor are they necessarily the most convenient for theoretical or empirical purposes. Assuming interior solutions, it is possible to express a subset of prices and wages as functions of their associated quantities and the remaining prices and wages, non-labor income, and other constraints.[2] More importantly, it is possible to give a different interpretation to these functions which makes them useful in cases where corner solutions exist, and the usual demand functions are not defined. In particular, we may interpret these prices as shadow prices or marginal values. It is well known that if positive quantities of a market good are purchased, a necessary equilibrium condition is that its price equals its marginal value, while if a good is not purchased, its price exceeds the marginal valuation at zero quantities of the good. For labor supply or the demand for leisure, a similar condition applies except that now there are two possible corners: given a fixed amount of time in the decision period, an individual may work no more than that amount of time, and cannot work less than zero hours. For equilibrium at the first type of corner, the marginal valuation at zero quantities of *leisure* is less than the market wage while at the second corner, the marginal valuation at the maximal quantity of leisure exceeds the market wage.

Working with the shadow price functions, it is possible to characterize both interior and corner solutions within a common theoretical framework because the shadow price functions are defined at corners where demand functions are not defined. In this paper, we apply this insight to develop a unified econometric methodology for estimating the

---

[2] *This requires the usual assumption of the non-vanishing of the appropriate Jacobian.*

parameters of both the hours of work and decision to work functions for married women. The problem of corner solutions is particularly pronounced in analyzing labor supply data for married women, and for this reason we focus on this group in this paper. Nonetheless, the methodology developed below is generally applicable to any situation where corner solutions are of practical importance.

The shadow price function for the wife's time may be written as

$$(1) \qquad\qquad W^* = g(h, W_m, P, A, Z)$$

where W^* is the shadow price, h is the hours of work, or alternatively, the amount of time the wife does not have available for her nonmarket activities, W_m is the wage of the husband, P is the vector of goods prices, A is the asset income of the household, and Z is a vector of constraints which arise from previous economic choices or chance events, such as the number of children, the education of the family members, and the state of household technology. W^* is the value the household places on marginal units of the wife's time in production and consumption.

The formal derivation of this function is relegated to Appendix 1. There we establish that if the ordinary labor supply function is a positive monotonic function of wage rates, equation (1) may be derived in a straightforward fashion, with the range of that function constituting the domain of the marginal valuation function. We further establish that equation (1) possesses a continuous partial derivative with respect to h at $h = 0$ if the household preference function is defined for quantities of leisure in excess of the total time currently available to the wife. Historical time-series and cross-section studies suggest that there is a monotonic *positive* relationship between wage rates and labor supply for married women (Mincer [18], Ashenfelter and Heckman [3]) so that excluding the "backward bending" case is not objectionable, at least for an analysis of this demographic group. However, in the empirical work presented below, the hypothesis of a positive relationship is tested rather than directly imposed on the data.

While there may be strong intuitive feelings about the direction of the relationship between W^* and other variables, the assumption of utility maximization yields no information on these signs. Nonetheless, previous empirical analysis suggests that children tend to increase W^* and that this effect is more pronounced the younger their ages. If leisure is a normal good, it is easy to show that increments in net worth raise W^*. Michael [17] argues that the education of the wife raises the wife's efficiency in producing domestic services. Thus, education might affect W^* but the direction of that effect is uncertain.

The determinants of the market wage rate (W) are better known. Education and years of labor force experience are expected to increase the wage (Mincer [19]). The market wage function may thus be written as

$$(2) \qquad\qquad W = B(E, S)$$

with S defined as the number of years of schooling, and E defined as the extent of labor market experience. Previous research suggests $B_E > 0$ and $B_S > 0$.

If a woman is free to adjust her working hours, a working woman will have $W = W^*$ as an equilibrium condition.[3] If she does not work, and hours of work cannot become negative, $W^* \geq W$. In this analysis, hours of work play the role of a slack variable in nonlinear programming and the basic condition $h(W^* - W) = 0$ applies to all women free to choose their working hours.

If a woman works, equations (1) and (2) become a recursive system determining hours worked. Just as in the Marshallian model of market demand where quantity adjusts to equate demand and supply prices, hours adjust in this model to equate offered and asking wages. Since the offered wage is assumed to be independent of hours worked, and the asking wage is assumed to increase with hours worked, a necessary condition for equilibrium to occur is that at zero hours of work, offered wages should exceed asking wages.

2. ESTIMATION

In order to estimate equations (1) and (2), we must specify their functional form and associated stochastic structure. Assuming that there exists a suitable monotonic transformation of the dependent variables so that each equation may be expressed as a linear function of its independent variables, and letting $l(\cdot)$ be that transformation, equations (1) and (2) for the ith observation may be written as

$$(3) \qquad l(W_i^*) = \beta_0 + \beta_1 h_i + \beta_2 (W_m)_i + \beta_3 P_i + \beta_4 A_i + \beta_5 Z_i + \epsilon_i,$$

$$(4) \qquad l(W_i) = b_0 + b_1 S_i + b_2 E_i + u_i.$$

We assume that ϵ_i and u_i are jointly normally distributed, each with mean zero, and correlation between these disturbances is allowed. The disturbances for each observation are assumed to be independent of the other disturbances, and the right-hand side variables. These disturbances reflect variations in functions known to the appropriate individual, but not known to the economist. Our results are not directly applicable to the case of labor market search where the wage is unknown to the individual before she enters the market.

The linearity of equation (3) does not necessarily imply that an exogenous wage increase causes a working woman to increase her working hours at a rate independent of the level of the wage rate. Only if $l(W_i) = W_i$ does the substitution effect remain constant for all values of wages and associated hours of work.

In applying the model, it is important to make a distinction between observed and hypothetical values for the variables. Thus, in equations (3) and (4), we assume that the

---

[3] Note, we dismiss the possibility of a corner solution where a woman works all available hours since it is empirically uninteresting.

disturbances are uncorrelated with the regressors. However, *observed* hours of work will depend on those disturbances.

To see this, consider a woman with $l(W) > l(W^*)$ at the zero hours of work position. If this condition holds for individual i, i.e., if

$$(5) \qquad b_0 - \beta_0 + b_1 S_i + b_2 E_i - \beta_2 (W_m)_i - \beta_3 P_i - \beta_4 A_i - \beta_5 Z_i > \epsilon_i - u_i,$$

hours of work adjust so that $W_i^* = W_i$. Then equations (3) and (4) become a recursive system determining working hours, and the particular adjustment of hours depends, in part, on the magnitude of the discrepancy $\epsilon_i - u_i$.

Given that condition (5) holds, the reduced form equations for observed wages and hours become

$$(6) \qquad h_i = \frac{1}{\beta_1}\left(b_0 - \beta_0 + b_1 S_i + b_2 E_i - \beta_2 \left(W_m\right)_i - \beta_3 P_i - \beta_4 A_i - \beta_5 Z_i\right) + \frac{u_i - \epsilon_i}{\beta_1}.$$

$$(7) \qquad l(W_i) = b_0 + b_1 S_i + b_2 E_i + u_i.$$

The crucial feature of the model is that we obtain observations on which to estimate equations (6) and (7) only if condition (5) holds. Thus, for a sample of working women, the distributions of the disturbances of equations (6) and (7) are conditional on inequality (5) and hence are conditional distributions. Since the same exogenous variables appear in condition (5) and equations (6) and (7), the mean and other characteristics of these conditional distributions, for a particular observation, depend on the values of the exogenous variables for the observation. Thus, it is not possible to obtain unbiased or consistent estimates of equations (6) and (7) using ordinary least squares since the regressors are correlated with the disturbances. The same remarks apply to any instrumental variable estimation technique such as two-stage least squares which uses the exogenous variables appearing in condition (5) as instruments.

However, it is possible to obtain consistent parameter estimates. Using the well known relationship between conditional and unconditional distributions, the joint distribution of *observed* hours and wages for the ith working woman may be written as

$$(8) \qquad j\left(h_i, l(W_i) \big| W_i^* < W_i\right)_{h=0} = \frac{n\left(h_i, l(W_i)\right)}{pr\left(\left[W_i > W_i^*\right]_{h=0}\right)},$$

where $n(h_i, l(W_i))$ is the unconditional distribution, $pr([W_i > W_i^*]_{h=0})$ is the probability that the woman works, and $j(\cdot)$ is the conditional distribution. Since ϵ_i and u_i are jointly normally distributed, $n(\cdot)$ is a multivariate normal density, and $pr(\cdot)$ is a univariate cumulative normal density function with many of the same parameters as $n(\cdot)$. These statements are proved in Appendix 2.

If a sample of T married women contains K who work, and $T - K$ who do not, the likelihood function for the entire T observations may be written as

$$L = \prod_{i=1}^{K} j\Big(h_i, l(W_i)\big|(W_i > W_i^*)_{h=0}\Big) \cdot \mathrm{pr}\Big([W_i > W_i^*]_{h=0}\Big) \times \prod_{t=K+1}^{T} \mathrm{pr}\Big([W_i > W_i^*]_{h=0}\Big).$$

Using equation (8), the likelihood function collapses to

(9)
$$L = \prod_{i=1}^{K} n\big(h_i, l(W_i)\big) \prod_{i=K+1}^{T} \mathrm{pr}\Big([W_i > W_i^*]_{h=0}\Big).$$

Maximizing this function with respect to the parameters of the model, including the variances and covariances of the disturbances in equations (3) and (4), yields consistent, asymptotically unbiased, and efficient parameter estimates which are asymptotically normally distributed.[4]

The likelihood function in equation (9) differs from Tobin's [23] in that $n(\cdot)$ is a multivariate normal density, while it is a univariate density in the Tobit model, and the parameter β_1 which appears in $n(h_i, l(W_i))$ does not appear in the cumulative density $\mathrm{pr}(W_i < W_i^*|_{h=0})$. Further differences are explored in Appendix 2.

If all women work, so that $T = K$, maximizing function (9) is equivalent to the full information maximum likelihood method (FIML). But if $K < T$, FIML applied to a subsample of working women will not be a maximum likelihood method with desirable properties as long as *any* parameter affects both the distribution governing the work decision ($\mathrm{pr}(W_i > W_i^*|_{h=0})$) and the density for hours of work and wages, $n(h_i, l(W_i))$.

The usual rules for identification of the parameters apply to this model. In the present case, identification is assured since labor market experience is excluded from the shadow price equation, and the effects of children, the husband's wage, and net assets are excluded from the market wage equation. Moreover, hours of work are excluded from the market wage equation.

Our system of equations expands Gronau's [11] work in several ways. By introducing the extent of work into the analysis, rather than focusing solely on the work participation decision inequality (5), we utilize the further information that, in equilibrium, working women equate offered and asking wages. Since Gronau works exclusively with inequality condition (5) to estimate the determinants of asking and offered wages by probit analysis,

---

[4] *The proof of these propositions follows from a straightforward extension of Amemiya's [2] valuable proof of the consistency and asymptotic normality of the Tobit estimator.*

he cannot identify the parameters of the wage functions associated with variables common to both wage equations since only the difference in these parameters enters inequality (5) and, indeed, equation (6). A further problem in utilizing probit analysis is that the coefficients in inequality (5) are estimated only up to a factor of proportionality.[5] By using Tobit analysis, which utilizes inequality (5) and equation (6), it is possible to estimate the factor of proportionality, but the problem of identifying parameters of variables common to both equations remains. Secondly, Gronau assumes that the disturbances across equations are uncorrelated, whereas we allow for correlation. Since the disturbances capture such omitted variables as ability, quality of schooling, and taste factors, it is plausible that they should be correlated and in fact the estimated correlation turns out to be quite high.

3. EMPIRICAL RESULTS

The model was estimated on a sample of 2,100 married white women age 30–44 from the 1967 National Longitudinal Survey. These data are described elsewhere in detail (Shea, et al. [22]). A novelty of these data is that information about retrospective labor market experience is asked of all women.

For empirical purposes, the class of monotonic transformations of the wage variables $l(W)$ is restricted to the "power transformations" suggested by Box and Cox [6]. This class may be written as

$$l(W) = \frac{W^\lambda - 1}{\lambda},$$

and λ may be estimated from the data. If $\lambda = 1$, the wage variable enters linearly. If $\lambda = 0$, the natural logarithm of the wage is the appropriate transformation. In practice, values of λ near zero were found whether hourly or weekly wages were used. As an empirical strategy, it was then decided to assume that $\lambda = 0$ to estimate wage functions more directly comparable to previous studies. In fact, Chiswick [8] and Mincer [19] have suggested theoretical reasons why natural logarithms should be used as dependent variables for the market wage equation. The natural logarithm has the additional desirable feature that the derived labor supply functions have an uncompensated substitution effect which varies depending on hours worked and wages.

Optimization of likelihood function (9) requires a numerical technique. In this paper, GRADX (Goldfeld and Quandt [23]) was used to perform the optimization. To test

---

[5] Gronau circumvents these difficulties by assuming that the market wage for working women is the appropriate market wage for nonworkng women of similar demographic characteristics. This implies that we know the portion of inequality (5) that corresponds to the market wage for all women, whether or not they work, and the probit coefficient for the market wage yields an estimate of the factor of proportionality. This procedure is equivalent to estimating a wage function on the subsample of working women and utilizing these estimates in a subsequent analysis. As we show in the text, such a procedure leads to inconsistent parameter estimates.

against the possibility of a local optimum a variety of initial values was used. In all cases, the function converged to the same general set of parameter values.[6]

The appropriate time unit for the empirical analysis is a matter of judgement. In this paper, a year is taken as the "current period." The appropriate measure of labor supply is also a matter for debate. It is possible that women can adjust their weeks worked much more freely than their hours per week. If this is so, weeks worked would be a more appropriate measure of labor supply than annual hours worked, since freedom to adjust is assumed in the model. In practice, both annual hours and weeks worked were used to quantify annual labor supply, and the results from each measure are presented below.

The number of children less than six years old was used to approximate the constraining effect of children. When additional children variables were introduced, such as the number of children 6–18 years old, they were insignificant using asymptotic normal tests.[7] To measure unearned income, the net worth of the household was estimated by summing over all components of debt and assets. The measure of work experience was the number of years respondents had worked at least six months. The wage rate of the husband was obtained by dividing his estimated annual hours worked into his annual earnings. This variable exerts income and cross substitution effects on the wife's asking wage. The education of the wife is measured in years. With all these variables, there is the serious possibility of correlation with the disturbances of equations (5) and (6), since many of these variables may be the result of previous choices partly dependent on previous disturbances which may be highly correlated with current disturbances. In a world of perfect certainty and unchanging tastes, this correlation may be quite large. On the other hand, the correlation will be weakened by the occurrence of unforeseen events and random changes in tastes, and the correlation would be expected to be weaker the greater the distance in time between the age when an "exogenous" variable was chosen and the current age. However, there is a possibility that our estimates are biased, but evaluating the importance of the bias is a non-trivial statistical and theoretical task.

The empirical results are presented in Tables I and II. In Table I, annual hours are used as a measure of annual labor supply, while in Table II weeks worked are employed. The results in Table I are "cleaner" because the labor supply measure is derived independently of the wage rate, since separate questions were asked to derive these measures. The weeks estimates rely on a weekly wage obtained by dividing weeks worked into annual earnings.

In both tables, the estimated effect of one child less than six years old is to raise the asking wage by roughly fifteen per cent. Increases in net assets increase the asking wage in both equations but the effect is only statistically significant in the annual hours table. A one dollar increase in the husband's wage rate raises the wife's asking wage by five per cent. Unit increases in the wife's schooling raise the asking wage by five per cent for

---

[6] *Readers interested in the results of all these iterations may obtain them from the author on request.*

[7] *This finding may be due to the unusual sample composition. Virtually all women in the sample had at least one child 6–18 years in age.*

TABLE I

ANNUAL HOURS WORKED*

	Intercept	Number of Children Less Than Six	Net Assets	Wage Rate of Husband	Experience	Education	Labor Supply	Standard Deviation
ln Asking Wage	-.623 (.088)	.179 (.019)	$.135 \times 10^{-5}$ $(.055 \times 10^{-5})$	.051 (.007)	—	.0534 (.007)	$.63 \times 10^{-3}$ $(.05 \times 10^{-3})$	.532 (.019)
ln Offered Wage	-.982 (.11)	—	—	—	.048 (.004)	.0761 (.0075)	—	.452 (.0121)

The estimated correlation of disturbances across equations is .6541 (.046)

* Asymptotic standard errors in parentheses.

TABLE II

ANNUAL WEEKS WORKED*

	Intercept	Number of Children Less Than Six	Net Assets	Wage Rate of Husband	Experience	Education	Labor Supply	Standard Deviation
ln Asking Wage	3.1 (1.36)	.149 (.022)	$.50 \times 10^{-6}$ $(.55 \times 10^{-6})$	.046 (.008)	—	.039 (.0124)	.02 (.003)	.671 (.021)
ln Offered Wage	2.75 (1.62)	—	—	—	.0445 (.0062)	.061 (.010)	—	.677 (.018)

The estimated correlation of disturbances across equations is .83 (.043)

* Asymptotic standard errors in parentheses. Data: National Longitudinal Survey of Work Experience for Women 30–44; 2,100 white married spouse present women.

hours worked, but only four per cent for weeks worked. In both tables, the effect of education is to raise the offered wage more than the asking wage and the differences are significant.[8] This implies that ceteris paribus more educated women work more frequently, and work longer hours than less educated women. An additional unit of labor market experience raises the market wage by 4.5 per cent in both tables.

As expected, increases in hours and weeks worked are associated with increases in the marginal value of remaining units of the wife's time used for consumption and home production. Since the sign of this coefficient is not imposed on the data by the estimation procedure, its positivity confirms the validity of our hypothesis about this sign made in Section 1. The estimated correlation between the disturbances of the two equations turns out to be quite large, and for both measures of labor supply is significantly different from zero and unity. The correlation is higher in Table II, possibly due to the way the market wage is derived for this measure of labor supply.

The estimated coefficients may be used to generate the probability that a woman works, and the actual hours worked for a working woman. An exogenous wage increase is equivalent to a shift in the intercept of the market wage equation. Using equation (6),

$$\frac{\partial h_i}{\partial b_0} = \frac{1}{\beta_1},$$

where b_0 is the intercept in market wage equation (7) measured in "units" of natural logarithms of wages

For the annual hours model, this partial is estimated to be 1,600. This implies that a unit increase in the natural logarithm of real hourly wages leads to 1,600 additional hours of work. This may seem to be disturbingly large until one recognizes that a unit change in the natural logarithm of wages represents almost a trebling of actual wages. A 10 per cent increase in real wages would be expected to increase work effort by 160 hours. For weeks worked the point estimate is 50, suggesting that a 10 per cent increase in the weekly wage rate raises weeks worked by 5. These coefficients are large, but not unreasonable.

To further assess the estimates of the model, we present the predicted probabilities of working for women with different characteristics. For a typical woman with four years of labor market experience whose husband makes $2.50 per hour, with net assets of $5,000, we present expected work participation rates, cross-classifying education with the number of children less than six. The estimates appear to be consistent with published statistics on labor force participation rates, and are also consistent with Bowen and Finegan's finding that labor force participation rate differentials by education narrow with the presence of pre-school children (Bowen and Finegan [5, p. 123]).

---

[8] *The estimated asymptotic standard errors for the difference in coefficients is .0052 for the hours case and .0055 in the weeks case.*

TABLE III

ESTIMATED PROBABILITIES OF WORKING

Number of Children Less Than Six	Years of Schooling				
	8	10	12	14	16
0	.30	.38	.47	.56	.66
1	.09	.13	.18	.25	.32
2	.013	.025	.04	.065	.09

Husband's wage rate is $2.50 per hour, net worth is $5,000, and the woman has four years of experience.

To contrast our results with those derived from conventional methods, we present full information maximum likelihood estimates of equations (5) and (6) based on a subsample of 804 working white women. Although we have argued that this procedure is inappropriate since it does not account for sample censoring, it is of some interest to determine whether application of the proposed method leads to any important differences in the estimates.

Table IV corresponds to Table I while Table V corresponds to Table II. The most pronounced differences arise in estimates of the effects of pre-school children. In Tables IV and V, the coefficients on the variable "number of children less than six" are considerably reduced in size, and become statistically insignificant using asymptotic normal tests at five per cent significance levels. The estimates of the market wage function derived from the subsample of working women give much lower estimates of the response of weekly or hourly wages to years of labor market experience, and somewhat lower estimates of the effect of years of schooling on these wages. The slope coefficients for education in each set of equations for either labor supply variable become virtually identical, suggesting that education has little effect on labor supply for women in this age group.

While it is impossible to conclude from this evidence that the proposed method gives better results, the comparisons show that it does lead to differences in empirical estimates. These differences, especially in the case of the determinants of market wages and effect of children on labor supply, would seem to favor the proposed method.

4. SUMMARY AND CONCLUSIONS

In this paper, we develop a model which generates the probability that a woman works, her hours of work, her asking wage, and her offered wage from a common set of parameters. These parameters allow us to estimate the value of time for nonworking women, and the wage rates they would face in the market. A method of estimating these parameters is proposed and applied. The model appears to give believable parameter estimates.

The method allows us to use an entire sample of women, whether or not they work, to estimate the hours of work equation. In this sense, our procedure is similar in spirit to the

TABLE IV

ANNUAL HOURS WORKED: FULL INFORMATION MAXIMUM LIKELIHOOD APPLIED TO THE SUBSAMPLE OF WORKING WOMEN*

	Intercept	Number of Children Less Than Six	Net Assets	Wage Rate of Husband	Experience	Education	Labor Supply	Standard Deviation
ln Asking Wage	-1.28 (.18)	.0703 (.09)	$.169 \times 10^{-5}$ $(.78 \times 10^{-7})$	.0376 (.01)	—	.0623 (.008)	$.83 \times 10^{-3}$ $(.95 \times 10^{-4})$	.469 (.012)
ln Offered Wage	-.36 (.086)	—	—	—	.0195 (.0025)	.0681 (.007)	—	.507 (.035)

The estimated correlation of disturbances across equations is .591 (.09)

* Asymptotic standard errors in parentheses.

TABLE V

ANNUAL WEEKS WORKED: FULL INFORMATION MAXIMUM LIKELIHOOD APPLIED TO THE SUBSAMPLE OF WORKING WOMEN*

	Intercept	Number of Children Less Than Six	Net Assets	Wage Rate of Husband	Experience	Education	Labor Supply	Standard Deviation
ln Asking Wage	1.55 (.31)	.046 (.03)	$-.36 \times 10^{-7}$ (1.0×10^{-6})	.022 (.012)	—	.0485 (.012)	.043 (.007)	.65 (.015)
ln Offered Wage	3.13 (1.21)	—	—	—	.026 (.0035)	.0561 (.0098)	—	.78 (.05)

The estimated correlation of disturbances across equations is .697 (.07)

* Asymptotic standard errors in parentheses. Data: National Longitudinal Survey of Work Experience for Women 30–44; 804 married spouse present women who worked in 1966.

procedure of Leibowitz [**15** and **16**] and others. However, we have shown that observations on nonworking women enter the sample likelihood function in a different way than observations on working women, since the former group gives information on many parameters of the asking and offered wage functions, but no information on the substitution effect ($1/\beta_1$ in equation (6)). Moreover, by posing the problem in the suggested way, we convert a "missing variable" problem (i.e., the problem that we do not observe wages for nonworking women) into a source of information about more fundamental parameters which underlie the labor supply and work decision equations.

Several important qualifications are in order. Throughout this paper, we assume that the individual faces a parametric wage that does not depend on the number of hours worked. This assumption is both convenient and conventional, but might be in conflict with the facts. It is possible to relax this assumption within our framework as long as consumer equilibrium is characterized by marginal equality conditions. However, if wage rates for a standard work year are suitably high because employers have incentives to economize on heads for a given number of manhours, consumer work equilibrium might no longer be characterized by the marginal equality condition we have exploited in the text. This possibility, if empirically important, would require an alternative model of binary choice.

In deriving the estimates, we assume that the disturbances for wages and shadow prices are normally distributed. Clearly, the statistical approach is more general, and estimates for alternative multivariate densities are both possible and desirable. More crucially, we must admit that our dichotomy between work and non-work should be replaced by a trichotomy: work, looking for work, and out of the labor force. To make this extension, it is necessary to develop a more complete model of labor supply under uncertainty than currently exists.

APPENDIX 1

For convenience, we change the notation from that of Section 1. Without loss of generality, we neglect the Z restrictions which may easily be reintroduced into the analysis. The household is assumed to possess a twice-differentiable quasiconcave utility function,

$$(A1.1) \qquad U(X_1, \ldots, X_n),$$

which is assumed to have positive first partial derivatives for all its arguments. For convenience, let X_1 be the wife's leisure. The argument presented below remains valid if there are many separate uses for the wife's leisure as discussed in Becker [**4**]. A is asset income, P_i is the price of good i, T is the amount of time available to the wife, and h is hours of work, $T - X_1$, with associated wage rate P_1. The household is assumed to maximize (A1.1) for a fixed h subject to

$$(A1.2) \qquad \sum_{i=2}^{n} P_i X_1 - A - P_1 h = 0$$

and

(A1.3)
$$T - X_1 - h = 0.$$

The LaGrangian may be written as

$$U(X_1, \ldots, X_n) - \lambda\left(\sum_{i=2}^{n} P_i X_i - A - P_1 h\right) - \mu(X_1 + h - T)$$

where λ and μ are LaGrange multipliers.

The first order conditions are

$$U_1 - \mu = 0,$$
$$U_2 - \lambda P_i = 0 \quad (i = 2, \ldots, n),$$

and (A1.2) and (A1.3). The assumption of an interior maximum is innocuous and is easily relaxed. In particular, (A1.3) will always hold if the marginal utility of leisure is positive.

From these conditions, a system of equations for $X_2, \ldots, X_n, \lambda$, and μ may be solved as functions of $P_2, \ldots, P_n$, and $P_1 h + A$.

The shadow price of time may be defined as

$$\frac{U_1}{\lambda} = \frac{\mu}{\lambda}.$$

This is the money value the household places on marginal units of the wife's time X_1. Note that we assume that the utility function is defined for quantities of leisure in excess of the amount T currently available.[9] This condition will be met if the household can "imagine" having more of the wife's time available than it currently possesses, just as it is conventionally assumed to be able to evaluate baskets of market goods not currently attainable with its money budget constraint. This assumption is not equivalent to the assumption that the preference map is defined for negative quantities of time or goods since hours of work indicate the *absence* of time to be used for leisure or home production, and do not enter as a direct argument in the utility function.

For any arbitrary P_1, we may write $U_1/\lambda = W^*$ as

(A1.4)
$$W^* = k(h, P_1 h + A, P_2, \ldots, P_n).$$

If the wife's leisure is a normal good, $k_2 > 0$. If the price weighted sum of all other goods and leisures (treated as a composite commodity) is a normal good, $k_1 > 0$. Assuming twice differentiability of the preference function, and a non-vanishing Hessian, (A1.4) will have continuous first partial derivatives.

---

[9] It is possible to imagine a household augmenting the wife's time by purchasing perfect substitutes for her home production time and defining these input hours as negative work.

It is important to notice that (A1.4) is defined whether or not labor supply functions exist. For a particular configuration of h, P_2, ..., P_n, A to be an equilibrium solution to the utility maximization problem with h voluntarily chosen, it is necessary that $P_1 = W^*$, i.e., that the income flow from the parametric wage P_1, given the value of A, P_2, ..., P_n, yield a value of the shadow price equal to the parametric wage. The relationship between the equilibrium values of W^* and h, if one exists, defines the labor supply relationship. Over the domain of h where equilibrium values exist, the continuity of k implies the continuity in the labor supply function. Note that under our assumption about preferences we can always adjoin the value of W^* at $h = 0$, or for that matter, values of W^* for suitably chosen values of $h < 0$, to the conventional labor supply function, and that continuity of k assures us that "adjoined labor supply" is continuous and differentiable in equilibrium wages.

If a labor supply function exists,[10] an "adjoined labor supply function" also exists. Assuming that the former is a positive monotonic relationship, we can solve out the latter relationship for equilibrium values of W^*, and hence we reach equation (1) in the text.

APPENDIX 2

Statistical Models

The joint distribution of ϵ_i and u_i, $M(\epsilon_i, u_i)$ is assumed to be a bivariate normal fully characterized by

$$E(\epsilon_i) = 0,$$
$$E(u_i) = 0,$$
$$E(u_i^2) = \sigma_u^2,$$
$$E(\epsilon_i^2) = \sigma_\epsilon^2,$$
$$E(u_i \epsilon_i) = \sigma_{\epsilon u} = \rho \sigma_u \sigma_\epsilon,$$

where ρ is the population correlation coefficient between u_i and ϵ_i.

The joint density may be written as

$$(A2.1) \qquad M(\epsilon_i, u_i) = \frac{\left(\sigma_\epsilon^2 \sigma_u^2 (1 - \rho^2)\right)^{-1/2}}{2\pi} \exp- \frac{1}{2(1-\rho^2)} \left(\frac{\epsilon_i^2}{\sigma_\epsilon^2} + \frac{u_i^2}{\sigma_u^2} - \frac{2\rho \epsilon_i u_i}{\sigma_\epsilon \sigma_u} \right),$$
$$-\infty < u_i < \infty, \quad -\infty < \epsilon_i < \infty.$$

The probability associated with condition (5) in the text, $\mathrm{pr}([W_i > W_i^*]_{h=0})$ comes to

$$(A2.2) \qquad \mathrm{pr}(b_0 - \beta_0 + b_1 S_i - \beta_2 (W_m)_i + b_2 E_i - \beta_3 P_i - \beta_4 A_i - \beta_5 Z_i > \epsilon_i - u_i).$$

---

[10] *It is tedious, but straightforward, to establish sufficient conditions for a labor supply function to exist. Since U is assumed to have positive first partials, $W^* > 0$ if $P_1 = 0$. If for all P_1, $k_2 h \leq 0$ a unique solution $\hat{W}^* = P_1$ exists for each h. If for all P_1, $k_2 h > 1$, no solution exists. If $0 < k_2 h < 1$ for all P_1, a solution might exist, and if it does, it is unique. A sufficient condition for a solution to exist is that $k_{22} h^2 \leq 0$ (i.e., the marginal rate of substitution between goods and leisure increases at a decreasing rate for increasing levels of utility). Note that at $h = 0$, a solution always exists.*

The distribution of $\epsilon_i - u_i$ may be obtained from (A2.1) by letting $t_i = \epsilon_i - u_i$, substituting $u_i + t_i$ for ϵ_i, and integrating out u_i, or by noting that sums and differences of normal variates are normal variates. Thus, $\epsilon_i - u_i$ is a normal variate with mean zero and variance $\sigma_\epsilon^2 + \sigma_u^2 - 2\rho\sigma_\epsilon\sigma_u$.

Using the standard normal, probability (A2.2) may be written

$$\mathrm{pr}\left(\frac{b_0 - \beta_0 + b_1 S_i - \beta_2(W_m)_i + b_2 E_i - \beta_3 P_i - \beta_4 A_i - \beta_5 Z_i}{\left(\sigma_\epsilon^2 + \sigma_u^2 - 2\rho\sigma_\epsilon\sigma_u\right)^{1/2}} > \frac{\epsilon_i - u_i}{\left(\sigma_\epsilon^2 + \sigma_u^2 - 2\rho\sigma_\epsilon\sigma_u\right)^{1/2}} \right)$$

so that

$$\mathrm{pr}\left(\left[W_i > W_i^*\right]_{h=0}\right) = \int_{-\infty}^{J_i} \frac{1}{\sqrt{2\pi}} \exp\left(-\frac{1}{2}r^2\right) dr$$

where

$$J_i = \frac{\left(b_0 - \beta_0 + b_1 S_i - \beta_2(W_m)_i + b_2 E_i - \beta_3 P_i - \beta_4 A_i - \beta_5 Z_i\right)}{\left(\sigma_\epsilon^2 + \sigma_u^2 - 2\rho\sigma_\epsilon\sigma_u\right)^{1/2}}.$$

Similarly,

$$\mathrm{pr}\left(\left[W_i < W_i^*\right]_{h=0}\right) = \int_{J_i}^{\infty} \frac{1}{\sqrt{2\pi}} \exp\left(-\frac{1}{2}r^2\right) dr.$$

The derivation of the distribution for $n(h_i, l[W_i])$ proceeds along similar lines. We may write equations (6) and (7) as

$$h_i - D_i = \frac{u_i - \epsilon_i}{\beta_1},$$

$$l[W_i] - F_i = u_i,$$

so that the distributions of the variables on the left are clearly linked to those on the right.

Now $(u_i - \epsilon_i)/\beta_1$ and u_i are jointly normally distributed:

$$E(u_i) = 0 = E\left(\frac{u_i - \epsilon_i}{\beta_1}\right),$$

$$E(u_i)^2 = \sigma_u^2,$$

$$E\left(\frac{u_i - \epsilon_i}{\beta_1}\right)^2 = \frac{\sigma_u^2 + \sigma_\epsilon^2 - 2\rho\sigma_\epsilon\sigma_u}{\beta_1^2},$$

$$\mathrm{cov}\left(\frac{u_i - \epsilon_i}{\beta_1}, u_i\right) = \frac{\sigma_u^2 - \rho\sigma_\epsilon\sigma_u}{\beta_1}$$

The joint density of h_i, $l[W_i]$ may be written as

$$n\big(h_i, l[W_i]\big) = |\beta_1| \frac{\big(\sigma_\epsilon^2 \sigma_u^2 (1 - \rho^2)\big)^{-1/2}}{2\pi} \exp\left(-\frac{G}{2(1 - \rho^2)}\right)$$

where $|\beta_1|$ is the absolute value of β_1, and where G is defined as

$$G = \big(h_i - D_i\big)^2 \left(\frac{\beta_1^2}{\sigma_\epsilon^2}\right) - 2\big(h_i - D_i\big)\big(l[W_i] - F_i\big)\left(\frac{1}{\sigma_\epsilon^2} - \frac{\rho}{\sigma_\epsilon \sigma_u}\right) + \big(l[W_i] - F_i\big)^2 \left(\frac{1}{\sigma_\epsilon^2} + \frac{1}{\sigma_u^2} - \frac{2\rho}{\sigma_\epsilon \sigma_u}\right).$$

If we let $l[W_i] = (W_i^\lambda - 1)/\lambda$ as Box and Cox [6] propose, then the joint density for h_i and W_i may be written as

$$q(h_i, W_i) = W_i^{\lambda-1} \cdot n(h_i, l[W_i]).$$

Using this transformation, we may estimate λ along with the other parameters of the model. Introducing this parameter creates another difference between our method and the Tobit method.

REFERENCES

[1] Aigner, D.: "An Appropriate Econometric Framework for Estimating a Labor Supply Function from the SEO File," Report No. 7124, Social Systems Research Institute, The University of Wisconsin, Madison, Wis., 1971.

[2] Amemiya, T.: "Regression Analysis When the Dependent Variable Is Truncated Normal," Technical Report No. 59, Stanford Institute for Mathematical Studies in the Social Sciences, Stanford, Calif., 1972.

[3] Ashenfelter, O., and J. Heckman: "The Estimation of Income and Substitution Effects in a Model of Family Labor Supply," Econometrica, 42 (1974), 73–85.

[4] Becker, G.: "A Theory of the Allocation of Time," The Economic Journal, 75 (1965), 493–517.

[5] Bowen, W., and T. Finegan: The Economics of Labor Force Participation. Princeton: Princeton University Press, 1969.

[6] Box, G., and D. Cox: "An Analysis of Transformations," Journal of the Royal Statistical Society, Series B, 26 (1964), 211–243.

[7] Boskin, M.: "Income Maintenance Policy, Labor Supply, and Income Redistribution," Research Memorandum No. 111, Research Center in Economic Growth, Stanford University, Stanford, Calif., 1971.

[8] Chiswick, B.: "An Interregional Analysis of Schooling and the Skewness of Income," in Education, Income, and Human Capital, ed. W. L. Hansen. New York: National Bureau of Economic Research, 1970.

[9] Council of Economic Advisers: Economic Report of the President, 1973. Washington, D.C.: U.S. Government Printing Office, 1973.

[10] Goldfeld, S., and R. Quandt: *Nonlinear Methods in Econometrics.* Amsterdam: North Holland, 1972.

[11] Gronau, R.: "The Effect of Children on the Housewife's Value of Time," *Journal of Political Economy,* Supplement, 81 (1973), 168–199.

[12] Heckman, J.: "Three Essays on Household Labor Supply and the Demand for Market Goods," Ph.D. Thesis, Princeton University, 1971.

[13] Hotelling, H.: "Demand Functions with Limited Budgets," *Econometrica,* 3 (1935), 66–78.

[14] Kalachek, E., and F. Raines: "Labor Supply of Low Income Workers," Technical Studies, President's Commission on Income Maintenance Programs, Washington, D.C., 1970.

[15] Leibowitz, A.: "Women's Allocation of Time to Market and Non-Market Activities: Differences by Education," Ph.D. Dissertation, Columbia University, 1971.

[16] ———: "Education and the Allocation of Women's Time," in *Carnegie Commission Essays on Education,* ed. T. Juster. New York: National Bureau of Economic Research, 1973.

[17] Michael, R.: *The Effect of Education on Efficiency in Consumption.* New York: National Bureau of Economic Research, 1972.

[18] Mincer, J.: "Labor Force Participation of Married Women," in *Aspects of Labor Economics.* New York: National Bureau of Economic Research, 1963.

[19] ———: "Schooling, Experience, and Earnings," mimeograph. National Bureau of Economic Research, New York, 1972.

[20] Pollak, R.: "Conditional Demand Functions and Consumption Theory," *Quarterly Journal of Economics,* 83 (1969), 209–227.

[21] Samuelson, P.: "Structure of Minimum Equilibrium Systems," in *Essays in Economics and Econometrics: A Volume in Honor of Harold Hotelling,* ed. R. W. Pfouts. Chapel Hill: University of North Carolina Press, 1960.

[22] Shea, J., R. Spitz, and F. Zeller: *Dual Careers: A Longitudinal Study of Labor Market Experience of Women.* Columbus, Ohio: Center for Human Resource Research, The Ohio State University, May, 1970.

[23] Tobin, J.: "Estimation of Relationships for Limited Dependent Variables," *Econometrica,* 26 (1958), 24–36.

ABOUT THE AUTHOR

James J. Heckman

James Heckman has spent the majority of his career at the University of Chicago. Jim was born in 1944, received his undergraduate degree in math from Colorado College, and his Ph.D. in economics from Princeton University. He began his career in 1970 at Columbia University and moved three years later to Chicago. He is now the Henry Schultz Distinguished Service Professor on the economics faculty at Chicago, as well as the director of the Center for Social Program Evaluation, which is a part of Chicago's Irving B. Harris Graduate School of Public Policy.

With the paper included in this volume, originally published in 1974, Jim founded a revolutionary empirical approach for understanding how decisions to participate in the labor force are behaviorally linked to the choices of how many hours employed persons work. Economists quickly recognized that his insights applied to a wide range of behaviors, including basic consumer demand, in which one needs to know not only how much consumers of a good purchase, but also who purchases this good at all. Building on this paper, Jim went on to develop a rich research literature for analyzing any empirical model involving jointly determined discrete and continuous variables. This body of work still defines the forefront of the field, and has become an integral part of the economics discipline.

Few economists match Jim's contributions to economics. He has published nearly 150 articles to date, with many considered to be seminal papers. In addition to the innovations first noted, he has fundamentally changed our thinking about how education and training influence earnings, what has happened to discrimination in the last fifty years, how economists can better understand life-cycle behavior, and what we can learn from social experiments. This does not even include all Jim's research integrating the fields of econometrics and statistics, which by itself would make for an impressive career. In recognition of these accomplishments, he received the John Bates Clark Medal in 1983, awarded to the best economist under the age of 40, and became a member of the National Academy of Sciences in 1992.

No one who meets Jim forgets him. He is an engaging conversationalist who can talk about almost anything. His command of economics is legendary, but his breadth of knowledge of other topics is no less extraordinary. You will meet many people who have stories about conversations that they have had with Jim that lasted several hours, and they will invariably be impressed by how much he knows and how much they learned. Jim sometimes worries about falling behind and not maintaining his productivity. Everyone else knows that there is no reason for concern.

Why Is There Mandatory Retirement?

EDWARD P. LAZEAR
University of Chicago and National Bureau of Economic Research

This paper offers an explanation of the use of mandatory-retirement clauses in labor contracts. It argues that the date of mandatory retirement is chosen to correspond to the date of voluntary retirement, but the nature of the optimal wage profile results in a discrepancy between spot wage and spot VMP (value of the worker's marginal product). This is because it is preferable to pay workers less than VMP when young and more than VMP when old. By doing so, the "agency" problem is solved, so the contract with mandatory retirement is Pareto efficient. A theory of agency is presented and empirical evidence which supports the hypothesis is provided.

Mandatory retirement has recently become an important issue. Congress has enacted legislation that extends coverage under the Age Discrimination in Employment Act to workers up to age 70 rather than to age 65 as it previously stood. This essentially outlaws the use of mandatory retirement at age 65, a common practice. Furthermore, Congress is considering the extension of the Age Discrimination Act such that exemption would be eliminated entirely. The current legislation already does this for federal workers. In order to understand whether or not legislation outlawing mandatory retirement would benefit society, it is first essential to ask why this institution exists. The primary task of this paper is to offer an analysis of that institution, with testable implications, and then to discuss policy proposals that are consistent with and implied by this analysis. As an outgrowth, a theory of agency is presented which provides insight on how to compensate an agent in a manner that creates a harmony of interest between the principal and the agent.

There are many defenses and explanations of mandatory retirement. Most rely on the notion that a worker's productivity declines significantly after some age, say 65, and that mandatory retirement is the employer's way to deal with this reduced productivity. Yet, there is a significant diversity of talent in the labor force. No one claims that only the most talented individuals are the ones who can find jobs. Instead, economists believe that differences in wage rates reflect differences in productivity. The same is true of older workers. If older workers are less productive than younger workers, employers in a competitive labor

The author wishes to thank Charles Brown, Dennis Carlton, Linda Edwards, Victor Fuchs, Nathaniel Gregory, Victoria Lazear, Jacob Mincer, Sam Peltzman, Melvin Reder, Sherwin Rosen, and Lester Telser for useful suggestions. Victoria Lazear provided substantial assistance in solving the problem discussed in Section IA of the text.

market would be forced to pay older workers a lower wage rate than they pay younger workers. There is no necessity to lay off the older workers simply because their productivity is not as high as the younger workers'. In fact, very young workers earn less than middle-aged workers as a reflection of their lower productivity. Yet, we do not find researchers arguing that the minimum age for employment should be 45. The correct question then is, Why does employment rather than wage adjust?

Some have argued that morale would be adversely affected by lowering the wages of older workers. But it is not obvious that terminating workers rather than lowering their wages will improve the morale of the remaining work force. A 60-year-old worker who is faced with approaching termination is not necessarily going to have a better attitude than one who knows his wage rate will be lowered 5 years from now. Another view often expressed is that one cannot judge the decrease in productivity so that it would be impossible to adjust wages accordingly. But laying off a worker adjusts his wage rate to zero. This is a poorer approximation of his true productivity decline than any smooth wage adjustment. Furthermore, employers face the problem of gauging productivity for all workers. There is nothing unique about 65-year-olds in this regard. Thus, a productivity decline is not a sufficient explanation for the existence of mandatory retirement. One must ask why the productivity decline is dealt with by terminating the worker rather than by reducing his wages.[1]

Another "explanation" is that a uniform retirement policy avoids the disadvantage of discrimination between employees. Two questions arise. First, there is nothing that requires that a uniform retirement policy be one that has a provision for mandatory retirement. One could easily set up a flexible retirement scheme, where payment varies with length of service, that is invariant across individuals but does not require mandatory retirement at any given age. The second problem is that employers discriminate between employees at every level: some are promoted, others are terminated, others experience wage gains while others do not, and the existence of differences between workers is dealt with in many ways. Why should employers or employees favor a system that reduces the ability of the employer to compensate workers differentially?

Another "explanation" is that mandatory retirement creates promotion possibilities for younger workers. This explanation ignores at least two factors: First, young workers know that they will become old workers at some date in the future. They care about the present value of some lifetime wage path rather than the present value of any segment of it. Although they would prefer to be promoted when young, they also would, if their retirement is truly mandatory, prefer to continue working when old. Second, promotion may be interpreted as an increase in one's wage rate (and perhaps a change in the accompanying job title) that occurs as one's productivity rises over the life cycle. The firm will, in competition, pay the worker his marginal product, no matter how old he is. Thus,

---

[1] *See Gordon (1960), Kreps (1961), National Industrial Conference Board (1964), and U.S. Department of Health, Education, and Welfare (1976) for some commonly offered explanations of mandatory retirement.*

there would be no incentive for a firm to mandatorily retire a worker whose marginal product was equal to or greater than his wage rate to "promote" a younger worker.

Needless to say, none of the so-called explanations satisfactorily describes why it is optimal to terminate a worker at a certain age rather than reduce his wages accordingly and in a continuous fashion. In fact, explanations of mandatory retirement suffer from the same drawback as explanations of layoffs. Economists have been puzzled by layoffs as an alternative to spot VMP payments as well. I suggest that the two phenomena are linked.

The purpose of this paper is to give a theoretical explanation for the existence of mandatory retirement that is consistent with economic theory and then to test this theory empirically. Before proceeding, it is important to make clear what is meant by "mandatory retirement." The phenomenon that we wish to explain has the following characteristics: First, there is a definite date when a contract (either explicit or implicit) ends. Second, at that date there will be some workers who will wish to remain with the firm at their previous wage rates, but whom the firm will not choose to employ at that wage.[2] Thus, mandatory retirement has the characteristic that at some time T, the worker earned some wage $\bar{W}$. But at $T + \epsilon$, the firm is no longer willing to employ the worker at wage $\bar{W}$, nor is the firm's wage-offer function continuous at that point (i.e., it takes a discrete jump downward for some workers). This story, by definition, implies that at T the firm is paying some workers more than the value of their marginal products. This is a necessary condition for the firm to desire to terminate the worker, and this is the bottom line to virtually all explanations of mandatory retirement. The argument here will be that, for reasons discussed below, it will be optimal for firms and workers to have a payment scheme such that the worker receives less than his marginal product when young and more than his marginal product when old. This implies that there be some date at which the firm is no longer willing to pay the worker his current wage. He is, therefore, mandatorily retired.

In some recent work, Feldstein (1976) has employed the notion that a worker's commitment to the firm tends to be permanent. He presents evidence which reveals that a large proportion of total job separations consist of layoffs, and, further, that layoffs are, in large part, temporary. That is, the worker is reemployed by the same firm which has laid him off in the first place. The lifetime commitment to the firm is the starting point from which we attempt to explain the existence of mandatory retirement. A sketch of that explanation follows.

---

[2] *Given this definition, the institution of term contracts with up-or-out employment arrangements (i.e., arrangements where the worker is either promoted or forced to leave the firm) is a form of mandatory-retirement contract. The model to be presented in this paper could be applied to the analysis of that problem as well. In a recent theoretical paper by S. Freeman (1977), retirement and promotion decisions are linked. His model will not, per se, yield mandatory retirement, however. The reason is that in his framework there is no reason to distinguish between lump sums at critical time points and smooth payment streams with the same present value. The former will not yield mandatory retirement as it is commonly used.*

Workers care about the present value of their wage stream over the lifetime (i.e., their wealth), whereas firms care about the present value of the worker's marginal product over his lifetime. Other things equal, a worker would be indifferent between a wage path which paid him a constant dollar amount over his lifetime and another one which had the same present value but paid him less when he was young and more when he was old. Other things equal, the firm would be indifferent between paying the two streams. But other things are not equal. It will be shown that a wage profile which pays workers less when they are young and more when they are old will allow the worker and firm to behave in such a way as to raise the present value of marginal product over the lifetime. For example, by deferring payment a firm may induce a worker to perform at a higher level of effort. Both firm and worker may prefer this high wage/high effort combination to a lower wage/lower effort path that results from a payment scheme that creates incentives to shirk. Thus, it may pay the firm and worker to set up a scheme such that the worker is paid less than his marginal product when he is young and more than his marginal product when he is old to compensate.

The efficiency condition for retirement is that the value of the worker's marginal product is just equal to his reservation wage. This will determine the optimal date of retirement. But if workers are paid less than their marginal products when they are young and more when old, their wage rate at T (the optimal retirement date) will exceed VMP and, therefore, the reservation wage. Although this is the efficient and equilibrium date of retirement (the date such that the present value of the lifetime marginal product equals the present value of the lifetime wage payment), the worker will not voluntarily retire at this date because wage exceeds reservation wage. Wage exceeds reservation wage at this point because that payment scheme produces a superior lifetime profile which workers prefer ex ante. Therefore, mandatory retirement is required to induce them to leave the firm at the optimal date. Thus, the existence of mandatory retirement is optimal from the worker's point of view. The worker is actually better off as the result of a contract which specifies a mandatory termination date. This allows the worker's present value of marginal product to be higher than it would be in the absence of such a contract, and these "rents" will spill over to the worker.

I. THE MODEL

Consider an individual who has a value of marginal product over his lifetime, $V^*(t)$, and a wage rate $W^*(t)$ as illustrated in figure 1. This worker is receiving an amount less than his VMP for $t < t^*$ and an amount greater than his marginal product for $t > t^*$. Let T be the point such that

$$V^*(T) = \tilde{W}(T), \tag{1}$$

where $\tilde{W}(t)$ is the individual's reservation wage at t. Any $W^*(t)$ path that satisfies the condition that

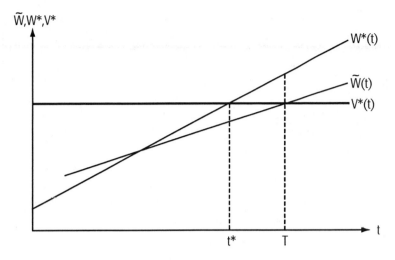

$$\int_0^T W*(t)e^{-rt}dt = \int_0^T V*(t)e^{-rt}dt \tag{2}$$

FIGURE 1

will be an equilibrium path.[3] That is, other things equal, a worker is indifferent between a path which pays him his spot VMP at each point in time and one which pays him a wage less than VMP initially and more than VMP later. As long as each path yields the same present value, workers have no preference. The argument in this paper, however, is that other things are not equal. A path which pays less than VMP when young and more than VMP when old may yield the worker a higher lifetime wealth. The reason is that a steeper path reduces the worker's incentive to cheat, shirk, and engage in malfeasant behavior. That is, it affects the amount of output per hour worked by altering the worker's incentive structure. This generates a preference for a path that has a wage greater than VMP at the date when VMP equals the reservation wage. Since this is the point when retirement should occur, and since workers would not voluntarily leave at this point (since $W*[T] > \tilde{W}[T]$), "mandatory" retirement is a necessary consequence. But what is important here is that retirement is "mandatory" only in an ex post sense. It is negotiated in advance and is part of an optimal contractual arrangement which ensures that firm-worker separation occurs at the appropriate time.[4]

---

[3] This assumes that the worker can borrow and lend at rate r. To the extent that this does not hold, a utility-maximizing framework must replace the wealth-maximizing one. The fundamental analysis and its conclusions, although somewhat more complex, remain essentially the same.

[4] That is, the worker is "mandatorily retired" at T. This is not the same as saying that the worker leaves the firm at T. He is retired from his old contract, but not necessarily from his old firm. For example, at age 65 many professors are mandatorily retired from their former contracts and

A. INCENTIVES-INDUCED MANDATORY RETIREMENT

A steeper-than-VMP wage path is generated when we consider the notion of optimal effort, honesty, and malfeasance on the job.[5] These are treated symmetrically because performing at a level of effort lower than expected is merely a special type of worker "cheating."

Let a worker's marginal product at time t be given by $V^*(t)$; his reservation wage is $\tilde{W}(t)$, and the optimal wage path is $W^*(t)$ (as defined above). Worker "cheating" is assumed to be detectable immediately and the worker is dismissed when he cheats.[6] A worker will cheat when the present value of cheating exceeds the cost of cheating. The major cost of cheating is the loss of the current job which carries with it earnings greater than the individual's reservation wage. This immediately suggests that if wage paths are steeper than VMP paths (and reservation wage paths as the result), this will discourage cheating by workers since it raises the costs of termination. Stated otherwise, a firm which withholds payment until the end of an individual's work life is less likely to experience worker cheating than one that pays workers more at the beginning and less at the end of the worker's career. But if the former path discourages cheating, it results in a higher expected lifetime value of the marginal product. Thus, workers produce more and are paid more if their wage paths are steeper than VMP. But this implies that $W^*(T) > \tilde{W}(T)$. Given that, the worker would not choose to retire at T. Since his VMP is equal to his reservation wage at T, however, it is optimal for him to leave the firm. Therefore, both worker and firm will, at $t = 0$, agree on a "mandatory" retirement date of T. I reiterate that it is only mandatory in the sense that, once at T, the worker would prefer to continue working at $W^*(T)$ if it were available. It is not available because his VMP is less than $W^*(T)$, his reservation wage equals his VMP at that point, and he has been paid exactly the full present value of his lifetime VMP at point T. Time T is the date of ex post mandatory, but ex ante voluntary, retirement.

In order to determine the exact shape of the $W^*(t)$ path, it is necessary to formalize the model: To make the model completely general, we start out with the possibility not only

---

renegotiate a new contract frequently called "emeritus." The wage rate changes, as do the working conditions. In this case, the worker stays with the former firm. In most cases, however, "mandatory retirement" will be coupled with firm-worker separation as well. The reason is that at T when renegotiation occurs, it is no longer necessarily the case that the worker-firm match and corresponding working conditions (hours, flexibility, effort, etc.) that were optimal between 0 and T will also be optimal between T and retirement (or death). For example, older workers may want shorter and more flexible hours with limited responsibility (or they may want zero hours of work, i.e., retirement). This is not necessarily the type of work conditions/wage trade-off that they would choose between 0 and T. If not, T will be characterized by a reshuffling of workers among firms. What is crucial is the termination of the former contract.

[5] Papers which have dealt with this issue are Becker and Stigler (1974) and Stiglitz (1975).

[6] This is a result rather than an assumption. It is true because any worker who finds it optimal to cheat at $t = t_0$ will cheat with certainty at $t > t_0$. Therefore, the firm gains by replacing him with a worker whose probability of cheating is less than one at that point.

of worker cheating, but of firm cheating as well. Firm "cheating" takes the form of promising a worker a stream $W^*(t)$ from 0 to T, but dismissing the honest worker at some $t < T$ and depriving him of the promised wage stream. The firm's cheating may be intentional or may be "unintentional," if, for example, the firm goes bankrupt before T.[7] Initially, let us assume that firm cheating is unintentional or exogenous and that the distribution of dates t at which the firm "cheats" on the worker is known and given by $\tilde{g}(t)$. Exogeneity of $\tilde{g}(t)$ will be dropped below, but it is useful to adopt the assumption for comparison's sake.

Let the ith worker be assigned a $\theta_i \sim f(\theta_i)$, where θ is defined as the benefit that the worker derives from cheating. It may reflect the utility increase he derives when he works at a low effort level rather than the high effort level promised, or it may reflect something as tangible as revenue from the sale of stolen merchandise. For simplicity, assume that θ_i is constant over the worker's lifetime. If the worker "cheats," assume that he is caught with certainty and that as a result he is terminated. (The problem is complicated somewhat if there is a time lag for detection. As it turns out, that will necessitate pensions as part of the optimal wage path. For now this is ignored.)[8] The expected rent to a worker at time t is

$$ R(t) = e^{rt} \int_t^T \left\{ W^*(\tau) - \tilde{W}(\tau) - \tilde{g}(\tau) e^{r\tau} \int_\tau^T \left[W^*(\delta) - \tilde{W}(\delta) \right] e^{-r\delta} d\delta \right\} e^{-r\tau} d\tau. \quad (3) $$

This rather complicated expression is the value in period t dollars of nominal rents to the worker $[W^*(t) - \tilde{W}(t)]$ minus the probability that the firm will cheat on the worker in the form of early termination $(\tilde{g}[\tau])$ times the cost to the worker of that cheating $(e^{r\tau} \int_t^T [W^*(\delta) - \tilde{W}(\delta)] e^{-r\delta} d\delta)$. The worker cheats at time t if $\theta_i > R(t)$. From this, $\tilde{f}(t)$, the probability of worker cheating at time t, is derived:

$$ \tilde{f}(t) = \begin{cases} F[R(0)] & \text{for } t = 0, \\ f[R(t)][R'(t)] & \text{for } R' < 0 \text{ and } t > 0, \\ 0 & \text{for } R' > 0 \text{ and } t > 0, \end{cases} \quad (4) $$

where $F \equiv 1 - \int_{-\infty}^R f(\theta) d\theta$. That is, at $t = 0$, some individuals, $F[R(0)]$, will have $\theta > R(0)$ and will choose to cheat. If $R'(t) > 0$, then those who did not cheat at $t = 0$ are even less likely to do so now or $\tilde{f}(t) = 0$. If $R'(t) < 0$, some individuals who did not cheat at zero, namely, $f[R(t)]$ $[R'(t)]$, will now find it profitable to cheat, so $\tilde{f}(t) = f[R(t)]$ $[R'(t)]$.

---

[7] "Unintentional" is in quotes because the value of bankruptcy depends upon how much the firm owes workers and so is at least in part endogenous.

[8] It is a trivial extension of the model to allow the worker a probability of detection less than one. In the terminology below, $R(t)$ is merely replaced by $R(t) \cdot P$, where P is the probability of detection.

The problem then for the firm is to choose T and $W^*(t)$ so as to maximize the payment to the worker subject to the constraints that lifetime earnings equal lifetime expected VMP and that T is efficient. This can be written:

maximize over T, $W^*(t)$

$$\text{wealth} = \int_0^T \left\{ W^*(t) + \tilde{f}(t) \left[\theta - e^{rt} \int_t^T W^*(\tau) e^{-r\tau} d\tau \right] - \tilde{g}(t) e^{rt} \int_t^T W^*(\tau) e^{-r\tau} d\tau \right\} e^{-rt} dt \qquad (5)$$

subject to

wealth = expected VMP

$$= \int_0^T \left[V^*(t) - \tilde{f}(t) e^{rt} \int_t^T V^*(\tau) e^{-r\tau} d\tau - \tilde{f}(t) c(t) - \tilde{g}(t) e^{-rt} \int_t^T V^*(\tau) e^{-r\tau} d\tau \right] e^{-rt} dt - \xi, \qquad (6)$$

where ξ are hiring costs and the boundary condition is

$$V^*(T) - \tilde{f}(T) c(T) = \tilde{W}(T). \qquad (7)$$

Equation (5) says wealth is equal to the wage rate ($W^*[t]$) plus the probability of worker cheating, $\tilde{f}(t)$, times the gain from worker cheating to the worker (θ) minus the cost to the worker ($e^{rt} \int_t^T W^*[\tau] e^{-r\tau} d\tau$), minus the probability of firm cheating, $[\tilde{g}(t)]$, times the cost to the worker ($e^{rt} \int_t^T W^*[\tau] e^{-r\tau} d\tau$). Expected VMP consists of nominal VMP, $[V^*(t)]$, minus the costs imposed by worker cheating equal to the sum of the loss of his output between t and T ($e^{rt} \int_t^T V^*[\tau] e^{-r\tau} d\tau$), and exogenous costs imposed on the firm, $c(t)$,[9] times the probability that the worker cheats, $[\tilde{f}(t)]$, minus the probability that the firm cheats, $[\tilde{g}(t)]$, times the effect on marginal product ($e^{rt} \int_t^T V^*[\tau] e^{-r\tau} d\tau$), minus hiring costs, ξ. Equation (7) says that net VMP at T must equal the reservation wage $W(t)$ for efficiency. The complete solution to the problem is complicated and relegated to an appendix.[10] We merely sketch the solution here.

If $\tilde{g}(t)$ is exogenous, that is, the probability of the firm cheating on the worker is independent of $W^*(t)$, the solution boils down to choosing $W^*(t)$ so as to set $\tilde{f}(t) = 0$, that is, completely eliminating worker cheating. Payment should be weighted sufficiently toward the end of the career so that at every point t it does not pay for the worker to cheat. The exact form of the solution depends upon the distribution of θ_i. In the simplest case, where all workers have $\theta_i = \bar{\theta}$, the solution is indeterminate, but it has the characteristic

---

[9] The $c(t)$ may be zero or positive. One example is the loss suffered when the worker takes customers with him upon his departure.

[10] Available from author upon request.

that at time T, $W^*(T) - \tilde{W}(T) \geq \bar{\theta}$, and that $V^*(T) = W(T)$.[11] The intuition behind this solution is clear: If the worker cheats, he imposes cost $c(t)$ on the firm, but receives $\bar{\theta}$. Therefore, the cheating lifetime net VMP and wealth is

$$\int_0^{t^*} V^*(t)e^{-rt}dt + \left[\bar{\theta} - c(t^*)\right]e^{-rt^*}$$ (8)

if the worker cheats at t^*. If he never cheats, his lifetime VMP and wealth is simply $\int_0^T V^*(t)e^{-rt}dt$. As long as $c(t) > \bar{\theta}$, the cost imposed on the firm by worker cheating exceeds the value of cheating to the worker (stolen machines sell at a price less than the replacement cost to the firm) and the zero-cheating path will be preferred. The zero-cheating equilibrium is produced by paths having $R(t) > \theta$ for all t.

Figure 2 illustrates some possible $W^*(t)$ paths. One path is ABP. Here the worker receives a constant amount less than his VMP over his lifetime, but receives a large lump sum at T to set present values of payment and marginal products equal. There is no worker cheating because $R(t)$ is always greater than $\bar{\theta}$; it never pays to cheat. Another possibility is the more conventional LQ curve. Again, there is no worker cheating, and at T the worker receives more than his marginal product. Again, of course, present values of

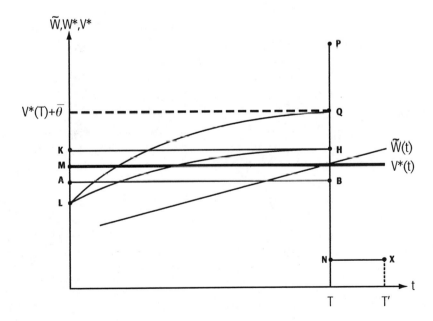

FIGURE 2

[11] The Becker-Stigler (1974) solution is a special case of this general form.

lifetime earnings and marginal products are equal. Another possibility is *LKHQ*. This is the Becker-Stigler (1974) solution where the worker posts a "bond" equal to *LM*, is paid interest on it (*KM*), and gets back the principal at *T* (*HQ = LM*). A fourth possibility is *LHNX*. Here the worker is paid less than his VMP initially, more at *T*, and receives a pension equal to *NX*. As long as the present value of remaining rent exceeds $\bar{\theta}$ and the present value of earnings equals present value of payments, this will be an optimal path. This path is probably the most typical.

The important point that comes out of the above analysis is that in all these cases, $W^*(T) > \bar{W}(T)$. That is, if the worker could continue to earn $W^*(T)$, he would not choose to retire. If he were paid $V^*(T)$, on the other hand, he would choose to retire. Mandatory retirement is warranted because it is optimal for the worker to retire at *T*, but paying him a wage that would induce him to do so voluntarily would result in more than the optimal amount of cheating. Thus, a path that is optimal from a cheating point of view coupled with mandatory retirement is superior for both worker and firm.

Without going into the details of the analysis, suffice it to say that when $\tilde{g}(t)$, the probability of firm cheating, is endogenous and influenced by the amount owed to the worker, the indeterminacy disappears (as it does for certain distributions of θ_i). The complete analysis is contained in an appendix.[12] The sense of the main result is this: As the amount owed to the worker above his marginal product increases, the gains to the firm from cheating on the worker increase. Therefore, minimizing the sum of cheating costs (which is essentially what [5] does) will trade off reduced worker cheating against increased firm cheating as $W^*(t)$ becomes more end weighted. This eliminates the indeterminacy and tends to reduce the end weighting of the payment stream. Mandatory retirement will still be required, however, since $W^*(T) > \bar{W}(T)$.

As an aside, it is interesting to ask whether or not $\tilde{g}(t)$ is endogenous. That is, does the firm have a greater incentive to cheat when it owes the worker more? In a world of perfect (or unbiased)[13] information and infinitely lived firms, the answer appears to be "No." In that case, any cheating by the firm would affect the next generation of workers' assessments of $\tilde{g}(t)$. This would raise the wage that the firm has to pay to attract workers, and this cost should just offset the benefit. However, if either of these assumptions is dropped, $\tilde{g}(t)$ may well become endogenous.[14]

A second result is that as firm cheating becomes more profitable and $\tilde{g}(t)$ increases, *T* declines. That is, mandatory retirement should occur at earlier ages in industries where the incentive for firms to cheat on their workers is higher. This is because the left-hand side of equation (7) is reduced as $\tilde{f}(t)$ increases and less end weighting of the wage path produces a higher $\tilde{f}(t)$.

---

[12] *Again, available from the author upon request.*

[13] *See Fama (1978) on this point.*

[14] *This suggests that a firm with an unanticipated decrease in its horizon will be more likely to cheat on workers. Thus, one may expect to find that the incidence of pension default and early termination is higher in declining industries.*

One final and important implication results from the analysis: Other things constant (including education, ability, etc.), workers who have steeper profiles are more likely to have entered a long-term contract designed to prevent cheating. A necessary consequence of this contract is mandatory retirement. Therefore, individuals whose lifetime wage growth rate is higher than anticipated are more likely to have mandatory retirement. This somewhat counterintuitive implication that the high-performing, honest workers, with high wage growth rates, are more likely to have mandatory retirement is tested in the empirical section. The prediction is unequivocally supported by that evidence.

Note that pensions are a possibility, but not a necessity up to this point. Path *LHNX* in figure 2, for example, is one possible path. Two added considerations make pensions part of the optimal determinate wage path. The first, and most obvious, is a progressive income tax structure which makes a lump-sum payment at T less desirable than a smooth pension flow from T to T'. The second is relaxation of the assumption that cheating is observed immediately. If there were a lag time required for detection, then it would be optimal to withhold some payment until after T, or until the results were in, as it were. Pensions would act as such a holdback. This argument is somewhat less compelling than the first, however, because it requires that firms be allowed to terminate pension payments after they have already begun to make them. As an empirical phenomenon, the significance of midstream termination is doubtful.[15]

B. STOCHASTIC VARIATION

Another consideration is important. There is a potential inefficiency in this model which is tied to the question of early retirement. One observes that individuals sometimes leave the firm before T, the date of mandatory retirement. Does this suggest a mistake or inefficiency implicit in the lifetime contract? The answer is no. Consider figure 3.

Suppose that we introduce a stochastic component to the analysis such that at time t^*, the worker receives an unexpected offer of $\overline{W}_{t^*}$ from another firm. Under these circumstances, the worker would not leave the original firm, because $W^*(t^*) > \overline{W}_{t^*}$. However, if $\overline{W}_{t^*}$ measures his VMP in the alternative firm, it is inefficient for him to remain with the original firm since $\overline{W}_{t^*} > V(t^*)$. That is, his social value is greater at the alternative firm, yet he remains with the original firm only because his wage rate is higher there. This is clearly inefficient, and it is unnecessary. An appropriate severance payment will eliminate the inefficiency which seems at first glance to be a necessary consequence of long-term contracts. At t^*, the original firm still "owes" the worker area *ABCD* as payment (with

---

[15] *An alternative justification for a wage profile which rises more steeply than VMP is risk aversion coupled with uncertainty about VMP. If some workers will have low VMPs in the future relative to others, but neither workers nor firms can identify these workers initially, workers will prefer to buy "insurance" from the firm. This notion, which is described in detail in an earlier version of this paper, is related to the insurance ideas of Baily (1974), Azariadis (1975), Grossman (1977), and the self-selection analyses of Rothschild and Stiglitz (1976) and Salop and Salop (1976). The empirical evidence, however, is at odds with this view and so I only mention it in passing.*

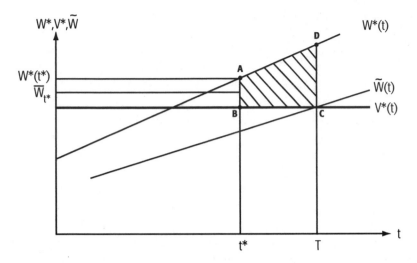

FIGURE 3

interest) for service rendered between 0 and t_0. If the firm were to make a lump-sum payment to the worker at t^* equal to area $ABCD$ in t^* dollars, the firm would have paid out over the worker's lifetime an amount exactly equal to the present value of his marginal product. This is the equilibrium condition for the firm's payment through T, so the firm suffers no loss by allowing the worker to quit at t^* with severance pay. The worker, however, is better off. As the result of taking the job at the alternative firm and receiving severance pay, he will receive the present value of $W^*(t)$ from 0 to T plus the present value of the difference $\tilde{W}(t^*) - V(t)$ from t^* to T. That is,

$$
\begin{aligned}
\text{the present value} \\
\text{of earnings}
\end{aligned}
\quad
\begin{aligned}
&= \int_0^{t^*} W*(\tau)e^{-r\tau}d\tau + \int_{t^*}^T \big[W*(\tau) - V*(\tau)\big]e^{-r\tau} + \int_{t^*}^T \overline{W}(t^*)e^{-r\tau}d\tau \\
&= \int_0^T W*(\tau)e^{-r\tau}d\tau - \int_{t^*}^T V*(\tau)e^{-r\tau}d\tau + \int_{t^*}^T \overline{W}(t^*)e^{-r\tau}d\tau \\
&= \int_0^T W*(\tau)e^{-r\tau}d\tau + \int_{t^*}^T \big[\overline{W}(t^*) - V*(\tau)\big]e^{-r\tau}d\tau,
\end{aligned}
$$

which exceeds his earnings at the original firm $[= \int_0^T \tilde{W}*(\tau)e^{-r\tau}d\tau]$ by the difference between $\tilde{W}(t^*)$ and V^* for the appropriate period. Thus, the worker and firm behave efficiently as long as severance pay is permitted.

One form that the severence-pay arrangement may take is increased pension benefits. Thus, we expect that workers who retire early would receive a larger expected pension than those who work through T. This is a characteristic of many pension plans (as will be discussed below).

The qualification raised in the last few paragraphs is an important one because it reconciles the phenomenon of early retirement with the lifetime payment scheme suggested earlier. It is also important because it means that unexpected changes either in the alternative use of time (as another employment offer or a change in the value of leisure, say, due to poor health) or in the value of the marginal product at the original firm (say, due to business-cycle conditions) do not result in an inefficiency. This long-term contract carries no immobility costs as long as severance pay (or pension adjustment) is permitted.

C. THE CHOICE OF T

The past few pages have argued that mandatory retirement is the necessary consequence of an optimal wage scheme which makes both workers and firms better off. There, the existence of some T or date of mandatory retirement was determined optimal. But one important issue remains: The formal model presented in Section A yields a solution for T given the parameters. However, one observes that the actual distribution of T is not as smooth as one might expect from that model. That is, the reservation wage functions are likely to be smooth, and this would imply a smooth distribution of T. The real world seems to be characterized by a set of T's that take particular values. One source (Banker's Trust 1975), which sampled firms which employed a total of 8.4 million workers (about 10 percent of the civilian labor force) in 1970–75, reports that of firms which stated an age of mandatory retirement, over 87 percent had that age equal to 65. This suggests that there is some exogenous factor which pulls T to age 65. An obvious candidate for prime mover is the social security provision which becomes available at age 65. Consider the reservation wage function in figures 1 and 2. If at 65 an individual becomes eligible for a social security subsidy to leisure, the reservation wage $\bar{W}(t)$ is likely to take a discrete jump upward at 65. This means that voluntary retirement takes a discrete jump at age 65 as well, which implies that the choice of T such that age equals 65 is most likely. An implication of this argument is that before social security, the distribution of mandatory-retirement ages among firms with mandatory retirement would have been more dispersed. Unfortunately, no data are available on this point.

Social security is one possible determinant of T. There may be others as well. Social security payments do not affect all individuals in the same way. High-wage workers, for example, may find the social security subsidy to leisure relatively less attractive than do low-wage workers. As a result, ages of mandatory retirement might vary by the characteristics of the workers. An obvious determinant of retirement date is education. If education increases the value of work by more than the value of leisure, one would expect more educated workers to retire later (Bowen and Finegan [1969] find this positive relationship). If, as this paper claims, mandatory retirement is the outgrowth of an optimal long-term contract, we might then expect that conditional upon having mandatory retirement, education and the age of mandatory retirement will be positively correlated. This is explored in the empirical analysis below. In addition, anything that affects $\tilde{f}(t)$ and $\tilde{g}(t)$ will affect the choice of T. If either probability of cheating is higher, T will be lower. Thus, the age of mandatory retirement will be negatively related to the probability of early termination.

II. SOME IMPLICATIONS OF THE MODEL

In the previous section, a model was presented which has implications for the incidence of mandatory retirement by job and demographic characteristics. In this section I will explore these implications in greater detail and outline the empirical tests which will be discussed in the next section.

The first and most important implication of the model is that mandatory retirement is more likely to be found where job tenure is long. That is, we portray mandatory retirement as the consequence of an optimal long-term contract between a worker and firm. If contracts are short term, say week by week or even year by year, profiles where wages are below VMP early in life and above VMP late in life are infeasible. Mandatory retirement is only useful in a long-term context.

Another implication, already discussed, is that unanticipated wage growth and the existence of mandatory retirement should be positively correlated. This, too, can be tested easily. By looking at an individual's work history and corresponding wage growth one can see how it relates to mandatory retirement. The argument on wage growth relates to the part that is unobservable at $t = 0$. Some differences are anticipated. We know, for example, from the outset that more educated workers learn more rapidly than the less educated. We therefore want to compare two individuals with the same observable characteristics.[16] The one with the most rapid wage growth, given these characteristics, is then the one with the higher probability of mandatory retirement under the incentives view. We therefore expect the probability of mandatory retirement to be positively related to the difference between actual wage growth and predicted (at time $t = 0$) wage growth.

Wage growth and job tenure are not exogenous variables. They are themselves the result of a choice process that is based on lifetime optimization. This suggests that mandatory retirement will be correlated with those variables that underlie wage growth and job tenure determination. That is, a reduced form, as well as structural approach, may prove interesting. For example, to the extent that whites have longer job tenure than nonwhites, whites should have a higher incidence of mandatory retirement. Similarly, if males enjoy longer job tenure than females, they will experience more mandatory retirement. Similarly, union workers, who have longer job tenure than nonunion workers (see Medoff 1976), should be more likely to experience mandatory retirement. It should be noted that these implications are the opposite of those derived from a queue or discrimination theory. If mandatory retirement were a way to reduce the labor force and make room for the younger, more desirable workers, one would expect that blacks, females, and the poorly educated would be the most affected. (They are the workers who suffer most from layoffs—the phenomenon that queue theory was formulated to explain.) The hypothesis in this paper, where mandatory retirement is viewed as the result of optimal

---

[16] *What is observable to the economist may be much more limited than that which is observable to the employer. It is the latter that is relevant. We are, unfortunately, restricted to the former.*

lifetime contracting, suggests that it is the more favored rather than least favored workers who face mandatory retirement.[17]

Pensions are one way to compensate the worker at T. It was argued above that if there is a progressive tax structure which taxes lump-sum payments at a higher rate than it does pensions, or if cheating is detected with a lag, pensions will be part of the optimal path. Thus, pensions should be positively correlated with mandatory retirement since they both are manifestations of the same contractual arrangement. Also important is that it is necessary to have some type of severance pay in order to avoid the inefficiencies of a long-term contract. As argued above, paying higher pensions to those who retire before T is one such arrangement. Burkhauser (1976) finds that workers who leave the firm before the normal retirement date receive a pension, the actuarial value of which is a monotonic increasing function of the years to normal retirement. This is strong support for the long-term contract view.

This model reinforces the implication of many firm-specific labor models that older workers, if laid off, will have a difficult time finding another job at the same wage. If wage exceeds VMP for older workers, a new firm will be unwilling to pick this worker up at his previous wage.

An additional implication comes from considering types of compensation. Since the steep wage path which necessitates mandatory retirement is seen as the result of an agency problem, piece-rate workers are unlikely to experience mandatory retirement. Mandatory retirement was the necessary consequence of a payment scheme which induced workers to perform optimally. A piece-rate compensation scheme is a substitute. Under this type of payment scheme, workers always have an incentive to reveal their true ability or effort.[18]

The explanation of mandatory retirement provided in this paper also suggests a particular life-cycle pattern of preference for mandatory retirement. In this scheme workers at $t = 0$ prefer the payment arrangement that implies mandatory retirement. Firms prefer this arrangement as well. At time T, however, given that the worker and firm have followed the mandatory-retirement plan, firms favor mandatory retirement for the old worker, but the worker may oppose it vehemently, even though he favored it when he was young. That is, his lifetime wealth is higher with the mandatory-retirement scheme than without it, but given the wage path, his wealth would be even higher if he could continue to work at $W^*(T)$ beyond T. Thus, firms will oppose laws that restrict the use of mandatory-retirement contracts (explicit or implicit). Labor, in general, will also oppose these laws. Old workers, however, will push for legislation that makes mandatory retirement illegal

---

[17] It has been suggested that this view explicitly characterizes the Japanese labor market. Mandatory retirement takes place at age 55 after a long-term contract with the firm has been completed. Often, renegotiation takes place and the worker remains with the firm after 55 (see, e.g., Hashimoto [1977]).

[18] Unfortunately, data on piece-rate vs. time-rae compensation are very difficult to obtain. They are unavailable in the data set used below in this study.

since they can increase their wealth levels by doing so, given that they enjoyed wage paths $W^*(t)$ from $t = 0$ to $t = T$. This closely parallels the demographic breakdown of support of revisions to the Age Discrimination in Employment Act. Both business and organized labor opposed raising the age of exemption to 70. Major support, however, came from lobbying groups which represent the interests of the elderly.[19]

III. An Empirical Model

In this section, the implications discussed above will be given specific functional form and will be tested empirically. Let *MR* be a dummy which equals one if the individual in question has a mandatory retirement provision on his current job, and zero otherwise.[20] Let *E* be the number of years that the worker has been employed with his current firm. Let *AWG* be the average level of wage growth over the individual's lifetime. Then the theory above predicts that

$$\text{prob}\left(MR = 1\right) = \frac{1}{1 + \exp\left\{-\left[\alpha_0 + \alpha_1 E + \alpha_2\left(AWG - A\hat{W}G\right)\right]\right\}}, \tag{9}$$

where $A\hat{W}G$ is the predicted level of wage growth from a wage growth regression. Further, there will be equations for the determination of *E* and *AWG* as well:

$$E = \beta_0 + \beta_1 \text{ Male} + \beta_2 \text{ White} + \beta_3 \text{ Ed} + \beta_4 \text{ Urban} + \beta_5 \text{ Married} + \beta_6 AFJ, \tag{10}$$

where Male, White, Urban, and Married are zero-one dummies, and Ed is the years of schooling completed; *AFJ* is the age of first job. (This corrects for vintage and inflation effects.)

$$AWG = \gamma_0 + \gamma_1 \text{ Male} + \gamma_2 \text{ White} + \gamma_3 \text{ Ed} + \gamma_4 \text{ Urban} + \gamma_5 \text{ Married} + \gamma_6 AFJ. \tag{11}$$

Alternatively, one can specify the following reduced-form equation:

---

[19] *It should be pointed out, however, that there are many other models of mandatory retirement which generate the same structure of preferences. On the other hand, Ehrenberg (1978) finds that firefighters and policemen who have mandatory-retirement provisions also obtain higher wages. This is consistent with this model.*

[20] *This variable actually understates the true incidence of mandatory retirement. Some retirement is mandatory as a result of pension schemes which essentially prevent anyone from continuing to work past 65. For example, mandatory retirement is likely to be unnecessary in a firm that offers no pension to individuals who leave the firm after age 65, and a full salary pension to those who leave at 65. This points out that the mandatory-retirement response is itself a function of price. Some attempt to deal with response bias is made below.*

prob $(MR = 1)$

$$= 1/\{1 + \exp[-(\eta_0 + \eta_1 \text{ Male} + \eta_2 \text{ White} + \eta_3 \text{ Ed} + \eta_4 \text{ Urban} + \eta_5 \text{ Married} + \eta_6 \text{ AFJ})]\}. \quad (12)$$

The signs of the coefficients in (12) should be the same as the sign on the corresponding variable in (10). This is because α_1 is positive and because $AWG - A\hat{W}G$ should not vary with any of these variables if (11) is specified correctly.

The same set of equations can be estimated with MR replaced by PP, where PP is a dummy equal to one if there is a pension plan. Thus,

$$\text{prob}\left(PP = 1\right) = \frac{1}{1 + \exp\left\{-\left[\delta_0 + \delta_1 \text{Ed} + \delta_2\left(AWG - A\hat{W}G\right)\right]\right\}}. \quad (13)$$

If δ_1 and δ_2 have the same signs as α_1 and α_2, we might expect a positive simple correlation between PP and MR.

The data used in this analysis came from the Longitudinal Retirement History Survey, 1969–71. This is a panel study of about 11,000 individuals who were 58–63 years old in 1969. A follow-up survey was done in 1971, and the data used in this analysis are derived from that wave. Only those working in 1971 were used so that data on wages could be obtained.

All were asked whether or not their firm had a mandatory-retirement provision which applied to them. An affirmative answer to this question was coded as $MR = 1$. The wage rate, W, is the hourly (actual or derived) wage rate on the current job. The measure of job tenure used, E, is the difference between the question date and the date at which the individual reports to have started his current job. Average wage growth, AWG, is constructed as follows: Individuals were asked what their wage rates were on their first full-time jobs. (The starting wage on their current job was not reported.) They also reported the age at which they took this job. Thus, define

$$AWG \equiv \frac{W_t - W_{t_0}}{t - t_0}, \quad (14)$$

where t_0 is the age of first job and t is the individual's current age. All other variables were defined above.

IV. RESULTS

First and most important, it should be noted that both job tenure and wage growth affect mandatory retirement positively. This is seen in equation (9) in table 1. Individuals who have longer job tenure and more rapid unanticipated wage growth are the ones who are most likely to face mandatory retirement. This finding, although consistent with the theory of this paper, is hard to reconcile in terms of queue or discrimination theories of mandatory retirement. Note that the effect of $AWG - A\bar{W}G$ is positive and substantial. This is consistent with the incentives or agency view of mandatory retirement. Second, note that the reduced-form coefficients in equation (12) go in the direction predicted by this theory but seem inconsistent with theories of discrimination. Note in particular that males and highly educated workers are the ones most likely to have mandatory retirement.[21]

It is interesting that the pension-plan equation (13) and the mandatory-retirement equation (9) are very similar and that the reduced-form versions are not very different. The theory related to lifetime labor force contracts predicts that this would be the case (note that the mean value of MR is .35 and the mean value of PP is .49). The exogenous variables seem to have virtually the same effect on the existence of mandatory retirement as they do on the existence of pension plans. Furthermore, the correlation between mandatory retirement and pension plans in a simple sense is extremely high. In this sample, 62 percent of those with a pension plan have mandatory retirement. Further, 86 percent of those who have mandatory retirement also have a pension plan. This finding is important. It is strong support for the coupling of mandatory retirement and pensions. The theory above suggests that they should be linked directly as each is the outcome of the same optimal contract. That is, in a world where the tax rate is higher on a lump-sum payment than on a smooth flow of income with the same present value, or in a world where cheating is detected with a lag, all wage paths that have mandatory retirement will also have pensions.

As mentioned above, there may be reporting bias associated with the MR variables. New workers, for example, may be less aware of the rules of the firm and less likely to report the existence of mandatory retirement. To treat this, individuals with tenure levels in the twentieth percentile were separated from the rest of the sample, and the estimation contained in table 1 was repeated for each group separately. (The low-tenure group had $0 \leq E \leq 4.3$; the high-tenure group had $4.3 \leq E \leq 59.0$.) The results, only summarized here for the sake of brevity, reveal the same basic story as table 1. Deletion of the low-tenure individuals leaves the results for the top 80 percent essentially unchanged. In addition, the results for the low-tenure group were similar to those for the high-tenure group. The only notable difference is that for this group, married workers were less likely to face mandatory retirement than unmarried ones.

Some empirical evidence can be obtained on variations in T, the age of mandatory retirement, across individuals. Earlier it was suggested that more highly educated individuals would have optimal dates of retirement later in their lifetimes. If the skills which they acquired in school were relatively more useful in the labor market, then they would

---

[21] *The reversal in signs on the urban variable may reflect the fact that information is easier to obtain in small towns and there is, therefore, less need for payment schemes which require mandatory retirement.*

TABLE 1

LOGIT AND OLS RESULTS

	Eq. (9): MR			Eq. (10): E	Eq. (11): AWG	Eq. (12): MR			Eq. (13): PP			PP		
	Logit	$\frac{\partial \overline{MR}}{\partial X_i}\frac{X_i}{\overline{MR}}$	$\frac{\partial \overline{MR}}{\partial X_i}$	OLS	OLS	Logit	$\frac{\partial \overline{MR}}{\partial X_i}\frac{X_i}{\overline{MR}}$	$\frac{\partial \overline{MR}}{\partial X_i}$	Logit	$\frac{\partial \overline{PP}}{\partial X_i}\frac{X_i}{\overline{PP}}$	$\frac{\partial PP}{\partial X_i}$	Logit	$\frac{\partial \overline{PP}}{\partial X_i}\frac{X_i}{\overline{PP}}$	$\frac{\partial PP}{\partial X_i}$
E	.02727 (.00249)	.31	.006	...	...	...	...	...	.02958 (.00249)	.28	.007	...	...	...
$AWG - A\hat{W}G$	2.8992 (.502)	*	.661	...	...	...	...	...	5.8557 (.5791)	*	1.46	...	...	...
Male	...	...	...	2.25 (.37)	.0640 (.0135)	.2268 (.1398)	†	.051	...	...	...	.3451 (.1345)	†	.086
White	...	...	...	1.00 (.77)	.0118 (.0119)	.0757 (.1299)	†	.017	...	...	...	.2650 (.1231)	†	.066
Ed	...	...	...	.153 (.062)	.0084 (.0009)	.0963 (.0100)	.655	.021	...	...	...	.0945 (.0097)	.51	.023
Urban	...	...	...	−.289 (.423)	.0183 (.0065)	.2254 (.0672)	†	.051	...	...	...	.3492 (.0652)	†	.087
Married	...	...	...	1.015 (.769)	−.0201 (.0118)	−.0244 (.1230)	†	−.007	...	...	...	.0221 (.1185)	†	.006
AFJ	...	...	...	−.174 (.130)	.0014 (.0004)	.0011 (.0049)	.014	.0002	...	...	...	−.0129 (.0048)	−.14	−.003
DMR	...	...	...	...	...	...	...	...	...	...	...	...	...	...
Constant	−1.1067 (.057)	...	...	16.1 (1.2)	−.0833 (.0194)	−1.9852 (.2105)	...	...	−.5582 (.0545)	...	...	−1.4727 (.200)	...	...
SEE	...	...	...	13.27	.205	...	...	...	...	...	...	...	...	...
N	4,123	...	...	4,123	4,123	4,123	...	...	4,123	...	...	4,123	...	...
−2 log λ	186.7	...	...	...	...	119.9	...	...	324.9	...	...	180.7	...	...
R^2	...	...	...	.025	.029	...	...	...	...	...	...	...	...	...

Note. Standard errors are in parentheses.

* $AWG - A\hat{W}G = 0$ by construction; $\overline{A\hat{W}G} = .088$.

† Dummy variables; $\overline{MR} = .352$, $\overline{PP} = .485$.

have an incentive to continue working longer than less educated workers. It follows, then, that if mandatory retirement is a manifestation of an optimal long-term contract, more educated workers should have older ages of mandatory retirement.

In table 2, a regression is presented in which the age of mandatory retirement is regressed on demographic variables, education, and job tenure. The sample contains only those who face mandatory retirement. The first point is that education has an important (in size and precision of estimate) effect on the age of mandatory retirement. It appears as though more educated workers make contracts which end at a later point in their life cycles. This is consistent with the notion that they choose to retire later voluntarily as well.

Second, note that job tenure has a negative effect on the age of mandatory retirement. In the context of this sample of old workers, all of whom are about the same age, job tenure is a proxy for the date at which the employment contract was made. Holding age about constant, those workers with fewer years of job tenure also have more recently made a "contract" with the employer than those with longer tenure. The results suggest that more recent contracts specify a later age of mandatory retirement. Individuals who have made more recent contracts may have done so either because the value of their leisure did

TABLE 2

REGRESSION AND LOGIT RESULTS

	MR Age OLS
Male	−.093 (.256)
White	−.387 (.246)
Ed	.118 (.017)
Urban	−.133 (.120)
Married	.198 (.225)
AFJ	−.005 (.009)
E	−.032 (.004)
Constant	66.4 (.4)
R^2	.066
N	1,429
SEE	2.25

Note. Standard errors are in parentheses.

not rise as rapidly as they expected ($\bar{W}[t]$ is flatter than had been anticipated) or because they ended up being more productive in the labor force than expected ($V^*[t]$ is higher than anticipated). In either case, it is optimal for them to be "bought out" of their previous contract (through severance pay or early pensions) and to negotiate a new one. The new one will have a later date of mandatory retirement because, as equation (6) shows, the higher is $V^*(t)$ or the flatter is $\bar{W}(t)$, the later will be the date of mandatory retirement.

Third, the coefficient on White is negative. Other things constant, whites have earlier ages of mandatory retirement than blacks. Although the explanation of this phenomenon is not obvious, let us conjecture. Even holding education and urbanization constant, whites have substantially higher income than blacks. This is especially true of nonwage income. Thus, if the education effect captures most of the wage variation, the white variable may well proxy higher property income. Since the income effect on leisure is positive, holding education constant yields an increase in the demand for leisure via income effects, so whites are richer individuals with the same wage rate. As such, whites prefer to work less and therefore set up contracts with earlier retirement dates.

V. SUMMARY AND CONCLUSIONS

This paper provides an explanation of the institution of mandatory retirement that is derived from optimizing behavior on the part of both workers and firms. The theory, simply stated, is that it pays both parties to agree to a long-term wage stream which pays workers less than their VMPs when young and more than the VMPs when old. By using this payment schedule, the worker's lifetime VMP is higher than it would be in the absence of that scheme because this provides valuable incentives to the worker which would otherwise be lost to moral hazard. A necessary consequence of this payment schedule is mandatory retirement, that is, a date at which the contract is terminated and the worker is no longer entitled to receive a wage greater than his VMP. Its mandatory nature is illusory, however. The date of mandatory retirement is the social and private optimum date of retirement.

This theory has some perhaps counterintuitive implications. It suggests that the long-tenured and most able workers will face mandatory retirement rather than the least tenured. It predicts that the highly educated, white, male workers are the ones most likely to be mandatorily retired. These predictions are borne out in the empirical section.

The most important implication of this theory is that workers and firms all benefit from the existence of mandatory retirement. Although older workers may be unhappy about this provision when the retirement day draws near, their lifetime wealth levels are increased as the result of being able to enter into these kinds of contracts. What they lose by being mandatorily retired is more than offset by what they have gained during working years as the result. As mandatory retirement is made illegal before age 70 and the social security payment age is not raised accordingly, there will be an efficiency loss as voluntary and mandatory retirement ages diverge. If the ability to enter into mandatory-retirement contracts is eliminated through legislation, this analysis argues that current older workers will enjoy a small once-and-for-all gain at the expense of a much larger and continuing efficiency loss that affects all workers and firms adversely.

REFERENCES

Azariadis, Costas. "Implicit Contracts and Underemployment Equilibria." *J.P.E.* 83, no. 6 (December 1975): 1183–1202.

Baily, Martin N. "Wages and Employment under Uncertain Demand." *Rev. Econ. Studies* 41 (January 1974): 37–50.

Banker's Trust Company. 1975 *Study of Corporate Pension Plans.* New York: Banker's Trust, 1975.

Becker, G., and Stigler, G. "Law Enforcement, Malfeasance, and Compensation of Enforcers." *J. Legal Studies* 3, no. 1 (1974): 1–18.

Bowen, W. G., and Finegan, T. A. *The Economics of Labor Force Participation.* Princeton, NJ.: Princeton Univ. Press, 1969.

Burkhauser, R. "Early Pension Decision and Its Effect on Exit from the Labor Market." Ph.D. dissertation, Univ. Chicago, 1976.

Ehrenberg, Ronald. "Retirement System Characteristics and Compensating Wage Differentials in the Public Sector." Unpublished paper, Cornell Univ., 1978.

Fama, Eugene. "Agency Problems and the Theory of the Firm." Mimeographed. Univ. Chicago, 1978.

Feldstein, Martin. "Temporary Layoffs in the Theory of Unemployment." *J.P.E.* 84, no. 5 (October 1976): 937–57.

Freeman, S. "Wage Trends as Performance Displays Productive Potential: A Model of Application to Academic Early Retirement." *Bell J. Econ.* 8, no. 2 (Autumn 1977): 419–43.

Gordon, M. S. "Older Workers and Retirement Policies." *Monthly Labor Rev.* 83, no. 6 (June 1960): 577–85.

Grossman, H. "Risk Shifting, Layoffs, and Seniority," Working Paper no. 76-7, Brown Univ., 1977.

Hashimoto, M. "Variable Wages, On-the-job Training, and Lifetime Employment in Japan." Unpublished paper, Univ. Washington, September 1977.

Kreps, J. "A Case Study of Variables in Retirement Policy." *Monthly Labor Rev.* 84, no. 6 (June 1961): 587–91.

Medoff, J. "Layoffs and Alternatives under Trade Unions in United States Manufacturing." Discussion Paper no. 525, Harvard Inst. Econ. Res., 1976.

National Industrial Conference Board, Inc. *Corporate Retirement Policies and Practices.* Studies in Personnel Policy, no. 190. New York: NICB, 1964.

Rothschild, Michael, and Stiglitz, Joseph. "Equilibrium in Competitive Insurance Markets: An Essay on the Economics of Imperfect Information." *Q.J.E.* 90, no. 4 (November 1976): 629–49.

Salop, Joanne, and Salop, Steven. "Self-Selection and Turnover in the Labor Market." *Q.J.E.* 90, no. 4 (November 1976): 619–27.

Stiglitz, J. "Incentives, Risk, and Information: Notes toward a Theory of Hierarchy." *Bell J. Econ.* 6, no. 2 (Autumn 1975): 552–79.

U.S. Department of Health, Education, and Welfare. *Reaching Retirement Age.* Social Security Administration Research Report no. 47. Washington: Government Printing Office, 1976.

ABOUT THE AUTHOR

Edward P. Lazear

Edward Lazear is Jack Steele Parker Professor of Human Resources Management and Economics in the Graduate School of Business, and Senior Fellow in the Hoover Institution, at Stanford University. Well known as a leader in research on the structure of human resource management, Lazear also founded, and remains editor of, the influential *Journal of Labor Economics*.

Lazear received A.B. and A.M. degrees from the University of California, Los Angeles in 1971. After obtaining his Ph.D. degree from Harvard University, Lazear joined the faculty of the Graduate School of Business of the University of Chicago, where he remained until he moved to Stanford in 1992. Lazear was elected president of the Society of Labor Economists in 1998.

Despite the time he devotes to his teaching (he was awarded a Distinguished Teaching Award by Stanford in 1994), Lazear is also known as an avid wind surfer and skier.

An Empirical Model of Labor Supply in a Life-Cycle Setting

THOMAS E. MACURDY

Stanford University and National Bureau of Economic Research

This paper formulates and estimates a structural intertemporal model of labor supply. Using theoretical characterizations derived from an economic model of lifetime behavior, a two-step empirical analysis yields estimates of intertemporal and uncompensated substitution effects which provide the information needed to predict the response of hours of work to life-cycle wage growth and shifts in the lifetime wage path.

INTRODUCTION

Over the past several years there has been considerable activity in formulating life-cycle models of labor supply. Most of this work has gone unnoticed in the empirical literature. This study develops an estimable model of labor supply that fully incorporates life-cycle factors, and it devises simple econometric procedures for estimating this model.

Most empirical work on labor supply assumes decision making in a one-period context. Typically, annual hours of work are regressed on the current hourly wage rate and some measure of property income. A worker, however, determines his current labor supply in a life-cycle setting. Unless credit markets are "perfectly imperfect" and there is no human capital accumulation, the supply of labor is a function of current and future discounted wage rates as well as wealth and constraints in other periods. Accordingly, regressions of hours of work on current hourly wage rates yield a wage coefficient that confuses the response of labor supply to wage changes of three types: those arising from movements along a given lifetime wage profile, those arising from shifts in the wage profile, and those arising from changes in the profile slope. As a result, the wage coefficient usually reported in empirical studies has no behavioral interpretation in the context of a life-cycle framework.

The theory underlying the model of lifetime consumption and hours of work in this paper represents a natural extension of Friedman's (1957) permanent income theory to a

This research was supported by NSF grant no. SOC77-27136 and grant no. 10-P90748/9-01 from the Social Security Administration. I have benefited from discussions with James Heckman, Robert Michael, and John Pencavel on the material in this paper. I am also grateful for comments from Douglas Brown, William Gould, and Dan Sumner.

situation in which the relative price of consumption and leisure varies over the life cycle. Theoretical characterizations of consumption and labor supply derived from this theory sharply distinguish between factors determining a consumer's dynamic behavior and factors determining differences in consumption and hours of work across consumers. This separation leads to a manageable empirical model that allows one to distinguish the responses of labor supply to wage changes attributable to movements along a lifetime wage profile from those responses attributable to parametric changes in this profile. In addition, one can estimate the effects of wealth and demographic characteristics on lifetime hours of work.

The organization of this paper is as follows. Section I outlines an economic model of life-cycle behavior. Section II develops and discusses an empirical model of labor supply. Section III interprets the parameters of this empirical model. Section IV contains the empirical analysis.

I. A Life-Cycle Model of Consumption and Labor Supply

The consumer is assumed to choose consumption and hours of leisure at each age to maximize a lifetime preference function that is strongly separable over time, subject to a wealth constraint. Let utility at age t be given by the concave differentiable function $U[C(t), L(t)]$, where $C(t)$ is the amount of market goods consumed and $L(t)$ is the number of hours spent in nonmarket activities at age t. The consumer starts life with assets $A(0)$ and operates in an environment of perfect certainty. At each age t he faces a real wage rate equal to $W(t)$ assumed to be exogenously given. The consumer can freely borrow and lend at a real rate of interest equal to $r(t)$ in period t, and his rate of time preference is ρ. A lifetime is assumed to consist of $T + 1$ periods with L^* being the total number of hours in each period.

Formally, the consumer's problem is to choose $C(t)$ and $L(t)$ at each age to maximize the lifetime preference function

$$G\left\{\sum_{t=0}^{T}\frac{1}{(1+\rho)^t}U[C(t), L(t)]\right\}\tag{1}$$

subject to the wealth constraint

$$A(0)+\sum_{t=0}^{T}R(t)N(t)W(t)=\sum_{t=0}^{T}R(t)C(t),\tag{2}$$

where $G(\cdot)$ is a monotonically increasing differentiable function, $N(t) \equiv L^* - L(t)$ is hours of work at age t, and $R(t) \equiv 1/\{[1 + r(1)][1 + r(2)] \cdots [1 + r(t)]\}$ is the discount rate which converts real income in period t into its period 0 equivalent with $R(0) = 1$.

Conditions for an optimum are satisfaction of the lifetime budget constraint and

$$U_1[C(t), L(t)] = R(t)(1 + \rho)^t \lambda, \qquad t = 0, \ldots, T, \tag{3}$$

$$U_2[C(t), L(t)] \geq R(t)(1 + \rho)^t \lambda W(t), \qquad t = 0, \ldots, T, \tag{4}$$

where subscripts denote partial derivatives and λ is defined by $\lambda = \lambda^*/G'$, where λ^* is the Lagrange multiplier associated with the wealth constraint (i.e., λ^* is the marginal utility of wealth in period 0) and G' is the derivative of G. According to condition (3), consumption is chosen so that the marginal utility of consumption equals the marginal utility of wealth after adjusting for a discount factor which depends on the rate of time preference and the rate of interest. Condition (4) determines the consumer's choice of leisure. If it is an equality, then a positive amount of labor is supplied to the market. If it is a strict inequality, then all time is devoted to nonmarket activities.

Using the definition of labor supply (i.e., $N[t] \equiv L^* - L[t]$) and the implicit-function theorem, it is possible to solve equations (3) and (4) for consumption and labor supply as functions of the form

$$C(t) = C[R(t)(1 + \rho)^t \lambda, W(t)], \qquad t = 0, \ldots, T, \tag{5}$$

$$N(t) = N[R(t)(1 + \rho)^t \lambda, W(t)], \qquad t = 0, \ldots, T. \tag{6}$$

The functions $C(\cdot,\cdot)$ and $N(\cdot,\cdot)$ depend only on the functional form of $U(\cdot,\cdot)$. As a consequence of concavity of U and the assumption that consumption and leisure are normal goods, they satisfy

$$C_1 < 0, N_1 \geq 0, N_2 \geq 0. \text{[1]} \tag{7}$$

These consumption and labor-supply functions allow for corner solutions for hours of work either at age t or at any other age t'. No matter what the consumer's labor-force participation pattern over his lifetime, consumption and labor-supply decisions at any age (including the decision to set hours of work equal to zero) are completely

---

[1] *See Heckman (1974, 1976) for proofs of these inequalities. Heckman develops and uses functions equivalent to those given by eqq. (5) and (6) in his analysis of the behavior of consumption and labor supply over the life cycle.*

determined by the functions $C(\cdot,\cdot)$ and $N(\cdot,\cdot)$ and the values of the variables $R(t)(1 + \rho)^t \lambda$ and $W(t)$.[2]

The relationships given by (5) and (6) hereafter will be referred to as the "λ constant" consumption and labor-supply functions. They represent the marginal utility of wealth constant demand functions for consumption and leisure for a particular form of the life-time preference function given by (1), namely, the one obtained when G is the identity transformation. For this particular choice of G, λ is the marginal utility of wealth in period 0. Given a choice of $U(\cdot,\cdot)$, it is theoretically possible to compute a unique value for λ using data on an individual's consumption, labor supply, and wage rate at a point in time. This fact receives much attention in the formulation of the empirical model which is discussed in the next section.

Substituting the λ constant consumption and labor-supply functions into the budget constraint given by (2) yields the equation

$$A(0) + \sum_{t=0}^{T} R(t)\left\{ C\left[R(t)(1+\rho)^t \lambda, W(t) \right] \right\} - W(t)\left\{ N\left[R(t)(1+\rho)^t \lambda, W(t) \right] \right\}. \tag{8}$$

This equation implicitly determines the optimal value of λ; λ, then, can be expressed as a function of initial assets, lifetime wages, interest rates, rates of time preference, and "consumer tastes." Concavity of preferences implies

$$\frac{\partial \lambda}{\partial A(0)} < 0 \quad \text{and} \quad \frac{\partial \lambda}{\partial W(t)} \le 0, \quad t - 0,\ldots,T. \tag{9}$$

Inspection of the λ constant functions reveals that consumption and labor-supply decisions at a point in time are related to variables outside the decision period only through λ. Thus, except for the value of the current wage rate, λ summarizes all information about lifetime wages and property income that a consumer requires to determine his optimal

---

[2] If it is optimal for the consumer to work at age t, then condition (4) is an equality and the functions $C(\cdot,\cdot)$ and $N(\cdot,\cdot)$ represent the solutions of eqq. (3) and (4) for the variables C(t) and N(t) = L* − L(t), respectively. If, on the other hand, the necessary condition given by (4) is an inequality, i.e., $U_2 [C(t), L^*] > R(t)(1 + \rho)^t \lambda W(t)$, then the consumer chooses not to work. In this case, $N(\cdot,\cdot) = 0$ and the function $C(\cdot,\cdot)$ is the solution of the equation $U_1 [C(t), L^*] = R(t)(1 + \rho)^t \lambda$ for C(t). In either case, $C(\cdot,\cdot)$ and $N(\cdot,\cdot)$ only contain the variables $R(t)(1 + \rho)^t \lambda$ and W(t) as arguments and their functional form depends only on the form of the period t utility function $U(\cdot,\cdot)$. For further discussion on this issue see Heckman and MaCurdy (1980). Introducing age dependence into the utility function does not change any of this analysis. If the utility function at age t is given by U[C(t), L(t), X(t)], where X(t) is a vector of time-varying determinants of "consumer tastes," then a third argument X(t) enters the consumption and labor-supply functions given by (5) and (6). These functions satisfy the restrictions given by (7), and they also allow for corner solutions.

[3] See Heckman (1974, 1976) for proof of these propositions.

current consumption and labor supply. At any age, any path of wages or property income over a consumer's lifetime that keeps λ and the current wage constant implies the same optimal current consumption and labor-supply behavior.

The λ constant functions represent an extension of Friedman's (1957) permanent income theory to a situation in which the relative price of consumption and leisure varies over the life cycle. According to these functions, current consumption and labor-supply decisions depend on a permanent component and the current wage rate. The variable λ is like permanent income in the theory of the consumption function. At each point in time it is a sufficient statistic for all historic and future information about lifetime wages and property income that is relevant to the current choice of consumption and labor supply. The usual concept of permanent income or wealth does not qualify as a sufficient statistic for this retrospective and prospective information.[4] Given knowledge of permanent income, a consumer also requires information on future wages to determine his optimal current consumption and labor supply. Only if wages are constant over the life cycle, or labor supply is exogenously determined, can λ be written as a simple function of permanent income or wealth.

The λ constant consumption and labor-supply functions fully characterize a consumer's dynamic behavior in a world of perfect certainty.[5] According to these functions, there are two reasons why a consumer might change his consumption or hours of work as he ages: (1) the real wage rate changes, or (2) the rate of interest varies and is not equal to the rate of time preference.[6]

II. AN EMPIRICAL MODEL

This section formulates an empirical model of labor supply that is based on the economic model described above. Specific functional forms are proposed for the λ constant labor-supply function and for the relationship between λ and such variables as lifetime wages and initial assets. The following discussion assumes the availability of panel data.

---

[4] *Permanent income here is defined as that stream of income whose discounted value equals the consumer's wealth in present value terms. Formally, permanent income in period 0, Y_p, is defined by the equation $A(0) + \Sigma_{t=0}^{T} R(t)N(t)W(t) = Y_p \Sigma_{t=0}^{T} R(t)$.*

[5] *See MaCurdy (1978, 1980, in press) for a discussion of the uncertainty case. It is shown in these papers that with minor modifications the empirical specifications of labor supply developed in this section and their implementation in the following sections are consistent with a world in which the consumer is uncertain about his future lifetime path of wages and property income.*

[6] *Changes in a consumer's tastes can also be a reason for adjustments in consumption and labor supply over the life cycle. As discussed in n. 2 above, if the period utility function is age dependent, the λ constant consumption and labor-supply functions will also be age dependent. It is still true, however, that the λ constant functions fully characterize a consumer's dynamic behavior.*

AN EMPIRICAL SPECIFICATION FOR THE λ CONSTANT LABOR-SUPPLY FUNCTION

Assume that consumer i at age t has utility given by

$$U_i[C_i(t), L_i(t)] = Y_{1i}(t)[C_i(t)]^{\omega_1} - Y_{2i}(t)[N_i(t)]^{\omega_2}, \tag{10}$$

where $0 < \omega_1 < 1$ and $\omega_2 > 1$ are time-invariant parameters common across workers, and $Y_{1i}(t)$, $Y_{2i}(t) > 0$ are age-specific modifiers of "tastes." The variables $Y_{1i}(t)$ and $Y_{2i}(t)$ depend on all of consumer i's characteristics which plausibly affect his preferences at age t; these characteristics may include such variables as the number of children present at age t, the consumer's education, and even age itself

Assuming an interior optimum,[7] the implied λ constant labor-supply function for consumer i at age t in natural logs is

$$\ln N_i(t) = \frac{1}{\omega_2 - 1}\left\{ \ln \lambda_i - \ln Y_{2i}(t) - \ln \omega_2 + \ln\left[R(t)(1+\rho)^t \right] + \ln W_i(t) \right\}. \tag{11}$$

Assuming that "tastes" for work are randomly distributed over the population according to the equation $\ln Y_{2i}(t) = \sigma_i - u_i^*(t)$, the labor-supply function can be written as

$$\ln N_i(t) = F_i + \delta \sum_{k=0}^{t}\left[\rho - r(k)\right] + \delta \ln W_i(t) + u_i(t), \tag{12}$$

where $F_i = [1/(\omega_2 - 1)](\ln \lambda_i - \sigma_i - \ln \omega_2)$, $\delta = 1/(\omega_2 - 1)$, $u_i(t) = \delta u_i^*(t)$, $r(0) = \rho$, and we have used the approximations $\ln[1 + r(t)] \approx r(t)$ and $\ln(1 + \rho) \approx \rho$. The unobserved variables σ_i and $u_i(t)$ represent the unmeasured characteristics of consumer i; σ_i is a permanent component, and $u_i(t)$ is a time-varying error term with zero mean. If we assume that the real rate of interest, $r(t)$ for $t \geq 1$, is constant over the life cycle and equal to r, then the λ constant hours of work function reduces to

$$\ln N_i(t) = F_i + bt + \delta \ln W_i(t) + u_i(t), \tag{13}$$

where $b = \delta(\rho - r)$.[8]

---

[7] *Since this study's empirical objective is to examine the labor-supply behavior of prime-age males, this assumption is not unreasonable.*

[8] *There are other forms of the utility function that have convenient empirical specifications for the λ constant consumption and leisure demand functions. Two such functions are*

The intercept term F_i in this equation represents a time-invariant component that is unique to individual i. This study treats F_i as a fixed effect. Since F_i contains $\ln \lambda_i$ as one of its components, one cannot assume that F_i is a "random factor" uncorrelated with exogenous variables of the model. Inspection of equation (8) reveals that λ depends on the values of variables and constraints in all periods. By construction, F_i is correlated with any exogenous variables used to predict a consumer's wages or wealth. Hence, treating F_i as part of the error term would result in biased parameter estimates of the labor-supply function. Treating F_i as a fixed effect, on the other hand, avoids this bias.

Estimating the parameters of equation (12) only requires variables observed within the sample period. Regressions of current hours of work on individual specific intercepts and current wage rates produce a full set of parameter estimates.[9] Because F_i captures the effect of $\ln \lambda_i$, its estimated value summarizes all of the retrospective and prospective information relevant to consumer i's current choices. As there is no need to forecast any life-cycle variables that are outside the sample period, the λ constant functions afford a considerable simplification of the empirical analysis.

Use of the λ constant functions allows one to estimate parameters needed to characterize dynamic behavior without introducing any assumptions regarding a consumer's behavior outside the sample period. To appreciate this point, consider the problem of predicting the additional hours of work a consumer will supply in response to observing a higher wage rate than he observed at a younger age. To obtain an estimate of this response using a traditional model of life-cycle labor supply, one must formally incorporate the worker's future plans in the model. For example, if the worker anticipates an early retirement, future wages corresponding to the retirement years do not influence current labor supply. Thus, the researcher must not include these wages as explanatory

---

$$U_i(t) = \kappa_i(t)\left[C_i(t) + \mu_i^*(t)\right]^{\omega^*}\left[L_i(t) + \mu_i(t)\right]^{\omega},$$

$$\kappa_i(t), \omega^*, \omega > 0, \omega^* + \omega < 1 \text{ or } \kappa_i(t), \omega^*, \omega < 0;$$

$$U_i(t) = \kappa_i^*(t)\frac{\left[C_i(t) + \mu_i^*(t)\right]^{\omega^*} - 1}{\omega^*} + \kappa_i(t)\frac{\left[L_i(t) + \mu_i(t)\right]^{\omega} - 1}{\omega},$$

$$\kappa_i^*(t), \kappa_i(t) > 0, \omega^*, \omega < 1,$$

where $\kappa_i^*(t)$, $\kappa_i(t)$, $\mu_i^*(t)$, $\mu_i(t)$, ω^*, and ω are all parameters. Both of these functions are concave. They include Cobb-Douglas, addilog, CES, and Stone-Geary as special cases. The λ constant functions for consumption and leisure are log linear in λ, wages, and the coefficients $\kappa_i^*(t)$ and $\kappa_i(t)$, which represent specific modifiers of tastes. This study uses the utility function given by (10) to formulate an empirical model because it implies a form for the labor-supply function which can be readily compared with labor-supply equations found in existing empirical work.

[9] *If utility at age t depends on measured characteristics of the consumer that vary over the sample period, then current values of these "taste-shifter" variables would also be included as regressors. A natural way to introduce such taste-shifter variables is to model the taste coefficient $Y_i(t)$ as a function of the form $\ln Y_i(t) = \sigma_i + X_i(t)\beta - u_i^*(t)$, where $X_i(t)$ is a vector of variables influencing tastes and β is a parameter. For this case, $X_i(t)\beta\delta$ enters as an additional linear term in the λ constant labor-supply equation given by (12) or (13).*

variables. Such considerations lead to difficult data requirements and complicated estimation procedures. Using equation (12), on the other hand, it is possible to analyze this problem without knowing anything about a worker's future plans; an individual constant term for each worker accounts for a worker's future plans in a parametrically simple way.

An Empirical Specification for Individual Effects

Estimation of the λ constant labor-supply function given by (12) does not directly estimate all of the parameters required to characterize all aspects of labor supply. Differences among individuals in initial wealth or lifetime wage paths affect the level of hours of work through F_i. To explain any aspect of labor supply other than dynamic behavior (e.g., how the hours of work of two individuals differ at a point in time), one must confront the problem of predicting individual effects.

From the theoretical analysis above, we know that the value of F, or more properly λ, is uniquely determined by the implicit equation given by (8). This equation does not admit an analytical solution for λ given the specific form of the utility function given by (10), even if it is known that this function applies to all ages and the consumer works in each period. The variable λ is a complicated function of initial assets, lifetime wages, the interest rate, the rate of time preference, and parameters representing unobserved "taste" variables.[10] Using such a relationship as an empirical specification is not feasible.

This study assumes that equation (8) implies a solution for λ in which $\ln \lambda$ can be approximated as a linear function of measured characteristics, the natural log of wages at each age, initial wealth, and an unobserved random variable representing unmeasured characteristics. With this assumption the implied equation for F_i is

$$F_i = Z_i\phi + \sum_{t=0}^{T^*} \gamma(t)\ln W_i(t) + A_i(0)\theta + a_i, \tag{14}$$

where Z_i is a vector of observed variables (e.g., family background variables), a_i is an error term, and ϕ, $\gamma(t)$, and θ are parameters assumed to be constant across consumers.[11] This structural relationship for F_i implicitly assumes that each consumer has a working life of $T^* + 1$ years. According to the theoretical restrictions given by (9), the $\gamma(t)$'s and θ should all be negative.

---

[10] *The equation determining λ_i is*

$$A_i(0) = \sum_{t=0}^{T} R(t)\left\{\left[\frac{1}{Y_{1i}(t)\omega_2}R(t)(1+\rho)^t\lambda_i\right]^{1/(\omega_1-1)} - W_i(t)\left[\frac{1}{Y_{2i}(t)\omega_2}R(t)(1+\rho)^t\lambda_iW_i(t)\right]^{1/(\omega_2-1)}\right\}.$$

[11] *The assumption that these parameters are constant across consumers is, of course, only an approximation. Formally, it can be shown that*

Unfortunately, to formulate an estimable version of an equation for F_i, we require additional assumptions concerning the forms of the lifetime wage and income paths. In contrast to the λ constant labor-supply function, estimating the parameters of equation (14) requires data which normally are not available. Most variables appearing in this equation are not directly observed, including the dependent variable F_i, wages outside the sample period, and initial wealth. While estimates of F_i are obtained as a by-product from estimating equation (12), we still require a mechanism for predicting wages outside the sample period and initial permanent income. We do this by introducing lifetime profiles for wages and income.

This study assumes that the lifetime wage path is

$$\ln W_i(t) = \pi_{0i} + t\pi_{1i} + t^2\pi_{2i} + V_i(t), \tag{15}$$

where π_{0i}, π_{1i}, and π_{2i} are linear functions of the form

$$\pi_{ji} = M_i g_j, \qquad j = 0, 1, 2, \tag{16}$$

M_i is a vector of exogenous determinants of wages which are constant over the consumer's lifetime (e.g., education and background variables), g_j, $j = 0, 1, 2$, are vectors of parameters, and $V_i(t)$ is an error term. This path assumes that wages follow a quadratic equation in age with an intercept and slope coefficients that depend on age-invariant characteristics of the consumer.[12]

$$\gamma(t) = \delta\frac{\partial \ln \lambda}{\partial \ln W(t)} = \delta\left[\frac{\partial \ln N(t)}{\partial \ln \lambda} + 1\right]\frac{\partial \ln \lambda}{\partial A(0)}E^*(t),$$

where $E^*(t) = N(t)W^*(t)$ and $W^*(t) = W(t)R(t)$ are the period 0 present value of earnings and wages in period t. This relationship for $\gamma(t)$ is derived by differentiating Roy's identity for N(t) with respect to A(0) to obtain the equation

$$\frac{\partial \lambda}{\partial W^*(t)} = \lambda\frac{\partial N(t)}{\partial A(0)} + N(t)\frac{\partial \lambda}{\partial A(0)} = \lambda N(t)\left[\frac{\partial \ln N(t)}{\partial \ln \lambda} + 1\right]\frac{\partial \ln \lambda}{\partial A(0)}$$

$$= \frac{\lambda}{W^*(t)}\left[\frac{\partial \ln N(t)}{\partial \ln \lambda} + 1\right]\frac{\partial \ln \lambda}{\partial A(0)}E^*(t).$$

Since the empirical specification for the λ constant hours of work function implies $[\partial \ln N(t)]/(\partial \ln \lambda) = \delta$, we see that we cannot formally have $\gamma(t) = \delta (\partial \ln \lambda)/[\partial \ln W(t)]$ and $\theta = \delta(\delta \ln \lambda)/[\partial A(0)]$ constant. Notice that the effects of the interest rate and time preference on F_i are absorbed into the coefficients of specification (14).

[12] In the following analysis it is assumed that this wage equation generates unbiased predictions for lifetime wages. These predictions need not be efficient nor do they need to be the same predictions used by consumers. It is possible to introduce many alternative forms for the wage equation, such as higher-order polynomials or polynomials with other functions of time (e.g., reciprocals) replacing t and t^2, with only minor modifications of empirical specifications used in the following analysis.

Predicting a consumer's initial wealth is complicated by the fact that most data sets do not contain extensive measures of even the consumer's current wealth. Some measure of the consumer's property or nonwage income during the sample period, however, is usually available.[13] Let $Y_i(t)$ and $A_i(t)$ denote the property income and assets of consumer i at age t. If $Y_i(t)$ is the income flow generated by investing assets $A_i(t)$ at a rate of interest equal to r, we have the relationship $Y_i(t) = A_i(t)r$. Assume that the following quadratic equation in age approximates the lifetime path for property income:

$$Y_i(t) = \alpha_{0i} + t\alpha_{1i} + t^2\alpha_{2i} + \nu_i(t), \tag{17}$$

where α_{0i}, α_{1i}, and α_{2i} are linear functions of the form

$$\alpha_{ji} = S_i q_j, \qquad j = 0, 1, 2, \tag{18}$$

S_i is a vector of measured age-invariant characteristics of consumer i (e.g., education and background variables), q_j, $j = 0, 1, 2$, are parameter vectors, and $\nu_i(t)$ is an error term.[14] The intercept α_{0i} can be thought of as a measure of consumer i's permanent income at age 0; that is, $\alpha_{0i} = A_i(0)r$.[15]

Combining the lifetime paths for wages and income with equation (14) creates an equation for F_i that can be estimated using data observed within the sample period. Substituting the wage process given by (15) and the relationship $\alpha_{0i} = rA_i(0)$ into equation (14) yields

$$F_i = Z_i\phi + \pi_{0i}\overline{\gamma}_0 + \pi_{1i}\overline{\gamma}_1 + \pi_{2i}\overline{\gamma}_2 + \alpha_{0i}\overline{\theta} + \eta_i, \tag{19}$$

or substituting relations (16) and (18) yields

$$F_i = K_i\psi + a_i, \tag{20}$$

where

$$\overline{\gamma}_j = \sum_{t=0}^{T^*} t^j\gamma(t) \quad j = 0,1,2, \quad \overline{\theta} = \theta/r, \tag{21}$$

---

[13] *These income measures seldom include imputed income generated by consumer durables, which is a major source of property income for most consumers.*

[14] *In contrast to W(t), Y(t) is determined endogenously in this model. Eq. (17) can be viewed as an approximation to the optimal lifetime path for Y(t) expressed as a function of the exogenous variables of the model.*

[15] *Formally, this relationship between α_{0i} and $A_i(0)$ is correct only in a continuous time framework. When modeling the problem in discrete time, one must distinguish assets held at the beginning, at the end of the period, and exactly when asset income is earned within the period.*

K_i is a vector including all age-invariant characteristics determining either wages, income, or λ (i.e., all the elements of M_i, S_i, and Z_i), ψ is a vector of coefficients, and η_i is a disturbance term which is randomly distributed across workers with zero mean. Equation (19) is a structural relationship between F and the characteristics of a consumer's wage and income profiles. The empirical analysis of this study focuses on estimating the parameters of this equation, ϕ, $\overline{\gamma}_0$, $\overline{\gamma}_1$, $\overline{\gamma}_2$, and $\overline{\theta}$. As we shall see shortly, these parameters have a sound economic interpretation. Equation (20) is essentially a reduced-form equation for (19). By estimating the parameters of this equation, it is possible to predict how F varies across consumers using only age-invariant characteristics of the consumer as explanatory variables.

III. INTERPRETATION OF PARAMETERS

In investigating the effect of changes in wages on labor supply, it is important to separate parametric change of the sort usually contemplated in comparative static exercises from evolutionary change due to movement along a life-cycle wage path.[16] A parametric wage change refers to shifts in a life-cycle wage profile (e.g., a shift from path II to path I in figure. 1), while an evolutionary wage change refers to movements along a given profile (i.e., along any path in figure 1). Thus, parametric wage changes refer to differences in wages across consumers, while evolutionary wage changes refer to differences in wages across time for the same consumer.[17]

Consider the behavior of labor supply over the life cycle. As a consumer ages, he adjusts his hours of work in response to the different wage rates he observes at each point in his lifetime. These labor-supply adjustments represent responses to evolutionary wage changes; they reflect the consumer's desire to supply more hours in those periods with highest wages. There is no wealth effect associated with this kind of wage variation since the wage profile is known to the consumer at the beginning of his lifetime and changes in wages are due only to movement along this given profile. It is apparent from the labor-supply function given by (12) that the value of the parameter δ determines the hours of work response to evolutionary wage changes. Hereafter, I will refer to δ as the intertemporal substitution elasticity. The theoretical prediction for its sign is positive. For the particular form of the utility function given by (10), δ is also the direct elasticity of substitution for hours of work in any two periods.

Now compare the labor-supply profiles of two consumers who face wage paths II and III, respectively. As illustrated in figure 1, the wage profiles for consumers II and III are

---

[16] *This distinction goes back to Ghez and Becker (1975).*

[17] *This statement is true only in an environment of perfect certainty. If there is uncertainty about the future, a consumer can experience parametric wage changes as he acquires new information about his lifetime wage path. For a discussion of these issues see MaCurdy (1980, in press).*

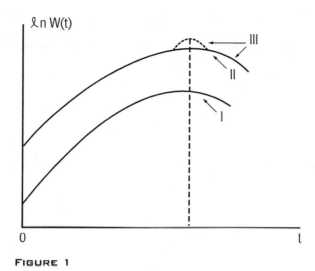

FIGURE 1

the same except at age t' when consumer III's wage rate is higher than consumer II's. Let Δ denote the absolute value of this difference in period t' wages. This wage difference represents a parametric wage change because it involves a shift in the lifetime path of wages. It causes the labor-supply profiles for consumers II and III to be different at all ages. Comparing these labor-supply profiles is the sort of problem usually considered in comparative static exercises. In terms of the empirical model outlined above, this higher wage rate has two effects on consumer III's labor supply. The first effect is on the value of F. According to equation (14), consumer III will set a value for F which is lower than the value of F for consumer II by an amount equal to $\gamma(t') \cdot \Delta$. This decline in F implies that at all ages other than t' consumer III's labor supply will be less than consumer II's by a constant fraction. At age t' there is a second effect of the wage difference. Neglecting the decline in F, consumer III's labor supply at age t' will be higher by an amount equal to $\delta \cdot \Delta$. Thus, the total impact on consumer III's hours of work at age t' is $[\delta + \gamma(t')] \cdot \Delta$. Since $\delta > 0$ and $\gamma(t') < 0$, there is no sign prediction for $\delta + \gamma(t')$, so consumer III's hours of work at age t' may be greater than or less than consumer II's.

The parameters $\gamma(t')$ and $\delta + \gamma(t')$, then, determine the difference in consumer II's and consumer III's labor-supply profiles which is due to the discrepancy in their wage rates at age t'. The quantities $\gamma(t')$ and $\delta + \gamma(t')$ correspond to the usual concepts of cross- and own-uncompensated substitution elasticities. These elasticities describe the response of labor supply to parametric wage changes. They can be used to predict differences in labor supply across consumers. These elasticities do not directly provide information on the response of labor supply to evolutionary wage changes, so they cannot be used to predict differences in a given consumer's labor supply over time. Since the intertemporal substitution elasticity exceeds the own-uncompensated substitution elasticities (i.e., $\delta > \delta + \gamma[t']$), one expects an evolutionary wage change to induce a larger labor-supply response than a comparable parametric wage change. The wealth effect associated with a parametric wage change accounts for the smaller labor-supply response.

Comparing the labor-supply profiles for consumers I and II also involves a parametric wage change. As illustrated in figure 1, consumer II's wage profile exceeds consumer I's by a constant fraction over the entire life cycle. The parametric wage change associated with moving from consumer I to consumer II's wage profile is analogous to increasing the value of the intercept of the lifetime wage path, π_0. This has two effects on labor supply in each period. First, a consumer adjusts his value of F in response to the profile shift. According to equation (19), F declines by an amount equal to $\bar{\gamma}_0 = \Sigma_{t=0}^{T^*} \gamma(t)$ times the increase in the value of π_0. This decline in F implies a fall in hours of work at each age. Second, there is a direct impact on each period's labor supply. Holding the value of F constant, a consumer increases his hours of work by an amount equal to δ times the increase in π_0. The implied total impact on each period's labor supply, therefore, is $\gamma_0 + \delta$ times the change in π_0. Because $\bar{\gamma}_0$ is unambiguously negative, there is no sign prediction for this total impact. Since $\bar{\gamma}_0 + \delta$ is less than $\gamma(t') + \delta$, however, the response of labor supply to a shift in π_0 should be less in algebraic value than the response to a shift in the wage profile only at age t'. The wealth effect associated with a shift in π_0 is greater. The labor-supply profile for consumer II, then, can lie above or below consumer I's labor-supply profile. It will lie above consumer I's if $\bar{\gamma}_0 + \delta$ is positive.

The empirical specification of life-cycle supply given by equations (12) and (19) provides a convenient framework for estimating the response of labor supply to the different kinds of wage changes described above. Estimation of the λ constant labor-supply equation produces an estimate of the intertemporal substitution elasticity δ. This elasticity can be used to predict the response of labor supply to evolutionary wage changes; it provides the information one needs to describe a consumer's dynamic behavior. Estimating the equation for F given by (19) produces estimates of the parameters $\bar{\gamma}_0$, $\bar{\gamma}_1$, $\bar{\gamma}_2$, and $\bar{\theta}$. These estimates provide the additional information one requires to predict the response of labor supply to parametric wage and wealth changes, and they can be used to explain labor-supply differences across consumers. Combining the estimates of $\bar{\gamma}_0$, $\bar{\gamma}_1$, and $\bar{\gamma}_2$ with the estimate of δ allows one to predict how labor-supply profiles adjust to changes in the wage-path coefficients π_0, π_1, and π_2. This includes both shifts and slope changes of the wage profiles. The estimate of $\bar{\theta}$ provides the information one needs to predict the response of labor-supply profiles to changes in a consumer's initial permanent income. Estimating the empirical model proposed in this paper, then, fully characterizes a consumer's lifetime labor-supply behavior.

THREE SUBSTITUTION ELASTICITIES

Nowhere in the above interpretation of parameters was there any mention of compensated substitution elasticities. In terms of the above notation, it can be shown using Slutsky's equation that the own- and the cross-compensated elasticities are $\delta + \gamma(t) - E(t)\theta$ and

$\gamma(t) - E(t)\theta$, respectively, where $E(t) \equiv N(t)W(t)$ is real earnings at age t.[18] In the analysis of life-cycle behavior, it is important to distinguish sharply compensated elasticities from the intertemporal elasticity (i.e., δ) and the uncompensated elasticities (i.e., own effects $\delta + \gamma[t]$ and cross effects $\gamma[t]$) discussed above.

Some researchers incorrectly infer that intertemporal and compensated substitution elasticities are the same.[19] The fact that an individual is at the same level of lifetime utility at all ages in a world of perfect certainty suggests that responses in hours of work to changes in the wage rate over the life cycle represent compensated substitution effects, which in turn suggests that the intertemporal and compensated elasticities are equivalent. These elasticities, however, are used to predict labor-supply responses to different kinds of wage changes. As discussed above, intertemporal elasticities determine hours of work responses to evolutionary wage changes. Compensated elasticities, on the other hand, are like uncompensated elasticities in the sense that they determine responses to parametric wage changes (i.e., wage changes due to shifts in wage profiles rather than movements along these profiles). Compensated elasticities, then, can be used to predict differences in hours of work across consumers whose wage profiles are different and whose lifetime utility is the same.

Formally, the intertemporal substitution effect can also be interpreted as an elasticity that is associated with a particular kind of parametric wage change. In particular, it determines the response of hours of work at age t to a shift in the age t wage rate holding λ or the marginal utility of wealth constant. Thus, whereas uncompensated elasticities hold financial wealth constant and compensated elasticities hold lifetime utility constant, the intertemporal elasticity is equivalent to a parametric wage elasticity that holds λ constant.

[18] According to Slutsky's equation,

$$\left.\frac{\partial N(t)}{\partial W(t)}\right|_U = \left.\frac{\partial N(t)}{\partial W(t)}\right|_{A(0)} - N(t)\frac{\partial N(t)}{\partial A(0)}.$$

So

$$\left.\frac{W(t)}{N(t)}\frac{\partial N(t)}{\partial W(t)}\right|_U = \left.\frac{W(t)}{N(t)}\frac{\partial N(t)}{\partial W(t)}\right|_{A(0)} - W(t)N(t)\frac{\partial \ln N(t)}{\partial A(0)} = \delta + \gamma(t) - E(t)\theta.$$

[19] There has been some confusion concerning the interpretation of wage coefficients estimated in labor-supply studies such as those of Ghez and Becker (1975) and Smith (1977), who use synthetic cohort data. Because these studies estimate the response of hours of work to life-cycle wage growth, the wage coefficient is an intertemporal substitution elasticity. While this elasticity constitutes an upper bound for compensated and uncompensated elasticities, it is not one of the familiar elasticities associated with parametric wage changes. Thus, without imposing nontrivial restrictions on preferences, wage coefficients estimated using synthetic cohort data cannot be used for policy analysis of the sort encountered in predicting labor-supply responses to negative income tax experiments or other proposed changes in tax policies. Elsewhere, Smith (1975) uses these estimated coefficients for exactly this purpose, namely, to predict the effect of income-maintenance programs on hours of work.

In the literature on consumer demand, this particular elasticity is known as the specific substitution effect.[20] This correspondence between intertemporal and specific substitution effects is a direct consequence of the assumption that utility is additive over periods.

While the three types of substitution elasticities are related, they are distinct and reduce to the same value only if income or wealth effects are zero. Assuming leisure is a normal good in all periods, these elasticities can be ordered as follows: $\delta > \delta + \gamma(t) - E(t)\theta > \delta + \gamma(t)$; that is, intertemporal responses are greater than compensated responses which are in turn greater than uncompensated responses.[21] It is also easy to show that intertemporal and compensated responses must be positive, while uncompensated responses may be either positive or negative. Intertemporal and uncompensated substitution effects, then, provide an upper and a lower bound for compensated substitution elasticities.

IV. EMPIRICAL ANALYSIS

The λ constant hours of work function given by (12) and the structural equation for F given by (19) provide a manageable empirical model for analyzing labor-supply behavior in a life-cycle setting. This model naturally suggests a two-step estimation procedure. In

[20] See Phlips (1974, pp. 47–50) for further discussion.

[21] We can relate these elasticities using solutions of what is known as the fundamental matrix equation in the literature on consumer demand (see, e.g., ibid.). For leisure demand, it can be shown that: (1) the intertemporal effect is

$$\left.\frac{\partial L(t)}{\partial W(t)}\right|_{\lambda} = \lambda \mu^{22},$$

where μ^{22} is the (2, 2) element of the inverse of the hessian matrix of $U[C(t), L(t)]$; (2) the compensated effect is

$$\left.\frac{\partial L(t)}{\partial W(t)}\right|_{U} = \left.\frac{\partial L(t)}{\partial W(t)}\right|_{\lambda} + \Omega\left[\frac{\partial L(t)}{\partial A(0)}\right]^{2},$$

where $\Omega = -\lambda\,[\partial\lambda/\partial A(0)]^{-1} > 0$; and (3) the uncompensated effect is

$$\left.\frac{\partial L(t)}{\partial W(t)}\right|_{A} = \left.\frac{\partial L(t)}{\partial W(t)}\right|_{U} + N(i)\frac{\partial L(t)}{\partial A(0)}.$$

So, if $L(t)$ is a normal good and U is concave, we have

$$\left.\frac{\partial L(t)}{\partial W(t)}\right|_{\lambda} < \left.\frac{\partial L(t)}{\partial W(t)}\right|_{U} < \left.\frac{\partial L(t)}{\partial W(t)}\right|_{A}.$$

The proposed restrictions on labor-supply elasticities follow immediately using this result.

the first step, one estimates the parameters of the λ constant labor-supply equation. This step provides an estimate of the intertemporal substitution elasticity and all the information a researcher requires to predict how the hours of work of a given consumer will differ at two points in time. In the second step, one uses estimated "individual effects" as dependent variables to estimate the structural equation for F which produces estimates of wealth effects and uncompensated substitution elasticities associated with shifts in the intercept and the slope of the lifetime wage path. This step provides the additional information one requires to predict how labor supply will differ across consumers. Using results from both steps, it is possible to compute the average own- and cross-uncompensated substitution elasticities associated with wage changes in a single year. These results also permit the calculation of upper and lower bounds for compensated elasticities. This two-step estimation procedure exploits the special characteristics of panel data to characterize life-cycle behavior with a minimal amount of computational burden.[22]

The empirical work reported here uses the randomly designed sample from the Michigan Panel Study of Income Dynamics. The sample consists of observations of 513 prime-age, white, married males for the years 1967–76. Only males continuously married to the same spouse during the period 1968–77 and who were 25–46 years old in 1967 were included in the sample.[23] The labor-supply variable used in the empirical analysis is annual hours of work. The wage variable is average hourly earnings deflated by the Consumer Price Index.

To avoid confusion in this section we must be careful to distinguish between age variables and indexes representing a sample period. As in the previous discussion, t denotes

---

[22] There is an alternative strategy for estimating this structural model of lifetime labor supply. Instead of the procedure suggested above, one could use a one-step procedure. Substituting the right-hand side of eq. (19) for F directly into the λ constant labor-supply equation given by either (12) or (13) produces a new equation containing all of the structural parameters of interest. It is possible to estimate this equation in a single step using constrained simultaneous-equation estimation procedures. The two-step procedure offers advantages over this one-step method when there exists misspecification of the equation for F. The presence of any misspecification errors in the F-equation leads to inconsistent estimators for all parameters of the labor-supply equation in the case of the one-step procedure. For the two-step estimation scheme, however, only the second-step estimators for the parameters of the F-equation are inconsistent.

Houthakker and Taylor (1970, chap. 5) and Phlips (1974, pp. 190–93, 250–60) have estimated marginal utility of wealth constant demand functions as an intermediate computational step toward estimating a system of ordinary demand functions. In contrast to their work, I directly estimate the λ constant demand functions as a means of characterizing a consumer's dynamic behavior. I treat λ as a fixed effect which summarizes the effect of historic and future information on current decisions. I thank James Heckman and Orley Ashenfelter for the Houthakker-Taylor reference.

[23] A worker had to satisfy the following criteria as well to be included in the sample: (1) He must be classified as employed or unemployed (i.e., permanently disabled and retired were deleted). (2) Wage and labor-supply data must be available for all years. (3) A worker must report less than 4,680 hours worked per year. The absolute value of the difference in his real average hourly earnings in adjacent years cannot exceed $16 or a change of 200 percent. The absolute value of the difference in the number of hours he works in adjacent years cannot exceed 3,000 hours or a change of 190 percent. The purpose of this last criterion is to minimize difficulties arising from the presence of outliers.

the age of a consumer; in particular, $t = 0$ when the consumer is 25 years old, $t = 1$ when he is 26, etc. The index j, on the other hand, denotes the sample period; $j = 1$ when the observation is from year 1967, $j = 2$ when it is from 1968, etc. The following analysis assumes that there are a total of τ sample periods ($\tau = 10$ for the sample used in this paper). Finally, the notation $t(j)$ denotes the consumer's age in sample period j. Thus, $\ln W_i(t)$ is consumer i's wage at age t, $\ln W_i(j)$ is his wage in period j, and $\ln W_i(t) = \ln W_i[t(j)] = \ln W_i(j)$.

ESTIMATES OF THE INTERTEMPORAL SUBSTITUTION ELASTICITIES

Estimating the parameters of the λ constant labor-supply equation is simplified by working with a first-differenced version of this equation. First differencing equation (12) yields

$$D \ln N_i(j) = \delta[\rho - r(j)] + \delta D \ln W_i(j) + \epsilon_i(j), \qquad j = 2, \ldots, \tau, \tag{22}$$

where D is the difference operator, that is, $D \ln N_i(j) = \ln N_i(j) - \ln N_i(j - 1)$, and $\epsilon_i(j) = Du_i(j)$ is a disturbance. This equation relates a consumer's labor-supply changes to changes in his wage rate. Notice that differencing eliminates individual effects, and thus it avoids the introduction of incidental parameters. Step one of the estimation procedure is to use this equation to estimate the intertemporal substitution elasticity, δ.

Combining these equations for a given worker into a single system of simultaneous equations creates a model that is particularly well suited for an empirical analysis. Stacking equation (22) for worker i according to the j index yields

$$
\begin{bmatrix}
D \ln N_i(\tau) \\
D \ln N_i(\tau - 1) \\
\cdot \\
\cdot \\
\cdot \\
D \ln N_i(3) \\
D \ln N_i(2)
\end{bmatrix}
=
\begin{bmatrix}
\beta_\tau \\
\beta_{\tau-1} \\
\cdot \\
\cdot \\
\cdot \\
\beta_3 \\
\beta_2
\end{bmatrix}
+
\begin{bmatrix}
D \ln W_i(\tau) \\
D \ln W_i(\tau - 1) \\
\cdot \\
\cdot \\
\cdot \\
D \ln N_i(3) \\
D \ln N_i(2)
\end{bmatrix}
\delta +
\begin{bmatrix}
\epsilon_i(\tau) \\
\epsilon_i(\tau - 1) \\
\cdot \\
\cdot \\
\cdot \\
\epsilon_i(3) \\
\epsilon_i(2)
\end{bmatrix},
\tag{23}
$$

where $\beta_j = \delta[\rho - r(j)], j = 2, \ldots, \tau$. Putting this system into vector notation, we have

$$D \ln N_i = \beta + D \ln W_i \delta + \epsilon_i, \qquad i = 1, \ldots, n, \tag{24}$$

where $D \ln N_i, \beta, D \ln N_i$, and ϵ_i are $(\tau - 1) \times 1$ vectors with $D \ln N_i' = [D \ln N_i(\tau), \ldots, D \ln N_i(2)], \beta' = (\beta_\tau, \ldots, \beta_2), D \ln W_i' = [D \ln W_i(\tau), \ldots, D \ln W_i(2)], \epsilon_i' = [\epsilon_i(\tau), \ldots, \epsilon_i(2)]$, and n is the total number of workers in the sample. The following analysis assumes that the error vectors ϵ_i are independently distributed across individuals once common time effects are removed with the inclusion of year dummies in the labor-supply equations. No restrictions are imposed on the covariance matrix of ϵ_i, which permits arbitrary forms of serial correlation.

The parameters of equation (24) are estimated using standard two-stage and three-stage least-squares procedures which permit the imposition of equality constraints across equations.[24] The wage-growth variables, $D \ln W_i(j), j = 2, \ldots, \tau$, are treated as endogenous variables. The set of instruments used to predict $D \ln W_i(j)$ includes family background variables,[25] education, age, interactions between education and age, and dummy variables for each year of the sample. Estimation of (24) using simultaneous equation methods takes advantage of the time-series aspect of panel data to estimate the intertemporal substitution elasticity δ with a minimal amount of computational burden. These methods avoid biases arising from pure reporting error in earnings and hours of work, and they offer a flexible framework for testing and estimating alternative functional forms.

Another equation that can be used to estimate δ is one that relates changes in hours of work to changes in earnings. Adding $\delta \cdot D \ln N_i(j)$ to both sides of (24) and solving this new equation for $D \ln N_i(j)$ yields

$$D \ln N_i(j) = \frac{\delta[\rho - r(j)]}{1+\delta} + \frac{\delta}{1+\delta} D \ln E_i(j) + \frac{\epsilon_i(j)}{1+\delta}, \quad j = 2,\ldots,\tau, \tag{25}$$

where $E_i(j) \equiv N_i(j)W_i(j)$ is real earnings in period j. Stacking these equations creates a model like (24), except that $D \ln W_i$, δ, and ϵ_i are replaced by $D \ln E_i$, $\delta/(1+\delta)$, and $[1/(1+\delta)]\epsilon_i$, respectively, and the elements of β become $\beta_j = \{\delta[\rho - r(j)]\}/(1+\delta), j = 2, \ldots, \tau$. Exactly the same procedures described above for estimating equations (24) are applied to estimate the parameters of the stacked representation of (25). Using the coefficient on earnings, $\delta/(1+\delta)$, it is possible to construct an estimate of δ.

Table 1 presents estimates of the intertemporal substitution elasticity. Two specifications of the labor-supply equation are considered. One assumes that the interest rate, $r(t)$, is constant over time, and it constrains intercepts in the labor-supply equations (i.e., the elements of β) to be equal over the sample. The other allows $r(t)$ to be different in each

TABLE 1

SIMULTANEOUS-EQUATION ESTIMATION OF FIRST-DIFFERENCED LABOR-SUPPLY-EQUATION ESTIMATES OF THE INTERTEMPORAL SUBSTITUTION ELASTICITY

Estimation Procedure	D(Log Wage)	D(Log Earnings)*	Intercept	Average of Year Dummies
2SLS	.23 (2.42)	. . .	−.009 (4.02)	. . .
3SLS	.14 (1.97)	. . .	−.008 (4.26)	. . .
2SLS	. . .	.35 (2.22)	−.006 (4.26)	. . .
3SLS	. . .	.25 (2.63)	−.006 (5.18)	. . .
2SLS	.15 (.98)	. . .	. . .	−.008
3SLS	.10 (.80)	. . .	. . .	−.008
2SLS	. . .	.45 (1.54)	. . .	−.007
3SLS	. . .	.30 (1.67)	. . .	−.007

Note: Absolute values of t-statistics are in parentheses.
* The estimates and t-statistics reported in the "Log Earning" column are for δ; they are computed using the coefficient on earnings, denoted ψ, and its t-statistics. We have $\hat{\delta} = \hat{\psi}/(1-\hat{\psi})$. To convert the t-statistics reported for ψ to those for δ requires division by the quantity $(d\delta/d\psi) = (1+\delta)^2$ evaluated at $\delta = \hat{\delta}$.

period by including dummy variables for each year without any constraints on their coefficients, which permits intercepts to be different each period. These alternative empirical specifications yield similar results. All of the implied estimates of the intertemporal substitution elasticity are positive. According to the estimates of the wage coefficients, δ lies in the range .10–.23. The earnings coefficients indicate a range of .25–.45 for δ. The earnings coefficients indicate a higher estimate for δ in all cases, but these differences are small relative to their standard errors. The estimates of the intercepts indicate that the real rate of interest exceeds the rate of time preference on average by about 2–4 percentage points.

A comparison of these results with others in the literature is difficult since most studies use cross-section data for their empirical analysis where differences in lifetime wage paths are the primary source of wage variation across observations. As a consequence, they do not estimate the intertemporal substitution elasticity. Estimating equation (13) using cross-section data is complicated by the presence of individual effects, F_i. As discussed above, economic theory implies that F_i is correlated with a consumer's wages and all of his other characteristics. Therefore, it is not reasonable to assume that F_i is a "random factor" uncorrelated with explanatory variables. One, then, cannot directly use observations on individuals from a cross section to estimate the parameters of (13) even if one uses simultaneous equation estimation procedures. Such procedures implicitly treat individual effects as random variables, and this leads to inconsistent parameter estimates. To estimate the intertemporal elasticity using cross-section data, one requires a specification of the labor-supply equation where variation in wages reflects evolutionary wage change.

One approach constructs synthetic cohorts to estimate equation (13) using cross-section data as implemented by Ghez and Becker (1975) and Smith (1977). A synthetic cohort is constructed by computing geometric means of wage rates and hours worked for each age group, and it is assumed to represent the life cycle of a typical individual. The basic assumption underlying this approach is that there are no cohort effects, so that group individual effects (i.e., the average of the F_i's for each age group) are the same for all age groups after adjusting for "smooth" vintage effects. In this case, least-squares estimation of equation (13) using synthetic cohort data produces consistent parameter estimates.[26] This approach allows for measured "taste-shifter" variables such as family size and age. In principle, this approach accounts for the endogeneity of wages and measured characteristics by using group averages as instruments. The problem of treating group effects as random variables does not arise since it is assumed that they are the same for all age groups.

The estimates of the intertemporal substitution elasticity obtained by Ghez and Becker and Smith are comparable to those estimates presented in table 1 of this paper. Becker forms synthetic cohorts using the 1960 U.S. Census, and he obtains estimates for δ ranging from $-.068$ to $.44$.[27] Smith, on the other hand, treats the family as the relevant decision unit and uses the 1967 Survey of Economic Opportunity to form his synthetic cohorts. He estimates δ to be about $.32$.[28] Comparing these estimates of δ and those reported in table 1 suggests that cohort effects do not seriously bias estimates based on synthetic cohort data.

ESTIMATES OF RESPONSES TO PARAMETRIC WAGE CHANGES

Estimating the structural equation for F given by (19) provides the additional information we require to predict a consumer's labor-supply response to parametric wage changes. Estimating this equation is not as difficult as it may first appear. It is true that all of the variables appearing in this equation (F_i, π_{0i}, π_{1i}, π_{2i}, and α_{0i}) are not directly observable. But it is possible to construct observable quantities that have expected values equal to these variables. If one replaces the unobserved variables by their observed counterparts,

---

[26] *Ghez and Becker and Smith do not interpret their parameter estimates as those of a* λ *constant labor-supply function. Given their log-linear specifications, however,* $\ln \lambda$ *is absorbed into the intercept of their regression specifications.*

[27] *Estimates obtained from Ghez and Becker (1975, pp. 112, 114).*

[28] *Estimates obtained from Smith (1977, p. 244).*

one can employ standard two-stage least-squares procedures to estimate the structural parameters of interest.

First consider the coefficients of the lifetime path for wages. Define the difference operator D_k as $D_k \ln W_i(j) = \ln W_i(j) - \ln W_i(j-k)$. Applying this operator to the wage equation given by (15) and dividing the result by k yields

$$\frac{D_k \ln W_i(j)}{k} = \pi_{1i} + \pi_{2i}\left[2t(j)-k\right] + \frac{D_k V_i(j)}{k}.$$

Subtracting $D_1 \ln W_i(2)$ from this equation and dividing the result by $1/(2j-k-3)$ creates a new equation:

$$\frac{1}{2j-k-3}\left[\frac{D_k \ln W_i(j)}{k} - D_1 \ln W_i(2)\right] = \pi_{2i} + \frac{D_k V_i(j)}{(2j-k-3)k} - \frac{D_1 V_i(2)}{2j-k-3}.$$

Notice that the dependent variable of this last equation has mean equal to π_{2i}. Replacing π_{2i} in the previous equation by this dependent variable allows one to create another observable variable whose mean is π_{1i}. Further substituting these two observable variables for π_{2i} and π_{1i} in the original wage equation allows one to create a third measurable variable whose expected value is π_{0i}. Following this strategy and taking averages to use all the available data, consider the following definitions:

$$\tilde{\pi}_{2i} = \frac{1}{\tau-2}\sum_{j=1}^{\tau-2}\frac{1}{j}\left[\frac{D_{j+1}\ln W_i(j+2)}{j+1} - D_1 \ln W_i(2)\right] \qquad (26)$$

$$\tilde{\pi}_{1i} = \frac{1}{\tau-1}\sum_{j=1}^{\tau-1}\left\{\frac{D_j \ln W_i(j+1)}{j} - \tilde{\pi}_{2i}\left[2t(j+1)-j\right]\right\} \qquad (27)$$

$$\tilde{\pi}_{0i} = \frac{1}{\tau}\sum_{j=1}^{\tau}\left\{\ln W_i(j) - \tilde{\pi}_{1i}t(j) - \tilde{\pi}_{2i}\left[t(j)\right]^2\right\}, \qquad (28)$$

where τ is the total number of sample periods. It can be shown that $E(\tilde{\pi}_{hi}) = \pi_{hi}$, $h = 0, 1, 2$. This is an important result because the $\tilde{\pi}_{hi}$'s are observable variables, and it is possible to use the $\tilde{\pi}_{hi}$'s as dependent variables in a simultaneous-equation analysis to estimate the π_{hi}'s consistently.

Similarly, given observations on consumer i's income over the sample period, one can construct the variable $\tilde{\alpha}_{0i}$ using definition (28) with $Y_i(j)$ replacing $\ln W_i(j)$; $\tilde{\alpha}_{0i}$, then, can be used in a simultaneous-equation analysis to predict the intercept of the lifetime income path, α_{0i}, which is a measure of consumer i's initial permanent income.

An analogous strategy can be used to construct a measurable variable to serve as a proxy for F_i. From equation (13) we see that an average of the quantities $\ln N_i(j) = bt(j) - \delta \ln W_i(j)$ has an expected value equal to F_i, but unfortunately, this average cannot be directly observed since it depends on unknown parameters b and δ. We have estimates of these parameters, however, from the first step of the empirical analysis. A logical alternative to the above average, then, is to form the variable

$$ \tilde{F}_i = \frac{1}{\tau} \sum_{j=1}^{\tau} \left[\ln N_i(j) - \hat{b}t(j) - \hat{\delta} \ln W_i(j) \right]. $$

Asymptotically, $\tilde{F}_i$ has an expectation equal to F_i.

Collecting the above results, we have a complete simultaneous-equations model given by

$$ \tilde{\pi}_{hi} = M_i g_h + \eta_h, \qquad h = 0, 1, 2, \tag{29} $$

$$ \alpha_{0i} = S_i q_0 + \eta_3, \tag{30} $$

$$ \tilde{F}_i = \phi + \tilde{\pi}_{0i} \bar{\gamma}_0 + \tilde{\pi}_{1i} \bar{\gamma}_1 + \tilde{\pi}_{2i} \bar{\gamma}_2 + \tilde{\alpha}_{0i} \bar{\theta} + \eta_4, \tag{31} $$

where the vectors of exogenous variables M_i and S_i and the coefficient vectors g_0, g_1, g_2, and q_0 are defined by (16) and (18), and the η_h's are disturbances. We have one set of equations for each consumer i. The endogenous variables in this model are $\tilde{F}_i$, $\tilde{\alpha}_{0i}$, and the $\tilde{\pi}_{hi}$'s; the exogenous variables are the elements of M_i and S_i; and the structural parameters of interest are $\bar{\gamma}_0$, $\bar{\gamma}_1$, $\bar{\gamma}_2$, and $\bar{\theta}$. The vectors M_i and S_i contain variables determining the coefficients of the lifetime wage and income paths. In the following empirical analysis, they include the consumer's education, his education squared, and family background variables.[29]

To estimate the parameters of the structural equation for F given by (31) consistently, one can employ a standard two-stage least-squares procedure. The standard errors reported

---

[29] Family background variables include the education of both the father and the mother of the consumer and dummy variables indicating parents' economic status at the time the consumer was growing up.

by this procedure are valid if the number of time-series observations for each consumer is sufficiently large.[30]

Table 2 presents estimates for the structural parameters of the individual effects equation given by (31), where $\tilde{F}_i$ is computed using three different sets of estimates for b and δ. The estimates of $\bar{\gamma}_0$, $\bar{\gamma}_1$, and $\bar{\gamma}_2$ are all negative as theory predicts. These estimates decrease monotonically as one uses a higher estimated value of δ to compute the proxy variable for individual effects, $\tilde{F}_i$. Since uncompensated substitution elasticities associated with permanent wage changes are calculated by adding the estimate of δ to the estimate of $\bar{\gamma}_0$, an inverse relationship between the estimates of δ and $\bar{\gamma}_0$ is required if uncompensated permanent wage elasticities are to remain constant for different choices of $\hat{\delta}$ in computing $\tilde{F}_i$.

All of the estimates of the initial permanent income coefficient, $\bar{\theta}$, are statistically insignificant and very small. The measure of property income (i.e., $Y_i[t]$) used in this empirical analysis is total family income minus husband's earnings in thousands of 1967 dollars. While the estimates of $\bar{\theta}$ are negative as theory predicts when low estimated values of δ are used to construct $\tilde{F}_i$, we see that the estimated effects of a change in income on hours of work are minute; a \$1,000 increase in initial permanent income leads to at most a .026 percent decrease in hours of work. Several other measures of property income were tried in the empirical analysis;[31] in every case the estimates obtained for $\bar{\theta}$ were of the order of magnitude reported in table 2.

Combining estimates of $\bar{\gamma}_0$ and δ allows one to form estimates of cross- and own-uncompensated substitution elasticities and bounds for compensated elasticities associated with wage changes in a single year. Dividing the estimate of $\bar{\gamma}_0$ by the length of the working life produces an estimate of the average cross-uncompensated elasticity. Using results from the second row of table 2 and assuming a working life of 40 years implies a cross elasticity equal to $-.0018$. Adding the estimate for δ (which is .15 for the second row of table 2) to this cross elasticity implies a value of .15 for the average own-uncompensated elasticity. Since the average own-compensated elasticity lies between the intertemporal and the average own-uncompensated elasticity, we conclude that this compensated elasticity is also approximately equal to .15. Increasing a consumer's wage rate in period t by 10 percent, then, leads to about a 1.5 percent increase in his hours of work in period t and approximately no change in his hours of work at other ages.

---

[30] If one does not have a sufficiently large number of these time-series observations, however, the usual standard errors are invalid. The problem lies in the fact that we use estimated values for b and δ to form the dependent variable F_i. In cases where the number of time-series observations is small, one must adjust the usual standard errors to account for errors in estimating b and δ. The precise form of this adjustment can be obtained from the author upon request. While this adjustment is not complicated, it does require the use of matrix operations. This adjustment was very minor in every instance for which it was used in this study, which suggests that even 10 observations per person is large enough to neglect making any adjustments in standard errors.

[31] One measure of income excluded wife's earnings. Others included imputed income for house ownership. Due to data limitations, it was not possible to include imputed income from other forms of consumer durables, which certainly constitute a major component of a consumer's nonwage income.

TABLE 2

SIMULTANEOUS-EQUATION ESTIMATION OF FIXED-EFFECTS EQUATIONS

$\hat{b}, \quad \hat{\delta}$	$\bar{\gamma}_0$	$\bar{\gamma}_1$	$\bar{\gamma}_2$	$\hat{\theta}$	Intercept
−.009, .1	−.05 (1.5)	−.83 (1.4)	−10.47 (1.2)	−.00026 (.48)	7.81 (157)
−.009, .15	−.07 (1.78)	−1.08 (1.65)	−13.03 (1.31)	−.0001 (.16)	7.77 (137)
−.009, .23	−.10 (2.13)	−1.46 (1.9)	−16.86 (1.4)	.0001 (.2)	7.68 (119)

Note: Absolute values of t-statistics are in parentheses. The dependent variable $\tilde{F}_i$ (i.e., the proxy variable for F_i) is computed using the estimates b and δ reported in the stub column. Income is measured in thousands of dollars.

Combining estimates of $\bar{\gamma}_0$, $\bar{\gamma}_1$, and $\bar{\gamma}_2$ with estimates of δ provides the information needed to predict a consumer's labor-supply response to shifts in his wage profile. In response to a uniform 10 percent increase in wages at all ages (i.e., a parallel shift in the log wage profile), the estimates of the second row of table 2 predict that a consumer will adjust his hours of work by an amount equal to $(\bar{\gamma}_0 + \hat{\delta})10\% = (-.07 + .15)10\% = .8$ percent at all ages. There is, then, a small positive response in a consumer's labor supply to parallel shifts in his log wage profile. If the slope of a consumer's wage profile is altered by changing the coefficient on the linear term (i.e., π_{1i}) by Δ percent, the estimates for $\bar{\gamma}_1$ and δ indicate that his hours of work at age t change by $(\bar{\gamma}_1 + \hat{\delta}t)\Delta\% = (-1.08 + .15t)\Delta\%$. Recall that t here measures a consumer's age and takes a value of 0 when the consumer is 25 years old. Hence, hours of work decline at early ages (i.e., prior to age 32) and they increase at later ages in response to this sort of increase in the slope of the wage profile. The same is true when the slope of the wage profile is altered by changing the coefficient on the quadratic term (i.e., π_{2i}) by Δ percent. Hours of work at age t adjust by an amount equal to $(-13.03 + .15t^2)\Delta\%$, which also implies a decline in hours of work at younger ages (i.e., prior to age 34) and an increase at older ages.

The estimates above of uncompensated elasticities are generally consistent with results found in cross-section studies and the popular notion that the lifetime labor-supply curve of prime-age males is not very responsive to permanent wage changes. If, in a cross-section analysis, one purges wages and income of their transitory components using a simultaneous-equation method and interprets the estimated coefficients as some sort of "lifetime average" relationship, then one finds small positive estimates for wage coefficients and negative or zero estimates for income coefficients for prime-age males,[32] which

---

[32] *Accounting for the endogeneity of* $\ln W_i(t)$ *and* $Y_i(t)$ *has been shown to have a significant effect on cross-section estimates. DaVanzo, Detray, and Greenberg (1976) find that treating both wages and income as endogenous variables leads to positive estimates for wage coefficients and negative or zero estimates for income coefficients for prime-age men, which are consistent with the empirical results reported above. Neglecting this endogeneity produces estimated coefficients with opposite signs.*

agrees with the results above. In contrast to previous work, however, the estimates above also indicate that to predict the response of labor supply to shifts in the lifetime wage path one must be careful to specify the particular shift involved and the time of the life cycle relevant for evaluating the response. The lifetime labor-supply curve for prime-age males is backward bending for some types of wage changes over part of the life cycle, and it is positively sloped for other age ranges and wage changes.

V. CONCLUSION

This study formulates a manageable empirical model of labor supply that fully incorporates life-cycle considerations. This model naturally divides the analysis into two steps. In the first step, the analysis concentrates on measuring parameters relevant for describing a consumer's dynamic behavior. Here one estimates the response of hours of work to evolutionary wage changes. In step two, the analysis focuses on measuring parameters relevant for explaining differences in labor supply across consumers. This step produces estimates of the impact of parametric changes in wealth and in wages on hours of work over the life cycle. This two-step analysis offers a very tractable estimation procedure with minimal data requirements.

We have seen that there are three types of substitution elasticities relevant for predicting the response of hours of work to changes in the wage rate. The existence of these three elasticities reflects the fact that the effect of a wage change depends on its source. The intertemporal elasticity determines the labor-supply response to wage changes resulting from life-cycle wage growth and movements over a perfectly foreseen business cycle. Uncompensated and compensated elasticities, on the other hand, determine the hours of work response to shifts in wage profiles. When specifying these latter elasticities one must identify not only the particular wage profile shift involved but also that part of the profile that is being held constant. While the three types of substitution elasticities are distinct, they are related with intertemporal and uncompensated elasticities providing an upper and lower bound for compensated elasticities.

This paper presents a full set of estimates required to describe the lifetime labor-supply behavior of prime-age males. Estimates of the intertemporal substitution elasticity indicate that a 10 percent increase in the real wage rate which is due to life-cycle wage growth induces a 1–5 percent increase in hours worked. The estimates of own-period uncompensated and compensated substitution elasticities range between .1 and .5, and cross-uncompensated elasticities associated with a 1-year wage change are approximately zero. Estimates of uncompensated elasticities associated with shifts in the entire wage profile indicate that a uniform 10 percent increase in wages at all ages leads to a 0.5–1.3 percent increase in hours of work, and an increase in the slope of the profile leads to a decline in hours of work at early ages and an increase at later ages. The interpretation of these empirical results is, of course, dependent upon strong theoretical assumptions. The analysis in this paper neglects the presence of taxes, and it assumes that capital markets are perfect. There is an implicit assumption that hours of work are perfectly flexible and chosen freely by the worker. This paper also ignores the role of human capital investment in measuring both the supply of labor and the returns to work.

The important point for an analyst to extract from this study is the following: Recognizing that individuals make their decisions in a life-cycle setting is crucial if one's objective is to estimate economically meaningful parameters. Creating an empirical model that accounts for such a setting need not complicate the analysis, and it generally leads to a more complete understanding of consumer behavior.

REFERENCES

DaVanzo, Julie; Detray, Dennis N.; and Greenberg, D. H. "The Sensitivity of Male Labor Supply Estimates to the Choice of Assumptions." *Rev. Econ. and Statis.* 55 (August 1976): 313–25.

Friedman, Milton. *A Theory of the Consumption Function.* Princeton, N.J.: Princeton Univ. Press (for Nat. Bur. Econ. Res.), 1957.

Ghez, Gilbert, and Becker, Gary S. *The Allocation of Time and Goods over the Life Cycle.* New York: Columbia Univ. Press (for Nat. Bur. Econ. Res.), 1975.

Heckman, James J. "Life-Cycle Consumption and Labor Supply: An Explanation of the Relationship between Income and Consumption over the Life Cycle." *A.E.R.* 64 (March 1974): 188–94.

———. "A Life-Cycle Model of Earnings, Learning and Consumption." *J.P.E.* 84, no. 4, pt. 2 (August 1976): S11–S44.

Heckman, James J., and MaCurdy, Thomas E. "A Life Cycle Model of Female Labour Supply." *Rev. Econ. Studies* 47 (January 1980): 47–74.

Houthakker, Hendrik S., and Taylor, Lester D. *Consumer Demand in the United States, 1929–1970.* 2d ed. Cambridge, Mass.: Harvard Univ. Press, 1970.

MaCurdy, Thomas E. "Two Essays on the Life Cycle." Ph.D. dissertation, Univ. Chicago, 1978.

———. "Using Multiple Time Series Analysis to Estimate a Dynamic Model of Labor Supply." Unpublished manuscript, Stanford Univ., 1980.

———. "An Empirical Model of Labor Supply in an Environment of Uncertainty." In *Longitudinal Studies of the Labor Market,* edited by B. Singer and James J. Heckman. New York: Academic Press, in press.

Phlips, Louis. *Applied Consumption Analysis.* Amsterdam: North-Holland, 1974.

Smith, James P. "On the Labor-Supply Effects of Age-related Income Maintenance Programs." *J. Human Resources* 10 (Winter 1975): 25–43.

———. "Family Labor Supply over the Life Cycle." *Explorations Econ. Res.* 4 (Spring 1977): 205–76.

ABOUT THE AUTHOR

Thomas E. MaCurdy

Tom MaCurdy is professor of economics and a senior fellow at the Hoover Institution at Stanford University, where he has been since 1978. He is also a research associate of the National Bureau of Economic Research and an adjunct fellow at the Public Policy Institute of California. Tom received his B.A. from the University of Washington and his Ph.D. in 1978 from the University of Chicago.

Known for his work on the economics of income transfer programs, human resources, and labor markets, MaCurdy has also been actively engaged in research and advice to a variety of federal and California state and county agencies. His recent studies investigate the consequences of governmental policies underlying welfare programs (e.g., AFDC and food stamps), unemployment compensation, social security, Medicare, Medicaid, and various forms of public assistance for low-income populations. Tom has been actively involved with several scholarly journals, serving in various editorial capacities for *Labor Economics,* the *Journal of Econometrics,* the *Review of Economics and Statistics,* and *Econometrica.*

Determining Participation
in Income-Tested Social Programs

ORLEY ASHENFELTER

Estimates of the number of participants to expect in income-tested social programs may be made from data on income distributions alone. These simple estimates will be biased if the social program induces incentive effects or if some eligible participants do not pursue their application for benefits. This article brings these issues together and sets out a statistical framework for testing whether the simple estimates are likely to be adequate in practice. The data used for the empirical work come from the Seattle and Denver Income Maintenance Experiments, the largest of several similar experiments thus far undertaken. The results imply that the simple estimates of program participation may be adequate if a program of the experimental type investigated here is implemented nationally.

1. INTRODUCTION

The overall costs of government welfare programs are determined both by the benefits received per participant and by the number of participants. In most social programs, individuals or families may participate in the receipt of benefits only if their income falls below a cutoff level specified by Congress or by the program's operators. Estimating the extent of program participation for different levels of income eligibility is thus an important factor in public discussions of the initiation and modification of these social programs.

At first blush it might seem that determining the extent of program participation is a straightforward statistical problem. The number of program participants could simply be estimated as the number of families or individuals in the relevant population with incomes at or below the proposed program cutoff income. The data required to produce these estimates are nothing more than a random sample of the incomes of the relevant population and the associated cumulative income distribution function. More generous social programs, which are those with higher income cutoffs determining eligibility, would naturally be expected to have a greater number of participants.

Orley Ashenfelter is Professor, Department of Economics, Princeton University, Princeton, NJ 08544. The author is grateful to the editor and two referees for helpful comments; to Robert Moffitt, John Pencavel, and Philip Robins for helpful discussions; and to Mark Plant and Michael Ransom for skillful assistance. Financial support for this research was provided in part by the Department of Health and Human Services through a contract with SRI International.

There are two potential difficulties with this approach to estimating program participation. First, some workers who would normally have incomes in excess of the program income cutoff may reduce their labor supply to make themselves eligible for program participation. To the extent that these incentive effects exist, estimates of program participation based on simple cumulative income distributions will systematically understate actual participation. For a given level of program generosity, however, the size of these incentive effects will vary with the implicit tax rate in the social program. The key to identifying these incentive effects is therefore to isolate the effects on program participation of variations in implicit social program tax rates that are independent of program generosity. Doing this requires data that contain variations in both program generosity *and* program tax rates. Estimating the size of these incentive effects is of considerable practical importance because they provide an indication of how and to what extent simple tabulations of the cumulative income distribution will understate program participation.

Second, estimates of the actual participation in existing U.S. welfare programs often indicate that many families who are eligible on the basis of their income do not participate. This raises the possibility that the incidence of information, reporting, or other unobserved nonpecuniary costs are a significant deterrent to actual program participation. The key to identifying the presence of these deterrent costs is the ability to compare actual program participation against the participation predicted for a group whose income distribution would otherwise have been identical to that of the participants. In an experimental setting the natural place to obtain these data is from a comparison of treatment and control groups. Estimating the size of these nonpecuniary participation effects is of considerable practical importance because they provide an indication of how and to what extent simple tabulations of the cumulative income distribution will *overstate* program participation.

The purpose of this article is to bring these three issues together in such a way that they may be explored empirically. The data used for this purpose are probably the best that will be available for some time and come from the Seattle and Denver Income Maintenance Experiments, the largest of several similar experiments thus far undertaken. The empirical strategy is to construct a statistical framework that treats the cross-sectional heterogeneity of incomes as an inevitable determinant of some correlation between program generosity and program participation, but that allows the data to confirm the further presence or absence of both economic incentives and unobserved nonpecuniary participation costs. The basic goal is to set out a convenient and tractable scheme for organizing the relevant data that nests all of the relevant hypotheses to be tested.

The first section of the article is expository and sets out the basic issues as clearly as possible. The natural focus is on the characteristics of families that make them eligible for benefits without changing their labor supply and how to distinguish these families from those that do change their behavior. Inevitably, the elementary empirical analysis it contains is instructive, but too simple.

The second section contains a correct but nevertheless easily implemented statistical framework based on a convenient specification of a model of labor supply. The empirical results are contained in the third section, and the conclusion contains a discussion of the further research that these results suggest may be useful.

2. ELEMENTARY DETERMINANTS OF PROGRAM PARTICIPATION

2.1 ELIGIBILITY FOR EXPERIMENTAL FAMILIES

In a negative income tax program, families receive an income guarantee of G dollars and face a tax rate of t on their nonwelfare income (y). If they claim it, they therefore receive a subsidy (D) of $D = G - ty$ dollars as long as their income (y) is less than G/t. If family income y is greater than the quantity G/t, the family cannot receive a subsidy. The income cutoff G/t is called the *breakeven income* for the program. Families with incomes below the breakeven are said to be eligible for program participation, whereas families with higher incomes are not eligible.

Suppose at the outset that families do not control their incomes, but that incomes differ among families. Suppose also that there are no unobserved nonpecuniary costs of program participation such as "welfare stigma." In this situation families whose incomes fall below the breakeven income would then choose to receive a subsidy, whereas other families would be ineligible for the program. The only economic behavior involved in this prediction is the trivial assumption that more is preferred to less.

To make things concrete suppose that the logarithm of income (henceforth called *log income*) is normal with mean μ and standard deviation σ. Under the assumptions just stated, the fraction of families eligible for benefits will be identical to the fraction who participate in the program (P) and will be

$$P = F[(\ln G/t - \mu)/\sigma] \tag{2.1}$$

where F indicates the value of the cumulative standardized normal distribution function. Now suppose several groups are randomly selected from the pool whose log income is normally distributed and that these groups are offered negative income tax plans with varying income guarantees and tax rates. This is a stylized description of the Seattle and Denver Income Maintenance Experiments. Equation (2.1) then describes a series of points relating the participation fraction (P) and the log of the breakeven of the offered plan. There are two observations to make about this relationship. First, higher income guarantees (G) and lower tax rates (t) are associated with greater participation. This relationship is purely mechanical in the sense that it merely reflects increased eligibility for program benefits as the breakeven of the plan increases and the program becomes more generous. Moreover, in this simple setup the elasticity of program participation across groups with respect to the program guarantee is equal but opposite in sign to the elasticity of program participation with respect to the tax rate. A regression of program participation on G and t does not, therefore, establish anything more than the fact that families offered programs with high breakevens are more likely to be eligible for program benefits even if they do not change their behavior.

Second, a plot of the participation fraction P against the log of the breakeven reveals the parameters of the log income distribution and can be used both to estimate those parameters and to test the normality assumption. Table 1 contains data from the Seattle/Denver experiments to illustrate this point. Column 1 lists the fraction of families initially offered a negative income tax program who received more than a nominal payment during any quarter of the second year of the experiment. The data are classified by the breakeven of the program offered to the experimental family. Since some of the programs have similar breakeven levels, I have aggregated those that were similar when it equalized cell sizes. All experimental families received at least $60 per quarter independently of their incomes as compensation for various administrative obligations. The number of families in the numerator of the participation fraction is the number of families receiving more than this nominal payment in at least one calendar quarter of the second year of the experiment. Families that drop out of the program are therefore included in the data as nonparticipants, and this classification is an enormous advantage for this analysis. After all, attrition is logically equivalent to nonparticipation and Pencavel and West (1978) have shown that it is highly correlated with the program breakeven to which a family is assigned. As one can see from Table 1, the participation proportion increases with the breakeven of the program, as expected. (There are several definitions of program breakeven that might be used for this analysis, but I have simply used the ratio of the nominal program income guarantee to the nominal tax rate as the breakeven throughout.)

Unfortunately, because of the setup of the Seattle/Denver experiments the participation proportions in Table 1 are not estimates of the cumulative values of the normal distribution given by (2.1). In these experiments, as in others, families were initially screened on the basis of their pre-experimental incomes before being assigned to an experimental program. To account for the truncation of the income distribution on the basis of pre-experimental incomes I have also reported the adjusted participation proportion in column 2 of Table 1. (The method of adjustment is contained in Appendix A.) The actual participation proportions observed in the sample are upward biased estimates of the participation proportions that would be observed in a national negative income tax program, because the experimental sample overrepresents families with low incomes in the pre-experimental year and incomes are positively correlated in subsequent years.

The dashed line in Figure 1 is a plot on normal probability paper of the adjusted participation fractions against the log of the breakeven for the six groups listed in Table 1. Although there is clearly considerable variation, these points do roughly coincide with a straight line and are not strong evidence against the normality assumption.

2.2 CONTROL FAMILIES

The design of the Seattle/Denver negative income tax experiments also includes provision for a control group of randomly selected families. A natural question arises as to what use

TABLE 1

DATA ON EXPERIMENTAL AND CONTROL FAMILIES IN THE SECOND YEAR OF THE SEATTLE/DENVER INCOME MAINTENANCE EXPERIMENT

Program Earnings Breakeven for Experimental Families $	The Proportion of Experimental Families Participating in the Receipt of Payments		Income Ordinate for Control Families $	The Cumulative Earnings Distribution for Control Group Families	
	Unadjusted for Truncation (1)	Adjusted for Truncation (2)		Unadjusted for Truncation (3)	Adjusted for Truncation (4)
5,430–6,850	.328	.29	6,850	.315	.28
7,366–7,600	.319	.29	7,600	.383	.34
8,000	.521	.45	8,000	.433	.39
8,001–8,821	.558	.48	8,821	.527	.46
9,600	.673	.57	9,600	.609	.53
11,200	.734	.64	11,200	.774	.66

the data from this group are for the analysis of program participation. The answer is that these data provide independent evidence on both the form of the cumulative distribution function of log income and the values of the parameters of that distribution.

To continue, suppose that the log incomes of control families are also normal with mean μ and standard deviation σ. The fraction of control families with log incomes below a value R is then

$$P = F\left[(R - \mu)/\sigma\right] \qquad (2.2)$$

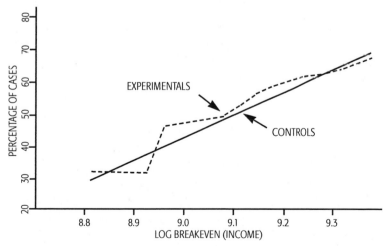

FIGURE 1

Cumulative Income Distribution (controls) and Probit Function (experimentals).

Choosing $R = \ln G/t$ gives a relationship between the values of the empirical cumulative distribution function of log income and the values of R among the control families that should be the same as the relationship between the participation fraction and the program breakeven among the experimental families. The unadjusted points on the cumulative income distribution for the control group are listed in column 3 of Table 1. The ordinates were selected to correspond with the six program breakevens for the experimentals. The numbers listed in column 3 are simple, distribution-free estimates of the actual participation fractions in column 1 that ignore both incentive and nonpecuniary deterrent effects in the determination of participation. Most (but not all) of these estimates seem reasonably accurate. In essence, improving on these benchmark estimates provides the basic challenge for any statistical model of participation.

As with the experimental families, the control families are selected in the Seattle/Denver experiments so as to overrepresent low income families and this requires an adjustment of the observed cumulative proportions $\tilde{P}$. The adjustment method for the control families is identical to that made for the experimental families. These adjusted proportions in column 4 of Table 1 are also plotted in Figure 1. As one can see from Figure 1, the estimated points of the cumulative distribution of log incomes for the control families do closely coincide with a straight line. This suggests that the normality assumption is reasonable. Moreover, the position of this line is close, but by no means identical, to the position of the similar relationship for experimental families. This suggests that the data for both control and experimental families are useful for the analysis of program participation, and that systematic labor supply behavior or the presence of nonpecuniary participation costs may partly account for the difference between the positions of the two lines in Figure 1.

2.3 Labor Supply Behavior and Participation

The analysis so far has emphasized the mechanical determinants of program participation by treating the family's income as exogenous. The spirit of the analysis of labor supply, however, is that by choosing their hours of work family members may manipulate their income so as to become eligible for negative income tax payments. To determine how many families will engage in this behavior it is necessary to recognize that a negative income tax offers a change, both harmful and beneficial, in the opportunity set that a family faces. The harmful aspect is the decrease in the wage rate from w to $(1 - t)w$ that a family member faces, but the beneficial aspect is the increase in the guaranteed (unearned) income level of G that the family now has. The family that is offered the opportunity to participate in a negative income tax program presumably will do so if the harmful effect of participating is outweighed by the beneficial effect. It is shown to a second-order approximation in Appendix B that all families whose earned incomes would have fallen below the quantity

$$y^0 = (G/t)(1 - .5et)^{-1} \qquad (2.3)$$

will perceive the net benefits of program participation to be greater than the net costs. In equation (2.3), e is the elasticity of labor supply and is assumed to be constant for purposes of estimation. The relaxation of this assumption could be easily handled by working out a third- or higher-order approximation to family behavior, and it would merely introduce powers of t into (2.3). As it stands, (2.3) demonstrates the intuitive proposition that the choice of program participation will vary from what it would be if there were no incentive effects to the extent that the labor supply elasticity (e) differs from zero. If $e = 0$, labor supply is insensitive to tax rates and participation is determined as if incomes were exogenously determined. The larger e is, the greater participation is, and the more sensitive participation is to variations in the tax rate.

It is a straightforward matter to use the criterion of (2.3) as the basis for a simple econometric model of participation. First, for reasonable values of e and t, the logarithm of (2.3) is

$$\ln y^0 \approx \ln G/t + .5et. \qquad (2.4)$$

Second, assume that however families determine their earnings in a given period, $\ln(y)$ is normal with mean μ and standard deviation σ. If the earned income that would be received in the absence of program participation, $\ln y$, turns out to be less than $\ln y^0$ in any period the family will choose to make itself eligible for program participation. The fraction of families that do choose participation when offered a program with breakeven G/t and tax rate t is thus

$$P = F\left[\left(\ln y^0 - \mu\right)/\sigma\right]$$
$$= F\left[\left(\ln G/t + .5et - \mu\right)/\sigma\right]. \qquad (2.5)$$

Equation (2.5) neatly separates the mechanical from the behavioral aspects of program participation. From (2.1), one finds that the mechanical component of participation is $F[(\ln G/t - \mu)/\sigma]$. This is the participation that would be expected if incomes were exogenously determined, or if $e = 0$. The participation induced by a change in labor supply behavior is thus the difference between (2.5) and (2.1): $F[(\ln G/t + .5et - \mu)/\sigma) - F[(\ln G/t - \mu)/\sigma]$.

2.4 NONPECUNIARY COSTS OF PARTICIPATION

A natural way to investigate the effect of nonpecuniary participation costs or inclinations toward program participation is to assume that each family behaves as if these were of a dollar quantity Q. The condition for participation in the program for the family is then that $\ln y < \ln y^0 + Q$. If $Q < 0$, the family has a distaste for participation, while if $Q > 0$, the family feels otherwise. Suppose that these inclinations are normally distributed and independent of $\ln y$ with mean μ^* and standard deviation σ^*. (Assuming $\ln y$ and Q are independent has no quantitative content here, since a correlation between Q and $\ln y$ would change the definition of $\hat{\sigma}$ in (2.6) by merely the subtraction of twice the covariance between $\ln y$ and Q. There would be no change in the form of (2.6), however.) The fraction of families that will choose participation, when offered a program with breakeven G/t and tax rate t, is then just the fraction for which $\ln y - Q < \ln y^0$, and is simply

$$P = F\left[\left(\ln y^0 - \left(\mu - \mu^*\right)\right)/\left(\sigma^2 + \sigma^{*2}\right)^{1/2}\right]$$

$$= F\left[\left(\ln G/t + .5et - \left(\mu - \mu^*\right)\right)/\hat{\sigma}\right], \tag{2.6}$$

where $\hat{\sigma} \equiv (\sigma^2 + \sigma^{*2})^{1/2}$. The difference between (2.5) and (2.6) is the amount by which program participation differs from what would be the case if there were no nonpecuniary participation costs or tastes. It seems plausible that the parameters of the distribution of these costs or tastes would differ according to the type of program and the manner of its administration, and (2.6) shows just how these differences will affect program participation.

Equation (2.6) leads naturally to a simple probit estimation scheme using the data on the experimental group. Not all of the parameters in (2.6) can be estimated from these experimental data alone, however. The importance of the data from a randomly selected control group is that they may be used to estimate μ and σ; using those estimates, one can then estimate μ^* and σ^* to test the importance of nonpecuniary participation costs as determinants of program participation. As a result, all of the parameters in (2.6) may be identified. After all, the observed distribution of log earnings for the experimental group does not provide data to estimate μ and σ by simple methods because it is contaminated by any experimental effects that exist.

It is now clear why the analysis whose results are pictured in Figure 1 is too simple. Equation (2.6) indicates that the dashed line portraying the fractional participation of the experimental group may differ from the solid line indicating the cumulative distribution of the log earnings of the control group for two different reasons. On one hand, the level and/or slopes of these lines may differ because of the presence of nonpecuniary program participation costs. On the other hand, in the absence of these costs the dashed line should lie above the solid line so long as $e \neq 0$, and the size of any systematic difference should depend on the tax rate in the negative income tax programs. We turn next to a simple estimation scheme for sorting out these effects.

3. STATISTICAL FRAMEWORK

3.1 LIKELIHOOD OF THE EXPERIMENTAL SAMPLE

Equation (2.6) gives the probability of observing a participant and leads directly to the likelihood of the experimental sample. Two preliminary issues require some discussion, however. First, as we have observed, the experimental families offered participation in the Seattle and Denver Income Maintenance Experiments were screened on the basis of their pre-experimental incomes. Assuming that the joint distribution of pre-experimental and experimental log earnings is bivariate normal, however, implies that the conditional log earnings distribution during the experimental period is normal with mean linear in pre-experimental log earnings. It follows that (2.6) applies directly with the understanding that μ in that equation is replaced by a linear function of pre-experimental earnings. Thus, the truncation of the sample on the basis of pre-experimental earnings may be handled by simply including an additional regressor and taking some care in the interpretation of the parameters μ and σ. (The precise interpretation is given in Appendix A.) Second, it is natural to suppose that μ and μ^* in equation (2.6) are not constants, but instead vary across individuals with a (row) vector of variables X_i'. This also causes no problem for the interpretation of (2.6) as $\mu - \mu^*$ may simply be replaced in (2.6) by putting $\mu = X_i'\beta$ and $\mu^* = X_i'\beta^*$, so that $\mu - \mu^* = X_i'(\beta - \beta^*)$, where β and β^* are vectors of coefficients. It should be understood that because of the pre-experimental screening on income, the vector X_i must contain, at a minimum, the value of pre-experimental income, but it may contain other variables as well. Since a primary concern is to obtain a consistent estimator for the parameters e and $\hat{\sigma}$ in (2.6), it is most important to include variables in the vector X_i that may be correlated with the assignment of families to the various programs.

It follows that if the first n experimentals participate and the next m do not, the (log) likelihood of the observed sample is

$$\mathcal{L}^1 = \sum_{i=1}^{n} \ln F_i + \sum_{i=n+1}^{n+m} \ln(1 - F_i), \qquad (3.1)$$

where $F_i = F[(\ln G/t_i + .5et_i - X_i'(\beta - \beta^*)/\hat{\sigma}]$. This is nothing more than the (log) likelihood function for a simple probit analysis. Indeed, the only difference between this analysis and a simple probit analysis is that here the parameter $\hat{\sigma}$ is identified because of the structure of the model. It follows that estimates of the parameter $1/\hat{\sigma}$ may be taken as the probit coefficient on $\ln G/t_i$ and that the coefficients e and $\beta - \beta^*$ are simple functions of the ratios of these probit coefficients. Standard computing routines may thus be used.

An important message of this analysis is that the presence of economic incentives to program participation may be identified from data on an experimental group alone because of variation in the tax rates t_i. On the other hand, the correlates or presence of nonpecuniary program participation costs cannot be identified from experimental data alone. Regressions of program participation on the variables X_i cannot distinguish whether a variable influences participation because it is a determinant of the conditional mean of the earnings distribution or because it is a determinant of the conditional mean of the distribution of nonpecuniary participation costs.

3.2 LIKELIHOOD OF THE CONTROL SAMPLE

The value of the control sample is that it provides information on μ and σ, or, equivalently, β and σ, and this information identifies β^* and σ^* as well. The (log) likelihood function for the control sample is equivalent to the conventional setup for a regression function and is

$$\mathcal{L}^2 = \sum \ln f_i / \sigma, \tag{3.2}$$

where $f_i = f[(\ln y_i - X_i'\beta)/\sigma]$ and f indicates the unit normal density function. The regression estimates of β and σ that result from the maximization of (3.2), taken with the probit estimates of $\beta - \beta^*$ and $\hat{\sigma}$ that result from the maximization of (3.1), then identify all of the parameters in this model.

The form of the likelihood functions (3.1) and (3.2) suggests an important test of this model. If there are no nonpecuniary participation costs, or if they are uncorrelated with the variables in X_i, then $\hat{\sigma} = \sigma$ or $\beta - \beta^* = \beta$. In this case the combined (log) likelihood of the experimental and control samples taken together is

$$\begin{aligned}
&= \mathcal{L}^1 + \mathcal{L}^2 \\
&= \sum_{i=1}^{n} \ln F_i + \sum_{i=n+1}^{n+m} \ln(1 - F_i) + \sum_{i=n+m+1}^{n+m+r} \ln f_i / \sigma,
\end{aligned} \tag{3.3}$$

where r indicates the number of control observations and $F_i = F[(\ln G/t_i + .5et_i - X_i'\beta)/\sigma]$. By examining the components of (3.3) it is clear that the parameters β and σ are common to all parts of the likelihood function. It is a relatively straightforward matter to maximize (3.3) with respect to these parameters and e by numerical methods and to compare the maximized value of (3.3) against the sum of the unconstrained values of (3.1) and (3.2) by a likelihood ratio test. The economic significance of this test is that the null hypothesis that $\beta - \beta^* = \beta$ and $\sigma = \hat{\sigma}$ is consistent with a model in which program participation is not influenced by "welfare stigma" or other nonpecuniary participation costs. If this null hypothesis is accepted it offers the opportunity of pooling the data from the control and experimental groups so as to increase the efficiency of the estimation of the effect of economic incentives on program participation by increasing the precision with which the parameter e may be estimated. If this null hypothesis is rejected, however, then these nonpecuniary participation costs must be judged important determinants of program participation and this raises questions about whether the results ought to be generalized to other populations without further investigation.

4. EMPIRICAL RESULTS

An important message from (2.5) is that it should be fitted to data on groups that come from homogeneous populations. Particularly, groups with differences in mean earnings may be pooled using dummy variables to account for these differences, but this is not sufficient to handle differences in variances because the value of σ affects every coefficient in (2.5).

As a preliminary effort, therefore, the data for the control group were stratified by location of experiment (Seattle or Denver) and the variance in log earnings was calculated for the separate parts of the control group. The ratio of these variances (Denver/Seattle) was 1.006 and clearly did not justify stratification. A similar calculation comparing the variance in log earnings for Chicanos and others also indicated no necessity for stratification, but the same variance ratio comparing whites to blacks was 1.27 and clearly was significantly different from unity at conventional test levels. Since the variance in the log earnings of whites is significantly larger than for blacks, it follows that σ in equation (2.5) differs for these two groups and that special care must be taken in pooling the data for them. As a consequence, the first set of results reported in the following subsections is for white families, who constitute about two-thirds of the sample.

4.1 RESULTS FOR WHITE FAMILIES

Column 1 of Table 2 contains estimates of the parameters σ and β obtained by maximizing (3.2). This is nothing more than a regression of log earnings on the variables indicated and the estimate of $1/\sigma$ is nothing more than the reciprocal of the estimated standard deviation of the regression disturbances. The variables in the vector X are a constant, pre-experimental log earnings, a dummy variable indicating location, a dummy variable indicating whether the experimental family was offered a three- or five-year treatment, and a set of dummy variables indicating a family's predicted income level. These latter variables were assigned values prior to the experiment based on pre-experimental data and were used for the purpose of assignment to the 11 different negative income tax programs with various combinations of income guarantee (G) and tax rate (t). (Families within predicted income groups were assigned randomly to the various negative income tax programs. Predicted income was defined by a procedure explained in Keeley et al. 1978.) As one can see from Table 2, most of these variables have very little explanatory power except for pre-experimental earnings.

Column 2 of Table 2 contains the estimates of $1/\hat{\sigma}$, $\beta - \beta^*$, and e obtained by the maximization of (3.1). This is nothing more than the fit of a probit equation to the explanation of participant status among the experimental group. As with the control group, the X variables other than pre-experimental earnings have very little explanatory power in this equation. The log of the breakeven, on the other hand, is a powerful predictor of participant status. As the data in Table 1 also indicate, it follows that the major determinant of participant status is the generosity of the negative income tax plan that an experimental family was offered. The estimate of the compensated substitution elasticity, e, is around .2,

TABLE 2

ESTIMATES OF THE DETERMINANTS OF PAYMENT RECEIPT FOR WHITE AND CHICANO
TWO-PARENT FAMILIES (ESTIMATED STANDARD ERRORS IN PARENTHESES)

	Controls (Regression) (1)	Experimentals (Probit) (2)	Combined (3)	Combined (4)
Estimates of:				
$1/\sigma$ (or $1/\hat{\sigma}$)	1.332	1.562	1.328	1.351
	(.038)	(.187)	(.036)	(.037)
e	—	.232	.134	.190
Coefficient of:		(.295)	(.278)	(.314)
Pre-Experimental	.395	.187	.309	.421
Earnings	(.046)	(.046)	(.035)	(.043)
3-Year Treatment	—	.108	.134	.118
		(.067)	(.057)	(.076)
enver Location	.004	−.102	−.050	−.039
	(.061)	(.065)	(.047)	(.048)
$E0$	−.383	−.224	−.352	−.339
	(.243)	(.269)	(.193)	(.189)
$E1$	−.085	.130	.163	.021
	(.539)	(.376)	(.343)	(.335)
$E2$	−.467	−.155	−.361	−.343
	(.145)	(.156)	(.115)	(.113)
$E3$	−.242	−.011	−.141	−.128
	(.101)	(.099)	(.074)	(.074)
$E4$	−.061	.079	−.006	.003
	(.081)	(.087)	(.068)	(.061)
$E6$	.033	.122	.061	.061
	(.086)	(.103)	(.070)	(.069)
Constant	5.493	7.295	6.220	5.243
		(.432)	(.312)	(.385)
Pre-Experimental				.171
Earnings*				(.037)
Constant*				7.420
				(.471)
Log-Likelihood	−701.7	−479.5	−1193.5	−1184.7
Number of Observations	624	800	1424	1424

Note. Coefficients with an asterisk are for experimentals.

which is certainly consistent with the other experimental and cross-sectional evidence available, but it is very poorly determined and has an estimated standard error of around .3. (See the summary of other experimental and cross-section results in Ashenfelter (1978), and the results in Keeley et al. 1978, for example.) This implies that the tax rate in the experimental plan has only a poorly determined effect on the family's participant status.

There is also very little evidence from the comparison of the estimates of $1/\sigma$ and $1/\hat{\sigma}$ in columns 1 and 2 of Table 2 that "welfare stigma" is at work in these data. Although the estimate of $1/\hat{\sigma}$ from the data for experimentals is larger than the estimate of $1/\sigma$ for controls, these estimates are clearly not significantly different. This lends remarkable support for the basic model of (2.5), especially when one recognizes that the results in column 2 are derived from observed dichotomous behavior that is based on a sample completely independent from that used to obtain the estimates in column 1 of Table 2.

The most efficient estimator of e may be that obtained from the combined evidence from the experimental and control groups and these results from the maximization of the combined likelihood function (3.3) are contained in column 3 of Table 2. (Maximization was carried out by Standard numerical methods by first using an algorithm due to Davidon and to Fletcher and Powell and then by an algorithm due to Goldfeld, Quandt, and Trotter. A standard reference for these methods is Goldfeld and Quandt (1972).) Although the estimated standard error of the estimate of e does decline slightly, the estimate of e does also. In neither case would the estimate of e be judged significantly different from zero at conventional test levels. Again, there is little evidence of a well-determined effect of the tax rate on participant status.

It is, of course, possible to test whether it is sensible to combine the data for controls and experimentals by contrasting the maximized likelihood in column 3 against the sum of the maximized likelihoods in columns 1 and 2. This gives an estimated test statistic (twice the difference between the unconstrained and constrained likelihood values) of 24.6 to be compared against the tabulated χ^2 distribution with 10 degrees of freedom. This comparison implies that the constraints would be rejected at the .01 significance level, but not at the .005 level. A comparison of the coefficients in columns 1 and 2 of Table 2 makes it clear why the constraints are rejected: The constants and coefficients of pre-experimental earnings are very different in the experimental and control samples. The difference in constants is perhaps not very surprising since the assignment to experimental and control status was based, in part, on estimates of permanent income. It follows that experimental and control families may very well have been drawn from populations with different mean earnings levels. The difference in coefficients on pre-experimental earnings might likewise reflect differences in the correlation coefficient between earnings in adjacent periods between the two groups and could also be a result of the method of assignment to experimental and control group status.

The results in column 4 of Table 2 combine the data on controls and experimentals, but allow the constants and coefficients on pre-experimental earnings to be different for the control and experimental groups. The χ^2 statistic comparing the sum of the likelihoods in columns 1 and 2 against the likelihood in column 4 now falls to 7.0 and would not be judged statistically significant at even the .10 level. Although the model in column 4 has a plausible a priori basis and obviously provides a satisfactory fit to the data, it is derived after an examination of the results in columns 1 through 3 of Table 2 and may simply be a case of overfitting. It should be made clear, therefore, that the model reflects the following fact in the data: Participant status is less highly (negatively) correlated with pre-experimental earnings than would have been predicted on the basis of data from the control group only. An alternative explanation, therefore, is that "welfare stigma" is significantly negatively correlated with pre-experimental earnings. Still, as the comparison of the likelihood values in columns 3 and 4 indicates, this modification does very little to improve the predictions of participant status, so that the results in column 3 are perhaps still the most useful summary of the data.

4.2 RESULTS FOR BLACK FAMILIES

Column 1 of Table 3 contains the results for black families from the maximization of the combined likelihood function (3.3). As expected, the estimate of $1/\sigma$ is larger for black families than for white families, indicating the smaller variance in the log earnings of black families. The estimates of e and the coefficients on pre-experimental earnings are very similar for black and white families, however. It seemed useful, therefore, to combine the data on both black and white families, duly allowing the estimates of $1/\sigma$ to differ between the two groups, to increase the precision of the estimate of the compensated labor supply elasticity e. These estimates for the full sample of 2,119 families are contained in column 2 of Table 3. As one can see from the table, the estimated standard error of the estimate of e is at its lowest there, although the estimate of e is still so imprecise that it would not be judged to be significantly different from zero in this table either.

TABLE 3

ADDITIONAL ESTIMATES* OF THE DETERMINANTS OF THE RECEIPT OF PAYMENTS IN A NEGATIVE INCOME TAX EXPERIMENT (ESTIMATED STANDARD ERRORS IN PARENTHESES)

	Black Families	All Families
Estimates of:		
$1/\sigma$ for Blacks	1.521	1.491
	(.060)	(.060)
$1/\sigma$ for Whites	—	1.332
		(.037)
$1/\sigma$	—	—
e	.132	.165
	(.349)	(.242)
Coefficient of Pre-Experimental Earnings	.323	.316
	(.053)	(.030)
Log-Likelihood	−562.7	−1768.6
Number of Observations	695	2119

* Other variables included in these equations whose coefficients are not reported are a dummy variable for the Denver site, the normal income variables, and a dummy indicating participation in a 3-year treatment.

5. CONCLUSION

The advantages of the econometric framework set out here for analysis of the discrete choice of participation in a negative income tax program are considerable. First, the purely mechanical fact that a more generous program will inevitably lead to greater receipt of program benefits is neatly separated from the behavioral responses the program may induce. The former behavior implies nothing more than that a family eligible for an income transfer will take it, while the latter emphasizes the importance of estimating the labor supply effects that are the traditional objects of study by economists. Second, the estimation of the parameters necessary for predicting the extent of participation or receipt of benefits is straightforward and can be carried out with familiar computational methods. At an empirical level, the results from the Seattle/Denver Income Maintenance Experiment suggest that differences in participation across negative income tax plans are due primarily to differences in program breakevens or generosity. Tax rate variations have only small additional effects on participation, although estimates of elasticities of labor supply are certainly consistent with previous research. Perhaps most important, the empirical results also suggest that in this experiment the receipt of benefits was not affected by welfare stigma or other nonpecuniary program participation costs. Taken with the weak tax rate effects in the data, this fact provides considerable evidence of the value of simple program participation estimates such as those in columns 3 and 4 of Table 1 that are based on simple uncontaminated estimates of the income distribution.

The analysis also opens up a considerable agenda for further research. First, it is natural to consider combining the discrete choice model of participation with an analysis of the actual labor supply responses of program participants. Program participation is clearly a choice variable and the analysis here provides one potential method for treating participation and labor supply response as jointly determined endogenous variables. Whether models that force a common economic structure to explain both the participation and hours variables are useful empirically is a matter that can be subject to test in further research. Likewise, the analysis can be generalized to deal with intertemporal choice and the time pattern of participation in a negative income tax program. Results of such an application are reported by Plant (1982), who works out a specialized multivariate probit analysis like (2.5) that emphasizes both the serial correlation in the stochastic determination of low earnings and the role of labor supply elasticities.

Finally, the analysis provides a simple scheme for building the information from experiments into the simulation of the aggregate determination of program enrollment. Such projections must use information on the characteristics of the relevant aggregate population, and (2.6) shows just how estimates of the parameters of the appropriate group's earnings distribution can be used for this purpose. The same methods could well have wide applicability to any situation where discrete choices are possible, ranging from block pricing for electricity to food or housing purchases under alternative subsidy arrangements.

APPENDIX A: ADJUSTMENT FOR INCOME TRUNCATION

The adjustment of the participation fractions reported in column 1 of Table 1 (for the fact that a truncated income distribution was being sampled) was accomplished as follows. Write the joint cumulative distribution function of experimental and pre-experimental log incomes as $F(\ln \tilde{y}_2, \ln \tilde{y}_1)$. The right side of (2.1) is then $F(\ln G/t, \infty)$, the marginal cumulative distribution function of experimental income evaluated at the log of the breakeven. Assuming that the log of the truncation point is T, the unadjusted participation fractions in Table 1 are estimates of $\tilde{P} = F(\ln G/t, T)/F(\infty, T)$. These may be converted to estimates of the adjusted participation fraction

$$P = F(\ln G/t, \infty) = F(\infty, T)\tilde{P} + [F(\ln G/t, \infty) - F(\ln G/t, T)],$$

if estimates of $F(\infty, T)$ and $F(\ln G/t, \infty) - F(\ln G/t, T)$ are available. To calculate these, it is necessary to estimate μ_2, μ_1, σ_2, σ_1, and ρ, the means and standard deviations of the untruncated log incomes in the experimental and pre-experimental years and the correlation (ρ) between them. The estimates of these parameters from the control group sample using a straightforward maximum likelihood scheme are $\hat{\mu}_2 = 8.993$, $\hat{\mu}_1 = 8.990$, $\hat{\sigma}_2 = .840$, $\hat{\sigma}_1 = .925$, $\hat{\rho} = .413$. These lead to an estimate of .72 for $F(\infty, T)$ and estimates of $F(\ln G/t, \infty) - F(\ln G/t, T)$ for the six breakeven incomes of Table 1 of .057, .063, .077, .081, .090, and .107.

In the probit and regression analyses described in subsections 3.1 and 3.2, the joint normality of $\ln y_1$ and $\ln y_2$ implies that the conditional distribution of $\ln y_2$ will be linear in $\ln y_1$. The parameters μ and σ in Equation (2.5), using the above notation, may then be interpreted as

$$\mu = [\mu_2 - (\sigma_2/\sigma_1)\sigma\mu_1] + (\sigma_2/\sigma_1)\rho \ln(y_1),$$

where $\ln(y_1)$ is the logarithm of earnings in the pre-experimental period, and $\sigma^2 = \sigma_2^2(1 - \rho^2)$.

APPENDIX B: ECONOMIC DETERMINANTS OF PROGRAM PARTICIPATION

The classical model of labor supply assumes that a worker chooses to consume goods (x) and leisure (l) as if maximizing a quasi-concave utility function $u(l, x)$ subject to the budget constraint $x = wh + z$, where w is the wage rate, h is hours at work (total time minus l), and z is income received independently of work. This maximization problem leads to the demand functions $l = l(w, z)$ and $x = x(w, z)$ that indicate the most desirable consumption levels for any given values of w and z. The maximized or indirect utility level $\hat{u} = u(l(w, z), x(w, z)) = v(w, z)$ indicates how a worker's welfare varies as w and z vary. The inverse function $z = v^{-1}(w, \hat{u})$ therefore gives the minimum unearned income required by a worker with wage rate w to reach the utility level $\hat{u}$. The function $E(w, \hat{u})$ is called an excess expenditure function, and its properties and uses in this context are explored by Ashenfelter (1978,1980) and by Deaton and Muellbauer (1980). This function is a particularly convenient representation of family behavior for determining whether a family's welfare will be increased by participation in a social program. If the family participates in the program, it needs unearned income of $E[(1 - t)w, \hat{u}]$ to reach the utility level $\hat{u}$, while it needs unearned income of only $E(w, \hat{u})$ to reach the same utility level if it remains a nonparticipant. On the other hand, as a participant, the family obtains an increase in its unearned income of G dollars. Clearly, the family will choose to participate in the program if $E[(1 - t)w, \hat{u}] - E(w, \hat{u}) < G$, that is, if the extra unearned income needed to compensate the family for the damaging effects of the tax rate is less than the extra unearned income actually transferred to the family as a result of the program.

A natural procedure is to approximate the difference $E[(1 - t)w, \hat{u}] - E(w, \hat{u})$ by a second-order Taylor series around the nonparticipant equilibrium. Using the properties of the excess-expenditure function in which $\partial E/\partial w = -h$, where h is nonparticipant hours of work, and in which $\partial^2 E/\partial w^2 = -s$, where $s > 0$ is the compensated or utility-constant derivative of the labor supply function, we then have

$$E\left[(1-t)w, \hat{u}\right] - E\left(w, \hat{u}\right) \approx \frac{\partial E}{\partial w}(-tw) + \frac{1}{2}\left(\frac{\partial^2 E}{\partial w^2}\right)(-tw)^2$$

$$= htw - \frac{1}{2}s(tw)^2.$$

A family will choose to participate and receive a subsidy if

$$D + \frac{1}{2}s(tw)^2 > 0. \tag{A.1}$$

Since $s > 0$, it follows immediately that any family eligible for a positive subsidy on the basis of its nonparticipant hours decision ($D = G - twh > 0$) will participate, but also that some families above the breakeven will too. Even though these latter families will have lower total incomes as a result of their choice to participate, their decline in consumption of goods is more than compensated by the increased leisure they consume.

The earned income level below which a family will choose to participate may be called the *opting-in income level* and is obtained by converting (A.1) to an equality and solving for

$$y^o = wh^o = (G/t)(1 - .5te)^{-1}, \tag{A.2}$$

where $e = s(w/h)$ is the compensated elasticity of labor supply. Equation (A.2) demonstrates that the choice of program participation varies from what it would be when total income and labor supply cannot be controlled by the family.

Several economists have observed that the assumption used in the empirical analysis in the text that e is a constant implies an excess expenditure function of the form $E = f(\hat{u}) - g(\hat{u})w^{1+e}$. For this particular constant-elasticity function

$$y^o = (1 + e)G/[1 - (1 - t)^{1+e}], \tag{A.3}$$

which differs from (A.2). This demonstrates that (A.2) is only an approximation. It is nevertheless a good approximation as long as e and t are small. For example, with $e < .6$ and $t < .9$ the ratio of (A.2) to (A.3) is never larger than 1.06. Despite this, it may be of interest to future researchers to replace (A.2) with (A.3) to see what effect this has on the results. Doing this will, of course, introduce nonlinearities into the estimation of the probit function (2.5).

REFERENCES

Ashenfelter, O. (1978), "The Labor Supply Response of Wage Earners," in *Welfare in Rural Areas: The North Caroline-Iowa Income Maintenance Experiment,* eds. J. L. Palmer and J. A. Pechman, Brookings Institution, Washington, D.C., 109–138, 131–137.

———— (1980), "Unemployment as Disequilibrium in a Model of Aggregate Labor Supply," *Econometrica,* 48, 547–564.

Deaton, A., and Muellbauer, J. (1980), *Economics and Consumer Behavior,* New York: Cambridge University Press.

Goldfeld, S., and Quandt, R. (1972), *Nonlinear Methods in Econometrics,* Amsterdam: North-Holland Publishing Company.

Keeley, M.C., Robins, P., Speigelman, R., and West, R. (1978), "The Estimation of Labor Supply Models Using Experimental Data," *The American Economic Review,* 68, 873–887.

Pencavel, J., and West, R. (1978), "Attrition and the Labor Supply Effects of the Seattle and Denver Income Maintenance Experiments," Menlo Park: SRI International.

Plant, M.W. (1982), "An Empirical Analysis of Welfare Dependency," Discussion Paper No. 237, Los Angeles: University of California, Department of Economics. [Published in 1984 in *The American Economic Review,* 74, 673–684.]

ABOUT THE AUTHOR

Orley Ashenfelter

Orley has been with the Department of Economics and the Industrial Relations Section at Princeton since 1968. He was, in fact, both awarded his Ph.D. and promoted to associate professor (with tenure) at the same meeting of the board of trustees in 1970.

His research over the past thirty years has covered a wide range of issues in applied labor economics. Indeed, this body of research has been reprinted en masse in *The Collected Essays of Orley C. Ashenfelter,* Volumes I–III, Elgar, 1997. Orley has served as the editor of the *American Economic Review* since 1985, a fellow of the American Academy of Arts and Sciences since 1993, and on numerous advisory boards. In addition, Orley has produced a steady flow of first-class graduate students, and these now compose a significant fraction of the stock of major labor economists.

No summary of Orley's career, however, would be complete without mentioning his contributions to oenological economics. From the reislings of the Czech Republic to the cabernets of South Australia, no nontrivial wine varieties have escaped the scrutiny of his hedonic regressions. Indeed, when the *Encyclopaedia Britannica* first writes up Ashenfelter, O.C. (1942–) in the mid-twenty-first century, the scholarly contribution they will stress is "Qualite des Millesimes et Conditions Meteorologiques: Les Cas Bordelais."

ECONOMICS OF IMMIGRATION

George J. Borjas

David Card

Self-Selection and the Earnings of Immigrants

GEORGE J. BORJAS

This paper analyzes the way in which the earnings of the immigrant population may be expected to differ from the earnings of the native population because of the endogeneity of the decision to migrate. The empirical study shows that differences in the U.S. earnings of immigrants with the same measured skills, but from different home countries, are attributable to variations in political and economic conditions in the countries of origin at the time of migration.

Immigrants in the United States do not make up a random sample of the population from the countries of origin. This is perhaps the most convincing finding in the literature that analyzes how immigrants perform in the U.S. labor market. In the "first-generation" studies of this literature (Barry Chiswick, 1978; Geoffrey Carliner, 1980; Gregory DeFreitas, 1980), cross-section earnings functions were estimated and two conclusions were reached: 1) the age-earnings profile of immigrants is steeper than the age-earnings profile of the native population with the same measured skills; and 2) the age-earnings profile of immigrants crosses the age-earnings profile of natives about ten to fifteen years after immigration. Thus, after a relatively short adaptation period, immigrant earnings "overtake" the earnings of comparable native workers. The first of these findings was often explained in terms of the human capital framework: Immigrants presumably have stronger investment incentives than native workers, and hence immigrant earnings grow at a faster rate than native earnings. The existence of the overtaking age, however, was explained in terms of the unobserved characteristics of the migrants: Immigrants are a self-selected group and, as a result, immigrants may be "more able and more highly motivated" (Chiswick, p. 900) than the native born.

Recently, the focus has shifted from analyses of single cross-section data sets to studies of cohort or longitudinal data (see my 1985 and 1987 papers; and Guillermina Jasso and Mark Rosenzweig, 1985, 1986). The departure point for these studies is the well-known fact that the analysis of a single cross section of data cannot separately identify aging and

Department of Economics, University of California, Santa Barbara, CA 93106, and National Bureau of Economic Research. I am grateful to Gary Becker, Stephen Bronars, Richard Freeman, Daniel Hamermesh, James Heckman, Larry Kenny, and Sherwin Rosen for comments on earlier drafts of this paper. The research was funded by a grant from the Ford Foundation to the NBER, and by the National Science Foundation (Grant No. SES-8604973). The data sets used in this paper are available on request from the author.

Reprinted with permission from George J. Borjas, "Self-Selection and the Earnings of Immigrants," American Economic Review, Vol. 77 No. 4 (September 1987), pp. 531–553.

cohort effects.[1] The cross-section finding that immigrant earnings and years since migration are positively correlated can be explained either in terms of an aging effect (i.e., assimilation) or it may be due to cohort differences in quality (caused by nonrandom return migration propensities and/or secular shifts in the skill mix of immigrants admitted to the United States). These recent studies, in effect, bring to the forefront the question of how cohort quality and immigrant self-selection are related. For example, are immigrants selected from the upper or lower tail of the ability (or income) distribution in the sending countries? Even if immigrants are drawn from the upper tail of the income distribution in the home country, does that ensure that they end up in the upper tail of the U.S. income distribution? Finally, if cohort quality has experienced a secular decline in the postwar period (as my 1985 analysis suggests), what factors are responsible for this change in the selection mechanism determining immigration?

This paper presents a theoretical and empirical study of these questions. It is assumed that individuals compare the potential incomes in the United States with the incomes in the home countries, and make the migration decision based on these income differentials (net of mobility costs). The use of this standard model allows a systematic analysis of the types of selection biases that are created by this behavior.[2] It will be seen that the common assumption that immigrants are drawn from the upper tail of the "home" income distribution requires a set of conditions that will not be generally satisfied. More importantly, this type of model suggests a few key variables (namely, the characteristics of the relevant income distributions) that "predict" the types of selection biases created by income-maximizing behavior on the part of potential migrants.

The empirical work presented in this paper analyzes the U.S. earnings of immigrants from forty-one countries using the 1970 and 1980 censuses. Not surprisingly, it is found that the variance in (relative) immigrant earnings across these countries is substantial. Using the theoretical insights, however, the analysis shows that the variance in various measures of the "quality" of immigrants can be explained to a large extent by a few key variables describing economic and political conditions in the countries of origin.

I. THEORETICAL FRAMEWORK

Suppose there are two countries: country 0 and country 1. For concreteness, country 0 denotes the home country or the country of origin, while country 1 denotes the United

---

[1] For a recent discussion of this identification problem, see James Heckman and Richard Robb (1983).

[2] The model is formally identical to that presented in A. D. Roy's (1951) study of the impact of self-selection in occupational choice on the income distribution. The wealth-maximization hypothesis is also the cornerstone of the human capital model by Larry Sjaastad (1962). However, both Sjaastad's work and the literature it engendered pay little attention to the selection biases that are at the core of the Roy model.

States or the country of destination.[3] Residents of the home country have earnings which are distributed as

$$(1) \qquad \qquad \ln w_0 = \mu_0 + \epsilon_0,$$

where $\epsilon_0 \sim N(0, \sigma_0^2)$. The earnings facing this population if they were to migrate to the United States are given by

$$(2) \qquad \qquad \ln w_1 = \mu_1 + \epsilon_1,$$

where $\epsilon_1 \sim N(0, \sigma_1^2)$, and ϵ_0 and ϵ_1 have correlation coefficient ρ.

Equations (1) and (2) describe the earnings distributions facing a given individual that is contemplating emigration to the United States. This framework, due to A. D. Roy, can be interpreted as decomposing individual earnings into a part due to observable socio-economic variables (μ_0 and μ_1); and a part due to unobserved characteristics (ϵ_0 and ϵ_1). The Roy model focuses on the impact of selection biases on the disturbances ϵ_0 and ϵ_1. Initially, therefore, variations in socioeconomic variables (which shift μ_0 and μ_1) are ignored, but their role will be discussed below.[4]

The parameter μ_1 is the mean income that residents from the home country would earn in the United States *if all* home country citizens were to migrate to the United States. In general, this level of income need not be the same as that of the U.S. native population since the average skills of the two populations—even in the absence of selection biases— may differ. For simplicity, in the remainder of the discussion it is assumed that these intercountry differences in skill (such as education and age) have been standardized, and hence μ_1 also gives the earnings of the average native worker in the United States.[5]

The migration decision for persons in country 0 is determined by the sign of the index function:

---

[3] *Two important problems are ignored by the two-country setup. First, it is likely that potential movers from any country j will have more than one possible country of destination. Second, the probability that U.S. native-born persons emigrate to other countries may not be negligible. These possibilities are ignored in order to focus on the essential aspects of the selection problem.*

[4] *The Roy model has been recently used by Robert Willis and Sherwin Rosen (1979) to analyze the types of selection biases created by the college attendance decision. Heckman and Guilherme Sedlacek (1985) present a generalization of the Roy model and apply it to the problem of estimating market wage functions.*

[5] *It is possible, of course, that the average person in country 0 has ethnic or racial characteristics which are favored or penalized by the U.S. labor market. Hence the mean income of (equally skilled) natives may not equal μ_1. This possibility is ignored in the discussion that follows, but it can be easily incorporated into the model.*

(3)
$$I = \ln\left(w_1 / (w_0 + C)\right)$$
$$\approx \left(\mu_1 - \mu_0 - \pi\right) + \left(\epsilon_1 - \epsilon_0\right),$$

where C gives the level of mobility costs, and π gives a "time-equivalent" measure of the costs of emigrating to the United States (i.e., $\pi = C/w_0$). Assume that π is constant across all individuals in the country of origin. Since migration to the United States occurs when $I > 0$, the emigration rate from the country of origin is given by

(4)
$$P = \Pr\left[v > -\left(\mu_1 - \mu_0 - \pi\right)\right]$$
$$= 1 - \Phi(z),$$

where $v = \epsilon_1 - \epsilon_0$; $z = -(\mu_1 - \mu_0 - \pi)/\sigma_v$; and Φ is the standard normal distribution function.

Equation (4) neatly summarizes the economic content of the theory of migration proposed by Larry Sjaastad. If follows from (4) that the emigration rate is: (a) a negative function of mean income in the home country; (b) a positive function of mean income in the United States; and (c) a negative function of the costs of emigrating to the United States. There are, however, a number of other implications in the theory that yield important insights into the kinds of selection biases generated by the endogenous migration decision. In particular, consider the conditional means $E(\ln w_0 | I > 0)$ and $E(\ln w_1 | I > 0)$. The first of these means gives the average earnings of emigrants in the country of origin, while the latter term gives the average earnings of these migrants in the United States. Under the normality assumptions these conditional means are given by

(5)
$$E\left(\ln w_0 | I > 0\right) = \mu_0 + \frac{\sigma_0 \sigma_1}{\sigma_v}\left(\rho - \frac{\sigma_0}{\sigma_1}\right)\lambda,$$

(6)
$$E\left(\ln w_1 | I > 0\right) = \mu_1 + \frac{\sigma_0 \sigma_1}{\sigma_v}\left(\frac{\sigma_1}{\sigma_0} - \rho\right)\lambda,$$

where $\lambda = \phi(z)/P$; and ϕ is the density of the standard normal. The variable λ is inversely related to the emigration rate, and takes on a value of zero when $P = 1$ (James Heckman, 1979). Assume initially that $P < 1$ so that at least part of the home country's population is better off by not emigrating. Then the second terms in (5) and (6) define the kinds of selection biases generated by income-maximizing behavior. Equation (5) shows that the average emigrant may be "better" or "worse" off than the average person in the country of origin depending on $\rho \gtrless \sigma_0/\sigma_1$. Similarly, equation (6) shows that the average immigrant in the United States may have higher or lower earnings than the average native person depending on $\sigma_1/\sigma_0 \gtrless \rho$. Let Q_0 be the income differential between the average emigrant and the average person in country 0, Q_1 be the income differential between the average immigrant and the average native person in the United States, and $k = \sigma_1/\sigma_0$. There are three cases that are of interest.[6]

Case 1. Positive Selection: $Q_0 > 0$ and $Q_1 > 0$. In this situation the "best" persons leave the country of origin and when they get to the United States, they outperform the native population. A reading of the literature on the earnings of immigrants suggests that this positive selection is most often assumed in the interpretation of those empirical results. Inspection of equations (5) and (6), however, shows that the necessary (and sufficient) conditions for positive selection to occur are

$$(7) \qquad\qquad \rho > \min(1/k, k) \quad \text{and} \quad k > 1.$$

Thus if ρ is sufficiently high *and*, if income is more dispersed in the United States than in the country of origin, the immigrants arriving in the United States are indeed selected from the upper tail of the home country's income distribution and will outperform the native born.

Case 2. Negative Selection: $Q_0 < 0$ and $Q_1 < 0$. In this type of selection the United States draws persons from the lower tail of the home country's income distribution and these immigrants do not perform well in the U.S. labor market. The necessary (and sufficient) conditions for negative selection to occur are

$$(8) \qquad\qquad \rho > \min(1/k, k) \quad \text{and} \quad k < 1.$$

Negative selection again requires that ρ be "sufficiently" positive but that the income distribution be more unequal in the home country that in the United States.[7]

Case 3. Refugee Sorting: $Q_0 < 0$ and $Q_1 > 0$. The United States draws below-average immigrants (in terms of the country of origin), but they outperform the U.S. native born upon arrival. The necessary (and sufficient) condition for this to occur is

$$(9) \qquad\qquad \rho < \min(1/k, k).$$

These three cases summarize the quality differentials between migrants and the native base in each of the two countries. It seems plausible to argue that for non-Communist

---

[6] *A fourth case where $Q_0 > 0$ and $Q_1 < 0$ is theoretically impossible since it requires $\rho > 1$.*

[7] *The generalization of the model to allow for variable mobility costs (π) shows that the necessary conditions for negative (positive) selection remain unchanged as long as mobility costs and earnings do not have an "excessive" negative (positive) correlation. In addition, the impact of variable mobility costs on the results of the analysis is negligible if the variance in mobility costs is small relative to the variance in the income distributions.*

countries, ρ is likely to be positive and large. After all, profit-maximizing employers are likely to value the same factors in any market economy. The quality of immigrants in the United States then depends *entirely* on the ratio of variances in the income distributions of the United States and the country of origin. Suppose, for example, that $\sigma_0^2 > \sigma_1^2$. The United States, in a sense, "insures" low-income workers against poor labor market outcomes while "taxing" high-income workers (relative to the country of origin). This opportunity set implies that low-income workers have much greater incentives to migrate than high-income workers, and thus leads to immigrants being negatively selected from the population. Conversely, if $\sigma_1^2 > \sigma_0^2$, the home country now protects low-income workers from poor labor market outcomes and taxes the high-income worker. This opportunity set generates a "brain drain" into the United States. Available data on the distribution of income (World Bank, 1986, pp. 226–27) suggest that income is more unequally distributed in the large number of Third World countries (for example, Mexico, India, etc.) which form the bulk of current immigration to the United States.[8] Income-maximizing behavior is inconsistent with the traditional assumption that the United States draws the "best" workers from a given country and that those workers will (eventually) outperform the U.S. native born.

On the other hand, ρ need not always be positive and strong. It is likely, in fact, that ρ is negative for countries that have recently experienced a Communist takeover. The change from a market economy to a Communist system is often accompanied by structural shifts in the income distribution and, in particular, the confiscation of the financial holdings of entrepreneurs. Immigrants from such systems will be in the lower tail of the "revolutionary" income distribution but will outperform the average U.S. native worker. This result signals the movement of persons who cannot match with the new political structure, but who "seek refuge" and match quite well in a market economy.

These insights are developed under the assumption that selection biases *do* exist (i.e., $P < 1$ and $\lambda > 0$). Since for most countries in Latin America and Asia the mean level of the U.S. income distribution greatly exceeds the mean level of the home country's income distribution, it is unclear why—in the context of an income-maximizing model—the entire population of country 0 does not emigrate to the United States.

There are two reasons why we do not observe wholesale migrations of entire populations to the United States. First, it is not the differences in mean income levels that determine the extent of migration, but the differences in mean income levels *net* of migration costs. These migration costs will be both monetary and psychic, and are likely to be large in countries that have different cultural and social backgrounds than the United States. Second, there are statutory restrictions on the number of legal immigrants the United States will accept from any given country. These quotas play the important role of increasing migration costs of emigrants (if the numerical constraints are binding), since

---

[8] *It must be noted, however, that these data on income inequality do not correspond exactly to the variances that are the primitive parameters of the Roy model. In particular, σ_0^2 and σ_1^2 describe the dispersion in "opportunities" (for a given socioeconomic characteristic).*

these individuals will presumably have to compete (and invest time and effort) to obtain the relatively scarce visas. Hence mobility costs ensure that only some persons in country 0 find it worthwhile to emigrate and thereby create the selection biases that are apparent in immigration data.

The model outlined above can be used to infer how the quality of immigrants in the United States will differ in the cross section (across different countries of origin) or over time (as economic conditions in the country of origin and in the United States change). The income-maximization hypothesis implies the existence of a reduced-form quality-of-immigrants equation given by

$$(10) \qquad Q_1 = Q_1(\mu_1 - \mu_0 - \pi, \sigma_0, \sigma_1, \rho).$$

To determine the restrictions implied by the behavioral assumption of income maximization it is instructive to recall that $Q_1 = \gamma\lambda$, where $\gamma = (\sigma_0\sigma_1/\sigma_v)(k - \rho)$. The parameter γ does *not* depend on the size of the flow, while λ does. The impact of any variable α on the quality of immigrants in the United States is given by

$$(11) \qquad \frac{\partial Q_1}{\partial \alpha} = \lambda\frac{\partial \gamma}{\partial \alpha} + \gamma\frac{\partial \lambda}{\partial \alpha}.$$

The first term in (11) holds the size of the flow constant and will be called the "composition" effect. It measures how a change in the ability mix of a constant-sized immigrant pool affects their quality (relative to the U.S. native population). The second term in (11) will be called the "scale" effect and captures what happens to the quality of U.S. immigrants as the size of the flow is changed for any given "mix" (i.e., for constant γ).

Consider what happens to immigrant quality as the mean of the home country's income distribution increases. It can be shown that

$$(12) \qquad \frac{\partial Q_1}{\partial \mu_0} = \frac{\sigma_1\sigma_0}{\sigma_v^2}(k - \rho)\frac{\partial \lambda}{\partial z}.$$

Shifts in μ_0 lead only to a scale effect on Q_1. In addition, it is easy to show that $\partial\lambda/\partial z > 0$.[9] As discussed earlier, the sign of $k - \rho$ determines whether immigrants fall in the upper or lower tail of the U.S. income distribution. Equation (12) shows that $k - \rho$ also determines what happens to the (U.S.) earnings of immigrants as mean income in the home country increases. If $k - \rho$ is negative (immigrants are coming from countries with significantly

---

[9] *This follows trivially from the fact that λ is defined as $E(x|x > z)$, where x is a standard normal random variable.*

more unequal income distributions and ρ is "sufficiently" positive), $\partial Q_1/\partial \mu_0 < 0$. The intuition for this result follows from the fact that as μ_0 increases the emigration rate falls. The increase in μ_0 improves the position of the "marginal" immigrant so that he no longer migrates. But this marginal immigrant was more productive than the average immigrant. The increase in μ_0, therefore, leads to a reduction in the average quality of the immigrant population. Since the mean of the home country's income distribution and mobility costs play identical roles in the model, equation (12) also predicts that increases in mobility costs will *decrease* immigrant quality if $k - \rho < 0$.

It is important to note that this result only captures the impact of changes in μ_0 (or migration costs) on the extent of selection bias (Q_1). The increase in μ_0, however, can be induced by either a shift in the skill distribution of the country of origin's population, or by an increase in the country's wealth that is unrelated to skills (for example, the discovery of a large inventory of natural resources). If μ_0 shifts because of the latter factor, equation (12) correctly predicts the change in observed immigrant earnings (which are given by $\mu_1 + Q_1$). However, if μ_0 shifts due to an increase in the skill level of the population, the change in immigrant earnings will also depend on the term $d\mu_1/d\mu_0$. This derivative will be positive if skills are transferable across countries, and this skill shift may dominate any changes that occur in Q_1 as μ_0 increases. Hence the (relative) earnings of immigrants in the United States may well be a positive function of μ_0 regardless of the sign of equation (12).[10]

The change in the quality of immigrants due to a mean-preserving increase in the income inequality of the home country is given by

(13)
$$\frac{\partial Q_1}{\partial \sigma_0} = \frac{\sigma_1^2 \sigma_0}{\sigma_v^3}\left(\rho^2 - 1\right)\lambda - \frac{\sigma_1 \sigma_0^2}{\sigma_v^3}\left(k - \rho\right)\left(1 - \rho k\right)\frac{\partial \lambda}{\partial z} z,$$

where the first term gives the composition effect and the second term gives the scale effect. Since $|\rho| \leq 1$, the composition effect will always be nonpositive. An increase in σ_0

---

[10] *This discussion illustrates how differences in skill characteristics can enter the Roy model. More generally, the earnings distributions in the two countries can be written as*

$$\ln w_0 = X\delta_0 + \epsilon_0, \quad \ln w_1 = X\delta_1 + \epsilon_1,$$

and the emigration rate (for given characteristics X) is given by

$$P = \Pr\{(\epsilon_1 - \epsilon_0) > -[X(\delta_1 - \delta_0) - \pi]\}.$$

Selection will occur not only on the basis of unobserved characteristics (ϵ), but also in terms of the socioeconomic variables X as long as the two countries value these skills differently. Although the empirical analysis below (by holding X constant) focuses on the selections in ϵ, it would be very interesting to also investigate the types of selections generated in X.

reduces the income of the poorest while it improves the position of the richest. Hence the mix of immigrants will include more persons from the lower tail of the distribution.

In addition, a change in σ_0 changes the rate of emigration. Equation (13) shows that the sign of the scale effect depends on the sign of three terms: $(k - \rho)$, $(1 - \rho k)$, and z. The first two of these terms are nothing but the restrictions in equations (7) and (8). Suppose, for concreteness, that there is negative selection: the least-able persons leave the home country and they perform below the U.S. native average. This implies $k - \rho < 0$ and $1 - \rho k > 0$. Inspection of (13) reveals that the direction of the scale effect depends on the sign of $z = -(\mu_1 - \mu_0 - \pi)/\sigma_v$. If $\mu_1 > \mu_0 + \pi$, so that mean U.S. incomes are higher than foreign incomes even after adjusting for mobility costs, z is negative, the scale effect is negative, and thus immigrants from countries with more income inequality will perform worse in the United States.

The intuition for the workings of the scale effect can be grasped by considering Figure 1, which is drawn with $z < 0$ and $\sigma_1 < \sigma_0$. As σ_0 increases, the worst-off persons in country 0 will still want to migrate, while the better-off persons become relatively better off and their migration incentives decline. The emigration rate drops due to the withdrawal of the "best" potential migrants from the market, and thus the quality of the pool that does reach the United States declines.

The last characteristic of the home country's income distribution which determines the quality of immigrants is ρ. It can be shown that

$$(14) \qquad \frac{\partial Q_1}{\partial \rho} = -\frac{\sigma_1 \sigma_0^3}{\sigma_v^3}(1 - \rho k)\lambda + \frac{\sigma_1^2 \sigma_0^2}{\sigma_v^3}(k - \rho)\frac{\partial \lambda}{\partial z}z.$$

Changes in the correlation coefficient also induce two effects. Consider first the composition effect. Its sign depends on $-(1 - \rho k)$, which is negative if there is negative selection.

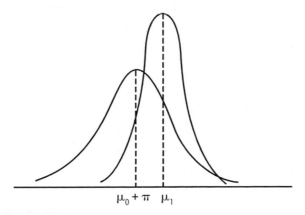

$\mu_0 + \pi \quad \mu_1$

FIGURE 1

An increase in ρ implies that a better match exists between performance in the United States and in the home country. Since $\sigma_0 > \sigma_1$ this decreases the profitability of migration for the best persons in country 0 and increases it for the worst persons.

In addition, changes in p have an impact on the emigration rate, and the scale effect is given by the last term in (14). If the conditions for negative selection hold, $k - \rho < 0$ and the sign of the scale effect will depend on the sign of $-z$. If, as before, we assume $z < 0$, the scale effect of an increase in the correlation coefficient on the quality of immigrants is seen to be positive.

A summary of the comparative statics results under the various regimes is provided in Table 1. One implication is immediately clear: generalizations about the quality of immigrants in the United States are hard to come by. The model does, however, isolate the key factors that determine the types of selections in the immigrant population and these factors shed some light on my 1985 finding that the quality of immigrants declined in the postwar period. Prior to the 1965 Amendments to the Immigration and Nationality Act, immigration to the United States from Eastern Hemisphere countries was regulated by numerical quotas. These quotas were based on the ethnic population of the United States in 1919 and thus encouraged immigration from (some) Western European countries and discouraged immigration from all other countries. The favored countries have one important characteristic: their income distributions are probably much less dispersed than those of countries in Latin America or Asia. The 1965 Amendments revamped the quota system, established a 20,000 numerical limit for immigration from any single country (subject to both hemispheric and worldwide numerical limits), and led to a substantial increase in the number of immigrants from Asia and Latin America. The new flow of migrants originate in countries that are much more likely to have greater income inequality than the United States. It would not be surprising, therefore, if the quality of immigrants declined as a result of the 1965 Amendments.[11]

II. EMPIRICAL FRAMEWORK

The quality measure Q_1 derived in the previous section is the standardized wage differential between immigrants and natives in the United States. In any given cross section, this wage differential is affected by two factors: 1) differences in the skill composition of the various immigrant cohorts; and 2) the rate of convergence between foreign- and native-born earnings (i.e., the rate of assimilation of immigrants). An empirical framework for measuring these effects thus begins with the specification of the regression model:

$$(15) \qquad \ln w_i(T) = X_i \theta_T + \delta I_i + \alpha_1 I_i y_i + \alpha_2 I_i y_i^2 + \beta_1 I_i C_i + \beta_2 I_i C_i^2 + v_i,$$

where $w_i(T)$ is the wage rate of individual i in cross-section year T; X_i is a vector of socio-economic characteristics; I_i is a dummy variable set to unity if the individual is foreign

---

[11] In addition, the 1965 Act changed the emphasis in the allocation of visas toward family reunification and away from occupational preferences. This shift may well lead to an even steeper decline in the quality of immigrants admitted to the United States.

TABLE 1

SUMMARY OF COMPARATIVE STATICS RESULTS

		Positive Selection $Q_0 > 0, Q_1 > 0$	Negative Selection $Q_0 < 0, Q_1 < 0$	Refugee Sorting $Q_0 < 0, Q_1 > 0$
$\partial Q_1/\partial\mu_0$:	Composition Effect	none	none	none
	Scale Effect	+	−	+
$\partial Q_1/\partial\sigma_0$:	Composition Effect	−	−	−
	Scale Effect, $z < 0$	−	−	+
	$z > 0$	+	+	−
$\partial Q_1/\partial\rho$:	Composition Effect	+	−	−
	Scale Effect, $z < 0$	−	+	−
	$z > 0$	+	−	+

born; y_i represents the number of years the immigrant has resided in the United States; and C_i is the calendar year of the immigrant's arrival. The parameters α_1 and α_2 capture the impact of assimilation on the (relative) earnings of immigrants, while β_1 and β_2 capture the cohort differentials.[12]

Of course, in a single cross section of data, equation (15) cannot be estimated since the variables C_i and y_i are related by the identity $T \equiv C_i + y_i$. Substituting this identity in (15) yields

$$(16) \quad \ln w_i(T) = X_i\theta_T + (\delta + \beta_1 T + \beta_2 T^2)\, I_i + (\alpha_1 - \beta_2 - 2\beta_2 T)I_i y_i + (\alpha_2 + \beta_2)I_i y_i^2 + v_i.$$

Equation (16) shows that the typical cross-section earnings function estimated in the immigration literature does not identify a single parameter of interest.[13] It is easy to show, however, that if another cross section is available in calendar year T' all the parameters in (15) can be identified.[14] Moreover, the comparison of the two cross-section regressions

---

[12] The parameters β_1 and β_2 capture two kinds of cohort effects: 1) differences in the skill composition of cohorts due to a secular trend in the quality of immigrants; and 2) differences due to selective emigration of foreign-born persons in the United States. Little is known, however, about the selection biases associated with return migration even though the Roy model can be generalized to account for the possibility that individuals make "mistakes." Unfortunately, U.S. data on the return migration of foreign-born persons is basically nonexistent, and hence this problem is ignored in what follows.

[13] Except perhaps for the coefficient of the immigrant dummy. This coefficient gives the wage differential between the most recent cohort of immigrants and the native-born population.

[14] Provided that period effects on the immigrant-native wage differential are negligible. This assumption is far from innocuous. Unfortunately, since only two cross sections are available, little can be done to test its validity.

provides interesting insights about the extent and direction of cohort-quality differentials. Let $\gamma_1 = \delta + \beta_1 T + \beta_2 T^2$, $\gamma_2 = \alpha_1 - \beta_1 - 2\beta_2 T$, and $\gamma_3 = \alpha_2 + \beta_2$, be the coefficients of the immigration variables in the cross section at calendar year T. This vector will shift over time since

(17)
$$\partial \gamma_1 / \partial T = \beta_1 + 2\beta_2 T$$

(18)
$$\partial \gamma_2 / \partial T = -2\beta_2$$

(19)
$$\partial \gamma_3 / \partial T = 0$$

The immigration vector in cross-section earnings functions (except for the coefficient of $I \cdot y^2$) is inherently unstable, though the direction of the instability provides insights into the underlying structural changes. For instance, γ_1 (the coefficient of the immigrant dummy) will be shifting down over time if the quality of immigrants is decreasing at the "margin" (i.e., in the cross-section year T). In addition, the age-earnings profile of immigrants (relative to natives) becomes steeper over time (i.e., γ_2 increases) if the decline in the quality of immigrant cohorts has accelerated over the sample period.

The empirical analyses below uses the 1970 and 1980 census cross sections to identify the parameters of interest (δ, α_1, α_2, β_1, and β_2). From these estimates it is possible to calculate measures of three alternative dimensions of cohort quality that underlie the discussion. The first of these dimensions is simply the wage of an immigrant cohort relative to the native base prior to any assimilation taking place; that is, a measure of the "raw" skills a given immigrant cohort brings to the United States. A second dimension is given by the extent to which the quality of successive immigrant cohorts is changing over time, while a third dimension is given by the extent to which the earnings of a specific immigrant cohort grow—above and beyond pure aging effects—in the U.S. labor market. Clearly, there are many ways of defining variables that capture these three facets of the "quality" of immigrants. However, since all possible definitions of a particular dimension of quality are based on the same underlying parameters, there is a high degree of correlation among the alternative measures. Thus, to some extent, the choice of the empirical representation of a given facet of quality is arbitrary. In the empirical analysis below, the three dimensions of quality are defined by

1) The predicted wage differential in 1979 between the most recently arrived immigrant cohort and the native base. This measure of the quality of a single cohort of immigrants—prior to assimilation taking place—is given by the coefficient of the immigrant dummy variable in the 1980 cross section.

2) The rate of wage growth (relative to natives) for an immigrant cohort that has resided in the United States for ten years. This is the assimilation effect evaluated at $y = 10$, and is given by $\partial \ln w/\partial y|_{y=10} = \alpha_1 + 20\alpha_2$.

3) The predicted wage differential immediately after immigration between the 1979 cohort and the 1955 cohort. This measure of the extent of cohort-quality change is designed to compare the typical immigrant that migrated prior to the 1965 Immigration and Nationality Act with the typical immigrant from the most recent wave. Using equation (15) it is easy to show that this change in cohort quality is given by $24\ (\beta_1 + 2\beta_2 T - 24\beta_2)$, where T indexes the 1980 cross section.

III. REGRESSION RESULTS FROM THE 1970–1980 CENSUSES

The data are drawn from the 1970 2/100 U.S. Census (obtained by pooling the 5% SMSA and County Group Sample and the 5% State Sample) and the 1980 5/100 A Sample.[15] The complete samples are used in the creation of the immigrant extracts, but random samples are drawn for the native "baseline" population.[16] The analysis is restricted to men aged 25–64 who satisfied four sample-selection rules: 1) the individual was employed in the calendar year prior to the census; 2) the individual was not self-employed or working without pay; 3) the individual was not in the Armed Forces (as of the survey week); and 4) the individual did not reside in group quarters.[17]

Since labor market conditions changed substantially between 1970 and 1980, the empirical framework derived in the previous section focused on the behavior of immigrant earnings *relative* to the earnings of natives. In this paper *all* immigrant groups will be compared to a single native base: the group of white, non-Hispanic, non-Asian men.

Forty one countries were chosen for analysis. The countries were selected on the basis that *both* the 1970 and 1980 censuses contained a substantial number of immigrants from the country. In particular, it is necessary to have at least 80 observations of persons born in a particular foreign country in the pooled 2/100 1970 Census to enter the sample of

---

[15] *The two 1970 samples that are pooled are essentially independent of each other. The only substantive difference between them—in the context of this study—is that the set of persons for whom SMSA residence is defined differs in the two samples. However, the coefficients of the SMSA dummy in earnings functions estimated separately in the two samples are not statistically different from each other.*

[16] *The native-born extract is a .001 sample in the 1970 census and a .00042 sample in the 1980 census.*

[17] *The analysis is restricted to men aged 25–64 in either census year. This differs from the more common methodology of tracking the "same" men over time. It can be shown (Heckman and Robb) that if the underlying parameters are constant over time, it is unnecessary to track specific cohorts across censuses in order to identify the structure. In addition, the samples exclude men who are self-employed. This restriction creates its own set of selection biases. However, an equally serious problem would arise if self-employed men were included in the study and their incomes were analyzed jointly with the wages of salaried men. Finally, the data exclude men who had annual earnings under $1,000 in either of the census years.*

the 41 countries.[18] The 41 countries under analysis account for 90.4 percent of all immigration to the United States between 1951 and 1980.

Summary statistics on the immigrant flow in the 1951–80 period are presented in Table 2. The first column of Table 2 gives the total number of immigrants from each country that arrived in the United States in that period. Although this number is interesting, it is more instructive if it is converted into a percentage of the country of origin's 1980 population. This statistic is presented in the second column and gives the percentage by which the country of origin's population would increase (in 1980) if all the persons who emigrated to the United States in the past three decades returned to their birthplace. This percent ranges from the trivially small (.04 percent of Brazil and the USSR) to the amazingly large (over 10 percent for Jamaica). Of the 41 countries in Table 2, 17 of them experienced emigration to the United States which exceeded 1 percent of that country's population.

TABLE 2

IMMIGRATION FLOWS TO THE UNITED STATES IN THE 1951–80 PERIOD

Country of Birth	1951-80 Immigration		1951–60 Immigrants as Percent of 1950 Population[a]	1971–80 Immigrants as Percent of 1970 Population[a]
	Total Number (in 1000s)	As Percent of 1980 Population[a]		
Europe:				
Austria	48.1	.6	.4	.1
Czechoslovakia	60.4	.4	.2	.1
Denmark	30.0	.6	.3	.1
France	90.1	.2	.1	.04
Germany	611.5	1.0	.7	.1
Greece	232.3	2.4	.6	1.1
Hungary	93.4	.9	.7	.1
Ireland	120.9	3.5	2.2	.5
Italy	524.8	.9	.4	.2
Netherlands	85.7	.6	.5	.1
Norway	45.1	1.1	.8	.1
Poland	244.9	.7	.5	.1
Portugal	204.2	2.1	.2	1.2

[18] *Only two of the countries in the analysis have between 80 to 100 observations in the 1970 census, an additional 11 countries have between 101 and 200 observations, 8 have between 201 and 300 observations, and 20 have more than 300 observations. Of course, the sample sizes in the 1980 census are significantly larger.*

TABLE 2 (CONTINUED)

IMMIGRATION FLOWS TO THE UNITED STATES IN THE 1951–80 PERIOD

Country of Birth	1951-80 Immigration		1951–60 Immigrants as Percent of 1950 Population[a]	1971–80 Immigrants as Percent of 1970 Population[a]
	Total Number (in 1000s)	As Percent of 1980 Population[a]		
Romania	49.8	.2	.1	.1
Spain	71.2	.2	.04	.1
Sweden	41.9	.5	.3	.1
Switzerland	40.1	.6	.4	.1
United Kingdom	562.9	1.0	.4	.2
USSR	105.4	.04	.02	.02
Yugoslavia	147.0	.7	.4	.2
Asia and Africa: China (Taiwan)	331.9	1.9	.4	1.4
Egypt	46.4	.1	.02	.1
India	211.1	.03	.001	.03
Iran	59.1	.2	.01	.2
Israel	48.1	1.3	.7	.9
Japan	131.1	.1	.05	.05
Korea	314.8	.8	.02	.8
Philippines	478.9	9	.1	1.0
Americas: Argentina	81.5	.3	.1	.3
Brazil	43.1	.04	.02	.01
Canada	676.4	2.8	2.0	.5
Colombia	165.5	.6	.4	.6
Cuba	611.9	6.3	1.5	3.2
Dominican Republic	251.9	4.3	.5	3.4
Ecuador	96.7	1.2	.3	.8
Guatemala	45.1	.7	.1	.5
Haiti	100.2	1.8	.1	1.3
Jamaica	221.7	10.3	.6	7.3
Mexico	1399.8	2.0	1.2	1.3
Panama	50.8	2.6	1.2	1.5
Trinidad & Tobago	88.0	8.0	.2	6.0

Source: U.S. Bureau of the Census (various issues).
[a] The population base refers to the country of origin.

The national composition of the flows received by the United States over the 1951–80 period did not remain constant over the three decades. The third column gives the flow of immigrants in the 1951–60 decade as a percent of the country's 1950 population; while the fourth column presents the flow of immigrants in 1971–80 as a percent of the country's 1970 population. These statistics document the declining importance of Western European countries as a source of immigrants and the increasing importance of Asia and Latin America. The fact that the characteristics of the sending countries changed drastically during the postwar period implies that the types of selections that distinguish the immigrant population from the native born also changed.

The 1970 and 1980 cross-section regressions were jointly estimated in each of the 41 samples (i.e., the group of immigrants from a specific country of origin pooled with the "white" native base), using the (ln) wage rate in the year preceding the census as the dependent variable. The socioeconomic vector of characteristics X included: years of completed schooling, age, age squared, whether health limits work, whether married, spouse present, and whether resident of an SMSA. The regression framework derived in Section II implies that the coefficient of the quadratic years-since-migration variable should be constant across censuses. This restriction was satisfied (at the 5 percent level of significance) by 32 of the 41 countries in the data, and hence was imposed on the analysis.

The restricted coefficients of the immigration vector in both the 1970 and 1980 census cross sections are presented in the first five columns of Table 3. The coefficients of the immigration variables in 1970 differ drastically from the coefficients of the immigration variables in 1980. This difference implies that cross-section regressions do not capture the "true" assimilation impact since cohort effects are confounding the analysis. Consider, for example, Colombia: In 1970, the most recent immigrants earned about 22 percent less than the native base, and their (relative) earnings increased by about 1.7 percent in the first year after immigration. By 1980, the most recent wave of Colombians earned 40 percent less than the *same* native base, and their earnings increased by about 2.2 percent in the first year after immigration. The tilting of the cross-section profile so that later cross sections are steeper and have a more negative constant term implies that the quality of the more recent Colombian immigrant waves is lower than that of the earlier waves. Conversely, consider the immigrants from France: In 1970, the typical French immigrant earned about 8 percent less than a comparable native person, and had earnings growth of about .2 percent during that first year after immigration. By 1980, the most recent immigrant earned about 10 percent *more* than the native base, and had earnings growth of minus .5 percent during that first year. The flattening of the cross-section profile implies that the quality of French immigrants increased over the sample period.

Three dimensions of cohort quality are implicit in these regression coefficients. The entry wage differential between the 1979 immigrant cohort and the native base is given by the coefficient of the immigrant dummy in the 1980 census cross section. Table 3 clearly shows that this coefficient has a large variance across countries. The last two columns of Table 3 present estimates of the other two dimensions of cohort quality: the assimilation rate defined by the slope of the earnings-assimilation path at $y = 10$; and the rate of

TABLE 3

ESTIMATES OF MODEL PARAMETERS[a]

Country of Birth	1970		1980			Rate of Assimilation at $y = 10$	1955–79 Change in Cohort Quality
	I	$I \cdot y$	I	$I \cdot y$	$I \cdot y^2$		
Europe:							
Austria	.0189	.0036	.0321	.0034	−.00003	.0040	.0287
	(.26)	(.75)	(.52)	(.82)	(−.45)	(.66)	(.20)
Czechoslovakia	−.1525	.0147	−.1441	.0127	−.00019	.0088	−.0143
	(−2.48)	(3.34)	(−2.79)	(3.23)	(−2.74)	(1.64)	(−.10)
Denmark	.0838	−.0033	.2018	−.0056	.00009	.0068	.2441
	(.82)	(−.44)	(2.14)	(−.81)	(.72)	(.78)	(1.21)
France	−.0785	.0020	.0999	−.0046	.00005	.0111	.3183
	(−1.28)	(.47)	(2.48)	(−1.33)	(.79)	(2.05)	(2.74)
Germany	.0999	−.0025	.1409	−.0047	.00007	−.0002	.0618
	(3.82)	(−1.37)	(5.40)	(−2.62)	(2.38)	(−.10)	(1.17)
Greece	−.2400	.0115	−.3092	.0141	−.00018	.0049	−.1231
	(−6.70)	(3.73)	(−11.28)	(5.42)	(−3.33)	(1.56)	(−1.75)
Hungary	−.1555	.0173	−.2082	.0145	−.00021	.0036	−.1744
	(−2.98)	(4.12)	(−4.30)	(4.23)	(−3.31)	(.86)	(−1.85)
Ireland	−.0732	.0019	−.0514	.0027	−.00002	.0050	.0666
	(−1.54)	(.53)	(−1.09)	(.78)	(−.28)	(1.26)	(.72)
Italy	.0133	.0060	−.0673	.0065	−.00009	−.0031	−.1855
	(.60)	(3.72)	(−3.45)	(4.58)	(−3.49)	(−1.55)	(−4.07)
Netherlands	.0127	−.0061	.1252	−.0074	.00015	.0062	.2487
	(.23)	(−1.45)	(2.71)	(−2.15)	(2.35)	(1.35)	(2.41)
Norway	.2245	−.0093	.2785	−.0096	.00015	.0013	.1241
	(2.54)	(−1.55)	(3.77)	(−1.76)	(1.58)	(−.17)	(.71)
Poland	−.1936	.0181	−.2734	.0184	−.00024	.0058	−.1865
	(−5.70)	(7.62)	(−11.08)	(9.61)	(−6.86)	(1.98)	(−3.08)
Portugal	.0797	.0032	−.0913	.0073	−.00012	−.0102	−.3418
	(1.95)	(.86)	(−3.25)	(2.47)	(−1.95)	(−2.77)	(−4.02)
Romania	−.3015	.0263	−.3161	.0229	−.00030	.0136	−.0929
	(−4.23)	(4.97)	(−7.02)	(5.47)	(−3.65)	(2.17)	(−.72)
Spain	−.3547	.0233	−.1920	.0134	−.00022	.0203	.2245
	(−6.15)	(4.32)	(−4.10)	(2.88)	(−2.39)	(3.98)	(1.92)
Sweden	.0128	.0119	.0465	.0099	−.00021	.0080	.0465
	(.13)	(1-90)	(.69)	(1.88)	(−2.14)	(.88)	(.24)
Switzerland	−.0201	.0132	.1467	.0067	−.00015	.0171	.2912
	(−.27)	(2.18)	(2.48)	(1.33)	(−1.56)	(2.56)	(1.97)
United Kingdom	.0607	−.0006	.1271	−.0023	.00002	.0038	.1303
	(2.70)	(−.34)	(7.38)	(−1.61)	(.67)	(1.84)	(2.81)
USSR	−.3509	.0277	−42.99	.0262	−.00035	.0105	−.2144
	(−6.70)	(8.34)	(−18.75)	(11.70)	(−7.67)	(2.22)	(−2.31)
Yugoslavia	−.0659	.0096	−.0920	.0097	−.00009	.0054	−.0608
	(−1.51)	(2.72)	(−2.82)	(3.52)	(−1.61)	(1.49)	(−.79)
Asia and Africa:							
China (Taiwan)	−.4525	.0227	−.5327	.0254	−.00037	.0114	−.1481
	(−14.34)	(9.43)	(−26.43)	(11.66)	(−8.22)	(4.01)	(−2.44)

TABLE 3 (CONTINUED)

ESTIMATES OF MODEL PARAMETERS[a]

Country of Birth	1970		1980			Rate of Assimilation at y = 10	1955–79 Change in Cohort Quality
	I	I · y	I	I · y	I · y²		
Egypt	−.4466 (−7.00)	.0421 (5.67)	−.4586 (−10.84)	.0396 (7.57)	−.00056 (−4.34)	.0260 (4.76)	−.0706 (−.57)
India	−.2847 (−7.09)	.0453 (9.71)	−.4340 (−21.41)	.0497 (16.75)	−.00096 (−11.03)	.0179 (5.33)	−.2845 (−3.84)
Iran	−.4078 (−4.71)	.0229 (3.03)	−.3101 (−10.19)	.0249 (5.45)	−.00031 (−2.47)	.0294 (4.13)	.2690 (1.88)
Israel	−.2998 (−4.19)	.0282 (4.54)	−.3397 (−8.44)	.0260 (5.74)	−.00041 (−3.84)	.0128 (2.11)	−.1314 (−1.00)
Japan	−.1314 (−2.65)	.0010 (.19)	.1016 (4.31)	−.0049 (−1.46)	.00002 (.18)	.0159 (3.60)	.4616 (4.78)
Korea	−.5450 (−8.69)	.0439 (5.72)	−.4481 (−19.44)	.0393 (9.68)	−.00071 (−5.40)	.0323 (6.31)	.1544 (1.37)
Philippines	−.4360 (−13.31)	.0265 (11.30)	−.3881 (−23.14)	.0266 (13.33)	−.00041 (−9.34)	.0233 (7.84)	.1158 (1.80)
Americas: Argentina	−.2099 (−3.81)	.0210 (3.58)	−.2427 (−5.80)	.0186 (4.13)	−.00032 (−3.11)	.0077 (1.65)	−.1191 (−1.12)
Brazil	−.1430 (−1.70)	.0114 (1.44)	−.0257 (−.45)	.0062 (1.00)	−.00015 (−1.11)	.0123 (1.66)	.1941 (1.19)
Canada	.0645 (2.86)	.0003 (.17)	.1165 (6.06)	−.0013 (−.91)	−.00000 (−.21)	.0030 (1.50)	.0988 (2.17)
Colombia	−.2247 (−4.33)	.0169 (2.74)	−.4030 (−12.67)	.0219 (5.78)	−.00036 (−3.71)	−.0007 (−.17)	−.3444 (−3.82)
Cuba	−.4612 (−22.20)	.0214 (8.89)	−.4517 (−18.26)	.0208 (9.24)	−.00025 (−5.20)	.0164 (9.74)	.0129 (.28)
Dominican Republic	−.3293 (−5.81)	.0141 (2.45)	−.4556 (−13.91)	.0142 (3.62)	−.00018 (−1.74)	−.0019 (−.44)	−.3020 (−3.01)
Ecuador	−.4041 (−6.06)	.0242 (3.28)	−.4195 (−9.77)	.0210 (4.13)	−.00026 (−1.98)	.0127 (2.58)	−.0906 (−.82)
Guatemala	−.5127 (−5.76)	.0408 (5.03)	−.4013 (−8.97)	.0298 (5.09)	−.00066 (−4.40)	.0222 (2.96)	.0828 (.51)
Haiti	−.3356 (−4.99)	−.0027 (−.34)	−.5234 (−13.95)	.0175 (3.39)	−.00011 (−.77)	.0064 (1.20)	−.1130 (−.94)
Jamaica	−.3322 (−6.75)	.0165 (4.06)	−.2594 (−9.33)	.0097 (2.92)	−.00020 (−2.77)	.0095 (2.24)	.0600 (.64)
Mexico	−.3307 (−16.57)	.0191 (14.80)	−.4037 (−34.72)	.0206 (22.25)	−.00031 (−15.94)	.0078 (4.16)	−.1497 (−3.61)
Panama	−.3438 (−3.52)	.0159 (2.31)	−.2516 (−4.35)	.0115 (2.07)	−.00010 (−.88)	.0165 (2.04)	.1476 (.84)
Trinidad & Tobago	−.3091 (−4.02)	.0187 (2.59)	−.3257 (−6.94)	.0211 (3.70)	−.00024 (−1.95)	.0158 (2.35)	.0013 (.03)

[a] The *t*-ratios are presented in parentheses. The cross-section regressions hold constant the individual's completed schooling, age, marital status, health, and SMSA residence.

change in cohort quality, defined by the earnings differential between the 1979 cohort and the 1955 cohort at the time of arrival in the United States. Since these estimated parameters are functions of the cross-section coefficients of Table 3, it is not surprising to find that there is a lot of variance in both of these variables across countries. Immigrants from some countries have high assimilation rates, while immigrants from other countries experience no assimilation at all. Similarly, the rate of cohort-quality change is sometimes positive (thus indicating quality increased between the 1955 and 1979 cohorts) and sometimes negative (thus indicating a quality decrease across cohorts). For example, the most recent immigrant wave from the United Kingdom has an earnings potential that is about 13 percent higher than the wave that arrived in 1955, while the most recent immigrants from India have 28 percent lower earnings than the earlier cohort.

The Roy model suggests that country-specific characteristics of the income distribution (and mobility costs) determine the quality of immigrants in the United States. The important task, therefore, becomes the identification of observable variables which can proxy for these theoretical parameters, and the determination of whether these country-specific variables "explain" the variance in the quality proxies presented in Table 3.

IV. DETERMINANTS OF IMMIGRANT QUALITY

Table 4 describes the construction and source of country-specific aggregate variables which portray the political and economic conditions (as well as some characteristics of the immigrant populations) of the 41 countries under analysis during the 1950–79 period. Table 4 also presents the mean and range of these variables and comparable statistics for the United States.

Three of these variables are designed to capture political conditions in the country of origin. These political measures are obtained from the Cross-National Time-Series Archive (CNTSA), a historical data set containing both political and economic variables for all sovereign countries since 1815 (up to 1973).[19] The CNTSA set contains a variable describing the extent of "party legitimacy," that is, whether or not there is competition among political parties in the electoral system. The measure of party legitimacy is interpreted as an index of political freedom, and is used to construct two variables: 1) a dummy variable set equal to unity if the immigrant's birthplace had a competitive political system during the *entire* 1950–73 period; and 2) a dummy variable set equal to unity if the immigrant's birthplace had a competitive political system at the beginning of the period, but lost its political freedom by the end of the period. The omitted dummy variable indicates whether the birthplace of the immigrant had a noncompetitive political system both at the beginning and at the end of the 1950–73 period.[20] The last index of

---

[19] *The CNTSA was created by Arthur Banks and is available through the Inter-University Consortium for Political and Social Research, Ann Arbor, MI 48106.*

[20] *There is also the possibility that a country gained its freedom during the 1950–73 period. Only one country, however, falls in this category (the Dominican Republic). To reduce the number of exogenous variables, this country was pooled with the countries that were "free" throughout the entire period.*

TABLE 4

DEFINITION OF COUNTRY-SPECIFIC VARIABLES

Variable	Definition and Source	Mean	Minimum	Maximum	U.S. Value
Politically Competitive System	= 1 if the country had a competitive party system during the entire 1950–73 period; 0 otherwise. *Source:* Cross-National Time-Series Archive (CNTSA)	.41	—	—	1
Recent Loss of Freedom	= 1 if the country had a competitive party system at the beginning of the period but had a non-competitive party system at the end of the period; 0 otherwise. *Source:* CNTSA.	.20	—	—	0
Number of Assassinations	Number of politically motivated murders or attempted murders of high government officials or politicians in 1950–73. *Source:* CNTSA.	3.27	0	22	12
Income Inequality	Ratio of household income of the top 10 percent of the households to the income of the bottom 20 percent of the households. *Source:* World Bank (various issues) and United Nations (1977).	7.50	1.42	30.0	5.91
Distance from U.S.	Number of air miles (in thousands) between the country's capital and the nearest U.S. gateway (Los Angeles, Miami, or New York). *Source:* Airline offices contacted by author.	3.37	.18	7.49	—
English Proficiency	Fraction of 1975–80 cohort of immigrants who speak English well or very well. *Source:* 5/100 A Sample of the 1980 U.S. Census.	.74	.24	1.00	—
Age at Migration	Mean age at migration. *Source* 5/100 A Sample of the 1980 U.S. Census.	24.56	12.40	32.40	—
ln (per capital GNP)	(ln) 1980 per capita GNP in dollars. *Source:* U.S. Arms Control and Disarmament Agency (1984).	8.17	5.42	9.62	9.39
Rate of Change in Per Capita GNP	Annual rate of change in per capita GNP between 1963 and 1980, defined by: $\ln(GNP_{1980}/GNP_{1963})/17$. *Source:* U.S. Arms Control and Disarmament Agency (1975, 1984).	.03	.004	.07	.02
Rate of Change in Central Government Expenditures	Annual Change in the Percentage of GNP that is accounted for by central government expenditures, defined by $(GOVT_{1980} - GOVT_{1950})/30$, where $GOVT_t$ is the percent of GNP attributable to central government expenditures in year t. *Source:* CNTSA and U.S. Arms Control and Disarmament Agency (1984).	.41	−1.69	2.08	.26
Change in Quota	Change in fraction of population eligible for migration to the U.S., defined by (20,000/1979 population) ÷ (QUOTA/1950 population), where 20,000 is the maximum number of visas allocated to the country after 1965, and QUOTA is the number of visas allocated prior to 1965. *Source:* U.S. Immigration and Naturalization Service (1965).	38.90	.28	149.67	—

political stability used is a variable measuring the number of political assassinations (defined as a politically motivated murder or attempted murder of a high government official or politician) that took place in the specific country during the 1950–73 period.

The country-specific vector also includes variables that describe economic conditions in the various countries of origin:

1) The logarithm of per capita Gross National Product in 1980 (in U.S. dollars). In addition, the analysis also uses the average annual percentage change in that variable over the 1963–80 period. These variables, of course, are designed to control for the mean level of the income distribution (as well as changes in that level) in the various countries of origin.

2) The ratio of household income accruing to the top 10 percent of the households to the income accruing to the bottom 20 percent of the households (circa 1970). Unfortunately, this measure of income inequality does not exist prior to the 1970's for most of the countries under analysis, and hence the change in the extent of income inequality during the last three decades cannot be documented. The empirical analysis below will proxy for the change in income inequality by using the change in the fraction of GNP that can be attributed to central government expenditures over that period. Presumably, the greater the role of the government the more taxation and income redistribution that occurs, and hence the less unequal the income distribution will be.

3) The level of mobility costs is proxied by the number of air miles between the country's capital and the nearest U.S. gateway.

Finally, the regressions also include variables that describe relevant characteristics of the immigrant population itself. The two variables in this category are the fraction of the most recently arrived immigrants who speak English well or very well, and the average age at migration. These variables are likely to affect the earnings of immigrants as well as their incentives to invest in human capital, and hence will be important determinants of immigrant quality.

A. DETERMINANTS OF THE ENTRY WAGE DIFFERENTIAL

In the last section a variable measuring the entry wage differential between the foreign born and the native born for the immigrant cohort arriving in 1979 was calculated for each of the 41 countries under analysis. Table 5 presents the generalized least squares regressions of this measure of immigrant quality on the country-specific aggregate variables.[21]

The simplest specification in column 1 shows that the variable measuring whether or not the country was politically competitive in the postwar period has a strong positive

---

[21] The dependent variables in the "second-stage" regressions presented in this section are themselves estimated regression coefficients (or linear combinations thereof). Hence the disturbances in these regressions are heteroscedastic. Let y_i be the true value of the dependent variable (for country i) in the second-stage regressions. The "true" model is given by $y_i = Z_i \beta + \epsilon_i$, where $E(\epsilon_i) = 0$ and $E(\epsilon_i^2) = \sigma_\epsilon^2$. The variable y_i is unobserved, but $\hat{y}_i$ is estimated from the regressions in Section III,

impact on the immigrant's entry wage. Immigrants from these countries have 27 percent higher relative earnings (at the time of entry into the United States) than immigrants from politically repressive countries. This basic regression also shows that the extent of income inequality has a weak negative impact on the relative quality of immigrants. Immigrants from countries with more income inequality are of lower quality. This result is consistent with the theoretical implications of the Roy model. As income inequality increases, the migration incentives for persons in the upper tail of the distribution decline, thus lowering the average quality of the immigrant population.

In column 2 of Table 5, the variables measuring mobility costs and the age and English proficiency of immigrants are added to the regression. The results suggest that persons migrating from countries that have 100 percent English proficiency rates have about 26 percent higher relative earnings at the time of entry than immigrants from countries with 0 percent English proficiency rates.[22] Table 5 also shows that age at migration has a significant *negative* impact on the initial relative earnings of immigrants in the United States. Hence persons who migrate as youths have an easier time in the U.S. labor market than older immigrants.

The third regression in Table 5 adds the level of *GNP* per capita to the list of exogenous variables. Its impact is strongly positive, and its inclusion increases the explanatory power of the regression to over 80 percent! A 10 percent increase in a country's GNP increases the relative earnings of immigrants by about 1.2 percent. This effect is likely to be caused by the fact that the higher the GNP in the country of origin, the greater the resemblance between that country's economic structure and that of the United States, as well as the greater the skills of the immigrant flow. Hence immigrants from those countries perform quite well in the U.S. labor market. The last regression in Table 6 adds continent dummies (the omitted continent is Europe) to control for continent-specific fixed

where $\hat{y}_i = y_i + v_i$, $E(v_i) = 0$, $E(v_i^2) = \sigma_i^2$, and ϵ_i and v_i are assumed to be independent. The heteroscedasticity arises because the estimated regressions are given by

$$\hat{y}_i = Z_i\beta + \left(\epsilon_i - v_i\right) = Z_i\beta + \mu_i,$$

where $E(\mu_i) = 0$ and $E(\mu_i^2) = \sigma_\epsilon^2 + \sigma_i^2$. The OLS regression of the second stage provides an estimate of μ_i, and combined with the estimates of $\hat{\sigma}_i^2$ available from the first-stage regressions, the parameter σ_ϵ^2 can be estimated by

$$\hat{\sigma}_\epsilon^2 = \left(SSE - \Sigma\hat{\sigma}_i^2\right)/\left(N - K\right)$$

where SSE is the error sum of squares from the OLS second-stage regression and $N - K$ is the number of degrees of freedom. The calculated $\hat{\sigma}_\epsilon^2$ is then used to reestimate the second-stage regression using generalized least squares.

[22] *These results are consistent with the estimated gains to English language proficiency reported in Walter McManus et al. (1983).*

TABLE 5

Determinants of the Entry Wage Differential Between the 1979 Immigrant Cohort and Natives[a]

Country of Origin Characteristics	Regression			
	1	2	3	4
Intercept	−.2214 (−3.88)	.1838 (1.06)	−.9934 (−3.41)	−.9469 (−3.30)
Politically Competitive System	.2743 (4.49)	.1306 (2.01)	.1101 (2.16)	.1264 (2.39)
Recent Loss of Freedom	−.0010 (−.01)	−.0511 (−.75)	−.0062 (−.12)	.0136 (.25)
Number of Assassinations	−.0072 (−1.20)	−.0028 (−.54)	.0021 (.51)	.0044 (.92)
Income Inequality	−.0084 (−1.78)	−.0038 (−.89)	.0039 (1.02)	.0046 (1.13)
Distance from U.S.	—	−.0114 (−.89)	−.0031 (−.31)	.0018 (.09)
English Proficiency	—	.2596 (2.20)	.1980 (2.12)	.2030 (2.21)
Mean Age at Migration	—	−.0217 (−3.55)	−.0149 (−2.99)	−.0119 (2.28)
ln (per capita GNP)	—	—	.1164 (4.57)	.1015 (3.77)
Country in Asia or Africa	—	—	—	−.1145 (−1.58)
Country in North or South America	—	—	—	−.0640 (−.73)
R^2	.504	.681	.808	.826

[a] The t-ratios are presented in parentheses.

effects. These additional controls do not have a major impact on the coefficient of the other variables.[23]

Table 5 shows that controlling for variations in per capita GNP across countries of origin has a major impact on the coefficient of the inequality variable: the latter turns positive (and insignificant). The reason for this shift lies in the very high negative correlation between the two variables ($r = −.6$). Since high-income countries (mostly in Western

---

[23] To further test the sensitivity of the results, two additional variables were introduced into the regression: the percent of the country's labor force that is in agriculture, and the per capita school enrollment rate. Both of these variables were highly correlated with GNP per capita, and in fact became insignificant once GNP was controlled for. Their impact on the other variables in the regression was negligible.

Europe) also tend to have the least amount of income inequality, the impact of per capita GNP on initial immigrant quality is likely capturing shifts in both the mean and the variance of the country of origin's income distribution.

The results in Table 5, therefore, are not entirely consistent with the theoretical predictions. Note, however, that these regressions do not truly constitute a "test" of the theory. The Roy model shows that selection biases will depend on a number of parameters which are not directly measurable. Table 5 attempts to explain intercountry differences in terms of variables which supposedly proxy for these primitive concepts. Clearly the errors introduced in the creation of these variables weaken the link between the theory and the empirical work. Nevertheless, it is important to note that these few country-specific variables "explain" a large fraction of the intercountry differences evident in census data.

B. DETERMINANTS OF THE RATE OF ASSIMILATION

The assimilation rate is defined by the rate of earnings growth of an immigrant cohort (relative to natives) evaluated at ten years after immigration. Table 6 presents the regressions of this variable on the various country-specific proxies.

Assimilation rates are determined by political factors. In particular, immigrants from free countries have lower assimilation rates than immigrants from countries with a long history of political repression, while immigrants from countries that recently lost their political freedom have the highest assimilation rates. These results are consistent with the hypothesis that the costs of return migration for immigrants from politically repressive countries are high, and therefore they have the most incentives to adapt to the U.S. labor market. The same reasoning can also explain the strong positive impact of the number of assassinations on the rate of immigrant assimilation: immigrants from politically unstable countries have greater incentives to assimilate in the U.S. labor market since their return migration may be costly.

The regression in column 2 shows that although distance between the United States and the country of birth has a positive impact on the assimilation rate, the effect is not significant. However, immigrants from countries with higher levels of English proficiency have much higher assimilation rates. In fact, the rate of earnings growth of immigrants from English-speaking countries is 1.4 percentage points higher than that of immigrants from countries with 0 percent English proficiency rates. Similarly, the age at immigration has a strong *positive* impact on assimilation rates. This result is consistent with the hypothesis that immigrants who migrate as youths have little to gain from assimilation per se. On the other hand, the adaptation period is likely to be important for persons who migrate at older ages.

The last two regressions in Table 6 include per capita *GNP* variable and the continent dummies in the list of regressors. These variables have a significant impact on the assimilation rate (in column 4). Immigrants from wealthier countries have higher assimilation rates, and Europeans (the omitted continent) have higher assimilation rates than immigrants from the Americas, but lower assimilation rates than immigrants born in Asia or

TABLE 6

DETERMINANTS OF THE RATE OF ASSIMILATION[a]

Country of Origin Characteristics	Regression			
	1	2	3	4
Intercept	.0076 (2.96)	−.0240 (−3.88)	−.0237 (−1.50)	−.0280 (−2.32)
Politically Competitive System	−.0029 (−1.06)	−.0068 (−2.66)	−.0068 (−2.60)	−.0091 (−4.28)
Recent Loss of Freedom	.0063 (1.81)	.0029 (1.21)	.0030 (1.15)	.0021 (1.06)
Number of Assassinations	.0008 (2.68)	.0006 (2.36)	.0006 (2.14)	.0008 (3.07)
Income Inequality	−.0001 (−.50)	−.00002 (−.11)	−.00002 (−.10)	.0002 (.90)
Distance from U.S.	—	.0003 (.74)	.0003 (.70)	−.0027 (−2.89)
English Proficiency	—	.0138 (3.27)	.0138 (3.20)	.0122 (3.70)
Mean Age at Migration	—	.0009 (4.28)	.0009 (3.95)	.0009 (4.72)
ln (per capita GNP)	—	—	−.00002 (−.01)	.0021 (1.83)
Country in Asia or Africa	—	—	—	.0151 (5.11)
Country in North or South America	—	—	—	−.0080 (−2.08)
R^2	.302	.704	.704	.842

[a] The t-ratios are presented in parentheses.

Africa. Despite the strongly significant impact of the continent dummies, the qualitative effect of most of the other variables in the regression is unaffected.

C. DETERMINANTS OF THE CHANGE IN COHORT QUALITY

Section III calculated a variable measuring the wage differential between the 1979 immigrant cohort and the 1955 immigrant cohort as of the date of immigration. The regressions analyzing the determinants of cohort quality change are presented in Table 7. It should be noted that the specification of these regressions differs slightly from those presented in Tables 5 and 6 since cohort quality change is likely to be determined by *changes* in the explanatory variables over the 1954–79 period.

The simple specification in column 1 reveals that cohort quality change is strongly influenced by practically all the variables in the regressions. For example, the quality of

TABLE 7

DETERMINANTS OF THE RATE OF CHANGE IN COHORT QUALITY[a]

Country of Origin Characteristics	Regression			
	1	2	3	4
Intercept	−.3194	−.9951	−1.1779	−2.2202
	(−3.19)	(−3.97)	(−4.08)	(−4.69)
Politically Competitive System	.1760	.1075	.0712	.0630
	(2.54)	(1.60)	(.97)	(.70)
Recent Loss of Freedom	.1256	.1468	.1272	.1310
	(1.67)	(2.16)	(1.81)	(1.33)
Number of Assassinations	.0077	.0156	.0122	.0256
	(1.19)	(2.32)	(1.69)	(2.00)
Rate of Change in Central Government Expenditures	.0698	.0699	.0641	−.0099
	(1.60)	(1.75)	(1.60)	(−.21)
Rate of Change in Per Capita GNP	4.7010	3.0956	1.1567	−1.5321
	(2.27)	(1.60)	(.46)	(−.50)
ln (per capita *GNP*)	—	.0889	.1186	.2443
		(1.93)	(3.22)	(4.15)
Country in Asia or Africa	—	—	.1374	—
			(1.42)	
Country in North or South America	—	—	.0274	—
			(.41)	
Change in Quota	—	—	—	.0034
				(2.26)
R^2	.284	.418	.453	.581

[a] The t-ratios are presented in parentheses.

cohorts from countries that experienced a shift from political competition to repression increased by about 13 percent (relative to the quality of cohorts from countries that were politically repressive throughout the period). This effect is consistent with the implications of the theory developed in Section I. The change in political structure can be viewed as a change in the correlation coefficient of the earnings of individuals between the home country and the United States. The change toward a repressive government may make the correlation coefficient in earnings across the two countries negative. Thus persons in the "revolutionary" lower tail of the home country's income distribution migrate to the United States and perform quite well in the U.S. labor market.

Table 7 also shows that cohort quality change is strongly affected by the average annual change in the percent of GNP that is attributable to expenditures by the central government. Presumably the greater the role of the government, the more income redistribution that takes place and the greater the *decrease* in income inequality over the postwar period. The coefficient of this variable in Table 8 is consistent with the theoretical implication.

The next two regressions in Table 8 add the level of per capita GNP to control for country-specific differences in wealth, and the continent dummies to control for continent-specific fixed effects. The continent dummies are not very significant, but per capita GNP variable does have a strong positive impact on cohort-quality change. Its positive coefficient confirms the finding suggested by the descriptive analysis in Section III: the quality of immigrants admitted to the United States has been increasing over time when the immigrants originate in Western Europe and has been declining over time when the immigrants originate in the less developed countries.

One factor causing systematic quality shifts across immigrant cohorts may have been the change in the quota system mandated by the 1965 Amendments to the Immigration and Nationality Act. Table 4 defined a variable that measures the change in the fraction of the home country's population "eligible" for emigration to the United States before and after the 1965 Amendments. Higher levels of this variable imply a reduction in the levels of "mobility costs" faced by potential emigrants. The Roy model suggests that its impact

TABLE 8

PROBIT REGRESSION ON THE EMIGRATION RATE[a]

Country of Origin Characteristics	Regression	
	1	2
Intercept	−.6060 (−1.30)	−1.1614 (−2.46)
Politically Competitive System	.1206 (1.13)	.0801 (.81)
Recent Loss of Freedom	.1096 (.95)	−.0365 (−.32)
Number of Assassinations	−.0245 (−2.65)	−.0337 (−3.65)
Income Inequality	−.0113 (−1.51)	−.0145 (−2.00)
Distance from U.S.	−.1332 (−6.11)	−.1271 (−2.68)
English Proficiency	.1661 (.94)	.0488 (.30)
ln (per capita GNP)	−.1130 (−2.14)	−.0441 (−.83)
Country in Asia or Africa	—	.3386 (2.19)
Country in North or South America	—	.2923 (1.52)
χ^2	98.45	108.82

[a] The dependent variable is the probability that an individual migrated to the United States in 1951–80, and is given by the second column of Table 2. The t-ratios are presented in parentheses.

on the rate of cohort-quality change is positive if the correlation coefficient between earnings capacities in the two countries is positive and if income is more unequally distributed in the countries of origin than in the United States. The last column of Table 7 adds the quota variable to the regression and shows that it indeed has a positive and significant impact on the rate of change in cohort quality. It is important to note that this regression is estimated on only 28 observations since the quota system prior to the 1965 Amendments was applicable only to countries that were in the Eastern Hemisphere.

D. Determinants of the Emigration Rate

The empirical analysis in this paper focuses on the determinants of the (relative) earnings of immigrants. It is worth noting, however, that the Roy model also implies that the emigration rate will be a function of the same characteristics of the income distribution, political conditions, and migration costs that determine the relative earnings of immigrants. Therefore, it is important to explore if the emigration rate from the various countries of origin is responsive to shifts in the country-specific variables that have been used throughout this section.

Table 8 presents two probit regressions on the emigration rate.[24] The dependent variable is obtained from the second column of the summary statistics presented in Table 2, and is the fraction of the country of origin's population that emigrated to the United States in the 1951–80 period. The first of the two regressions includes the political variables, the distance variable (to measure migration costs), and the inequality variable, while the second regression adds the continent dummies.[25]

As expected, the distance between the country of origin and the United States has a negative impact on the emigration rate. The emigration rate is also lower for countries that have high levels of GNP per capita. These results, of course, are consistent with the predictions of the wealth-maximization framework. More interestingly, the second moment of the income distribution (as predicted by the Roy model) plays an important role in the determination of the emigration rate. In particular, countries with more income inequality have lower emigration rates. This negative coefficient is implied by the wealth-maximization framework if there is negative selection in the immigrant pool. Negative selection requires that the correlation between earnings in the United States and in the sending countries be sufficiently positive *and* that the United States has less income inequality than the sending countries. If, in addition, mean income in the United States exceeds mean income in sending countries (adjusted for mobility costs), as income

---

[24] *The probits were estimated using generalized least squares. The estimator, therefore, is minimum chi-squared and efficient.*

[25] *The regressions in Table 8 exclude the age at migration from the list of regressors since this variable was calculated in the subsample of immigrants and may have little relationship to the age distribution of the population in the country of origin.*

inequality in the home country increases, the migration incentive of the most able decreases while the poorest will still migrate. Hence the emigration rate *declines* due to the withdrawal of high-income persons from the pool of emigrants. The analysis of the emigration rate, therefore, leads to results that are generally consistent with the types of selection biases that have been documented in this paper.

V. SUMMARY

What determines the (labor market) quality of foreign-born persons in the United States? Most of the literature addresses this question simply by assuming that immigrants are a "select" group, and that the selection mechanism somehow sends the most able and the most ambitious persons in any country of origin to the United States. This paper is an attempt to analyze both the conceptual and empirical foundations for this type of assertion. Among the major findings of the study are:

1) If potential emigrants are income maximizers, foreign-born persons in the United States need not be drawn from the most able and most ambitious in the country of origin. Two conditions must be satisfied in order for positive selection to take place: a) there is a strong positive correlation between the earnings a worker may expect in the home country and the earnings the same worker may expect in the United States; and b) the United States has a more unequal income distribution than the home country. If the income distribution in the sending country is more unequal than that of the United States (and the correlation in earnings is positive and strong), emigrants will be chosen from the *lower* tail of the income distribution in the country of origin.

2) The empirical analysis of the earnings of immigrants from 41 different countries using the 1970 and 1980 censuses shows that there are strong country-specific fixed effects in the (labor market) quality of foreign-born persons. In particular, persons from Western European countries do quite well in the United States, and their cohorts have exhibited a general *increase* in earnings (relative to their measured skills) over the postwar period. On the other hand, persons from less developed countries do not perform well in the U.S. labor market and their cohorts have exhibited a general *decrease* in earnings (relative to their measured skills) over the postwar period.

3) The empirical analysis of the variance in various dimensions of immigrant incomes shows that a few variables describing political and economic conditions in the various countries of origin explain over two-thirds of the intercountry variance in the mean U.S. incomes of immigrants with the same measured skills. Immigrants with high incomes in the United States relative to their measured skills come from countries that have high levels of GNP, low levels of income inequality, and politically competitive systems.

REFERENCES

Borjas, George J., "Assimilation, Changes in Cohort Quality, and the Earnings of Immigrants," *Journal of Labor Economics,* October 1985, *3,* 463–89.

———, "Immigrant and Emigrant Earnings: A Longitudinal Analysis," *Economic Inquiry,* January 1989, *27,* 21–37.

Carliner, Geoffrey, "Wages, Earnings, and Hours of First, Second and Third Generation American Males," *Economic Inquiry,* January 1980, *18,* 87–102.

Chiswick, Barry R., "The Effect of Americanization on the Earnings of Foreign-Born Men," *Journal of Political Economy,* October 1978, *86,* 897–921.

DeFreitas, Gregory, " The Earnings of Immigrants in the American Labor Market," unpublished doctoral dissertation, Columbia University, 1980.

Heckman, James J., "Sample Selection Bias as a Specification Error," *Econometrica,* January 1979, *47,* 153–61.

——— and Robb, Richard, "Using Longitudinal Data to Estimate Age, Period, and Cohort Effects in Earnings Equations," in H. Winsborough and O. Duncan, eds., *Analyzing Longitudinal Data for Age, Period, and Cohort Effects,* New York: Academic Press, 1983.

——— and Sedlacek, Guilherme, "Heterogeneity, Aggregation, and Market Wage Functions: An Empirical Model of Self-Selection in the Labor Market," *Journal of Political Economy,* December 1985, *93,* 1077–125.

Jasso, Guillermina and Rosenzweig, Mark R., "How Well Do U.S. Immigrants Do? Vintage Effects, Emigration Selectivity, and Occupational Mobility," *Research in Population Economics,* 1988, *6,* 229–53.

——— and ———, "Family Reunification and the Immigration Multiplier: U.S. Immigration Law, Origin-Country Conditions, and the Reproduction of Immigrants," *Demography,* August 1986, *23,* 291–311.

McManus, Walter, Gould, William, and Welch, Finis, "Earnings of Hispanic Men: The Role of English Language Proficiency," *Journal of Labor Economics,* April 1983, *1,* 101–30.

Roy, A. D., "Some Thoughts on the Distribution of Earnings," *Oxford Economic Papers,* June 1951, *3,* 135–46.

Sjaastad, Larry A., "The Costs and Returns of Human Migration," *Journal of Political Economy,* October 1962, Suppl., *70,* 80–93.

Willis, Robert J. and Rosen, Sherwin, "Education and Self-Selection," *Journal of Political Economy,* October 1979, Suppl., *87,* S7–S36.

United Nations, *Compendium of Social Statistics,* New York: UN, 1977.

U.S. Arms Control and Disarmament Agency, *World Military Expenditures and Arms Transfers, 1972–1982,* Washington: USGPO, 1984.

———, *World Military Expenditures and Arms Trade, 1963–1973,* Washington: USGPO, 1975.

U.S. Bureau of the Census, *Statistical Abstract of the United States,* Washington: USGPO, various issues.

U.S. Immigration and Naturalization Service, *Annual Report of the Immigration and Naturalization Service,* Washington: USGPO, 1965.

World Bank, *World Development Report,* New York: Oxford University Press, various issues.

ABOUT THE AUTHOR

George J. Borjas

George Borjas is currently Pforzheimer Professor of Public Policy at the Kennedy School of Government at Harvard University. An originator and key contributor to the modern economic analysis of the economics of immigration, Borjas is himself an immigrant to the United States from Cuba.

Borjas began his academic career as a student at St. Peter's College in Jersey City, New Jersey, in 1971. He crossed the Hudson River to Columbia University for a Ph.D. in 1975 and began his teaching career at Queens College of the City University of New York in the same year. Following a postdoctoral year at the University of Chicago, Borjas moved to the University of California at Santa Barbara in 1978, where he spent 12 very productive years and, in fact, wrote the paper that appears in this volume. After five years teaching at the University of California at San Diego, Borjas moved to his present position at Harvard University in 1995.

George Borjas's scholarly career provides a remarkable example of the orderly progression that many economists wish was more common in the academic profession. Full of good humor, Borjas does not shy away from confrontation when the public policy issues related to his research are debated. To contribute to public discussion on the immigration debate, for example, Borjas has written widely for popular media like the *Wall Street Journal, The New York Times,* and, especially, the *National Review.*

The Impact of the Mariel Boatlift on the Miami Labor Market

DAVID CARD

Using data from the Current Population Survey, this paper describes the effect of the Mariel Boatlift of 1980 on the Miami labor market. The Mariel immigrants increased the Miami labor force by 7%, and the percentage increase in labor supply to less-skilled occupations and industries was even greater because most of the immigrants were relatively unskilled. Nevertheless, the Mariel influx appears to have had virtually no effect on the wages or unemployment rates of less-skilled workers, even among Cubans who had immigrated earlier. The author suggests that the ability of Miami's labor market to rapidly absorb the Mariel immigrants was largely owing to its adjustment to other large waves of immigrants in the two decades before the Mariel Boatlift.

One of the chief concerns of immigration policy-makers is the extent to which immigrants depress the labor market opportunities of less-skilled natives. Despite the presumption that an influx of immigrants will substantially reduce native wages, existing empirical studies suggest that the effect is small. (See the survey by Greenwood and McDowell [1986] and studies by Grossman [1982], Borjas [1987], and Lalonde and Topel [1987].) There are two leading explanations for this finding. First, immigrants have, on average, only slightly lower skills than the native population. Thus, econometric studies based on the distribution of the existing stock of immigrants probably understate the effect of unskilled immigration on less-skilled natives. Second, the locational choices of immigrants and natives presumably depend on expected labor market opportunities. Immigrants tend to move to cities where the growth in demand for labor can accommodate their supply. Even if new immigrants cluster in only a few cities (as they do in the United States), inter-city migration of natives will tend to offset the adverse effects of immigration.

The author is Professor of Economics, Princeton University. He thanks George Borjas, Alan Krueger, Bruce Meyer, and seminar participants at Princeton University for their comments.

A data appendix with copies of the computer programs used to generate the tables in this paper is available from the author at the Industrial Relations Section, Firestone Library, Princeton University, Princeton, NJ 08544.

These considerations illustrate the difficulty of using the correlation across cities between wages and immigrant densities to measure the effect of immigration on the labor market opportunities of natives. They also underscore the value of a natural experiment that corresponds more closely to an exogenous increase in the supply of immigrants to a particular labor market.

The experiences of the Miami labor market in the aftermath of the Mariel Boatlift form one such experiment. From May to September 1980, some 125,000 Cuban immigrants arrived in Miami on a flotilla of privately chartered boats. Their arrival was the consequence of an unlikely sequence of events culminating in Castro's declaration on April 20, 1980, that Cubans wishing to emigrate to the United States were free to leave from the port of Mariel.[1] Fifty percent of the Mariel immigrants settled permanently in Miami. The result was a 7% increase in the labor force of Miami and a 20% increase in the number of Cuban workers in Miami.

This paper summarizes the effects of the Boatlift on the Miami labor market, focusing on wages and unemployment rates of less-skilled workers. The analysis is based on individual micro-data for 1979–85 from the merged outgoing rotation group samples of the Current Population Survey (CPS).

Three features of the Mariel incident and the Census data greatly facilitate the analysis. First, the CPS sample of the Miami metropolitan area is relatively large: roughly 1,200 individuals per month. Second, a comprehensive picture of the Miami labor market in the months just before the Mariel Boatlift is available from the 1980 Census, which was conducted on April 1, 1980. Finally, unlike most other ethnic groups, Cubans are separately identified in the CPS questionnaire. Thus, it is possible to estimate wage rates, unemployment rates, and other economic indicators for both Cubans and non-Cubans in the Miami labor market, and to measure the effects of the Mariel immigration on the two groups separately.

OVERVIEW OF THE MIAMI LABOR MARKET BEFORE THE BOATLIFT

For at least a decade prior to the Mariel Boatlift, Miami was the most immigrant-intensive city in the country. Tabulations from the 1980 Census indicate that 35.5% of residents in the Miami Standard Metropolitan Statistical Area (SMSA) were foreign-born,[2] compared to 22.3% in Los Angeles, the city with the next-highest immigrant fraction, and 6.1% nationwide. At the time of the Census, 56% of immigrants in Miami were of Cuban origin. The

---

[1] See Masud-Piloto (1988, chaps. 6–7) for an overview of the political developments that led to the Mariel Boatlift.

[2] See U.S. Department of Commerce (1983). The Miami SMSA consists of Dade County, and includes Miami City as well as a number of smaller towns and cities. Throughout this paper, I use "Miami" to refer to this broader geographic region.

remaining foreign-born residents, who accounted for 16% of the Miami population, included other Hispanic groups and a broad selection of Caribbean and European nationals.

Miami also has a significant black population. The fraction of black residents was 15.0% in 1970 and had increased to 17.3% by the time of the 1980 Census. The large concentrations of both immigrants and blacks makes Miami ideal for studying the effect of increased immigration on the labor market opportunities of black natives.

Table 1 describes the four major groups in the Miami labor force in 1979: white non-Hispanics; black non-Hispanics; Cubans (foreign-born and native-born); and other Hispanics. For simplicity, I have restricted attention to individuals age 16–61, a group that represents roughly 60% of the Miami population. The fractions of Cubans and blacks in the 16–61 age group are 27.2% and 26.3%, respectively, and the fractions of white non-Hispanics and non-Cuban Hispanics are 34.4% and 11.1%. Overall, 73% of 16–61-year-olds participated in the labor force, with somewhat higher rates among whites and Cubans and lower rates among blacks and other Hispanics. Education levels in Miami are somewhat below the national average: the mean of completed education for 16–61-year-olds in 1979 was 11.8 years in Miami, compared with 12.2 years nationwide.

The occupation distributions in rows 7–17 of Table 1 give a crude indication of the degree of labor market competition among the four groups. Cubans and other Hispanics have very similar occupation distributions, with a higher representation in craft and operative occupations than either whites or blacks. Blacks are more highly concentrated in laborer and service-related occupations, and are significantly under-represented in managerial occupations.

A useful summary measure of the overlap in the occupation distributions of the different groups is the average percent increase in labor supply in occupations held by one group that would result from a one percentage point increase in the overall fraction of workers in a second group.[3] This index has the simple form $\Sigma_j s_{1j} s_{2j}/s_j$, where s_{1j} is the fraction of workers of group 1 in occupation j, s_{2j} is the fraction of workers of group 2 in occupation j, and s_j is the fraction of all workers in occupation j. Based on the distributions in Table 1, an inflow of immigrants resulting in a one percentage point increase in the fraction of Cubans in Miami would lead to a weighted average increase of .95% in the supply of labor to occupations held by whites. Under the same conditions the increase would be .99% for blacks, 1.02% for non-Cuban Hispanics, and 1.06% for Cubans themselves. These calculations suggest that the overlap between the occupational distributions of the four groups is relatively high.

THE MARIEL IMMIGRATION

Due to the unauthorized nature of the Boatlift, no exact count of the number of Mariel immigrants is available, and there is little precise information on the characteristics or

---

[3] This index is derived in Altonji and Card (1989:15–16).

TABLE 1

CHARACTERISTICS OF 16–61-YEAR-OLDS IN MIAMI, 1979.

Characteristic	Whites	Blacks	Cubans	Hispanics	All
Characteristics of Population Age 16–61					
1. Estimated Number (1000's)	319.3	244.1	252.4	102.9	928.4
2. Mean Education	12.8	11.4	11.0	11.6	11.8
3. Percent in Labor Force	75.6	68.3	77.2	68.8	73.1
Characteristics of Those in Labor Force					
4. Estimated Number (1000's)	241.3	166.6	194.7	70.8	678.2
5. Mean Education	13.1	11.8	11.3	11.9	12.1
6. Percent Age 16–24	21.1	24.1	22.0	26.0	22.8
Occupation Distribution (Percent of Employed)					
7. Professional and Technical	19.1	10.9	9.5	10.1	13.2
8. Managers	15.7	2.8	8.6	8.1	9.4
9. Sales	6.2	4.4	7.8	7.6	6.5
10. Clerical	21.9	21.0	19.1	20.9	20.9
11. Craftsmen	13.3	9.4	15.1	12.7	12.8
12. Operatives	4.4	8.4	19.4	16.7	11.1
13. Transportation Operatives	2.6	8.1	5.4	5.9	5.2
14. Laborers	5.1	10.5	4.7	4.0	6.3
15. Farm Workers	1.1	0.1	0.4	0.8	0.6
16. Less-Skilled Service Workers	5.0	13.3	6.1	10.2	8.0
17. More-Skilled Service Workers	5.7	10.9	4.0	3.0	6.2

Notes: White and black groups exclude Hispanics. Hispanic group includes all Hispanics other than Cubans. Less-skilled service workers include cleaning and food service workers. More-skilled service workers include health service, personal service, and protective service workers.
Source: Based on samples of employed workers in the outgoing rotation groups of the Current Population Survey in 1979.

final destinations of the immigrants. This section summarizes some of the available information, including data from the March 1985 Mobility Supplement to the Current Population Survey, which allows Mariel immigrants to be distinguished from other Cubans.

Most sources estimate the number of Mariel immigrants at between 120,000 and 125,000. A recent Census Bureau report (U.S. Department of Commerce 1988:9) states that 126,000 refugees entered the United States as "Cuban Entrants" (the special immigration status awarded to the Mariel refugees) between April 1980 and June 1981. Based on the settlement pattern of earlier Cubans, it is widely assumed that about one-half of these refugees settled permanently in Miami. The Census Bureau "Experimental County Population Estimates" file shows an increase of 80,500 in the Dade County population between April 1 and July 1 of 1980; 59,800 of these new entrants were age 16–61. My own tabulations from the CPS indicate that the Cuban share of the 16–61 age group increased from 27% in 1979 to 33% in 1981.[4] A similar increase is registered in CPS-based estimates of the Cuban share of the 16–61-year-old labor force, which changed from 37.2% in 1979 to 44.8% in 1981. Assuming that the Cuban share of the labor force would have remained constant between 1979 and 1981 in the absence of the Boatlift, these figures suggest that the Mariel immigration added approximately 45,000 to the Miami labor force—an increase of 7%.

From the first days of the Boatlift, the characteristics of the Mariel immigrants (hereafter referred to as Mariels) have been a subject of controversy. Among those who were permitted to leave Cuba were several hundred inmates of mental hospitals and jails. Many of these individuals were arrested by immigration officials upon their arrival in the United States, and over 1,000 were sent to a special prison facility in Atlanta to await deportation back to Cuba.[5] A similar number were arrested for crimes committed in the United States, and they still await determination of their ultimate immigration status.[6] Contemporary reports indicate that the Mariels included a relatively high fraction of less-skilled workers and a high fraction of individuals with low English ability (*Business Week* 1980).

Although the regular Current Population Survey questionnaire does not distinguish Mariels from other foreign and native-born Cubans, the March 1985 Mobility Supplement survey asked each respondent where he or she lived in March 1980 (one month before the start of the Boatlift). Table 2 presents a descriptive summary of the Cuban population interviewed in this survey, classified by whether the respondent claimed to be living abroad or in the United States five years earlier. The sample sizes, particularly of post-1980 entrants, are small.[7] Nevertheless, these data confirm the general impression that Mariels, on average, have less education, are somewhat younger, and are more likely to be male than other Cubans. The figures in Table 2 also suggest that the Mariels have lower labor force attachment and lower occupational attainment than other Cubans. Mariels are more heavily concentrated in laborer and service occupations, and are less likely to hold sales, clerical, and craft jobs.

The unadjusted wage gap between Mariels and other Cubans is 34%. Part of this differential is clearly attributable to the lower education levels and younger ages of the

---

[4] These tabulations are presented in greater detail in an earlier version of this paper (Card 1989, Table 2).

[5] See Masud-Piloto (1988:100–103). Under a 1984 agreement a total of 2,700 Mariel immigrants were to be returned to Cuba.

[6] Mariel immigrants were blamed for, and indeed seem to have committed, many crimes in the first few months after the Boatlift. Wilbanks (1984) reported that 38 of the 574 homicides in Miami in 1980 were committed by Mariel immigrants. Disaffected Mariels were involved in 6 airline highjacking attempts in August 1980. See Masud-Piloto (1988:95–96).

[7] The weighted count of all Cubans in the March 1985 CPS who entered the United States after 1980 is 85,800, which is only 69% of the estimated 125,000 Mariel refugees.

TABLE 2.

CHARACTERISTICS OF MARIEL IMMIGRANTS AND OTHER CUBANS: TABULATIONS FROM MARCH 1985 CPS.

Characteristic	Mariel Immigrants	All Other Cubans
Educational Attainment (Percent of Population in Each Category):		
No High School	56.5	25.4
Some High School	9.1	13.3
Completed High School	9.5	33.4
Some College	6.8	12.0
Completed College	18.1	15.8
Percent Male	55.6	50.7
Percent Under 30 in 1980	38.7	29.6
Mean Age in 1980 (Years)	34.9	38.0
Percent in Miami in 1985	53.9	52.4
Percent Worked in 1984	60.6	73.4
Mean Log Hourly Earnings	1.37	1.71
Occupation Distribution (Percent Employed in Each Category):		
Professional/Managers	19.3	21.0
Technical	0.0	1.5
Sales	4.5	11.2
Clerical	2.5	13.5
Craftsmen	9.5	19.9
Operatives	19.1	13.8
Transportation Ops.	3.8	4.3
Laborers	10.8	3.3
Farm Workers	0.0	1.8
Less-Skilled Service	26.0	7.4
More-Skilled Service	4.6	2.3
Sample Size	50	528
Weighted Count	42,300	476,900

Note: The sample consists of all Cubans in the March 1985 Current Population Survey age 21–66 (i.e., age 16–61 in 1980). Mariel immigrants are identified as those Cubans who stated that they lived outside the United States 5 years previously.

Mariels. A simple linear regression for the logarithm of average hourly earnings fitted to the sample of Cubans with earnings in 1984 suggests that the Mariels earned 18% lower wages than other Cubans, controlling for education, potential experience, and gender (the standard error of this estimate is .08). This gap presumably reflects the combination of lower language ability and a shorter assimilation time in the United States among the Mariels, as well as any differences in ability or motivation between the earlier and later Cuban immigrants.

THE EFFECT OF THE MARIEL IMMIGRATION ON THE MIAMI LABOR MARKET

Observers in Miami at the time of the Boatlift noted the strain caused by the Mariel immigration. The homicide rate increased nearly 50% between 1979 and 1980 (see Wilbanks 1984:142). On the weekend of May 17, 1980, a three-day riot occurred in several black neighborhoods, killing 13. A government-sponsored committee that was set up to investigate the riot identified other long-standing grievances in the black community as its cause, but cited the labor market competition of Cuban refugees as an important background factor (Governor of Florida 1980: 14–15).

Another widely cited indicator of the labor market pressure created by the Mariel influx is the Miami unemployment rate, which rose from 5.0% in April 1980 to 7.1% in July. Over the same period state and national unemployment rates followed a similar pattern, suggesting that the changes in Miami were not solely a response to the Mariel influx. Nevertheless, widespread joblessness of refugees throughout the summer of 1980 contributed to a perception that labor market opportunities for less-skilled natives were threatened by the Mariel immigrants.[8]

Tables 3 and 4 present simple averages of wage rates and unemployment rates for whites, blacks, Cubans, and other Hispanics in the Miami labor market between 1979 and 1985. For comparative purposes, I have assembled similar data for whites, blacks, and Hispanics in four other cities: Atlanta, Los Angeles, Houston, and Tampa-St. Petersburg. These four cities were selected both because they had relatively large populations of blacks and Hispanics and because they exhibited a pattern of economic growth similar to that in Miami over the late 1970s and early 1980s. A comparison of employment growth rates (based on establishment-level data) suggests that economic conditions were very similar in Miami and the average of the four comparison cities between 1976 and 1984.

The wage data in Table 3 reveal several features of the Miami labor market. Perhaps most obvious is that earnings are lower in Miami than in the comparison cities. The differentials in 1979 ranged from 8% for whites to 15% for blacks. More surprising is that real earnings levels of whites in both Miami and the comparison cities were fairly constant between 1979 and 1985. This pattern contrasts with the general decline in real wages in the U.S. economy over this period (see Bound and Johnson 1989:5–6) and underscores the relatively close correspondence between economic conditions in Miami and the comparison cities.

---

[8] *For example, a Florida State Employment Service official and a Department of Labor Wage and Hours Division official noted downward pressure on wages and working conditions in the unskilled segment of the Miami labor market (Business Week 1980).*

TABLE 3

LOGARITHMS OF REAL HOURLY EARNINGS OF WORKERS AGE 16–61 IN MIAMI AND FOUR COMPARISON CITIES, 1979–85.

Group	1979	1980	1981	1982	1983	1984	1985
Miami:							
Whites	1.85	1.83	1.85	1.82	1.82	1.82	1.82
	(.03)	(.03)	(.03)	(.03)	(.03)	(.03)	(.05)
Blacks	1.59	1.55	1.61	1.48	1.48	1.57	1.60
	(.03)	(.02)	(.03)	(.03)	(.03)	(.03)	(.04)
Cubans	1.58	1.54	1.51	1.49	1.49	1.53	1.49
	(.02)	(.02)	(.02)	(.02)	(.02)	(.03)	(.04)
Hispanics	1.52	1.54	1.54	1.53	1.48	1.59	1.54
	(.04)	(.04)	(.05)	(.05)	(.04)	(.04)	(.06)
Comparison Cities:							
Whites	1.93	1.90	1.91	1.91	1.90	1.91	1.92
	(.01)	(.01)	(.01)	(.01)	(.01)	(.01)	(.01)
Blacks	1.74	1.70	1.72	1.71	1.69	1.67	1.65
	(.01)	(.02)	(.02)	(.01)	(.02)	(.02)	(.03)
Hispanics	1.65	1.63	1.61	1.61	1.58	1.60	1.58
	(.01)	(.01)	(.01)	(.01)	(.01)	(.01)	(.02)

Note: Entries represent means of log hourly earnings (deflated by the Consumer Price Index—1980 = 100) for workers age 16–61 in Miami and four comparison cities: Atlanta, Houston, Los Angeles, and Tampa-St. Petersburg. See note to Table 1 for definitions of groups.
Source: Based on samples of employed workers in the outgoing rotation groups of the Current Population Survey in 1979–85. Due to a change in SMSA coding procedures in 1985, the 1985 sample is based on individuals in outgoing rotation groups for January–June of 1985 only.

In contrast to the pattern for whites, the trends in earnings for nonwhites and Hispanics differ somewhat between Miami and the comparison cities. Black wages in Miami were roughly constant from 1979 to 1981, fell in 1982 and 1983, and rose to their previous level in 1984. Black earnings in the comparison cities, on the other hand, show a steady downward trend between 1979 and 1985. These data provide no evidence of a negative impact of the Mariel immigration on black wages in Miami. The data do suggest a relative downturn in black wages in Miami during 1982–83. It seems likely, however, that this downturn reflects an unusually severe cyclical effect associated with the 1982–83 recession. (I return to this issue in Table 6, below.)

Wage rates for non-Cuban Hispanics in Miami were fairly stable between 1979 and 1985, with only a slight dip in 1983. In contrast, Hispanic wage rates in the comparison cities fell about 6 percentage points over this period. Again, there is no evidence of a negative effect in Miami, either in the immediate post-Mariel period or over the longer run.

Table 3 does indicate a decline in Cuban wage rates relative to the wage rates of other groups in Miami. Relative to the wages of whites, for example, Cuban wages fell by 6–7 percentage points between 1979 and 1981. Assuming that the wages of earlier Cuban immigrants were constant, this decline is consistent with the addition of 45,000 Mariel workers to the pool of Cubans in the Miami labor force, and with the 34% wage differential between Mariels and other Cubans noted in Table 3. A more thorough analysis of Cuban wages is presented in Table 7, below.

The unemployment rates in Table 4 lead to the same general conclusions as the wage data in Table 3. There is no evidence that the Mariel influx adversely affected the unemployment rate of either whites or blacks. The unemployment rates suggest a severe cyclical downturn in the black labor market in Miami in 1982–83. Black unemployment rates in Miami, which had been 2–4 points lower than those in the comparison cities from 1979 to 1981, equalled or exceeded those in the comparison cities from 1982 to 1984. The 1985 data indicate a return to the pre-1982 pattern, although the sampling errors are large enough to prevent precise inferences.

Unlike the situation for whites and blacks, there was a sizable increase in Cuban unemployment rates in Miami following the Mariel immigration. Cuban unemployment rates were roughly 3 percentage points higher during 1980–81 than would have been expected on the basis of earlier (and later) patterns. Assuming that the unemployment rates of earlier Cuban immigrants were unaffected by the Mariel influx, this effect is consistent with unemployment rates of around 20% among the Mariels themselves. Although far from conclusive, this simple calculation suggests that the increase in Cuban unemployment rates could easily be explained as a result of the addition of the Mariel refugees to the Cuban population, with little or no effect on earlier immigrants.

The simple averages of wages and unemployment rates in Tables 3 and 4, which combine workers of all ages and education levels, do not directly address the question of whether the Mariel immigration reduced the earnings of less-skilled natives in Miami. A more direct answer is provided by the data in Table 5. In order to identify "less-skilled" workers, I fit a linear regression equation for the logarithm of hourly earnings to workers in the comparison cities. The explanatory variables in this regression included education, potential experience, squared potential experience, indicator variables for each gender and race group, and interactions of the gender-race indicators with potential experience and squared potential experience. I then used the estimated coefficients from this equation to form a predicted wage for each non-Cuban worker in Miami, and sorted the sample from each year into quartiles on the basis of predicted wage rates.

This procedure provides a simple way to identify more- and less-skilled workers in the Miami labor market. Means of actual log wages for each quartile and year are presented in the first four columns of Table 5. The difference in mean wages between the first and fourth quartiles, which provides an index of the spread in the wage distribution, is presented in the fifth column of the table.

If the Mariel immigration reduced the wages of less-skilled natives, one would expect to observe a decline in the wage of workers in the lowest skill quartile, at least relative to workers in the upper quartile. The actual averages show no evidence of this effect. Apart from the temporary increase in relative wages of workers in the lowest quartile between 1979 and 1981, the distribution of non-Cubans' wages in the Miami labor market was remarkably stable between 1979 and 1985. Taken together with the data in Table 3, these

TABLE 4

UNEMPLOYMENT RATES OF INDIVIDUALS AGE 16–61 IN MIAMI AND FOUR COMPARISON
CITIES, 1979–85. (STANDARD ERRORS IN PARENTHESES)

Group	1979	1980	1981	1982	1983	1984	1985
Miami:							
Whites	5.1	2.5	3.9	5.2	6.7	3.6	4.9
	(1. 1)	(0.8)	(0.9)	(1. 1)	(1. 1)	(0.9)	(1.4)
Blacks	8.3	5.6	9.6	16.0	18.4	14.2	7.8
	(1.7)	(1.3)	(1.8)	(2.3)	(2.5)	(2.3)	(2.3)
Cubans	5.3	7.2	10.1	10.8	13.1	7.7	5.5
	(1.2)	(1.3)	(1.5)	(1.5)	(1.6)	(1.4)	(1.7)
Hispanics	6.5	7.7	11.8	9.1	7.5	12.1	3.7
	(2.3)	(2.2)	(3.0)	(2.5)	(2.1)	(2.4)	(1.9)
Comparison Cities:							
Whites	4.4	4.4	4.3	6.8	6.9	5.4	4.9
	(0.3)	(0.3)	(0.3)	(0.3)	(0.3)	(0.3)	(0.4)
Blacks	10.3	12.6	12.6	12.7	18.4	12.1	13.3
	(0.8)	(0.9)	(0.9)	(0.9)	(1. 1)	(0.9)	(1.3)
Hispanics	6.3	8.7	8.3	12.1	11.8	9.8	9.3
	(0.6)	(0.6)	(0.6)	(0.7)	(0.7)	(0.6)	(0.8)

Note: Entries represent means of unemployment indicator variable for individuals age 16–61 in Miami and four comparison cities: Atlanta, Houston, Los Angeles, and Tampa-St. Petersburg. Samples are based on individuals in the labor force. See notes to Table 3 for definitions of groups and data sources.

TABLE 5

MEANS OF LOG WAGES OF NON-CUBANS IN MIAMI BY QUARTILE OF PREDICTED WAGES,
1979–85. (STANDARD ERRORS IN PARENTHESES)

Year	Mean of Log Wage by Quartile of Predicted Wage				Difference of
	1st Quart.	2nd Quart.	3rd Quart.	4th Quart.	Means: 4th − 1st
1979	1.31	1.61	1.71	2.15	.84
	(.03)	(.03)	(.03)	(.04)	(.05)
1980	1.31	1.52	1.74	2.09	.77
	(.03)	(.03)	(.03)	(.04)	(.05)
1981	1.40	1.57	1.79	2.06	.66
	(.03)	(.03)	(.03)	(.04)	(.05)
1982	1.24	1.57	1.77	2.04	.80
	(.03)	(.03)	(.03)	(.04)	(.05)
1983	1.27	1.53	1.76	2.11	.84
	(.03)	(.04)	(.03)	(.05)	(.06)
1984	1.33	1.59	1.80	2.12	.79
	(.03)	(.04)	(.04)	(.04)	(.05)
1985	1.27	1.57	1.81	2.14	.87
	(.04)	(.04)	(.04)	(.05)	(.06)

Note: Predicted wage is based on a linear prediction equation for the log wage fitted to individuals in four comparison cities; see text. The sample consists of non-Cubans (male and female, white, black, and Hispanic) between the ages of 16 and 61 with valid wage data in the earnings supplement of the Current Population Survey. Wages are deflated by the Consumer Price Index (1980 = 100).

data provide little evidence of a negative effect of the Mariel influx on the earnings of natives.

A final check is provided in Table 6, which contains more detailed information on wages, employment rates, and unemployment rates for blacks in Miami between 1979 and 1985. I separately analyzed the set of all blacks and the set of blacks with less than 12 years of education in order to isolate any stronger effect on the less-skilled segment of the black population. For both groups I calculated the differential in wages between Miami and the comparison cities (both the unadjusted difference in mean log wages and a regression-adjusted differential that controls for education, gender, marital status, part-time status, private/public employment, and potential experience) and the differentials in the employment-population rate and the unemployment rate between Miami and the comparison cities.

As indicated in Table 3, the wage differential for blacks in Miami relative to those in the comparison cities decreased slightly between 1979 and 1981. The differential increased substantially in 1982, but then began a steady downward trend after 1983. By 1985, the wage gap was less than 5% for all black workers, and was actually positive for less-educated blacks. The magnitudes of the regression-adjusted wage differentials are not significantly different from the unadjusted wage differentials, and show no evidence of any effect of the Mariel immigration on black wages.

A similar conclusion emerges from the pattern of differentials in employment-population ratios and unemployment rates.[9] Among all blacks, there is some evidence of a relative decline in the employment-to-population ratio in Miami between 1979 and 1985.[10] This effect seems to have started in 1982, and is less pronounced among low-education blacks than among those with more education. As noted in Table 4, the series of unemployment rate differentials indicates a sharp downturn in labor market opportunities for blacks in 1982. Given the lag between the arrival of the Mariels and the emergence of this unemployment gap, however, the gap seems more likely to have resulted from the 1982 recession than from the influx of less-skilled immigrants.

The effects of the Mariel immigration on Cuban labor market outcomes are examined in detail in Table 7. The first column of the table reproduces the means of log wages in each year from the third row of Table 3. The second column gives predicted log wages of Cubans in Miami, using estimated coefficients from a regression equation fit to Hispanics

---

[9] I also computed regression-adjusted employment-population and unemployment gaps using simple linear probability models. The explanatory power of the statistical models is so low, however, that the adjusted differentials are almost identical to the unadjusted differentials.

[10] Although they are not reported in Table 6, I have also constructed differentials in the labor force participation rate between Miami and the comparison cities. For blacks as a whole these show a decline in relative participation rates in Miami starting in 1982, although the decline is only temporary for the low-education group. The differential in labor force participation rates is approximately equal to the differential in the employment-population rate plus the differential in the unemployment rate multiplied by the average labor force participation rate (.7 for the overall group, .55 for the low-education group).

TABLE 6

COMPARISON OF WAGES, UNEMPLOYMENT RATES, AND EMPLOYMENT RATES FOR BLACKS IN MIAMI AND COMPARISON CITIES. (STANDARD ERRORS IN PARENTHESES)

	All Blacks				Low-Education Blacks			
	Difference in Log Wages, Miami − Comparison		Difference in Emp./Unemp., Miami − Comparison		Difference in Log Wages, Miami − Comparison		Difference in Emp./Unemp., Miami − Comparison	
Year	Actual	Adjusted	Emp. − Pop. Rate	Unemp. Rate	Actual	Adjusted	Emp. − Pop. Rate	Unemp. Rate
1979	−.15 (.03)	−.12 (.03)	.00 (.03)	−2.0 (1.9)	−.13 (.05)	−.15 (.05)	.03 (.04)	−.8 (3.8)
1980	−.16 (.03)	−.12 (.03)	.05 (.03)	−7.1 (1.6)	−.07 (.05)	−.07 (.05)	.03 (.04)	−8.2 (3.5)
1981	−.11 (.03)	−.10 (.03)	.02 (.03)	−3.0 (2.0)	−.05 (.05)	−.11 (.05)	.04 (.04)	−7.7 (4.2)
1982	−.24 (.03)	−.20 (.03)	−.06 (.03)	3.3 (2.4)	−.17 (.05)	−.20 (.05)	−.04 (.04)	.6 (4.7)
1983	−.21 (.03)	−.15 (.03)	−.02 (.03)	.1 (2.7)	−.13 (.06)	−.11 (.05)	.04 (.04)	−3.3 (4.7)
1984	−.10 (.03)	−.05 (.03)	−.04 (.03)	2.1 (2.4)	−.04 (.06)	−.03 (.05)	.05 (.04)	.1 (4.7)
1985	−.05 (.04)	−.01 (.04)	−.06 (.04)	−5.5 (2.6)	.18 (.07)	.09 (.07)	.00 (.06)	−4.7 (5.6)

Notes: Low-education blacks are those with less than 12 years of completed education. Adjusted differences in log wages between blacks in Miami and comparison cities are obtained from a linear regression model that includes education, potential experience, and other control variables; see text. Wages are deflated by the Consumer Price Index (1980 = 100). "Emp. − Pop. Rate" refers to the employment: population ratio. "Unemp. Rate" refers to the unemployment rate among those in the labor force.

in the four comparison cities. The gap between actual and predicted wages is presented in the third column of the table. These series show that the 9 percentage point decline in Cuban real wage rates in Miami between 1979 and 1985 was a result of two complementary factors: a 6% relative decline in the "quality" of the Cuban labor force in Miami, as measured by the decline in their predicted wages, and a 3 percentage point increase in the quality-adjusted wage gap between Cuban workers in Miami and Hispanic workers in the comparison cities. Two-thirds of the wage decline is therefore attributed to the changing productivity characteristics of the Cuban labor force, and one-third to a decrease in the return to skills for Cubans in the Miami labor market.

The next four columns of Table 7 give the means of log wages for Cuban workers in each quartile of the distribution of predicted wages (using the same prediction equation as was used to form the means in column 2). These means suggest that real wage rates of Cubans in the lowest quartile of the wage distribution declined by 11–12 percentage points between 1979 and 1985. The decline is smaller for workers in the higher quartiles, but there is some variation between 1984 and 1985, and in light of the sampling errors it is difficult to draw precise inferences. The difference between the means of the first and

TABLE 7

MEANS OF LOG WAGES OF CUBANS IN MIAMI: ACTUAL AND PREDICTED, AND BY QUARTILE OF PREDICTED WAGES.
(STANDARD ERRORS IN PARENTHESES)

Year	Mean of Log Wages Log in Miami			Mean of Log Wages by Quartile of Predicted Wages				Mean Log Wage of Cubans Outside Miami	Difference in Cuban Wages Miami – Rest-of-U.S.	
	Actual	Predicted	Actual – Predicted	1st	2nd	3rd	4th		Actual	Adjusted
1979	1.58 (.02)	1.73 (.02)	–.15 (.03)	1.31 (.02)	1.44 (.03)	1.64 (.04)	1.90 (.05)	1.71 (.04)	–.13 (.04)	–.10 (.04)
1980	1.54 (.02)	1.68 (.02)	–.14 (.03)	1.25 (.02)	1.49 (.05)	1.59 (.04)	1.81 (.05)	1.66 (.03)	–.12 (.04)	–.06 (.03)
1981	1.51 (.02)	1.68 (.02)	–.17 (.03)	1.23 (.03)	1.43 (.03)	1.55 (.04)	1.80 (.05)	1.63 (.03)	–.13 (.04)	–.09 (.03)
1982	1.49 (.02)	1.68 (.02)	–.19 (.03)	1.27 (.03)	1.43 (.04)	1.50 (.04)	1.77 (.06)	1.71 (.03)	–.22 (.04)	–.12 (.03)
1983	1.48 (.03)	1.65 (.02)	–.17 (.03)	1.16 (.02)	1.41 (.04)	1.56 (.04)	1.80 (.06)	1.62 (.03)	–.14 (.04)	–.08 (.03)
1984	1.53 (.03)	1.69 (.02)	–.17 (.03)	1.20 (.03)	1.40 (.04)	1.65 (.05)	1.88 (.06)	1.63 (.03)	–.10 (.04)	–.08 (.03)
1985	1.49 (.04)	1.67 (.03)	–.18 (.05)	1.19 (.06)	1.43 (.06)	1.53 (.08)	1.80 (.09)	1.77 (.06)	–.27 (.07)	–.19 (.05)

Notes: Predicted wage is based on a linear prediction equation for the log wage fitted to individuals in four comparison cities; see text. Predicted wages for Cubans in Miami are based on coefficients for Hispanics in comparison cities. The adjusted wage gaps between Cubans in Miami and Cubans in the rest of the U.S. are obtained from a linear regression model that includes education, potential experience, and other control variables; see text. Wages are deflated by the Consumer Price Index (1980 = 100).

fourth quartiles is 9 percentage points higher in 1984 than 1979, but the gap narrows to only 2 points in 1985. These figures are consistent with a larger decline in earnings at the low end of the Cuban wage distribution after the Mariel immigration, as might be expected from the addition of a large group of relatively unskilled workers to the pool of Cubans. The extent of the decline, however, is not precisely measured.

An alternative method to assess the effect of the Mariel immigration on the earnings of Cubans in the Miami labor market is to compare Cuban wages in Miami to the wages of Cubans elsewhere in the United States. Since the fraction of Mariels in the Cuban labor force is roughly the same inside and outside Miami, this comparison controls for any unobservable differences in skill between the Mariels and other Cubans (due to language ability, for example).[11] The ninth and tenth columns of Table 7 contain estimates of the wage differential for Cubans in Miami relative to those elsewhere in the country, both unadjusted and adjusted for education, gender, part-time status, private sector/public sector employment, marital status (interacted with gender), and potential experience.

The earnings differentials computed in this way are roughly constant between 1979 and 1984. The 1982 unadjusted wage differential is 10 percentage points larger than earlier or later ones, but the regression-adjusted differential is not significantly different from any of the other differentials. The 1985 data also indicate a slightly higher Cuban wage rate outside Miami. In any case, a comparison of Cuban wages inside and outside the Miami labor market shows no evidence of a widening gap in the years immediately following the Mariel immigration. On the assumption that the Mariel influx had no effect on the wage rates of other Cubans *outside* Miami, this finding suggests that the observed downturn in Cuban wages in Miami can be attributed solely to the "dilution" of the Cuban labor force with less-skilled Mariel workers.

INTERPRETATION OF THE FINDINGS

The data in Tables 3–7 point to two conclusions. First, the Mariel immigration had essentially no effect on the wages or employment outcomes of non-Cuban workers in the Miami labor market. Second, and perhaps even more surprising, the Mariel immigration had no strong effect on the wages of other Cubans. The observed decline in average Cuban wage rates in Miami after 1980 is no larger than would be expected by simply adding the Mariel immigrants to the pool of Cuban workers, assuming that the Mariels earned about one-third less than other comparable Cubans (as the March 1985 data suggest). This conclusion is confirmed by a comparison of Cuban wage rates inside and outside Miami, which shows no relative change over the period.

These conclusions lead naturally to the question of how the Miami labor market was able to absorb a 7% increase in the labor force with no adverse effects. One possible answer is that the Mariels displaced other immigrants and natives who would have

---

[11] This proposition is strictly true only if the unobservable differences have a constant proportional effect on all Mariels, independent of the level of observed skills or location choice.

moved to Miami in the early 1980s had the Boatlift not occurred. Some evidence on this hypothesis is provided by comparing population growth rates in Miami to those in other Florida cities. From 1970 to 1980, the Miami population grew at an annual rate of 2.5% per year while the population of the rest of Florida grew at a rate of 3.9%. After April 1, 1980, the growth rate in Miami slowed to 1.4% per year while that in the rest of the state decreased to 3.4%.[12] The greater slowdown in Miami suggests that the Boatlift may have actually held back long-run population growth in Miami. In fact, the population of Dade County in 1986 was about equal to the pre-Boatlift projection of the University of Florida Bureau of Economic and Business Research under their "low population growth" scenario (see *Florida Statistical Abstract* 1981, Table 1.24).

Nevertheless, data from the March 1985 Current Population Survey suggest that Miami continued to attract new foreign-born immigrants after 1980. A total of 2.7% of all non-Cuban immigrants who arrived in the United States after March 1980 were living in Miami in March 1985. At the time of the 1980 Census, however, only 1.8% of all non-Cuban immigrants in the United States lived in Miami. Thus, Miami attracted "more than its share" of new non-Cuban immigrants to the country in the five-year period after the Mariel immigration. The implication is that the slowdown in the rate of growth of the Miami SMSA after June 1980 occurred because of a change in the net migration rate of natives and older cohorts of immigrants, rather than because of a change in the inflow rate of new immigrants. This finding is consistent with the pattern of domestic migration between 1970 and 1980 identified by Filer (1988), who found a strong negative correlation across SMSAs between the net immigration rate of natives and the immigration rate of immigrants.

A second explanation for the rapid absorption of the Mariel immigrants is the growth of industries that utilize relatively unskilled labor. Altonji and Card's (1989) tabulations from the 1970 and 1980 Censuses indicate that a small set of industries employ a large fraction of immigrants, and that these industries expanded more rapidly between 1970 and 1980 in cities with large immigrant populations than in other cities. The immigrant-intensive industries identified in their analysis are apparel and textiles, agriculture, furniture, private household services, hotels and motels, eating and drinking establishments, and business services. These are relatively low-wage industries that employ large numbers of semi-skilled operatives and laborers.

A comparison of the industry distributions of employment in Miami and the entire country before and after the Mariel Boatlift shows little change in the relative importance of immigrant-intensive industries in Miami.[13] Nevertheless, these tabulations suggest that the industry distribution in Miami in the late 1970s was well suited to handle an influx of unskilled immigrants. Textile and apparel industries were particularly prominent in

---

[12] *These figures are obtained from U.S. Department of Commerce (1971, Table 32, and 1988, Table 1).*

[13] *These tabulations are reported in Card (1989, Table 9). Pre-Boatlift data are based on the 1979 and 1980 March Current Population Surveys. Post-Boatlift data are based on the March 1984 and March 1985 CPS.*

Miami, with 5.5% of total employment in these industries as compared to only 2.3% nationwide. Seventy-five percent of workers in textiles and apparel and 45% of workers in other manufacturing industries were Cubans. Although employment in immigrant-intensive industries did not expand after the Boatlift, and the Cuban share of employment in these industries was relatively stable, the Mariels may have simply replaced earlier cohorts of Cuban immigrants as the latter moved to more desirable jobs.

CONCLUSIONS

The experiences of the Miami labor market in the aftermath of the Mariel Boatlift provide a natural experiment with which to evaluate the effect of unskilled immigration on the labor market opportunities of native workers. The Mariel immigrants increased the labor force of the Miami metropolitan area by 7%. Because most of these immigrants were relatively unskilled, the proportional increase in labor supply to less-skilled occupations and industries was much greater.

Yet, this study shows that the influx of Mariel immigrants had virtually no effect on the wage rates of less-skilled non-Cuban workers. Similarly, there is no evidence of an increase in unemployment among less-skilled blacks or other non-Cuban workers. Rather, the data analysis suggests a remarkably rapid absorption of the Mariel immigrants into the Miami labor force, with negligible effects on other groups. Even among the Cuban population there is no indication that wages or unemployment rates of earlier immigrants were substantially affected by the arrival of the Mariels.

Despite the clear-cut nature of these findings, some caution is required in their interpretation, since the Miami labor market is far from typical of other local labor markets in the United States. Although the arrival of some 60,000 refugees in only a six-month period occasioned problems for the Mariel immigrants, in many respects Miami was better prepared to receive them than any other city. In the two decades before the Mariel Boatlift Miami had absorbed a continuing flow of Cubans, and in the years since the Boatlift it has continued to receive large numbers of Nicaraguans and other Central Americans. Thus, the Mariel immigration can be seen as part of a long-run pattern that distinguishes Miami from most other American cities.

Two factors that may have been especially important in facilitating the absorption of the Mariel immigrants are related to the distinctive character of the Miami labor market. First, Miami's industry structure was well suited to make use of an influx of unskilled labor. This structure, and particularly the high concentration of textile and apparel industries, evolved over the previous two decades in response to earlier waves of immigrants, and may have allowed the Mariel immigrants to take up unskilled jobs as earlier Cuban immigrants moved to better ones. Second, because of the high concentration of Hispanics in Miami, the lack of English-speaking ability among the Mariels may have had smaller effects than could be expected for other immigrants in other cities.

A final factor in the Mariel immigration is the response of domestic migration. A comparison of Miami growth rates to those in the rest of Florida suggests that the net migration rate of natives and earlier immigrants into the Miami area slowed considerably after the Boatlift. To some extent the Mariels may have displaced other migrants from within the United States who could have been expected to move to Miami.

REFERENCES

Altonji, Joseph, and David Card. 1989. "The Effects of Immigration on the Labor Market Outcomes of Natives." Princeton University Industrial Relations Section Working Paper Number 256, August.

Borjas, George. 1987. "Immigrants, Minorities, and Labor Market Competition." *Industrial and Labor Relations Review,* Vol. 40 (April), pp. 382–92.

Bound, John, and George Johnson. 1989. "Changes in the Structure of Wages During the 1980's: An Evaluation of Alternative Explanations." National Bureau of Economic Research Working Paper Number 2983, May.

Business Week. 1980. "The New Wave of Cubans Is Swamping Miami." No. 2651 (August 25), pp. 86–88.

Card, David. 1989. "The Impact of the Mariel Boatlift on the Miami Labor Market." National Bureau of Economic Research Working Paper Number 3069, August.

Filer, Randall. 1988. "The Impact of Immigrant Arrivals on Migratory Patterns of U.S. Workers." Unpublished manuscript, Hunter College and the Graduate Center, City University of New York, October.

Governor of Florida. 1980. *Report of the Governor's Dade County Citizen's Committee.* Miami.

Greenwood, Michael, and John McDowell. 1984. "The Factor Market Consequences of U.S. Immigration." *Journal of Economic Literature,* Vol. 34 (December), pp. 1738–72.

Grossman, Jean. 1982. "The Substitutability of Natives and Immigrants in Production." *Review of Economics and Statistics,* Vol. 64 (November), pp. 596–603.

Lalonde, Robert, and Robert Topel. 1987. "Labor Market Adjustments to Increased Immigration." Unpublished manuscript, University of Chicago Graduate School of Business, September.

Masud-Piloto, Felix Roberto. 1988. *With Open Arms: Cuban Migration to the United States.* Totowa, NJ.: Rowman & Littlefield.

United States Department of Commerce, Bureau of the Census. 1971. *1970 Census of Population—Number of Inhabitants: United States Summary* (PC1-A1). Washington, D.C.: GPO.

———. 1983. *1980 Census of Population—Characteristics of the Population: Detailed Population Characteristics.* Vol. 1, Chap. D, Part 2, Florida: PC80-1-D11. Washington, D.C.: GPO.

———. 1988. *Current Population Reports—Population Estimates and Projections: United States Population Estimates by Age, Sex, and Race: 1980 to 1987.* Series P-25, No. 1022. Washington, D.C.: GPO, March.

———. 1988. *Current Population Reports—Local Population Estimates: South 1986 Population and 1985 Per Capita Income Estimates for Counties and Incorporated Places.* Series P-26, No. 86-S-SC. Washington, D.C.: GPO, March.

University of Florida Bureau of Economics and Business Research. 1981. *Florida Statistical Abstract.* Gainesville: University Presses of Florida.

Wilbanks, William. 1984. *Murder in Miami: An Analysis of Homicide Patterns and Trends in Dade County Florida, 1917–1983.* Lanham, Md.: University Press of America.

ABOUT THE AUTHOR

David Card

David Card, who received a bachelor's degree from Queens University in Canada and a Ph.D. from Princeton University in the United States, is an empirical labor economist par excellence. His work has generated important and in some instances controversial findings on major issues in economic analysis and public policy, ranging from the intertemporal life cycle model, to the effect of wage indexation clauses in collective bargaining contracts, to the effects of school resources on earnings, to the employment of minimum wage workers. Card is a native Canadian who analyzes Canadian as well as U.S. economic issues and often contrasts developments between the two economies. What characterizes David Card's work is creative use of statistical evidence to make inferences about how the economy operates. David reports his results in an objective manner that resembles a laboratory scientist reporting an experiment, giving the findings and the statistical or interpretative problems that he could not fully address. He reports results that support standard economic models and results that reject them with equanimity. Among David's important findings are (1) that the U.S. minimum wage has modest or negligible effects on employment, (2) that the life-cycle labor supply model has only limited ability to explain micro supply behavior, (3) that unanticipated changes in real wages due to inflation affect employment, and (4) that much of the rise in Canadian unemployment relative to U.S. unemployment is due to an increase in the proportion of people without jobs who report themselves as unemployed, in part because of Canada's unemployment insurance system.

David's paper on the Mariel boatlift, which shows little effect of this immigration shock on native earnings and employment in the Miami labor market, is an example of how to illuminate an issue by finding an appropriate "natural experiment."

WAGE INEQUALITY

Charles Brown

Richard B. Freeman

Lawrence F. Katz and Kevin M. Murphy

John Bound and George Johnson

Equalizing Differences in the Labor Market

CHARLES BROWN

The theory of equalizing differences asserts that workers receive compensating wage premiums when they accept jobs with undesirable nonwage characteristics, holding the worker's characteristics constant. Previous research provides only inconsistent support for the theory, with wrong-signed or insignificant estimates of these wage premiums fairly common. An oft-cited reason for these anomalies is that important characteristics of the worker remain unmeasured, biasing the estimates.

In this paper, longitudinal data are used to test this conjecture. Although such data improve the control for worker characteristics, the plausibility of the estimates is not markedly improved. Alternative explanations for these results are considered.

> *"It's indoor work and no heavy lifting."*
>
> Senator Robert Dole,
> *explaining why he wanted to be*
> *Vice President.*

The theory of equalizing differences—that individuals are induced to accept less attractive jobs by compensating differences in their wage rates—is an important tool in economists' attempts to understand the labor market. Both as a test of the theory and in order to improve the measurement of compensation, researchers have attempted to estimate "prices" for nonwage characteristics. Despite evidence from studies of the internal wage policies of firms that equalizing differences are present [Doeringer and Piore, 1971, pp. 66–68; and

I have benefited from comments on earlier versions of this paper by C. Clotfelter, G. Duncan, R. Freeman, E. Lazear, J. Medoff, J. Quinn, W. Vroman, R. Weiss, an anonymous referee, and seminar participants at Boston College, Harvard University, the University of Maryland, and the U.S. Department of Labor. I am indebted to the General Research Board and the Computer Science Center at the University of Maryland for financial support and computer time. Ollie Ballard provided skillful research assistance. The paper was completed while the author was an economist at the Office of Research Methods and Standards, Bureau of Labor Statistics. The views expressed are those of the author and do not reflect the policies of the BLS or the views of other BLS staff members.

Reynolds 1974, p. 210] recent research on the determinants of individual earnings has provided rather limited support for the theory (see Table I).[1]

Lucas [1977, pp. 554–55] found evidence of significant compensation for repetitive work and somewhat smaller (though statistically significant) compensation for jobs with bad working conditions (hazards, extreme temperatures, etc.). Jobs requiring physical strength appeared to command lower wages, other things equal, and these differences were "significant" statistically. Neither Bluestone [1974, pp. 132–222] nor Quinn [1975, pp. 112, 115] nor Hamermesh [1977, p. 65] found consistent evidence of wage compensation for jobs requiring physical strength or involving hazards or extreme temperatures.

Smith [1973] found that "the probability of [work-related] death may be fully reflected in wage rates, but evidence of compensating differentials related to nonfatal injuries is scant." Thaler and Rosen [1975, pp. 289–94] concluded that, for workers in the most hazardous occupations, occupation-specific mortality rates do exert a positive influence on wage levels. Even here, the point estimates of this premium and their statistical significance are sensitive to the other variables included in the estimating equation and the functional form (linear or log-linear) employed.

Taubman [1975, pp. 51–52] analyzed the relationship between wages and the reasons that individuals in the NBER-TH sample of above-average ability males gave for choosing their occupation. Interpreting the latter as reflecting differences in their actual job characteristics, he found that most had statistically significant, plausibly signed, and often substantial coefficients. Duncan [1976, p. 472] found substantial compensating differentials for some job characteristics (freedom to control hours worked, safe working conditions, and employment and income stability);[2] however, the probability of observing such estimated differences by chance was not explored. Duncan and Stafford [1977, p 15] reported positive premiums for work effort and for jobs that restrict "opportunities to choose an individual or flexible work schedule and an individual work pace"—but these differences become statistically insignificant when a theoretically preferable wage measure is

---

[1] *Studies included in Table I were those using micro-data to explain the wages of broad groups of workers. Interesting studies excluded by this criterion were Antos and Rosen [1975], and Toder [1972] (both dealt only with teachers) and Mixon [1975] (who used time series data on 3-digit SIC industries). Each of these studies focused on job characteristics quite different from those in Table I. Antos and Rosen found that "equalizing wage differentials on working conditions are important sources of teacher wage variation." Toder found that communities with high proportions of nonwhites must pay a wage premium to attract teachers of given quality, but there was no analogous differential for teaching children in poor communities. Mixon reported that increases in the minimum wage led to statistically significant revision in at least one (out of five) nonwage characteristics in fifteen out of twenty low-wage industries studied.*

[2] *Because Duncan reported standardized weights from canonical correlation rather than unstandardized regression coefficients, his results were adjusted to make them more comparable to others in Table I. The unstandardized weight as a fraction of the mean wage equals the standardized weight times the coefficient of variation of the wage divided by the standard deviation of the job characteristics. However, the latter was adjusted so that the range of the job characteristic was zero to one in all cases, making them more nearly comparable to the dummy variables used by other authors in Table I.*

TABLE I

SUMMARY OF PREVIOUS MICRO-DATA STUDIES

Author	Source of individual data	Source of job data	Sample	Dependent variable	Job characteristic	Expected sign	Coefficient (std. error)	Notes
Lucas [1977] Table 1	Survey of Econ. Oppy.	Dict. of Occ. Titles	White males 12 yrs ed	ln (wage/hr)	Repetitive work	+	0.103* (0.043)	
					Requires phys. strength	+?	-0.170* (0.038)	
					Bad working conditions	+	0.068* (0.028)	
					Supervise people	+	0.152* (0.053)	
Bluestone [1974] Table 5.8, col. 2	Survey of Econ. Oppy	Dict. of Occ. Titles	White males	wage/hr (in $)	Requires phys. strength	+?	-0.13* (0.04)	Measured on 1 to 5 scale Insignificant
					Bad working conditions	+		
Quinn [1975] Table 5–9	Longitud. Retirement History Survey	Dict of Occ. Titles	White males Age 58–63	ln (wage/hr)	Work under stress or phys. strength	+	0.058* (0.031)	
					Other phys. demands	+	-0.015 (0.030)	
					Bad working conditions	+	0.005 (0.030)	
Hamermesh [1977] Table 3 col. 2	ISR Survey of working conditions	ISR Survey of working conditions	White males age 21–65	ln (annual) earnings)	Noise	+	0.151 (0.10)	Jointly insignificant ($F = 0.091$)
					Weather and heat	+	0.075 (0.07)	
					Dirt	+	-0.007 (0.77)	
					Hazardous materials	+	0.037 (0.03)	
					Hazardous equipment	+	0.033 (0.07)	
					Misc. hazards	+	0.029 (0.04)	

(continued on following page)

TABLE I (CONTINUED)

SUMMARY OF PREVIOUS MICRO-DATA STUDIES

Author	Source of individual data	Source of job data	Sample	Dependent variable	Job characteristic	Expected sign	Coefficient (std. error)	Notes
Thaler-Rosen [1975] Tables 3 & 4, col. D	Survey of Econ. Oppy.	Society of Actuaries	Adult males in risky occupations	wage/week (in $) / ln (wage/week)	Deaths per 1,000 manyears / Deaths per 1,000 manyears	+ / +	3.52* (2.10) / 0.0206 (0.0167)	
Smith [1973] Table 1, col. D	Current Pop. Survey	U.S. Dept. of Labor	White males	ln (wage/hr)	Deaths per 1,000 manyears / Lost workyrs per 1,000 manyears	+ / +	0.360* (0.151) / −.0011* (0.0005)	
Taubman [1975] Table III-5	NBER-TH	NBER-TH	Above-avg. IQ men age 44–52	Annual earnings	Prefer salaried / Teacher / Reason took job: Pros. finan. suc. / Independ. work / Interper. contact / Help others / Was a challenge / Job security / Provide free time	− / − / + / − / − / − / + / − / −	−0.10* / −0.18* / 0.17* / −0.11* / −0.01 / −0.08* / 0.17* / −0.13* / 0.02	Coefficients expressed as fraction of avg. earnings of not self-employed high school grads
Duncan [1976] Table 1	Quality of Employment Survey	Quality of Employment Survey	Males age 21–65 working full time	(wage + est. fringe benefits)/hr	Safe and healthy working conditions / Control of overtime / Employment stability	− / − / −	−0.21 / −0.56 / −0.20	Expressed as fraction of mean wage. Based on standardized weights from canonical correlation (see text fn. 2). No tests of significance
	Panel Study of Income Dynamics	Panel Study of Income Dynamics	Male hshd. heads in same job in 1970 and 1971	wage/hr	Free to increase work hours / Freedom to reduce work hours / Income stability	− / − / −	−0.23 / −0.23 / −0.14	

Study	Data source	Sample	Dependent variable	Independent variable	Sign	Coefficient	Notes
Duncan-Stafford [1977] Table 2	Time Use Survey	Adult blue-collar workers	ln (wage/hr)	Works with machines	+	0.169* (0.086)	
				Not free to take time off	+	0.031 (0.092)	
				ln (index of work effort)	+	0.066* (0.032)	
			ln (wage/hr)	Works with machines	+	0.157 (0.099)	"hours" = time at work – break time – training time
				Not free to take time off	+	0.098 (0.105)	
				ln (index of work effort)	+	0.000 (0.037)	
Lazear [1977] Table 1	NLS Young Men	Men 14–24 in 1966	Change in ln (wage/hr)	Change in enrollment status	–	–0.132* (0.025)	
Schiller-Weiss [1977] Table 1	Social Security LEED file	Employees of 133 large firms	ln (annual earnings)	Eight pension-plan characteristics			Jointly significant for 26–34 and 35–39 age cohorts; not for older cohorts

* = Statistically significant at the 0.05 level.

employed. Lazear [1977, p. 175] reports significantly lower wages for young men enrolled in school, "consistent with an equalizing-difference explanation which argues that students optimally choose more flexible and easier jobs at the cost of lower wages."

Evidence on other important job characteristics is more limited. For example, human capital theorists maintain that individuals gain entry into occupations with prospects of higher future wages only by accepting lower current wages. Empirical support for this proposition has been rather indirect (e.g., inferences from the pattern of the variance of earnings by age [Mincer, 1974, pp. 58–59], or differences in age-earnings profiles between groups [Lillard, 1977, p. 521].[3] Schiller and Weiss [1977, p. 17] investigated the relationship between pension benefits and wages in a sample of workers in large firms. They found support for the equalizing-differences hypothesis among younger workers but not among those nearing retirement. The relationship between wages and other fringe benefits (vacations, health insurance, etc.) has not been examined, although the existence of a tradeoff is often asserted in collective bargaining contexts [Reynolds, 1974, p. 217].

The overall pattern that emerges from Table I is one of mixed results: some clear support for the theory but an uncomfortable number of exceptions. Among the studies that fail to find equalizing differences, the most common explanation is the omission of important worker abilities, biasing the coefficients of the job characteristics.

The purpose of this paper is to provide a more appropriate test of the theory. In Section I a model of labor-market choice that emphasizes equalizing differences is presented. The model formalizes the omitted variable argument and suggests that even "favorable" results could underestimate the magnitude of these differences. Moreover, the analysis in Section II suggests that a more appropriate test of the model can be conducted when longitudinal data are available.

In Section III the data are described. The National Longitudinal Survey (NLS) Young Men's sample provides seven years' data on the labor market experiences of males age 14–24 in 1966. Data on occupational characteristics are taken from several sources and matched to individuals on the basis of their occupation or industry. The results are presented and discussed in Section IV. Concluding observations are offered in Section V.

I. THE MODEL

The central focus of the theory of equalizing differences is the choice made by individuals *with given personal characteristics* (X) among jobs with different wages (w) and differing nonwage attributes (Z). In order to attract labor of a given quality, an employer offering jobs that are hazardous or otherwise undesirable must pay higher wages than employers offering jobs with more desired nonwage characteristics. Therefore, an individual faces a set of jobs with differing combinations of w and Z, and is assumed to choose among these opportunities in order to maximize utility.

---

[3] *Hause's [1973] study of the covariance between earnings at different points in time (using Swedish data) is an exception.*

Formally, let Z be the vector of nonwage characteristics, measured so that larger values of Z represent less desired jobs. ("Less desired" is understood to reflect the preferences of the marginal individual.) If $f(w,Z;X)$ is the function relating wages to nonwage job characteristics for persons with personal characteristics X, the theory asserts that $\partial w/\partial Z_j > 0$ for all j.

This prediction can be tested once the function $f(w,Z;X)$ is specified. Unfortunately, theory provides no guidance in the choice of functional forms, at least for most Z's.[4] A convenient specification is the semi-log equation,

$$(1) \qquad\qquad W \equiv \ln(w) = XB + ZA + u,$$

where u is a random disturbance.[5]

Equation (1) is the estimating equation used in most of the studies mentioned earlier, where the estimates of the A's were often insignificantly different from zero and sometimes "significant" but wrong-signed.

It is not difficult to explain this result, even if the theory is correct ($A > 0$). Consider what happens to the estimate of A when some of the X's are omitted from equation (1). For simplicity, suppose that

$$(2) \qquad\qquad W = B_0 + X_1 B_1 + X_2 B_2 + ZA + u,$$

where B_1, B_2, and A are scalars, X_1 and X_2 are orthogonal, and data on X_2 are unavailable. The bias in the estimate of A will have the same sign as the correlation between X_2 and Z. If the people with more X_2 "spend" some of their greater earning capacity on reducing Z, this correlation will be negative,[6] and the estimate of A will be biased toward (or even

---

[4] For a discussion of the relationship of f to production relationships and workers' tastes, see Thaler and Rosen [1975, pp. 268–86].

[5] Equation (1) has been estimated by ordinary least squares in previous studies. Several readers of earlier drafts of this paper have questioned the appropriateness of such estimation, arguing that u and Z are inevitably correlated. Ordinary least squares might be appropriate if all the systematic determinants of earning capacity were included among the X's; one might then argue that transitory variation (due, for example, to measurement error in reported wages) was independent of Z. Of course, X is never fully specified; but the resulting difficulties are more easily understood from the "omitted variable" discussion in the text than from a simultaneous-equations-bias perspective. In any case, finding instruments for the Z's that are not themselves X's would be extremely difficult.

[6] Evidence in Lucas [1974] on the relationship between observable determinants of earning capacity (schooling and age) and nine job characteristics is consistent with this hypothesis. Bowles [1972, p. S238] argues that this positive relationship holds for social class and nonmonetary job characteristics generally. Bailey and Schwenck [1972, p. 15] report "an increasing emphasis [on employer-financed retirement and insurance plans] accompanying higher levels of earning power." Duncan [1976], however, found that, controlling for education, other determinants of earning capacity (e.g., experience, SES, tenure, test score) were not significantly related to nonpecuniary job characteristics.

beyond) zero. The omitted-variable argument is the most frequently encountered explanation for insignificant or wrong-signed coefficients [e.g., Lucas 1977, p. 555; Toder, 1972, p. 440; Quinn, 1975, p. 103; and Duncan and Stafford, 1977, p. 3]. Moreover, it implies that even right-signed estimates may be too small [Antos and Rosen, 1975, p. 137].

Rigorous generalization of this argument to cover more than one Z does not appear possible.[7] However, in general, the bias in estimating A_k will have the same sign as the coefficient of Z_k in a hypothetical regression of the omitted X on the included X and all of the Z's. If that hypothetical coefficient is negative, the estimate of A_k is biased toward (or beyond) zero.[8]

II. THE IMPORTANCE OF LONGITUDINAL DATA

Clearly, it is important that the determinants of earning capacity be specified as completely as possible. However, the data usually available are deficient in that they provide no information on many potentially important personal characteristics. For example, the Survey of Economic Opportunity (the source of wage and personal characteristics data used by Lucas, Bluestone, and Thaler and Rosen) contains no measures of intelligence or fluency in oral communication, and its measures of social background are far from ideal.[9]

To the extent that most of the omitted dimensions are individual-specific (i.e., do not change over time), they can be summarized by an individual-specific intercept. With cross-sectional data, including individual-specific intercepts among the X's would be impossible, since there would be one such "variable" for each observation. Given data on wages and

---

[7] With two Z's, equation (2) would become

(2')
$$W = B_0 + B_1 X_1 + B_2 X_2 + Z_1 A_1 + Z_2 A_2 + u.$$

The bias in estimating, say, A_2 has the same sign as

$$[\text{cov}(X_1,Z_1)\,\text{cov}(X_1,Z_2) - \text{var}(X_1)\,\text{cov}(Z_1,Z_2)]\,\text{cov}(X_2,Z_1)$$
$$+ [\text{var}(X_1)\,\text{var}(Z_1) - \text{cov}(X_1,Z_1)^2]\,\text{cov}(X_2,Z_2).$$

Assuming that $\text{cov}(X_i,Z_j)$ is negative for all i and j, the sign of the bias is still indeterminate, since we cannot rule out the possibility that the first term in brackets is negative and large enough to make the bias positive. A moderately helpful assumption is that $r(X_1,Z_i) = r(X_2,Z_i)$, $i = 1,2$, where r is the simple correlation. In this case, the bias has the same sign as $r(X_1,Z_2) - r(X_1,Z_1)r(Z_1,Z_2)$, which will be negative unless $r(Z_1,Z_2)$ is positive and both $r(Z_1,Z_2)$ and $r(X_1,Z_1)$ are substantially larger than $r(X_1,Z_2)$ in absolute value.

[8] Given two individuals with identical observed X's and identical Z's (except for Z_k) and even-money odds, would you bet that the individual with greater Z_k had more or less of the unmeasured X? This question elicits one's subjective expectation of the hypothetical coefficient: betting that the individual with greater Z_k will have less unmeasured X is equivalent to expecting that A_k is biased toward zero.

[9] See Bowles [1972, section III].

jobs of individuals at several points in time, the use of individual-specific intercepts is a feasible strategy for controlling for individual characteristics that do not change over time.

Of course, some determinants of earnings capacity do change over time (e.g., an individual's age, work experience, formal job training, and marital status). To the extent that such dimensions remain unmeasured, the omitted-variable problem persists, albeit (hopefully) reduced. Fortunately, the NLS data include fairly detailed information on many of these characteristics.

Including several hundred individual-specific intercepts in the X-matrix would exceed the capacity of almost any computer program that calculates regressions. Fortunately, there is a computationally feasible alternative.
Define

$$\tilde{W}_{it} = W_{it} - \frac{1}{T}\sum_{t=1}^{T} W_{it}, \quad i = 1, 2, \ldots, \left(\text{number of individuals}\right), \quad t = 1, 2, \ldots, T$$

$$(3) \qquad \tilde{X}_{ijt} = X_{ijt} - \frac{1}{T}\sum_{t=1}^{T} X_{ijt}, \quad j = 1, 2, \ldots, \left(\text{number of } X\text{'s}\right)$$

$$\tilde{Z}_{ikt} = Z_{ikt} - \frac{1}{T}\sum_{t=1}^{T} Z_{ikt}, \quad k = 1, 2, \ldots, \left(\text{number of } Z\text{'s}\right).$$

It can be shown[10] that regressing $\tilde{W}$ on $\tilde{X}$ and $\tilde{Z}$ gives the same estimates of B and A as regressing W on X, Z, and the set of individual specific intercepts.

Equation (3) emphasizes that, with individual-specific intercepts, it is changes in W, X, and Z over time for each individual that identify B and A. This would cause difficulties if individuals remained in the same occupation, since the changes in Z would presumably be negligible. Fortunately, occupation-changing is the rule rather than the exception for young men. In the sample analyzed below, 85 percent of the individuals changed 3-digit occupations at least once between 1966 and 1973, and 60 percent moved to a new broad (one-digit) occupational group.[11]

III. THE DATA

The NLS Young Men's sample provided data in each of the seven years 1966–1971 and 1973. Eliminating individuals who were college graduates, were in school at any of the

[10] *The key is to partition the independent variable matrix so that the set of individual intercepts is in one block and the X's and Z's are in the other. Note that the standard errors for each coefficient calculated by standard computer programs from the transformed data must be corrected to reflect the loss of degrees of freedom due to the (swept-out) intercepts. See Pacific Consultants [1976, pp. 202–15].*

[11] *Individuals who do not change jobs are still "useful" observations, in that they help to determine the coefficients of the individual characteristics.*

survey dates, or did not provide usable data on wages, industry, occupation, or the other variables described below reduced the sample from 5,225 (roughly 2,000 of whom were out of school in 1966) to 470. The subsample studied here was older, had more stable labor force attachment, and came from less "advantaged" backgrounds than the larger sample.

Given the individual-intercept strategy, only determinants of earning capacity that change over time need be (or can be)[12] included explicitly in equation (1). The effects of those determinants of earning capacity that do not change over time (e.g., schooling or race) are reflected implicitly in the intercepts.

The Young Men's surveys provide information on seven determinants of earning capacity that change over time:

1. Six dummy variables (which equal one for observations from the 1967, 1968, 1969, 1970, 1971, and 1973 surveys, respectively, and zero otherwise) were included. These dummies capture the general growth in wages due to technical progress, price inflation, etc., and the effects of time spent not working.

2. Three types of variables reflect human capital investments. The first is the cumulative time spent in civilian formal training programs, measured in hours of training/(40×52). Three types of training programs could be distinguished: company training, part-time school courses, and "other."[13] The second is cumulative work experience since 1965, measured in weeks employed/52. Presumably, this variable measures the productive effect of past on-the-job investments associated with informal "learning by doing" rather than formal training programs. Finally, tenure with current employer, measured in months/12, is included to capture differences in firm-specific human capital investments.

3. Two measures of unionization were employed. First, the fraction of workers unionized in the individual's (3-digit Census) industry was coded separately for office and production workers, based on data in Freeman and Medoff [1980]. Second, the probability that the individual worker was himself covered by a collective bargaining agreement was included. For 1969–1971, this was a dummy variable (1 = covered, 0 = not covered) from the NLS file. Whether the worker was covered by a collective bargaining agreement was not ascertained in the remaining years. If the worker was working with the same employer in, say, 1968 as in 1969, the 1969 dummy was coded for 1968. If the worker was with a different employer, the probability of his being covered in 1968 was taken to be the fraction of (office or production) workers in his industry who were covered.

4. Marital status was represented by a dummy variable that equals one whenever the respondent is currently married and zero otherwise.

---

[12] *Including a characteristic that did not change over time would make that characteristic an exact linear combination of the individual-specific intercepts.*

[13] *Part-time school included business and technical school, regular school, and correspondence courses. Because formal apprenticeships are coded separately only in 1966 and 1973, they were included in the "other" category.*

5. Geographic variation in wage rates is reflected in three dummy variables, which equal one whenever an individual works in an SMSA, lives in the South, or lives in the West, respectively, and zero otherwise.

6. The effect of involuntary job separation was represented (crudely) by the cumulative number of times an individual has been fired or laid off.

7. The effect of health problems on earning capacity was represented by a dummy variable that equals one whenever the respondent reported a health problem that interfered with work activities.

In order to compare the results presented here to those of other researchers, conventional determinants of workers' wages that do not change over time were included *instead of* the individual-specific intercepts in some regressions. These variables were years of schooling, months of military training programs, labor-market experience in 1965, knowledge of the world of work, an index of the socioeconomic status in which the individual grew up, and race.

An important source of data on job characteristics was the Dictionary of Occupational Titles (DOT) file. Originally, each of over 13,000 DOT occupations was assigned a dummy variable for each characteristic (1 = present, 0 = absent). These 13,000 occupations were then aggregated into the nearly 300 3-digit Census occupations using a conversion matrix based on the October 1966 Current Population Survey. Thus, the "score" for each occupation represents the probability that a randomly selected individual in that 3-digit occupation has the given job characteristic. For details see Lucas [1974]. Both "laborers, not elsewhere classified," and "operatives, not elsewhere classified," are subdivided according to Census industry, in order to reflect the heterogeneity of these important "residual" categories.

Four characteristics were selected for study here:

1. the job requires performing repetitive functions;
2. the job requires working under stress;
3. the job requires physical strength;
4. the job involves bad working conditions (extremes of cold or heat, humidity, vibrations, or hazards).

An alternative, more specific measure of bad working conditions, the increase in the actuarial probability of death associated with hazardous occupations [Society of Actuaries, 1967] was also used. Since these data measure the *extra* risk from working in such occupations, occupations not covered were assigned a value of zero. This made it imperative that Society of Actuaries' occupations be matched to Census occupations (or occupation-industry pairs) whenever possible. These annual extra-mortality probabilities have been multiplied by 1,000 as a scaling factor; thus, we have the extra deaths per thousand man-years in each occupation. (Among all males age twenty-five, about two out of 1,000 die each year; thus, the coefficient of this variable may be interpreted as the compensation for increasing the normal risk of death by one-half.)

Data were available from various sources on four other potentially important job characteristics:

1. The number of hours usually worked by the individual was recorded each year by the NLS. The logarithm of hours worked and a separate dummy variable for part-time work (less than thirty-five hours per week) were used.

2. A dummy variable that equals one whenever the individual worked for a federal, state, or local government, and zero otherwise, was constructed. It was intended to reflect the greater job security of government employment [Blechman, Gramlich, and Hartman, 1975, p. 68], although other interpretations are possible.

3. When an individual was currently enrolled in a formal training program (e.g., company training program), the NLS file gives the number of hours per week the individual spends in training. The ratio of training hours to usual hours worked was coded as a measure of self-investment opportunities of the job. The NLS did not determine whether the firm paid the employee for time spent in training, or for tuition, or other expenses. This seems almost certain for company training, unlikely for part-time schooling, with "other" training in between. Given Lazear's argument that students select more flexible, less demanding jobs while enrolled, one would expect a negative sign even for part-time schooling, but the interpretation of this coefficient is unclear. Finally, workers who reported their occupations as being in Census "apprentice" categories often did not report themselves to be enrolled in formal training.[14] Whatever the "formality" of apprenticeship, there is strong reason to believe that substantial on-the-job training occurs in these occupations. Therefore, a dummy variable that equals one whenever the respondent's occupation is one of the Census apprentice categories, and zero otherwise, was created. Human-capital theory leads one to expect a negative sign for this variable.

4. Ideally, total compensation (including fringe benefits) would be used as the dependent variable. Lack of appropriate data has precluded this in the past, and the NLS data are no exception. However, data on total expenditures for labor compensation, divided into wage and nonwage components, are available for 2-digit SIC industries.[15] Annual data from 1965 to 1669 were averaged, and the values assigned to each Census industry were those of the 2-digit SIC industry to which it belonged. For manufacturing industries these estimates were refined using data on a 3-digit SIC level for 1967 from the *Annual Survey of Manufacturers* [1973]. From these data the ratio of nonwage compensation to wages was calculated, and matched to each individual according to his Census industry. If the logarithm of total compensation is some function of X and the other job characteristics (i.e., $h(X,Z)$), then

---

[14] *For example, in 1966 and 1973 (the only years in which formal apprenticeship programs were recorded separately), only half of those who were in apprentice occupations were recorded as being in apprenticeship programs.*

[15] *Unpublished data, Bureau of Economic Affairs.*

$$\ln(\text{wage}) = h(X,Z) - \ln(1 + \text{nonwage compensation/wages})$$
$$\simeq h(X,Z) - (\text{nonwage compensation/wages})$$

so that the coefficient of our measure of nonwage compensation to wages would be -1.0.

Two other "job characteristics" taken from the DOT file were also included in some regressions: GED (general educational development) and SVP (specific vocational preparation). Their inclusion, in addition to the other determinants of earning capacity described above, can be justified in several ways: as measuring omitted productive characteristics of individuals; as reflecting perceived productivity differences among individuals that are not explained by the other X's; as reflecting wage differentials that workers in some jobs receive over identical workers in other jobs.

IV. RESULTS

Estimates of the parameters of equation (1) appear in Table II. Columns 5 to 8 include individual-specific intercepts, while columns 1 to 4 do not.

In columns 1–4, coefficients of the individual characteristics are generally in line with expectations and previous research using these data [e.g., Griliches, 1977; Kohen, 1972]. The human capital variables are generally significant. The exceptions are cumulative company training and tenure; the near-zero coefficient for tenure probably reflects the fact that job search and consequent job changes are important for workers in their twenties. If anything, the cumulative experience variable has an implausibly large effect. The unionization variables, marital status, and geographic variables have the expected impacts. The (crudely constructed) layoff-discharge variable has no effect on wages; health problems have a small negative impact, but the coefficient is about the same size as its standard error. Race, knowledge of the world of work, early experience, and years of schooling have the expected effects on wages, while military experience has little impact.

The individual characteristics in columns 1 to 4 are more comprehensive than those typically included in the studies in Table I. However, the coefficients of the job characteristics in columns 1–4 display the same inconsistent relationship to theoretical predictions one observes in Table I. The government worker coefficient is significantly negative and reasonable in magnitude. The supplements variable is wrong-signed and very significantly different from -1.0. Time spent in school or "other" training programs has a fairly large negative impact on current wages, but time in company training or being an apprentice does not. The four DOT variables are either "significant" and wrong-signed (repetitive work in columns 1 and 2, and bad working conditions) or insignificant. A zero coefficient for jobs requiring physical strength is sensible for workers in their twenties, but the other three characteristics should generate positive wage differentials. The risk of death variable has a statistically significant positive coefficient that is roughly three times as large as that reported by Thaler and Rosen. Part-time workers receive lower wages (in line with analogous results for females; see Rosen [1976]) but otherwise longer

TABLE II

Estimates of Equation (1)

Variable	Mean (st. dev.)	1	2	3	4	5	6	7	8
Constant	1.00 (0.00)	5.71 (0.127)	5.66 (0.126)	5.71 (0.126)	5.68 (0.125)				
Year = 1967	0.143 (0.350)	−0.013 (0.023)	−0.015 (0.022)	−0.007 (0.022)	−0.009 (0.022)	0.003 (0.013)	0.003 (0.013)	0.004 (0.013)	0.004 (0.013)
Year = 1968	0.143 (0.350)	0.012 (0.033)	0.009 (0.032)	0.026 (0.032)	0.023 (0.032)	0.035* (0.018)	0.035* (0.018)	0.036* (0.018)	0.036* (0.018)
Year = 1969	0.143 (0.350)	0.013 (0.045)	0.006 (0.045)	0.031 (0.044)	0.025 (0.044)	0.035 (0.024)	0.034 (0.024)	0.035 (0.024)	0.035 (0.024)
Year = 1970	0.143 (0.350)	−0.011 (0.058)	−0.022 (0.057)	0.014 (0.057)	0.005 (0.057)	0.018 (0.031)	0.017 (0.031)	0.019 (0.031)	0.018 (0.031)
Year = 1971	0.143 (0.350)	−0.049 (0.071)	−0.061 (0.070)	−0.019 (0.070)	−0.029 (0.070)	−0.020 (0.038)	−0.021 (0.038)	−0.020 (0.038)	−0.021 (0.038)
Year = 1973	0.143 (0.350)	−0.071 (0.098)	−0.090 (0.097)	−0.027 (0.097)	−0.043 (0.097)	−0.042 (0.053)	−0.043 (0.053)	−0.041 (0.053)	−0.043 (0.053)
Cum company train school	0.078 (0.467)	−0.003 (0.011)	−0.003 (0.011)	−0.005 (0.011)	−0.006 (0.011)	−0.001 (0.011)	−0.001 (0.011)	0.000 (0.011)	−0.001 (0.011)
Cum part-time school	0.100 (0.368)	0.035* (0.014)	0.036* (0.014)	0.033* (0.014)	0.034* (0.014)	0.026 (0.016)	0.026 (0.016)	0.026 (0.016)	0.026 (0.016)
Cum other school	0.096 (0.459)	0.049* (0.011)	0.047* (0.011)	0.043* (0.011)	0.042* (0.011)	−0.007 (0.013)	−0.008 (0.013)	−0.008 (0.013)	−0.009 (0.013)
Cum work exper. since 1965	3.91 (2.17)	0.103* (0.014)	0.105* (0.014)	0.096* (0.014)	0.097* (0.014)	0.101* (0.008)	0.102* (0.008)	0.102* (0.008)	0.102* (0.008)
Years tenure current job	3.06 (2.85)	0.000 (0.002)	0.001 (0.002)	0.001 (0.002)	0.002 (0.002)	0.006* (0.002)	0.006* (0.002)	0.006* (0.002)	0.006* (0.002)
Prob resp covered by union	0.378 (0.448)	0.130* (0.013)	0.126* (0.013)	0.134* (0.013)	0.132* (0.013)	0.081* (0.016)	0.080* (0.016)	0.080* (0.016)	0.080* (0.016)
Union coverage, office	0.015 (0.073)	0.274* (0.074)	0.332* (0.073)	0.233* (0.074)	0.271* (0.073)	0.178* (0.076)	0.201* (0.074)	0.176* (0.076)	0.210* (0.074)

Union coverage, nonoffice	0.396 (0.326)	0.223* (0.023)	0.178* (0.022)	0.207* (0.023)	0.172* (0.021)	0.200* (0.027)	0.190* (0.026)	0.203* (0.027)	0.190* (0.026)
Currently married	0.750 (0.433)	0.132* (0.012)	0.133* (0.012)	0.129* (0.012)	0.130* (0.012)	0.065* (0.013)	0.065* (0.013)	0.064* (0.013)	0.064* (0.013)
Job in SMSA	0.678 (0.467)	0.135* (0.011)	0.135* (0.011)	0.135* (0.011)	0.135* (0.011)	0.105* (0.020)	0.105* (0.020)	0.104* (0.020)	0.104* (0.020)
Residence in South	0.440 (0.496)	-0.106* (0.012)	-0.107* (0.012)	-0.107* (0.012)	-0.109* (0.012)	-0.003 (0.045)	-0.002 (0.045)	-0.004 (0.045)	-0.002 (0.045)
Residence in West	0.095 (0.293)	0.034 (0.018)	0.031 (0.018)	0.040* (0.018)	0.038* (0.018)	0.135* (0.064)	0.138* (0.064)	0.133* (0.064)	0.137* (0.064)
Cum layoff + discharge	0.439 (0.888)	0.001 (0.006)	0.000 (0.006)	0.002 (0.006)	0.002 (0.006)	0.013 (0.007)	0.013 (0.007)	0.011 (0.007)	0.012 (0.007)
Health limits work	0.069 (0.253)	-0.021 (0.020)	-0.022 (0.019)	-0.020 (0.019)	-0.022 (0.019)	-0.009 (0.019)	-0.010 (0.019)	-0.007 (0.019)	-0.009 (0.019)
Race = White	0.760 (0.427)	0.125* (0.014)	0.128* (0.014)	0.110* (0.014)	0.111* (0.014)				
Knowledge of World of Work	33.9 (8.50)	0.0053* (0.0008)	0.0055* (0.0008)	0.0051* (0.0008)	0.0053* (0.0008)				
SES Index	91.3 (20.9)	0.0016* (0.0003)	0.0017* (0.0003)	0.0016* (0.0003)	0.0016* (0.0003)				
Cum experience in 1965	3.07 (2.34)	0.012* (0.002)	0.011* (0.002)	0.012* (0.002)	0.011* (0.002)				
Years schooling completed	11.0 (2.00)	0.031* (0.004)	0.032* (0.004)	0.031* (0.004)	0.031* (0.004)				
Cum military training	0.150 (0.635)	0.005 (0.008)	0.006 (0.008)	0.005 (0.008)	0.006 (0.008)				
Government worker	0.091 (0.287)	-0.074* (0.019)	-0.091* (0.019)	-0.060* (0.019)	-0.071* (0.019)	-0.076* (0.024)	-0.080* (0.024)	-0.074* (0.024)	-0.079* (0.024)
Sup/wages in industry	0.110 (0.051)	0.010 (0.119)	0.185 (0.117)	0.050 (0.118)	0.178 (0.116)	0.170 (0.163)	0.223 (0.161)	0.161 (0.163)	0.217 (0.161)
Time now in company train	0.008 (0.067)	-0.009 (0.079)	0.003 (0.079)	0.003 (0.078)	0.012 (0.078)	-0.036 (0.061)	-0.033 (0.061)	-0.032 (0.061)	-0.029 (0.061)

(continued on following page)

TABLE II (CONTINUED)

ESTIMATES OF EQUATION (1)

Variable	Mean (st. dev.)	1	2	3	4	5	6	7	8
Time now in part-time school	0.008 (0.058)	-0.357* (0.088)	-0.360* (0.088)	-0.361* (0.087)	-0.360* (0.087)	-0.200* (0.071)	-0.204* (0.071)	-0.205* (0.071)	-0.209* (0.071)
Time now in other training	0.008 (0.063)	-0.193* (0.082)	-0.181* (0.082)	-0.191* (0.082)	-0.182* (0.081)	-0.116 (0.065)	-0.112 (0.065)	-0.117 (0.065)	-0.113 (0.065)
Occupation = apprentice	0.018 (0.132)	-0.007 (0.039)	-0.005 (0.039)	-0.028 (0.039)	-0.030 (0.039)	-0.098* (0.034)	-0.097* (0.034)	-0.098* (0.034)	-0.098* (0.034)
Repetitive work	0.395 (0.361)	-0.137* (0.015)	-0.143* (0.016)	-0.036 (0.024)	-0.029 (0.023)	-0.049* (0.016)	-0.050* (0.017)	-0.056* (0.025)	-0.048* (0.025)
Work under stress	0.067 (0.176)	0.041 (0.031)	-0.005 (0.032)	-0.012 (0.033)	-0.043 (0.034)	0.028 (0.040)	0.027 (0.040)	-0.019 (0.043)	-0.017 (0.043)
Physical strength required	0.188 (0.252)	-0.006 (0.023)	-0.036 (0.022)	0.030 (0.023)	0.011 (0.022)	-0.028 (0.025)	-0.036 (0.024)	-0.009 (0.026)	-0.018 (0.025)
Bad working conditions	0.561 (0.353)	-0.067* (0.018)		-0.044* (0.019)		-0.031 (0.020)		-0.037 (0.021)	
Deaths/1,000 manyears	0.225 (0.448)		0.060* (0.012)		0.057* (0.012)		0.009 (0.012)		0.007 (0.012)
Ln (usual hours)	3.77 (0.198)	-0.375* (0.031)	-0.381* (0.030)	-0.368* (0.030)	-0.369* (0.030)	-0.254* (0.028)	-0.255* (0.028)	-0.254* (0.028)	-0.255* (0.028)
Part-time worker	0.028 (0.164)	-0.095* (0.037)	-0.105* (0.037)	-0.087* (0.037)	-0.089* (0.036)	-0.052 (0.032)	-0.053 (0.032)	-0.053 (0.032)	-0.053 (0.032)
Low GED requirement	0.584 (0.387)			-0.044 (0.024)	-0.067* (0.022)			0.044 (0.024)	0.033 (0.024)
Low SVP requirement	0.158 (0.222)			-0.212* (0.030)	-0.204* (0.030)			-0.075* (0.030)	-0.075* (0.030)
Standard error of estimate		0.277	0.276	0.274	0.274	0.202	0.202	0.202	0.202
R-squared		0.635	0.636	0.641	0.643	0.833	0.833	0.834	0.834
Number of observations		3,290	3,290	3,290	3,290	3,290	3,290	3,290	3,290

* = Statistically significant at the 0.05 level.

workweeks generate lower hourly wages. Including GED and SVP makes the coefficients of repetitive work and bad working conditions less negative, but has little additional impact.

Individual-specific intercepts are included in columns 5 to 8. The coefficient of cumulative part-time schooling is reduced, and the effect of cumulative "other" training is eliminated. The impacts of the regional dummies are less in line with those in earlier studies. The coefficients of the unionization variables decline, but this was predictable. If some firms pay above-market wages, they should attract better qualified workers, thus offsetting part of the initial wage differential. If the individual-specific intercepts do in fact provide a superior control for variation in worker quality, their inclusion should reduce the impact of unionization.

The impacts of the intercepts on the coefficients of the job characteristics vary considerably, and there is no marked improvement in the correspondence between these coefficients and a priori predictions. The government worker and supplements/wages variables are nearly unaffected. The time in company training variable remains negligible, the coefficients of the part-time school and other training variables are reduced in absolute value, but the apprentice dummy acquires a significant negative coefficient. The effects of repetitive work and bad working conditions become less negative (the former remaining "significant"), while stress and strength are unaffected. The risk of death variable, however, loses its significant positive effect. The coefficients of the continuous workweek and the part-time dummy variables have become less negative.

The lack of consistent improvement in coefficients of the job characteristics due to the intercepts might be attributed to a lack of variation in the transformed variables (see equation (3)), leading to imprecise parameter estimates. In fact, however, the standard errors of these coefficients are not substantially raised by the addition of the intercepts. This reflects the fact that occupation-changing among young workers is common, so that "within-individual" variation in job characteristics is substantial.

Several experiments with the estimating equation are not reported in Table II. First, the cumulative training variables were coded using months rather than hours of training (i.e., neglecting hours spent per week). Second, the extra risk of death variable was replaced by a variable that took the values used by Thaler and Rosen in their subset of risky occupations, and zero otherwise, to test whether the coding of the additional occupations was responsible for the differences from their results. Third, rates of growth in employment in the individual's industry and occupation from 1960 to 1970 were added as explanatory variables, to test the idea that employers in growing industries or occupations might offer both higher wages and better working conditions to attract more employees. None of these changes led to results appreciably different from those in Table II.

Various restrictions of the basic sample were also considered. The sample was divided by race, and also by years of schooling (did/did not graduate from high school). While some of the job characteristics (government worker, time currently in training) were more often significant for whites and high school graduates, there was no clear pattern to the disaggregated equations. Next, the sample was restricted to those with scores of at least 28 (out of a possible 56) on the "knowledge of world of work" test. The motivation was to exclude those with the least information about the job market. Unfortunately, the test emphasizes questions that would be verifiable from Census tabulations rather than reflecting detailed knowledge about the individual's local labor market. In any case, the results for the resulting 2,639 observations were not markedly different from those in Table II. Finally, the sample was restricted to individuals who had been out of school for at least two years at the 1966 survey (2,674 observations), to check whether individuals finding their way in the labor market were obscuring the more systematic behavior of other workers. However, the results were qualitatively similar to those in Table II.

V. CONCLUSIONS

The hypothesis that the inconsistent support for the theory of equalizing differences that characterized previous studies was due to the omission of important dimensions of worker quality was not supported by the data. Despite reasonably adequate measures of those worker characteristics that change over time and a statistical technique for holding constant differences that do not, the coefficients of job characteristics that might be expected to generate equalizing differences in wage rates were often wrong-signed or insignificant.

One is left with several explanations for this failure, none of which is entirely convincing.

1. "Labor markets are simply not as competitive as the theory of equalizing differences assumes." While the assumptions of the perfect-information profit- and utility-maximizing model most often used to explain the equalizing difference hypothesis—and relate it to applied welfare economics [Thaler and Rosen, 1975]—may be too strong, considerably weaker assumptions still imply such differences. Suppose that wages and working conditions are determined by collective bargaining without the threat of extinction compelling these decisions to conform to cost-minimizing outcomes. Suppose that workers lack information about working conditions and underestimate the differences in working conditions among firms. As long as workers prefer better working conditions and higher wages, and employers hire the applicants they perceive to be most qualified, the relationship between wages and unpleasant job characteristics holding worker quality constant should still be positive—though weaker than the stronger set of assumptions would imply.

2. "The *marginal* worker's tastes may be different from those assumed in the a priori signing of the coefficients." For example, while some workers abhor physical labor, others prefer it to more sedentary endeavors; thus, jobs requiring physical strength may not be unpleasant for the marginal worker, and no equalizing difference would be required. However, this conjecture is much less convincing for most of the other job characteristics in Tables I and II.

3. "The job characteristics are not well-measured." Undoubtedly, there is a large element of truth to this assertion, particularly for characteristics "matched" on the basis of

occupation rather than being reported directly by the worker. It would be an attractive explanation for coefficients that fell a little short of plausible magnitude or statistical significance. But it is difficult to construct a measurement-error rationale for coefficients that are wrong-signed and significantly different from hypothesized values (e.g., repetitive work or supplements/wages).

4. "Omitted variables—both individual characteristics that change over time and job characteristics—may be biasing the results." Admittedly, some determinants of changes in individual productivity (e.g., intensity of informal on-the-job training) remain unmeasured. However, the results were little improved when individual-specific "abilities" were controlled. The omission of some job characteristics raises a more complicated issue. One might expect good job characteristics to be positively correlated in general. However, controlling for all X's, the partial correlation among job characteristics is more difficult to assess. It may be, for example, that individuals who do repetitive work have more freedom to work overtime or require less (costly) job search to find jobs. Lacking data to hold these omitted characteristics constant, one can only speculate.

5. "Testing the hypothesis on a sample in their early and mid-twenties is inappropriate." It is not obvious why workers in this age range should provide weaker support for the hypothesis than older workers. After all, the common stereotype of youth is one who is *overly* sensitive to working conditions, insufficiently willing to put up with repetitive, stressful, or otherwise unpleasant work in order to "make something" of himself.[16] In any case, as reported in Section IV, deleting the least experienced fifth of the sample failed to provide clearer support for the hypothesis.

One could undoubtedly construct a more convincing case for each of these explanations, but it is doubtful that it would be fully satisfactory, explaining the "successes" in Tables I and II as well as the failures. While the present paper provides little support for an oft-used explanation, the task of choosing (or combining) the alternatives remains.

REFERENCES

Antos, Joseph R., and Sherwin Rosen, "Discrimination in the Market for Public School Teachers," *Journal of Econometrics,* III (May 1975), 123–50.

Bailey, William R., and Albert E. Schwenk, "Employer Expenditures for Private Retirement and Insurance Plans," *Monthly Labor Review,* XCV (July 1972), 15–19.

Blechman, Barry M., Edward M. Gramlich, and Robert W. Hartman, *Setting National Priorities: The 1976 Budget* (Washington: The Brookings Institution, 1975).

Bluestone, Barry, "The Personal Earnings Distribution: Individual and Institutional Determinants," Ph.D. thesis, University of Michigan, 1974.

---

[16] *Moreover, using older workers would make it likely that current wages would be quite different from the wages anticipated by those workers when they made their career decisions.*

Bowles, Samuel, "Schooling and Inequality from Generation to Generation," *Journal of Political Economy,* LXXX (supplement) (May/June 1972), S219–S255.

Doeringer, Peter, and Michael Piore, *Internal Labor Markets and Manpower Analysis* (Lexington, MA: D. C. Heath, 1971).

Duncan, Greg, "Earnings Functions and Nonpecuniary Benefits," *Journal of Human Resources,* XI (Fall 1976), 462–83.

———, and Frank Stafford, "Pace of Work, Unions, and Earnings in Blue Collar Jobs," unpublished manuscript, March 1977.

Freeman, Richard, and James Medoff, *What Do Unions Do?,* forthcoming. 1980.

Griliches, Zvi, "Wages of Very Young Men," *Journal of Political Economy,* LXXXIV (supplement) (Aug. 1976), S69–S86.

Hamermesh, Daniel S., "Economic Aspects of Job Satisfaction," in Orley Ashenfelter and Wallace Oates, eds., *Essays in Labor Market and Population Analysis* (New York: John Wiley and Sons, 1977), pp. 53–72.

Hause, John C., "The Covariance Structure of Earnings and the Job Training Hypothesis," unpublished manuscript, December 1973.

Kohen, Andrew I., "Determinants of Early Labor Market Success Among Young Men: Ability, Quantity, and Quality of Schooling," Ph.D. thesis, Ohio State University, 1973.

Lazear, Edward. "Schooling as a Wage Depressant," *Journal of Human Resources,* XII (Spring 1977), 164–76.

Lillard, Lee, "Inequality: Earnings vs. Human Wealth," *American Economic Review,* LXVII (March 1977), 42–53.

Lucas, Robert E. B., "Working Conditions, Wage-Rates, and Human Capital: A Hedonic Study," Ph.D. thesis, M.I.T., 1972.

———, "The Distribution of Job Characteristics," *Review of Economics and Statistics,* LVI (Nov. 1974), 530–40.

———, "Hedonic Wage Equations and Psychic Wages in the Returns to Schooling," *American Economic Review,* LXVII (Sept. 1977), 549–58.

Mincer, Jacob, "The Distribution of Labor Incomes: A Survey with Special Reference to the Human Capital Approach," *Journal of Economic Literature,* VIII (March 1970), 1–26.

———, *Schooling, Experience, and Earnings* (New York: Columbia University Press, 1974).

Mixon, J. Wilson, "The Minimum Wage and the Job Package," B.L.S. Working Paper No. 67, January 1977.

Pacific Consultants, *The Impact of Win II: A Longitudinal Evaluation,* processed, 1976.

Quinn, Joseph, "The Microeconomics of Early Retirement," Ph.D. thesis, M.I.T., 1975.

Reynolds, Lloyd G., *Labor Economics and Labor Relations,* sixth edition (Englewood Cliffs, N.J.: Prentice Hall, 1974).

Rosen, Harvey, "Taxes in a Labor Supply Model with Joint Wage-Hours Determination," *Econometrica,* XLIV (May 1976), 485–508.

Schiller, Bradley, and Randall Weiss, "Pensions and Wages: A Test of the Equalizing Differences Hypothesis," unpublished manuscript, January 1977.

Smith, R. S., "Compensating Wage Differentials and Hazardous Work," Technical Analysis Paper No. 5, Office of Evaluation, U. S. Department of Labor, August 1973.

Society of Actuaries, *1967 Occupation Study* (Chicago: Society of Actuaries, 1967).

Taubman, Paul, *Sources of Inequality in Earnings* (New York: American Elsevier Publishing Company, 1975).

Thaler, Richard, and Sherwin Rosen, "The Value of Saving a Life: Evidence from the Labor Market," in Nestor E. Terleckyj, ed., *Household Production and Consumption* (New York: N.B.E.R., 1975).

Toder, Eric, "The Supply of Public School Teachers to an Urban Metropolitan Area: A Possible Source of Discrimination in Education," *Review of Economics and Statistics,* LIV (Nov. 1972), 439–43.

U. S. Census Bureau, *Annual Survey of Manufacturers: 1968 and 1969* (Washington: U. S. Government Printing Office, 1973).

ABOUT THE AUTHOR

Charles Brown

Charles Brown is a professor of economics at the University of Michigan. He received his Ph.D. in economics from Harvard University in 1974. After one year as an assistant professor at Boston College, he spent a decade at the University of Maryland. Since 1985, he has been a professor of economics at the University of Michigan, where he now is chair of the department. Charlie Brown currently serves on the editorial boards of the *American Economic Review* and the *Journal of Economic Literature* and has been a research associate at the National Bureau of Economic Research since 1979. His main research interests include the economic effects of minimum wages, the survey measurement of labor market outcomes, the influence on pay of firm size, racial and gender disparities in the labor market, and the effects of affirmative action.

An important theme of Brown's work has been attempting to document and understand the wage premiums associated with working in firms of different sizes. These firm-size wage differentials tend to be quite substantial, with large firms paying considerably more than smaller firms do [see "The Employer Wage Size Effect," *Journal of Political Economy,* Oct. 1989 (with James Medoff)]. The firm-size wage differential appears to be both sizable and omnipresent. In particular, it remains even after adjusting for observable measures of worker quality, industry, occupation, unionization, and working conditions. The firm-size wage premium remains a well-established fact that awaits a link with a compelling theoretical explanation.

In an often-cited article, Brown (with Curtis Gilroy and Andrew Kohen) wrote an important survey summarizing the literature to that time about the employment and unemployment effects of minimum wages (see "The Effect of Minimum Wage on Employment and Unemployment," *Journal of Economic Literature,* June 1982). Brown's survey quickly became the consensus professional view that minimum wages had modest negative (positive) effects on employment (unemployment). For example, they concluded that the estimated effects on teenage employment (the most studied population group) implied that a 10% increase in the minimum wage reduced employment by 1 percent to 3 percent.

A third theme of Brown's research concerns the quality and accuracy of measurement of incomes and work in surveys. To assess the quality of measurement, Brown and his colleagues validated survey reports in the Panel Study of Income Dynamics (PSID) against reports obtained from a single firm (see "Evidence on the Validity of Cross-Sectional and Longitudinal Labor Market Data on Earnings," *Journal of Labor Economics,* July 1994). On the whole, their evaluations are reasonably positive. Annual earnings, as well as its first difference, are reported with high accuracy. However, considerably more bias exists in derived measures of hourly wages, especially when computed by dividing earnings by hours worked.

Longitudinal Analyses of the Effects of Trade Unions

RICHARD B. FREEMAN

Harvard University and California Institute of Technology

This paper examines how measurement error biases longitudinal estimates of union effects. It develops numerical examples, statistical models, and econometric estimates which indicate that measurement error is a major problem in longitudinal data sets, so that longitudinal analyses do not provide the research panacea for determining the effects of unionism (or other economic forces) some have suggested. There are three major findings: (1) The difference between the cross-section and longitudinal estimates is attributable in large part to random error in the measurement of who changes union status. Given modest errors of measurement, of the magnitudes observed, and a moderate proportion of workers changing union status, also of the magnitudes observed, measurement error biases estimated effects of unions downward by substantial amounts. (2) Longitudinal analysis of the effects of unionism on nonwage and wage outcomes tends to confirm the significant impact of unionism found in cross-section studies, with the longitudinal estimates of both nonwage and wage outcomes lower in the longitudinal analysis than in the cross-section analysis of the same data set. (3) The likely upward bias of cross-section estimates of the effect of unions and the likely downward bias of longitudinal estimates suggest that, under reasonable conditions, the two sets of estimates bound the "true" union impact posited in standard models of what unions do.

But union members are different from nonmembers in unobserved ways, biasing your estimates. You should . . . make a selectivity bias correction . . . simultaneously determine union status and economic outcomes . . . develop an unobservables model . . . USE LONGITUDINAL DATA. [Archetypical comment on virtually any study of the economic effects of unionism, or suitably modified, on any other empirical subject.]

I have benefited from comments of seminar participants at the University of Chicago, Caltech, Australia National University, and the University of California, and the suggestions of John Abowd, Gary Chamberlain, and H. Gregg Lewis.

Reprinted with permission from Richard Freeman, "Longitudinal Analysis of the Effects of Trade Unions," Journal of Labor Economics: (1984), vol. 2, no. 1, pp. 1–26. © 1984 by The University of Chicago.

Longitudinal data, which follow the same worker over time, offer researchers a potentially valuable way to examine often-raised objections to the findings of cross-section studies. Unlike complex "structural model" approaches to cross-section data problems, which often yield unstable and uninformative results (Freeman and Medoff 1981), longitudinal data offer a distinctively different "experiment" for uncovering the effects of changes in economic variables. In the case of unions, what is a more natural way to study what unions do than to compare economic outcomes for workers (firms) before and after they change union status?

This paper presents a critical analysis of the "natural experiment." In contrast to the archetypical comment cited above, it argues that longitudinal analyses do not provide a research panacea for determining the effects of unionism (or other economic forces). The main reason for this is the substantial impact of measurement or misclassification error of the union (other economic) variable on longitudinal work.

The paper is divided into four sections. Section I develops briefly the statistical models used in this (and other) longitudinal investigations of what unions do. Section II examines the effect of measurement error in union status on estimated effects of unionism in cross-section and longitudinal studies. Section III presents the results of estimating the effect of unionism on outcomes in four longitudinal and cross-section data sets. In contrast to other empirical analyses using longitudinal data, it treats two market outcomes which are at the center of the "voice-response" face of unionism, dispersion of wages and provision of fringe benefits, as well as wages. Section IV considers the argument that cross-section and longitudinal estimates of union effects "bound" the true impact of unionism.

There are three basic findings: (1) The difference between the cross-section and longitudinal estimates is attributable in large part to random error in the measurement of who changes union status. Given modest errors of measurement, of the magnitudes observed, and a moderate proportion of workers changing union status, also of the magnitudes observed, measurement error biases downward estimated effects of unions by substantial amounts. (2) Longitudinal analysis of the effects of unionism on nonwage and wage outcomes tends to confirm the significant impact of unionism found in cross-section studies, with the longitudinal estimates of both nonwage and wage outcomes lower in the longitudinal analysis than in the cross-section analysis of the same data set. (3) The likely upward bias of cross-section estimates of the effect of unions and the likely downward bias of longitudinal estimates suggests that, under reasonable conditions, the two sets of estimates bound the "true" union impact posited in standard models of what unions do.

All told, the paper concludes that because of measurement error and likely selectivity of who changes union status, longitudinal analysis is a useful tool for "checking on" the result of cross-section studies but may very well yield worse estimates of the parameters of interest.

I. LONGITUDINAL MODELS OF WHAT UNIONS DO

The standard cross-section analysis of the impact of collective bargaining on the economic outcome or behavior of individual workers (or firms) involves a multivariate statistical analysis of an equation of the form

$$O_i = a + bU_i + cX_i + u_i, \tag{1}$$

where O_i = outcome for person i, U_i = dichotomous unionization variable (1 = covered, 0 = not covered), X_i = control variables (education, sex) assumed constant over time, and u_i = error term. The recurrent objection to estimates based on (1) is that because of selectivity of union workers u_i is likely to be positively correlated with U_i, leading to an overstatement of the union effect. Since, as Abowd and Farber (1982) have stressed, who gets a union job results from the decisions of both employers and workers, the selectivity argument depends on whose decision dominates the hiring process. In the case of wages it is generally assumed that, given high union wages, firms select more able workers from the queue facing them, producing $E(u_i U_i) > 0$. In the case of nonwage outcomes, it is often claimed that workers sort themselves in such a way that those who have strong desires for union-type work conditions and modes of compensation (and would thus obtain more of those outcomes in nonunion settings than the randomly chosen worker) choose union jobs. In this case firms either are indifferent or prefer those workers as well (since they will be more satisfied).

Longitudinal data provide a way to deal with the correlation between unionism and the error term. Assuming that the part of u_i that is correlated with U_i is an individual effect constant over time, so that $u_{it} = \alpha_i + \epsilon_{it}$ with $E(\epsilon_{it} U_{it}) = 0$, addition of individual constants (which can be viewed as a form of differencing) will eliminate the correlation between u_{it} and U_{it}. In a two-period linear model one obtains

$$\Delta O_{it} = b\Delta U_{it} + \Delta \epsilon_{it}, \tag{2}$$

where ΔU_{it} takes the values $-1, 0, 1$. A multivariate analysis of (2) will yield the desired b as long as the change in union status is properly measured and is uncorrelated with the change in the random part of the error term.

Equation (2) can be readily generalized to exploit more fully the longitudinal data by allowing different changes in union status to have different effects on wages. In particular, we can allow changes in outcomes to differ among workers who join unions, leave unions, stay union, and stay nonunion:

$$\Delta O_{it} = \alpha_1 UU + \alpha_2 UN + \alpha_3 NU + \alpha_4 NN + \Delta \epsilon_{it}, \tag{3}$$

where UU, UN, NU, and NN are dummy variables that take the values 1 or 0 depending on the union status in the two periods: $UU = 1$, if union in both periods; $UN = 1$, if union in period 1, nonunion in period 2; $NU = 1$, if nonunion in period 1, union in period 2; $NN = 1$, if nonunion in each period; and where the constant term has been suppressed.

Equation (3) shows that the before/after nature of the experiment permits calculation of three different union effects, each answering a somewhat different question: (1) What happens to nonunion workers who join unions compared to nonunion workers who remain nonunion (obtained as the difference between the coefficients on *NU* and *NN*, *NU − NN*, for short)? (2) What happens to union workers who leave the union compared to those who remain union (*UN − UU*)? (3) Among workers who change, what happens to those who join a union as compared to those who leave a union ((*UN − NU*)/2 or some other such average)?

It can be readily seen that when union differential is constant over time (*UU = NN*) and when the effects of joining and leaving unions are the same in absolute value (|*NU − NN*| = |*UN − UU*|), equation (3) collapses into equation (2). Less restrictively, if the only reasons for (3) to differ from (2) are changes in union differentials over time, the estimated parameters will fulfill the equality in absolute values given above; that is, the only difference between the gains of workers who join unions versus those who leave is the changed union differential over time.

Equations (2) and (3) can be readily generalized to analyze data covering more than two periods. The natural extension of (2) is to a fixed effects model with individual constants (differences from mean values) for each person. The natural extension of (3) is to a model with dummy variables for all possible classifications of changes in status. For ease of exposition in this paper I treat only the two-period case.

INTERPRETING LONGITUDINAL RESULTS

Assuming that $E(\alpha_i U_i) > 0$, the longitudinal estimates of union impact should be lower than cross-section estimates. In fact, empirical analyses of wages do indeed show a lower impact of unionism in longitudinal than in cross-section data, providing support for the "omitted ability bias" model given above (among the panel studies are Duncan 1977, 1979; Brown 1980; Mellow 1981; Mincer 1981; Chamberlain 1982). In Chamberlain's analysis, for example, addition of individual constants reduces the union coefficient by 32%–44%, indicating "a substantial heterogeneity (ability) bias." The union wage effect still stands, but its magnitude is smaller than in traditional cross-section analysis. As the archetypical comment at the beginning of the paper indicates, many have interpreted the smaller longitudinal estimates as providing better estimates of the true union effects than the larger cross-section estimates. Indeed, under the fixed-effect assumptions that changes in union status are properly measured and that selectivity of changers does not produce a correlation of the error in the change-in-outcome equation with changes in status, the longitudinal estimate is unbiased.

Are these assumptions likely to be valid in empirical work? What does their violation do to longitudinal estimates of union effects? This paper argues that neither assumption is likely to be valid and that, under reasonable conditions, measurement error and selectivity of changers will bias *downward* longitudinal estimates of union effects. Because in practice measurement error appears to be the principal econometric problem in analysis of longitudinal data, I focus largely on the measurement error issue.

II. THE PROBLEM OF MEASUREMENT ERROR

In cross-section studies of unionism, one generally ignores measurement error in the union status variable on the assumption that only a small number of workers are likely to be misclassified and thus that any bias in the estimated union coefficient due to measurement error is modest. Misclassification of a small number of workers will, however, produce a much larger error in longitudinal than in cross-section analysis and thus cannot be readily ignored. The reason for the greater error is twofold. On the one hand, random misclassification of workers in two periods will produce a larger number of misclassified workers than random misclassification in one period. On the other hand, by obtaining information on union effects from generally small numbers of changers, the longitudinal analysis will contain a smaller number of correct observations. As a result the proportion of observations in error will be much larger in the longitudinal analysis than in the cross-section analysis, producing a larger bias.

A numeric example illustrates the dramatically different effect of modest misclassification on cross-section and longitudinal estimates. Assume we have a sample of 100 workers, of whom 25 are union members and 75 are not. Assume measurement error is such that 2 union workers are misclassified and 2 nonunion workers are misclassified.[1] Then we have the situation shown in table 1A. If the true value of the outcome variable is 1.00 for nonunion workers and 1.30 for union workers, our estimated means would be 1.28 and 1.01, giving an estimated differential of 27%, a value that is 10% below the true impact of unionism.

Assume that 20 workers switch union status in the period, 10 joining and 10 leaving unions. With 4 workers misclassified in each period, so that 8% of union workers and 2.7% of nonunion workers are incorrectly classified, it can be demonstrated (see eq. [12]) that the longitudinal data set will be approximately as shown in table 1B. There are three points to note about this data set. First, the longitudinal estimates of the union effect from *NU* and *UN* comparisons are the same: 1.25/1.03 or 21%, which is 30% below the true impact of unionism—an attenuation that is three times as large as that in the cross-section analysis. Second, measurement error produces a pattern of differences in levels of wages between the four sets: for example, workers measured as leaving unions have a lower wage in period 1 than workers who remain union, workers measured as joining unions have a higher wage in period 1 than workers who remain nonunion, and so on. Third, the best estimate of the difference in wages in the data is the comparison of the mean level of wages for the *UU* set with the mean level for the *NN* set, which yields essentially the correct 30% differential. For this to be the best estimate of the union effect, however, workers in the two sets would have to be otherwise identical, contrary to the assumed $E(a_i U_i) > 0$.

---

[1] *The assumption that equal numbers of workers are misclassified implies that the observed proportion union is an unbiased estimate of the true proportion. It is a useful simplifying assumption that appears consistent with actual measurement error (see table 3) but is not critical to the numeric example or to the ensuing statistical analysis.*

TABLE 1

EXAMPLE OF MEASUREMENT ERROR EFFECT
A. CROSS-SECTION DATA SET

Observed	True	Number
U	U	23
U	N	2
N	U	2
N	N	73

B. LONGITUDINAL DATA SET

	Observed	Consisting of True	With Observed Means of 1	2
UU	13	13 UU	1.30	1.30
UN	12	9 UN, 1 UU, 2 NN	1.25	1.03
NU	12	9 NU, 1 UU, 2 NN	1.03	1.25
NN	63	61 NN, 1 UN, 1 NU	1.004	1.004

More formally, I compare what measurement error in the dichotomous union status variable does to the estimated union coefficient in cross-section equation (1) to what measurement error in the change in union status variable does to the estimated union coefficient in longitudinal equation (2). Because of the restricted values of union status or change in status, the measurement error is correlated with the workers' true status, so that the standard measurement error in regression analysis must be modified, along lines set out by Aigner (1973) and by Marquis et al. (1981).[2]

Consider first measurement error in a dichotomous variable. Let M = measured union status, U = actual status, and e = error. Then

$$M = U + e \tag{4}$$

where possible errors are: -1, if a person's true status is union ($U = 1$), producing a nonunion classification ($M = 0$), and 1, if a person's true status is nonunion ($U = 0$), producing a union classification ($M = 1$).

Now let r_U be the probability that a union worker is misclassified and r_N be the probability that a nonunion worker is misclassified and $1 - r_U$ and $1 - r_N$ be the corresponding probabilities that the workers are correctly classified. Then the relation between the expected error and the true status is

---

[2] Much of what follows is based on Marquis et al. (1981). I have also benefited from Aigner (1973).

$$E(e) = r_N + (-r_U - r_N)U, \tag{5}$$

so that from (4)

$$E(M) = r_N + (1 - r_U - r_N)U. \tag{6}$$

Hence we can write M as

$$M = r_N + (1 - r_U - r_N)U + \nu \tag{6'}$$

where ν is a random variable with mean zero and variance σ_ν^2.

The effect of regressing an outcome O on M rather than on U can be evaluated by substituting (6') into the true equation (1) and treating the random component of measurement error as an omitted variable. Substitution yields

$$O_i = (b/1 - r_U - r_N)M_i + cX_i - b\nu_i/(1 - r_U - r_N) + u_i, \tag{7}$$

where I have suppressed the constant term.

The bias on the coefficient on M_i from omitting ν_i is the coefficient of ν_i in (7) times the regression coefficient of ν_i on M_i, holding the X's fixed. Assuming, for ease of presentation, that M is uncorrelated with the X's in (7), we obtain the coefficient of ν_i on M from (6') as σ_ν^2/σ_M^2, the random measurement error component of the measured variance. Then the regression for (7) yields for the coefficient on M_1 ($\hat{b}$)

$$\begin{aligned}
E(\hat{b}) &= \left[b/(1 - r_U - r_N)\right]\left(1 - \sigma_\nu^2/\sigma_M^2\right) \\
&= \left[b/(1 - r_U - r_N)\right](1 - r_U - r_N)^2 \sigma_U^2/\sigma_M^2 \\
&= b(1 - r_U - r_N)\sigma_U^2/\sigma_M^2.
\end{aligned} \tag{8}$$

Since union status is binomial, $\sigma_U^2 = \bar{U}(1 - \bar{U})$, where $\bar{U}$ = mean proportion union. If, as in our numeric example, we assume that $\bar{M} = \bar{U}$, which holds whenever $r_U U = r_N(1 - U)$, equation (8) simplifies to

$$E(\hat{b}) = b(1 - r_U - r_N). \tag{9}$$

When M is correlated with X (r_{MX}) and when the random component of the measured error is independent of $X[E(\nu X) = 0]$, the comparable equation is

$$E(\hat{b}) = b\frac{\left[1 - r_U - (r_N)\right] - b_{UX}b_{XM}}{1 - r_{MX}^2} \tag{10}$$

where b_{UX}, and b_{XM} are the simple regression coefficients. Here the bias depends on the relation between the X's and both observed and true union status. If we assume that the random component of the measurement error is independent of $X[b_{UX} = 0]$ then, noting that $b_{UX}b_{XM} = r_{MX}^2$, (10) becomes

$$E(\hat{b}) = b \frac{(1 - r_U - r_N) - r_{MX}^2}{1 - r_{MX}^2}. \tag{10'}$$

Since the bias in (10') is greater than the bias in (9), we conclude that as long as the random component of measurement error is uncorrelated with the X's the cross-section estimate of the union effect is biased downward by at least $1 - r_U - r_N$ percent.[3]

Turning to the effect of measurement error on longitudinal estimates, we proceed in a similar manner to the preceding analysis. In this case, the equation relating measured and true changes in union status is

$$\Delta M = \Delta U + e, \tag{11}$$

where ΔM = measured change in union status $(=1, 0, -1)$, ΔU = true change $(=1, 0, -1)$, and e = error $(2, 1, 0, -1, -2)$.

When r_U and r_N are independent over time, the relationship between the true changes and the measured changes can be written as functions of r_U and r_N and of the true changes from one state to the other T_{ij} $(i, j = U$ or $N)$ as follows:

$$
\begin{aligned}
M_{NN} &= (1 - r_N)(1 - r_N)T_{NN} + (1 - r_N)r_U T_{NU} + (1 - r_U)r_N T_{UN} + r_U r_U T_{UU} + \nu_{NN} \\
M_{NU} &= (1 - r_N)r_U T_{NN} + (1 - r_U)(1 - r_N)T_{NU} + r_N r_U T_{UN} + (1 - r_U)r_U T_{NN} + \nu_{NU} \\
M_{UN} &= (1 - r_N)r_N T_{NN} + r_N r_U T_{NU} + (1 - r_U)(1 - r_N)T_{UN} + (1 - r_U)r_U T_{UU} + \nu_{UN} \\
M_{UU} &= r_N r_N T_{NN} + (1 - r_U)r_N T_{NU} + (1 - r_U)r_N T_{UN} + (1 - r_U)(1 - r_U)T_{UU} + \nu_{UU},
\end{aligned}
\tag{12}
$$

where ν_{ij} is a random error.

Equation (12) is the critical equation in our analysis. The three terms in each equation in which an r_i or r_j is multiplied by a $(1 - r_j)$ represent misclassification errors. The terms in which $(1 - r_i)$ is multiplied by $(1 - r_j)$ represent true changes in the measured observations. As before, the error term can take on only a limited set of values, dependent on the value of the true change. The relation between the true values of ΔU and the possible error is defined as in table 2 below. But from this array it can be seen that

---

[3] We ask if the following inequality holds:

$$1 - r_U - r_N > \frac{1 - r_U - r_N - r_{MX}^2}{1 - r_{MX}^2}.$$

Multiply by $(1 - r_{MX}^2)$ to obtain $(1 - r_U - r_N)(1 - r_{MX}^2) > 1 - r_U - r_N - r_{MX}^2$. But simplifying we obtain $(r_U + r_N)r_{MX}^2 > 0$, which proves the inequality.

TABLE 2

RELATION BETWEEN TRUE VALUE OF ΔU AND POSSIBLE ERROR

	Frequency of Error Assuming True Value of ΔU		
Error	1	0	−1
2	0	0	$r_U r_N$
1	0	$(1-r_N)r_N+(1-r_U)r_U$	$r_N(1-r_U)+r_U(1-r_N)$
0	$1-(r_N+r_U-r_U r_N)$	$1-2((1-r_N)r_N-(1-r_U)r_U)$	$1-(r_N+r_U-r_U r_N)$
−1	$r_N(1-r_U)+r_U(1-r_N)$	$(1-r_N)r_N+(1-r_U)r_U$	0
−2	$r_U r_N$	0	0

$$E(e) = -(r_U + r_N)\Delta U, \tag{13}$$

so that

$$e = -(r_U + r_N)\Delta U + \nu \tag{13'}$$

and

$$\Delta M = -(r_U + r_N)\Delta U + \nu, \tag{14}$$

where ν is a random measurement error. Substituting (14) into (2) and applying the omitted variable bias formula for omission of ν yields for the expected value of the estimated longitudinal impact of unionism $(\hat{b}_L)$,

$$E(\hat{b}_L) = b/(1 - r_U - r_N)(1 - \lambda), \tag{15}$$

where λ is the ratio of random variance (σ_ν^2) to measured variance $(\sigma_{\Delta M}^2)$. From (14) $\sigma_{\Delta M}^2 = (1 - r_U - r_N)^2 \sigma_{\Delta U}^2 + \nu^2$, yielding

$$E(\hat{b}_L) = b(1 - r_U - r_N)\sigma_{\Delta U}^2 / \sigma_{\Delta M}^2. \tag{16}$$

According to (16) the downward bias in the longitudinal analysis will exceed the downward bias in the cross-section analysis as long as $\sigma_{\Delta U}^2 < \sigma_{\Delta M}^2$. Calculating variances we find that

$$\sigma_{\Delta U}^2 = (T_{UN} + T_{NU}) + (T_{UN} - T_{NU})^2 \tag{17}$$

and

$$\sigma_{\Delta M}^2 = (M_{NU} + M_{UN}) + (M_{UN} - M_{NU})^2. \tag{17'}$$

For ease of analysis, assume that the true mean of unionism, $\bar{U}$, is constant over time and that there is no constant response bias, $E(\bar{M}) = \bar{U}$. But it can be shown (Marquis et al. 1981, p. 101) that M_{UN} depends on T_{UN},

$$E(M_{UN}) = (1 - r_U - r_N)^2 T_{UN} + \delta_M^2$$

$$E(M_{NU}) = (1 - r_U - r_N)^2 T_{NU} + \delta_M^2,$$

(18)

where $\delta_M^2 = (1 - r_U)r_U\bar{U} + (1 - r_N)r_N(1 - \bar{U})$, the average variance of the measurement error.

With constant $\bar{U}$, $T_{UN} = T_{NU}$. Now let T_C be the proportion of workers changing union status in the sample ($T_C = T_{UN} + T_{NU}$). Then (17) simplifies to

$$\sigma_{\Delta M}^2 = T_C,$$

(19)

while substitution of (18) into (17′) yields

$$\sigma_{\Delta M}^2 = (1 - r_U - r_N)^2 T_C + 2\delta_M^2.$$

(19′)

Equation (19′) is an approximation due to the absence of terms reflecting the equation-specific error terms (ν_{UN}, ν_{NU} of [12]).

The key question is, will $\sigma_{\Delta U}^2$ always be less than $\sigma_{\Delta M}^2$? Examination of (19)–(19′) shows the answer to be negative. When measurement error is large so that $(1 - r_U - r_N)^2$ is close to zero and when T_C is large $\sigma_{\Delta U}^2 > \sigma_{\Delta M}^2$. For example, let $r_U = r_N = .40$ and $\bar{U} (= r_U/r_U + r_N) = .50$. Then $\sigma_{\Delta M}^2 = .04 \, T_C + .48$, so that for $T_C > .5 \, \sigma_{\Delta U}^2 > \sigma_{\Delta M}^2$. In this case, measurement error biases the cross-section estimate more than the longitudinal estimate.

On the other hand, when measurement error is modest—as in our earlier numeric example—$\sigma_{\Delta U}^2$ will be less than $\sigma_{\Delta M}^2$ for moderate values of T_C, producing a greater downward bias in the longitudinal calculation. Since the effect of measurement error on longitudinal as opposed to cross-section analysis thus depends on the magnitudes of the various parameters in the measurement error formula, I turn next to estimates of the critical magnitudes.

EVIDENCE ON MEASUREMENT ERROR

The first parameters needed to evaluate the importance of measurement error are the actual errors themselves—r_U and r_N. I have identified two surveys which provide the type of information needed to estimate r_U and r_N: separate measures of the union status of the same workers at essentially the same time. The first survey is a special supplement to the January 1977 Current Population Survey, which asked workers whether or not they were covered by collective bargaining and then asked their employers the same question. The second is the May 1979 Current Population Survey, which asked workers about their collective bargaining status on the "dual job" supplement and on the "pension" supplement. While there are differences in the timing of the questions in both surveys, the time differences are sufficiently slight so that differences in answers provide us with a reasonable first-order approximation to random measurement error in union status.

Table 3 tabulates the responses to these two surveys. It shows that while r_U and r_N are, as stated, modest in value, they are sufficiently nonnegligible to produce potentially large response error bias in longitudinal data. In the 1979 CPS sample 6.4%–8.1% of workers in the union category and 1.9%–2.3% of those in the nonunion category are misclassified, giving a value of 8.7%–10.0% for the critical $r_U + r_N$ figure. In the 1977 matched employer-employee sample, 7.5% of workers in the union category and 2.3% of those in the nonunion category are misclassified giving a 9.8% value to $r_U + r_N$.

To check whether the differences in classification on the samples can, in fact, be interpreted as resulting from random measurement error, I have estimated union wage equations for the sample of workers for whom there are conflicting estimates of union status and for the sample for whom there are no such conflicts. If the conflict in responses is due to random misclassification, one would expect no significant union wage effect for persons in the sample in which estimates conflict, compared to a sizable union effect in the sample for which there are no conflicts in whether a person is union or not. As can be seen in the unnumbered table below, estimates of standard log wage equations (with the usual demographic and human capital controls) for the samples yield the expected results where the + before the coefficient reflects the change in sign depending on which estimate of unionism is used as the independent variable.[4]

	Union Status	
	Agreement	Disagreement
January 1977 sample estimated union coefficient (standard error)	.26 (.02)	±.05 (.07)
May–June 1979 sample estimated union coefficient (standard error)	.21 (.01)	+.06 (.07)

Finally, taking the magnitudes of the estimated misclassification errors in table 3 as valid, we can apply the formulas given earlier to evaluate the impact of measurement error on regression estimates of union impacts, given different proportions of workers truly changing union status. As can be seen in table 4, when only 5% of workers change status the longitudinal estimate is less than half the cross-section estimate and just 40% of the true b, whereas if 15%–20% change status the estimates are closer together. Consistent with the preceding analysis, when the proportion changing union status rises to relatively high levels, the longitudinal estimates exceed the cross-section estimates.

Table 5 turns to the next obvious issue: the proportion of workers who actually change union status in a longitudinal data set. It examines the proportions *measured* as changing

---

[4] *In the January survey there are two reported wages: one from the individuals, the other from employers. I have used the wage reported by the individuals in this analysis.*

TABLE 3

MISCLASSIFICATION OF UNION STATUS ON TWO SURVEYS
A. CURRENT POPULATION SURVEY, MAY 1979

Covered by Collective Bargaining on Main Survey	Covered by Collective Bargaining on Pension Supplement		
	Yes	No	Total
Yes	3,976	272	4,248
Row (%)	93.6	6.4	
Column (%)	91.9	1.9	23.2
No	321	13,688	14,009
Row (%)	2.3	97.7	
Column (%)	8.1	98.1	76.8
Total	4,297	13,950	18,257
Row (%)	23.5	76.5	100

B. EMPLOYER—EMPLOYEE MATCHED SURVEY, JANUARY 1977

Covered by Collective Bargaining, by Employers	Covered by Collective Bargaining by Employees or Household Respondent		
	Yes	No	Total
Yes	707	57	764
Row (%)	92.5	7.5	
Column (%)	92.5	2.3	23.2
No	57	2,476	2,533
Row (%)	2.3	47.8	76.8
Column (%)	7.5	97.8	
Total	764	2,533	3,297
Row (%)	23.2	76.8	100

Source. A, tabulated from May matched sample, CPS; B, tabulated from January 1977 Employee Employer Matched Sample.

TABLE 4

POTENTIAL IMPACT OF MEASUREMENT ERROR ON ESTIMATES OF UNION EFFECTS

Proportion of Workers Truly Changing Union Status (%)	Estimated Bias in Cross-Section Estimate (a)	Estimated Bias in Longitudinal Estimate (b)	Relative Bias (a/b)
5	.90	.40	.45
10	.90	.59	.66
15	.90	.70	.78
20	.90	.77	.86
25	.90	.82	.91
30	.90	.86	.95
80	.90	1.00	1.12

Source. Calculated using formulas (9) and (19′) assuming $r_U = 7.5\%$, $r_N = 2.5\%$, and $\bar{U} = .25$, so $\delta_M^2 = .036$.

TABLE 5

PROPORTION OF WORKERS MEASURED AS CHANGING UNION STATUS IN DIVERSE SURVEYS

Status	Survey (Sample Size)			
	May 1974–75 CPS (7,887)	Michigan Panel Survey of Income Dynamics 1970–79 (635)	National Longitudinal Survey 1970–78 (1,905)	Quality of Employment Survey 1970–77 (543)
NN	.714	.400	.609	.595
NU	.028	.098	.160	.057
UN	.034	.094	.087	.101
UU	.225	.408	.149	.247
M_C(*UN* or *NU*)	.062	.192	.242	.158
$\bar{U}_1$ (*UU* or *UN*)	.259	.502	.231	.348
$\bar{U}_2$ (*UU* or *NU*)	.253	.506	.309	.304
Estimated T_C (true *UN* or *NU*)	. . .	.117	.210	.091

Source. Tabulated from relevant survey estimates of true *UN* or *NU* as described in the text with $r_U + r_N = .10$ and that $r_N/(r_U + r_N)$ equal the average rate of unionization in the period; thus, for the NLS, I set $r_N/(r_U + r_N) = 1/2 (.231 + .309) = .27$ and obtain $r_N = .027$, $r_U = .073$. The same procedure is used for the other data sets. Note the Michigan PSID includes all of the "poverty" sample, producing a large proportion of union workers.

status in four major longitudinal surveys: the May 1974–75 Current Population Survey (CPS), the National Longitudinal Survey of Men Aged 14–24 in 1966 (NLS) for the period 1970–78, the Michigan Panel Survey of Income Dynamics (PSID) for 1970–79, and the Quality of Employment Panel Survey (QES), 1973–77, and also records estimates of the true proportion changing. The estimates of the true proportions changing are obtained by summing the expected values of M_{UN} and M_{NU} from (18), which yields

$$E(M_C) = (1 - r_U - r_N)^2 T_C + 2\delta_M^2, \qquad (20)$$

where T_C is the proportion of true changers, and solving for T_C. In the cases where $\bar{U}$ changes over time, equation (20) is still applicable because the impact of changes in *U* has offsetting effects on $E(M_{UN})$ and $E(M_{NU})$.[5]

---

[5] *Specifically, the formulas with changes in the value of U between the periods are (Marquis et al. 1981, p. 101)* $E(M_{NU}) = r_U(-\Delta U) + (1 - r_U - r_N)^2 T_{NU} + \delta_U^2$ *and* $E(M_{UN}) = r_U(\Delta U) + (1 - r_U - r_N)^2 T_{UN} + \delta_U^2$, *so that the sum becomes* $E(M_C) = E(M_{NU}) + E(M_{UN}) = (1 - r_U - r_N)^2 T_C + 2\delta_U^2$.

In three of the samples, the calculations yielded reasonable estimates of the true proportion changing, and those figures are reported in the table. In the May CPS sample, however, the formulas yielded no estimate, because under the assumptions, measurement error by itself should have produced virtually the proportion of changers observed.

The key finding in table 5 is that whether one looks at the measured proportion of changers or at the estimated true proportion the values are on the low side of the figures in table 4. The measured changes (M_C) range from 6.2% (CPS) to 24.2% (NLS) while the "true" proportion changing varies from 9.1% (QES) to 21% (NLS). With these changes, measurement error biases downward the longitudinal estimates by 14% (NLS) to 29% (PSID) to 34% (QES) and by even larger amounts in the CPS, according to the estimates in table 2.

In sum, given measurement errors in union status that produce values of $r_U + r_N$ of about .10, and true proportions of workers changing status below .20, the analysis in this section suggests that longitudinal estimates of the effect of unionism on economic outcomes will be below cross-section estimates and, more important, below the true effect of unionism as well.

III. COMPARISONS OF LONGITUDINAL AND CROSS-SECTION ESTIMATES OF UNION EFFECTS

As noted Section I, there have been several studies of union wage effects using longitudinal data. These studies have found lower union effects than are found in comparable cross-section studies. By contrast, while there is a large and growing cross-section literature on the effects of unions on outcomes other than level of wages, such as dispersion of wages, labor turnover (notably quit behavior), fringe benefits, and the like (see Freeman and Medoff [1981] for a summary), there has been little longitudinal evidence regarding the effect of union membership on these outcomes. This section provides evidence that for two important "nonwage" outcomes, the dispersion of wages and fringe benefits, and for wages, longitudinal analysis yields smaller estimated union effects than does cross-section analysis, but that the estimated effects are still fairly sizable and economically significant. This finding leads us to reject criticisms that the results of cross-section studies of the nonwage outcomes are more subject to "heterogeneity" or fixed effects bias than are the results of wage studies. As measurement error should reduce the estimated impact of unionism on all outcomes, this is consistent with the models given in Section II.

The analysis treats the four data sets set out in table 5. In each case I sought the largest possible sample for which the outcome variables and the union variable were reported. In the Michigan PSID sample, in which one has a number of possible years to examine, I report the results from a relatively long time span, 1970–79, though I examined shorter spans as well. In contrast to some studies, I include all of the special "poverty" sample as well as the random sample in the survey. In the NLS sample I also chose a relatively long time span to examine. As the May CPS sample covers one year and the QES covers three years, the result is significant variation in the time span covered and, as seen in table 5, significant variation in the proportion of persons changing union status as well.

WAGES

Table 6 presents the results of my longitudinal analysis of union wage effects in the four data sets.[6] It records the log wages for the four union-change groups before and after the change, the change in log wages, and the implied union effects and, for comparison, the cross-section estimates of the union wage effect in the same data. While there is some variation among the three types of longitudinal estimates, the general pattern of results is clear: the longitudinal calculations yield lower estimates of the union effects than do cross-section calculations. As many longitudinal analyses focus on the difference in changes in wages between those joining and those leaving unions, the most significant comparison is between the $(NU - UN)/2$ estimates and the cross-section estimates.[7] Consistent with the results of Mellow (1981), they show a great reduction in the estimated union effect in the May 1974–75 CPS. As this is the group with the smallest measured proportion of changers, this is to be expected from measurement error. There is, however, one aberrant case in the table: in the QES, the $(NU - UN)/2$ comparison yields a larger rather than smaller estimated union effect than does the cross-section analysis. In this case, the cross-section difference in wages was only moderately above the longitudinal difference (UU and NN differ by .17 and .15) so that inclusion of regression controls reduced the cross-section estimate to the lower level. Note also that the pattern of differences in the log wages themselves, before and after the change, are also generally, although not always, in line with the impact of measurement error. The before-change log wages show that union leavers have lower wages than union stayers, which agrees with the Section II numerical example. The after-change log wages also show that union joiners have lower wages than union stayers in all cases. By contrast, the before and after comparisons of changers with nonunion stayers show a less consistent pattern.

Finally, if we assume that the estimates of measurement error used in table 5 apply to these data, we can calculate the proportion of the difference between cross-section/longitudinal coefficients due to measurement error. To do this we estimate the relative bias of longitudinal to cross-section estimates from table 4, using the estimated true proportion of changers from table 5, and multiply the resulting statistic by the cross-section estimate in table 6. This yields .24 for the NLS and .16 for the PSID as the expected estimates from

---

[6] *The measurement of wages varies across the data sets. In the CPS I measure wages by the ratio of usual weekly earnings to usual weekly hours; in the PSID, I use average hourly wages; in the NLS, I use the reported hourly rate; while in the QES wages are annual earnings from work divided by hours worked times 52.*

[7] *In regression analyses which impose NU = UN, the coefficient is a weighted average dependent on relative numbers changing status. The reader can readily calculate weighted averages for contrast, if desired.*

TABLE 6

LOG WAGES, CHANGES IN LOG WAGES ASSOCIATED WITH CHANGING UNION STATUS, AND ESTIMATED UNION EFFECTS

Group and Survey	Log Wage			Group	Estimated Union Effects
	Before	After	Δ		
A. May CPS, 1974–75:					
NN	1.24	1.34	.10	NU − NN	.09
NU	1.28	1.47	.19	UU − UN	.08
UU	1.58	1.67	.09	(NU − UN)/2	.09
UN	1.46	1.47	.01	Cross-section	.19
B. National Longitudinal Survey of Young Men, 1970–78:					
NN	.97	1.84	.87	NU − NN	.12
NU	.94	1.93	.99	UU − UN	.09
UU	1.34	2.05	.71	(NU − UN)/2	.19
UN	1.22	1.84	.62	Cross-section	.28
C. Michigan PSID, 1970–79:					
NN	.95	1.61	.67	NU − NN	.08
NU	1.06	1.81	.75	UU − UN	.26
UU	1.29	2.02	.73	(NU − UN)/2	.14
UN	1.16	1.63	.47	Cross-section	.23
D. QES, 1973–77:					
NN	1.38	1.85	.48	NU − NN	.19
NU	1.24	1.91	.67	UU − UN	.11
UU	1.55	2.00	.45	(NU − UN)/2	.16
UN	1.35	1.70	.34	Cross-section	.14

Source. Calculated from the surveys. Cross-section estimates based on multivariate regression model with standard set of controls for demographic and human capital variables.

the longitudinal analyses, if measurement error were the only factor operating. Comparing these figures to the actual longitudinal estimates in table 6, we see that measurement error explains 44% (NLS) to 77% (PSID) of the cross-section/longitudinal differences. While further analysis is required to pin down the specifics of the misclassification effects in each data set, our analysis suggests that measurement error can explain much of the difference between cross-section and longitudinal estimates of union wage effects.

This conclusion, while at odds with the widely used fixed-effects interpretation of the difference between longitudinal and cross-section analysis, is consistent with recent evaluations by other researchers. Chowdhury and Nickell (1982), who correct for measurement error bias in standard covariance estimates by instrumenting unionization on lagged unionization (on the grounds that serial correlation in the U variable is strong but is absent from measurement error), found that a longitudinal estimate of the union effect of .10 increased to .30 in the instrumental analysis. Their conclusion was that "omitted quality variables bias the union effect upwards by about as much as measurement error problems bias it downwards and the 'old-style' cross section estimates are of the right order of magnitude after all." H . Gregg Lewis (1983), in an evaluation of the effect of measurement error on union wages estimates, has also reached a conclusion similar to mine.

DISPERSION OF WAGES

The proposition that trade union wage policies are designed to reduce inequality of wages within firms and across firms for workers doing similar work has a long history in labor economics, stretching back to the Webbs. Numerous cross-section comparisons of wage inequality have found that inequality is less in union than in nonunion settings (see, e.g., Hyclak 1977, 1979; Freeman 1980, 1982; Hirsch 1982; Plotnick 1992). Standard wage regressions provide corroborating evidence, showing that for the most part the impact of most wage-determining variables is smaller on the wages of union than on the wages of nonunion workers. The magnitude of the estimated union impact is sufficiently sizable to suggest that, despite the increase in dispersion due to union monopoly wage effects, unionism reduces overall inequality of wages.

Do comparisons of dispersions of wages in a longitudinal framework confirm the cross-section results? How much smaller, if at all, is the estimated union effect on dispersion? To answer these questions I have tabulated the standard deviation of the log of earnings for workers by their change in union status in the four data sets referred to earlier. The resulting calculations are given in table 7, which follows the same format as table 6. As can be seen, the longitudinal calculations confirm the cross-section finding of lower wage dispersion under unionism. Dispersion tends to fall when workers join unions and increase when they leave, confirming the reduction in dispersion under unionism. There are, however, notable differences in the magnitude and consistency of the effects by group, with $NU - NN$ and $(NU - UN)/2$ comparisons showing larger union effects than $UU - UN$ comparisons and with the PSID and QES showing more variable results than the other samples. To compare the longitudinal estimates to cross-section estimates, I have made some crude calculations of what a full cross-section analysis (which involves correcting observed differences in variances by observed differences in characteristics) might yield by reducing the difference in standard deviations between UU and NN workers in the before and after data by 30%, a figure consistent with a full analysis of May 1973–75 CPS data (Freeman 1980, table 4). Without the adjustment the impact of unionism on dispersion estimated with the longitudinal data is much smaller than the impact estimated with the cross-section data. With the adjustment, the longitudinal estimate is still noticeably smaller, by magnitudes comparable to those obtained in table 6 for wages.

TABLE 7

STANDARD DEVIATION OF LOG WAGES, CHANGES IN STANDARD DEVIATIONS ASSOCIATED WITH CHANGING UNION STATUS, AND ESTIMATED UNION EFFECTS

Group and Survey	Standard Deviation in Log Wages			Group	Estimated Union Effects
	Before	After	Δ		
A. May CPS 1974–75:					
NN	.59	.58	−.01	NU − NN	−.08
NU	.52	.43	−.09	UU − UN	−.05
UU	.38	.35	−.03	(NU − UN)/2	−.06
UN	.46	.48	.02	Cross-section	−.15
B. National Longitudinal Survey of Young Men, 1970–78:					
NN	.47	.53	.06	NU − NN	−.10
NU	.39	.35	−.04	UU − UN	−.13
UU	.29	.30	.01	(NU − UN)/2	−.09
UN	.32	.46	.14	Cross-section	−.14
C. Quality of Employment Survey, 1973–77:					
NN	.55	.55	.00	NU − NN	−.23
NU	.52	.32	−.20	UU − UN	.03
UU	.38	.36	−.02	(NU − UN)/2	−.07
UN	.54	.49	−.05	Cross-section	−.13
D. Michigan PSID 1970-79:					
NN	.46	.53	.07	NU − NN	−.15
NU	.45	.37	−.08	UU − UN	.01
UU	.31	.30	−.01	(NU − UN)/2	−.03
UN	.40	.38	−.02	Cross-section	−.13

Source. Tabulated from the various surveys. The cross-section effect is estimated by taking 70% of the difference in standard deviations between UU and NN (averaged for before and after). This is an approximate correction for differing characteristics of union and nonunion workers.

Finally, note that comparisons of the levels of the standard deviations among groups tell a stronger story than did the comparison of the levels of wages.[8] In the before data, workers who leave unions have larger dispersions than those who stay, and workers who join unions have larger dispersions than nonunion workers who remain nonunion. In the after data, workers joining unions have greater dispersion than workers who were always union members while workers leaving unions have less dispersion than workers who remain nonunion. While these patterns could be due to factors other than error in measuring union membership, they are consistent with a pure measurement error interpretation.

---

[8] *A full analysis of the effect of measurement error on dispersion differs somewhat from that of analysis of measurement error in the regression format, but the qualitative effects of error are the same.*

TABLE 8

NUMBERS OF FRINGES, AND PRESENCE OF PENSIONS, CHANGES IN NUMBERS OF FRINGES, AND PRESENCE OF PENSIONS ASSOCIATED WITH CHANGING UNION STATUS AND ESTIMATED UNION EFFECTS, QES, 1973–77

Group	Before	After	Δ	Group	Estimated Union Effects
Number of fringes:					
NN	3.01	2.56	−15%	NU − NN	32%
NU	2.59	3.02	17%	UU − UN	0%
UU	3.64	3.28	−10%	(NU − UN)/2	13%
UN	3.16	2.55	−10%	Cross-section	13%
Proportion of workers with pensions:					
NN	.65	.70	.05	NU − NN	.34
NU	.55	.90	.35	UU − UN	.02
UU	.95	.96	.01	(NU − UN)/2	.18
UN	.78	.77	−.01	Cross-section	.25

Source. Tabulated from Quality of Employment Panel, 1973–77. Pension figures based on 429 *NN*'s, 185 *UU*'s, 66 *UN*'s, and 48 *NU*'s.

Taking all these factors into consideration, I conclude that, as with wages, the impact of unions on dispersion found in cross-section studies is confirmed in a longitudinal analysis and that the magnitude of the effect is commensurably lower, at least partly as a result of error in measuring union status.

FRINGE BENEFITS

The third cross-section finding which I examine with longitudinal data in this paper is the finding that unionism increases the fringe component of compensation, particularly those fringe benefits that are most desired by older workers, such as pensions (for studies of fringe benefits, see Duncan 1976; Goldstein and Pauly 1976; Donsimoni 1978; Solnick 1979; Leigh 1980; Viscusi 1980; Freeman 1981, 1983). As the QES is the only data set which provides fringe benefit figures over time, my longitudinal analysis is limited to that data set. I consider two measures of fringes, the number of fringes reported by workers and the proportion with pensions.

Table 8 presents the results of a longitudinal analysis for these two variables, again following the table 6 format. While changes in the list of fringes in the surveys causes the number of fringes reported for the majority of workers to fall, the evidence shows that workers who went from nonunion to union gained fringes, while those going from union to nonunion lost relative to those who remained union. The implied union effects are all positive, with, however, considerable difference in magnitude. The *UN − NN* estimate, in particular, greatly exceeds *UN − UU*. The pension coverage figures show a similar pattern, with a sizable increase in the proportion with pensions for workers joining unions but no real change for those leaving unions. Comparisons of the longitudinal with the cross-section estimates show no difference for number of fringes but the usual diminution of the union effect for provisions of pensions.[9] Finally, note that the pattern of differences in levels of fringes is similar to that found in dispersion for comparisons of *UN*'s or *NU*'s with *UU*'s but is mixed in comparisons of changes with *NN*'s.

Taking the results of tables 6–8 as a whole, a reasonable generalization is that longitudinal analyses confirm the qualitative findings of cross-sectional analyses, with, however, smaller estimated union effects, possibly due in large part to the greater impact of errors of measurement on longitudinal than on cross-section statistics.

IV. BOUNDING THE TRUE IMPACT?

If, as researchers usually assume, there is a substantial selectivity problem in cross-section analysis, which dominates any problems of measurement error, then cross-section estimates of union effects overstate true union effects. The preceding sections show that if there is a substantial measurement error problem in longitudinal analysis, and if there is no countervailing problem of selectivity of changers, other longitudinal estimates of union effects understate true union effects. When both of these statements are true, we have an important "bounding" result:

> THEOREM: Under reasonable assumptions about the impact of measurement error and of selectivity of persons into unions, cross-section estimates of union effects provide an upper bound and longitudinal estimates provide a lower bound on the "true" union impact in the model under study.

To prove the theorem, it is necessary to show that (*a*) measurement error biases longitudinal estimates downward to a greater extent than it does cross-section estimates, which is done in Section II; (*b*) selectivity of unionists in a cross-section biases cross-section estimates upward more than measurement error biases those estimates downward, which I shall assume on the basis of the modest estimated effect of measurement error; in the cross-section; and (*c*) selectivity of who changes union status in longitudinal data either biases longitudinal estimates downward or biases them upward by less than measurement error biases them downward.

In this section I consider proposition *c*. I examine the likely impact of selectivity in who changes union status on longitudinal estimates of union effects. I shall argue that under plausible models of the economics of unionism, selectivity of changers biases longitudinal estimates of union effects *downward*, reinforcing rather than weakening or offsetting the effects of measurement error. Hence, as long as *b* holds, the bounding theorem will be valid.

---

[9] *The cross-section regression for number of fringes is based on regressions using 635 persons with 10 occupation, 6 industry, tenure, tenure squared, education, race, sex, years of schooling, and marital status controls. The regression for proportion with pensions is based on the same sample and model.*

MODELING SELECTIVITY[10]

There are two types of selectivity involved in who becomes union or nonunion: workers' choice of working union (nonunion) jobs and employers' choice of workers. I model selectivity on the part of workers, then examine how the analysis changes when employers select workers from the queue desiring union jobs.

Consider the workers' decision to switch from union to nonunion status when the outcomes are determined by

$$O_{Uij} = \bar{d} + d_j + \alpha_j + \epsilon_{Uij}$$
$$O_{Nij} = \alpha_j + \epsilon_{Nij}, \tag{21}$$

where O_{Uij} = outcome for jth worker in ith period ($i = 1, 0$) when $\bar{d}$ = average union differential, d_j = differential for jth worker relative to average differential with $E(d_j) = 0$, α_i = individual "ability" effect, and ϵ_{Uij} (ϵ_{Nij}) = error when j works union (nonunion) with expected values 0 and variances σ_U^2 and σ_N^2. A worker will choose to accept a union job when

$$O_{U1j} - O_{N1j} > K, \tag{22}$$

where K measures cost of mobility. Assume a bivariate normal distribution of the outcome variables. Then the truncated mean gain from working union is

$$E\left(O_{U1j} - O_{N0j} \middle| O_{U1j} - O_{N1j} > K\right) = \bar{d} + \frac{\sigma_d^2 + \sigma_U^2}{\sigma^*} \frac{f\left[(K - \bar{d})/\sigma_*\right]}{1 - F\left[(K - \bar{d})/\sigma_*\right]}, \tag{23}$$

where $\sigma_*^2 = \sigma_d^2 + \sigma_U^2 + \sigma_N^2$ and where $f/(1 - F)$ is the "inverse Mills" ratio correction for truncation. Equation (23) overstates the union differential because it averages only over workers with especially high gains.

Similarly, for workers leaving unions, we obtain

$$E\left(O_{U1j} - O_{U0j} \middle| O_{N1j} - O_{U0j} > K\right) = -\bar{d} + \frac{\sigma_d^2 + \sigma_N^2}{\sigma^*} \frac{f\left[(K + \bar{d})/\sigma_*\right]}{1 - F\left[(K + \bar{d})/\sigma_*\right]}, \tag{24}$$

as the expected mean change.

---

[10] I have benefited immensely from the comments of John Abowd in this section. The statistical analysis which follows relies extensively on John Abowd (1983).

As our estimate of the union effect we take (½) $(NU - UN)$, which in the present context is ½ of (23) minus ½ (24). This yields

$$\bar{d} + \left[\frac{\sigma_U^2 f\left[(K - \bar{d})/\sigma^*\right]}{\sigma^* 1 - F\left[(K - \bar{d})/\sigma^*\right]} - \frac{\sigma_N^2 f\left[(K + \bar{d})/\sigma^*\right]}{\sigma^* 1 - F\left[(K + \bar{d})/\sigma^*\right]} \right] \Big/ 2, \tag{25}$$

where $\bar{d}$ is the union effect and the remaining components reflect selectivity of changers. Assume, for simplicity, that $\sigma_U^2 = \sigma_N^2$ and that there is a true union effect $\bar{d} > 0$. Then the selectivity bias is negative since $f[(K - \bar{d})/\sigma^*]/[1 - F(\cdot)] < f[(K + \bar{d})/\sigma^*]/[1 - F(\cdot)]$ because $K + \bar{d} > K - \bar{d}$. If, as is plausible given our findings on dispersion, $\sigma_U^2 < \sigma_N^2$, the negative bias is enhanced. If, by contrast, $\bar{d} = 0$ and $\sigma_U^2 = \sigma_N^2$, selectivity has—logically enough— no such bias effect.[11]

In this model if there is a union effect, the selectivity of changers biases longitudinal estimates of that effect downward. Even if there is not, we have established that selectivity on the part of workers does *not* bias upward the longitudinal estimate and thus cannot offset the predicted downward bias from measurement error.

What about selectivity by employers? Rather than providing a detailed analysis of this question (which involves complex double integrals), let us simply evaluate the qualitative impact of such selectivity on our previous results. Since only union firms have a queue of workers outside their plants, I assume that the only firm selectivity is selection of workers into union jobs. Firms will choose to hire workers with low d_j's—that is, those for whom the true union effect is smallest (with a fixed union wage effect, this involves picking workers with the highest productivity)[12]—and try to displace those with high d_j's.

With respect to workers who join unions, employer selectivity will augment the downward bias in the longitudinal estimate. This is because firms will be selecting lower values of d_{NUj} from the sample of workers for whom $d_{NUj} > K + \epsilon_{Nij} - \epsilon_{Nij}$. This will reduce the inverse Mills ratio component of (23).

With respect to workers who leave union jobs, the easiest assumption is that because of seniority rules, firms have no selectivity, leaving (24) as is. If firms are able to select who leaves, however, there is an additional negative bias component to (24), so that we can no longer sign the net effect of selectivity in (25). For the bias in (25) to remain negative, it is necessary that the effect of firm selectivity on who joins a union dominate the effect of firm selectivity on who leaves. This is plausible given that firms are free to hire whom they want but not to fire or lay off.

---

[11] We can also compare the bias in the $NU - NN$ and $UU - UN$ estimates. Following the analysis in the text, we find that the mean for NN is σ_N^2/σ^*. $(f[(K - \bar{d})/\sigma^*]/[1 - F[(K - \bar{d})/\sigma^*]]$, so that the mean for $NU - NN = \bar{d} + \{[(\sigma_d^2 + \sigma_U^2 - \sigma_N^2)/\sigma^*]f\}/(1 - F)$, which is less than $\bar{d}$ when $\sigma_d^2 + \sigma_U^2 < \sigma_N^2$, which is likely since the dispersion of wages is less than the dispersion of nonunion wages. Hence, here too we have an underestimate.

[12] That is, a reasonable specification is $d_j = -\lambda \alpha_j$, where α_j is our ability indicator with $E(\alpha_j) = 0$.

All told, our analysis of selectivity in who changes union status suggests that, under reasonable selection criteria but simplified statistical assumptions, the longitudinal estimates of union effects will be biased downward, establishing the bounding theorem.

V. CONCLUSION

In this paper I have tried to show that measurement error is a significant problem in analysis of longitudinal data. I have developed some models of measurement error, examined numerical examples, and estimated the impact of measurement error in four data sets. My analysis has not been complete. I gave only cursory treatment to issues of the correlation between the random component of measurement error and control variables and ignored completely the potential impact of standard exclusion rules (such as requiring positive wages and sensible values of explanatory variables) on longitudinal as opposed to cross-section analyses. These errors of omission aside, the analysis suggests that longitudinal analysis is not the research panacea it is sometimes seen to be. While omitted fixed effects bias cross-section estimates of union effects upward, measurement error and possibly selectivity of changers bias longitudinal estimates downward. Under reasonable conditions, the two sets of estimates bound the true impact of unionism and thus should be viewed as complementary research tools. While neither is likely to yield the true parameter, together they enable us to estimate the magnitude of the effects of unionism, which appear to be quite substantial in empirical work.

REFERENCES

Abowd, John M. "Comments on the Effects of Selectivity Biases on Estimates of Union/Nonunion Effects in a Panel Setting." Review of "Longitudinal Analyses of the Effects of Trade Unions" by Richard Freeman. Mimeographed. Chicago: University of Chicago, 1983.

Abowd, John M., and Farber, Henry S. "Job Queues and the Union Status of Workers." *Industrial and Labor Relations Review* 35 (April 1982): 354–67.

Aigner, Dennis J. "Regression with a Binary Independent Variable Subject to Errors of Observation." *Journal of Econometrics* 1 (1983): 49–60.

Brown, Charles. "Equalizing Differences in the Labor Market." *Quarterly Journal of Economics* 94 (February 1980): 113–34.

Chamberlain, Gary. "Multivariate Regression Models for Panel Data." *Journal of Econometrics* 18 (1982): 5–46.

Chowdhury, G., and Nickell, S. "Individual Earnings in the U.S.: Another Look at Unionization, Schooling, Sickness and Unemployment Using Panel Data." Discussion Paper no. 141, Centre for Labour Economics, London School of Economics, November 1982.

Donsimoni, Marie-Paule Joseph. *An Analysis of Trade Union Power: Structure and Conduct of the American Labor Movement.* Ph.D. thesis, Harvard University, 1978.

Duncan, Greg J. "Earnings Functions and Nonpecuniary Benefits." *Journal of Human Resources* 10 (Fall 1976): 462–83.

———. "Paths to Economic Well-Being." In *Five Thousand American Families—Patterns of Economic Progress,* edited by Greg J. Duncan and James N. Morgan. Vol. 5. Ann Arbor: Institute for Social Research, 1977.

———. "An Empirical Model of Wage Growth." In *Five Thousand American Families—Patterns of Economic Progress,* edited by Greg Duncan and James N. Morgan. Vol. 7. Ann Arbor: Institute for Social Research, 1979.

Freeman, Richard B. "Unionism and the Dispersion of Wages." *Industrial and Labor Relations Review* 34 (October 1980): 3–23.

———. "The Effect of Trade Unionism on Fringe Benefits." *Industrial and Labor Relations Review* 35 (July 1981):489–509.

———. "Union Wage Practices and Wage Dispersion within Establishments." *Industrial and Labor Relations Review* 36 (October 1982): 3–21.

———. "Unionism, Pensions, and Union Pension Funds." Paper presented to National Bureau of Economic Research Conference on Pensions, Labor, and Individual Choice, March 23–26, 1983. [Published in *Pensions, Labor, and Individual Choice,* David Wise, ed. Chicago: University of Chicago Press for NBER, 1985.]

Freeman, Richard B., and Medoff, James L. "The Impact of Collective Bargaining: Illusion or Reality?" In *U.S. Industrial Relations 1950–1980: A Critical Assessment,* edited by Jack Steiber, Robert McKersie, and Quinn Mills. Madison, Wis.: Industrial Relations Research Association, 1981.

Goldstein, Gerald, and Pauly, Mark. "Group Health Insurance as a Local Public Good." In *The Role of Health Insurance in the Health Services Sector,* edited by Richard N. Rosett. New York: National Bureau of Economic Research, 1976.

Hirsch, Barry. "The Interindustry Structure of Unionism, Earnings and Earnings Dispersion." *Industrial and Labor Relations Review* 36 (October 1982): 22–39.

Hyclak, Thomas. "Unionization and Urban Differentials in Income Inequality." *Journal of Economics* 3 (1977): 205–7.

———. "The Effect of Union on Earnings Inequality in Local Labor Markets." *Industrial and Labor Relations Review* 33 (October 1979): 77–84.

Leigh, Duane E. "The Effect of Unionism on Workers' Valuation of Future Pension Benefits." *Industrial and Labor Relations Review* 34 (July 1981): 510–21.

Lewis, H. Gregg. "Fixed Effects or Measurement Errors in Panel Data?" Durham, N.C.: Duke University, Graduate School of Business, June 1983.

Marquis, K. H.; Duan, N.; Marquis, M. S.; Polich, J. M.; with Meslkoff, J. E.; Shwartzbach, D. S.; and Stasz, C. M. "Response Errors in Sensitive Topic Surveys: Estimates, Effects, and Correction Options." Rand/R-2710/2-HHS. Santa Monica, Calif: Rand Corporation, April 1981.

Mellow, Wesley. "Unionism and Wages: A Longitudinal Analysis." *Review of Economics and Statistics* 63 (February 1981): 43–52.

Mincer, Jacob. "Union Effects: Wages, Turnover, and Job Training." NBER Working Paper no. 808, November 1981. [Published in *Collected Essays of Jacob Mincer. Volume 2. Studies in Labor Supply* (Economists of the Twentieth Century Series). Aldershot, UK: Elgar, 1993, pp. 262–99. (Distributed in U.S. by Ashgate, Brookfield, Vt.)]

Plotnick, Robert D. "Trends in Male Earnings Inequality." *Southern Economic Journal* 48 (January 1982): 724–32.

Solnick, Loren M. "Unionism and Employer Fringe Benefit Expenditures." *Industrial Relations* 17 (February 1978): 102–7.

Viscusi, W. Kip. "Unions, Labor Market Structure and the Welfare Implications of the Quality of Work." *Journal of Labor Research* 1 (Spring 1980):175–92.

ABOUT THE AUTHOR

Richard B. Freeman

Richard Freeman's research spans a remarkable array of topics. First among these is improving our understanding of the role of labor unions in the economy. One much-studied aspect of unions' impact is the effect of unions on wages, and the paper reprinted here has been a regular item on my graduate reading list. Unions also affect working conditions in ways studied more often by those in industrial relations than by labor economists; Richard's work shows quite clearly that labor economists have much to add to these discussions. He has also been an early and influential voice on the importance of the challenges of unions' organizing in the private sector, and their public-sector success.

Richard's career began with important work on higher education and discrimination. He showed that enrollments respond to rates of return—not just in the decision to enroll but in the choice of major. He was an early voice on the importance of the Civil Rights Act of 1964, particularly for younger and more highly educated blacks, and stuck with the topic as the news from the front grew less encouraging. More recently, he has turned to the study of inequality, immigration, and homelessness. His interest in and knowledge of developments outside the United States have added a valuable dimension to his work on many of these topics. If there is a fountain of youth for academics, it is a willingness to tackle new topics and find new collaborators; Richard has remained forever young.

It would be interesting to count how many different data sets appear in Richard's research. He was among the first labor economists to make cross checking across independent data sources a standard feature of his work. While he is quite willing to address important econometric issues (and "Longitudinal Analysis" offers a very nice example), one also sees a clear preference for judging the impact of omitted variables by finding a data set in which the variable in question is available.

Large as the direct impact of his research has been, Richard's indirect effect on the practice of labor economics has been even larger. As Program Director for Labor Studies at the National Bureau of Economic Research, he has organized major projects on youth unemployment and the special problems of black youth, public sector unionization, trade and immigration, wage inequality, and cross-national comparisons of labor-market and social-welfare institutions. Most important, he has provided guidance and encouragement to a generation of labor economists: he enjoys economics, he shares ideas, and he clearly enjoys the sharing.

Richard B. Freeman is currently also Ascherman Professor of Economics at Harvard University and Direcor of the Programme in Discontinuous Economics at the London School of Economics.

Charles Brown

Changes in Relative Wages, 1963–1987: Supply and Demand Factors

LAWRENCE F. KATZ

KEVIN M. MURPHY

A simple supply and demand framework is used to analyze changes in the U. S. wage structure from 1963 to 1987. Rapid secular growth in the demand for more-educated workers, "more-skilled" workers, and females appears to be the driving force behind observed changes in the wage structure. Measured changes in the allocation of labor between industries and occupations strongly favored college graduates and females throughout the period. Movements in the college wage premium over this period appear to be strongly related to fluctuations in the rate of growth of the supply of college graduates.

I. INTRODUCTION

Wage inequality among both men and women increased substantially in the United States during the 1980s. Changes in the wage structure along three primary dimensions played an important role in rising inequality. First, there was an increase in wage differentials by education with a particularly sharp rise in the relative earnings of college graduates. Second, the average wages of older workers increased relative to the wages of younger workers for those with relatively low levels of education. The combination of these two changes generated an increase in the weekly wages of young male college graduates by approximately 30 percent relative to young males with twelve or fewer years of schooling from 1979 to 1987. Third, earnings inequality also increased greatly within narrowly defined demographic and skill groups. Although the male and female wage structures widened considerably, differences in earnings between men and women narrowed

We thank John Bound, Richard Freeman, Claudia Goldin, Lawrence Summers, Finis Welch, and participants at several seminars and NBER conferences for helpful comments. We are also grateful to Chinhui Juhn, Brooks Pierce, and Boris Simkovich for expert research assistance. Financial support was provided by NSF Grant No. SES-9010759. The final data sets used in this paper are available upon request.

throughout the 1980s. The average wage of women increased by about 8 percent relative to the average wage of men from 1979 to 1987.

Although the pattern of movements in the U. S. wage structure in the 1980s is well documented,[1] much disagreement remains concerning the fundamental causes of the changes. Several explanations have received much attention. One class of explanations postulates that changes in the U. S. wage structure during the 1980s are driven primarily by shifts in the relative demand for labor favoring more-educated and "more-skilled" workers over less-educated and "less-skilled" workers and favoring females over males. One variant emphasizes technological changes (possibly associated with the computer revolution) that are likely to have raised the relative demand for more-educated and flexible workers and reduced the demand for physical labor [Davis and Haltiwanger, 1991; Krueger, 1991; Mincer, 1991]. A second hypothesizes that shifts in product demand largely associated with large trade deficits in the 1980s have led to a sharp decline in manufacturing employment and a shift in employment toward sectors that are education and female intensive [Murphy and Welch, 1991]. Alternative explanations focus on changes in wage-setting institutions such as the decline in unions [Freeman, 1991], changes in pay norms [Mitchell, 1989], and the erosion of the real value of the minimum wage [Blackburn, Bloom, and Freeman, 1990].

In this paper we examine how far one can go toward explaining recent changes in relative wages in the United States using a simple supply and demand framework. Rather than focusing on changes in relative wages during the 1980s in isolation, we analyze relative wage movements over the longer 25-year time period from 1963 to 1987. By examining this longer time period, we are able to evaluate the ability of competing explanations to explain a wide range of wage observations (such as both falling college wage premiums in the 1970s and rising college wage premiums in the 1980s) as well as differences in timing in changes in wage differentials.

The paper is organized as follows. Section II describes the data from the March Current Population Surveys that we use throughout the paper. Section III uses these data to describe the basic patterns of change in real and relative wages in the United States over the 1963 to 1987 period. Section IV outlines the simple factor demand model that we use to interpret these relative wage data and evaluates the ability of simple demand shift stories to explain the observed patterns of changes in relative factor prices and supplies. Section V expands the basic model to incorporate both within- and between-industry components of relative factor demands. Section VI uses the basic framework to examine changes in education and experience differentials. Section VII summarizes our conclusions.

We conclude that rapid secular growth in the relative demand for "more-skilled" workers is a key component of any consistent explanation for rising inequality and

---

[1] *See, for example, Blackburn, Bloom, and Freeman [1990]; Bound and Johnson [1992]; Juhn, Murphy, and Pierce [1989]; Karoly [1990]; Katz and Revenga [1989]; Levy and Murnane [1991]; and Murphy and Welch [1992].*

changes in the wage structure over the last 25 years. Although much of this shift in relative demand can be accounted for by observed shifts in the industrial and occupational composition of employment toward relatively skill-intensive sectors, the majority reflects shifts in relative labor demand occurring within detailed sectors. These within-sector shifts are likely to reflect skill-biased technological changes. Differences in the time pattern of rising education differentials and rising within-group inequality suggest that they are distinct phenomena. Our results indicate that observed fluctuations in the rate of growth of the relative supply of college graduates combined with smooth trend demand growth in favor of more-educated workers can largely explain fluctuations in the college/high school differential over the 1963-1987 period. Steady demand growth in favor of more highly-skilled workers over the last twenty years appears consistent with both movements in education differentials and within-group inequality.

II. THE DATA

The data we use in this paper come from a series of 25 consecutive March Current Population Surveys (CPSs) for survey years 1964 to 1988. These CPS data are from the March Annual Demographic Supplement and provide information on earnings and weeks worked in the calendar year preceding the March survey. These surveys provide wage and employment information on approximately 1.4 million workers for the 1963 to 1987 period. From these CPS data we create two samples: (1) a wage sample that we use to measure weekly wages of full-time workers by demographic group and (2) a count sample that we use to measure the amount of labor supplied by each of these demographic groups. The taxonomy we use divides the data into 320 distinct labor groups, distinguished by sex, education (less than 12, 12, 13–15, and 16 or more years of schooling), and 40 single-year potential experience categories (corresponding to the first 40 years since the estimated age of labor market entrance).[2]

The wage measure that we use throughout the paper is the average weekly wage of full-time workers (computed as total annual earnings divided by total weeks worked) within a gender-education-experience cell.[3] Our wage sample includes full-time wage and salary workers who participated in the labor force for at least 39 weeks in the calendar year prior to the March survey, worked at least one week, and did not work part year due to school, retirement, or military service. Self-employed workers and those working

---

[2] Potential experience is calculated as min(age − years of schooling − 7, age − 17) where age is the age at the survey date.

[3] Weeks worked are available only on a bracketed basis for survey years prior to 1976. To impute weeks worked for the 1964–1975 surveys, we divided the wage sample for the later survey years into cells defined by the weeks worked brackets used in the earlier surveys and sex. We used the means of weeks worked for these cells from the 1976–1988 surveys as our estimates of weeks worked for individuals in the corresponding cells in the earlier surveys.

without pay were excluded from the wage sample. The sample includes individuals for whom the Census imputed wages but makes a correction for the fact that the imputation procedures changed between the 1975 and 1976 March CPS surveys.[4] Workers with top coded earnings were imputed annual earnings at 1.45 times the annual topcode amount. This correction is based on our estimates of the conditional average earnings of those with earnings above the topcode. In addition, we excluded workers with real weekly earnings below $67 in 1982 dollars (equal to one half of the 1982 real minimum wage based on a 40-hour week). As best as we can ascertain from experimentation, our results are not highly sensitive to these exclusion criteria.

The count sample includes all individuals who worked at least one week in the preceding year (regardless of whether they were wage and salary workers, self employed, or otherwise). We compute total hours worked for each cell in each year by computing the product of total annual hours (weeks worked times usual weekly hours) and the individual CPS sample weight for each individual in the cell and then summing over all the individuals in the cell.[5] We use these total hours measures as estimates of the total labor supplied to the U. S. market by individuals with given characteristics. The total hours calculations for each cell are then deflated by the sum of total hours worked over all cells so that hours for each cell in each year are expressed as a fraction of total annual hours that year.

The use of two separate samples, one for measuring supplies and one for measuring prices, reflects the different criteria each sample must meet. The primary concern with the wage sample is to obtain data on a group that maintains a reasonably constant composition through time thus providing estimates of the prices received by workers of given skills. In this regard, our goal was to maximize the comparability through time. This is why we tried to focus on full-time workers with reasonably strong labor force attachment.

---

[4] *The Census began using a finer classification of observables to impute wages for workers who failed to report wages in the 1976 survey. Since information on which workers had imputed wages is not available for the years 1963–1966, one cannot construct a wage series using only workers without imputed wages for our entire sample period. To adjust group average wages for changes in the imputation procedures, we multiplied the average wages in each cell for the years 1963–1975 by a time-invariant, cell-specific adjustment factor. The adjustment factors were picked to impose the condition that the average percentage wage difference between the wages of all workers and those of workers without wage imputations were the same in the 1967–1975 and 1975–1987 periods. Our qualitative findings for the 1967–1987 period are quite similar when we use our adjusted series including workers with imputed wages and when we use only workers without wage imputations. See Lillard, Smith, and Welch [1986] for a discussion of the changes in techniques to impute missing data implemented with the 1976 survey.*

[5] *Total hours worked for group j in year t is given by $\sum_i h_{ijt}\omega_{ijt}$, where i indexes individuals, h is annual hours worked, and ω is the CPS sample weight. Usual weekly hours for the previous year are only available in the CPS since 1976. For survey years 1964–1975 we use hours worked during the survey week to measure usual weekly hours in the previous year. For individuals who did not work during the survey week, we imputed usual weekly hours using the mean of hours worked last week for individuals of the same sex and same full-time/part-time status who reported hours worked last week on that year's survey.*

For purposes of computing supply, the desire for homogeneity is overridden by the requirement of measuring an aggregate quantity.

Our wage data can be summarized by the (320×25) matrix W which contains the average weekly wage from the wage sample for each of our 320 groups in each year from 1963 to 1987. When we describe wages for more aggregated groups, we use a fixed-weight aggregation scheme where the fixed weights are given by the 320-element vector of average employment shares over the 1963 to 1987 period which we denote N. In addition, we use this same vector of fixed-weights to construct wage indices for each year as $N'W$. Deflating wages in each year by the value of this index for the year generates a time series of relative wages by groups (where each group's wage is indexed to the wages for a fixed bundle of workers). The average of these relative wages through time provides an estimate of the average relative wage of a given group and hence provides a natural basis for aggregating quantities of labor supplied across groups in terms of *efficiency units*. Accordingly, when we measure quantities of labor in efficiency units, we compute more aggregate supplies from the individual cell supplies by weighting hours worked in each cell contained in the aggregate by the average relative wage of that cell and summing.

III. REAL AND RELATIVE WAGE CHANGES, 1963–1987

Table I describes changes in the real weekly wages of the full labor force and of individual demographic groups for the 1963–1987 period and for three periods, 1963–1971, 1971–1979, and 1979–1987.[6] Over the entire period average real weekly wages increased by 16.1 percent.[7] This growth in real wages breaks down into a 19.2 percent increase between 1963 and 1971 and small declines during the 1971–1979 and 1979–1987 subperiods. The major difference between these computations and more standard measures of average real wages is that the measures in Table I refer to wages for a fixed demographic distribution (the average employment distribution over the 1963 to 1987 period) and hence do not reflect changes in the level of wages arising from shifts in the education, gender, or experience composition of the labor force.

The next two rows of the table indicate that wages of women increased by 9 percent relative to the wages of men over the entire period. This reduction in the overall gender gap in earnings was concentrated in the 1980s. In fact, the earnings of women increased relative to those of men in almost all experience-education cells during the 1980s. Panel A of Figure I contrasts the time pattern of changes in the female/male wage ratio for high

---

[6] *We compute real wages by deflating nominal wages in each year by the implicit price deflator for personal consumption expenditures from the National Income and Product Accounts.*

[7] *We refer to 100 times log changes as percentage changes in this section.*

TABLE I

U. S. REAL WEEKLY WAGE CHANGES FOR FULL-TIME WORKERS, 1963–1987[a]

Group	Change in log average real weekly wage (multiplied by 100)			
	1963–1971	1971–1979	1979–1987	1963–1987
All	19.2	−2.8	−0.3	16.1
Gender:				
Men	19.7	−3.4	−2.4	13.9
Women	17.6	−0.8	6.1	22.9
Education (years of schooling):				
8–11	17.1	0.3	−6.6	10.9
12	16.7	1.4	−4.0	14.1
13–15	16.4	−3.4	1.5	14.4
16+	25.5	−10.1	7.7	23.1
Experience (men):				
1–5 years	17.1	−3.5	−6.7	6.8
26–35 years	19.4	−0.6	0.0	18.8
Education and Experience (men):				
Education 8–11				
Experience 1–5	20.5	1.5	−15.8	6.2
Experience 26–35	19.3	−0.4	−1.9	17.0
Education 12				
Experience 1–5	17.4	0.8	−19.8	−1.6
Experience 26–35	14.3	3.2	−2.8	14.7
Education 16+				
Experience 1–5	18.9	−11.3	10.8	18.4
Experience 26–35	28.1	−4.0	1.8	25.9

[a] The numbers in the table represent log changes in mean weekly wages using data from the March Current Population Surveys for 1964–1988. Mean weekly wages for full-time workers in each of 320 sex-education-experience cells were computed in each year. Mean wages for broader groups in each year represent weighted averages of these cell means using a fixed set of weights (the average employment share of the cell for the entire 1963–1987 period). All earnings numbers are deflated by the implicit price deflator for personal consumption expenditures.

school and college graduates from 1963 to 1987.[8] Although the narrowing of the gender gap in wages started earlier for college graduates than for high school graduates, the increase in the female/male wage ratio is much more substantial in the 1980s for high school graduates.

The next four rows of Table I show real wage changes by education level. For the full period, real wage changes are monotonically increasing in education level, reflecting a

---

[8] The female/male wage ratios reported in the figure are computed by first sorting the data into cells defined by education level and five-year potential experience intervals. The reported female/male wage ratios are fixed-weighted averages of the ratios of the average weekly wage of females to the average weekly wage of males in each cell where the fixed weight for each cell is the cell's average share of total employment over the entire 1963–1987 period. The wage ratios reported in the other panels of Figure I are analogous fixed-weighted averages of wage ratios for cells defined by gender, education level, and five-year experience interval.

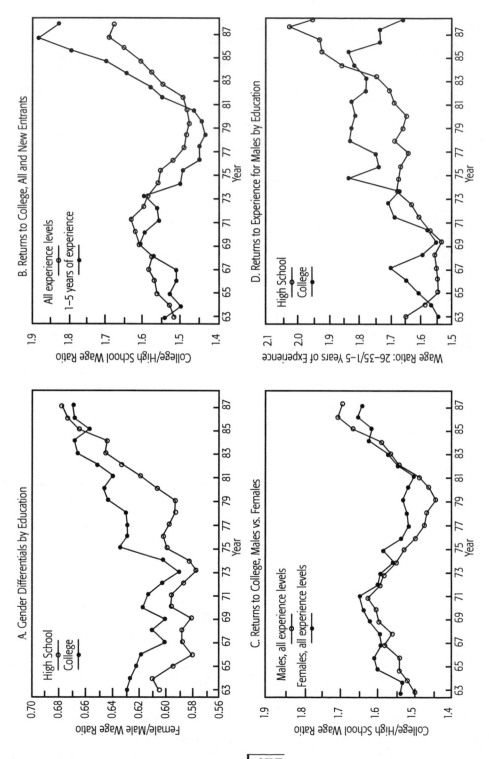

FIGURE I
Major U. S. Relative Wage Changes, 1963–1987

rise in education-based wage differentials. The timing of the growth in education returns is very uneven, however. From 1963 to 1971 college graduates gained about 8 percent on other groups. Between 1971 and 1979 real wages fell the most for college graduates, by 10.1 percent, and actually increased slightly for the two least-educated groups. In contrast, from 1979 to 1987 college graduates gained 14.1 percent on high school dropouts and 11.7 percent on high school graduates. Since these changes more than make up for the decline in the relative wages of college graduates over the 1970s, the college wage premium was higher in the late 1980s than at any other time during our sample and most likely at any other time during the postwar period [Goldin and Margo, 1992].

Panels B and C of Figure I further illustrate changes in the earnings of college graduates relative to high school graduates. Panel B documents movements in the fixed-weighted average college/high school wage ratio for all workers and for workers with one to five years of experience. The figure highlights much larger swings in educational differentials for young workers than for older workers in the 1970s and 1980s. In fact, the college/high school wage ratio for young workers fell from 1.61 in 1969 to 1.44 in 1979 and then increased sharply to 1.82 in 1987. Panel C shows that fluctuations in the college wage premium were quite similar for men and women.

The next two rows of Table I examine real wage changes by experience level for males. Over the entire sample period the wage gap between older and younger workers expanded with peak earners, those with 26 to 35 years of experience, gaining 12 percent on new entrants, those with 1 to 5 years of experience. Although experience differentials for men expanded throughout the period, they increased most substantially during the 1980s.

The final rows of Table I present real wage movements for education by experience cells for males. Two distinct patterns emerge. First, high school graduates and high school dropouts show the largest increases in experience differentials (16.3 and 10.8 percent, respectively) and for both groups this increase is accounted for entirely by the rise in experience returns in the final time interval. For college graduates the time series of experience returns is quite different. Experience differentials increase sharply in both of the first two time intervals so that from 1963 to 1979 experienced college graduates gained 16.5 percent on new entrants. However, during the 1980s the relative wages of young college graduates increased sharply. The differences in the patterns of changes in experience differentials for high school and college graduates are graphed in Panel D of Figure I.

We have so far referred to changes in real wages for groups distinguished by sex, education, and experience. However, given that these factors account for only about one third of the differences in wages across workers, there is significant room for relative wage changes within these categories as well. We use the dispersion of relative wages within our gender-education-experience cells as a measure of the spread in relative wages across different skill levels within the cells. Empirically we do this by looking at the distribution of residuals from a regression of log weekly wages on a quartic in experience fully interacted with sex and four education-level dummies, and linear terms in education within these categories. The distribution of residuals from this regression essentially captures the dispersion of wages within the demographic groups.

We summarize these results in panel A of Figure II where we plot the differences in the log wage residuals of those at the ninetieth and at the tenth percentiles of the distribution of log wage residuals for men and women. Within-group (residual) wage inequality has expanded enormously for both women and men from 1963 to 1987. The log wage gap between the ninetieth and tenth percentile worker within experience-education groups increased by approximately 0.26 for men and 0.21 for women from 1963–1987. This striking increase in wage inequality within groups means that not only have the less-educated and less-experienced workers lost out over our sample period but so too have the "least-skilled" or "least-lucky" workers within each category.

An examination of the time series displayed in Panel A of Figure II shows that residual inequality started to expand in the early 1970s and continued increasing rather smoothly in the 1980s. This time pattern contrasts sharply with the pattern for education differentials. We conclude from these differences in timing that the general rise in within- group inequality and the rise in education premiums over the 1963–1987 period are actually somewhat distinct economic phenomena. The earlier increase in within-group inequality suggests a rise in the demand for "skill" that predates the recent rise in returns to education.

We next examine changes in overall wage inequality by sex. Panel B of Figure II plots movements in overall wage dispersion as measured by the log wage differential between workers at the ninetieth and tenth percentiles of the wage distribution for men and for women. The 90–10 log wage differential for males remained stable in the 1960s, increased substantially from 1.18 in 1970 to 1.29 in 1979, and then expanded sharply by 0.18 log points from 1979 to 1987. Wage inequality for females remained fairly stable in the 1960s and 1970s, and then increased sharply from 1.08 in 1979 to 1.32 in 1987. The log wage gap between the ninetieth and tenth percentile workers increased by 0.26 for men and by 0.25 for women from 1963 to 1987. The pattern of changes in overall wage inequality over our sample period is quite similar if one uses alternative summary measures such as the variance of log wages, the interquartile range, or a gini coefficient [Juhn, Murphy, and Pierce, 1989; Karoly, 1990; Levy and Murnane, 1991]. In fact, the weekly and hourly wage distributions for both men and women appear to have spread out fairly evenly across all percentiles from 1963 to 1987.

We conclude that all major relative wage differentials with the exception of the male/female differential increased from 1963 to 1987. These basic changes in the U. S. wage structure can be summarized as follows.

1. The college wage premium rose from 1963 to 1971, fell from 1971 to 1979, and then rose sharply from 1979 to 1987. The changes in the college/high school wage ratio were greatest for the youngest workers in the 1970s and 1980s and greatest for prime age workers in the 1960s.

2. Experience differentials expanded substantially from 1963 to 1987. The most dramatic increases in experience differentials occurred for less-educated males from 1979–1987.

3. Overall and residual weekly wage inequality for both men and women (as measured by the 90–10 log wage differential) were stable during the 1960s and then increased by

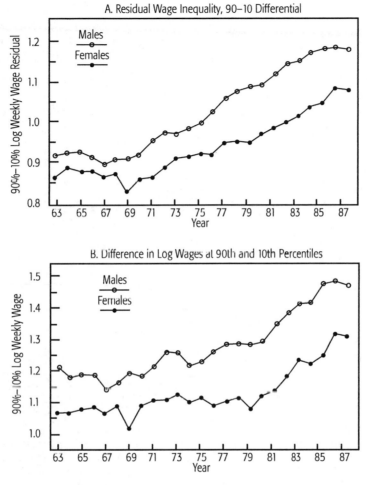

FIGURE II

Changes in Overall and Residual Wage Inequality

almost 30 percent from the late 1960s to 1987. The increase in residual inequality has been quite steady since the early 1970s, while the growth in overall inequality accelerated in the 1980s.

4. After remaining fairly stable in the 1960s and 1970s, male/female wage differentials narrowed substantially from 1979 to 1987.

IV. A SIMPLE SUPPLY AND DEMAND FRAMEWORK

We begin our examination of the between-group relative wage changes documented in the previous section using a simple supply and demand framework in which different demographic groups (identified by sex, education, and experience) are treated as distinct labor inputs. We think of the relative wages of demographic groups as being generated by the interaction of the relative supplies of the groups and an aggregate production with its associated factor demand schedules. To the extent that these different demographic groups are imperfect substitutes in production, we can view changes in relative wages as being generated by shifts in relative supplies and shifts in the factor demand schedules. The framework is distinctly partial equilibrium in that we do not specify the determinants of relative factor supplies. We only require that observed prices and quantities must be "on the demand curve."

A. THE BASIC FRAMEWORK

Our basic framework involves an aggregate production function consisting of K types of labor inputs. We assume that the associated factor demands can be written as

$$(1) \qquad X_t = D(W_t, Z_t),$$

where

$X_t = K \times 1$ vector of labor inputs employed in the market in year t

$W_t = K \times 1$ vector of market prices for these inputs in year t

$Z_t = m \times 1$ vector of demand shift variables in year t.

The demand shifters Z_t reflect the effects of technology, product demand, and other non-labor inputs on demands for labor inputs.

Under the assumption that the aggregate production function is concave, the $(K \times K)$ matrix of cross-price effects on factor demands, D_w, is negative semidefinite. Equation (1) can be written in terms of differentials as

$$(2) \qquad dX_t = D_w dW_t + D_z dZ_t.$$

The negative semidefiniteness of D_w implies that

$$(3) \qquad dW_t'(dX_t - D_z dZ_t) = dW_t' D_w dW_t \le 0.$$

Changes in factor supplies (net of demand shifts) and changes in wages must negatively covary.

One hypothesis that has attracted much attention in previous related research (e.g., Freeman [1979] and Welch [1979]) is whether shifts in relative supplies are the driving force behind observed changes in relative wages. A test of an extreme version of this hypothesis is to examine whether the data are consistent with stable factor demand. In this case, wage changes are generated by relative supply changes arising from changing demographics and school completion rates. In the case of two inputs the basic implication of stable relative factor demand is that an increase in the relative supply of a group must lead to a reduction in the relative wage of that group. More generally, if factor demand is stable (Z_t fixed), equation (3) implies that $dW_t'dX_t \leq 0$. We use our estimates of the time series, (X_t, W_t), $t = 1963, \ldots, 1987$, and a discrete version of this equation to test for stable demand. Specifically, we test for fixed factor demand between the year t and year τ by evaluating whether

$$(4) \qquad (W_t - W_\tau)'(X_t - X_\tau) \leq 0.$$

This inequality provides a natural way in which to evaluate the pure supply shifts story. Periods of time in which the inequality in (4) is satisfied (i.e., the inner product of changes in wages and changes in factor supplies is nonpositive) have the potential to be explained solely by supply shifts. When this inequality is not satisfied, no story relying entirely on supply shifts is consistent with the data. In this case, we can evaluate alternative hypotheses concerning relative demand shifts (alternative proxies for Z_t) using the discrete version of (3) given by

$$(5) \qquad (W_t - W_\tau)'[(X_t - X_\tau) - (D(W_\tau,Z_t) - D(W_\tau,Z_\tau))] \leq 0,$$

where we compute the inner product of the change in wages from year τ to year t with the changes in net supplies (equal to the actual change in supply less the change in demand for X that would have happened at fixed factor prices).

In our implementation of this framework, we are concerned with explaining *relative* wage changes as a function of *relative* supply and *relative* factor demand shifts. We abstract from changes in absolute wages arising from factor-neutral technological change and from neutral demand shifts associated with changes in the scale of the economy. To do so, we use a relative wage measure (actual wages W_t deflated by the wage index $N'W_t$, where N is the ($K \times 1$) vector of average employment shares over the entire sample for the K labor inputs) and a relative supply measure (actual supplies X_t deflated by the total supply of labor in the economy measured in efficiency units $\Omega'X_t$, where Ω is the ($K \times 1$) vector of average relative wages over the entire sample) when we empirically evaluate (4) and (5).[9]

---

[9] *The use of these relative wage and quantity measures can be formally justified as follows. We first assume that the aggregate production function can be written as $y_t = \phi_t F(X_t)$ where ϕ_t indexes the state of technology of the economy and $F(\ )$ is concave. The concavity of $F(\ )$ implies that*

$$[F_x(X_t) - F_x(X_\tau)]'(X_t - X_\tau) \leq 0,$$

where F_x is the $K \times 1$ vector of derivatives of F with respect to the K inputs. Under the assumption that marginal products are set equal to factor prices, we have $W_t = \phi_t F_x(X_t)$ for all t so that the inequality can be rewritten as

B. RELATIVE SUPPLY CHANGES

Table II summarizes changes in relative factor supplies (where each group's supply is measured relative to the total supply in efficiency units) over the 1963–1987 period and the subperiods 1963–1971, 1971–1979, and 1979–1987 for the same aggregates used to analyze changes in wages in Table I. The table illustrates that there has been substantial long-run growth in the relative supply of more-educated workers, younger workers, and women. The increase in the average educational attainment of the labor force is particularly striking. The share of aggregate hours worked contributed by college graduates increased from 13.0 to 26.3 percent from 1963–1987, while the share for high school dropouts fell from 39.2 to 12.6 percent over the same period. Since the relative supplies and wages of more-educated workers and women increased over the sample, relative demand changes favoring these groups are necessary to explain the observed data.

On the other hand, the table does illustrate the possibility that differences in the rate of growth in the relative supply of college graduates may help explain the time pattern of changes in the college wage premium. The largest increase in the supply of college graduates comes during the 1971–1979 period in which the college wage premium declined, and the smallest growth of supply comes during the 1979–1987 period in which the college wage premium expanded sharply. A smooth secular increase in the relative demand for college graduates combined with the observed fluctuations in the rate of growth of relative supply could potentially explain the movements in the college wage premium from 1963 to 1987.

An analogous story emphasizing smooth trend growth in the relative demand for women and relative supply growth variation seems less likely to provide a complete story for changes in the gender gap in earnings. The rate of growth of the share of the labor force accounted for by women is more rapid in the 1970s than in the 1960s or 1980s. The deceleration in the rate of growth of female labor supply in the 1980s combined with a secular growth in the relative demand for industries and occupations in which women have been concentrated may help explain the greater earnings gains made by women in the 1980s than in the 1970s. On the other hand, the acceleration in the growth rate of relative supply from the 1960s to the 1970s bodes poorly for an explanation based on supply growth fluctuations since the relative earnings of women declined in the 1960s.

$$[(W_t/\phi_t)-(W_\tau/\phi_\tau)]'(X_t - X_\tau) \le 0.$$

If we further assume that there are constant returns to scale in production so that F( ) is a linear homogeneous function, then $F_x(k_t X_t) = F_x(X_t)$ for any scalar k_t. Thus $W_t = \phi_t F_x(k_t X_t)$ and $W_\tau = \phi_\tau F_x(k_\tau X_\tau)$ for any scalars k_t and k_τ. This implies that the inequality,

$$[(W_\tau/\phi_t) - (W_\tau/\phi_\tau)]'(k_t X_t - k_\tau X_\tau) \le 0,$$

also holds for any scalars k_t and k_τ. This final inequality is the form of (4) that we use in our empirical tests. We approximate the level of productivity at time t, ϕ_t, using the value of our wage index $N'W_t$, and we multiply the factor quantities X_t in year t by one over the total supply in efficiency units.

TABLE II

RELATIVE SUPPLY CHANGES, 1963–1987[a]

Group	Change in log share of aggregate labor input (multiplied by 100)			
	1963–1971	1971–1979	1979–1987	1963–1987
Gender:				
Men	−2.9	−4.9	−4.2	−12.0
Women	11.2	15.7	11.2	38.2
Education (years of schooling):				
8–11	−35.2	−48.6	−41.9	−125.7
12	7.6	−4.8	−4.8	−2.0
13–15	20.3	23.3	6.7	50.3
16+	17.8	24.1	15.6	57.5
Experience (men):				
1–5 years	30.3	16.3	−27.9	18.6
6–10 years	14.2	19.5	−10.4	23.4
11–15 years	−4.3	6.9	17.5	20.1
16–20 years	−17.8	−6.6	22.7	−1.7
21–25 years	−15.5	−16.9	0.0	−32.3
26–35 years	−5.5	−23.8	−17.4	−46.7
Experience and education (men):				
Education 8–11				
Experience 1–5	−21.1	1.5	−53.3	−72.9
Experience 26–35	−34.8	−59.8	−65.3	−159.8
Education 12				
Experience 1–5	16.2	18.7	−40.9	−6.0
Experience 26–35	4.0	−26.9	−10.9	−33.8
Education 16				
Experience 1–5	52.7	17.1	−12.7	57.1
Experience 26–35	19.8	18.9	−5.8	32.9

[a] The numbers in the table represent log changes in each group's share of total labor supply measured in efficiency units (annual hours times the average relative wage of the group for the 1963–1987 period) using data from the March Current Population Surveys for 1964–1988. Supply measures include all workers in the count sample described in the text.

Changes in the age structure of the labor force may be an important part of an explanation for secular increases in the relative earnings of older workers. The share of labor supply (measured in efficiency units) accounted for by workers with one to ten years of experience increased rapidly from 18.9 percent in 1963 to a peak of 30.8 percent in 1980 and then decreased to 27.4 percent in 1987. The secular increase in the share of young workers consisted of dramatic increases in the relative supply of new entrants from the mid-1960s to the late 1970s as the baby boom cohorts entered the labor force combined with a sharp decline in the share of new entrants in the 1980s with the passage of the baby boom cohorts into mid-career. This pattern of changes in relative supplies can help explain increases in experience differentials in the 1970s, but it has some difficulties with the sharp increases in experience differentials for less-educated males in the 1980s.

C. CAN RELATIVE SUPPLY CHANGES EXPLAIN RELATIVE WAGE CHANGES?

To more formally examine how relative supply changes line up with the relative wage changes, we implement the framework outlined above. For the analysis in this section we divide our data into 64 distinct labor groups, distinguished by sex, 4 education categories (8–11, 12, 13–15, and 16+ years of schooling), and 8 experience categories (1–5, 6—10, 11–15, 16–20, 21–25, 26–30, 31–35, and 36–40 years). We begin with equation (4) and compute the inner products of changes in relative wages with changes in relative factor supplies between time periods. To reduce the number of computations and minimize the impact of measurement error, we aggregate our 25 years into 5 five-year intervals and compute average relative wages (relative to our wage index) and average relative supplies for each of our 64 groups within these subperiods. We then compute the inner products of the changes in these measures of wages and supplies between each pair of these five intervals.

The results of these calculations are given in the top part of Table III. The data appear to be reasonably consistent with the stable demand hypothesis for the 1965–1980 period. Five of the six comparisons for this period are negative, and the positive one is quite small and might be difficult to distinguish from sampling error. In contrast, all comparisons involving the interval centered in 1985 are positive and thereby reject a stable factor demand structure. Our findings are quite similar when we limit the analysis to men.

Figure III illustrates these patterns by plotting changes in log relative supplies against changes in log relative wages for the 64 labor groups for the period as a whole and for the three subperiods. The lines drawn in the figures represent predicted values from weighted least squares regressions of the changes in log wages on the changes in log factor supplies for each interval with the weights being the employment shares of each group in the initial period. The four graphs shown in the figure reinforce the findings from the inner products: for the 1963–1987 period as a whole and most strongly for the 1980s, the groups with the largest increases in relative supplies tended to have the largest increases in relative wages. Thus, when looking across groups, differential supply growth alone seems like an unlikely candidate to explain the observed changes in relative wages for the entire period. In fact, we find a negative relationship between growth in factor supplies and in relative wages only during the 1971–1979 period. These findings indicate that demand growth was an important component of the change in factor prices over the period as a whole and particularly during the 1980s. Delineating the time pattern and nature of these relative demand shifts is our next goal.

We first examine whether the observed wage changes can be made consistent with the observed pattern of relative quantity changes simply by allowing for smooth trend changes in relative demands. Such trend demand shifts might reflect a steady pace on nonneutral technological changes or steady changes in the industrial composition of employment. To do this, we regress the time series of relative wages and of quantities for each of our 64 groups on a constant and a linear time trend. We then average the residuals over five-year centered intervals for each group and compute the inner products in

TABLE III

INNER PRODUCTS OF CHANGES IN RELATIVE WAGES WITH CHANGES IN RELATIVE
QUANTITIES FOR 64 DEMOGRAPHIC GROUPS

5-year centered interval	5-year centered interval			
	1965	1970	1975	1980
Inner products of actual changes				
1970	0.0128			
1975	−0.1129	−0.1084		
1980	−0.0893	−0.1605	−0.0040	
1985	0.3813	0.1704	0.2224	0.1421
Inner products of changes in detrended data:				
1970	−0.0251			
1975	−0.0423	−0.0351		
1980	0.0074	−0.0201	−0.0070	
1985	−0.0028	−0.0037	−0.0402	0.0138

changes in detrended relative prices and relative quantities. The results of this procedure
are shown in the bottom half of Table III. Comparing these numbers with those obtained
without correcting for trend changes, we see that many more of the comparisons now
show negative inner products. We infer from this that trend demand growth alone can
make almost all of the observed price and quantity changes consistent with otherwise stable demand, although the remaining positive inner product for the 1980s in detrended
changes suggests some acceleration in the rate of growth of demand for women and
more-educated workers in the 1980s appears necessary.

V. MEASURING CHANGES IN THE RELATIVE DEMAND FOR LABOR

It is clear that substantial shifts in relative labor demand are necessary to explain
observed changes in the wage structure since the early 1960s as reflecting changes in relative competitive wage levels. Changes in the structure of product demand, increased
international competition, and skill-biased technological change have attracted much
attention as possible reasons for shifts in labor demand against less- educated males. We
find it useful to think of relative labor demand shifts as coming from two types of
changes: those that occur within industries (i.e., shifts that change the relative factor
intensities within industries at fixed relative wages) and those that occur between industries (i.e., shifts that change the allocation of total labor demand between industries at
fixed relative wages). Important sources of within-industry shifts include factor nonneutral technological change, changes in prices of nonlabor inputs (e.g., computer services),

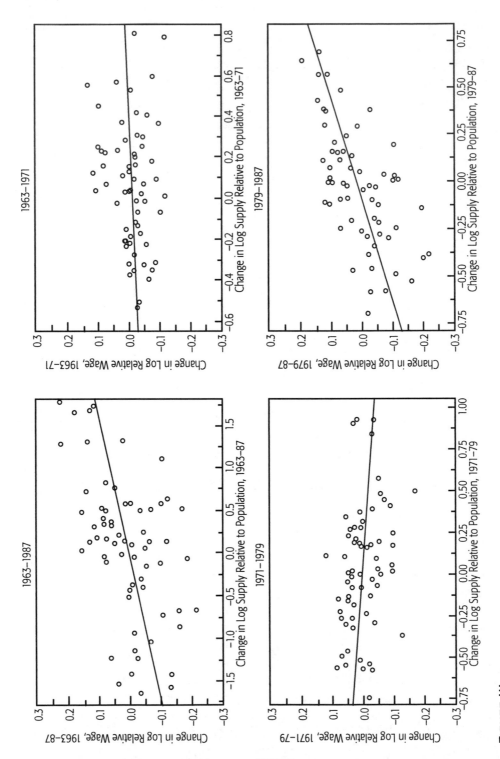

FIGURE III

Price and Quantity Changes for 64 Groups

and "outsourcing" (shifts of portions of industry production out of the United States). Between-industry shifts in demand may be driven by shifts in product demand across industries, sectoral differences in factor-neutral total factor productivity growth, and shifts in net international trade which change the domestic share of output at fixed relative wages.

The effect of between-industry shifts in labor demand on the relative demands for different demographic groups depends on group differences in industrial employment distributions. Table IV presents the distributions of employment among twelve broad industries and three major occupational categories of six gender-education groups.[10] The distributions in the table are the average distributions for each group over the 1967 to 1987 period.[11] The substantial differences in employment distributions indicate that shifts in labor demand across industries and occupations may greatly affect the relative wages of these groups.

Table V illustrates that large changes occurred in the industrial and occupational distribution of total employment over the 1967–1987 period. The shift over the entire period in the industrial employment distribution out of "low tech" and "basic" manufacturing and into professional and business services is suggestive of a trend demand shift in favor of college graduates and of women and against less-educated males. The substantial decline in importance of production worker jobs points toward similar demand shifts.

If within-industry relative factor demand is stable so that changes in the wage structure are entirely explained by between-industry shifts in labor demand and relative supply changes, then the shares of industrial employment of groups whose relative wages have increased should tend to fall inside every industry. Thus, the hypothesis of stable within-industry demand implies that the shares of women and college graduates should have declined in all industries. Since the share of aggregate employment of women and college graduates increased over this period, this scenario requires a substantial shift in employment into industries that intensively employ women and more-educated workers. In fact, an examination of our CPS data indicates that the shares of employment (measured either in total hours or efficiency units) accounted for by women and by college graduates increased in almost every two-digit industry both from 1963 to 1987 and during the 1980s.[12] This finding indicates that within-industry demand shifts favoring these groups must have occurred. On the other hand, the finding that within-industry shifts must have occurred does not rule out the possibility that the between-industry shifts suggested by Table V are an important factor in explaining relative wage changes. We next

---

[10] *We focus on gender-education groups because differences in industrial distributions by sex and education are much more significant than differences by experience level.*

[11] *Because of incompatibilities between the industry and occupation codes available in the 1964–1967 CPS surveys and those in the later surveys, we limit our analysis of shifts in labor demand arising from shifts across industry and occupation cells to the 1967–1987 period.*

[12] *Davis and Haltiwanger [1991] and Gottschalk and Joyce [1991] similarly report for the 1980s that the within-industry employment shares of groups increased with increases in relative wages.*

TABLE IV

AVERAGE INDUSTRIAL AND OCCUPATIONAL DISTRIBUTIONS OF SIX DEMOGRAPHIC
GROUPS, 1967–1987[a]

	Percentage employment shares					
Years of schooling: Gender:	8–11 Men	8–11 Women	12 Men	12 Women	16+ Men	16+ Women
Industry						
Agriculture and mining	9.8	3.0	6.4	1.8	3.0	1.0
Construction	14.1	0.7	11.2	1.4	3.4	0.6
Manufacturing:[b]						
Low tech	12.2	18.3	7.2	6.7	2.8	1.2
Basic	19.0	13.9	19.6	11.0	11.4	4.1
High tech	2.8	2.6	4.2	2.7	5.4	1.4
Communications, trans., and utilities	9.5	1.8	10.8	5.3	4.7	2.7
Wholesale trade	4.2	1.8	5.4	3.1	5.4	2.0
Retail trade	12.6	21.7	14.2	19.5	7.3	7.2
Professional, medical, and bus. services and FIRE	4.8	15.5	7.2	28.0	28.0	26.8
Education and welfare	2.2	5.9	1.9	7.6	19.0	45.5
Public administration	3.0	1.8	6.7	5.7	7.4	5.1
Other services	5.8	12.9	5.2	7.2	2.3	2.5
Occupation						
Professional, technical, and managers	9.3	6.8	19.7	15.2	77.3	76.9
Sales and clerical	5.6	19.8	12.3	52.2	12.6	17.5
Production and service workers	85.1	73.4	68.0	32.6	10.1	5.6

[a] The numbers in the table for each demographic group represent the average share of employment (measured in total annual hours) of that group in the corresponding industry or occupation with the average taken over the 1967–1987 period.
[b] Low tech manufacturing includes the lumber, furniture, stone, clay, glass, food, textiles, apparel, and leather industries. Basic manufacturing includes the primary metals, fabricated metals, machinery, electrical equipment, automobile, other transport equipment (excluding aircraft), tobacco, paper, printing, rubber, and miscellaneous manufacturing industries. High tech manufacturing includes the aircraft, instruments, chemicals, and petroleum industries.

more formally develop and implement a procedure for assessing the magnitude of between- and within-industry shifts in relative labor demands.

A. CONCEPTUAL FRAMEWORK

One widely used measure of the effect of between-sector demand shifts on relative labor demands is the fixed-coefficient "manpower requirements" index (e.g., Freeman [1975, 1980]). This index measures the percentage change in the demand for a demographic

TABLE V

OVERALL INDUSTRY AND OCCUPATION EMPLOYMENT DISTRIBUTIONS, 1967–1987[a]

	Percentage employment shares				Full period change
	1967–1969	1973–1975	1979–1981	1985–1987	
Industry					
Agriculture and Mining	5.4	4.5	4.4	3.8	−1.6
Construction	6.2	6.8	6.6	6.7	0.5
Manufacturing:[b]					
Low tech	8.7	7.5	6.4	5.5	−2.8
Basic	17.1	15.0	14.4	12.0	−5.1
High tech	4.3	3.6	3.5	3.4	−0.9
Commun., trans., and utilities	7.3	7.2	7.3	7.1	−0.2
Wholesale trade	3.7	4.4	4.6	4.6	−0.9
Retail trade	13.7	13.9	13.6	14.3	−0.6
Prof., med., and bus. serv. and FIRE	13.4	16.7	18.9	21.5	8.1
Education and welfare	7.9	9.3	9.2	9.4	1.5
Public admin.	6.2	5.9	5.9	6.0	−0.2
Other services	6.0	5.1	5.3	5.9	−0.1
Occupation					
Prof/tech and managers	28.1	29.6	32.0	35.4	7.3
Sales and clerical	21.3	21.8	22.5	22.4	1.1
Production and service workers	50.6	48.6	45.5	42.2	−8.4

[a] The numbers in the table are percentage shares of total employment measured in total annual hours.
[b] Low tech manufacturing includes the lumber, furniture, stone, clay, glass, food, textiles, apparel, and leather industries. Basic manufacturing includes the primary metals, fabricated metals, machinery, electrical equipment, automobile, other transport equipment (excluding aircraft), tobacco, paper, printing, rubber, and miscellaneous manufacturing industries. High tech manufacturing includes the aircraft, instruments, chemicals, and petroleum industries.

group as the weighted average of percentage employment growth by industry where the weights are the industrial employment distribution for the demographic group in a base period.[13] In this section we clarify the interpretation of these demand shift measures. These simple demand shift indices provide appropriate demand shift measures for implementing equation (3) to determine whether within-sector relative demand shifts are necessary to explain observed shifts in relative wages. Although they provide biased

[13] *This proxy for the percentage change in demand for demographic group k can be written as $\sum_j \lambda_{jk}(\Delta E_j/E_j)$, where j indexes industry, E_j is total employment of all demographic groups in industry j, $\lambda_{jk} = E_{jk}/(\sum_j E_{jk})$ in a base year, and E_{jk} is the employment of group k in industry j.*

measures of "true" between-sector relative demand shifts if relative wages are not stable, the nature of the bias can be determined. These demand shift indices tend to understate the relative demand shift favoring groups with increases in relative prices.

We begin our formal analysis by considering an economy that consists of J sectors (which can be thought of as industries or as industry-occupation cells) and K labor inputs. We denote output in sector J by Y_j and assume that production takes place under constant returns to scale in all sectors. We can write the $(K \times 1)$ vector of factor demands in sector j, X_j, as

$$(6) \qquad X_j = C_w^j(W)Y_j,$$

where $C_w^j(W)$ is the $(K \times 1)$ vector of unit factor demand curves (i.e., the partial derivatives of the unit cost function in sector j with respect to each group's own wage). Equation (6) can be written in terms of differentials as

$$(7) \qquad dX_j = C_w^j(W)dY_j + Y_jC_{ww}^j(W)dW,$$

under the assumption that within-sector demand is stable. Premultiplying by W and using the result that unit factor demands are homogeneous of degree zero in factor prices, we derive

$$(8a) \qquad W'dX_j = W'X_j(dY_j/Y_j)$$

or

$$(8b) \qquad \frac{dY_j}{Y_j} = \frac{W'dX_j}{W'X_j}$$

so that we can measure the percentage change in outputs by the value weighted percentage change in inputs.

This result is particularly useful, since aggregating (7) across sectors yields

$$(9) \qquad dX = \sum_j X_j \frac{dY_j}{Y_j} + C_{ww}dW = \sum_j X_j \frac{W'dX_j}{W'X_j} + C_{ww}dW,$$

where dX is the $(K \times 1)$ vector of employment changes and C_{ww} is the $(K \times K)$ matrix that corresponds to the production-weighted average of the Hessians (second partial derivatives) of the unit cost functions for the J industries and is negative semidefinite. Equation (9) implies that

(10)
$$dW'\left(dX - \sum_j X_j \frac{W'dX_j}{W'X_j}\right) = dW'C_{ww}dW \le 0.$$

Equation (10) is of the form given in equation (3). Thus, an appropriate between-sector demand shift measure to evaluate whether the data are consistent with stable demand within sectors is the $(K \times 1)$ vector;

(11)
$$\Delta D = \sum_j X_j \frac{W'dX_j}{W'X_j},$$

which is simply the vector of weighted sums of sector employments for each factor with the weights given by the percentage changes in the value of inputs in each sector. This demand shift index is exactly the standard fixed-coefficients index with sectoral employment changes measured in efficiency units rather than in raw hours. The intuitive interpretation of the index is that those inputs employed heavily in expanding sectors will have increased demand, while those inputs employed mostly in contracting sectors will have falling demand.

It is important to note at this point that all quantities in equation (11) are the equilibrium changes in factor employments and are thereby directly measurable. No presumption has been made as to the source of the changes in employments other than the fact that the sector-specific unit cost functions are being held fixed.[14] Although the demand index given in equation (11) can be directly inserted into equation (10) to test for the stability of demand within sectors, this demand index does not provide an unbiased measure of "true" between-industry demand shifts when relative wages are changing.

The reason for this bias is that changes in relative wages can affect the distribution of sectoral outputs so that ΔD will not measure the effects of changes in the allocation of labor demand across sectors at fixed relative wages. The output shares of sectors that intensively employ groups with relative wage increases are likely to fall relative to what they would have been at stable relative wages. Thus, ΔD is likely to be a downward biased measure of demand shifts in favor of groups with relative wage increases.

More formally, we can write the $(J \times 1)$ vector of changes in relative outputs, dY_j, as

(12)
$$dY = dY^* + Y_p dP = dY^* + Y_p C_w dW,$$

---

[14] Katz and Murphy [1990] show that this demand measure is appropriate even in the presence of within-sector, factor-neutral technological change.

where dY^* is the ($J \times 1$) vector of "true" product demand shifts computed at fixed factor prices, P is the ($J \times 1$) vector of sector output prices, Y_p is the ($J \times J$) matrix of derivatives with respect to the price vector of the sectoral demand functions, and C_w is the ($J \times K$) matrix of derivatives of the unit cost function with respect to own wages. The second equality arises from the assumption of constant returns to scale which implies that $dP = C_w(W)dW$. Using equations (6), (8a), (11), and (12), we can write our demand index as

$$(13) \qquad \Delta D = \sum_j C_w^j(W)dY_j = \left(C_w\right)' dY = \left(C_w\right)' dY^* + \left(C_w\right)' Y_p C_w dW.$$

Equation (13) gives our demand shift measure in terms of the true factor demand shift $(C_w)'dY^*$ and a bias term $(C_w)'Y_p C_w dW$. If $(C_w)'Y_p C_w$ is negative semidefinite (as will be the case in the absence of income effects), this bias term will be inversely related to wage changes on average (i.e., the inner product of dW and the bias term will be nonpositive). In the two-factor case the between-sector demand index given in equation (11) will understate the demand increase for those groups with rising relative wages. More generally, our demand shift index will tend to understate the magnitude of the true relative demand shifts favoring groups with increases in relative wages.

B. Measured Demand Shifts, 1967–1987

To implement this approach to measuring demand shifts, we divide the economy into 50 two-digit industries and 3 occupation categories and take the resulting 150 industry-occupation cells as our sectors. The advantage of adding occupations to the industry taxonomies used in most previous work is that doing so allows us to look at some dimensions of within-industry shifts in labor demand, as well as between-industry shifts. In this framework we can think of occupations as producing intermediate goods within industries.

Empirically we construct our demand shift measure to correspond to the index ΔD defined in equation (11). We specify our index of the between-sector change in demand for group k measured relative to base year employment of group k in efficiency units, E_k, as

$$(14) \qquad \Delta X_k^d = \frac{\Delta D_k}{E_k} = \sum_j \left(\frac{E_{jk}}{E_k}\right)\left(\frac{\Delta E_j}{E_j}\right) = \frac{\sum_j \alpha_{jk}\Delta E_j}{E_k}$$

where j indexes sector, E_j is total labor input in sector j measured in efficiency units, and $\alpha_{jk} = (E_{jk}/E_j)$ is group k's share of total employment in efficiency units in sector j in the base year. This measure expresses the percentage change in demand for each group as a weighted average of the percentage changes in sectoral employments (measured in efficiency units) in which the weights are group-specific employment distributions. We turn equation (14) into an index of relative demand shifts by normalizing all employment measures so that total employment in efficiency units in each year sums to one. We choose the average of the 1967–1987 sample period to be our base period.[15] Thus, we use the average share of total employment in sector j of group k over the 1967–1987 period as our measure of α_{jk}, and the average share of group k in total employment over the 1967–1987 period as our measure of E_k.

We define our overall (industry-occupation) demand shift index for group k, ΔX_k^d, as the index given in (14) when j indexes our 150 industry-occupation cells. We also decompose this index into between- and within-industry components. The between-industry demand shift index for group k, ΔX_k^b, is given by the index in (14) when j refers to 50 industries. We define our within-industry demand shift index for k, ΔX_k^w, as the difference between the overall demand shift index and the between-industry demand shift index (i.e., $\Delta X_k^w = \Delta X_k^d - \Delta X_k^b$). These within-industry demand shifts reflect shifts in employment among occupations within industries.

Table VI presents our relative demand shift estimates for eight demographic groups for the entire 1967–1987 period and for three subperiods. The overall measure of demand shifts for the entire period is monotonically increasing in education level for both men and women. The overall measure also shifted in favor of women relative to men within every education group from 1967 to 1987. Since education differentials expanded and gender differentials narrowed over the 1967–1987 period, the actual between-sector demand shifts toward more-educated workers and women that would have occurred at fixed-factor prices are likely to have been even greater than the increases indicated in Table VI. The overall measure indicates that between-sector shifts in employment increased the demand for male college graduates by over 30 percent relative to males with twelve or fewer years of schooling. Demand shifts in favor of women are much greater for high school graduates and those with some college than for high school dropouts and college graduates. These differences reflect the concentration of males but not females with 12 to 15 years of schooling in production occupations and manufacturing industries.

Although the measured demand shifts toward more-educated workers and toward women have been substantial, they are significantly smaller than the observed relative supply changes documented in Table II. Thus, changes in relative wages and changes in relative supplies net of changes in the between-sector demand shift index positively covary over the 1967–1987 and the 1979–1987 period. Demand shifts within our industry-occupation cells are required to explain the observed extent of positive covariation in changes in relative wages and relative supplies.

Table VI also suggests that the pace of overall demand growth for college graduates appears to have been relatively steady over the 1967–1987 period. On the other hand, there are some differences in the time pattern of shifts in the demand for female and male college

---

[15] Our basic qualitative findings concerning measured demand shifts are insensitive to choice of base year.

TABLE VI

INDUSTRY AND OCCUPATION BASED DEMAND SHIFT MEASURES, 1967–1987[a]

Group	Between industry				Change in log relative demand (multiplied by 100) Within industry				Overall (industry and occupation)			
	67–71	71–79	79–87	67–87	67–71	71–79	79–87	67–87	67–71	71–79	79–87	67–87
Males												
Dropouts (8–11 years)	-3.3	-4.8	-6.0	-14.1	0.7	-2.4	-2.9	-4.7	-2.6	-7.2	-8.9	-18.7
HS graduates (12 years)	-2.5	-3.0	-3.6	-9.0	0.3	-1.6	-1.7	-3.1	-2.2	-4.6	-5.3	-12.1
Some college (13–15 years)	-1.0	-0.6	0.4	-1.2	-0.2	0.5	0.9	-1.2	-1.2	-0.1	1.2	-0.0
College graduates (16+ years)	3.5	4.3	2.9	10.7	-1.1	2.6	4.3	5.8	2.4	6.9	7.2	16.5
Females												
Dropouts (8–11 years)	-5.0	-6.4	0.3	-11.1	0.4	-2.9	-3.3	-5.7	-4.5	-9.3	-3.0	-16.8
HS graduates (12 years)	0.4	1.1	4.3	5.8	1.1	0.2	-3.1	-1.8	1.5	1.3	1.2	4.0
Some college (13–15 years)	3.7	5.6	5.9	15.2	0.8	2.5	-0.9	2.4	4.5	8.1	5.0	17.6
College graduates (16+ years)	8.3	6.4	3.0	17.7	-0.4	1.8	1.8	3.1	7.8	8.2	4.7	20.8

[a] The overall and between-industry demand shift measures for group k are of the form $\Delta D_k = \sum_j \alpha_{jk} (\Delta E_j / E_k)$ where α_{jk} is the average share for group k of employment in sector j over the 1967–1987 period, E_j is the share of aggregate employment in sector j, and E_k is the average share of total employment of group k for 1967–1987. The reported numbers are of the form $\log(1 + \Delta D_k)$. In the overall measure, j indexes 150 industry-occupation cells. In the between-industry measure, j indexes 50 industries. The within-industry index for group k in year t is the difference of the overall and between-industry measures for group k in year t. In all calculations, employment is measured in efficiency units.

graduates. The magnitude of relative demand shifts favoring college males appears to have increased in the 1980s, while demand shifts favoring female college graduates are smaller in the 1980s than in the earlier periods. These differences reflect the rapid growth of the professional and business services in the 1980s and the decline in relative employment in education and the public sector in this same period. Furthermore, the overall demand shift index masks important differences in the between- and within-industry measures of demand shifts. Between-industry shifts for college graduates appear to have decelerated in the 1980s, while within-industry demand shifts (largely reflecting an accelerating rate of decline in the share of production jobs within industries) have accelerated throughout the period.

C. Demand Shifts Arising from Changes in International Trade

We next examine the importance of changes in net international trade in manufactured goods as a source of relative labor demand shifts.[16] Many have argued that increased import competition particularly with the large U. S. trade deficits of the 1980s has played an important role in shifting employment out of manufacturing sectors and shifting relative demand against less-educated workers.

To estimate the labor supply equivalents of trade, we transform trade flows into equivalent bodies on the basis of the utilization of labor inputs in the domestic manufacturing industries that constitute the bulk of the traded goods sector. We do this by estimating the direct labor supply embodied in trade, ignoring indirect input-output effects. Thus, the implicit labor supply in trade is the labor input required to produce traded output domestically. Formally, we let I_{it} be net imports in industry i in year t, Y_{it} be domestic output of industry i in year t, and E_{it} be the share of total efficiency units in the U. S. economy in year t employed in sector i ($\Sigma_i F_{it} = 1$). The implicit supply of labor embodied in net imports in industry i in year t measured as a fraction of total U. S. labor input is given by $(E_{it}/Y_{it})*I_{it}$. The implicit supply of labor of demographic group k contained in net trade in year t as a fraction of total domestic labor supply of k is given by

$$(15) \qquad L_t^k = \sum_i e_i^k E_{it}\left(\frac{I_{it}}{Y_{it}}\right),$$

where e_i^k is the average proportion of employment (measured in efficiency units) in industry i made up of workers in group k over the 1967–1987 period.

We measure the effect of trade on relative demand for demographic group k in year t as

$$(16) \qquad T_t^k = -\left(\frac{1}{E^k}\right)\sum_i\left[e_i^k E_{it}\left(\frac{I_{it}}{Y_{it}}\right)\right] + \sum_i\left[E_{it}\left(\frac{I_{it}}{Y_{it}}\right)\right],$$

---

[16] See Borjas, Freeman, and Katz [1992] and Murphy and Welch [1991] for more detailed treatments of the effects of international trade flows on relative labor demands.

where E^k is the average share of total employment in efficiency units of group k for the 1967–1987 period. The first term is simply the implicit supply of the labor of group k contained in trade normalized by base year employment of k with the sign reversed to convert this supply shift measure into a demand shift measure. The second term adjusts the demand shift measure so that trade affects only relative demands for labor.[17]

In equation (16) we assume that trade-induced changes in an industry's output alter the employment of production and nonproduction workers in that industry in the same manner as would domestic-induced changes in output. Alternatively, however, it is plausible that exports and imports may affect quite different portions of an industry and may have differential impacts on the employment of production and nonproduction workers. In particular, while exports and production for domestic consumption may create employment for both kinds of workers in a similar manner, imports may displace production workers to a far greater extent than they displace nonproduction workers. In fact, many activities of nonproduction workers (e.g., marketing, sales, accounting) may be relatively complementary with production workers overseas. To take into account this issue, we provide two estimates of the effects of trade on employment. Under the first method which we denote "equal allocation," we directly employ equation (16) and treat net imports in a manner analogous to domestic production for domestic consumption. Under the second method which we denote "production worker allocation," we modify the first term in equation (16) so that exports are allocated to all workers in the same manner as domestic production for domestic consumption, but imports are allocated to production workers only.[18]

We use data on imports, exports, and output from the NBER Immigration, Trade, and Labor Market Data Files to compute the trade ratios used in the construction of our indices of demand shifts arising from trade.[19] These data cover four-digit SIC manufac-

---

[17] *This demand shift index has the property that $\Sigma_k T_i^k E^k = 0$. Murphy and Welch [1991] provide a formal justification for this type of demand shift index.*

[18] *We replace the first term on the right-hand side of the equation (16) with*

$$-\left(\frac{1}{E^k}\right)\sum_i\left\{\left[e_i^k E_{it}\left(\frac{X_{it}}{Y_{it}}\right)\right]-\left[p_i^k E_{it}\left(\frac{M_{it}}{Y_{it}}\right)\right]\right\},$$

where X measures exports, M measures imports, and p_i^k is group k's average share of production worker employment in industry i over the 1967–1987 period. We classify as production workers those workers in the manufacturing sector in the following broad occupational categories: craft workers, handlers and laborers, operatives, transport operatives, and service workers.

[19] *Abowd [1991] provides a detailed discussion of this data set and the construction of trade data on a four-digit SIC industry basis. The data on output and employment in each industry given by the NBER data set are from the Annual Survey of Manufactures.*

TABLE VII

CHANGES IN RELATIVE LABOR DEMAND PREDICTED BY CHANGES IN INTERNATIONAL TRADE IN MANUFACTURES, 1967–1985[a]

Group	Change in relative labor demand from trade by group measured as percent of group base-year employment[b]					
	Equal allocation[c]			Production worker allocation[d]		
	67–73	73–79	79–85	67–73	73–79	79–85
Males						
Dropouts (8–11 years)	−0.16	0.07	−0.63	−0.50	−0.25	−1.48
HS graduates (12 years)	−0.08	0.08	−0.28	−0.27	−0.10	−0.71
Some college (13–15 years)	0.04	0.05	0.07	0.16	0.21	0.42
College graduates (16+ years)	0.18	0.02	0.55	0.58	0.42	1.50
Females						
Dropouts (8–11 years)	−0.48	−0.25	−2.22	−0.76	−0.32	−4.00
HS graduates (12 years)	−0.08	−0.15	−0.16	−0.11	−0.21	−0.27
Some college (13–15 years)	0.12	−0.15	0.08	0.17	−0.23	0.11
College graduates (16+ years)	0.22	−0.20	1.26	0.24	−0.25	1.50

[a] Data on trade flows are from the NBER Immigration, Trade, and Labor Market data files. Labor input data are from the March CPS files.
[b] Base-year employment for each group is that group's average share of total employment from 1967–1985.
[c] Imports and exports are assumed to affect production and nonproduction workers in the same manner as production for domestic consumption.
[d] Imports are assumed to affect production workers only, and exports are assumed to affect all workers in the same manner as does production for domestic consumption.

turing industries for each year from 1967 to 1985. We aggregate these data into 21 two-digit manufacturing industries.

Table VII presents the changes in relative labor demand predicted by changes in international trade in manufactures for the 1967–1973, 1973–1979, and 1979–1985 periods. The table indicates that the effects on relative labor demands of trade were quite moderate until substantial trade deficits developed in the 1980s. The adverse effects of trade on relative labor demand are concentrated on high school dropouts. Female dropouts who have traditionally been employed intensively as production workers in import-competing industries such as apparel and textiles are the group most affected by trade. In fact, demand changes from trade are larger for female high school dropouts in the 1980s than are domestic sources of between-sector demand shifts. The table also indicates that the effects of trade on relative labor demand are substantially larger when imports are assumed to disproportionately affect production workers. Although trade-induced changes in relative demand move in the correct direction to help explain rising education differentials in the 1980s, they are quite small relative to the increases in the relative supplies of more-educated workers over the same period.

VI. UNDERSTANDING CHANGES IN EDUCATION AND EXPERIENCE DIFFERENTIALS

A. EDUCATION DIFFERENTIALS

The college/high school wage premium increased from 1963 to 1971, fell from 1971 through 1979, and then rose sharply after 1979. There are two primary types of explanations for these movements in the college/high school wage differential. The first interprets these changes in relative earnings as representing changes in the relative market price of skills possessed by college and high school graduates.

The second type of explanation focuses on changes in the composition of college and high school graduates that affect the relative skill levels of the two groups. This type of explanation interprets the decline in the college wage premium in the 1970s as reflecting a decline in the relative quality of college graduates and the rise in education returns in the 1980s as reflecting a decline in the relative quality of high school graduates. Because within-cohort comparisons are likely to hold the relative quality of college and high school graduates relatively constant, this hypothesis suggests one should not find important within-cohort changes in the college wage premium. Since movements in the college/high school wage differential are quite similar within cohorts and within experience levels over our sample period [Blackburn, Bloom, and Freeman, 1990; Katz and Murphy, 1990], we conclude it is appropriate to view differences in the movement in the college wage premium in the 1960s, 1970s, and 1980s as largely reflecting changes in the relative price of college skills rather than as primarily reflecting changes in the relative quality of college graduates. Thus, we turn to evaluating supply and demand explanations for changes in the relative price of college skills.

We take the overall college/high school wage ratio for males and females combined as the relative price to be explained.[20] We amalgamate our 320 groups into two labor aggregates: college equivalent workers and high school equivalent workers. We use the relative quantity of college and high school equivalents as our relative supply variable in assessing explanations for movements in the college/high school wage ratio.

We create our measures of college and high school equivalents as follows. We construct aggregate labor inputs (using a fixed-weight total supply measure with weights proportional to average wages over the 1963–1987 period) for each of our four education groups (8–11, 12, 13–15, and 16+ years of schooling). We treat high school graduates (those with twelve years of schooling) as pure high school equivalents, and we treat college graduates as pure college equivalents. We allocate other categories of workers (those with less than twelve years of schooling and those with some college) to our two aggregate groups on the basis of regressions determining the extent to which their wages move

---

[20] In this section we measure the college/high school wage ratio as the fixed-weight average of the ratio of the average weekly wage of college graduates to the average weekly wage of high school graduates for sixteen cells defined by sex and five-year experience brackets. The fixed weight for each cell is the cell's average share of total employment over the 1963–1987 period. This series is plotted in Panel B of Figure I as the college/high school wage ratio for all experience levels.

with the wage of high school graduates and college graduates, respectively. For those with less than a high school degree and those with some college, we regress the average wage series for each of these two groups on the wage series for high school graduates and for college graduates over the 1963–1987 period.[21] (The implicit assumption is that each group is a linear combination of college and high school graduates). The regression results suggest that one person with some college is equivalent to a total of 0.69 of a high school graduate and 0.29 of a college graduate, while a high school dropout is equivalent to 0.93 of a high school graduate and −0.05 of a college graduate. We use these coefficients to allocate the corresponding quantities of high school dropouts and those with some college to the high school and college quantities to form the supplies of high school and college equivalents.

We consider the simplest CES technology with two factors (college and high school equivalents) so that relative wages in year t, $w_1(t)/w_2(t)$, and relative supplies in year t, $x_1(t)/x_2(t)$, satisfy the relationship

$$(17) \qquad \log\left(\frac{w_1(t)}{w_2(t)}\right) = \left(\frac{1}{\sigma}\right)\left[D(t) - \log\left(\frac{x_1(t)}{x_2(t)}\right)\right],$$

where σ is the elasticity of substitution between college and high school equivalents and $D(t)$ is the time series of relative demand shifts measured in log quantity units. Given that there are other inputs in the production function, this is a conditional factor demand framework which requires that demand shifts be defined to include the effects of changes in the prices (or equivalently the supplies) of these other inputs.

The elasticity of substitution is an unknown parameter, and the time series of $D(t)$ is unobservable. Under the assumption that the economy operates on the demand curve given by equation (17), a given value of the elasticity of substitution between factors ($\sigma = \sigma_0$) implies a time series of demand shifts:

$$(18) \qquad D(t) = \sigma_0 \log(w_1(t)/w_2(t)) + \log(x_1(t)/x_2(t)).$$

The greater the elasticity of substitution between the two factors, the smaller the impact of shifts in relative supplies on relative wages and the greater must be the fluctuations in $D(t)$ to explain any given time series of relative prices for a given time series of observed relative quantities.

We take two approaches to developing stories consistent with the observed time series on prices and quantities. The first is to estimate σ by running (17) by ordinary least squares under the assumption that $D(t)$ is approximated by a simple linear time trend. We are somewhat skeptical of estimates of σ recovered from 25 nonindependent time series observations.

---

[21] *The regressions do not contain intercept terms.*

Our second approach is to use equation (18) to impute $D(t)$ conditional on a choice for the value of σ. For any given value of σ, we can evaluate the implied explanation by examining whether the implied time series for $D(t)$ matches well with the measures of between- and within-industry demand shifts developed in the previous section.

The basic movements in our relative price and relative quantity measures over our sample period are summarized in the top part of Table VIII. The relative supply of college equivalents grew tremendously over this period, and the college wage premium increased substantially. A regression of the log of the ratio of the supply of college to high school equivalents on a linear time trend for the 1963–1987 period yields a coefficient of 0.045 ($t = 41.5$), and the log relative price series is almost orthogonal to trend. Hence the relative demand for college equivalents has grown by about 4.5 percent per year on average over the sample period.

The key question to be addressed is the degree to which the time series of the college wage premium has been driven by fluctuations in the growth of supply versus the extent to which it has been driven by fluctuations in demand-side factors. Figure IV graphs the detrended wage and price series (in Panels A and B). Since the price series has little trend, the series in Panel A is quite similar to the overall returns to college series. The quantity series plotted in Panel B and summarized in Table VIII reveals some important features, however: supply grew more slowly than average from 1963–1971, faster than average from 1971 until about 1979, and then more slowly than average again in the 1980s. It appears that an explanation emphasizing fluctuations in supply growth has the potential to explain observed fluctuations in the college wage premium.

Thus, the model in equation (17) in which $D(t)$ is proxied by a linear time trend may fit the data reasonably well. OLS estimation of this equation for the 1963–1987 period yields

$$(19) \qquad \log(w_1/w_2) = - \underset{(0.150)}{0.709} \log(x_1/x_2) + \underset{(0.007)}{0.033} \text{ time} + \text{constant},$$

with an R^2 of 0.52. The estimate of σ in (19) implies an elasticity of substitution between college and high school labor of about 1.41. The actual time series of college returns and the fitted values from this regression are shown together in Panel C of Figure IV. The figure shows that this model does a tolerable job of explaining the movements in the college wage premium except for the period from the late 1970s to the early 1980s.

Panel D in Figure IV shows the implied demand series derived from (18) for elasticities of substitution of 0.5, 1.41, and 4 with demand normalized to equal 0 in 1963. The figure illustrates that there is a one-dimensional family of implied demand shifts (indexed by σ) that are consistent with the observed price and quantity time series. The implied demand shifts range from relatively steady demand growth when σ is small (0.5 to 1) to demand growth which slows significantly in the 1970s and accelerates greatly during the 1980s when σ is moderate to high.

To see how alternative demand shift scenarios compare with the observed pattern of between-sector demand shifts calculated in the previous sections, we aggregate the

TABLE VIII

COLLEGE/HIGH SCHOOL RELATIVE WAGES, QUANTITIES, AND DEMAND SHIFTS

Variable	Log Change (multiplied by 100)					
	1963–1971	1967–1971	1971–1979	1979–1987	1963–1987	1967–1987
College/high school weekly wage ratio[a]	7.7	3.0	−10.4	12.8	10.0	5.4
Relative supply of college to high school equivalents	31.4	16.6	40.8	25.5	97.6	82.9
Measured relative demand shifts—college/high school[b]						
Overall (industry-occupation)	—	4.6	10.2	9.9	—	24.8
Between industry	—	5.9	6.7	4.6	—	17.2
Within industry	—	−1.3	3.6	5.2	—	7.6

[a] The college/high school weekly wage ratio is the fixed-weight average of the ratio of the average weekly wage of full-time college graduates to full-time high school graduates for sixteen gender-experience groups. The fixed weights for each group are the average shares of that group in total employment for the 1963–1987 period.
[b] These demand shift measures are the corresponding measures from Table VI aggregated to measure shifts in the demand for college equivalents relative to high school equivalents.

demand shift measures by education-gender groups presented in Table VI into demand shifts for college equivalents relative to high school equivalents. Table VIII compares these shifts with movements in the relative supply of college equivalents. Our demand shift index implies that the relative demand for college graduates increased by 10.2 per cent from 1971–1979 and by 9.9 percent from 1979–1987. There is little direct indication of an acceleration in the growth of the relative demand for more highly educated workers from these demand shift indices. On the other hand, our analysis of the nature of the bias in these indices indicates that the demand shift index understates the "true" between-sector growth for college graduates relative to high school graduates in the 1980s and overstates the shifts in the 1970s. Furthermore, the overall demand shift measure masks a combination of a deceleration in measured between-industry demand shifts and an acceleration in measured within-industry demand shifts from the 1970s to the 1980s. The measured demand shifts explain about one third of the implied trend demand shifts consistent with the observed time series of prices and quantities.

B. EXPERIENCE DIFFERENTIALS

We next examine explanations for movements in experience differentials for males over the 1963–1987 period. We focus on males, since our measure of potential experience is likely to be a worse indicator of actual experience for women than for men. We take the ratio of the wage of males with 26 to 35 years of experience (old workers or peak earners) to the wage of males with 1 to 5 years of experience (young workers or new entrants) as the relative price to be explained.

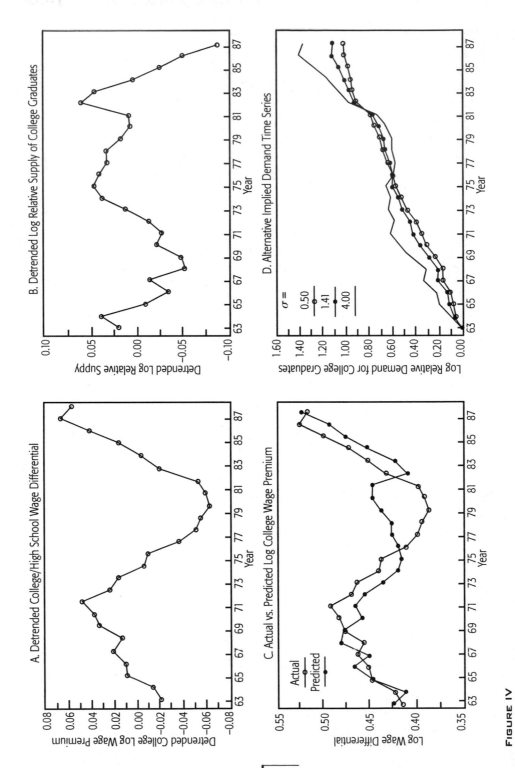

FIGURE IV
Education Differentials: Supply and Demand Analysis

The path of the log old/young wage differential for all males over our sample period is presented in Panel A of Figure V. The overall old/young wage differential for males was reasonably constant from the mid-1960s to 1970, increased sharply in the early 1970s, remained stable in the late 1970s, and increased greatly in the 1980s. The log old/young wage differential increased by approximately 0.12 over the entire period. The time pattern of the changes in experience differentials for all men is dominated by changes for those with less than sixteen years of schooling. Panel D of Figure I showed that experience differentials increased markedly from 1979 to 1987 for high school graduates and actually fell for college graduates over the same period. These sharp differences in a period of rising education differentials are suggestive of the "active labor market" hypothesis of Freeman [1975] in which changes in the labor market show up most sharply for new entrants because more senior workers are insulated by labor market institutions, such as seniority layoff systems, and valuable firm-specific capital. In particular, the collapse of new employment opportunities for less-educated workers in the manufacturing sector in the 1980s is likely to have had its most severe impact on young less-educated males.

We first examine the ability of changes in the relative supply of more- to less-experienced workers to explain changes in experience differentials. Table II indicates that the relative supply of workers with one to ten years of experience increased greatly over the entire 1963–1987 period but actually declined in the 1980s as the baby boom cohort workers became more experienced and the baby bust cohort entered the labor market. This suggests that the growth in relative supply of young workers can help explain the secular growth in experience differentials but will have trouble explaining changes in the 1980s. On the other hand, the fraction of workers with eleven to twenty years of experience grew rapidly in the 1980s, and it is a priori unclear how an expansion of the supply of workers in this group affects the earnings of new entrants relative to peak earners.

We attempt to deal with the issue of how multidimensional changes in the age structure of the labor force affect the relative earnings of old to young workers by using a relative supply variable that aggregates all experience groups into two groups (old and young equivalents). The construction of this variable is exactly analogous to the construction of college and high school equivalents above. We treat workers with 26 to 35 years of experience as pure old equivalents and those with 1 to 5 years of experience as pure young equivalents. We allocate workers in the five other five-year experience brackets (6–10, 11–15, 16–20, 21–25, 36–40 years) to our two aggregate groups on the basis of regressions (without intercepts) of their wages on the wages of those with 26–35 and 1–5 years of experience.[22]

---

[22] On the basis of these regressions, we define the number of old (N_0) and of young equivalents (N_y) as

$$N_y = n_1 + 0.92n_2 + 0.86n_3 + 0.53n_4 + 0.38n_5 + 0.07n_6 - 0.07n_7 - 0.01n_8$$

$$N_0 = 0.23n_2 + 0.39n_3 + 0.66n_4 + 0.77n_5 + 0.97n_6 + 1.037n_7 + 0.98n_8,$$

where n_j is the fixed-weight total supply of workers in the jth five-year experience group (i.e., n_1 is the supply of those with one to five years of experience, etc.).

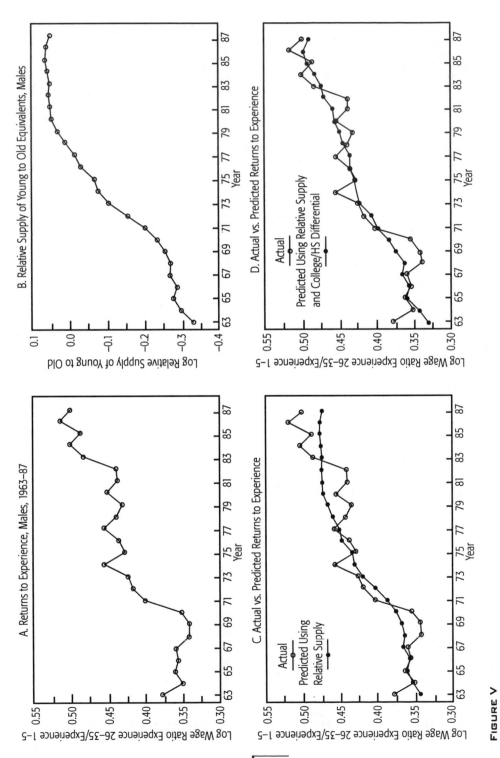

Figure V

Experience Differentials for All Males: Supply Factors

We display the time path of the log relative supply of young to old equivalents in panel B of Figure V. The basic movements in the relative supply of young to old equivalents look quite similar to a smoothed version of the changes in the old/young wage ratio illustrated in panel A of the figure. In particular, the long-term growth in experience differentials is quite consistent with the long-term increase in the share of young equivalent workers. Yet the timing of the changes in experience differentials (particularly movements in the mid-1970s and the 1980s) does not match up well with the smoothly declining rate of growth of the relative supply of young equivalents.

These points are brought out by a comparison of movements in actual experience differentials and the predicted values from a regression over the 1963–1987 of the log old/young wage ratio on the log relative supply of old to young equivalents.[23] The actual and predicted values from this regression are contrasted in panel C of Figure V. The regression does a good job of explaining the secular growth in experience differentials but fails to explain the sharp increase in the 1980s. The active labor market hypothesis suggests that a weak market for less-educated workers may help explain widening experience differentials for less-educated workers since young less-educated workers will bear the brunt of adjustment to changing market conditions. The addition of the log of the overall college/high school wage ratio to our specification (essentially as a proxy for relative demand shifts in favor of older workers) improves the ability of the regression to explain movements in overall experience differentials as is illustrated in panel D of Figure V.[24] Relative supply movements combined with the state of the labor market for educated workers go a long way toward explaining changes in experience differentials for men.

VII. CONCLUSIONS

A simple supply and demand framework helps illuminate many aspects of changes in the U. S. wage structure. The relative wages and quantities of more-educated workers and women increased substantially from 1963 to 1987. Within-group and overall wage inequality also increased sharply over this period. Substantial secular growth in the demand for more-educated workers, females, and "more-skilled" workers within groups is necessary to interpret the observed changes in relative wages as changes in competitive skill prices. Measured changes in the allocation of labor demand between sectors (150 industry-occupation cells) can account for a large minority of the secular demand shifts in favor of groups with rising relative wages. Demand shifts arising from changes in international change in manufacturing only start to be of quantitative significance with the

---

[23] *This regression yielded a coefficient (standard error) of −0.342 (0.032) on the log relative supply variable and an R^2 of 0.83.*

[24] *The regression of the log relative earnings of old to young males (RE) on the log relative supply of old to young equivalents (RSUP) and the log of the overall college/high school wage premium (CHSPREM) yields a coefficient (standard error) of −0.348 (0.028) on RSUP and of 0.292 (0.106) on CHSPREM and has an R^2 of 0.87.*

appearance of large trade deficits in the 1980s. The majority of the required demand shifts in favor of more-educated workers and females reflect difficult to measure changes in within-sector relative labor demand. Recent work by Krueger [1991] suggests that the spread of computers in the workplace may be an important component of these within-sector changes in the composition of labor demand.

The pattern of changes in the wage structure differed substantially in the 1960s, 1970s, and 1980s. The college wage premium increased moderately in the 1960s, declined in the 1970s, and expanded dramatically in the 1980s. Differences across the three decades in the rate of the growth of the supply of college graduates as a fraction of the labor force appear to play an important role in explaining these large differences in the behavior of the relative earnings of college graduates. Fluctuations in the rate of growth of relative supply do not greatly help illuminate differences across decades in changes in the male/female wage differential. Within-group earnings inequality was stable in the 1960s and has increased steadily since the early 1970s. The differences in the time pattern of rising education differentials and rising within-group inequality suggest that they are at least partially distinct economic phenomena.

Much recent work indicates that economic pressures toward increased inequality and skill differentials arising from between-industry shifts in labor demand and skill-biased technological change appear important in most OECD economies in the 1980s (e.g., Gottschalk and Joyce [1991]; Katz and Loveman [1990]). Although wage structures appear to have started to expand in almost all OECD countries by the middle of the 1980s, the magnitude of the changes varies substantially. The extent to which this divergence in wage structure changes across countries is explained by differences in the supply and demand factors emphasized in this paper as opposed to differences in wage-setting institutions is an important topic for future research.

REFERENCES

Abowd, John, "Appendix: The NBER Immigration, Trade, and Labor Market Data Files," in *Immigration, Trade and the Labor Market*, J. Abowd and R. Freeman, eds. (Chicago: University of Chicago Press, 1991), pp. 407–21.

Blackburn, McKinley, David Bloom, and Richard B. Freeman, "The Declining Position of Less-Skilled American Males," in *A Future of Lousy Jobs?* Gary Burtless, ed. (Washington, DC: The Brookings Institution, 1990), pp. 31–67.

Borjas, George J., Richard B. Freeman, and Lawrence F. Katz, "On the Labor Market Effects of Immigration and Trade," in *The Economic Effects of Immigration in Source and Receiving Countries*, G. Borjas and R. Freeman, eds. (Chicago: University of Chicago Press, 1992), pp. 213–44.

Bound, John, and George Johnson, "Changes in the Structure of Wages During the 1980s: An Evaluation of Alternative Explanations," *American Economic Review*, LXXXII (1992), pp. 371–92.

Davis, Steven J., and John Haltiwanger, "Wage Dispersion between and within U. S. Manufacturing Plants, 1963–86," *Brookings Papers on Economic Activity: Microeconomics* (1991), 115–80.

Freeman, Richard B., "Overinvestment in College Training?" *Journal of Human Resources*, X (Summer 1975), 287–311.

————, "The Effect of Demographic Factors on the Age-Earnings Profile in the United States," *Journal of Human Resources,* XIV (Summer 1979), 289–318.

————, "An Empirical Analysis of the Fixed Coefficient 'Manpower Requirements' Model, 1960–1970," *Journal of Human Resources,* XV (1980), 176–99.

————, "How Much Has De-Unionisation Contributed to the Rise in Male Earnings Inequality?" NBER Working Paper No. 3826, August 1991.

Goldin, Claudia, and Robert A. Margo, "The Great Compression: The Wage Structure in the United States at Mid-Century," *Quarterly Journal of Economics,* CVII (1992), 1–34.

Gottschalk, Peter, and Mary Joyce, "Changes in Earnings Inequality: An International Perspective," mimeo, Boston College, June 1991.

Juhn, Chinhui, Kevin M. Murphy, and Brooks Pierce, "Wage Inequality and the Rise in the Returns to Skill," mimeo, University of Chicago, November 1989.

Karoly, Lynn A., "The Trend in Inequality Among Families, Individuals, and Workers in the United States: A Twenty-Five Year Perspective," mimeo, The Rand Corporation, May 1990.

Katz, Lawrence F., and Gary Loveman, "An International Comparison of Changes in the Structure of Wages: France, the United Kingdom, and the United States," mimeo, Harvard University, December 1990.

Katz, Lawrence F., and Ana L. Revenga, "Changes in the Structure of Wages: The United States vs Japan," *Journal of the Japanese and International Economies,* III (December 1989), 522–53.

Katz, Lawrence F., and Kevin M. Murphy, "Changes in Relative Wages, 1963–1987: Supply and Demand Factors," mimeo, Harvard University, April 1990.

Krueger, Alan B., "How Computers Have Changed the Wage Structure: Evidence from Microdata, 1984–89," mimeo, Princeton University, August 1991.

Levy, Frank, and Richard Murnane, "U. S. Earnings Levels and Earnings Inequality: A Review of Recent Trends and Proposed Explanations," mimeo, Harvard University, July 1991.

Lillard, Lee, James Smith, and Finis Welch, "What Do We Really Know About Wages? The Importance of Nonreporting and Census Imputation," *Journal of Political Economy,* XCIV (June 1986), 488–506.

Mincer, Jacob, "Human Capital, Technology, and the Wage Structure: What Do Time Series Show?" NBER Working Paper No. 3581, January 1991.

Mitchell, Daniel J. B., "Wage Pressures and Labor Shortages: The 1960s and 1980s, *Brookings Papers on Economic Activity* (1989:2), 191–232.

Murphy, Kevin M., and Finis Welch, "The Role of International Trade in Wage Differentials," in *Workers and Their Wages,* M. Kosters, ed. (Washington, DC: The AEI Press, 1991), pp. 39–69.

————, and ————, "The Structure of Wages," *Quarterly Journal of Economics,* CVII (1992), 285–326.

Welch, Finis, "Effects of Cohort Size on Earnings: The Baby Boom Babies' Financial Bust," *Journal of Political Economy,* LXXXVII (October 1979), S65–S98.

ABOUT THE AUTHORS

Lawrence F. Katz

Larry Katz is professor of economics at Harvard University. He is especially well known for his research on wage inequality and his evaluation of the effects of government programs on the labor market, and since 1991 has served as an influential editor at the *Quarterly Journal of Economics*.

After receiving his A.B. degree in economics at the University of California at Berkeley in 1981, Katz completed a Ph.D. in economics at the Massachusetts Institute of Technology in 1986. Katz spent a year as an assistant professor in the School of Business Administration at the University of California at Berkeley before he moved to Harvard University in 1986.

In January of 1993 Katz was selected for the newly created position of Chief Economist in the U.S. Department of Labor. He held this position until August 1994, when he returned to Harvard.

Despite his important roles as editor, public policy advisor, and teacher, Katz creates the time to follow his keen interest in bird watching and has been spotted in some very exotic locales pursuing his avocation.

Kevin M. Murphy

Kevin Murphy is George P. Shultz Professor of Business Economics and Industrial Relations at the University of Chicago. Well known for his research on wage inequality, Murphy has also written on a diverse set of topics that includes the economics of taste formation and growth.

Murphy received an A.B. in economics from the University of California at Los Angeles in 1981 and a Ph.D. in economics from the University of Chicago in 1986. He joined the faculty of the Graduate School of Business at the University of Chicago in 1983, where he has since remained.

In 1997 Murphy was awarded the John Bates Clark Medal, given to the outstanding American economist under the age of 40, by the American Economic Association.

Changes in the Structure of Wages in the 1980's: An Evaluation of Alternative Explanations

JOHN BOUND

GEORGE JOHNSON

During the 1980's, a period in which the average level of real wage rates was roughly stagnant, there were large changes in the structure of relative wages, most notably a huge increase in the relative wages of highly educated workers. This paper attempts to assess the power of several alternative explanations of the observed relative wage changes in the context of a theoretical framework that nests all of these explanations. Our conclusion is that their major cause was a shift in the skill structure of labor demand brought about by biased technological change. (JEL J31)

During the 1980's, there were three major changes in the structure of wages in the United States. First, there was a precipitous rise in the relative wages and earnings of workers with high levels of education. The average wage of a college graduate increased relative to the average wage of a high school graduate by over 15 percentage points from 1979 to 1988. The high-school/elementary-school wage differential also increased substantially. Second, for those in the labor force who had not completed college there was a large increase in the average wage of older workers relative to younger workers. Third, the average wage of women relative to the average wage of men increased by about 8 percent, resulting in a fall in the average wage disadvantage of women from 30 percent of men's wages in 1979 to 24 percent in 1988.

The fact that there have been large changes in the distribution of wages and income has been widely documented (see e.g., Kevin Murphy and Finis Welch, 1991; McKinley Blackburn et al., 1990/91; Marvin Kosters, 1989). There is, however, less consensus concerning the *causes* of these phenomena than about the changes themselves. There are four—not necessarily exclusive—explanations that have received recent attention. The first attributes the wage-structure changes to the decline in manufacturing employment, in large part associated with the increase in the trade deficit during the 1980's, which may

Both authors are members of the Department of Economics, The University of Michigan, Ann Arbor, MI 48109, and are affiliated with the National Bureau of Economic Research. They are indebted for suggestions to participants in numerous seminars, especially C. Brown, and to two anonymous referees.

Reprinted with permission from John Bound and George Johnson, "Changes in the Structure of Wages in the 1980's: An Evaluation of Alternative Explanations," American Economic Review, Vol. 82 No. 3 (June 1992), pp. 371–392.

have increased the relative demand for better-educated workers and female workers (Murphy and Welch, 1991). The second explanation concentrates on the loss of wage premia paid to blue-collar males in certain industries because of the declines of manufacturing employment and the power of unions (Barry Bluestone and Bennett Harrison, 1988). The third attributes the wage-structure changes to changes in technology, brought on in large part by the computer revolution (Jacob Mincer, 1991). The fourth attributes the rise in the relative wages of college graduates to a slowdown in the rate of growth of the college-educated population, caused in turn by the drop in the size of the cohort entering the labor market during the 1980's (Murphy and Welch, 1989).

While some work has been done evaluating each of the above explanations, such work has usually involved assessing the merits of each in isolation. The purpose of this paper is to evaluate comprehensively the explanatory power of each of the explanations. Our major conclusion is that, while each of the other three contributed slightly to the explanation of observed relative wage movements, their primary cause was technical change.

The remainder of the paper is organized as follows. Section I describes the major changes in the wage structure during the 1970's and 1980's. Section II sets out a simple model from which the testable implications of the alternative explanations are obtained. Section III reports the results of the tests, and Section IV summarizes our major conclusions.

I. CHANGES IN THE STRUCTURE OF WAGES

Our first task is to document the changes in the wage structure that occurred during the 1980's as well as, for comparative purposes, the changes in the structure of wages that occurred in the 1970's. The analysis is based on imputed wage rates from questions on usual weekly earnings and hours from the Current Population Survey (CPS) for 1973–1974, 1979, and 1988. Each sample eliminates all workers in agriculture, forestry, and fisheries, as well as private household service and individuals with imputed hourly wages less than $1.00 or greater than $100 in 1979 dollars.[1] Each sample included only persons between the ages of 18 and 64 who reported employment as their major normal weekly activity.

Each of the resultant samples (66,808 for 1973–1974, 145,744 for 1979, and 149,011 for 1988) was then split into 32 subsamples based on four values of completed years of schooling, S (dropouts: $S < 12$; high school: $S = 12$; some college: $12 < S < 16$; and college: $S \geq 16$), four levels of potential labor-market experience, X (0–9, 10–19, 20–29, and 30+ years), and two sexes. For each subsample in each of the three periods, the logarithm of the wage rate for each individual was regressed on X and dummy variables for educational attainment

---

[1] *A problem with the CPS data is that weekly earnings are capped at $999, which introduces a downward bias in wage rates, especially for prime-age men with high levels of education in the 1988 sample. To deal with this, we used the unedited weekly-earnings measure, which is "top-coded" at $1,923, for observations that were at the $999 cap. Very few respondents, even among the critical groups, exceeded this higher cap. For the approximately 20 percent of the relevant observations for whom earnings were not available in the unedited file, we assigned the geometric mean among the top-capped individuals.*

(where relevant), nonwhite, part-time employment, residence in an SMSA, four major regions, and employment in 17 major industries (a list of which are given in Table 2). From the estimated regression coefficients we then calculated the estimated mean log wage in each period of workers in the ith education/experience/sex group, Y_i, evaluated for whites working full time in SMSA's in the mean region and industry for the group at particular years of schooling (8 for dropouts, 12 for high school, 14 for some college, and 16 for college) and at the midpoints of the experience ranges ($X = 5$, 15, 25, and 35).[2]

The estimated values of the real average hourly wage rates of the 32 groups [$\exp(Y_i/P)$, where P is the value of the CPI relative to its value in 1988] are reported in columns (i)–(iii) of Table 1. A striking feature of these results is the downward trend in most real wage rates over the entire period. The average per annum growth of real wages between 1973 and 1979 was -0.010,[3] and the equivalent rate of growth between 1979 and 1988 is -0.008. Fringe benefits are not included in CPS wages, but from aggregate data on the ratio of supplements to wages and salaries to total compensation (*Economic Report of the President,* 1990 table C-24), our estimates should be adjusted upward by 0.006 and 0.001 for, respectively, the 1973–1979 and 1979–1988 periods to reflect total per annum compensation growth. This yields annualized (fixed-weight) rates of growth of real wages of -0.4 percent and -0.7 percent over the two periods.

A graphical illustration of the three major stylized facts about the wage structure that are the focus of this paper is provided in Figures 1 and 2. Here, the estimated wage rates in 1979 and 1988 for the four educational categories (dropouts, high school graduates, those with some college, and college graduates) are plotted against the midpoints of the four labor-market experience intervals, separately for men and women. Columns (iv) and (v) of Table 1 report the fixed-weight proportional relative wage changes for each of the 32 demographic groups in the two time periods.[4] [For example, the wage of male college graduates relative to high school graduates with five years of experience increased from $11.38/8.96 = 1.27$ in 1979 to $12.16/7.31 = 1.66$ in 1988, and the change in the logarithm of this relative wage is the difference in the two groups' relative wage changes in column (v), $0.136 - (-0.134) = 0.270$.]

---

[2] *A dummy variable for 1974 was included in the 1973–1974 regressions (the two years having been merged in order to yield an adequate sample of employment by industry), and this was set equal to zero for the computation of the Y_i's.*

[3] *This is equal to $\Sigma_i[Y_i(1979) - Y_i(1973)]k_i(1973)/6 - \ln[P(1979)/P(1973)]/6$, where $k_i(1973)$ is group i's share of total employment in 1973–1974.*

[4] *The value of each of the relative wages in Figures 1 and 2 is $rel_i = \exp(Y_i - \Sigma_i Y_i k_i)$, and the fixed-weight proportional wage change of each group is $\Delta Y_i - \Sigma_i Y_i k_i$. The change in rel_i (as well as the average real wage change with variable weights) also depends on the value of $\Sigma_i(y_i + \Delta Y_i)\Delta k_i$, the change in the average wage in the economy due to changes in the demographic composition of the work force. The value of this term was 0.004 over the 1973–1979 interval (the mean worker was more educated but was younger and more likely to be female), but over the 1979–1988 interval its value was 0.042 (because the labor force got older).*

TABLE 1

ESTIMATED AVERAGE REAL HOURLY WAGE RATES (IN 1988 DOLLARS), RELATIVE WAGE CHANGES, AND EMPLOYMENT DISTRIBUTIONS BY EXPERIENCE, EDUCATION, AND SEX FOR 1973, 1979, AND 1988

Experience (years)	Education	Real wage levels			Fixed-weight relative wage changes		Employment distributions		
		1973 (i)	1979 (ii)	1988 (iii)	1973–1979 (iv)	1979–1988 (v)	1973 (vi)	1979 (vii)	1988 (viii)
Men:									
0–9	dropouts	7.52	7.20	5.54	0.020	−0.192	0.027	0.023	0.015
	high school	9.69	8.96	7.31	−0.015	−0.134	0.077	0.079	0.060
	some college	10.61	9.89	8.51	−0.008	−0.080	0.041	0.043	0.034
	college	12.69	11.38	12.16	−0.046	0.136	0.043	0.048	0.041
10–19	dropouts	9.96	9.61	7.45	0.027	−0.185	0.033	0.021	0.018
	high school	12.69	12.09	10.31	0.014	−0.089	0.062	0.057	0.067
	some college	14.60	13.43	12.06	−0.021	−0.037	0.023	0.031	0.036
	college	16.95	15.29	14.81	−0.040	0.038	0.028	0.036	0.050
20–29	dropouts	11.37	10.25	8.53	−0.041	−0.113	0.037	0.024	0.014
	high school	13.92	12.81	11.91	−0.020	−0.003	0.046	0.040	0.045
	some college	15.33	14.37	13.93	−0.002	0.039	0.020	0.016	0.022
	college	18.62	17.10	17.08	−0.022	0.069	0.020	0.022	0.028
30+	dropouts	11.30	10.74	10.17	0.012	0.015	0.078	0.054	0.029
	high school	13.65	13.02	12.05	0.015	−0.007	0.051	0.051	0.042
	some college	15.39	14.60	14.27	0.010	0.047	0.014	0.015	0.014
	college	18.26	16.88	17.64	−0.016	0.114	0.011	0.015	0.016
Women:									
0–9	dropouts	5.80	5.48	4.82	0.005	−0.058	0.014	0.012	0.008
	high school	7.14	6.87	6.18	0.024	−0.035	0.066	0.069	0.055
	some college	8.91	7.79	7.52	−0.071	0.034	0.028	0.038	0.038
	college	10.42	9.29	10.00	−0.052	0.144	0.027	0.036	0.040
10–19	dropouts	6.68	5.96	5.11	−0.051	−0.084	0.016	0.013	0.011
	high school	8.21	7.74	7.60	0.004	0.052	0.040	0.049	0.058
	some college	10.11	9.21	9.29	−0.052	0.079	0.011	0.019	0.034
	college	11.29	10.64	11.38	0.003	0.138	0.011	0.017	0.036
20–29	dropouts	6.17	6.31	5.81	0.085	−0.013	0.022	0.015	0.011
	high school	8.22	7.96	7.74	0.030	0.042	0.040	0.038	0.049
	some college	9.23	8.90	9.64	0.027	0.150	0.009	0.012	0.022
	college	12.04	10.54	11.25	−0.070	0.135	0.010	0.011	0.019
30+	dropouts	6.38	6.59	6.20	0.095	0.009	0.040	0.029	0.019
	high school	8.39	8.07	7.96	0.024	0.056	0.045	0.048	0.046
	some college	9.59	9.12	9.59	0.012	0.121	0.009	0.012	0.013
	college	12.50	10.52	11.15	−0.110	0.128	0.008	0.008	0.009

The first stylized fact, the increase in the relative wages of more-educated workers during the 1980's, is very clearly seen from inspection of Figures 1 and 2. With very few exceptions, the change in the average relative wage position of more-educated workers, experience and sex held constant, was higher than that for less-educated workers. The average proportionate change in the wages of college graduates relative to those of high school graduates was 0.163 for men and 0.118 for women. Over the 1973–1979 period, on the other hand, the college relative wage fell (by 0.035 for men and 0.073 for women).[5] The increase in the wages of high school graduates relative to those of dropouts during the 1980's was also very large except for the highest experience category; for $X \leq 30$, the proportionate change in the average high-school/dropout relative wage was 0.072 for men and 0.060 for women. These differentials changed very little during the 1970's.

The second fact about the wage structure in the 1980's is that for those who did not complete college there was an increase in the relative earnings of older workers, especially for men. This is reflected in an increase in the slopes of the relevant relative-wage profiles in Figures 1 and 2. For noncollege workers (all except college graduates) the average proportionate wage change of those with more than 19 years of experience exceeded that of younger workers by 0.107 for men and by 0.043 for women. During the 1973–1979 period, this relative wage was constant for men, but it increased by 0.058 for women.

The third major wage-structure development is reflected in the fact that the 1988 relative wage profiles for women in Figure 2 tend to be higher relative to their 1979 values than is true for men in Figure 1. The average fixed-weight proportional wage change for women was 0.076 greater than that for men, which represented an acceleration of the 1973–1979 difference in wage changes by gender of 0.016. Indeed, the average logarithmic wage advantage of men (at the demographic weights for each year) declined from 0.392 in 1973 to 0.363 in 1979 and to 0.280 in 1988, which means that the relative wages of women (based on geometric means) were 0.675, 0.696, and 0.756 over the three periods.[6]

---

[5] The social rate of return to a four-year college program for men behaved in a similar manner from 1973 to 1988. Assuming a 2,000-hour work year, average retirement at age 61, and that the resource cost of each year of college equals average tuition at private universities, the real internal rate of return fell from 4.8 percent to 4.1 percent from 1973 to 1979 and then increased to 7.3 percent in 1988. If tuition had not risen during the 1980's at 5.1 percent per annum in real terms, the rate of return in 1988 would have been 8.4 percent, or double its 1979 value. Interestingly, the steep decline in the real wages of young high school graduates in concert with the rise in real tuition costs caused the average ratio of opportunity costs (lost earnings) to total costs to fall from 0.73 in 1973 to 0.58 in 1988.

[6] The value of the gross average log wage of women relative to men increased by slightly more than did their fixed-weight relative wages relative to those of men primarily because of an increase in their average educational attainment relative to men in the work force. An additional source of the wage gap between men and women, which is netted out of our figures, is the fact that women are more likely to be employed part-time (15.5 percent versus 5.5 percent in 1988). Since there is a negative effect on individual wages of being employed part-time (15 percent for women and 22 percent for men in 1988), this adds approximately two percentage points to the gender differential in each of the years.

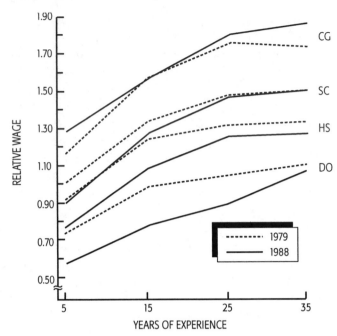

FIGURE 1

Estimated Relative Wage Rates by Education for Men by Years of Experience, 1979 and 1988

Notes: CG = college graduates, SC = some college, HS = high school, and DO = dropouts.

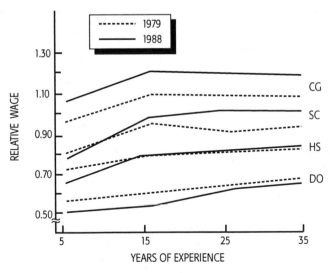

FIGURE 2

Estimated Relative Wage Rates by Education for Women by Years of Experience, 1979 and 1988

Notes: CG = college graduates, SC = some college, HS = high school, and DO = dropouts.

A major problem in the interpretation of the wage-structure developments of the 1980's, which has been noted in previous work on this topic (e.g., Murphy and Welch, 1992), is that there were large increases in the relative supplies of most of the demographic groups whose relative wages increased. (The correlation between the proportional change in relative wages across the 32 demographic groups [column (v) in Table 1] and the proportional change in relative supply [the logarithm of the ratio of column (viii) to column (vii)] is +0.51.) Other things equal, there should have been a *decrease* in the relative wages of these groups, for the work force got more educated and more female during the 1980's. The obvious strategy for explaining the wage-structure developments of the 1980's is to look for the set of demand-shift factors that were sufficiently powerful to overcome the effects of demographic changes that would have caused the wage structure to move in the opposite direction.

II. A CONCEPTUAL FRAMEWORK FOR EVALUATING ALTERNATIVE EXPLANATIONS

In order to perform an empirical analysis of the reasons for the observed relative changes of the 1980's, it is useful to set out a simple theoretical model that incorporates all of the major explanations. The aggregate work force is composed of I demographic groups (defined by age, education, and sex). The wage rate of group-i workers in industry j is W_{ij}, and this is conveniently defined as the product of the "competitive" wage, W_{ic}, and a relative rent, μ_{ij}. If the nonpecuniary attributes of employment in all industries were identical and there were no unions or other factors causing wage rates to deviate from their competitive norm, the μ_{ij}'s would be identically equal to 1. Whatever the reasons, however, there is substantial evidence that quality-adjusted wage levels vary across industries (Sumner Slichter, 1950; Alan Krueger and Lawrence Summers, 1988).

Defining Y_{ij} and M_{ij} as the logarithms of W_{ij} and μ_{ij}, the geometric mean of the wage rate for group-i workers is

$$(1) \qquad Y_i = Y_{ic} + \sum_j M_{ij}\phi_{ij}$$

where $Y_{ic} = \ln(W_{ic})$ and $\phi_{ij} = N_{ij}/N_i$ is the proportion of group-i workers who are employed in industry j.

This suggests an initial classification of explanations of relative wage movements into those that focus on market factors (changes in relative demand or supply that affect the W_{ic}'s) and those that focus on institutional factors (changes in the values of the μ_{ij}'s or their incidence), for the change in the relative average log wage of each group i is

$$(2) \qquad dY_i = dY_{ic} + \sum_j \left(\phi_{ij}dM_{ij} + M_{ij}d\phi_{ij}\right).$$

The change in the relative average wage for group-i workers is (2) less its weighted average across all I groups. This can change for a particular group either because its competitive wage grows faster or slower than average or because of changes in the average level or average incidence of industry wage premia, represented by the two parts of the second term on the right-hand side of (2).

Estimation of the initial relative wage impact of changes in average group premia is straightforward. The task of devising tests of alternative explanations of changes in competitive wage levels is more challenging. To do this, we utilize a conventional model of the determination of competitive wages for each of the I demographic groups and the employment level for each group in each of J industries (N_{ij}). There are five (admittedly simplifying) assumptions made in the model (the equations of which are set out in the Appendix) so that it can be used for purposes of testing. First, output in each industry is a function of efficiency units of employment, $b_{ij}N_{ij}$, of each of the demographic groups, where b_{ij} is an index of the technical efficiency of group-i workers in industry j. The single intrafactor elasticity of substitution, σ, is assumed to be constant and equal across industries (with, following Daniel Hamermesh [1986], $1 < \sigma < \infty$), but different industries may employ the different groups in different proportions.[7] Second, the demand for the output of each industry is a function of its relative price and an exogenous shift parameter. Third, the employment levels of all groups in each industry (the N_{ij}'s) are determined by equations setting the marginal revenue products of the I labor inputs equal to their competitive wage rates.[8] Fourth, the economy is at full employment in the sense that the total effective aggregate labor supply (i.e., measured labor force minus frictional unemployment) of each labor group (N_i) is employed in the J industries in the economy. The final assumption is that the N_i's are exogenous. In particular, the aggregate supply of each demographic group does not depend on its relative average wage.

---

[7] *A more general specification, which would allow partial elasticities of complementarity among labor groups to vary (rather than assume that all cross-elasticities are equal to $1/\sigma$) can be set out theoretically but is intractable empirically. It turns out, however, that the proportional changes in the supplies of groups that might be considered a priori to be substitutable for each other to some extent (e.g., men and women dropouts in the youngest experience interval) are highly correlated. Thus, it does not make much difference exactly how the labor groups are aggregated.*

[8] *This assumption can be justified theoretically on the grounds that (a) the μ_{ij}'s result from the effects of trade unions on relative wages and that (b) unions and management bargain over both wages and employment. These assumptions imply that the competitive wage (W_{ic}), rather than the negotiated wage ($\mu_{ij}W_{ic}$), figures in the determination of employment levels by industry (see Henry Farber [1987] for an extensive discussion of this); in other terms, changes in the μ_{ij}'s yield solutions that are off the conventional demand curves. The alternative assumption is that employment is set in each industry such that marginal revenue products are equal to negotiated wages. In this case, an increase in a particular μ_{ij} will lower W_{ic} because of employment effects, and the sign of the effect of a change in μ_{ij} on the average wage for that group is ambiguous. Our simplifying assumption thus implies a possible bias in our empirical results toward acceptance of the explanation involving changes in the $\sum_j \mu_{ij}\phi_{ij}$'s.*

The model leads to the conclusion that the change in the competitive wage of group-i workers (relative to the change in the aggregate wage) depends positively on their average rate of technical change (relative to all groups) $d(\ln b_i)$, negatively on their relative supply change $d(\ln N_i)$, and positively on the change in their relative product-demand-shift index $d(\ln D_j)$. Substituting Appendix equation (A9) for dY_{ic} in (2), we have

$$(3) \quad dY_i = \left(1 - 1/\sigma\right)d\left(\ln b_i\right) - \left(1/\sigma\right) \times d\left(\ln N_i\right) + \left(1/\sigma\right)d\left(\ln D_i\right) + \sum_j \left(\phi_{ij}dM_{ij} + M_{ij}d\phi_{ij}\right).$$

The four alternative explanations of the wage-structure changes of the 1980's are nested in this equation, and three of them (all but that dealing with technical change) can be directly confronted by the data.

To illustrate the operation of the model, consider the possible explanations of the increase in the relative wage of college graduates during the 1980's. Figure 3 shows the relative-demand and relative-supply functions for college-educated labor, with w the wage and n the supply of college-educated workers relative to other labor. The initial values of w and n are w_0 and n_0. We know that w increased to w_1'' in the face of an increase in n to n_1 [in fact, from the data in Table 1, $\Delta(\ln w) = 0.111$ and $\Delta(\ln n) = 0.139$ for the 1979–1988 period]. If the initial equilibrium were at point a in Figure 3 with the demand curve n_d (which means that average relative rents $[\Sigma_j \mu_{ij}\phi_{ij}]$ for college and noncollege workers were equal), we would expect w to fall to w_1' through the operation of the $-(1/\sigma)d(\ln N_i)$ term in (3). That w rose to w_1'' implies, in the absence of a change in relative rents, that the relative-demand function shifted to n_d'. This, according to (3), could

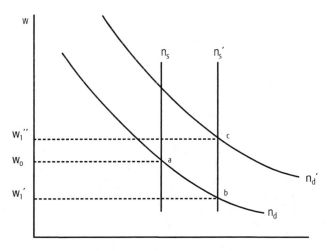

FIGURE 3

Shifts in the Relative Demand for (n_d) and Relative Supply of (n_s) College-Educated Labor

have been caused by shifts in product demand [the $d(\ln D_i)$ term in (3)] or changes in technology [the $d(\ln b_i)$ term in (3)] that were relatively favorable to college-educated workers.

The other possible explanation of the increase in w is that the initial relative-demand function was n'_d but that noncollege workers received higher rents (through the effects of unionism) such that the equilibrium of the economy was point a in Figure 3. The increased relative supply of college graduates would have driven w down to w'_1, but the rents disappeared during the 1980's, resulting in an increase in the college relative wage to w''_1, an amount equal to the distance between points b and c in Figure 3 above what it would have been in the absence of whatever institutional changes occurred.

III. EVIDENCE ON ALTERNATIVE EXPLANATIONS

We now apply the model developed in Section II to the question of the causes of the wage structure that was described in Section I, examining in turn explanations that focused on changes in average rents, changes in the structure of product demand, and technical change. These explanations are, of course, not mutually exclusive.

A. CHANGES IN THE INDUSTRIAL WAGE STRUCTURE

In order to discern how much of the observed wage-structure change was due to changes in the demographic composition of employment between high- and low-wage industries and how much was due to changes in industry wage differentials, it is necessary to estimate group-average wage rates by industry, the Y_{ij}'s. These can be obtained from the estimated parameters of our original 32 regressions for each of the three years in which log CPS wages were regressed on experience and dummy variables for education, part-time status, nonwhite, area size, region, and major industry of employment. The average log wage for group-i workers in industry j is the predicted value for the particular educational level (8, 12, 14, or 16) and experience level (5, 15, 25, or 35) for white, full-time workers residing in SMSA's in the average region for that group with the relevant industry coefficient in effect.[9]

The next step is to estimate average industry wage effects across all groups in each period. For each of the three years these were obtained from a weighted (by $[k_i\phi_{ij}]^{0.5}$) regression of the 32×17 Y_{ij}'s on dummy variables for (all but one of) the 32 groups and 17 industries. This decomposes each Y_{ij} into a group effect and a common-industry effect, and the deviations of the estimated value of the latter from its mean in the three years are reported as M_j (the estimated value of the log of μ_j) in columns (iv)–(vi) of Table 2. For

---

[9] Tables reporting the relevant Y_{ij}'s as well as the industry distribution of employment, the ϕ_{ij}'s, are available from the authors upon request.

TABLE 2

ESTIMATED AGGREGATE WEIGHTS (ϕ_j) AND WAGE EFFECTS (M_j) FOR 17 CPS INDUSTRIES IN 1973, 1979, AND 1988

Industry	Weight (ϕ_j)			Wage effect (M_j)		
	1973 (i)	1979 (ii)	1988 (iii)	1973 (iv)	1979 (v)	1988 (vi)
Construction	0.067	0.059	0.059	0.206	0.137	0.112
Durables/mining	0.190	0.179	0.141	0.073	0.089	0.099
Nondurables	0.119	0.107	0.088	0.018	0.020	0.025
Transport	0.041	0.042	0.039	0.112	0.122	0.069
Utilities	0.035	0.035	0.034	0.151	0.147	0.166
Wholesale trade	0.041	0.041	0.041	0.014	0.000	−0.004
Retail trade	0.137	0.141	0.147	−0.202	−0.150	−0.175
Finance	0.054	0.065	0.075	0.029	0.012	0.079
Business services	0.028	0.032	0.054	−0.079	−0.072	−0.051
Personal services	0.019	0.019	0.024	−0.282	−0.179	−0.218
Entertainment	0.007	0.008	0.010	−0.133	−0.098	−0.120
Medical	0.025	0.031	0.039	−0.068	−0.063	−0.058
Hospitals	0.044	0.048	0.048	−0.006	0.015	−0.049
Welfare	0.014	0.017	0.024	−0.282	−0.222	−0.252
Education	0.096	0.090	0.084	−0.103	−0.107	−0.055
Professional services	0.019	0.023	0.028	0.084	0.044	0.104
Public administration	0.065	0.064	0.068	0.126	0.070	0.093

example, in 1973 the estimated average hourly wage in construction relative to education, other things held constant, was $\exp[0.206 − (−0.103)] = 1.36.$[10]

The estimated contribution of changes in average industry wage effects to the relative wage change of each demographic group can then be calculated as $\Sigma_j M_j \Delta\phi_{ij} + \Sigma_j (\phi_{ij} + \Delta\phi_{ij})\Delta M_j$. The first term is the part due to changes in the industry weights, and the sec-

---

[10] *The estimates of these industry wage effects are based on the specification that the proportionate effect of working in industry j is the same for all I groups (i.e., $\mu_{ij} = \mu_j$). This is, of course, testable, and it turns out that there are a few exceptions to the assumption. For example, noncollege men earned about 3-percent more than other groups in the first five industries listed in Table 2 (the location of the majority of blue-collar unionism). College women earned 20-percent more than other groups in 1973 in the four "public service" industries (hospitals, welfare and religious, education, and public administration), possibly reflecting a combination of discrimination in other industries and self-selection, but this coefficient fell to insignificance in the later years. Although these exceptions to the assumption of identical industry effects are interesting, they have virtually no effect on the quantitative contribution of industry wage effects to the explanation of wage-structure changes and, therefore, are ignored.*

ond term represents the parts due to changes in industry wage effects (evaluated at the weights at the end of the period). The values of the estimated contribution of the two sources of change in average industry wage effects to the summary relative wage changes for 1973–1979 and 1979–1988 discussed in Section I are reported in Table 3. Columns (i) and (v) give the relative wage changes in the 1970's and 1980's, (ii) and (vi) give the effects of changes in industry weights, and (iii) and (vii) give the effects of industry wage effects. For example, of the 0.163 proportional increase in the wage of male college graduates relative to high school graduates during the 1980's, 0.016 can be attributed to differential movements between high- and low-wage industries and 0.022 can be attributed to changes in industry wage effects, or a total of 0.038/0.163 = 22 percent of the change. All of the estimated changes in net average industry effects for the 1980's are in the right direction, but they do not explain a very large part of any of the summary relative wage changes.[11]

An alternative way of looking specifically at the question of whether workers' relative rents changed is to examine changes in the incidence of unionism. Between 1979 and 1988, the fraction of all workers in our sample who were union members fell from 27 percent to 19 percent, a slight acceleration of the decline in union membership that has been occurring since the mid-1950's.[12] Assume that the wage of each worker is equal to the competitive wage for the relevant demographic group times the union/nonunion relative wage if the worker is a union member ($U = 1$), that is, $W_{ic}\exp(\lambda U)$. Then the geometric average of the wages of demographic group i is $Y_i = Y_{ic} + \lambda U_i$, where λ is the logarithmic union/nonunion wage differential and U_i is the proportion of group-i workers who are unionized. Holding λ constant and assuming no feedback from the extent of unionization to the competitive wage, the contribution of changes in unionization to the wage of each group is $\lambda \Delta U_i$.

Using the upper-bound estimate of λ by H. Gregg Lewis (1986), 0.15, estimates of the contribution of changes in unionism to the relative wage change of each demographic group in each of the two time periods of this analysis can then be calculated. These calculations for the summary relative wage changes are reported in columns (iv) and (viii) of Table 3. For example, the fraction of male high school graduates (with no college) who

---

[11] The use of only 17 industries in our analysis, which is done for purposes of consistency with the rest of the paper, raises the possibility of downward aggregation bias. To check for this, we ran regressions for all men and all women (instead of separate regressions for 16 education/experience groups) in each period, using 45 detailed industries instead of the 17 major industries in the above analysis. The results implied that most of the total industry wage-structure effects (the sum of the compositional and wage-change effects) were picked up by the dummy variables for 17 industries. The major exceptions to this were confined to noncollege men during the 1980's, for whom the use of detailed industry dummies increased the total industry wage effects by up to one-half. However, this still falls far short of a full explanation of the relevant wage-structure changes.

[12] Our union-membership data were taken from the May version of the CPS for 1973, 1979, and 1988. For an analysis of the causes of the overall decline in unionization in the United States see Henry Farber (1987).

TABLE 3

ESTIMATED EFFECTS OF CHANGES IN INDUSTRY WAGE EFFECTS AND IN UNION
MEMBERSHIP ON RELATIVE WAGE CHANGES DURING 1973–1979 AND 1979–1988

		Relative wage change (i)	Industry effects		Union effect (iv)
Comparison groups	Sex		Weights (ii)	Wages (iii)	
A. 1973–1979:					
College/high school	men	−0.035	0.009	−0.002	0.012
	women	−0.073	0.005	−0.007	0.016
High school/dropout ($X < 30$)	men	−0.006	0.007	−0.001	0.004
	women	−0.002	−0.003	−0.010	0.004
Old/young (noncollege)	men	−0.004	0.007	−0 004	0.001
	women	0.058	0.012	−0.001	0.003
Women/men		0.011	0.002	0.012	0.004
		(v)	(vi)	(vii)	(viii)
B. 1979–1988:					
College/high school	men	0.163	0.016	0.020	0.013
	women	0.118	0.010	0.005	−0.006
High school/dropout ($X < 30$)	men	0.072	−0.001	0.003	0.002
	women	0.060	0.002	0.009	0.006
Old/young (noncollege)	men	0.107	0.010	0.005	0.010
	women	0.043	0.009	0.004	0.002
Women/men		0.076	−0.001	0.006	0.007

were union members fell from 0.385 in 1979 to 0.270 in 1988, and the corresponding figures for male college graduates were 0.174 and 0.146. Thus, the estimated contribution of changes in union incidence to the male college/high-school relative wage for the 1980's was $0.15 \times [-0.028 - (0.115)] = 0.013$. It is clear from inspection of column (viii) that the decline of unionism in the United States during the 1980's had *at most* a small effect on overall relative wage changes.

B. CHANGES IN THE STRUCTURE OF PRODUCT DEMAND

It is clear that not very much of the wage changes of the 1980's can be explained—even with perhaps unrealistically favorable assumptions—by changes in the industrial wage structure or in the incidence of unionism. It is necessary to focus (as other investigators, such as Murphy and Welch [1991], have concluded) on changes in relative competitive wage levels.

Changes in the structure of product demand can in principle shift the relative labor-demand functions for different groups, and the presumption of this explanation is that in the 1980's these demand shifts were both in the right direction and large. As can be seen from inspection of columns (ii) and (iii) of Table 2, there was a significant shift during the 1980's in the fraction of total employment ($\phi_j = \Sigma_i \phi_{ij} k_i$) from industries that were the traditional employers of male blue-collar labor (like manufacturing) toward industries that employ larger fractions of women and highly educated labor (like finance and profes-sional services). In addition to lowering the average wages of blue-collar males because wage levels are higher in manufacturing than in the expanding industries (the weights effect, $\Sigma_j M_j \Delta \phi_{ij}$, in Table 3), such a shift would also have lowered their wage levels in, say, hardware stores because they are less scarce.

One index of the influence of product demand shifts on relative labor-demand func-tions, which has been used by Richard Freeman (1975), Murphy and Welch (1991), and Lawrence Katz and Murphy (1992), is the average employment growth by industry weighted by the initial employment distribution of each demographic group. This is

$$(4) \qquad \text{EMP}_i = \sum_j \Delta\left(\ln \phi_j\right) \phi_{ij}$$

where $\Delta(\ln \phi_j)$ is the proportionate change in the logarithm of industry j's share of aggre-gate employment in each period. The calculated values of $\Delta(\ln \phi_{ij})$ for each of 17 major industries for 1973–1979 and 1979–1988 are reported under $\Delta\phi$ in columns (i) and (iv) of Table 4. EMP_i can be considered as a rough proxy for the discrete version of $d(\ln D_i)$ in (3). The presumption of the demand-shift explanation of the wage-structure changes of the 1980's is that the EMP_i's were both in the right direction (i.e., toward more-educated, older, and female labor) and sufficiently large to overwhelm the "perverse" effect of increased relative supplies of most of the demographic groups whose relative wages increased.

In fact, the values of EMP_i are positively correlated with changes in relative supply for the 1979–1988 period (the slope coefficient of a weighted regression of EMP_i on the change in the log change in supply across the 32 demographic groups was 0.049 with a standard error of 0.020). Although the size of these shifts is not sufficiently large to con-stitute the whole explanation, they at least have the right sign, so previous studies have concluded that part of the explanation of the wage-structure phenomena is found in product demand shifts.

A problem with this conclusion is that it is necessary to net out the effect of changes in the relative supply of the different groups. If, for example, there were a very large increase in the relative supply of college-educated labor over some time interval, we would expect, other things equal, a tendency for industries that are the most skill-intensive to grow relative to other industries. The use of total relative-employment changes by indus-try as a proxy for product demand shifts, therefore, may confound product demand shifts with relative-supply changes.

An alternative approach that gets around this possible bias is to estimate a discrete ver-sion of Appendix equation (A10), and the resultant estimated demand-shift indexes by industry for the two periods are reported under Δx_1, in columns (ii) and (v) of Table 4. Because the estimated value of $\Delta(\ln x_j)$ picks up employment growth in each industry as

TABLE 4

PROPORTIONATE EMPLOYMENT CHANGES ($\Delta[\ln \phi_j]$) AND DERIVED DEMAND INDEXES ($\Delta[\ln x_j]$) BY INDUSTRY, FOR 1973–1979 AND 1979–1988

Industry	1973–1979			1979–1988		
	$\Delta\phi$ (i)	Δx_1 (ii)	Δx_2 (iii)	$\Delta\phi$ (iv)	Δx_1 (v)	Δx_2 (vi)
Construction	−0.126	0.000	0.037	0.014	0.148	0.182
Durables/mining	−0.057	0.034	−0.041	−0.224	−0.171	−0.270
Nondurables	−0.096	−0.034	−0.109	−0.179	−0.125	−0.221
Transport	0.035	0.096	0.021	−0.070	−0.027	−0.135
Utilities	−0.004	−0.019	0.092	−0.007	−0.079	−0.201
Wholesale trade	−0.004	0.002	0.045	−0.023	0.044	0.099
Retail trade	0.036	0.050	0.087	0.061	0.167	0.203
Finance	0.178	0.075	0.120	0.156	0.112	0.117
Business services	0.128	0.133	0.173	0.534	0.573	0.617
Personal services	−0.023	−0.013	0.005	0.252	0.365	0.399
Entertainment	0.210	0.132	0.173	0.211	0.265	0.310
Medical	0.215	0.105	0.152	0.241	0.195	0.252
Hospitals	0.080	−0.036	0.013	0.018	−0.123	−0.060
Welfare	0.230	0.055	0.117	0.355	0.237	0.320
Education	−0.057	−0.215	−0.146	−0.059	−0.286	−0.198
Professional services	0.242	0.087	0.140	0.199	0.123	0.200
Public administration	−0.008	−0.056	−0.006	0.072	−0.027	0.048

a deviation from the weighted rates of growth across demographic groups of its initial employment distribution, $\Delta(\ln x_j)$ is greater than $\Delta(\ln \phi_j)$ in industries (like construction) that tended to hire low-educated and male labor and smaller in industries (like education) that have the opposite demographic composition.

The next step is to calculate a derived demand-shift index, $\text{DEM}_{1i} = \Sigma_j \Delta(\ln x_j)\phi_{ij}$, which is analogous to the calculation of the EMP_i index in (4). For the 1979–1988 period, however, this index exhibits a small *positive* correlation with relative-supply changes, which is not favorable to acceptance of the product-demand-shift explanation as an important source of the wage-structure developments of the 1980's. What is in fact happening is that, while the traditional employers of males with low education were declining during the 1980's, so were some industries that traditionally employ a large fraction of college graduates, notably education and public administration.

TABLE 5

PROPORTIONATE SUPPLY CHANGES, ALTERNATIVE PRODUCT-DEMAND-SHIFT INDEXES, AND SPECIFIC-INDUSTRY TECHNICAL CHANGE BY AGGREGATED GROUPS FOR 1973–1979 AND 1979–1988

Comparison groups	Sex	Supply (i)	Demand-change indexes			Specific technical change (v)
			EMP (ii)	DEM$_1$ (iii)	DEM$_2$ (iv)	
A. 1973–1979:						
College/high school	men	0.204	0.033	−0.051	−0.014	0.016
	women	0.172	−0.039	−0.132	−0.091	0.004
High school/dropout	men	0.304	0.013	−0.002	−0.001	−0.012
($X < 30$)	women	0.316	0.042	0.005	0.028	−0.006
Old/young	men	−0.154	−0.002	−0.006	−0.010	0.028
(noncollege)	women	−0.212	−0.014	−0.012	−0.012	0.043
Women/men		0.119	0.038	−0.021	0.005	−0.023
		(vi)	**(vii)**	**(viii)**	**(ix)**	**(x)**
B. 1979–1988:						
College/high school	men	0.176	0.048	−0.032	0.022	0.033
	women	0.334	0.001	−0.127	−0.082	0.016
High school/dropout	men	0.338	0.006	−0.007	−0.006	0.031
($X < 30$)	women	0.310	0.042	0.021	0.048	0.061
Old/young	men	−0.109	−0.019	−0.035	−0.039	0.109
(noncollege)	women	0.012	−0.008	−0.029	−0.029	0.052
Women/men		0.164	0.053	0.011	0.046	−0.037

The average values of the alternative demand-shift indexes for the summary demographic groups are reported in Table 5, in columns (ii) and (vii) under EMP for the index based on industry employment changes and in columns (iii) and (viii) under DEM$_1$ for the index based on estimated derived demand changes. For example, the proportional change in the relative supply of male college graduates relative to high school graduates [from column (vi)] was 0.176, which, by (3), implies that their relative wages should have decreased by $(1/\sigma) \times 0.176$ (instead of rising by 0.163). Use of the EMP index of relative-demand changes suggests that $(1/\sigma) \times 0.048$ of the failure of this relative wage to fall could be accounted for by product demand shifts. Use of the DEM$_1$ index, however, only deepens the mystery, for that index suggests that demand shifts were on balance slightly unfavorable to highly educated labor.

C. INTRA-INDUSTRY EMPLOYMENT SHIFTS

It is clear from the results thus far that the major wage-change phenomena of the 1980's are *not* adequately accounted for by explanations based on institutional factors or changes in the structure of product demand. This leads us to the consideration of the remaining possibility, that the 1980's were characterized by major changes in technology that were nonneutral with respect to different types of labor. Variations across demographic groups in the ceteris paribus effects on wages of technical change or changes in average group quality are reflected in the $(1 - 1/\sigma)d(\ln b_i)$ term in (3). Given the maintained assumption that $\sigma > 1$, the wage-structure facts are attributable to this set of explanations if the relative values of the b_i's for the more educated, older, and female demographic groups increased during the 1980's. The major difficulty with this explanation, unlike the explanations involving industry wage effects, supply, and product demand, is (as in the analysis of the sources of economic growth) that it involves the residuals of the intrafactor demand function rather than directly observable phenomena.

It has long been argued that in periods of rapid technical change the relative demand for highly educated workers may increase because of their superior ability to adapt to and refine new methods of production (see Richard Nelson and Edmund Phelps, 1966).[13] The 1980's, as well as the 1970's to some extent, have been characterized popularly as a period in which computer technology was adopted throughout most of the U.S. economy, and there have been several case studies that suggest that changes in production methods have been favorable to professional and technical workers relative to blue-collar workers (see e.g., Jerome Mark, 1987). To the extent that this technical change was common across most industries in the economy, we would expect that the $d(\ln b_i)$'s for certain demographic groups would have risen relative to others.[14]

If it were true, however, that the rate of growth of the technical-efficiency parameter for group-i workers in industry j, $d(\ln b_{ij})$, were equal to the weighted mean for that group, $d(\ln b_i)$, plus a random error, all that is predicted by the model in Section II is that the relative wages of those groups most favored by the technical change would rise. Since changes in the b_i's are not observed, there is no way to test this. The thrust of the recent literature on technical change, however, is that the effects of spurts of innovation on the relative demand for skilled labor may vary across industries. If this is so, some of the variation in the values of $d(\ln b_i)$ can be identified.

To make this concrete, suppose that there is a subset of industries, say J', in which the rate of growth of the efficiency parameters for a subset of the demographic groups, say I', differs from their average growth in other industries. Specifically,

---

[13] *Several implications of the complementarity between human capital and the rate of technical change were tested by Welch (1970) and more recently by Ann Bartel and Frank Lichtenberg (1987) and Jacob Mincer (1989).*

[14] *It is difficult to argue that the 1970's and 1980's were a period of rapid growth in overall labor productivity, for, as pointed out in Section I, the average real wage has been essentially stagnant since 1973 as compared to its 1.5–2-percent annual growth over the preceding 150 years. An alternative interpretation of recent technical developments, in terms of the CES production function given by (A1), is that the new computer technology caused a relative shift in the δ_{ij}'s toward highly skilled demographic groups. Given $\sigma > 1$, this is observationally equivalent to relative increases in the b_i's for highly skilled demographic groups. In a time-series analysis of CPS earnings differentials, Mincer (1991) provides some direct evidence that the partial productivity rebound of the 1980's was skill-biased.*

$$(5) \qquad d\left(\ln b_{ij}\right) = \begin{cases} c_{0i} + c_{1i} & i \text{ in } I' \text{ and } j \text{ in } J' \\ c_{0i} & \text{otherwise} \end{cases}$$

This implies that the average change across all industries in the efficiency parameters for a group in I' is $d(\ln b_i) = c_{0i} + c_{1i}T_i$, where T_i is the proportion of group i's employment that is in the J' industries. To estimate the extent of this group/industry specific technical change, note that

$$(6) \qquad d[\ln(b_{ij}/b_i)] = c_{1i}D_{I'}(D_{J'} - T_i)$$

where $D_{I'}$ and $D_{J'}$ are dummy variables for the relevant groups and industries. Following Appendix equation (A12), equation (6) should be substituted for $d[\ln(b_{ij}/b_i)]$ in the regression equation to estimate industry demand shifts, and the coefficient on this variable is an estimate of $(\sigma - 1)c_{1i}$. The resultant proportional change in the average value of b_i for each group can then be calculated as

$$(7) \qquad d(\ln b_i) = c_{0i} + c_{1i}T_i.$$

In other words, the change in the average-efficiency parameter for group-i workers equals a *general* component c_{0i}, which applies to all industries (and is unobservable), plus a specific component $c_{1i}T_i$, which applies only to certain industries.

Looking at the underlying data on the industry distributions of employment for the 32 demographic groups (the ϕ_{ij}'s), it is clear that in both the 1973–1979 and 1979–1988 periods there was a greater shift out of manufacturing and similar industries for younger and less-educated workers than for those with the opposite characteristics. For example, the fraction of male dropouts with $X < 10$ who were employed in durable goods and mining fell from 0.252 in 1979 to 0.157 in 1988, but the fraction of male college graduates with $X < 10$ employed in this sector increased from 0.148 to 0.150 during this period. Further analysis of the data suggested a similar pattern in four of the five traditional blue-collar industries (durables/mining, nondurables, transportation, and public utilities, but *not* in construction). These four industries were aggregated into the J' sector (that in which there was differential technical change by demographic group). The group characteristics that were selected to be included as dummy variables included those that were seen in Section 1 to have had an important influence on relative wage changes in the 1979–1988 period: the four educational groups and the four experience groups separately for men and women, the four experience groups for those who had not completed college separately for men and women, and gender by itself.

The test of the null hypothesis that the 13 dummy variables that represent the above characteristics did not add to the explanation of $\Delta(\ln \phi_{ij})$ was rejected in both periods at better than the 0.001 level. The results show that there was a major shift in the employment structure in this blue-collar sector toward more-educated workers and, for those who had not completed college, older workers. Further, these shifts were slightly stronger in the 1980's than in the 1970's.

The summary values of $(\sigma - 1)c_{1i}T_i$ for the aggregated comparison groups are reported under SPEC in columns (v) and (x) of Table 5. It is clear that the intra-industry shifts represented by the variable were an important source of the relative demand shifts for high-school/dropout and the non-college old/young comparisons, but they were unfavorable for women relative to men in the aggregate. Inclusion of the dummy variables to capture intra-industry employment shifts also changes the estimated derived demand indexes, the $\Delta(\ln x_j)$'s, which are reported under Δx_2 in columns (iii) and (vi) of Table 4. These estimates are generally between the $\Delta(\ln \phi_j)$'s and the original $\Delta(\ln x_j)$'s, and the resultant indexes of the estimated effect of product demand shifts on labor demand, which are reported for the summary comparison groups under DEM_2 in columns (iv) and (ix) of Table 5, are usually between EMP and DEM_1.

An alternative interpretation of the positive effect of experience on the employment shares of workers who had not finished college in the blue-collar sector concerns the effect of seniority systems in the face of declining employment in these industries. Since these industries pay relatively high wages (see Table 2) and thus have low rates of labor turnover, a reduction in their relative importance in the economy (from a 0.385 share of nonagricultural employment in 1973 to 0.363 in 1979 and then to just 0.302 in 1988) must have caused a reduction in their hiring of young workers. Thus, the employment share of younger noncollege workers in the blue-collar sector fell, not because of a decline in the productivity of less-experienced relative to more-experienced workers, but because older workers had the right to retain their "good" jobs.[15]

D. GENERAL TECHNICAL CHANGE

Variation in the other component of the proportionate change in the average-efficiency parameter for each group, c_{0i}, is not directly observable. It is, however, clear from inspection of the summary measures in Table 5 that the addition of relative specific technical change to the other explanations does not add enough to outweigh the perverse effects of relative supply changes for the 1980's. Obviously, something else is going on, and the only remaining candidate within our structure is variation in the c_{0i}'s. Fortunately, it appears that other things appear also to have been affecting wage changes in the 1970's, and this permits us to estimate the c_{0i}'s indirectly.

Following (3), the per annum growth of the relative wage of group-i workers over each period ($t = 1$ for 1973–1979 and $t = 2$ for 1979–1988) may be written as

$$(8) \qquad dY_{ai}(t) = -(1/\sigma)dN_{ai}(t) + (1 - 1/\sigma)c_{0i}(t)' + u_i(t)$$

---

[15] *The fact that there was no perceptible change in the age composition of employment in the construction industry is consistent with this seniority interpretation of the results. Construction is characterized by very high rates of labor turnover, so seniority is much less important than in the other blue-collar industries.*

where $dY_{ai}(t)$ is the annualized proportionate change in the relative wage of group-i workers adjusted for the change in total average industry wage effects, $dN_{ai}(t)$ is the per annum proportionate change in relative supply adjusted for product demand shifts and industry-specific technical change, $c_{0i}(t)'$ is the per annum value of general technical change, and $u_i(t)$ is a random error term. It then follows that the difference between the rates of growth of adjusted relative wages in the two periods is

$$(9) \qquad d^2Y_{ai} = -(1/\sigma)d^2N_a + (1 - 1/\sigma)[c_{0i}(2)' - c_{0i}(1)'] + u_i,$$

where $d^2Y_{ai} = dY_{ai}(2) - dY_{ai}(1)$, $d^2N_{ai} = dN_{ai}(2) - dN_{ai}(1)$, and $u_i' = u_i(2) - u_i(1)$.

We now specify that the growth in each group's efficiency parameter relating to all industries in the 1979–1988 period equals its value in the 1973–1979 period plus a difference A_i, that is,

$$(10) \qquad c_{0i}(2)' = c_{0i}(1)' + A_i.$$

It is assumed initially that A_i is uncorrelated with either $c_{0i}(1)'$ or d^2N_{ai}, which is equivalent to assuming that the pattern of general technical change in the two periods was (more or less) identical. If these assumptions are correct, the reciprocal of the elasticity of intrafactor substitution can be estimated by regressing d^2Y_{ai} on d^2N_{ai}, for the influence of general technical change disappears as a fixed effect. The estimated slope coefficient of a regression (weighted by $[k_i(1979)]^{0.5}$) of d^2Y_{ai} on d^2N_{ai} is -0.588 (SE $= 0.127$), which implies a value of σ of 1.70. This is approximately the midpoint of past estimates of that parameter (see the surveys by Hamermesh and James Grant [1979] and Richard Freeman [1986]).[16] It is then possible to obtain an estimate of the effect (common to both periods) of general technical change on the per annum growth rate of group-i workers, $(1 - 1/\sigma)c_{0i}'$, by computing the average of the residuals, $dY_{ai}(t) + (1/\sigma)dN_{ai}(t)$, over the two periods.[17]

To test for the possibility that the pace of general technical change for some groups may have risen or fallen from the 1970's to the 1980's (i.e., that certain A_i's were not zero) we added several dummy variables for sets of demographic groups to the right-hand side of (9). The only one that yielded a statistically significant result was that for five young,

---

[16] *The estimated coefficients of dY_{ai} on dN_{ai} for the 1973–1979 and 1979–1988 periods are, respectively, -0.077 (SE $= 0.023$) and $+0.094$ (SE $= 0.044$). The first of these yields an estimate of the intrafactor substitution elasticity that is implausibly large (the implicit σ is $1/0.077 \approx 13$), and the second has the wrong sign. Obviously the dN_{ai}'s in both periods are positively correlated with some omitted variable.*

[17] *A lower-bound estimate of the standard error of $(1 - 1/\sigma)c_{0i}'$ is the standard error of estimate of the second-difference demand function, which equals 0.0284 divided by two. This implies that the standard errors of the estimated effects of general technical change on relative wage changes are (at least) 0.085 and 0.128 for the 1973–1979 and 1979–1988 periods, respectively.*

low-education groups.[18] Inclusion of this dummy variable, YNGLO, yielded an estimated coefficient on d^2N_{ai} of -0.571 (SE = 0.128) and a coefficient on YNGLO of -0.026 (SE = 0.012). This result is consistent with $\sigma = 1.75$, and it implies that the relative wages of young workers with low levels of education fell by 2.6 percent per annum faster than they would have in the absence of the acceleration of technical change against them. With this modification, the estimated common values of $(1 - 1/\sigma)c_{0i}$ were recalculated. The estimated effects of general technical change on relative wage changes are $GEN_i(1) = 6 \times (1 - 1/\sigma)c_{0i}$ for the 1973–1979 period and $GEN_i(2) = 9 \times [(1 - 1/\sigma)c'_{0i} - 0.026\ YNGLO_i]$ for the 1979–1988 period. The average relative values of these estimates for the summary comparison groups are reported under GEN in columns (vi) and (xiii) of Table 6.

It is apparent from inspection of the estimated values of GEN for the 1980's that our major conclusion, which will be discussed more completely below, is that the principal cause of the significant wage-structure changes of the past decade was a shift in the structure of the b_i's that were extremely favorable to certain groups, especially women and the highly educated. We have interpreted the source of this shift as an exogenous change in technology, but the basic result has other interpretations.

First, the average value of GEN of women relative to men during the 1980's was 0.145, which means that, relative rents, supply, product demand, and intraindustry composition held constant, women's wages grew 1.6 percent per year faster than men's wages because of relative proportional changes in average b_i's. (The corresponding value for the 1973–1979 period was 1.4 percent.) Some of this may have been attributable to changes in production technology that were relatively favorable to women,[19] but much of the decline in the gender gap may reflect an improvement in the unobserved labor quality of women (see James Smith and Michael Ward, 1984; June O'Neill, 1985). Since our results are based on CPS data, which do not measure actual as opposed to potential labor-market experience, we cannot identify how much of the decline in the gender differential was due to technical change versus an increase in the average extent of labor-market attachment on the part of women (or other explanations, such as a gradual decline in labor-market discrimination against women).[20]

---

[18] *The five groups with unit values of YNGLO include both men and women dropouts and high school graduates in the lowest experience interval and male dropouts with $X = 10$–19. Several other dummy variables were added to this regression (all women, all college graduates, and so forth), but the estimated coefficients on these variables were small and statistically insignificant, indicating that their per annum c_{0i}'s did not change between the 1970's and 1980's.*

[19] *Compared to men, women tend to work in occupations that on average impose higher intellectual, as opposed to physical, demands (see Johnson and Gary Solon, 1986). Changes in production practices brought about by the introduction of computers would thus tend to favor "women's jobs" vis-à-vis "men's jobs."*

[20] *Using data from the Panel Study on Income Dynamics, which has detailed information on respondents' work histories, Allison Wellington (1991) reports that nearly half of the observed increase in wages of women relative men from 1976 to 1985 can be attributed to changes in job- and labor-market-attachment variables. This still leaves a great deal of women's improvement unexplained.*

TABLE 6

DECOMPOSITION OF ESTIMATED SOURCES OF 1973–1979 AND 1979–1988 RELATIVE WAGE CHANGES

		Relative wage change (i)	Source of relative wage change					
						Technical change		
Comparison groups			Rents (ii)	Supply (iii)	Demand (iv)	Specific (v)	General (vi)	Unexplained (vii)
A.	1973–1979:							
	College/high school men	−0.035	0.007	−0.117	−0.008	0.009	0.073	0.001
	women	−0.073	−0.002	−0.098	−0.052	0.002	0.120	−0.043
	High-school men	−0.006	0.006	−0.174	0.000	−0.007	0.153	0.016
	dropout (X < 30) women	−0.002	−0.013	−0.181	0.016	−0.004	0.158	0.022
	Old/young men	−0.004	0.003	0.088	−0.006	0.016	−0.104	−0.001
	(noncollege) women	0.058	0.011	0.121	−0.007	0.024	−0.076	−0.015
	Women/men	0.016	0.013	−0.066	0.003	−0.013	0.086	−0.007
		(viii)	(ix)	(x)	(xi)	(xii)	(xiii)	(xiv)
B.	1979–1988:							
	College/ men	0.163	0.036	−0.100	0.013	0.019	0.196	−0.001
	high school women	0.118	0.015	−0.191	−0.047	0.009	0.270	0.062
	High school/ men	0.072	0.002	−0.193	−0.003	0.018	0.267	−0.019
	dropout (X < 30) women	0.060	0.011	−0.177	0.027	0.035	0.202	−0.038
	Old/young men	0.107	0.015	0.062	−0.022	0.062	−0.023	0.013
	(noncollege) women	0.043	0.013	−0.007	−0.016	0.030	−0.006	0.029
	Women/men	0.076	0.005	−0.094	0.026	−0.021	0.145	0.015

A second problem of interpretation involves the large negative values of GEN for younger workers with low levels of education, especially in the 1980's. The discussion of this section has been in terms of an exogenous change in technology that lowered the b_i's of this group, but this is also subject to other explanations. The first of these is the possibility that workers with low levels of education who entered the labor market in the 1980's had a much lower level of innate ability than their older counterparts who entered the labor market in the 1970's. If this were true, the low relative values of the $d(\ln b_i)$'s would be a reflection of a recent decline in the effectiveness of precollege education rather than an exogenous change in technology.[21] Another possible explanation of the decline in the relative wages of young workers with low skill levels is that they were the most susceptible to competition from undocumented immigrants. In this case, the low

---

[21] John Bishop (1991) reports evidence of a widening in academic achievement scores between college and noncollege youth during the 1980's. Perhaps more importantly, Bishop also reports a sharp increase in the fraction of college students majoring in relatively remunerative fields such as business. It is therefore possible that the more-educated members of the youngest cohort in our analysis are relatively more motivated (in the acquisitive sense) than was true of the older cohorts.

$d(\ln b_i)$'s for these groups would be reflecting the underestimation of the "true" $d(\ln N_i)$'s applying to this type of labor.[22]

There is, on the other hand, some direct evidence in favor of the interpretation of variation in the $d(\ln b_i)$'s across demographic groups as reflecting changes in technology. The first concerns the effect on individual wages of the use of computers. Respondents of supplementary surveys of the CPS in 1984 and 1989 were asked whether they used computers on their jobs, and Krueger (1991) has estimated that the proportional ceteris paribus effect on wages of computer use was 0.170 in 1984 and 0.188 in 1989. The fraction of all workers who reported using computers on the job rose from 25 percent to 37 percent in 1989, other determinants held constant, and both the incidence of computer use and its absolute increase over the five-year period were greater for women than for men (43 percent versus 32 percent in 1989) and greater for more-educated workers (8, 29, and 59 percent in 1989 for dropouts, high school graduates, and college graduates, respectively). Further, Krueger estimates that from one-third to two-thirds (depending on model specification) of the 1984–1989 increase in the estimated effect of education is directly attributable to the use of computers.[23]

A second piece of direct evidence in favor of the technical-change interpretation of variation in the $d(\ln b_i)$'s concerns the effect of "high-tech" capital on the structure of labor demand within manufacturing industry. Using Bureau of Economic Analysis data, Ernst Berndt and Catherine Morrison (1991) report estimates of the effects of this type of capital, which includes computer, communications, and photocopy equipment and instruments, as distinct from other producers' durable equipment and structures. They report a dramatic increase in the ratio of high-tech to total capital stock in manufacturing from 0.095 in 1976 to 0.257 in 1986. Further, within two-digit manufacturing industries, increases in the high-tech intensity of capital are associated with both shifts in labor demand from production toward nonproduction workers and increases in the average educational attainment of production workers.[24]

[22] For evidence that the recent wave of immigration has had a negative effect on the wages of "native" workers with low skill levels, see Joseph Altonji and David Card (1991). The potential impact of undocumented immigration on relative wages in the context of our model can be assessed by assuming that (a) these immigrants are perfect substitutes for the demographic groups in YNGLO and (b) their labor force was equal to 3 million in 1979 (but not enumerated in official statistics). In order to have been responsible for all of the relative specific-industry and general technological change against the YNGLO groups from 1979 to 1988, the employment of undocumented immigrants would have to have increased over this period by 26.6 million (compared to the native YNGLO work force of 19.2 million).

[23] Krueger's estimates of the fraction of the increase in the educational differential explained by computers refer only to their direct effect on wages. There was also an indirect effect, due to the reduced supply for other functions (e.g., managing) of those groups that had the largest increases in use of computers. There is no way to resolve with current data sets how large these indirect effects might have been, but our results suggest that it is possible that they were very large.

[24] Berndt and Morrison (1991) also find a complementarity between skill and the other forms of capital, which is consistent with the hypothesis of Zvi Griliches (1969). They find, however, that high-tech capital is more complementary with skill than are the other types.

E. DECOMPOSITION OF RELATIVE WAGE CHANGES

We have now accumulated evidence on each of the potential explanations of the dramatic changes in the wage structure in the 1980's and can summarize the results. Following (3), the proportionate relative wage change of each demographic group equals the change in total industry wage effects plus the effects of relative supply changes, product demand shifts, and average technical change, which we have separated into that arising in specific industries and in general. Estimates of the contribution of each of these effects for the comparison groups are reported for 1973–1979 in columns (ii)–(vi) of Table 6 and for 1979–1988 in columns (ix)–(xiii). Columns (vii) and (xiv) are the amounts of these relative wage changes that remain unexplained.

The decompositions for the 1980's suggest a fairly consistent story. First, total changes in average industry wage effects [column (ix)] were in the right direction but accounted for a small fraction of relative wage changes. Second, for the comparisons involving education and gender, relative supply changes [column (x)] were large and in the wrong direction. The relative decrease in the supply of older relative to younger noncollege males, however, does account for a large proportion of the increase in the slope of the age/earnings profile for that group. Third, our estimates of the effects of product demand shifts (based on DEM_2 in Table 5) on relative wages are small and of uneven direction. Fourth, the two forms of technical change, SPEC and GEN, comprise the principle source of the increase in educational differentials and the decrease in the gender differential, and the large positive values of SPEC for older noncollege workers account for a large amount of the increase in their relative wages.

An alternative way to explain the wage changes of the 1980's, an approach followed most recently by Katz and Murphy (1992), is to focus on the deceleration of changes in the demographic composition of the labor force from the 1970's to the 1980's. For example, during the 1970's the per annum rate of growth of college graduates relative to high school graduates for males was $0.204/6 = 0.034$, but this fell to $0.176/9 = 0.019$ in the 1980's. If the 1973–1979 trend had continued during 1979–1988, other things held constant, the male college/high-school proportional relative wage would have increased by $9 \times (1/\sigma) \times (0.034 - 0.019) = 0.077$ less than the actual increase of 0.163. Similar results apply to the high-school/dropout and old/young differentials for both men and women, but not to the college/high-school differential for women or to the gender differential.

The shortcoming of the approach dealing with the deceleration of relative-supply changes is that it does not explain why the structure of relative demand is changing. The approach does, however, suggest that the 1970's would have been characterized by the sorts of wage-structure changes that prevailed in the 1980's if there had not been large increases in enrollment rates starting in the 1960's.

IV. CONCLUSIONS

We have attempted to evaluate the evidence concerning several alternative explanations of the dramatic wage-structure developments in the United States during the 1980's. Our analysis points strongly to the conclusion that the principal reason for the increases in wage differentials by educational attainment and the decrease in the gender differential is a combination of skilled-labor-biased technical change and changes in unmeasured labor quality. Interestingly, these sources of wage change applied to the 1970's as well as the 1980's, but they did not cause major changes in the wage structure in the 1970's because of the abnormally large increases in the relative supply of educated labor during that time. The extremely large relative-wage decrease of young workers with low educational attainment during the 1980's is more difficult to explain, because a large part of the source of this decrease did not apply in the 1970's.

It is interesting to speculate about what the results imply about the course of relative wages in the future. Given a continuation of the increase in the relative demand within industries for highly educated labor, wage differentials by education are likely to continue to increase unless there is a sharp rise in college attendance and completion rates. Such an increase does not appear to be likely in the near future (see Bishop and Shani Carter, 1990) in the absence of drastic changes in educational policy at all levels.

APPENDIX

THE DETERMINATION OF COMPETITIVE WAGE RATES

Assume that output of each of J industries (Q_j) depends on employment of each of the I demographic groups (N_{ij}) according to the CES (constant elasticity of substitution) function

(A1)
$$Q_j = a_j \left[\sum_i \delta_{ij} \left(b_{ij} N_{ij} \right)^{(\sigma-1)/\sigma} \right]^{\sigma/(\sigma-1)}$$

where b_{ij} is an index of the technological efficiency of group-i workers in industry j, a_j is a parameter representing the (neutral) technological efficiency of the industry and the effect of capital intensity, and σ is the elasticity of intrafactor substitution, which is assumed to be equal across industries. The relative demand for the output of industry j relative to some reference industry r is assumed to be

(A2)
$$Q_j/Q_r = \theta_j P_j^{-\epsilon} \qquad j \neq r$$

where P_j is the price of Q_j relative to Q_r, θ_j is an exogenous parameter reflecting consumer tastes and other factors (such as foreign competition) relative to good r, and ϵ is the absolute price elasticity of product demand for each industry. The marginal conditions for each industry are given by

(A3)
$$P_j \partial Q_j / \partial N_{ij} = P_j a_j \delta_{ij} b_{ij}^{1-1/\sigma} \left(Q_j / N_{ij} \right)^{1/\sigma} = W_{ic}.$$

Finally, it is assumed that the economy is at full employment, such that the effective (fixed) labor force of each group is allocated among the J industries, that is,

$$(A4) \qquad N_i = \sum_j N_{ij}.$$

The $2J - 1 + I \times (J - 1)$ equations represented by (A1)–(A4) comprise a model in which the $J Q_j$'s, $I W_{ic}$'s, $J - 1 P_j$'s and $I \times J N_{ij}$'s are determined as functions of the $J - 1 \theta_j$'s, $I \times J b_{ij}$'s, $J a_j$'s, and $I N_i$'s. The model is easily manipulated to obtain a few useful results. First, the share of total group-i employment in industry j is

$$(A5) \qquad \phi_{ij} = \delta_{ij}^\sigma (b_{ij}/b_i)^{\sigma-1} x_j / D_i$$

where b_i is the average value of the technological-efficiency parameter for group-i workers across industries and

$$(A6) \qquad D_i = \sum_j \delta_{ij}^\sigma \left(b_{ij}/b_i \right)^{\sigma-1} x_j$$

$$(A7) \qquad X_j = a_j^{\sigma-1} \theta_j^{\sigma/\epsilon} Q_j^{1-\sigma/\epsilon}.$$

Second, the ratio of the competitive wage for group-i workers to that of some other group s is

$$(A8) \qquad W_{ic}/W_{sc} = (b_i/b_s)^{1-1/\sigma} (D_i/D_s)^{1/\sigma} (N_i/N_s)^{-1/\sigma}$$

where D_i is an index of the effects of the θ_j's, a_j's, and Q_j's, and proportional changes in its values are referred to as a "product-demand-shift index." Holding constant the variables that affect W_{sc}, the total logarithmic derivative of (A8) is

$$(A9) \qquad d(\ln W_{ic}) = (1 - 1/\sigma) d(\ln b_i) + (1/\sigma) d[\ln(D_i/N_i)].$$

The third useful result from the model concerns the estimation in the demand-shift variable in (A9), $d(\ln D_i)$, which reflects changes in the θ_j's and a_j's. Total differentiation of (A6) yields the product-demand-shift index

$$(A10) \qquad d\left(\ln D_i\right) = \sum_j \phi_{ij} d\left(\ln x_j\right)$$

for $\sum_j \phi_{ij} d[\ln(b_{ij}/b_i)] = 0$. The $d(\ln x_j)$'s are not directly observed, but the total derivative of (A5) is

(A11) $$d\left(\ln\phi_{ij}\right) = \left(1-\phi_{ij}\right)d\left(\ln x_j\right) - \sum_{k\neq j}\phi_{ik}d\left(\ln x_k\right) + \left(\sigma-1\right)\left[d\left(\ln\left(b_{ij}/b_i\right)\right)\right]$$

which may be rewritten in matrix form as equation (A12),

(A12) $$\begin{bmatrix} d\left(\ln\phi_{11}\right) \\ d\left(\ln\phi_{12}\right) \\ \vdots \\ d\left(\ln\phi_{IJ}\right) \end{bmatrix} = \begin{bmatrix} 1-\phi_{11} & -\phi_{12} & \cdots & -\phi_{1J} \\ -\phi_{11} & 1-\phi_{12} & \cdots & -\phi_{1J} \\ \vdots & \vdots & & \vdots \\ -\phi_{I1} & -\phi_{12} & \cdots & 1-\phi_{IJ} \end{bmatrix} \begin{bmatrix} d\left(\ln x_1\right) \\ d\left(\ln x_2\right) \\ \vdots \\ d\left(\ln x_J\right) \end{bmatrix} + \begin{bmatrix} d\left[\ln\left(b_{11}/b_1\right)\right] \\ d\left[\ln\left(b_{12}/b_1\right)\right] \\ \vdots \\ d\left[\ln\left(b_{IJ}/b_I\right)\right] \end{bmatrix}.$$

In the absence of any information about the pattern of industry/group-specific technical change, the $d[\ln(b_{ij}/b_i)]$'s are treated as an error term, and the $d(\ln x_j)$'s may be estimated by ordinary least squares and then substituted back into (A10) to obtain estimates of the product-demand-shift index.

REFERENCES

Altonji, Joseph and Card, David, "The Effect of Immigration on the Labor Market Outcomes of Natives," in J. Abowd and R. Freeman, eds., *Immigration, Trade, and the Labor Market,* Chicago: University of Chicago Press, 1991, pp. 201–34.

Bartel, Ann P. and Lichtenberg, Frank R., "The Comparative Advantage of Educated Workers in Implementing New Technology," *Review of Economics and Statistics,* February 1987, *69,* 343–59.

Berndt, Ernst R. and Morrison, Catherine J., "High-Tech Capital, Economic Performance and Labor Composition in U.S. Manufacturing Industries: An Exploratory Analysis," mimeo, Massachusetts Institute of Technology, 1991.

Bishop, John, "Achievement, Test Scores, and Relative Wages," in M. Kosters, ed., *Workers and Their Wages,* Washington, DC: American Enterprise Institute, 1991, pp. 146–86.

———— and Carter, Shani, "The Worsening Shortage of Graduate Workers," mimeo, Cornell University, 1990.

Blackburn, McKinley L., Bloom, David E. and Freeman, Richard, B., "An Era of Falling Earnings and Rising Inequality?" *Brookings Review,* Winter 1990/91, *9,* 38–43.

Bluestone, Barry and Harrison, Bennett, *The Great U-Turn: Corporate Restructuring and the Polarization of America,* New York: Basic Books, 1988.

————, "The Analysis of Union Behavior," in O. Ashenfelter and R. Layard, eds., *Handbook of Labor Economics,* Amsterdam: North-Holland, 1986, pp. 1039–89.

Farber, Henry S., "The Recent Decline in Unionization in the United States," *Science,* 13 November 1987, *238,* 915–20.

Freeman, Richard B., "Over Investment in College Training?" *Journal of Human Resources,* Summer 1975, *10,* 287–311.

————, "Demand for Education," in O. Ashenfelter and R. Layard, eds., *Handbook of Labor Economics,* Amsterdam: North-Holland, 1986, pp. 357–86.

Griliches, Zvi, "Capital-Skill Complementarity," *Review of Economics and Statistics,* November 1969, *51,* 465–8.

Hamermesh, Daniel S., "The Demand for Labor in the Long Run," in O. Ashenfelter and R. Layard, eds., *Handbook of Labor Economics,* Amsterdam: North-Holland, 1986, pp. 429–71.

―――― and Grant, James, "Econometric Studies of Labor-Labor Substitutions and Their Implications for Policy," *Journal of Human Resources,* Fall 1979, *14,* 518–42.

Johnson, George and Solon, Gary, "Estimates of the Direct Effects of Comparable Worth Policy," *American Economic Review,* December 1986, *76,* 1117–25.

Katz, Lawrence F. and Murphy, Kevin M., "Changes in Relative Wages in the United States: Supply and Demand Factors," *Quarterly Journal of Economics,* 1992 (forthcoming).

Kosters, Marvin H., "Wages and Demographics," mimeo, American Enterprise Institute, Washington, DC, November 1989.

Krueger, Alan B., "How Computers Have Changed the Wage Structure: Evidence from Microdata, 1984–89," mimeo, Princeton University, 1991.

―――― and Summers, Lawrence H., "Efficiency Wages and the Inter-Industry Wage Structure," *Econometrica,* March 1988, *56,* 259–93.

Lewis, H. Gregg, "Union Relative Wage Effects," in O. Ashenfelter and R. Layard, eds., *Handbook of Labor Economics,* Amsterdam: North-Holland, 1986, pp. 1139–81.

Mark, Jerome S., "Technological Change and Employment: Some Results from BLS Research," *Monthly Labor Review,* April 1987, *110,* 26–9.

Mincer, Jacob, "Human Capital Responses to Technical Change," National Bureau of Economic Research (Cambridge, MA) Working Paper No. 3207, 1989.

――――, "Human Capital, Technology, and the Wage Structure: What Do the Time Series Show?" National Bureau of Economic Research (Cambridge, MA) Working Paper No. 3581, 1991.

Murphy, Kevin M. and Welch, Finis, "Wage Premiums for College Graduates: Recent Growth and Possible Explanations," *Educational Researcher,* May 1989, *18,* 17–26.

―――― and ――――, "The Role of International Trade in Wage Differentials," in M. Kosters, ed., *Workers and Their Wages,* Washington,. DC: American Enterprise Institute, 1991, pp. 39–69.

―――― and ――――, "The Structure of Wages," *Quarterly Journal of Economics,* 1992 (forthcoming).

Nelson, Richard R. and Phelps, Edmund S., "Investment in Humans, Technological Diffusion, and Economic Growth," *American Economic Review,* May 1966 (*Papers and Proceedings*), *56,* 69–75.

O'Neill, June, "The Trend in the Male–Female Gap in the United States," *Journal of Labor Economics,* January 1985, *3,* S91–S116.

Slichter, Sumner H., "Notes on the Structure of Wages," *Review of Economics and Statistics,* February 1950, *32,* 89–91.

Smith, James and Ward, Michael, *Women's Wages and Work in the Twentieth Century,* Santa Monica: Rand Corporation, 1984.

Welch, Finis, "Education in Production," *Journal of Political Economy,* January/February 1970, 78, 35–59.

Wellington, Allison, "Changes in the Male/ Female Wage Gap: 1976–1985," mimeo, Davidson College, 1991.

Council of Economic Advisors, *Economic Report of the President,* Washington, DC: U.S. Government Printing Office, 1990.

ABOUT THE AUTHORS

John Bound

John Bound was born in 1948 and grew up in Westchester County, New York. A little known fact about John is that he is the grandson of Cuban immigrants, making him at least the second "high-quality" ethnic Cuban represented in this volume. John's early interests were not in economics, but in education and in low-income populations. Indeed, his first reaction to economics courses taught at Harvard College was that they were "silly." Instead, he majored in philosophy. After graduating in 1971, he spent several years teaching in an alternative public school in Philadelphia. He returned to Harvard in the late 1970's to dabble in the social sciences and to obtain a master's degree in education. During his second stint at Harvard, John discovered that he loved anthropology but was not very good at it and turned to economics as a last resort. His whole view of the subject changed after sitting in on an undergraduate labor course taught by Richard Freeman. In Richard's hands, the subject did not seem so silly anymore. After some determined arm twisting by James Medoff, John agreed to enroll in the Ph.D. program and completed his dissertation in 1987 under the supervision of Zvi Griliches and Richard Freeman.

Since joining the faculty at the University of Michigan in 1986, John has proven to be a prolific and versatile researcher. He has compiled an impressive record that extends beyond conventional topics in labor economics to cover topics in sociology and public health. The paper reprinted here is one of several that examine the causes underlying the changes in the structure of wages and in the distribution of skills in the U.S. labor market. Students interested in this line of his research might also like to see his paper with Eli Berman and Zvi Griliches on "Changes in the Demand for Skilled Labor Within U.S. Manufacturing Industries."

If someone were to tell you, however, that one of John's papers had been selected for this volume because of its frequent appearance on graduate labor reading lists, it would be difficult to guess which paper or even the topic. He is also well known for his work on disability and labor force attachment, the economic progress of African-Americans, the connection between schooling inputs and academic achievement and wages, and measurement error in survey data. In addition, his paper with David Jaeger and Regina Baker on "A Cautionary Tale Regarding Instrumental Variables" caused quite a stir when it appeared as a National Bureau of Economic Research working paper.

John has also compiled an impressive list of publications in the area of public health, including a recent publication in the prestigious *New England Journal of Medicine*. Much of this research has been co-authored with his wife, Arline Geronimus, who is a prominent scholar in her own right and a member of the public health faculty at the University of Michigan. Many labor economists know of her provocative work on the labor market consequences of out-of-wedlock births among the economically disadvantaged.

John and Arline live in Ann Arbor, Michigan, with 3 children, Miriam and their twin boys Aidan and Charlie. The experience of raising twins has given John some new insights into twin studies, a fact that should make proponents of this literature uncomfortable!

Robert LaLonde

George Johnson

George Johnson was born in 1940; he obtained his undergraduate education at Babson College and his Ph.D. in economics from the University of California, Berkeley, in 1966. He has been on the faculty at the University of Michigan since 1966, and obtained policy experience both as a senior staff economist in the Council of Economic Advisors (1977–78) and as a Director in the Office of the Assistant Secretary for Policy, Evaluation, and Research in the U.S. Department of Labor (1973–74).

George's research interests span the spectrum of modern labor economics, including unionization, labor demand, human capital investments, and labor market discrimination. The Ashenfelter-Johnson model of the determinants of strike activity is a standard part of the toolkit taught to budding labor economists (*AER,* March 1969); and the Bound-Johnson analysis of the changes that occurred in the U.S. wage structure in the 1980's was one of the first attempts to make some sense of these changes, rather than to simply describe them (*AER,* June 1992).

George's research papers often have a great pedagogical advantage: they clearly define the problem and provide an answer that can be quickly grasped by newcomers to the field as well as appreciated by the aficionado. His work also illustrates the power of an approach that consistently combines economic theory with empirical evidence. This approach not only helps to uncover new evidence, but also provides a useful framework for interpretation and prediction.

In addition to his scholarly contributions, George Johnson is the funniest man in the profession. He is well known for his (biting) wit and contempt for the pomposity that many economists (and others) attach to their work. At a 1974 meeting in Washington, George made some typically outrageous remarks. A high-level bureaucrat complained, "Now back up a minute there, George." George stood up, backed out of the room, and was not seen for the rest of the meeting.

George is also famous for making lists of awards that he regularly grants at meetings and conferences. More often than not, the winner lives in blissful ignorance because George's awards often single out such things as the worst paper presented at the conference. An exceptionally memorable award ceremony occurred at an NBER labor studies meeting some years ago, when George presented the "Best Comment on a Paper" award to Genie (Walter Oi's seeing-eye dog) for growling loudly during a particularly bad presentation.

George Johnson has also done substantial work on the labor economics of economists, including widely cited studies of faculty salaries and of the correlation between salaries and citations. In view of the impact of George's research, a George Johnson clone would quip that a strong motivation for this work was to show the regression line linking salaries and citations to his department chair.

One of George Johnson's lesser-known papers asks: "Is Labor Economics Useful?" In George's hands, it sure is!

George J. Borjas

ECONOMICS OF DISCRIMINATION

Claudia Goldin

James P. Smith and Finis R. Welch

Monitoring Costs and Occupational Segregation by Sex: A Historical Analysis

CLAUDIA GOLDIN

University of Pennsylvania and National Bureau of Economic Research

Female manufacturing workers around 1900 were far more likely to be paid by the piece and were rarely employed at the same occupation in the same firm as males. These and related aspects of work organization can be understood through a model in which workers shirk, monitoring is costly, and males and females have different turnover rates. Employers adopt either piece rates or deferred payment. Occupational segregation by sex and differences in earnings result even if workers are equally productive. Establishment-level data on supervising male and female workers in time- and piece-rate positions are examined.

I. INTRODUCTION

An index of sex segregation across about 300 occupations in the United States has remained roughly constant at 66 from the beginning of this century, implying that two-thirds of either the male or the female labor force would have to change occupations to achieve occupational equality (Gross [1968], Blau and Hendricks [1979], and Beller and Han [1984] note a decline in the index during the 1970s). The origins and persistence of occupational segregation by sex have been explained within two general frameworks, one comprising a set of market forces and another a set of norms and ideologies circumscribing female roles. Neither paradigm, however, has yielded a universally accepted framework. It is the contention of this paper that both fail to explain certain aspects of male and female jobs, such as various differences in manufacturing occupations for males and females around the turn of this century and the swift emergence of females in the clerical sector somewhat later. Aspects of supervisory and monitoring costs are explored to understand long-term trends in occupational segregation.

This research has benefited from the comments of Stanley Engerman, Robert Margo, and William Sundstrom. The paper took form during informal discussions with Beth Hayes and would have been substantially improved had it not been for her untimely death. An early version was written when the author was a member of the Institute for Advanced Study; a grant from the National Science Foundation has provided support for a larger project on historical aspects of women's work, of which this is a part. This paper has been circulated as NBER Working Paper no. 1560.

According to the human capital model (Mincer and Polachek 1974; Polachek 1975, 1979, 1981; Zalokar 1982; but see England 1982), individuals choose occupations consistent with their life-cycle labor force participation. Because of their more abbreviated and discontinuous labor force activity, women opt for occupations with lower investment costs and less depreciation with time away from the job than men do. This framework can explain a substantial portion of observed differences in occupations by sex across broadly defined categories, such as professionals and personal service workers. But it does less well in explaining occupational arrangements within groupings.

In terms of long-term trends, the following questions seem to remain only partly answered by the human capital model. Why was there segregation by sex across certain jobs within manufacturing that required similar training and ability? Why were 47% of all female operatives in manufacturing paid by the piece (or some variant of incentive pay), while only 13% of all male operatives were paid so in 1890? Why were males and females invariably paid by the piece and rarely by time when both worked at the same job in the same firm? Why were males, but rarely females, employed in teams within manufacturing? And of related interest, why do females frequently complain that they are excluded from certain occupations when there are no obvious reasons for entry barriers? Finally, if, as will be demonstrated below, the returns to specific human capital in clerical work were approximately equal for females and males, what accounted for the swift feminization of the clerical sector in the first three decades of this century?

A variant of a shirking model of the Salop and Salop (1976) and Lazear (1979, 1981) variety will be employed, although an incentive pay model of the Lazear and Rosen (1981) type is complementary to the analysis. (The model will be contrasted later to a sorting model of the Lazear [in press] variety.) Workers differ only by the amount of time they intend to stay on the job; males remain for two or more periods, but females only for one. In all other respects, with the possible exception of reservation wages, these workers are identical. The high cost of supervising the output of workers leads employers to adopt one of two solutions to avoid shirking—piece rates and deferred payment. Because females are not employed in period 2, only piece rates can be used for them; males, however, could prefer deferred payment, which causes their earnings profile to be steeper than otherwise.

Occupational segregation by sex results even if workers are homogeneous with regard to their ability and there are no costs of job investment. Because the monitoring of piece rates may be costlier to use in comparison with deferred payment, but may be cheaper than with ordinary time rates, males can receive higher wages in equilibrium than females.[1] Life-cycle labor force participation differences between males and females dictate

---

[1] *Added production costs might result from using piece rates. The production process would have to be altered to divide the good into component parts that could be easily counted and checked for quality. The model below will assume that these costs (or benefits in the case of economies from division of labor) are zero.*

the final result, but individual choice of occupations does not.[2] Under a reasonable set of assumptions, females would want to be employed in the male sector but would be barred from doing so. The exclusion of females from this sector would be efficient.

Establishment-level and more highly aggregated data for manufacturing around the turn of this century are examined with regard to the costs of supervising and monitoring male and female workers in time- and piece-rate positions. Evidence on piece-rate workers across industries is presented to explore the predictions of the model.

Even though the entire occupational distribution has been widely segregated by sex, certain occupations have "changed sex" over time, and their study can reveal factors fostering segregation. Occupations in the clerical sector underwent this transformation in the early part of this century. The clerical sector was "routinized," as had occurred earlier in manufacturing, enabling employers to hire females (see Goldin and Sokoloff [1982] for a discussion of the division of labor in early nineteenth-century manufacturing). Qualitative and empirical evidence is presented indicating that the cost of supervising workers was reduced, but not the firm-level specificity of human capital as has been claimed. General training, acquired off the job, substituted for on-the-job training and enabled employers to homogenize their labor forces based on various preemployment tests. Secretarial services were thus supervised without the use of more costly piece rates.

II. A MONITORING MODEL OF OCCUPATIONAL SEGREGATION

Assume that good Q is the only good produced in the manufacturing sector, and that it can be produced by one of two processes: (1) Q can be divided into $n - 1$ parts and put together in an nth operation. Each of the parts is made separately, and a piece-rate system of payment can be used to pay labor when output quantity is easily monitored and output quality is not an important variable. (II) Alternatively, Q can be made in one process, possibly using a time-rate system of payment particularly when input quantity can be easily monitored and output quality cannot be ascertained cheaply. Thus there will be $n + 1$ occupations if both processes coexist. Examples of goods that have been made by both types of processes simultaneously are coats and cigars, but it is generally the case that when both processes coexist, the goods vary by quality with the higher-quality good made on time. It will be assumed at present, but considered in more detail later, that the nature of the good is independent of the production process.

---

[2] Turnover, not life-cycle labor force participation, is the actual variable of importance. Women could have discontinuous and abbreviated life-cycle labor force participation but lower turnover than men; that is, their length of time with firms could be longer. Most empirical evidence indicates, however, that women have considerably higher turnover and lower lengths of stay with firms than do men. Lower lengths of stay are evident from late nineteenth-century data on labor market experience (Hannon 1977; Goldin 1980, 1984); lower turnover was evident in the 1920s (see, e.g., Rogers 1929); and lower lengths of stay with firms are observed in 1980s data from the Current Population Surveys.

Also assume that there are two types of labor, L_f (female) and L_m (male), homogeneous and identical except that L_f is in the labor force for only 1 period and L_m is in for more than 1 period. They can also differ in their labor supply functions to this industry. It is critical, however, that both types of labor will shirk if their inputs or outputs go unsupervised.

Three combinations of payment and supervision can be used: (1) time rate with supervision of input; (2) piece rate with supervision of output; and (3) time rate with an incentive pay structure having a rising pay scale with time on the job (Salop and Salop 1976; Lazear 1979, 1981; Guasch and Weiss 1981).[3] Method 3 involves the supervision of input and a monitoring of output. It will be assumed now, and explored empirically later, that the monitoring costs of method 3 are lower than those of method 2, and that the monitoring costs of method 1 are the most expensive. In the model below it is implicitly assumed that there are neither costs nor benefits to dividing the good into component parts; that is, it is costless to invent piece rates and there are no gains from such further division of labor.

The first production process (1) for good Q can be represented by

$$q_i = f_i(L_i, R_i, S_i) \qquad i = 1, \ldots, n-1,$$

where L = labor, R = raw materials, and S = supervision. Assume, as well, that this production process is constant returns to scale in L, R, and S, fixed proportions, and identical across all i. Each q_i is part of Q such that the joining of the component parts of Q is defined as the nth process, $nQ = q$.

Each laborer on piece rates gets paid the following for each unit of output, under zero profit conditions: $w_p = p - s - r$, where s = per unit costs of supervision, and r = per unit costs of raw materials. The price of each piece, p, is the price of Q, P, divided by n, $p = P/n$. It will be assumed that the price of Q, P, is fixed exogenously.

Assume that the supply of labor function for L_f, defined in terms of the number of pieces produced at each piece rate, is $q = h(w_p)$, where $h' > 0$, and gives the number of pieces produced per period. As shown in figure 1, when $P = P^*$ and the equilibrium piece

---

[3] *The models in each of these articles differ from that presented below because each assumes that workers are heterogeneous in some factor relating to work effort or quitting and that the firm cannot determine this difference prior to hiring. The workers in the model below are homogeneous in their productivity and all will shirk if not monitored or given some incentive. But they differ in their turnover, which can be easily determined by the firm. Salop and Salop (1976) assume that workers differ by turnover and that firms cannot distinguish between slow and fast quitters before hiring. Their incentive compatible scheme is to withhold a fraction of earnings from workers in one period that is returned in the next. Guasch and Weiss (1981) assume that workers differ in ability and that, for risk-neutral workers, there always exists a self-selection mechanism in which workers pay for a test that, if passed, gives workers a known return. Lazear (1979) considers the impact of these types of implicit contracts on the date of voluntary retirement and generates a model of optimal mandatory retirement. Note that there is a close relationship between the results of these models and those of internal labor market theory, although the motivation for each of the constructs might differ.*

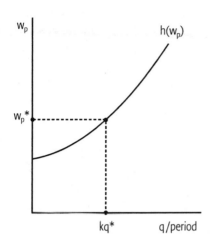 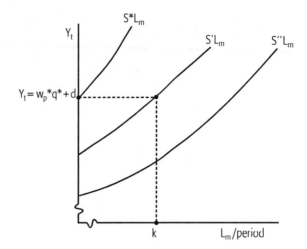

FIGURE 1

rate is w_p^*, production will be q^* per worker or kq^* for all piece workers, if each has an identical piece supply function. That is, $(q^*/n)k = kQ^*$ units of the good will be produced. There will be n occupations and k/n persons per occupation. Each worker receives an income of $Y_p = q^*w_p^*$ per period worked.

Alternatively, or in conjunction with process I, the industry can use process II, $Q = g(L, R, S)$, also assumed to be constant returns to scale and fixed proportions. In order to compare this production process with that given by process I, we must know the output per period produced by time workers. One assumption is that k time workers, given an amount of monitoring derived below, produce on average exactly what k piece workers do at a wage equivalent to a piece rate of w_p^*. In this case each time worker would have an accepted output standard of $Q^*n = q^*$ units per time period.

The zero profit condition implies that each time worker will receive $Y_t = (P - nr - s')(q/n) - t$, where s' is the per unit output supervision cost and t is the per time period input supervision cost. The first term in parentheses is the per unit (short-run) profit and the second is the amount of final output produced. The last term, t, is the cost per time period of supervising a time worker.[4] The standardization of the two methods implies that at the existing price of the output, P^*, there is an s' and a t such that q^* per worker is elicited per period. At that s' and t, firms would be indifferent between hiring time and piece-rate workers.

In general, therefore, $Y_t = Y_p + [sq - (s'q/n) - t]$, and the difference in the earnings of time and piece workers, to be denoted d, depends on the degree to which supervisory costs differ between the two methods. While it seems reasonable that $sq > s'q/n$, or that

---

[4] Note that while one could use the time workers to produce using the piece-rate technology, it would generally be more expensive to do so because of the added number of pieces to monitor. That is, if $s' = s$, supervision costs would be higher employing time workers on the piece-rate technology.

the monitoring of output is cheaper for time workers because there are fewer pieces, it is not clear that the magnitude of t will not swamp this difference. Furthermore, it is not clear whether the costs of monitoring a unit of the piece-rate good are less than the costs of monitoring a unit of the time-rate good, that is, the relationship between s and s'.

Consider only the first two types of payment and supervision. The costs of monitoring for type 1, time rate with only input supervision, could be sufficiently high that all workers would opt for piece-rate work. That is, s' per unit and t per person as supervision costs to elicit q^* might be high enough so that $Y_t < Y_p$, and then all workers would prefer to work on piece. An alternative to piece rates, however, is to hire only the L_m workers, all of whom will be in the labor force for at least 2 periods, and pay them $Y_{t1} = (w_p^* q^* + d - e)$ $< Y_p + d$ for period 1, and $Y_{t2} = (w_p^* q^* + d + e) > Y_p + d$ for period 2, where $d = q^* [s - (s'/n)] - t = (Y_t - Y_p)$, e = an optimal deferred payment, and there are zero rates of interest and time preference.

The incentive scheme of facing workers with an upward-sloping wage profile succeeds because employers can easily screen individuals who will not remain in the labor force for 2 periods, and there is sufficient monitoring of output that shirking can be detected prior to period 2. If time workers do not produce the required output level, they are dismissed after the first period and can only be hired in the piece-rate sector in the second period. Because workers value only income, they would rather work in the time-rate sector for both periods when $d > 0$. The firm promises to pay workers Y_{t2} in the second period, giving workers an incentive to produce the required level of output in the first period.

The time-rate experience profile rises with time on the job even though productivity does not. When $d > e$, the L_f's would want to enter the first period time-rate job but are prevented from doing so because the threat of firing them would be of no consequence. The size of e can be determined in a more comprehensive model by two sets of factors, the stability and reputation of the firms and the cost of effort to the workers (see Lazear [1979, 1981] for the determinants of the optimal profile). Note that when $d > 0$, the L_m's receive higher lifetime average income than do the L_f's, when all $n + 1$ occupations exist. This result holds even though all labor is intrinsically of equal productivity and even if $d < e$ or the deferred payment is greater than the difference in supervision costs.

A final issue concerns the conditions under which both types of workers, and thus both processes (comprising the $n + 1$ occupations), will coexist and, if so, which workers are assigned to which processes. The answer depends on the supply of labor. In the piece-work case, it was assumed that all labor was identical, and thus that $h(w_p)$, as drawn in figure 1, was an aggregate of the individual functions, all identical. For time work, however, the simplest case would be one in which the reservation wage for each worker differs, and thus the supply function gives the number of laborers supplied per time period at each Y. Because only the L_m's will ever be chosen to work on the time-rate jobs when $d > 0$, time-rate workers will be called L_m's. In the case drawn in figure 1, the supply function $S'L_m$ happens to lead to an equal number of L_m and L_f workers; $S''L_m$ leads to more L_m workers; and $S*L_m$ results in no L_m workers. Thus the ratio L_f/L_m depends on the position of the male labor supply function and the level of d, given the piece-rate supply function.

When both processes are used and $d > 0$, the following results will obtain:

(1) complete occupational segregation by sex;

(2) females will all be paid by the piece and males by time;

(3) the ratio of female to male earnings will be $[Y_p/(Y_p + d)] < 1$, on average, although for first-period employees it could be >1 if $d < e$; and

(4) if $d > e$, females would want to enter the entry-level L_m occupation but will be prevented from doing so.

III. MONITORING AND SUPERVISION IN MANUFACTURING, CIRCA 1890

Only one type of good existed in the monitoring model, and the method of payment for labor was solely determined by the costs of monitoring and differences in life-cycle employment across workers. In the real world, however, there are other reasons for using different methods of payment that determine the types of goods made by piece and time, the types of workers that will be employed in each process, and their remuneration. Three additional complementary reasons for piece rates must be added concerning the division of labor, the quality of the good, and the variance of required skill across workers. Another rationale for piece rates, distinct from the monitoring explanation set forth here, is that they enable the sorting of heterogeneous workers (Lazear in press). This alternative hypothesis will be explored in the empirical section.

Certain types of goods might be divided into pieces more easily than others, and in these the division of labor itself might reduce per unit costs. In these cases the piece-rate technology might dominate even in the absence of monitoring costs. Alternatively or in conjunction, goods may differ by quality. It is generally presumed that one can monitor output quality more cheaply in low quality goods than in high quality goods (Pencavel 1977). In the latter, one may want to screen workers and hire only those who will produce goods of uniformly high quality output and then supervise only by input. Such was the case in the manufacture of clothing at the turn of this century; high quality coats, for example, were made by skilled tailors working on time, while lower quality coats were made by less skilled operatives working by the piece (see the study of men's ready-made clothing, U.S. Senate [1910–11, vol. 87]).

The last reason for the method of payment concerns the variance in skill level across the various pieces or stages in the production process. When the variation in necessary skill is high, one may want to use the lower skilled operations to screen workers for the higher skilled operations. The method of screening might be more complex than merely monitoring the output of workers, the only observable aspect of piece-rate work. It may, instead, entail judging the inventiveness of workers, their ability to give orders and respond in a variety of situations. Ranking individuals in an ordinal sense may be far cheaper than grading them absolutely. It has been shown that when workers are risk neutral a rank-order system of prizes can elicit the same effort as a piece-rate system (Lazear and Rosen 1981). Both this variant of the model and that elaborated above imply that males will have a higher variance in earnings than will females (holding productivity constant), and thus it would be true even if males and females were equally productive in a deterministic or expected-value sense.

The relative use of piece work across industries and among firms within an industry may be determined by factors complementing those in the simple supervisory-cost model. The question is whether the division of workers between the two types of payment is determined primarily by differences in supervising workers that arise from differences in life-cycle labor force participation. Within the context of the formal model above, one might observe females producing goods that are cheaper to divide into pieces while males produce other goods by time. Similarly, males might produce the higher quality good, and males might also be employed on time-rate pay in industries that screen workers at one level of production for jobs at another.[5] How male and female workers are sorted across industries might be related to the costs of supervision given these complementary factors. What are the facts concerning the employment of males and females in industries around the turn of this century?

The data in table 1 indicate that 54% of all adult male employees in manufacturing in 1890 were in industries in which adult males were over 94% of the labor force. (Adult males were 79% of the total manufacturing labor force.) Because virtually all the remaining 6% who were not adult males were boys, 54% of all adult male employees in manufacturing could not possibly have been in an occupational-industrial classification in which there were women.

At the same time, 74% of all female employees were in the industries classified in table 1 as female intensive, those in which adult women were over 30% of all employees; adding the mixed industries raises the figure to 83%. (Adult women were 18% of the total manufacturing labor force and children were 3%.) It is only in the mixed industries, such as tobacco and printing, and very few of the female-intensive industries, such as cotton textiles, that one finds any overlap in male and female occupations within late nineteenth-century industries. In what ways did the female-intensive and mixed industries differ from the others?

In looking at the industries in table 1 that were exclusively male domains, several factors seem apparent in limiting the presence of females. Many of these industries required substantial apprenticeships (e.g., cooperage, masonry, plumbing, shipbuilding, custom

---

[5] *Other factors that might influence the cost effectiveness of using piece rates, as opposed to time rates, have been suggested in Pencavel (1977), Roummaset and Uy (1980), and Lazear (1981, in press). Piece-rate payment might also dominate when technical change is not very rapid, when there is a large luck component in production or sales, and when there is low variability in the efficiency of complementary inputs.*

TABLE 1

SEX SEGREGATION AND PIECE WORK AMONG 48 LARGE INDUSTRIES, 1890

	% Total Manufacturing Labor Force	% Adult Males in Labor Force*	% Adult Workers on Piece Rates†
"Male-intensive" industries:‡§			
Agricultural implements	.93	98	20.59
Blacksmithing and wheelwrighting	1.08	100	2.65
Boots and shoes, custom work	.75	98	36.34
Brick, tile, clay, and pottery	2.75	94	3.80
Carpentering	2.97	100	1.62
Carriages, wagons, and cars	3.07	99	10.81
Cooperage	.52	98	41.26
Flouring and grist mill	1.35	99	2.13
Foundry and machine shop	5.26	99	10.01
Furniture, factory	1.36	95	12.79
Iron and steel	3.24	99	0
Leather, includes morocco	.90	98	10.89
Liquors, malt	.74	98	1.27
Lumber and other mill products	6.07	98	3.47
Lumber, planing	1.84	98	1.70
Masonry, brick, and stone	2.30	100	1.76
Painting and paper hanging	1.19	100	4.94
Plumbing and gas fitting	.90	98	.74
Saddlery and harness	.64	95	21.59
Shipbuilding	.55	100	4.58
Slaughtering and meat packing	.86	96	3.53
Timber products	.98	99	21.51
Tin and coppersmithing	.82	94	6.38

	% Total Manufacturing Labor Force	% Adult Females in Labor Force*	% on Piece Rates†	
			Females	Males
"Female-intensive" industries:‡"				
Boots and shoes, factory	3.00	29	60.0	53.5
Boxes	.40	65	55.6	23.0
Carpets	.60	45	17.8	14.9
Clothing, men's	3.32	49	68.1	49.2
Clothing, women's	.09	63	46.8	43.2
Confectionary	.06	39	16.7	5.8
Corsets	.02	81	63.5	53.4
Cotton goods	4.70	52	73.4	31.7
Dressmaking	1.43	97	...	...
Fruits and vegetables, canning	1.08	48	49.9	19.8
Furnishing goods, men's	.05	74	65.7	51.7
Gloves and mittens	.02	59	78.0	39.7
Hats and caps	.06	34	70.2	55.3
Hosiery and knit goods	1.30	67	63.0	21.3
Millinery and lace goods	.03	73	41.4	29.7
Millinery, custom	.05	98	...	...
Shirts	.07	79	69.4	52.6
Silk	1.08	57	75.6	39.8
Woolen goods	1.68	38	76.6	26.3
Worsted goods	.09	46	...	...

(continued on following page)

TABLE 1 (CONTINUED)

SEX SEGREGATION AND PIECE WORK AMONG 48 LARGE INDUSTRIES, 1890

	% Total Manufacturing Labor Force	% Adult Females in Labor Force*	% on Piece Rates†	
			Females	Males
"Mixed" industries:				
Clothing; men's custom	1.83	23	54.0	56.1
Paper	.63	23	31.4	.5
Printing, book and job	1.23	17	15.0	9.3
Printing, newspaper and periodical	1.22	11	19.8	18.4
Tobacco	2.75	27	64.8	65.5

Source. United States Census Office (1895).
Note. Three dots indicate that the figure for the percentage on piece rates is vastly understated. The understated figure was used in the computation of the percentage of all workers on piece rates biasing downward that for females in particular. The data for cotton goods, silk, and woolens are adjusted for the undercount of pieceworkers in these industries using the more detailed, firm- and occupation-level data in the U.S. Department of Labor (1897). The procedure involved merely counting the number of workers by sex and their method of payment. Tobacco includes cigars and cigarettes; boots and shoes, factory includes rubber. Adult females are > 15 years old and adult males are > 16 years old.
* Male and female children comprise a separate category, not included here, and the figures for percent adult males and females do not exhaust the entire labor force.
† The percentage of workers on piece rates includes only operatives and nets out clerical workers and other nonoperatives.
‡ Male-intensive, female-intensive, and mixed refer to the actual percentage of males or females in each industry and not to an inherent characteristic of the industry.
§Total % manufacturing labor force in these 23 industries = 38; % adult males across all industries = 79; % total adult male workers in these 23 industries = 54; % adult male workers on piece rates across all industries = 12.9 (adjusted for the undercount of pieceworkers in the cotton goods, silk, and woolen industries in the 1890 Census of Manufacturing; see Note to this table for procedure).
" Total % manufacturing labor force in these 25 industries = 27; % adult females across all industries = 18; % total adult female workers in these 25 industries = 83; % adult female workers on piece rates across all industries = 46.9 (adjusted for the undercount of pieceworkers in the cotton goods, silk, and woolen industries in the 1890 Census of Manufacturing; see Note to this table for procedure).

boot and shoe making). Still others were physically demanding (e.g., slaughtering, iron and steel, milling). Yet these considerations alone might not explain the almost complete exclusion of females from the list. The method of work organization may also have contributed to the exclusivity of these industries. It should also be pointed out that male earnings were not higher in the male-intensive industries, even adjusting for the more rural location of the male-intensive industries.

It was the method of payment and not the absolute level of wages that differed for males across the three groups of industries. All laborers in the female-intensive industries were more frequently paid by the piece. Females were overwhelmingly paid by the piece in comparison with male manufacturing laborers in both the female-intensive and the mixed industries. Finally, the distribution of all male and female manufacturing labor by form of payment underscores the results of the separate industry comparisons.

Firms were surveyed by the 1890 Census of Manufacturing (U.S. Census Office 1895) concerning the number of full-time equivalent workers by sex, age group (adult and child), as well as type of position (clerical, skilled operative, unskilled operative, and piece-rate worker). It is not until 1960 that we again have comparable data for the entire manufacturing sector. The data in the 1890 Census of Manufacturing indicate that 37% of all adult female manufacturing workers (> 15 years) were paid by the piece, but that only 13% of all adult males (> 16 years) were paid so.

But the procedure used in the 1890 census to categorize piece-rate workers severely understates their number. Because so many occupations in the cotton goods, silk, and woolens industries, among others, were piece-rate jobs, the census did not record them as such but instead grouped these employees in the operative category. Only 10.1% of female employees were listed as being employed on piece-rates in cotton goods. The true figure is considerably higher.[6]

Correcting the incentive-pay employment figures for only three industries reveals that at least 47% of all female operatives across all industries were paid by the piece while only 13% of males were.[7] Females were therefore 3.5 times more likely than were males to be employed on piece rates. Furthermore, piece-rate payment almost always prevailed when males and females occupied the same position in the same firm. Examples from the textile industry are instructive. In only one out of the six predominantly male occupations in cotton textiles was payment generally made by the piece, but among four in which both men and women were found only one was paid by time.

Female workers predominated in those industries in which piece-rate work was common for all workers. The piece-rate percentages in table 1 are generally low for all the male-intensive industries, but the piece-rate percentages are relatively high for males in the female-intensive industries. Females were also employed on piece-rate work with

---

[6] Stanley Lebergott's chapter in Davis, Easterlin, and Parker (1972) also cites the 1890 Census of Manufacturing figures on piecework without corrections. Pencavel (1977), in turn, uses the Lebergott figures, although with reservations. On the undercount in the census, see U.S. Census Office, Manufacturing Industries, Part 1 (1895, p. 173), which states that "an arbitrary rule was adopted that all pieceworkers whose earnings are limited by the speed of machinery were to be included with those paid a specific amount by the week, the day, or the hour."

[7] Corrections to the cotton goods, silk, and woolens industries were made for both males and females by using data in U.S. Department of Labor (1897), which includes information on certain female-intensive and mixed industries. Male-intensive industries may also have suffered from an under-reporting of piece-rate employment. A comparison between data arrayed by industry in the 1885 Census of Massachusetts (Massachusetts Bureau of Statistics of Labor 1888) and those for Massachusetts in the 1890 Manufacturing Census (U.S. Census Office 1895) indicate that certain male-intensive industries did underreport incentive-pay work in the federal census. But the male-intensive industries that had the largest differences between the two censuses were relatively unimportant from a national standpoint (arms, clocks, and instruments). The overall figure for the percentage of all manufacturing laborers employed by incentive pay in Massachusetts was 38.7% in the 1885 Massachusetts census but only 22.7% in the 1890 Manufacturing Census. However, the 22.7% figure increases to 33.3% when corrections are made for the three industries (plus worsteds) listed above, and additional corrections for other female-intensive and mixed industries could well close the remaining gap between these two censuses.

greater frequency than were males within the same industry, and they were invariably employed on piece rates when males occupied the same job title.[8]

Certain institutional mechanisms, such as teams and inside contracting, also distinguish male-intensive industries from female-intensive ones. It appears that the length of stay in the labor force and on the job may have been critical in limiting the employment of women in those industries in which such institutions reduced supervisory costs. Teams were groups of workers organized by a contractor who dealt directly with the firm's managers or owners and who was contracted to produce a certain amount of output or paid by the final piece. The agent in turn hired workers, who were frequently well known to the contractor and to the other members of the team. The type of work performed fell somewhere between an intricate division of labor and a single production process for the good. Teams conserved on supervision costs for management because the contractors had knowledge of the productivity of individual workers and were able to increase effort because of personal friendships and kin ties. Teams were generally found only in the male-intensive industries or among male workers in other industries. (See Buttrick [1952], who notes that contractors were frequently paid by the piece; Montgomery [1979], who discusses teams among molders, tailors, and miners; U.S. Senate [1910–11, vol. 87], on male teams within men's ready-made clothing.)

In certain industries, in which virtually no women were employed, various aspects of the process could have been done by unskilled workers, and indeed were done by women during periods of labor shortage, such as World War I. In railroad foundries, for example, women were employed during the war in the production of cores and as machinists. The railroad union protested such employment after the war, claiming that such tasks were an integral part of the apprenticeship program, and that while women could be effectively employed in these areas, they undermined the training and screening of skilled workers (Greenwald 1981, pp. 116–17).

The division of workers into piece- and time-rate work, in the formal model of Section II, was a function of the costs of supervision and monitoring. Do supervision costs differ in the manner predicted by the observed differences in the form of payment by sex? That is, are supervision costs lower for piece-rate than time-rate workers in female-intensive industries but higher in male-intensive industries where other methods of monitoring and supervising were available?

Two sets of data having information on the form of payment and the costs of supervision are used to explore this issue. One set, from the 1895–96 Report of the Commissioner

---

[8] *Why were females and males both employed at piece rates when they were given the same occupational title? One reason may be that males were more productive than were females because the existing technology rewarded their greater strength, or because males had a greater incentive to work more intensively than females. Data from the 1895–96 Report of the Commissioner of Labor (U.S. Department of Labor 1897) indicate that the average ratio of earnings for females to males, when both worked at piece rates at the same firm and at the same occupation, was about 0.8. If these same workers were employed on time, their earnings would have differed (for a given occupation, at the same experience level, and so on). Even in the late nineteenth century unequal payment by gender for identical work would have damaged labor relations within the firm.*

of Labor (U.S. Department of Labor 1897), contains firm-level data on female-intensive and mixed industries.[9] Another, from the 1890 Census of Manufactures (U.S. Census Office 1897, pt. 2), contains city-level observations across all industries. The first set of data has been used for the female-intensive industries and the second for the male-intensive ones, of which only foundries had enough observations and large average firm size by city to be usable.[10]

Six industries—boxes, cigars, clothing, cotton, food, and shoes—were selected from the 1895–96 Report for the female-intensive industries. These industries differed considerably in the degree to which female workers advanced in jobs over the course of their employment and in the variance in female wages across occupations. Clothing and cotton textiles had the highest variance in wages and, it appears from the qualitative evidence, the greatest degree of occupational shift. Because of these differences, industry form-of-payment dummies have been added to the female-intensive industry regression equation explaining supervisory inputs.

The estimation in table 2 explaining supervisory inputs across firms in female-intensive industries indicates that supervisory costs were lowest for male and female piece-rate workers (except in the clothing and cotton textile industries). Male time workers and female time workers were next in order of lowest supervisory cost. A female time worker, on the margin, required almost eight times the supervisory input as did a female piece-rate worker. A male time worker required just one-third the supervisory input of a female time worker, but almost three times that of a male or female piece-rate worker.

These findings are consistent with the conclusions of the model. Female-intensive industries used piece-rate workers to conserve on supervisory costs. The absolute costs of supervision were nontrivial. The average weekly wage of a male supervisor was about $25.00. The marginal female time-rate worker required $0.0440 \times (\$25.00) = \$1.10$ worth of supervision per week or somewhere between 15% and 20% of per weekly earnings (assuming a range of $5.50 to $7.30).[11] The marginal female piece-rate worker required $0.00578 \times (\$25.00) = \$0.145$ or only 2%–3% of her weekly earnings.

---

[9] The 1895–96 Report includes information on approximately 68,000 male and 80,000 female employees, and of the 364 industries listed in the 1890 Census of Manufacturing, 57% were included in the report. The industries represented in the survey included, on a national scale, 40% of all male operatives but 96% of all female operatives, not a surprising finding given that the directive was "to investigate . . . the conditions attending the employment of women and children" (p. 11).

[10] In small artisanal firms, such as existed in cooperage, there was insufficient division of labor to measure the supervisory input. There were often no supervisors or managers enumerated because the artisans supervised themselves.

[11] The weekly wage across all (adult) female workers in manufacturing was $5.30 in 1890 and about $6.30 adjusted for full-time work (Brissenden 1929). The absolute values of the coefficients for the female-intensive equation may be too low because of a downward bias to the dependent variable. The 1895–96 Report of the Commissioner of Labor listed foremen, overseers, inspectors, and so on who were paid wages but rarely listed managerial personnel, presumably salaried, who were engaged in supervision. Such personnel, however, may have been a constant factor across firms and thus downwardly bias only the constant term and not the coefficients of interest.

TABLE 2

SUPERVISORY COSTS AND THE FORM OF PAYMENT, MANUFACTURING CIRCA 1890
(DEPENDENT VARIABLE: NUMBER OF SUPERVISORY PERSONNEL PER FIRM)

	Female-Intensive Industries		Male-Intensive Industries, Foundries
Constant	.6538		1.277
	(1.67)		(10.98)
Number of workers per firm:			
Male piece rate	.00506		.0115
	(.92)		(2.40)
Male time	.0142		
	(1.76)		
Skilled			.00679
			(2.81)
Unskilled			.00697
			(2.02)
Female piece rate	.00578		
	(1.95)		
Female time	.0440		
	(3.28)		
Industry dummies:			
Boxes	.313	(.54)	
Clothing	.070	(.11)	
Food	−1.261	(1.78)	
Shoes	.517	(.70)	
Cigars	.019	(.03)	
Industry-worker interactions:			
Cotton male piece	−.0019	(1.75)	
Cotton male time	.0425	(1.08)	
Cotton female piece	.0047	(.69)	
Cotton female time	−.0508	(2.81)	
Clothing male piece	.0021	(.28)	
Clothing male time	.0441	(3.91)	
Clothing female piece	.0028	(.54)	
Clothing female time	−.0537	(3.38)	
R^2	.936		.203
Number of observations	289		152

Note. Male-intensive industry, from U.S. Census Office (1895), pt. 2: *City Totals*. The observations are city-industry cells and have been weighted by $\sqrt{n}$, where n = the number of firms in the city. Female-intensive industries are from U.S. Department of Labor (1897), where the observation is a firm. t-statistics are in parentheses.

Are female earnings lower than those of males because of their higher supervisory costs? In terms of the predictions of the model, what is the value of $d = (Y_t - Y_p)$ and (Y_t/Y_p)? If all female workers are identical, then they must all receive the same net wage, and the choice between employing them on piece or on time must involve whether the piece-rate process is more expensive to employ in terms of dividing the good into its component parts. Under this assumption one can use the value of $\$1.10$ ($= 0.044 \times \$25.00$) as the total weekly supervisory (and/or added production) costs to employing a female and compare it with the value of supervision for a male time worker.

In the female-intensive industry sample, the difference between the marginal requirements of a female and a male time worker was $(0.044 - 0.0142 = 0.0298) \times (\$25.00) =$
\$0.745 or between 10% and 14% of the female weekly wage.[12] That is, $d = 0.745$, and the
ratio of earnings of an identically productive female to male would be between 88% and
91% (e.g., $5.50/(5.50 + 0.745) = 88\%$). The divergence from one is due entirely to the
higher costs of supervising female workers. Because males in female-intensive industries
may have been different from males in male-intensive industries in terms of turnover
rates, these percentages are probably lower-bound measures of the extent to which differences in monitoring costs widen the male-female earnings gap. Furthermore, when
differences in strength or work intensity correlated with gender are accounted for, monitoring costs explain about one-third of the remaining difference between male and female
wages.[13]

Consider now the two special female-intensive industries, cotton textiles and clothing.
The coefficients for these two industries differ from those of the other four industries in
two important ways. Female time workers were relatively inexpensive to supervise but
male time workers were considerably more expensive to supervise. Cotton textiles and
men's factory-made clothing, like the male-intensive industries, utilized screening on the
job. Here screening appears to have taken place within the piece-rate positions. These
industries, however, did not offer much job advancement for their male workers, and the
supervisory input, therefore, was high for male time-rate jobs.[14]

The results from the male-intensive industry are different from those for most of the
female-intensive industries. Supervisory costs were greatest, at the margin, for the piece-
rate workers and were only slightly higher for the unskilled than for the skilled workers.

---

[12] *The coefficients in the male-intensive industry sample are not exactly comparable to those in the
female-intensive sample and therefore have not been used in this example.*

[13] *The overall ratio of female to male earnings in manufacturing was about 0.6 in 1890. The ratio of
female to male earnings in piece-rate work (for the same occupations in the same firms) was about
0.8 (U.S. Department of Labor 1897, printing and tobacco industries). The ratio of 0.8 measures
actual physical productivity differences between male and female workers. Thus the true gap between
the sexes not accounted for by the physical productivity differences revealed in the piece-rate data is
$1 - (0.6/0.8) = 25\%$, rather than the initial 40%. The piece-rate ratio gives us a reason for handicap-
ping female workers and using a basis ratio of 0.8 instead of 1. Of the initial gap of 40 percentage
points, 15 are due to these differences in physical output and 25 remain. Monitoring costs account for
about another eight percentage points of the remaining 25. An example is instructive: say female
earnings are \$6.00 per week and male earnings are \$10.00 across all workers, but female and male
piece-rate workers earn \$6.00 and \$7.50. Monitoring costs narrow the unexplained portion even further. On average the difference in monitoring costs between males and females was \$0.75, thus
increasing the augmented female wage of \$7.50 to \$8.25. Therefore, a gap of 17.5 percentage points
remains, $1 - 8.25/10$, to be explained by a host of other factors.*

[14] *The male workers in these industries may very well have been less able or had high turnover and
may have been sorted out of the male-intensive industries and those in the female-intensive sector
that allowed advancement in wages and position. It should be noted that the firms in the 1895–96
Report were generally large and therefore did not include the outside contracting shops in men's
clothing that hired skilled tailors organized into teams.*

In the male-intensive industry an additional male piece-rate worker added about the same number of supervisors as did a male time-rate worker in the four female-intensive industries. A male time-rate worker in the male-intensive industry added about the same number of supervisors as did a female or male piece-rate worker in the four female-intensive industries. This reversal of the costs of supervision suggests that the formal model may have captured some of the intrinsic differences between the nature of production and work supervision in the two sets of industries.[15] Male time workers in male-intensive industries may have been supervised less expensively than were time workers in other industries because they were offered an incentive-compatible contract or worked in teams or were given prizes at certain intervals.

It might also be asked whether the supervisors were male or female and whether the costs of obtaining able supervisors varied across industries. The first question can be easily addressed, but the second will have to await the collection of additional data on the earnings of both the supervisors and the workers. Regression results using the number of supervisors of each gender as the dependent variables indicate that both female and male supervisors were used in the female-intensive industries, but, as might be expected, female supervisors were used almost exclusively to supervise female workers and male piece-rate workers. Female supervisors, however, did not oversee the male time-rate workers, a position, it appears, that was reserved for the male supervisors.

One alternative reason for piece rates is that they are a mechanism for sorting workers on the job. The predictions of the monitoring and the sorting models are somewhat different, and the data in the reports just cited enable some empirical tests of them. Lazear (in press) develops a sorting model of piece rates in which workers are heterogeneous with regard to productivity (q), but each has an identical, alternative wage. In the symmetric form of the model only the distribution of productivity is known to both employee and employer; in the asymmetric form the employee knows q. Piece-rate work entails an added cost of monitoring. The predictions of the model, in general, are that firms will sort workers on piece-rate work and then move them to time, saving the cost of monitoring; in the asymmetric case, the worst workers will opt out of the sorting process and will be employed on time. In the monitoring version of piece-rate work, the workers with the highest turnover (and thus the highest costs of supervising) are put on piece.

While it is difficult to formulate a decisive test of these alternative theories, the employment of almost one-half of all female manufacturing workers on piece rates supports the

---

[15] *Because of problems in scaling the dependent variable, a more cautious interpretation would use only the relative magnitudes of the coefficients. The problem is that the proxy for supervisors in the male-intensive industry data probably excludes a group of foremen and overseers, because it includes only managerial personnel involved in supervision (see also n. 11 above on the biases in the female-intensive industry data). The remaining supervisors were included with the skilled, time workers. Because the census gave a distribution of these workers by earnings, one method for estimating the number of total supervisors would be to use the number of workers above a particular level of earnings. Results using this procedure yield coefficients having the same relative magnitudes as those in table 2 (that is piece > unskilled time > skilled time), but all coefficients are substantially larger.*

monitoring-cost story, as does the lower frequency of young and inexperienced workers being hired on piece.[16] Furthermore, in only very few occupations were both time and piece workers hired by the same firm, while in many more occupations time- and piece-rate workers were hired by different firms. But even in the occupations having both time and piece in separate firms, one form of payment appears to have dominated.

In the tobacco industry, in which piece-rate work was very common, only one non-clerical occupation out of 10 had both piece and time workers being employed together by more than one firm. Piece and time workers were employed in six out of 10 occupations by different firms, although the form of payment was evenly divided in only two of these cases. In the printing industry, in which piece-rate work was less common but the employment of males more extensive, only three out of 28 occupations had both piece and time workers being employed together by more than one firm. Piece and time workers were employed in 11 out of 28 occupations by different firms, although the form of payment was unevenly divided in all these cases.[17] The monitoring-cost story implies that individual firms would not hire both piece and time workers; the sorting story implies that some firms might hire only time workers but certain firms would have both. Because of the infrequency of occupations having both piece and time workers employed within the same industry, let alone within the same firm, it is difficult to test the predictions of the two models with regard to earnings.

The implications of the formal model also concerned the shape of the female and male earnings functions. The male earnings function would be expected to rise over the two periods while that for females is defined only over one period. Because piece work involves a degree of on-the-job learning, but not necessarily what is usually termed investment, the female earnings profile might be expected to rise initially and then become flat, as assumed in the model.

Empirical work substantiates the claim that male earnings rose more continuously with time on the job but female earnings rose more steeply during the early period of employment. In a study of native-born male manufacturing workers in Michigan around 1890 (Hannon 1977), earnings rose for almost 30 years with time on the job. Studies of female earnings around that period (Goldin 1980; Eichengreen 1984) indicate that earnings rose

---

[16] *The 1885 Massachusetts Manufacturing Census (Massachusetts Bureau of Statistics of Labor 1888, pp. 1093–95) contains a somewhat better disaggregation of workers by age than does the federal census, and indicates that 18.6% of all "day hands" were between 14 and 21 years but that 17.7% of all "piece hands" were. The volume on the glass industry in a U.S. Senate report on women and child workers (U.S. Senate Documents 1910–11, pp. 419–20) stated that "whenever the work is of a more or less delicate character, and capable of great variations in quality and speed, the piece system is generally preferred. . . . Commonly at such work beginners are paid by the time, but, if adaptability is shown, the piece rate is shortly substituted. It is to this latter fact primarily that the higher earnings of pieceworkers as a class is to be attributed. Their earnings are higher than those of time workers in the same occupation, not so much because of more favorable terms of employment, but because it is the more capable workers who are placed on piece rates."*

[17] *The data are from U.S. Department of Labor (1897) and include both male and female workers 18 years old and over.*

more steeply for females than for males but peaked considerably earlier. While these findings are consistent with the monitoring model, they are also consistent with a human capital model of occupational segregation. Males may accumulate human capital over a longer period of time than do females, with their wages following their rising productivity. Females, on the other hand, could learn considerably in their early working lives, but decide not to invest in human capital having a longer gestation period. The true test between the two hypotheses, that of human capital and that of monitoring, is whether male productivity advances with their earnings. This test cannot be accomplished for the historical period being studied, but there is evidence for the current period that wages do not necessarily follow marginal products (Lazear and Rosen 1981; Medoff and Abraham 1981).

IV. THE "FEMINIZATION" OF THE CLERICAL SECTOR

The clerical sector was rapidly feminized in the early part of this century and ranks today as one of the major employers of women. In 1870 fewer than 3% of all clerical employees were women, but as early as 1900, 30% were, and by 1930 over 50% were women. It has been frequently claimed that this "feminization" was the result of technological changes, such as the mechanization of the office. A direct extension of this view is that the firm-specific component of clerical skills declined, particularly with the adoption of the typewriter (Rotella 1981). Nineteenth-century clerks were managers in training, but twentieth-century office typists had very limited occupational advancement. It seems clear that the new techniques and machinery, changed the nature of the job and opened the way for the employment of females.

But was the "feminization" of the office a function of the reduced level of skill required with the division of office work into tasks, or was it a function of a reduced level of supervision needed to elicit some level of output? Here again the human capital model and the monitoring model have similar implications and could provide complementary explanations. But several implications of each are distinct. One is to be found in the history of typing and the attempts by managers to avoid expensive piece-rate payments. The second concerns the returns to specific human capital. If the human capital-model of office "feminization" is correct, one should find that females accumulated less firm-specific human capital than did males. Data from a 1940 survey of clerical workers indicate approximately equal returns to time spent with the current firm.

In the early history of the modern office various tasks were paid by the piece. Typewriters in the Graton and Knight Manufacturing Company, for example, were equipped with cyclometers, "240 depressions of the typewriter keys or space bar [were] equivalent to one point . . . 600 points [were] considered base production and each point produced in excess [was] allowed for at the rate of one and one-half cents a point" (Coyle 1928, pp. 23–24). The use of these cyclometers increased the cost of labor, and other cost-saving methods were explored. Piece rates did not prevail, and their decline was a tribute to the ability of employers to pretest employees whose training in commercial and high school courses was completed before job entry.[18]

Monitoring in the office became simpler and cheaper than in the factory, despite the general expectation in the 1920s that the office would develop along factory lines. Employers divided workers into groups and paid each a set day rate. Standardization enabled employers to screen workers prior to employment. Commonwealth Edison Company, for example, claimed that its stenographers, typists, and dictaphone operators were "classed by temperament and ability. A dictator when he needs a girl telephones to the central bureau and one is sent who is adapted to his kind of work" (Coyle 1928, p. 23). At the same time, however, managers were aware that the benefits of easily supervised tasks cost them the ability to screen workers for higher level positions and cost them the accumulated human capital necessary to produce such workers. "The modern clerk knows one operation. . . . He is, therefore, less prepared for larger responsibility. . . . The stenographer from a centralized bureau has no . . . continuous and responsible relationship to any one person" (Coyle 1928, p. 27).

Data from the original surveys of a 1940 Women's Bureau Bulletin of male and female clerical workers are used to analyze the returns to training and education in the context of the earnings function.[19] The findings in table 3 indicate that the earnings function for females is similar to that thought typical today (Mincer and Polachek 1974). Earnings rise gradually with experience without peaking in the relevant range, education measured in years increases earnings, and "home time" decreases earnings by about 1.5% per year.

The comparisons with the male-earnings function reveal that returns to total experience in clerical work were far greater for men, while returns to experience with the present firm were lower. Years of education were less valuable for men, although an advanced or special degree was worth more. That is, men accumulated relatively more general human capital on the job than did women, and women accumulated a relatively larger amount of specific human capital. Consider a man and a woman with five continuous years with their first employer, thus only five years of experience. The woman's earnings would increase by 13.4% because of an increase in general skills, and she would receive an additional 6.6% because of skills specific to her current firm. The man would receive a 24.5% increase because of augmented general skills, but a 5.8% increase because of skills specific to his current firm.[20]

---

[18] Various studies published in the 1920s, utilizing Taylor's scientific methods, indicated the clerical jobs for which managers could effectively screen workers prior to employment and those they could not. See the discussion in Davies (1982), chap. 6.

[19] These data were retrieved from the National Archives. For a discussion of the Women's Bureau Bulletin and the survey from which these data were obtained, see Goldin (1984).

[20] Note that these results are the most generous to the alternative hypothesis. Those using the regressions that exclude the schooling dummies indicate a barely significant and smaller coefficient on the tenure variable for men.

TABLE 3

EARNINGS FUNCTIONS FOR FEMALE AND MALE CLERICAL WORKERS, 1940 (DEPENDENT VARIABLE: LOG FULL-TIME SALARY)

	Females		Males	
Constant	6.078* (.069)	6.085* (.083)	6.474* (.095)	6.518* (.085)
Totexp	.0290* (.0033)	.0290* (.0033)	.0518* (.0042)	.0535* (.0041)
Totexp^2	−.000453* (.000078)	−.000447* (.000080)	−.000848* (.000083)	−.000889* (.000081)
ExpFirm	.0135* (.0024)	.0133* (.0024)	.0081** (.0042)	.0115* (.0027)
Contin	.142* (.030)	.139* (.030)	−.0576 (.0615)	−.0781 (.0599)
Furlough	−.0224* (.0097)	−.0234* (.0098)	−.0413* (.0189)	−.0471 (.0186)
Married	.0131 (.0213)	.0149 (.0214)	.131* (.030)	.119* (.030)
YrsEduc	.0380* (.0049)	.0371 (.0075)	.0260* (.0052)	.0171 (.00472)
CCDum		.031 (.026)		−.014 (.046)
VocGrad		.046 (.034)		.149* (.063)
CollDum		.054 (.046)		.165* (.037)
HSDum		−.007 (.028)		.067* (.030)
HomeTime	−.0147* (.0051)	−.0151* (.0051)		
R^2	.464	.468	.643	.665
Number of Obs	724	724	481	481

Source. See Goldin (1984). These data are a sample of original schedules from U.S. Department of Labor, Women's Bureau. "Office Work in Philadelphia, 1940." Women's Bureau Bulletin no. 188–5 (1942). Record Group 86. Boxes 472–86. National Archives.

Notes. Standard errors are in parentheses; * indicates significant at least at the 0.05 level;** indicates significant at least at the 0.10 level.

Variable Definitions:

Totexp	=	years since individual began first clerical job
ExpFirm	=	years since individual began work with current employer
Contin	=	1 if years worked with current employer has been continuous
Furlough	=	number (or proportion) of years individual had been furloughed
Married	=	1 if married
CCDum	=	1 if has a commercial course degree
VocGrad	=	1 if graduated from a vocational school
CollDum	=	1 if graduated from college
HSDum	=	1 if graduated from high school
HomeTime	=	number of years unaccounted for, presumably spent out of the labor force; variable is defined as: Totexp − ExpFirm − years spent at other clerical jobs.

Analyses of the occupations of clerical workers in 1940 and at the time of their first clerical job reinforce the findings on earnings. Men typically began as clerks and rose through the ranks with experience. If they had college degrees, they began and remained in skilled positions. Women, however, were initially placed in jobs by years of education, far more so than were males, and generally remained in their first positions or ones very similar, independent of experience. For example, 70% of all females who began as stenographers and dictaphone operators remained so to 1940; 57% who began as machine operators also stayed in that position. Both findings are invariant to years of office experience. One important exception to the absence of job advancement is secretaries, who frequently rose through the ranks beginning first as general office clerks. Among males, the situation seems much the reverse. Fully one-third of all the men in 1940 were classed in skilled positions (only 6% of the females were). One-third of these began in skilled positions, typically those with college educations, but another 40% rose through the ranks beginning as general office clerks.

The presence of machinery and more task-oriented jobs did not eliminate the accumulation of specific human capital among clerical workers, female or male, but did allow for a finer division of labor. This finer division of labor had two effects. It reduced the amount of on-the-job training, at least compared with that apparently required of nineteenth-century clerks. But the manner by which jobs were divided and the use of prejob tests suggest that monitoring costs were reduced and that the employment of women in clerical jobs was furthered because such costs were conserved. Thus it appears that women began to be employed in the clerical sector when its jobs could be more finely divided and its output more cheaply monitored.

V. CONCLUDING REMARKS

The literature on occupational segregation by sex has focused on differences in the types of jobs held by males and females, particularly on those in different sectors of the economy and with emphasis on the degree and nature of the human capital required. But within various industries and even within certain occupations, male and female jobs have differed by the method of payment and the nature of the supervisory and monitoring input necessary to elicit output. The model offered in Section II explored the implications of various types of supervisory and monitoring methods, for which expected time on the job was an important determinant. These implications were explored with data from 1890 to 1940 regarding manufacturing and clerical work. Data from a wide variety of sources were consistent with the notion that females were employed in occupations and paid by methods, in particular piece rates, that conserved on monitoring costs.

During the first half of this century the majority of female workers did have rather abbreviated labor force experiences. The labor force participation rate for white married women was low for all age groups until the 1950s. Most women entered the labor force sometime before they married but at the time of marriage exited the labor force permanently. Thus it appears that the assumption of the model concerning the relative length of stay with firms for the majority of males and females was reasonable.

Because so many women exited from the labor force at the time of marriage in the 1920s and 1930s various firms instituted prohibitions against their female employees marrying and had stated policies against hiring married women. One interpretation of such prohibitions is that they served a screening function. Firms wanted to attract women who would remain in the labor force for some period of time, and these prohibitions led to the self-selection of those who planned to marry late if at all. These prohibitions emerged at the time the clerical sector was expanding and were used to a great extent in the insurance and banking segments of this industry, a finding consistent with the notion that there were large fixed hiring costs in this sector.

But sometime after 1950 an expanding portion of the female population had rather continuous and lengthy stays in the labor force even after marriage (Goldin 1983; Smith and Ward 1984). The female labor force began to be populated by a more heterogeneous group with regard to life-cycle labor force participation, and an extension of the work here would involve exploring the screening or revealing mechanisms that have been used to ascertain this aspect of employment where hiring costs, shirking, or specific human capital paid, in part, by the employer are important.

REFERENCES

Beller, Andrea H., and Han, Kee-ok Kim. "Occupational Sex Segregation: Prospects for the 1980s." In *Sex Segregation in the Workplace: Trends, Explanations, Remedies,* edited by Barbara F. Reskin. Committee on Women's Employment and Related Social Issues. Washington, D.C.: National Academy Press, 1984.

Blau, Francine, and Hendricks, Wallace. "Occupational Segregation by Sex: Trends and Prospects." *Journal of Human Resources* 14 (1979): 197–210.

Brissenden, Paul F. *Earnings of Factory Workers, 1899 to 1927: An Analysis of Pay-roll Statistics.* Washington, D.C.: Government Printing Office, 1929.

Buttrick, John. "The Inside Contract System." *Journal of Economic History* 12 (Summer 1952): 205–21.

Coyle, Grace. *Present Trends in the Clerical Occupations.* New York: Woman's Press, 1928.

Davies, Margery W. *Woman's Place Is at the Typewriter: Office Work and Office Workers, 1870–1930.* Philadelphia: Temple University Press, 1982.

Davis, Lance; Easterlin, Richard; and Parker, William. *American Economic Growth.* New York, 1972.

Eichengreen, Barry. "Experience and the Male-Female Earnings Gap in the 1890s." *Journal of Economic History* 46 (September 1984): 822–34.

England, Paula. "The Failure of Human Capital Theory to Explain Occupational Sex Segregation." *Journal of Human Resources* 17 (1982): 358–70.

Goldin, Claudia. "The Work and Wages of Single Women, 1870 to 1920." *Journal of Economic History* 60 (March 1980): 81–89.

———. "Life-Cycle Labor Force Participation of Married Women." National Bureau of Economic Research Working Paper no. 1251. Cambridge, Mass.: NBER, December 1983.

———. "The Historical Evolution of Female Earnings Functions and Occupations." *Explorations in Economic History* 21 (January 1984): 1–27.

Goldin, Claudia, and Sokoloff, Kenneth. "Women, Children, and Industrialization in the Early Republic: Evidence from the Manufacturing Censuses, 1820 to 1850." *Journal of Economic History* 42 (December 1982): 741–74.

Greenwald, Maurine Weiner. *Women, War, and Work: The Impact of World War I on Women Workers in the United States.* Westport, Conn.: Greenwood Press, 1981.

Gross, Edward. "Plus ça Change . . . : The Sexual Structure of Occupations over Time." *Social Problems* 16 (Fall 1968): 198–208.

Guasch, J. Luis, and Weiss, Andrew. "Self-Selection in the Labor Market." *American Economic Review* 71 (June 1981): 275–84.

Hannon, Joan. "The Immigrant in the Promised Land: Human Capital and Ethnic Discrimination in the Michigan Labor Market." Ph.D. dissertation, University of Wisconsin, 1977.

Lazear, Edward P. "Why Is There Mandatory Retirement?" *Journal of Political Economy* 87 (December 1979): 1261–84.

———. "Agency, Earnings Profiles, Productivity, and Hours Restrictions." *American Economic Review* 71 (September 1981): 606–20.

———. "Salaries and Piece Rates." *Journal of Business* (in press).

Lazear, Edward P., and Rosen, Sherwin. "Rank-Order Tournaments as Optimum Labor Contracts." *Journal of Political Economy* 89 (October 1981): 841–64.

Massachusetts Bureau of Statistics of Labor. *Census of Massachusetts. 1885.* Vol. 2, *Manufactures, the Fisheries, and Commerce.* Boston, 1888.

Medoff, J. L., and Abraham, K. G. "Are Those Paid More Really More Productive?" *Journal of Human Resources* 16 (Spring 1981): 186–216.

Mincer, Jacob, and Polachek, Solomon "Family Investments in Human Capital: Earnings of Women." *Journal of Political Economy* 82 (March/April 1974): S76–S108.

Montgomery, David. *Workers' Control of America: Studies in the History of Work, Technology, and Labor Struggles.* Cambridge: Cambridge University Press, 1979.

Pencavel, John. "Work Effort, on-the-Job Screening, and Alternative Methods of Remuneration." *Research in Labor Economics* 1 (1977): 225–58.

Polachek, Solomon. "Differences in Expected Post-school Investment as a Determinant of Market Wage Differentials." *International Economic Review* 16 (June 1975): 451–70.

———. "Occupational Segregation among Women: Theory, Evidence, and a Prognosis." In *Women in the Labor Market,* edited by C. Lloyd et al. New York: Columbia University Press, 1979.

———. "Occupational Self-Selection: A Human Capital Approach to Sex Differences in Occupational Structure." *Review of Economics Statistics* 63 (February 1981): 60–69.

Rogers, Thomas Wesley. "A Comparison of Labor Turnover among Men and Women in Two Large Chicago Companies." *Monthly Labor Review* 28 (January 1929): 39–41.

Rotella, Elyce. *From Home to Office: U.S. Women at Work, 1871–1930.* Ann Arbor, Michigan: UMI Research Press, 1981.

Roummaset, James A., and Uy, Marilou. "Piece Rates, Time Rates, and Teams: Explaining Patterns in the Employment Relation." *Journal of Economic Behavior and Organization* 1 (December 1980): 343–60.

Salop, J., and Salop, S. "Self-Selection and Turnover in the Labor Market." *Quarterly Journal of Economics* 90 (November 1976): 619–28.

Smith, James P., and Ward, Michael P. "Women's Wages and Work in the Twentieth Century." Rand Corp. Report. October 1984.

U.S. Census Office. *Report on Manufacturing Industries at the Eleventh Census: 1890.* Pt. 1, *Totals for States and Industries.* Pt. 2, *Statistics of Cities.* Washington, D.C.: Government Printing Office, 1895.

U.S. Department of Labor. *Eleventh Annual Report of the Commissioner of Labor, 1895–96: Work and Wages of Men, Women, and Children.* Washington, D.C.: Government Printing Office, 1897.

———. Women's Bureau. "Office Work in Philadelphia, 1940." Women's Bureau Bulletin no. 188–5 (1942). Record Group 86. Boxes 472–86. National Archives.

U.S. Senate. *Report on the Condition of Woman and Child Wage-Earners in the United States in Nineteen Volumes.* 61st Cong., 2d Sess. S. Docs. 86–104. Washington, D.C.: Government Printing Office, 1910–11.

Zalokar, Catherine Nadja. "A Human Capital Model of Sex Differences in Occupational Distribution and Wages." Ph.D. dissertation, Princeton University, 1982.

ABOUT THE AUTHOR

Claudia Goldin

Claudia Goldin, professor of economics at Harvard University, is best known for her sharp, analytic mind and for an ability to bring a long, historical perspective to issues in labor economics. She has written on a large number of topics, including the family, women in the economy, immigration, and inequality and education. In addition, she has researched a variety of issues in economic history. She has studied slavery, emancipation, the post-bellum South, and New Deal policies.

Goldin's most recent research explores the increase in secondary and higher education and the effect of the change in levels and distribution of education on income inequality. She is currently writing a book that examines the relation between technological change and investments in human capital.

Claudia Goldin received her B.A. from Cornell University and her Ph.D. in economics from the University of Chicago. She was an assistant professor at the University of Wisconsin and at Princeton University. She was a professor of economics at the University of Pennsylvania from 1985 to 1990, when she moved to Harvard.

Goldin is on the editorial boards of four journals and served as editor of the *Journal of Economic History* from 1984 to 1988. She was vice-president of the American Economic Association and of the Economic History Association and is currently president-elect of the Economic History Association. She is a fellow of the Econometric Society and of the American Academy of Arts and Sciences. In addition to having received the Irving Kravis Teaching Award and a Guggenheim Fellowship, she holds an honorary doctorate from the University of Nebraska.

Ms. Goldin has authored or edited five books and has approximately fifty published papers.

Edward Lazear

Black Economic Progress After Myrdal

James P. Smith
The RAND Corporation

Finis R. Welch
University of California, Los Angeles, and Unicon Research Corporation

I. Introduction

Forty-five years ago, Gunnar Myrdal published his masterwork on race relations in America, *An American Dilemma.* He began his chapter on the economic situation of blacks with the following summary:

> The economic situation of the Negroes in America is pathological. Except for a small minority enjoying upper or middle class status, the masses of American Negroes, in the rural South and in the segregated slum quarters in Southern cities, are destitute. They own little property; even their household goods are mostly inadequate and dilapidated. Their incomes are not only low but irregular. They thus live from day to day and have scant security for the future. Their entire culture and their individual interests and strivings are narrow. (p. 205)

In the 45 years since Myrdal's bleak assessment, this country has undergone a series of dramatic and far-reaching changes—economically, demographically, and politically. These changes have had important implications for the economic status of blacks, especially relative to the status of whites. This essay presents a reassessment of the relative long-term economic progress of black men, focusing on trends over those 45 years and the reasons for them.

The Issues and the Research

During the time period we cover, the American economy grew rapidly. It also shifted from its traditional agricultural and manufacturing base to one that is service and technology oriented. Part of this shift was the elimination of black sharecropping in cotton, which had been the primary economic activity of Southern blacks since the Civil War. This change motivated large numbers of Southern rural blacks to migrate into the inner cities of the North, eventually transforming the black population from predominately rural to largely urban.

The authors would like to thank Joyce Peterson for her help in writing this essay. Financial support was provided by grants from the Sloan, Olin, Russell Sage, and Ford Foundations.

Reprinted with permission from James P. Smith and Finis R. Welch, "Black Economic Progress After Myrdal," Journal of Economic Literature, Vol. XXVII (June 1989), pp. 519–564.

During the 1970s, the American economic structure suffered additional shocks. Increased international competition hit the older industrialized sectors of the Northeast and North Central states particularly hard. And these were the areas where blacks had made hard-won advances.

Racial tensions have persisted throughout this forty year period. The civil rights movement achieved stunning judicial and legislative successes in the 1950s and 1960s, partly by appealing to the moral conscience of the nation. The Civil Rights Act of 1964 and subsequent executive orders prohibited employment discrimination on the basis of race. Today, many believe that the civil rights movement has lost its way as it has attempted to move beyond guaranteed civil and political rights to strive toward economic equity. Others charge that it has also lost the moral high ground because of repeated accusations that it has defended reverse discrimination.

Postwar progress in race relations has been marred by race riots in American cities. In reaction to these riots, 25 years after Myrdal, a presidential commission issued the Kerner Report. Its portrait of black America was as bleak as that of Myrdal two decades earlier. Its pessimism about the economic status of blacks was compounded by its sense of hopelessness about the prospects for the future.

That pessimism and the pervasiveness of black poverty prodded the government to devise an elaborate system of publicly financed assistance that in some way now touches a majority of blacks. The primary aim was to provide a safety net, protecting black families from the worst ravages of poverty; but critics have charged that the safety net evolved into a web, trapping blacks into a self-perpetuating culture of poverty.

We take up several issues in this essay. Our most basic concern is whether the economic lot of black men has improved significantly since Myrdal's day.[1] We go beyond that issue by also examining whether economic progress has touched all parts of the black community. Finally, we deal with the thorny problem of isolating the underlying causes of black economic progress. We sought to determine, for example, the extent to which education and its quality, migration to cities and the North, and affirmative action have affected the economic progress of blacks.

In an attempt to identify some possible underlying causes, we limited our search to those factors that have become the grand themes of the economic literature. Among those themes, black schooling stands in the first rank. Waves of pessimism and optimism have occurred periodically in assessing schooling's role in promoting black economic mobility. Similarly, disagreement still persists concerning how fundamental a role the historical patterns of black migration played in shaping black economic history.

A number of prominent scholars have also argued with some persuasion that the deteriorating state of black employment negates any theme of progress that may emerge from looking at wages alone. Finally, controversy about affirmative action continues to divide economic scholars. Many scholars now question whether affirmative action has even

---

[1] We limit our focus to black men because including black women and the black family raises a number of issues that, although important, are ancillary to our main thesis.

achieved its primary aim of improving wages and employment for minorities. Meaty questions all, they constitute our agenda in this essay.

Before we begin, some honest advertising: By no means will our essay be a literature review in the traditional sense. First, we rely heavily on evidence from our own research from a recently completed project to document our claims.[2] It is this evidence and our interpretation of it that drive us to conclusions. An alternative path, with an honorable tradition to recommend it, would be to weigh the evidence from a balanced and comprehensive literature review. We use the literature instead to frame the big questions, and then let the data from the five decennial Censuses speak to these questions. (Note that this project made extensive use of the Public Use Tapes of the decennial Censuses from 1940 to 1980. All data in this article are from these sources unless otherwise indicated.)

Section II describes major trends in black-white male wage ratios from 1940 to 1980 and identifies the distribution of wage gains among important subgroups in the black population. Sections III, IV, and V attempt to isolate some causes of these trends: Section III describes differential racial trends in schooling and the income benefits associated with that schooling. Section IV deals with the influence of two dimensions of geographic location: black migration from the South to the North and the increasing urbanization of the black population.

Section V discusses two historical developments that were not included in our statistical model but that many people believe have played a significant role in recent black economic history: the declining work force participation rates of low-income blacks during the 1970s and affirmative action. The final section discusses changes that have occurred in the 1980s and speculates about future trends in the racial wage gap.

II. CLOSING THE RACIAL WAGE GAP

Since 1940, black men made a significant and quantitatively large improvement in their economic status relative to the status of white men. In this section, we summarize the principal trends in black-white male incomes across the 1940–80 time period. We describe trends in the average weekly wages of black men relative to white men's wages, the distributional effects within the black population, and the career wage growth of black men compared with the growth for white men. In the final section of this essay, we discuss the changes that have occurred in the 1980s and offer our assessment of what the future holds.

BLACK-WHITE MALE WAGES 1940–80

Since 1940, the American economy has enjoyed substantial economic growth, and inflation-adjusted incomes of all its citizens have risen dramatically.[3] Table 1 lists yearly

---

[2] *This essay is adapted from James P. Smith and Finis Welch (1986).*

[3] *On a national scale, Americans were first surveyed regarding their incomes as part of the 1940 decennial Census. Similar income questions were asked in each succeeding Census. The resulting data allow us to monitor trends that occurred between 1940 and 1980 in income disparities between black and white Americans.*

TABLE 1

MEAN MALE INCOME BY RACE, 1940–80
(IN CONSTANT 1987 DOLLARS)

Census Year	White Men	Black Men
1980	28,212	20,480
1970	28,075	18,078
1960	21,832	12,561
1950	15,677	8,655
1940	11,441	4,956

Note: Yearly incomes are weekly wages multiplied by an assumed workyear of 50 weeks.

incomes of men of both races. To adjust for the sevenfold inflation that has occurred since 1940,[4] all incomes are expressed in constant 1987 dollars.

Real incomes of white men expanded two-and-one-half-fold between 1940 and 1980— but earnings growth was even more rapid among black men. Real incomes of black men have more than quadrupled over these 40 years. In 1940, the typical black male employed for a full workyear earned almost $5,000; by 1980 he earned over $20,000.

The standard of living of today's black men has improved not only as measured against earlier black generations, but also relative to their white contemporaries. While incomes of white men were growing at a 2.2 percent rate throughout these 40 years, black men were enjoying an income growth of 3.5 percent per year. Table 2 depicts our estimates of black-white male weekly wage ratios from each of the decennial Census tapes.[5] The final row in this table contains relative wages aggregated across all experience classes. In addition, ratios are listed for five-year intervals of years of work experience.[6]

---

[4] For convenience, we will refer throughout this essay to the year the Census was taken, although all income statistics actually correspond to the calendar year preceding the Census.

[5] Our numbers are ratios of arithmetic means of weekly wages. Income is defined as the sum of wages and salary and self-employment income. Weekly wages are calculated as income divided by weeks worked. Our sample consists of men 16 to 64 years old who were U.S. citizens and who did not live in group quarters. A number of additional sample restrictions were imposed. We excluded men (1) who worked less than 50 weeks in the previous year and were attending school; (2) who worked 26 weeks or less in the previous year; (3) who were in the military; (4) who were self-employed or working without pay if they were not employed in agriculture; (5) whose weekly wages put them below the following values: 1940 = $1.50, 1950 = $3.25, 1960 = $6.25, 1970 = $10.00, 1980 = $19.80; (6) whose computed weekly wages put them above the following values: 1940 = $125, 1950 = $250, 1960 = $625, 1970 = $1,250, 1980 = $1,875; (7) who were in the open-ended, upper-income interval and who did not work at least 40 weeks last year. In addition, in the 1950 Census only sample line people (who were asked income questions) were included.

[6] Years of market experience is defined as current age minus assumed age at leaving school. The mapping from years of schooling completed and school leaving age is as follows: ed 0–11 = age 17, ed 12 = 18, ed 13–15 = age 20, ed 16 or more = age 23.

TABLE 2

BLACK MALE WAGES AS A PERCENTAGE OF WHITE MALE WAGES, 1940–80

Years of Market Experience	Census Years				
	1940	1950	1960	1970	1980
1–5	46.7	61.8	60.2	75.1	84.2
6–10	47.5	61.0	59.1	70.1	76.6
11–15	44.4	58.3	59.4	66.2	73.5
16–20	44.4	56.6	58.4	62.8	71.2
21–25	42.3	54.1	57.6	62.7	67.8
26–30	41.7	53.2	56.2	60.6	66.9
31–35	40.2	50.3	53.8	60.0	66.5
36–40	39.8	46.9	55.9	60.3	68.5
All	43.3	55.2	57.5	64.4	72.6

Table 2 points to a very impressive rise in the relative economic status of black men over this 40-year time span. Between these 40 years, black male wages increased 52 percent faster than those of whites. In 1940, the typical black male worker earned only 43 percent as much as his white counterpart. By 1980, the average black man in the labor force earned 73 percent as much as the typical white man.

The pace at which blacks were able to narrow the wage gap was far from uniform. The largest improvement occurred during the 1940s, a decade that witnessed a 24 percent expansion in the relative wages of black men.[7] These advances slowed considerably during the 1950s, but the pace picked up again in the years after 1960. During both the 1960s and 1970s, the rise in black wages was more than 10 percent higher than for whites.

Obviously, there has been impressive improvement in the relative economic status of blacks since 1940. It is largely an untold story that belies widely held views of black stagnation. However, one must remember that even today black male incomes still lag well behind those of whites. We are left then with a dual message: Considerable progress has been made in narrowing the wage gap between the races—but race is still an important predictor of a man's income.

---

[7] *Throughout this essay, the 1940 statistics include only wage income. In the 1940 Census, individuals were asked only the amount of their wage and salary incomes. In addition, we know whether they had $50 or more of other income, but not the amount. Those men without any wage income are not included in our 1940 sample. As a result, the 1940 sample is not strictly comparable to the other Census years. However, the trends we describe in the text are not affected to any large degree by this limitation. For example, if we similarly restrict the 1950 sample to men with positive wages and base the wage ratio only on wage income, our aggregate wage ratio in 1950 would be 59.0. This is even a larger wage improvement for blacks than we measure in Table 2.*

THE DISTRIBUTION OF BLACK WAGE GAINS

To this point, we have contrasted the average black and white worker. But such comparisons do not address the question of whether all segments of the black community shared in this black economic renaissance. Some scholars have argued that blacks have become increasingly divided into two economic worlds. The first includes members of the emerging black middle class, whose income gains have been real and substantial. The second group consists of the black underclass, increasingly left out and left behind. To address this issue, we now examine the extent of black economic progress across all parts of the economic spectrum.

While average white incomes are well in excess of those achieved by the average black, income distributions of the black and white populations have always overlapped. Table 3 summarizes the extent of this overlap. The left-hand side of the table measures the proportion of black men with income exceeding three critical values in the white income distribution: the bottom quartile, the median, and the top quartile. To illustrate, 29 percent of black men had incomes larger than that of the median white man in 1980. The right-hand side of Table 3 has a parallel set of numbers indicating the fraction of white men with incomes that exceed the same critical values within the black income distribution.

The overlap between the two income distributions was small in 1940. If income is the measuring rod, black and white men were indeed divided into two separate and unequal societies in 1940. In that year, only one in twelve black men earned more than the average white, and the upper segment of the income distribution resembled an exclusive white club. For black men, the chances were one in a hundred of being admitted to that club, the membership requirement being an income equivalent to one in the top 25 percent of the white population. The view from the other side was equally stark: 70 percent of white men earned more than the top 25 percent of blacks.

While by no means identical, these two income distributions have converged sharply across these 40 years. By 1980, 29 percent of working black men earned more than the median white. Nowhere were these changes more dramatic than in the circles of the economic elite. Even within the upper parts of the income distribution, black men are now more commonplace. Fully 10 percent of black men now rank higher than the white

TABLE 3

EXTENT OF OVERLAP BETWEEN BLACK AND WHITE INCOME DISTRIBUTIONS

Year	Percent of Black Men Whose Income Exceeds White Income at the			Percentage of White Men Whose Income Exceeds Black Income at the		
	Bottom Quarter	Median	Top Quarter	Bottom Quarter	Median	Top Quarter
1980	56	29	10	87	70	45
1970	45	22	5	90	78	57
1960	38	12	1	92	81	66
1950	36	12	2	92	82	66
1940	31	8	1	95	84	70

worker whose income puts him among the wealthiest 25 percent. This black penetration into the economic elite has been accomplished largely during the last 20 years. Between 1960 and 1980, the probability that a black man's income would fall in the top 25 percent white income bracket increased tenfold.

The expanding size of the black middle class[8] is illustrated in Table 4. In this table, each race is divided into three income classes. The middle column for black men lists the percentages of blacks whose incomes equate them with the white middle class. The columns to the left and right list the percentages of blacks with incomes below (i.e., the poor) and above (i.e., the elite) white middle-class income. This table simultaneously illustrates the persistence of black poverty, the growth of the black middle class, and more recently the emergence of a nonnegligible black upper class.

In 1940, three quarters of all blacks were below the white middle class. By any reasonable definition, the overwhelming majority were poor. Three quarters were destitute, with little hope that their lot or even that of their children would soon improve. The small black middle class in 1940 comprised only one in five black men. At the other extreme, the economic elite resembled an exclusive white club. In 1980, fully 20 percent of black working men still languished in the poor underclass, a reminder (if any of us needed it) that many blacks remain left out and left behind. But placed in historical perspective, such figures still represent enormous progress toward eradicating black poverty.

However, the real story of the period from 1940 to 1980 has been the emergence of the black middle class, whose income gains have been real and substantial. The growth in the size of the black middle class has been so spectacular that as a group it outnumbers the black poor. By 1980, more than two-thirds (68 percent) of blacks had incomes that met the criteria for middle class.

Nowhere are those changes more dramatic than when we focus on the contemporary economic elite. For the first time in American history, a sizable number of black men are

---

[8] *From the first attempts to measure poverty, debate has continued on whether poverty is an absolute or relative concept. The official government statistic is based on an absolute concept, so that the income necessary to escape poverty is adjusted upward over time only by the rate of inflation. At the other extreme, critics of the official statistics contend that poverty is a relative concept, so that poverty should be defined relative to the average income in that year. Using this concept, the bottom quarter of the income distribution would always be classified as poor. If the absolute income standard had been set 100 years ago, virtually no one would be poor today. Similarly, the relative concept of defining as poor the bottom quarter of Ugandans and Americans does not allow economic growth to reduce poverty at all.*

To count the poverty population, we have followed Smith (1988) by adopting a middle ground using elements of both absolute and relative definitions. It turns out that Smith's poverty definition also corresponds more closely to people's notions of what poverty means. When asked in surveys over time about the income required not to be poor, the poverty threshold has increased fifty cents by every dollar increase in real income. Based on that observation, Smith's definition increases the poverty threshold income by half a percent of every 1 percent growth in real income.

More technically, we originally separated the population into the three groups in Table 4 by defining the 1940 middle class as those whose income lies between two-thirds and four-thirds of the median white male income. The lower-income threshold for entering the middle class is adjusted upward by half the rate of white real income growth. Our definition of the elite is asymmetric. To be a member of the elite, one must have an income of four-thirds of the white median in that year.

TABLE 4

PERCENTAGE OF MEN IN THE MIDDLE CLASS

Year	White Men			Black Men		
	Below	Middle Class	Above	Below	Middle Class	Above
1980	11	60	29	20	68	12
1970	9	66	25	24	71	5
1960	12	64	24	39	59	2
1950	18	49	23	48	50	2
1940	30	40	30	76	22	2

economically better off than white middle-class America. During the last 20 years alone, the odds of a black man penetrating the ranks of the economic elite increased tenfold.

Table 5 summarizes the extent to which blacks made economic progress at different segments of the complete income distribution. To produce this table, incomes of working black men at each percentile of the black income distribution were calculated relative to the incomes of white men at the same percentile of the white income distribution. Virtually all parts of the working black population, no matter what their original position in the income distribution, participated in the black economic resurgence over this 40-year period. The principal exception relates to blacks within the bottom 10 percent. While even those black men gained relative to the lowest-income whites, the size of the wage improvement is much smaller.

Another way of identifying those blacks who gained more than others is to examine wage changes within age or schooling groups. To facilitate the age comparison, Table 6 lists percentage rates of growth in black-white weekly wage ratios by experience groups between successive Censuses. Table 7 presents the percentage growth in wage ratios by education level.[9]

As is evident from the last column of Table 6, over the full 40-year period, younger blacks gained more relative to whites than did experienced black workers. However, with the exception of those in the first five years of work, post-1940 relative black wage gains were fairly uniform across experience cells; but between 1960 and 1980, relative black wage gains were largest among younger workers. As a consequence, the cross-sectional decline with experience in black relative wages in Table 2 became steeper in 1980 than it was in 1960. This tilt in favor of younger blacks is an optimistic harbinger of the future. It implies that the pace at which blacks were able to narrow the racial wage gap accelerated over time.

While the overall trend favored young black workers, between-decade changes were very erratic. The 1940s established the tendency of larger relative wage gains among younger black workers. The principal anomaly occurred during the 1950s, when younger blacks suffered economic setbacks compared with young white workers. However, these

---

[9] *The percentage growth rates by age are derived from the ratios contained in Table 2.*

TABLE 5

PERCENTAGE INCREASE IN BLACK ANNUAL INCOME COMPARED WITH WHITES
AT SELECTED PERCENTILES: 1940–80

Percentile	Percentage Increase	Percentile	Percentage Increase
2	4.8	60	54.9
4	8.4	70	57.4
6	30.7	80	49.0
8	36.9	90	46.2
10	48.1	92	50.6
20	48.2	94	48.1
30	50.2	96	51.6
40	45.2	98	54.7
50	45.5		

TABLE 6

PERCENTAGE GROWTH IN BLACK-WHITE MALE RATIOS OF WEEKLY WAGES

Years of Work Experience	Growth Between				
	1950–40	1960–50	1970–60	1980–70	1980–40
1–5	28.1	−2.7	22.1	11.5	58.9
6–10	25.1	−3.2	17.1	8.8	47.8
11–15	27.1	1.9	10.9	10.4	50.3
16–20	24.4	3.1	7.3	12.5	47.3
21–25	24.6	6.3	8.6	7.7	47.2
26–30	24.2	5.6	7.5	9.9	47.2
31–35	22.5	6.6	10.8	10.4	50.3
36–40	16.4	17.5	7.5	12.7	54.2
All experience classes	24.2	4.1	11.3	12.0	51.6

losses were more than recouped in the next decade. During the 1960s, the relative wage increases achieved by younger blacks were three times the size of those of most experienced black workers.[10] The last decade is probably best described as one of relatively uniform black wage gains across experience classes.

We examine the education dimension of the distribution of racial wage gains in Table 7. Black male wages rose relative to whites between 1940 and 1980 at every schooling level. Table 7 indicates that the distribution of wage gains is slightly U-shaped, with the least and best educated blacks receiving the largest benefits.

---

[10] We analyzed the 1960–70 decade in depth in Smith and Welch (1977).

TABLE 7

PERCENTAGE GROWTH IN BLACK-WHITE WEEKLY WAGE RATIOS BY EDUCATION

	Years of Schooling						
Decade	0–4	5–7	8–11	12	13–15	16+	All
1940–80	35.5	36.5	30.8	32.8	45.0	44.8	51.6
1940–50	5.0	14.4	16.6	22.3	14.4	10.8	24.2
1950–60	12.9	5.5	−2.2	−6.8	6.9	10.4	4.1
1960–70	2.5	8.5	7.0	8.7	17.6	19.3	11.3
1970–80	15.1	8.1	7.4	8.6	6.2	4.3	12.0

Among those with eight or more years of schooling, there exists a distinct pro-skill bias in the rate of black wage improvement. For example, wages of black college graduates grew 45 percent faster than those of whites between 1940 and 1980; in contrast, black wages grew a third more rapidly than whites among men with terminal high school diplomas. This pro-skill bias was especially pronounced between 1950–70. During these 20 years, the relative wage gains of black college graduates were four times larger than those achieved by black high school graduates.

TRACKING BLACK-WHITE CAREERS

Schooling is one major theme of the human capital literature. On-the-job training remains its other main face. The evidence we have accumulated confirms that black men made larger wage gains than white men during the period from 1940 to 1980. Although accepting this conclusion, some observers fear that much of the gain may eventually evaporate as competition between the races intensifies over job careers. Such fears are misplaced.

One pattern that characterizes all five Census years in Table 2 is that black-white wage ratios decline with years of work experience. For example, in 1950, among men who had spent 36 to 40 years in the labor market, black wages were 47 percent of white. In the same year, among men in their first five years of work experience, black wages were 62 percent of white. For a long time, the cross-sectional decline in wage ratios with experience, as in Table 2, was the principal statistical evidence that led to widespread scientific and popular acceptance of a particular theory of labor market discrimination. According to this theory, an important mechanism of discrimination was that blacks were systematically denied access to jobs with more favorable future prospects or larger wage growth. Because of discrimination, blacks tend to be relegated to secondary labor markets and to jobs with little potential for career advancement (see, for example, Paul Osterman 1975; Michael Piore 1971; Michael Reich 1984; and Russell Rumberger and Martin Carnoy 1980).

Such cross-sectional data, however, do not speak directly to life-cycle realities for any group of workers. Men who have more labor market experience in any calendar year belong to older generations. The 47 percent ratio for the 36 to 40 experience interval, for example, may be lower than the 62 percent ratio for the first five years of experience in 1950 because the more experienced workers were born 35 years earlier. Relative to their white contemporaries, these older blacks had less schooling and attended poorer quality schools than their black successors would 35 years later.

Table 8 isolates the actual labor market experiences of labor market cohorts by re-arranging the items in Table 2. This rearrangement involved centering the original data by the initial year of labor market entry. For example, men in their first five years of work in 1940 first entered the labor market, on average, in 1938. Among these men, blacks earned 46.7 percent as much as whites. These same men by 1950 had spent 10–15 years in the labor market; blacks in this cohort now earned 58.3 percent as much as whites. By reading across any row in Table 8, we can follow the actual life-cycle path of relative wages of the labor market cohorts indexed in the first column.

The message of Table 8 is unambiguous. In contrast to the cross-sectional implication of deterioration in the relative economic status of blacks across labor market careers, the reality is that, if anything, black men actually improved their situation relative to whites. Black men narrowed the gap between their incomes and those of their white contemporaries as their careers evolved in virtually every instance depicted in Table 8. The cross-sectional decline in each Census year that characterized Table 2 is not the result of any increasing life-cycle differentiation by race. Instead, improvement in the quality of black workers relative to white workers across successive birth cohorts accounts for the cross-sectional decline.[11]

As the discussion has shown, the racial gap in men's wages has narrowed considerably over the 40-year period—but why? If blacks are to sustain or increase their economic gains, we need to identify and understand the major reasons for those gains. In the sections that follow, we examine some of these reasons.

III. CAUSES OF THE CLOSING WAGE GAP: EDUCATION
CAUSES OF THE CONVERGENCE IN RACIAL WAGE RATIOS

In this section and the next, we examine reasons for the substantial narrowing of the racial wage gap over time. Our aim here is to quantify how much of the closing was due to gains in education, and in the next section how much should be attributed to migration and the resurgence of the Southern economy. The 40-year horizon we employ permits decade-specific changes to be placed in a broader perspective. This emphasis on education and location does not imply that they are the only forces at work. Indeed, Section V discusses two more factors that might have some influence: the falling labor force participation rates of black men and affirmative action.

---

[11] *This more rapid cohort improvement for blacks has been called "the vintage hypothesis" in the literature. It is an issue that we addressed in a number of earlier papers. See Welch (1974), Smith and Welch (1977), and Smith (1984).*

TABLE 8

BLACK MALE WAGES AS A PERCENTAGE OF WHITE MALES BY LABOR MARKET COHORT

Median Year of Initial Labor Market Work	Census Year				
	1940	1950	1960	1970	1980
1978					84.2
1973					76.6
1968				75.1	73.5
1963				70.1	71.2
1958			60.2	66.2	67.8
1953			59.1	62.8	66.9
1948		61.8	59.4	62.7	66.5
1943		60.0	58.4	60.6	68.5
1938	46.7	58.3	57.6	60.0	
1933	47.5	56.6	56.2	60.3	
1928	44.4	54.1	53.8		
1923	44.4	53.2	55.9		
1918	42.3	50.3			
1913	41.7	46.9			
1908	40.2				
1903	39.8				
All	43.4	55.2	57.5	64.4	72.6

THE STATISTICAL FRAME

Our results are based on a statistical analysis of male weekly wages in the five micro data files from the 1940 to the 1980 Censuses. Regressions were estimated separately within eight five-year experience intervals, ranging between 1 to 5 and 36 to 40 years of work experience.[12] Separate analyses were conducted for each race and within each of the five decennial Censuses. The dependent variable in each specification was the logarithm of the weekly wage.[13] Explanatory variables fall into five groups: (1) years of schooling; (2) dummy variables indicating residence in the South; (3) standard metropolitan statistical

---

[12] Our results are derived from statistical analysis of male weekly wages in the five micro data files from the 1940 to the 1980 Censuses. The sample restrictions used in the analysis and the definition of work experience appear in Footnotes 5 and 6.

[13] Weeks worked were coded continuously from 1 to 52 weeks in the 1940, 1950, and 1980 Census. In the 1960 and 1970 Census, however, weeks worked were coded into broad intervals. To maintain comparability, the same intervals in all Census years were used. The following within-interval means, as calculated from the 1980 Census, were assigned: 1–13 = 6.50; 14–26 = 21.73; 27–39 = 33.08; 40–47 = 42.67; 48–49 = 48.29; 50–52 = 51.82. We checked this assumption by rerunning the analysis using continuous weeks worked. The differences were trivial.

areas (SMSAs);[14] (4) the central cities of these SMSAs, and (5) a set of single-year experience dummies within each experience interval.[15]

Our regression estimates will be used to partition change in the racial wage gap into education and location components. The idea is to quantify the extent to which the narrowing is due to gains in education, and how much should be attributed to migration and the growth of the Southern economy. To understand our procedure, define $ln\ R$ as the percentage gap in incomes between the races and let x refer to characteristics affecting wages with associated parameter vectors b. The subscripts 1 and 3 refer to current-year and base-year black male values, while 2 and 4 denote a corresponding index for whites. It follows that

$$\Delta\ ln\ R = [(x_1 - x_2)' - (x_3 - x_4)']\ b_4 \tag{1.i}$$

$$+\ (x_1 - x_3)'\ (b_3 - b_4) \tag{1.ii}$$

$$+\ (x_1 - x_2)'\ (b_2 - b_4) \tag{1.iii}$$

$$+\ x_1\ [(b_1 - b_2) - (b_3 - b_4)]. \tag{1.iv}$$

These equations measure the rate by which the racial income gap is narrowing ($\Delta\ ln\ R$). The first term (1.i), the main effect, measures the predicted change in black-white weekly wages that occurs because black and white men are becoming more similar in attributes that are valued at base-year white parameter values.[16] For example, if education differences between the races diminished over time, the black-white wage gap would narrow.

Each Census contained an open-ended upper-income interval. For each Census year and each open-ended income category (indicated in parentheses next to the Census year), the following values were assigned: 1940 (5,000) = 8,900; 1950 (10,000) = 22,500; 1960 (25,000) = 42,500; 1970 (50,000) = 80,000; 1980 (75,000) = 115,000. These top code values were calculated assuming that the upper part of the income distribution followed an exponential distribution.

[14] *The definition of SMSAs has changed periodically over the 40 years in the 1940 and 1950 Censuses, the Standard Metropolitan Area (SMA) concept was used. Starting in 1960, the SMSA definition has been employed. Some of these changes simply reflect the increasing urbanization of the American population. Others, however, are more troublesome analytically. For reasons of confidentiality in 1960, SMSAs were not reported in a number of low-population states. To maintain comparability, we imposed a similar restriction on the other Census years. Therefore, SMSAs in the following states were not included in our definition: Arizona, Colorado, Delaware, Hawaii, Idaho, Maine, Mississippi, North Dakota, Rhode Island, South Dakota, and Utah. A similar restriction applies for the central city variable.*

[15] *Our full regression estimates and associated standard errors are presented in Appendix Tables A.1 and A.2.*

[16] *The parameterization in equation (1) is clearly not unique. For example, base-year black parameter values (b_3) could weight the main effects with an appropriate reparameterization of the other three terms. However, in the interpretation in the text, this parameter weight reflects variation in market prices for skills. This view argues strongly for using the white (majority) parameter estimates. Similarly, under our parameterization, white parameter changes index changes in market price of attributes. The issue here is not one of uniqueness, but the interpretation one places on a particular parameterization. We find that our parameterization is the most useful in separating forces into components that correspond most closely to the debates that have dominated the economics literature.*

The second term measures race interaction. If blacks are paid less than whites for a given characteristic $[(b_3 - b_4) < 0]$, then blacks will lose relative to whites when mean attribute levels rise. For example, racially equal secular growth in levels of schooling favors whites if the income benefits from an additional year of schooling are higher for whites than for blacks.

The third term measures year interaction. If the estimated coefficient attached to a characteristic increases over time $[(b_2 - b_4) > 0]$, black/white wages will decline if blacks have less of the characteristic than whites. For example, if the income benefits from schooling rose between two Censuses, white men benefit more than black men because they have more schooling.

The fourth term measures race-year interaction. If racial differences in estimated coefficients become smaller $[(b_1 - b_2) - (b_3 - b_4)] > 0)$ over time, black wages will rise relative to whites. This term would capture the positive relative wage benefits accruing to blacks as race differences in schooling coefficients have declined.

Because we have separate estimates for each Census year, the regressions are first run across each of the four pairwise Census comparisons: 1940–50, 1950–60, 1960–70, and 1970–80. Linearity insures that effects over the 40 years can be obtained by summing these 10-year comparisons. The single-decade estimates alongside the 40-year summary help isolate the timing of effects.

THE ROLE OF EDUCATION

Controversy has always surrounded the prominence that should be assigned to black schools in shaping the economic history of blacks. The early analysis of the 1940 and 1960 Census led many scholars to conclude that the educational route to economic mobility was apparently closed for blacks. Morton Zeman's (1955) initial study of the 1940 Census suggested that white men received three times as much income as black men for each additional year of schooling.[17] Initial microlevel studies based on the 1960 Census (Giora Hanoch 1965 and Lester Thurow 1969) did little to amend this view. This work painted a consistent picture of low returns to schooling for blacks, as well as a sharp deterioration in relative black economic potential over job careers.

This pessimism was deepened by studies, especially those of Christopher Jencks and his coauthors (1972), claiming that attributes of schools matter little in future economic success. As a result, improving the quality of black schools was similarly viewed as having marginal payoffs in improving the economic status of blacks.

Along with discrimination, the historical role of black education has been the most debated issue among economic scholars. In particular, the historical importance of black schooling has been discounted by many scholars (see Orley Ashenfelter 1977 and William A. Darity 1982). They pointed out that blacks' long-term advances in education did not produce any closing of the racial income gap, at least until the mid-1960s. They

[17] *Zeman's research was based on tabulated aggregated data published in reports of the Census Bureau.*

also pointed to the series of studies cited above showing that blacks derived far less income benefit from their education than did whites.

In short, this consensus of early research implied that even if blacks got more and better education, the racial wage gap would persist. The historical record now strongly challenges this view: It shows that black education has risen relative to white education, that the wage return on black educational investment has risen over time. These factors, together, have significantly narrowed the racial wage gap.

TRENDS IN EDUCATIONAL DIFFERENCES

The first step in documenting this claim involves tracking racial trends in years of school completed. The number of grades completed is a crude summary index of the amount of learning and skill acquired in American classrooms. But if education plays a significant role in closing the racial wage gap, the most elementary evidence must rely on monitoring the extent to which black educational accomplishments are catching up to those of whites. Table 9 demonstrates that this is happening. Table 9 lists the average years of schooling completed for both races, as derived from the Census files.

Not surprisingly, the education levels of each new generation of workers increased between 1940 and 1980, but the increase was much greater for black men. Educational differences still persist between the races, but they are far less today than at any time in our history. Between 1940 and 1980, 40 percent of the racial education gap disappeared.

A simple way of depicting how these changes transformed the educational makeup of the work force is to examine racial disparities in the schooling of male workers at 20-year intervals. Begin this examination in 1980, when the majority of all workers of both races were high school graduates. Three-quarters of younger male workers (those aged 26–35) of both races were high school graduates in 1980, but blacks lagged more than a year behind whites. For the first time in our history, a sizable number of young black men were college graduates. One in nine blacks aged 26–35 completed college, compared to three in ten young white men.

It is easy to forget how little schooling the average black male worker had, even as late as 1960, and how large black-white education differences were in that year. Across the full age distribution, white men had a 2.7 year educational advantage over black men in 1960. If a high school graduate typified the 1980 black male worker, our average 1960 black worker competed in the labor market with only his elementary diploma. Fully 80 percent of the 1960 black male work force had not finished high school, and less than 3 percent of all black male workers had college degrees. The average level of schooling of young black workers in 1960 was about 9 years; the typical older black worker had not even completed the sixth grade. In contrast, the majority of white workers in 1960 still had completed high school, and one in ten were college graduates.

As dismal as these 1960 numbers seem, they represent substantial improvement over those for 1940. In that year, 80 percent of the 1940 black male work force had only elementary schooling and 40 percent had less than five years of education. Only 1 in 14

TABLE 9

AVERAGE YEARS OF SCHOOLING FOR BLACK AND WHITE MEN, 1940–80

	Census Year				
	1940	**1950**	**1960**	**1970**	**1980**
White Men					
Ages 26–35	9.89	10.77	11.49	12.36	13.56
Ages 36–45	9.15	9.98	10.93	11.78	13.02
Ages 46–55	8.54	9.20	9.96	11.15	12.20
Ages 56–64	8.07	8.47	9.06	10.16	11.45
Ages 16–64	9.38	9.99	10.65	11.51	12.47
Black Men					
Ages 26–35	5.97	7.60	9.01	10.54	12.15
Ages 36–45	5.40	6.41	7.84	9.49	11.26
Ages 46–55	4.84	5.54	6.51	8.19	9.85
Ages 56–64	4.36	4.92	5.51	6.81	8.48
Ages 16–64	4.70	6.83	8.00	9.47	10.96
White Minus Black					
Ages 26–35	3.92	3.17	2.48	1.82	1.41
Ages 36–45	3.75	3.57	3.09	2.29	1.76
Ages 46–55	3.70	3.66	3.45	2.96	2.35
Ages 56–64	3.71	3.55	3.55	3.35	2.97
Ages 16–64	3.68	3.16	2.65	2.04	1.51

black men in 1940 had graduated from high school and 1 in 100 received a college degree. Matters were little better among younger blacks in that year. Among black men 26 to 35 years old, four out of five failed to go beyond elementary school and the mean schooling level was less than six years.

While the 1940 education credentials of white workers were far less than those of today's workers, white men had a decidedly larger educational advantage over their black contemporaries. In that year, the average white worker completed 9.4 grades, 3.7 more than their black rivals. The majority of white men had at least some high school training and one in four were high school graduates.

An important pattern emerges when we examine trends across age groups within each Census year in Table 9. Since 1960, the smallest racial difference occurs among the younger workers. However, this pattern disappears among older workers in 1950 and is nonexistent in the 1940 data. This age relation contains important clues about the reasons why the rate by which blacks were able to catch up in education has accelerated.

The reasons become apparent when we track generational changes in schooling. Table 10 shows how much black education rose relative to white education over this 40-year period at different experience levels. More experienced black workers narrowed their education disparity by a year or two. In contrast, black men in their first five years of work had narrowed the gap by four years. Among men born in this century, there has been a substantial narrowing of racial difference in years of school completed. Moreover, this convergence has accelerated as each new cohort arrived in the labor market.

TABLE 10

BLACK-WHITE CONVERGENCE IN AVERAGE SCHOOLING: 1940–80

Experience Interval	Decline in Racial Disparity in Years of Schooling
1–5	4.05
6–10	3.17
11–15	2.57
16–20	2.30
21–25	2.09
26–30	1.76
31–35	1.58
36–40	1.10

THE WAGE GAINS FROM SCHOOLING

In examining the role of education, the key issues are (a) whether blacks have been able to translate better schooling into higher incomes and (b) whether blacks realize the same return as whites on educational investment. Our analyses indicate that education has translated into higher incomes for blacks and has helped narrow the racial wage gap. However, the interracial payoff for education has not been equal until very recently and even then only for younger workers.

Black-White Wages Ratios by Education. Table 11 lists black-white male weekly wage ratios within education classes.[18] This table reveals large racial wage disparities within education groups. Black men earned 50 to 55 percent as much as comparably educated whites in 1940. While these racial wage differences narrowed substantially over time, they remained at levels of 70 to 80 percent in 1980. These within-education wage ratios should be contrasted to the aggregate ratios of 43 percent in 1940 and 73 percent in 1980 (see Table 2). The difference informs us that education does play a significant role in explaining the racial wage gap. However, it also warns us that simply equalizing the number of years of schooling alone would leave a sizable racial wage gap.

The figures shown in Table 11 also confirm the belief that black men have historically received far less income benefit than white men did from more education. Controlling for the numbers of years of work experience, black-white income ratios in the earlier Censuses decline with years of schooling. This decline is particularly sharp in the high school and college groups and is accentuated among more experienced workers. To illustrate, consider men with 30 to 40 years of work experience in 1940. Black wages average about

---

[18] These weekly wage ratios are averages within ten-year experience intervals. These ratios are arranged by year of initial labor market entry in a manner similar to Table 8 to facilitate career tracking of work cohorts.

TABLE 11

BLACK-WHITE WEEKLY WAGE RATIOS BY EDUCATION

Median Year of First Labor Market Entry	Census Year				
	1940	1950	1960	1970	1980
Education = 0–7 years					
1975					83.9
1965				73.5	85.1
1955			66.4	72.1	79.7
1945		66.7	68.2	72.6	80.4
1935	63.0	65.4	68.4	74.5	
1925	59.3	64.9	67.5		
1915	56.1	59.1			
1905	53.0				
All	54.5	63.6	67.0	73.9	82.5
Education = 8–11 years					
1975					87.1
1965				83.9	78.2
1955			70.9	73.5	76.9
1945		75.6	71.0	73.3	78.9
1935	68.2	72.4	71.3	73.2	
1925	61.1	74.2	68.3		
1915	58.5	63.6			
1905	54.8				
All	59.7	70.9	70.1	78.8	74.8
Education = 12 years					
1975					83.0
1965				80.9	80.2
1955			72.8	75.0	78.2
1945		82.3	68.8	72.4	77.8
1935	70.4	73.8	68.2	68.8	
1925	58.8	65.1	61.7		
1915	48.3	53.2			
1905	36.2				
All	56.5	66.5	66.2	72.2	78.8
Education = 13–15 years					
1975					89.1
1965				91.2	81.0
1955			75.0	76.8	75.3
1945		84.2	66.4	67.6	73.5
1935	66.5	56.4	58.4	61.8	
1925	51.2	49.5	50.0		
1915	37.4	46.2			
1905	42.0				
All	47.4	55.8	62.9	75.0	79.8
Education = 16+ years					
1975					87.8
1965				84.7	80.8
1955			69.4	74.7	70.9
1945		68.4	62.1	67.6	65.0
1935	64.8	59.5	52.7	58.0	
1925	45.4	41.0	47.5		
1915	39.4	37.4			
1905	35.9				
All	48.7	50.4	60.2	73.0	76.2

one-half of white wages for those with 11 years of schooling or less. In contrast, black wages are little more than a third of white wages among high school and college graduates.

However, also note that this pattern of falling black-white wage ratios by education has been eliminated by the latter Censuses among workers in their first 20 years in the work force. This pro-skill bias in black economic gains is documented by the more rapid wage improvement among college graduates between 1940 and 1980.

The final pattern of note concerns career wage evaluation within schooling classes. The cross-sectional decline with work experience that characterized aggregate black-white wage ratios (in Table 2) also exists within education groups, especially in the earlier Censuses. Consider men with high school diplomas who were in their first 10 years of work in 1940. Among such men, blacks earned 70 percent as much as whites. If these men extrapolated their future based on the observed 1940 cross-section, they would anticipate that by the time they had been in the labor force 30 to 40 years, the blacks among them would earn only 36 percent as much as whites. If true, this would indeed suggest severe wage deterioration for blacks over their careers.

However, by tracking changes within cohorts in Table 11, the reality turns out to be quite different. The actual wage ratio of high school graduates in the 30- to 40-year experience interval was 69 percent, little different from the initial wage ratio that prevailed in 1940. Among men with 12 or less years of schooling, black male wage growth (at a minimum)[19] kept up with comparably educated whites as their careers proceeded.[20]

During the time period we are analyzing, most blacks did not go beyond high school. Therefore, this pattern of blacks maintaining their relative position across careers characterizes the typical black male as well. Among the more educated, the situation is less easy to summarize. Within some work cohorts, whites appear to have the advantage while blacks have an edge in others. In either case, the cross-sectional decline in black-white weekly wages is far weaker than the actual career reality. Taken as a whole, the evidence suggests that black wages did rise as rapidly as did white wages over careers, even among these more educated workers.

ESTIMATED INCREASE IN WAGES ASSOCIATED WITH INCREASED SCHOOLING

To understand the historical trend, we need to know how much another year of schooling has raised labor market earnings over time. We obtained estimates for each race of schooling coefficients—the proportionate increase in weekly wages associated with an additional year of schooling. Given our regression specification, separate estimates exist for each of our experience intervals from all five Census tapes.

---

[19] *After 20 years on the job, black-white wage ratios of these less educated men jumped sharply in the 1980 Census. The size of this jump and its timing late in the life-cycle suggest that it was not the result of any normal career progression. We return to this issue below.*

[20] *The principal exceptions were high school graduates with their first ten years of experience in 1950.*

Tables 12 and 13 present our estimated schooling coefficients from each of the Census tapes, arranged by market entry cohorts. There are two messages from these tables that we want to highlight: (1) trends in the value of skill, and (2) racial differences in the benefits from schooling.

Because blacks and whites differ in quantities of skills, they are differentially affected by variation in the price of skill. We can monitor secular trends in the price of skill by comparing schooling coefficients for different periods. Because white men are the dominant majority group, trends in the value of skill are most easily monitored from the white coefficient. As the tables show, there is considerable fluctuation across the decades in these coefficients. The amplitude of these fluctuations is much larger among less experienced workers, indicating that younger workers more keenly bear the brunt of aggregate market forces impacting on the price of skill. Schooling coefficients fell sharply between 1940 and 1950, increased gradually from 1950 to 1970—and then declined once again between 1970 to 1980. While differing in amplitude, secular trends for blacks follow those for white men.

We interpret the high returns to schooling in 1940 as a reflection of the lingering effects of the Great Depression. Skill-income ratios are well known to be procyclic, with less educated workers bearing more than their proportionate share of the economic penalties of recessions. It should not be surprising if incomes in 1939 also reflect this reality.

Forces operating on both the demand and supply side of the market are consistent with the increasing income benefits from education between 1950 and 1970 and the subsequent decline during the 1970s. Between 1950 and 1970, new workers were members of the relatively small birth cohorts of the 1920s and 1930s. Consequently, the supply of new college graduates into the labor market was not large. At the same time, according to Richard Freeman (1976), the demand for college-trained manpower accelerated sharply during those years, which is consistent with the rise in schooling coefficients. During the 1970s, however, supply and demand forces were precisely the reverse. Large numbers of college graduates, members of the baby boom generations, entered the labor market just as the demand for college-trained manpower was declining.[21]

Table 13 highlights some very dramatic secular changes by race. Of the 40 numbers in this table, there is but one instance where trends in the returns to schooling favored whites (the 1–5 experience interval between 1950 and 1960). In all other cases, we find a persistent narrowing of racial differences in schooling coefficients.

The end result of this 40-year persistence is that the magnitude of the change eventually became quite large. For example, among those in their first five years of work in 1940, white men's income increased 5 percent more than did black men's for each additional year of school attended. This white advantage declined as each new cohort of workers entered

---

[21] There is also a distinct experience component to these education coefficients within each of the cross-sectional surveys. For example, our estimated black schooling coefficient in 1970 was 7.97 percent for those with 1 to 5 years of work experience, but only 3.70 for black men with 36 to 40 years of experience. While this cross-sectional pattern exists for white men, it is far more acute among black men, particularly after the first experience interval. Most important the black attenuation with experience has increased sharply in more recent Census surveys.

TABLE 12

WHITE AND BLACK SCHOOLING COEFFICIENTS BY MARKET ENTRY COHORTS

Median Year of Work Cohorts	Experience Interval (Years)							
	1–5	6–10	11–15	16–20	21–25	26–30	31–35	36–40
White Schooling Coefficients								
1902								8.10
1907							7.93	
1912						8.52		5.98
1917					8.52		5.83	
1922				8.69		6.17		6.16
1927			8.76		6.08		6.62	
1932		8.93		6.05		6.64		6.36
1937	9.78		6.24		6.64		6.66	
1942		5.51		6.55		6.74		5.48
1947	6.09		6.65		7.04		6.19	
1952		6.94		7.38		6.45		
1957	8.93		7.14		6.92			
1962		7.44		6.94				
1967	9.99		6.78					
1972		6.13						
1977	8.53							
Black Schooling Coefficients								
1902								3.64
1907							3.12	
1912						3.69		2.38
1917					3.44		2.34	
1922				3.88		3.12		2.81
1927			4.67		1.79		3.18	
1932		5.14		3.18		4.00		3.70
1937	4.70		4.04		4.06		3.55	
1942		3.27		4.71		4.24		3.39
1947	4.03		4.66		5.36		4.46	
1952		5.32		5.96		5.11		
1957	5.81		6.26		5.64			
1962		6.69		6.12				
1967	7.97		7.24					
1972		7.31						
1977	9.62							

the labor market. In fact, among men who first entered the labor market during the 1970s, the income benefits that blacks received from schooling now exceed those of white men.

Alternative explanations can be offered for this racial convergence in education coefficients. One obvious candidate is the civil rights movement (and its associated legislation) during the 1960s. A number of studies, including our own (for one example, see Smith and Welch 1984), demonstrated that black male college graduates were among the primary beneficiaries of affirmative action pressures. This view is supported by a racial convergence in education coefficients that was twice as large in the 1970s as in the 1960s.

However, this cannot be the whole story nor, for that matter, a very large part of it. Table 13 also indicates that the general pattern of rising relative returns to black schooling emerged long before the civil rights activism of the 1960s. The root cause of the improvements in relative black returns apparently lies within long-term improvements across

TABLE 13

RACIAL DIFFERENCES IN EDUCATION COEFFICIENTS ARRANGED BY BIRTH COHORTS

Median Year of Work Cohorts	Years of Work Experience							
	1–5	6–10	11–15	16–20	21–25	26–30	31–35	36–40
1902								4.46
1907							4.81	
1912						4.89		3.60
1917					5.08		3.49	
1922				4.81		3.05		3.35
1927			4.09		4.30		3.43	
1932		3.78		2.88		2.64		2.66
1937	5.08		2.21		2.58		3.11	
1942		2.25		1.84		2.50		2.08
1947	2.06		1.99		1.68		1.73	
1952		1.63		1.42		1.34		
1957	3.12		0.88		1.27			
1962		0.75		−0.47				
1967	2.02		−0.47					
1972		−1.18						
1977	−1.09							

birth cohorts that enabled blacks to translate an incremental year of schooling into more income. The evidence we have accumulated in earlier research clearly points to improving quality of black schools as the most plausible explanation for this cohort improvement. We found dramatic changes in such basic indices as number of days attended, pupil-teacher ratios, the education accomplishments of teachers.[22] This evidence, combined with the coefficients in Table 13, suggests why blacks were able to translate a year of schooling into increasingly higher incomes over time.

QUANTIFYING EDUCATION'S EFFECT ON THE RACIAL WAGE GAP

Across the 40-year period, education dominated our regression accounting. Based on the equations (1.i) to (1.iv) above, Table 14 gives our regression accounting for schooling across the full period.[23] Combining all effects in the first four columns, education predicts an increase of relative black wages ranging from 17 to 84 percent. The two dimen-

---

[22] We document the evidence in detail in Welch (1974) and Smith (1984).

[23] With exceptions that we will note below, the decade by decade timing of education effects is not crucial.

TABLE 14

BLACK-WHITE RATIOS OF AVERAGE WEEKLY WAGES BY SCHOOLING AND WORK EXPERIENCE FOR SELECTED YEARS

Years out of School	Main Effects	Interaction with Race Effects	Interaction with Year Effects	Interaction with Race-Year Effects	Schooling Total
1-5	36	−21	5	65	84
6–10	22	−12	8	52	70
11–15	18	−14	7	45	56
16–20	16	−15	6	35	42
21–25	14	−18	6	32	35
26–30	11	−16	7	28	31
31–35	10	−18	5	25	23
36–40	6	−14	9	17	17

sions that served to close the racial wage gap were the narrowing of education disparity between the races and the improving economic benefits from black schooling.

The main effects column in Table 14 summarizes the influence of narrowing disparities in levels of schooling. Measured at white 1940 parameter values, the wage gap closed by 6 to 36 percent because blacks were more similar to whites in levels of school completion in 1980 than in 1940.

This influence of education is clearly largest among younger workers. This attenuation with age partly reflects declining education coefficients with years of market experience. However, it results principally from increased school completion for blacks. Table 10 demonstrated that the narrowing of racial differences in schooling levels was far more pronounced among less experienced workers than among older workers.

Race effects adjust the influence of converging schooling levels to accommodate the lower income returns blacks receive for each year of schooling. To catch up, black schooling levels must actually rise faster than those of whites. The full effect of changing levels of schooling is obtained by adding the main and race effects columns in Table 14. The narrowing of education differences failed to improve black-white wage ratios among older workers, but led to a net gain of 15 percent for younger men.

In addition to a smaller schooling disparity, blacks also began to experience higher economic benefits of schooling (i.e., race-year effects). Since 1940, there has been a spectacular rise in the income that blacks receive from a year of schooling, a phenomenon we attribute largely to the improving relative quality of black schools. According to Table 14, gains in the payoff to schooling increased relative wages of black men from 11 to 38 percent, young men being at the high end of that range.

The year effects summarize how secular changes in the price of skill affect the wage gap. Between 1940 and 1980, these year effects actually helped black men; this reflects the uncharacteristically high income returns from schooling in 1940, a depression year. The subsequently lower rate of return to schooling throughout the remaining 40 years also narrowed the wage gap because white men were affected more adversely. However, compared with the other factors related to schooling, secular swings in the market for skilled labor played a minor role in closing the wage gap.[24]

IV. CAUSES OF THE CLOSING WAGE GAP: GEOGRAPHIC LOCATION

Americans have always tried to improve their economic lot by moving to places where prospects for their economic advancement were better. Since the end of slavery, large numbers of black men exercised their freedom to choose the place where they lived and worked. For many decades, most of this black migration took place within the South. Beginning in 1910, the great black migration northward started, a movement that accelerated after 1940.

While migration has been changing residential patterns, the regional structure of the American economy has also changed—to the point that it bears little resemblance to that of 1940. The agriculture-based economy of the South, for example—characterized by low productivity and little technological advance—was viewed as a drag on black economic progress in 1940. The situation now is far different. Today, the smokestack industries of the North Central and Northeastern states are in decay while the restructured Southern economy is booming.

In this section, we investigate the impact of these changing patterns of regional location on trends in black-white male wage ratios. We will concentrate on the three regional issues that loom most important in the economic literature—the large-scale black South to North migration, the increasing urbanization of the black population, and differential interregional economic growth.

CHANGING PATTERNS OF RESIDENTIAL LOCATION

Two geographic factors stand out in shaping the economic status of blacks: their concentration in the Southern states and their increasing urbanization. During the period that we are studying, important changes were occurring across both dimensions that would radically transform the geography of the black population.

Table 15 illustrates one of these dimensions—the percentage of males who live in the South. Throughout American history, the economic welfare of blacks has been tied closely

---

[24] These swings were, however, far more important in shaping short-run changes across successive Census years. For example, the sharp drop in the economic benefits of schooling from the depression year 1940 to the more normal economic conditions of 1950 did contribute to the sharp rise in black incomes during the 1940s (raising black relative incomes by 7.8 percent). Similarly, the improving labor market for college graduates between 1950 and 1970 raised white men's incomes more than black incomes (a decline of 1.7 percent in black wages). Finally, relative to whites, black men received positive but small benefits (0.44 percent) from the difficult labor market faced by college graduates during the 1970s. The numbers used in this footnote are averages across the eight experience groups.

to events in the South. Fully nine out of ten blacks were Southerners in 1790, a proportion that changed but little over the next 120 years. Since 1910, the fraction of blacks living in the South has steadily declined. Spurred in part by the cutoff in European immigration, the great Northern black migration spanned the next two decades, 1910–30. When completed, it transformed the geographic and economic character of black America.[25]

Even so, three-quarters of all blacks still lived in the Southern states in 1940 (see Table 15), but with the end of the Depression, the movement North resumed with renewed force. During each decade between 1940 and 1970, a million and a half Southern blacks migrated to the North. The end result was to leave only slightly more than half of all black men Southern residents in 1970. The flow then reversed during the 1970s: As it did for white Americans, the net movement of blacks turned southward. A slightly larger proportion of blacks lived in the South in 1980 than lived there ten years earlier.

In contrast to these very dramatic changes, Table 15 indicates a remarkable stability in the distribution of the white population between the South and North. Slightly less than 30 percent of white men lived in the South, a proportion that has roughly prevailed for decades. There was an upward blip to over 30 percent during the 1970s, a reflection of the widely noted move to the Sunbelt.

The great northern migration had profound effects. The culture, laws, and economy of the South would no longer play so exclusive a role in shaping the economic position of blacks. However, it is also easy to exaggerate the extent of this change. Even today, the majority of blacks remain citizens of the South. Compared with the situation for whites, black economic well-being is still closely tied to the robustness of the Southern economy.

Moreover, geographical shifts in the place where blacks currently live shroud the continuing legacy of the South. Place of birth being immutable, the effects of migration on place of birth appear with a generational lag when the Northern-born children of migrants finally enter the labor force. Table 15 illustrates the slow-moving nature of these changes: Three-quarters of all black men were Southern-born by as late as 1970—another reminder that black roots in the South still run deep.

Besides migration, the geography of black people altered in another fundamental way. After the Civil War, nine of ten blacks lived in rural farm areas, especially in the rural counties of the Southern black belt. This century has witnessed the transition of the black people from largely rural to predominately urban. Although it began in the early decades of the twentieth century, this transition was completed during the 40-year period after 1940.

Whites were still more urbanized than blacks in 1940 (see Table 15). Urbanization affected both races, but blacks far more so than whites. By 1980, four out of every five men of both races lived in urban areas. Today, the principal difference between them is where they live within urban areas: whites in the suburban fringes, blacks in the central

---

[25] *During the First World War, the number of black Northern migrants trebled relative to the previous decade. This rate doubled again in the 1920s when three-quarters of a million blacks made their way to Northern cities.*

TABLE 15

REGIONAL DISTRIBUTION OF THE POPULATIONS

	1940	1950	1960	1970	1980
Black Men					
Live in South	74.8	63.8	57.5	52.1	53.1
Born in South	90.6	87.3	84.6	75.2	NA
SMSA	44.1	52.0	60.3	69.4	79.0
Central cities	29.8	40.0	49.8	55.5	58.5
White Men					
Live in South	28.2	28.4	28.6	29.5	31.8
SMSA	51.0	55.2	56.7	60.4	79.0
Central cities	26.7	26.9	25.8	24.2	29.8

cities. Fully 75 percent of all black SMSA residents resided in the central cities, compared with only 38 percent of whites.[26]

BLACK-WHITE WAGE DIFFERENCES BY GEOGRAPHIC LOCATION

Even among men who have the same amount of education and job experience, large geographic wage differentials prevail among regions. Identifying their underlying causes is a complex empirical problem. Some of these wage disparities may simply reflect cost-of-living differences between regions, or compensating payments for the relative attractiveness or undesirability of locational attributes (e.g., climate, crime, and density).[27] Given the magnitude of the regional wage differentials we estimate, it is also likely that they proxy unobserved indices of skill. Finally, the large black-white wage gap in the South may well reflect the historically more intense racial discrimination there.

Whatever the causes, it is fair to say that despite the growing amount of good work on this subject, the underlying sources of geographic wage differentials have not been adequately documented. Nor do we attempt to do so here. Our less ambitious goal is to measure how much of the change in the racial wage gap can be attributed to two geographical facts: (1) that blacks and whites live in different regions of the country, and (2) that the black-white wage gap varies across regions. As wages between regions change over time—whatever the underlying causes—we can measure the impact of such changes on the aggregate black-white wage gap.[28]

---

[26] In the North, blacks have always been more urbanized than whites. Even in the South a roughly equal fraction (one-third) of blacks and whites lived in urban areas. The overall difference between the races was largely due to the black concentration in the South, which was much more rural than the rest of the nation. The more rapid pace of urbanization of blacks documented in Table 15 reflects two factors. First, the South, a black-intensive region, urbanized more rapidly than the rest of the nation. Second, blacks left the relatively rural region of the South to live in the more urban North.

[27] For an attempt to price these attributes, see Sherwin Rosen (1979). To the extent that local labor markets are distinct, they also capture short- and long-run wage differentials among markets.

[28] Even for this much simpler problem, the results must be interpreted with caution. Calculations based on redistributing population between areas without compensating adjustments in average wages between regions are at best crude indicators. Historically, it is doubtful whether migrants have been representative either of region of origin or of destination, an issue we turn to below.

Table 16 presents our estimated wage difference associated with living in the Southern states. Traditionally, men of either race earned less in the South than in the North. Until the last decade, Southern white men received about 10 percent lower wages than white men located elsewhere; black weekly wages were approximately 30 percent lower in the South than elsewhere. Our estimates confirm that wages were lower in the South for both races, but the penalty for blacks was simply much larger.

No long-term trend exists between 1940 and 1970 in these geographic wage differences. After 1970, however, wages of both races increased faster in the South, particularly among younger workers, most likely reflecting the economic resurgence of the South.

Table 16 also shows the additional black-white wage gap associated with living in the South. Between 1940 and 1960, there was remarkable stability in these racial wage differences, with a 20 percent larger racial wage gap in the South than in other parts of the country. The southern racial wage disparity narrowed for younger workers between 1960 and 1970, but remained at historical levels among mature male workers. However, the truly dramatic story occurred between 1970 and 1980. A sharp decline occurred during the 1970s as the racial wage gap in the South fell by as much as two-thirds of their 1970 levels.

What accounts for this rapid movement toward the national norm in the Southern racial gap in the 1970s? Two explanations are possible. First, black-white skill differences may have converged in the South as the post-World War II cohorts entered the labor market. To illustrate this point, assume that Southern schools were effectively desegregated in 1960, six years after the Brown decision. The first class of Southern black children who had attended entirely desegregated schools would have first entered the labor market in the early to mid-1970s. Some of the improvement in black incomes during the 1970s may have been due to the skills acquired through this improved schooling. However, that is unlikely to be the whole story because there was a substantial erosion in racial wage disparities even among older workers in the 1970s (see Table 16). A more plausible explanation may well be that racial discrimination is waning in the South.

One issue that cross-sectional estimates such as those contained in Table 16 cannot answer is whether the wage disparity between regions correctly measures the potential income gain from migration. If they proxy unobserved skill differences, cross-sectional wage differentials would not represent the wage gain an individual would receive by moving from the South to the North.[29] Table 17 lists estimated wage differentials associated with place of residence and birth.[30]

---

[29] Some of the wage differences may reflect cost-of-living differences between regions, or compensatory payments for the relative attractiveness of places. To the extent that they do, regional wage differentials would not translate into real income differences.

[30] In the regressions on which these estimates are based, the excluded group are men both born and currently living in the North. As a result, these estimated wage differences in Table 17 are all relative to wages of Northern-born Northern residents. Only the results obtained from the 1960 Census are presented in the text. The estimates from the other Census years were qualitatively similar to those in 1960.

TABLE 16

REGIONAL WAGE DIFFERENTIALS

	Experience Interval							
Sample	1–5	6–10	11–15	16–20	21–25	26–30	31–35	36–40
Regression Coefficients for Southern Residence								
Black Men								
1940	−24.6	−25.8	−27.5	−30.0	−28.8	−33.3	−31.0	−32.1
1950	−26.2	−27.7	−27.3	−26.9	−37.7	−37.8	−34.6	−29.0
1960	−33.7	−31.7	−28.4	−29.6	−29.8	−31.2	−37.5	−35.3
1970	−20.9	−27.3	−28.4	−27.7	−27.1	−30.7	−29.3	−29.3
1980	−9.1	−11.8	−10.3	−17.5	−17.3	−16.1	−18.8	−22.9
White Men								
1940	−1.8	−9.3	−10.7	−10.6	−10.8	−11.5	−10.4	−9.5
1950	−8.0	−12.0	−7.9	−12.6	−13.9	−13.7	−11.8	−18.7
1960	−9.9	−12.1	−11.3	−9.4	−9.2	−10.8	−12.8	−14.3
1970	−5.7	−9.0	−10.0	−10.0	−9.6	−8.6	−8.0	−9.4
1980	−1.8	−5.1	−6.0	6.0	−7.9	−9.4	−7.6	−7.8
Racial Difference in Southern Residence Coefficients								
1940	−22.8	−16.5	−16.9	−19.5	−18.0	−21.8	−20.6	−22.5
1950	−18.2	−15.6	−20.4	−14.3	−23.9	−24.1	−22.9	−10.3
1960	−23.8	−19.7	−17.1	−20.2	−20.6	−20.5	−24.6	−21.0
1970	−15.2	−18.3	−18.3	−17.9	−17.6	−22.1	−21.3	−19.9
1980	−7.3	−6.8	−4.4	−11.5	−9.5	−6.7	−11.2	−15.1

TABLE 17

WAGE DIFFERENTIALS ASSOCIATED WITH REGION OF RESIDENCE AND BIRTH
(MEASURED RELATIVE TO MEN BOTH BORN AND CURRENTLY LIVING IN THE NORTH)

Place of Birth and Residence	Experience Interval							
	1–5	6–10	11–15	16–20	21–25	26–30	31–35	36–40
1960 Black Men								
Southern birth—Southern residence	−33.9	−30.0	−25.7	−28.1	−27.7	−21.5	−33.3	−32.7
Northern birth—Southern residence	−28.1	−24.2	−12.3	−13.2	−17.5	−7.0	−0.8	−16.8
Southern birth—Northern residence	−0.8	2.7	5.3	2.4	3.1	12.5	5.1	2.1
1960 White Men								
Southern birth—Southern residence	−9.9	−13.2	−12.6	−11.1	−10.8	−12.6	−14.1	−15.2
Northern birth—Southern residence	−4.9	−3.5	−2.8	0.8	0.4	1.7	3.8	−1.7
Southern birth—Northern residence	9.2	5.1	5.0	5.4	5.2	4.8	3.9	3.6

The most surprising result from the table is that Southern-born blacks who now live in the North earn more than blacks born and living in the North. Even after adjusting for education and labor market experience, it remains possible that Southern-born black men who now live in the North are far more able than those blacks who remained in the South. However, the magnitude of these wage differentials seems too large to be associated with selectivity of migrants alone. This dominance of place of residence over place of birth suggests to us that real wage disparities between the South and North were indeed historically quite large. Moreover, turning the question on its head, wage differences must have been large to generate the observed volume of migration. For example, between 1940 and 1950, more than one-third of all young blacks (16–25 years old) migrated from the four Southern states of Alabama, Georgia, Mississippi, and South Carolina.

The important role of place of residence should not be misunderstood as a refutation of our emphasis on quality of Southern schooling, an issue that involves an interaction of location with education. It is necessary to separate schooling quality from regional differences in the market for skilled labor. Because skilled labor is relatively scarce in the South, the premium to skill may be higher there even though Southern schools are of lower quality.

To separate effects, we interact years of education with dummy variables for Southern residence and Southern birth. The former captures regional differences in the returns to skill, and the latter measures regional differences in quality of schooling.

The estimates (see Table 18) show that the South is characterized by a larger wage premium to skill for both races. The fact that schooling demands a premium in the South may well be the basis for the migration of skilled labor to the South during the post–World War II era. However, Southern birth (and, presumably, attendance at Southern schools) lowers the wage premium to schooling for both races. If there is evidence of quality of schooling here, it is that Southern schools were inferior for both whites and blacks.

We complete our summary with a brief discussion of wage disparities between urban and rural areas. Men who live in SMSAs earn higher wages, a fact well documented in the literature (see Table 19). Among whites, this urban wage premium has declined over time. In 1980, white men in SMSAs earned 20 percent more than other whites; in 1940 this wage premium was 33 percent. A similar negative drift occurs among black men, and the size of the secular change is of approximately the same magnitude. Over time, the income benefits from living in SMSAs have simply eroded.

Among white men, the secular trend has been that white men living in central cities earn less than other white residents of SMSAs—by 1980, 10 percent less. In contrast, black men who lived in central cities traditionally have had higher wages, but this wage premium has declined significantly over time. In 1940, central city blacks earned 10 percent more than other black urban dwellers; by 1980, they earned 10 percent less. The long-term economic decline of the central cities is the most likely cause of the deteriorating wages for black central city residents.

TABLE 18

REGIONAL RETURNS TO SCHOOLING

Place of Birth and Education	Experience Interval							
	1–5	6–10	11–15	16–20	21–25	26–30	31–35	36–40
Black Men								
Southern birth ×education	−.031	−.035	−.022	−.019	−.028	−.017	−.037	−.014
Southern residence ×education	.007	.025	.027	.032	.029	.035	.030	.031
White Men								
Southern birth ×education	−.019	−.010	−.014	−.013	−.017	−.012	−.010	−.002
Southern residence ×education	.024	.026	.025	.021	.029	.028	.028	.025

Note: These results were obtained from the 1960 Census. Qualitative results from other Census years were quite similar.

TABLE 19

ESTIMATED SMSA AND CENTRAL CITY REGRESSION COEFFICIENTS

Sample	Experience Interval							
	1–5	6–10	11–15	16–20	21–25	26–30	31–35	36–40
SMSA Regression Coefficients								
Black Men								
1940	26.4	28.1	35.3	27.8	36.9	33.5	36.9	33.6
1950	24.8	36.2	36.0	40.7	33.7	46.4	34.7	41.4
1960	6.7	21.7	20.0	25.3	25.5	22.8	34.0	32.4
1970	−1.6	5.2	7.2	11.8	11.6	14.7	14.5	20.5
1980	10.1	19.9	22.3	24.7	20.6	19.7	19.5	30.8
White Men								
1940	28.9	30.5	31.1	33.2	36.5	33.8	34.3	37.2
1950	20.4	21.6	21.8	23.3	23.9	27.4	31.4	31.8
1960	17.6	18.1	19.6	22.5	23.3	26.0	29.6	33.4
1970	11.6	13.3	17.1	18.2	17.7	20.2	19.8	24.1
1980	2.7	13.2	18.0	19.8	20.6	20.2	20.5	21.1
Central City Regression Coefficients								
Black Men								
1940	17.7	16.0	9.1	8.9	7.8	5.7	6.8	9.0
1950	11.6	3.2	3.4	−0.0	−3.4	−5.9	5.6	2.8
1960	15.3	6.3	9.0	6.4	10.6	13.5	8.7	14.4
1970	10.0	8.6	4.6	2.8	4.2	4.2	7.7	5.3
1980	−4.1	−9.1	−12.1	−9.3	−11.7	−8.7	−5.9	−11.6
White Men								
1940	5.5	3.0	2.6	3.9	2.6	4.1	6.9	4.1
1950	1.3	0.1	−0.0	−1.3	−0.1	0.0	1.3	6.4
1960	−1.3	−4.9	−7.5	−7.1	−7.0	−5.3	−5.0	−2.0
1970	−3.6	−5.1	−6.7	−7.7	−8.1	−6.0	−4.8	−4.9
1980	−6.2	−9.9	−11.9	−12.8	−11.7	−11.0	−10.6	−9.1

QUANTIFYING THE ROLE OF LOCATION

In this section, we have identified a number of important residential changes that could affect the size of the racial gap. These changes included black migration, the recent erosion of the Southern wage gap, and differential economic growth across regions. What was the relative quantitative significance of these trends? To answer this question, Tables 20 and 21 summarize the results from our regression accounting for geographic factors. They focus on the three key aspects of residential location discussed above: the direct wage gains due to migration, the erosion of geographic dispersion in the racial wage gap, and the effect of differential economic growth across regions.

The size of migration's direct effect is shown in Table 20.[31] The direct effect measures the increase in relative wages resulting from the migration of blacks from low-wage southern rural areas to higher-wage northern urban centers. The data show that migration was important in closing the wage gap. Depending upon the specific experience level considered, migration increased black-white wage ratios by 11 to 19 percent between 1940 and 1980.[32] Overall, these direct wage benefits from migration rival education's role in closing the racial wage gap. Migration and schooling were the two key investments made by black men that drive their economic advances.

The single-decade comparisons in Table 20 show that black income gains from migration have declined steadily over time. The largest benefits were concentrated between 1940 and 1960, diminished during the 1960s, and were no longer an important source of black economic improvement during the 1970s.[33] Similarly, as urban and Southern racial wage ratios converged to the national norm, especially during the 1970s, migration's potential in raising black incomes ended. Consistent with the disappearance of geographic wage disparities, the era of large-scale black interregional migration is probably over.

The second quantitatively important locational influence we identified was the narrowing racial wage gap in the South. Whatever the cause, this change had a significant effect on black relative economic status. The improving situation in the South closed the racial wage gap at the nationwide level by 4 to 10 percent between 1940 and 1980 (see the last column of Table 21). Virtually all of the change occurred during the 1970s, the only decade where the racial wage disparity declined significantly.

---

[31] This direct effect of migration is obtained by adding the main and race terms in equation (1) above. Using equations (1.i) and (1.ii), the sum of these two terms is $B_3 (X_1 - X_3 - B_4(X_2 - X_4))$. $B_3(X_1 - X_3)$ measures the black gain from migration (using base-period wage geographic wage differences); $B_2 (X_2 - X_4)$ is the corresponding gain to white migration.

[32] It is of some interest to separate the gains into an urbanization and an interregional effect. The movement north raised relative black incomes from 5 to 8 percent; slightly larger black wage gains are attributed to going to urban areas. When they left the rural areas of the South for the northern cities, most blacks, of course, received both wage increases.

[33] Blacks were essentially transformed from their rural Southern base to a predominately urban group during the 20 years after 1940. As a consequence, the positive black benefits from going to urban places were largely completed by 1960. The wage gains achieved from moving north would last another decade. Then, with the end of the black migration to the North, these migration gains stopped.

TABLE 20

MIGRATION'S DIRECT CONTRIBUTION TO 1940 TO 1980 GROWTH
OF BLACK-WHITE WAGE RATIOS
(Units Are Changes in Natural Logarithms of Wages × 100)

Years of Market Experience	Time Period				Total 1940–80
	1940–50	1950–60	1960–70	1970–80	
1–5	9.3	6.5	4.2	−0.9	19.3
6–10	9.9	5.0	3.5	−1.7	17.7
11–15	10.9	4.0	1.7	−1.5	14.8
16–20	5.0	4.2	2.6	−1.1	10.7
21–25	5.4	4.4	2.3	0.0	12.0
26–30	3.2	2.3	5.1	0.1	10.6
31–35	4.3	3.5	3.7	1.3	12.5
36–40	1.8	5.0	1.9	2.4	11.0

TABLE 21

EFFECTS OF NARROWING IN REGIONAL RACIAL WAGE DIFFERENCES
ON THE GROWTH OF BLACK-WHITE WAGE RATIOS
(Units Are Changes in Natural Logarithms of Wages × 100)

Years of Market Experience	Years		Total 1940–80
	1940–70	1970–80	
1–5	−1.6	10.9	9.3
6–10	−5.5	11.1	5.6
11–15	−8.7	12.6	3.9
16–20	2.2	8.3	10.5
21–25	−2.5	2.0	−0.5
26–30	−0.3	7.2	6.9
31–35	−0.4	3.8	3.4
36–40	4.6	5.3	9.9

   The final geographic dimension we examined was the net effect of differential wage growth. This proved to be relatively unimportant, producing a net loss of 3 to 6 percent in blacks' relative incomes. Most of this loss is due to declining wages in central cities. The rising economic position of the South had little effect across the full 40-year period, partly because it is limited to the last 15 years. The recent Southern growth raised black incomes, relative to whites, by only 2 percent. Apparently, the economic revival of the South largely benefited black and white men alike.

In summary, our work identifies two geographic sources of long-term relative black economic improvement: the direct wage gains received from migration, and the erosion of the Southern racial wage gap during the 1970s. Migration raised black wages 11 to 19 percent between 1940 and 1980; the closing of the Southern wage gap added another 4 to 10 percent. While the decline of central cities had negative consequences for blacks, and the resurgence in the Southern economy positive ones, the overall net effect of these regional developments was small.

V. LABOR FORCE PARTICIPATION AND AFFIRMATIVE ACTION

Our regression analyses focused on those factors that are most likely to have narrowed the racial wage gap. However, other developments may well have affected black wages during the 40 years in question. The most notable among these are the decline in labor force participation rates of less educated and low-income black males between 1970 and 1980 and affirmative action.

THE DECLINING BLACK PARTICIPATION IN THE LABOR FORCE

Trends in wage rates are the primary focus of our essay. But our portrait of the changing economic status of black men is incomplete without a brief summary of parallel trends in employment and unemployment. In spite of the improvement in their labor market opportunities, an increasing number of black men have dropped out of the labor force in the middle of their careers. In addition, rising rates of unemployment, for young blacks especially, raise serious concerns about the labor force young blacks face.

To document long-term trends in black male employment, Table 22 lists the percentages of black and white men who worked at least one week during the previous year. For both races, those percentages remained basically stable from 1940 to 1970. After 1970 they declined sharply, and did so at a much faster rate among black men. Similarly, young blacks experienced a sustained rise in their unemployment rates relative to the rates for young whites. Unemployment rates of blacks 16–25 years old were 1.45 times those of whites in 1950. By 1980, the black youth unemployment rate was 22 percent, more than double the rate for young white men.[34]

Because conventional labor force statistics give a misleading portrait of activities of young men, we have divided activity status into two groups.[35] SEM (the "good activity") includes schooling, employment, and the military, while UOJ (unemployment, out of the labor force, and jail) are the bad ones (see Table 23).

---

[34] *The causes of this long-term deterioration in black youth unemployment are not well understood. According to John Cogan (1982), most of the decline before 1970 was due to the elimination of agriculture as the primary employer for young blacks. But the reasons for the post-1970 changes remain elusive.*

[35] *For a fuller discussion of this division, see Smith and Welch (1987).*

TABLE 22

PERCENTAGES OF BLACK AND WHITE MEN WHO WORKED AT LEAST ONE WEEK
IN THE PRECEDING YEAR, BY EDUCATION LEVEL

	Years of Education					
Year	0–7	8–11	12	13–15	16+	All
Blacks: Ages 36–45						
1980	74.5	81.9	87.2	90.4	93.4	85.1
1970	86.8	89.7	93.9	95.8	97.3	90.7
1960	89.8	91.4	93.8	95.0	98.8	91.4
1950	90.6	91.9	92.4	87.4	97.0	89.1
1940	90.2	88.9	88.9	96.3	93.6	90.0
Blacks: Ages 46–54						
1980	66.7	76.4	83.4	86.2	91.9	97.9
1970	84.1	86.6	92.6	92.1	95.9	87.7
1960	88.0	90.6	93.3	92.3	97.7	89.4
1950	88.8	88.2	88.8	98.0	94.6	89.8
1940	88.4	86.9	86.1	94.3	98.7	88.3
Whites: Ages 36–45						
1980	78.5	92.4	96.3	96.7	98.4	95.6
1970	89.1	96.1	98.1	97.9	99.0	96.9
1960	91.2	97.0	98.5	98.4	99.1	97.1
1950	91.0	95.1	95.9	96.6	96.7	94.7
1940	90.3	94.3	95.7	95.2	94.7	93.2
Whites: Ages 46–54						
1980	75.9	87.7	93.0	93.5	96.5	91.2
1970	85.3	94.1	96.6	96.9	98.3	94.7
1960	90.1	95.5	96.9	96.9	98.0	95.0
1950	87.8	91.8	93.2	94.3	94.8	91.3
1940	90.3	93.6	94.9	95.0	95.9	90.2

It may come as a surprise to many that there exists no negative secular trend for black male teenagers. Between 1940 and 1980 roughly one in five black male teenagers was confined to unproductive activities. In fact, the principal secular trend among black male teenagers was within the SEM group, where the fraction in school increased by 35 percent largely at the expense of the fraction at work. Because this is arguably a positive development, there is nothing on the employment side of the labor market that counteracts the positive wage story for black teenagers.

Although the seeds of the problem are certainly sown earlier, the secular deterioration, instead, is concentrated among somewhat older black men. More important, it is confined entirely to the 1970s; 28 percent of 24-year-old black men are in the unproductive group in 1980, a jump of 7 percentage points since 1970. In this age group in 1980, 1 in 9 black men were unemployed, another 1 in 9 were out of the labor force, and 1 in 20 were in jail. Similarly, 1 in 5 black men aged 35–36 are now assigned to our unproductive activities class, with half of them completely absent from the labor market.

To highlight this critical 1970s period for older black men, Table 24 lists changes in labor force participation that occurred between 1970 and 1980. Among men 36–45 years

TABLE 23

ACTIVITY STATUS OF BLACK MEN

	1980	1970	1960	1950	1940
18 Years Old					
SEM	79.3	79.5	78.6	82.1	78.3
UOJ	20.6	20.4	21.4	17.9	21.7
24 Years Old					
SEM	71.8	78.9	80.2	86.2	82.7
UOJ	28.2	21.1	19.8	13.8	17.3
35–36 Years Old					
SEM	79.7	86.3	82.9	86.5	85.3
UOJ	20.3	13.7	17.1	13.5	14.7

Note: SEM = school, employment, military; and UOJ = unemployment, out of the labor force, jail

TABLE 24

PERCENTAGE DECLINES IN LABOR FORCE PARTICIPATION, BOTH RACES, 1970–80

	Years of Education					
Race	0–7	8–11	12	13–15	16+	All
Ages 36–45						
Black	12.3	7.8	6.7	5.4	3.9	5.6
White	10.6	3.7	1.8	1.2	0.6	1.3
Ages 46–54						
Black	10.2	10.2	9.2	5.9	4.0	9.8
White	6.4	6.4	3.6	3.4	1.8	3.5

old, black participation rates fell by almost 6 percentage points, four times the decline among whites. The drop is even steeper among those 46–54 years old; once again, the fraction of black men who withdrew far exceeds that of white men. Among men 46–54 years old, black participation rates fell by 10 percentage points.

This deterioration in the employment side of the black male labor market raises two critical research questions: (1) What caused the decline in black employment? and (2) What implications does this recent decline in black employment have for the optimistic wage story we have been telling?

Causes of the Decline in Black Employment. In our view, one of the major unsettled research questions on race centers around the reasons for the growing fraction of persistently disengaged black men from the labor market. The competing hypotheses are not new, but a convincing case has not been made on either side. William Wilson (1988) and others have emphasized the demand side, claiming that the substantial restructuring of the economy in the last 15 years eliminated jobs that were disproportionately held by inner-city blacks.

The supply-side counterpoint, Charles Murray (1984), swayed in part by the coincidence in timing, directed attention toward the host of social programs now subsumed under the popular label, the "safety net." It is argued that these programs are an attractive alternative to work for many black men whose market rewards are meager. The political rhetoric surrounding this issue is obviously intense, but it has not yet been matched by scientific precision in settling the question.

There have been two recent attempts to tackle the difficult question of black youth employment.[36] Glen Cain and Ross Finnie (1989) adopt the demand-side view. Using aggregate SMSA level data from the 1980 Census, they assume that the level of average hours of work by white males 16–21 in an SMSA is an adequate indicator of the demand for youth labor. Their regression models do indicate a significant positive correlation of the average number of hours worked by black youth with their youth demand proxy. Welch (1989) champions instead the supply-side interpretation. He argues that the main culprit is that the reservation wage of black youth (the minimum wage they are willing to accept) has increased faster than the rising market wage of black youth.

A strict demand-supply–side confrontation is probably misplaced on this question. The pre-1970 stable black Labor Force Participation Rates (LFPR) indicate that supply and demand factors must have acted in concert. Before 1970, cross-sectional (i.e., across SMSAs) and time series variations in the demand for black labor existed. However, these demand shocks produced little variation in black LFPRs until the 1970s. This suggests that prior to 1970 the black supply curve (especially for mature workers) was relatively inelastic. The key event was that during the 1970s the black male supply function became much more elastic as opportunities in the nonmarket sector improved (i.e., welfare, crime). This supply-initiated change now allows demand variation to affect participation rates.

Effects of Declining Black Employment on the Wage Series. Fortunately, the other question we posed is more easily answerable, although there is often considerable confusion about precisely what the question is. The question we raise is this: Did the sharp decline in the black LFPRs during the 1970s and early 1980s distort the positive wage story?[37]

Table 24 illustrates an important dimension of this phenomenon that helps us address the wage issue. For both races, declines in LFPR are far steeper among the less educated. The concentration of these declines among blacks and among the less educated strongly suggests that the men who dropped out of the labor force had lower incomes than those

---

[36] In a series of papers, Donald Parsons (1980a, 1980b) has argued that the most likely course of the declining participation rates of older black males was the result of a single program. According to Parsons, the Social Security Disability (SSD) program accounted for the bulk of the declining participation rates. For a contrary view, see Robert Haverman and Barbara Wolfe (1984).

[37] A related but different question is: Do these declines in LFPR play a role in expanding levels of black poverty? The answer to this question can easily be "yes" without having any appreciable effect on the average black-white male wage.

who remained. Because of this correlation with income, these declining participation rates could have important implications for trends in black-white wages during the 1970–80 period. In particular, in an important paper, Richard Butler and James Heckman (1977) have argued that these supply-side reductions in the relative number of working black men were an important cause of the post-1965 rise in the relative income of blacks. The potential importance of their argument is illustrated in the within-cohort comparisons presented earlier (and repeated in the third and fourth column of Table 25). They show a sharp jump in black-white wages for older men as they accumulate an added 10 years of work experience between 1970 and 1980.

The Butler-Heckman hypothesis rests on compositional changes in the labor force. To assess the practical importance of their argument, 1980 wages were corrected for two compositional changes. The first reflects the more rapid declines in labor force participation among blacks and the less educated. To do this, we substituted observed 1970 labor force participation rates by education level for the 1980 rates.

We also adjusted for the fact that within schooling classes wages of dropouts are typically less than the wages of those who remained in the labor force by 1980. To do this, we use alternative assumptions about the wage of dropouts relative to those who remain in the labor force. We first calculate relative wages of dropouts using matched Current Population Survey (CPS) files across the years 1977–84.[38] The results of this selectivity correction are presented under the CPS Fully Adjusted column in Table 25. We simulate potential effects using a range of alternative values of the ratios of wages of dropouts to labor force stayers; these results appear in the last four columns of Table 25.

Using the CPS-based estimates, the total impact of changes in labor supply on black-white wage contrasts is small. The adjusted ratio for the youngest group is 96.3 percent of the observed ratio. For the two older groups, the adjusted and observed ratios are virtually identical. The simulated adjustments confirm what the CPS calculation shows. Even if we assume that dropouts would earn only half as much as those who remain in the labor force (see the column in Table 25 marked .5), the simulated black-white wage ratios remain similar (within 5 percent) to the observed ratios. Evidently, supply censoring explains at most a minor part of the observed increase in black-white male wages between 1970 and 1980.

AFFIRMATIVE ACTION

The next issue we address is affirmative action,[39] which still dominates the debate over government labor-market policy regarding race. Modern efforts at affirmative action began with the 1964 Civil Rights Act, aimed at eliminating employment discrimination against minority groups. Because of the historically intense discrimination against them, American blacks were the principal group this legislation was meant to protect. In the last

---

[38] Because of the sample rotation on the CPS, half of the March CPS samples are common between adjacent years. Within this matched sample of workers in year t, wages of those who dropped out of the labor force by year t + 1 were estimated relative to those who remained in the labor force in year t + 1.

[39] This section is derived from Smith and Welch 1984.

TABLE 25

SELECTIVITY CORRECTIONS ON BLACK-WHITE MALE WAGE RATIOS*

Years of Labor Market Experience in		Observed Black Wages as a Percentage of Whites		1980 Selectivity Corrected Wages				
				CPS Fully Adjusted	Simulated Adjustment Ratios			
1970	1980	1970	1980		0.8	0.5	0.3	0.1
15–20	25–30	62.8	66.9	64.4	66.1	65.0	64.3	63.5
21–25	31–35	62.7	66.5	66.1	65.6	64.5	63.8	63.0
26–30	36–40	60.6	68.5	68.1	67.7	65.7	65.7	64.8

* Let a_i represent the fraction of those in (age and education) group i who drop out of the labor force between 1970 and 1980 and let r_i represent the wage of dropouts relative to stayers. If y_i is the observed mean for stayers then the full mean including dropouts would be $y_i = y_i(1 + a_i(r_i - 1))$. The composite dropout adjusted average is $s_i y_i$ where s_i is the 1970 labor force share of group i. Since s_i, a_i, and y_i are observed, the adjustment focuses on r_i. In the column headed "CPS Fully Adjusted" r_i is computed from adjacent-year matches where individuals working in year t are divided according to their labor force status in year $t + 1$. The numbers used in the adjustment are averages from seven matches beginning with 1977–78 and ending with 1983–84. In the remaining four columns r_i is set to a constant (shown in each column) ranging from 0.8 to 0.1.

two decades, an extensive legal and federal administrative enforcement structure has been set up to enforce affirmative action. Title VII of the Civil Rights Act of 1964 established the Equal Employment Opportunity Commission (EEOC) to monitor compliance with its provisions. These provisions prohibited discrimination on the basis of race and sex—in pay, promotion, hiring, training, and termination.

The second major federal enforcement agency was the Office of Federal Contract Compliance Program (OFCCP)[40] This agency was established by a 1965 executive order (No. 11246) that prohibited discrimination by race among government contractors (amended in 1967 by No. 11375 to include sex).

Our discussion of affirmative action focuses on two questions: First, has affirmative action significantly altered the types and locations of jobs that blacks can obtain? Second, how has affirmative action affected the incomes of black men?

Employment Effects. To detect discriminatory behavior, EEOC has set up an extensive monitoring system. Since 1966, all firms in the private sector with 100 or more employees, and federal contractors with $50,000 contracts and with 50 or more employees, have been required to report annually on their total employment in each of nine broad occupation categories, reporting separately for each race-sex group. Firms are also required to indicate their federal contractor status on their EEO-1 reports.[41] These reports give enforcement agencies their initial opportunities to detect employment deficiencies.

[40] Initially, the agency was called OFCC. In 1978, the OFCCP incorporated the OFCC as well as eleven other separate compliance agencies of the federal government.

[41] In addition to these EEO-1 reports, non-private-sector firms must submit similar reports for their occupation-employment distribution. Since 1973, all local and state government units with 15 or more employees have been required to file an EEO-4 report, and all elementary and secondary

Because of these reporting requirements, only about half of the nongovernment, non-education work force is directly covered by affirmative action.[42] Federal contractors employed 35 percent of all nongovernment, noneducational institution workers in 1980, and 70 percent of all EEOC-covered workers.

We test for employment effects by measuring whether affirmative action has altered the location of black employment.[43] If affirmative action is effective and is adequately enforced, minority representation should expand more among firms that are required to report to EEOC than among firms that are not. Because federal contractors have more to lose, the greatest relative gains in employment and wages should occur among those EEO-1–reporting firms that are federal contractors.

While such relocation of black workers should be discernible in total employment figures, the largest minority gains should appear within certain occupation groups. We anticipate that the greatest black gains should occur in professional and managerial jobs for firms that are reporting to EEOC. Once again, these changes should be even larger among those firms that are federal contractors.[44]

Table 26 lists the relative probability that blacks are employed in EEOC-covered employment, and strongly supports the employment-response hypothesis.[45]

The basic test of affirmative action is its effect on employment trends in minority representation over time. On these grounds, the message of Table 26 is unambiguous. Black men were almost 10 percent less likely than white men to work in covered firms in 1966. By 1980, they were 25 percent more likely to work in EEOC-reporting firms.[46] Compared

---

school systems are required to file an EEO-5 report. Annual reports are required for units with 100 or more employees, with less frequent filing for smaller units. Similarly, all postsecondary schools with 15 or more full-time students are required to file reports (EEO-6), beginning in 1975. Because our data files contain only EEO-1 reports, all employment comparisons in the next section eliminate those who are self-employed and employees of the government or educational institutions.

[42] We estimate that half of all workers were in covered employment in both 1966 and 1980 (see Smith and Welch 1984).

[43] A number of other studies have used EEO data to measure employment effects. Among the more prominent are Ashenfelter and Heckman (1976), George Burman (1973), Morris Goldstein and Robert S. Smith (1976), Heckman and Kenneth Wolpin (1976), and Jonathan Leonard (1984). Generally speaking, they also find small employment effects.

[44] Our EEO-1 data were derived from firm EEO-1 reports for 1966, 1970, 1974, 1978, and 1980. For each race-sex group, employers were asked to list the number of employees in nine broad occupation categories. For each sex, the numbers of employees are listed separately by race: white—not of Hispanic origin, black, Hispanic, Asian, and American Indian. Because we could not devise a sensible separation using Census occupational data, we combined two occupations ("professionals" and "technicians"). Thus, we use eight occupational groups in this research.

[45] More precisely, these numbers are the share of total black male employment in EEOC-covered employment divided by the share of all white men in covered EEOC employment. See Smith and Welch (1984) for the original numbers.

[46] Leonard (1984) also reports that black employment grew most rapidly among firms that had a compliance review.

TABLE 26

REPRESENTATION OF BLACK MEN AND WOMEN IN COVERED EEOC EMPLOYMENT
COMPARED WITH WHITE MEN
(IN PERCENT)

Occupation	1966	1970	1974	1978	1980
Total Employment					
Black men	91.8	112.5	123.1	128.4	126.4
Black women	91.5	118.7	141.2	144.8	154.4
Officials and Managers					
Black men	53.3	80.0	104.0	101.1	106.8
Black women	61.4	10.5	142.3	178.5	154.4
Professionals and Technical					
Black men	62.8	82.9	137.8	117.2	97.6
Black women	74.5	63.4	84.3	104.3	118.7

with the 48 percent in 1966, fully 60 percent of all black men worked in covered firms by 1980.[47]

As large as those changes in total employment seem, they pale next to changes within the managerial and professional jobs. Black managers and professionals were half as likely as white managers and professionals to work in covered firms in 1966. By 1980, black managers and professionals were equally likely to be found in covered firms.[48]

The biggest employment changes clearly occurred between 1966 and 1970 (the first four years of reporting). Among black men, the trend continued at a diminished pace until 1974, and then apparently stabilized. The growth was greater for black women and persisted throughout the 1970s.

Wage Effects. The economic literature has now reached a consensus that affirmative action significantly altered the industrial location of minority employment. But have these shifts been accompanied by an improvement in the incomes of blacks? Here there exists much less consensus. Early time-series studies by Richard Freeman (1973) and Wayne Vroman (1974) relied on time-series analysis and essentially found a break in the relative wage series when affirmative action laws were enacted. A number of other studies (Charles Link 1975; Leonard Weiss and Jeffrey Williamson 1973; Joan Haworth, James Gwartney, and Charles Haworth 1975) assign a major role to affirmative action. Unfortunately, the standard practice was to deduce the impact of government as a component of the residual—all changes in black-white images not explained by the explanatory variables.

---

[47] The total employment numbers for black women are even more striking. Starting from nearly the same base as black men, 48 percent of black women were in covered employment in 1966, but that figure reached 75 percent by 1980. Black females changed from being 10 percent less likely (than white men) to work in covered firms in 1966 to more than 50 percent more likely in 1980.

[48] Once again, black women managers represent an even more dramatic relocation of employment. From 40 percent less likely to work in covered firms, black women were 50 percent more likely to work in EEOC-covered jobs by 1980.

To avoid exaggerated claims about the wage effects of affirmative action, we need to place them in historical perspective. The Civil Rights Act was passed in 1964 and the powers of two enforcement agencies, EEOC and OFCCP, were slowly put into place during the next decade. As a result, affirmative action is only relevant as an explanation for any post-1965 closing of the racial wage gap.

Table 27 helps illustrate our point. It lists the percentages by which the wage gap for black males narrowed between 1940 and 1960 and between 1960 and 1980. Wage effects attributed to affirmative action must occur in the second 20-year interval.[49] The lesson of Table 27 is clear. While some experience groups were favored in one 20-year period, and some in the other, the general pattern reveals that the racial wage gap narrowed as rapidly in the 20 years prior to 1960 (and before affirmative action) as during the 20 years afterward. This suggests that the slowly evolving historical forces we have emphasized in this essay—education and migration—were the primary determinants of the long-term black economic improvement. At best, affirmative action has marginally altered black wage gains around this long-term trend.

Examined with these more limited expectations, affirmative action did alter the pattern of minority wages. These patterns are isolated in Table 28, which lists black-white male wages at key points during affirmative action's existence.

The key impact on wages relates to timing. During the initial phases of affirmative action, there was a remarkable surge in incomes of young black males. The abrupt jump in relative wages for young black men from 1967–68 to 1971–72 in Table 28, especially for college graduates, is remarkable. According to our estimates, the racial wage gap for young college graduates jumped from 76 percent in 1967–68 to complete wage parity by 1971–72. A similar, but less sharp, surge exists among young high school graduates. In this group, black men earned 82 percent as much as comparable whites in 1967–68; four years later, they earned 91 percent as much.

These black wage gains, however, did not prove to be permanent. By mid-1975–76, Table 28 indicates that the racial wage gap had returned to more normal levels. Wages of young black college graduates were now 89 percent of those of whites, compared with the 1971–72 peak of 101 percent. Similarly, young black high school graduates in 1975–76 earned 83 percent as much as whites, a wage gap little different from the one that prevailed in 1967–68. The timing pattern resembles a wage bubble, with a sharp increase in black male incomes from 1967 to 1972, followed by the bursting of the bubble during the next five years.

In our view, affirmative action is the most plausible cause of this wage bubble. First, the timing of the wage bubble is consistent with the timing of the employment effects. The large shift in black employment was concentrated during the years 1966–70 and was largely completed by 1974. During these early years, EEOC-covered firms rapidly

---

[49] *This two-way equal division assigns too much weight to affirmative action, because the legislation was not effective in the first five years (1960–65).*

TABLE 27

PERCENTAGE NARROWING OF THE RACIAL WAGE GAP BY YEARS OF SCHOOLING, 1940–80

| Period | Years of Experience | | | | |
	1–10	11–20	21–30	31–40	All
16+ Years of Schooling					
1940–60	6.8	31.3	29.0	29.0	21.2
1960–80	23.5	26.3	29.7	31.3	23.5
12 Years of Schooling					
1940–60	3.3	15.7	34.5	53.3	15.8
1960–80	13.1	15.3	13.7	23.1	17.4
8–11 Years of Schooling					
1940–60	3.9	14.0	19.8	24.0	20.6
1960	23.4	22.0	15.3	17.5	20.8

Source: Table 9.

TABLE 28

WEEKLY WAGES OF BLACK MALES AS A PERCENTAGE OF WHITE MALE WAGES, STRATIFIED BY SCHOOLING AND EXPERIENCE

| Year | Years of Experience | | | | |
	1–5	6–10	11–20	21–30	31–40
All Schooling Classes					
1967–68	69.5	66.1	61.9	59.7	57.7
1971–72	82.1	72.0	66.1	62.5	64.0
1975–76	81.4	74.0	70.2	67.8	68.8
1979	84.2	76.5	72.0	69.3	64.1
16 Years of Schooling					
1967–68	75.7	66.5	59.8	55.3	53.7
1971–72	101.1	84.6	65.3	62.0	69.5
1975–76	89.1	84.1	72.7	67.2	70.9
1979	91.1	87.0	77.9	69.9	64.5
12 Years of Schooling					
1967–68	81.8	76.8	71.2	68.4	68.4
1971–72	90.7	82.3	76.2	71.0	73.8
1975–76	83.1	81.8	77.2	76.7	73.6
1979	84.2	80.4	80.2	78.2	77.8

Source: Yearly Current Population Survey Public Use Tapes for 1967–68, 1971–72, 1975–76. Public Use Tapes of the decennial Census were used for 1979.

increased their demand for black workers, bidding up their wages. However, once the stock of black workers had reached its new equilibrium, this short-run demand increase was completed and wages returned to their long-run levels.[50]

---

[50] These wage effects are consistent with black workers being relatively indifferent between covered and uncovered employment in the long run.

Two other characteristics of this wage bubble argue that affirmative action was the principal cause. First, most of the new hiring takes place among younger workers, whose skills have not yet been matched closely to specific firms and industries. Consistent with this observation, almost all the black wage increases in Table 28 took place among younger workers. Second, in analyzing employment shifts, we found that the largest changes for black employment took place among the more skilled—in the managerial and professional ranks. Consistent with these employment shifts, the wage bubble was larger among college graduates.

This last observation also points to the final wage effect of affirmative action—its apparent pro-skill bias. The essential purpose of affirmative action is to increase employment of blacks in jobs where they had previously been scarce. Because there are an abundance of blacks in low-skill jobs, the main pressures will be concentrated in the skilled jobs, where blacks had previously been scarce. Thus, if there is a story to be told of effects of affirmative action on relative wages of black men, its main plot must be one of non-neutrality with respect to education, with strong positive effects for college graduates and less strong, not necessarily positive effects at lower educational levels. If we make end-point comparisons in Table 28, we find that this indeed is what occurred. For high school graduates, the final wage gap in 1979 appears consistent with long-term secular trends. For young college graduates, black male wages have increased at a more rapid rate than was historically the case.

VI. GLIMPSES INTO THE FUTURE

Looking back on a 40-year record of black economic progress, we have seen a substantial narrowing of the racial wage gap. The 40 years between 1940 and 1980 have brought a partial American Resolution to Mydral's American Dilemma. But what of the future? Will black progress continue at the pace of the period from 1940 to 1980 or are we entering, instead, an era of black stagnation or even retrogression? Our research provides one perspective on those questions. By identifying the sources of past improvement, we have established the requisites for future progress. The lessons that history teaches give us both optimistic and pessimistic glimpses into black America's future.

THE BEGINNING OF THE END?

Before our exercise in forecasting, it is helpful to update our story to include the Reagan years. Table 29 lists inflation-adjusted male incomes from 1970 to 1986. In real dollars, incomes of men of either race changed little since 1970. In terms of racial economic progress, the first six years of the Reagan era are perhaps best characterized as treading water. Whether we use incomes of all men or only those of full-time workers, the black-white wage gap changed little over these years.

The structure of the racial wage gap, however, was altered during the 1980s in ways that raise real concern about the future. The reasons for concern are illustrated in Table 30,

TABLE 29

MALE INCOMES BY RACE: 1970-86
(IN 1987 DOLLARS)

Year	White Men	Black Men	Black-White Ratio
Mean Personal Income			
1970	22,954	13,711	59.7
1975	22,848	13,911	61.2
1980	22,060	13,566	61.6
1982	21,270	13,005	61.1
1984	22,161	13,256	59.8
1986	23,567	14,361	60.9
Mean Personal Income, Full-Time Workers			
1970	31,135	19,830	63.7
1975	31,830	21,521	67.6
1980	30,297	20,838	68.8
1982	29,911	20,596	68.9
1984	30,570	21,076	68.9
1986	32,095	21,873	68.2

Source: Current Population Surveys, Series P-60, various issues.

which lists black-white male income ratios by age during the 1980s.[51] The sharp deterioration in racial wage ratios with age that has always characterized cross-sectional data clearly became less pronounced during this decade. The racial wage gap actually widened somewhat from those under age 35, while it continued to narrow for those over 44 years old.

The 1980s represent a sharp departure from the historical record. If anything, that record is one where the expanding wage gap with age became more pronounced with each new decade, a reflection of accelerating across-cohort improvement in the relative skills of new black workers. If Table 30 signals a permanent shift, this process did not continue into the 1980s. This table does suggest that the wage gains achieved by the black labor market cohorts of the 1950s and 1960s were maintained in the 1980s. As their careers proceeded, black workers in their thirties and forties held on to their wage advances relative to whites. The problem lies instead with young black men, a disturbing harbinger of the future.

Should these recent trends raise serious concerns about future progress? The answer depends on what we see as the underlying causes, a question to which we now turn. There are three critical issues: economic growth, changes in the value of skill, and what is happening in the black schools.

ECONOMIC GROWTH

Across the 40 years between 1940 and 1980, the United States experienced tremendous economic growth that increased the incomes of both races dramatically. For example,

---

[51] *To smooth this series, three-year averages of income ratios were computed centered on the years listed in the first column. The 1985 entry represents an average of the 1985 and 1986 ratios.*

TABLE 30

BLACK-WHITE MALE INCOME RATIOS BY AGE, 1980–85

Year	Age Group 20–24	25–34	35–44	45–54	55–64
1985	69.1	69.2	61.9	64.8	55.9
1983	62.9	69.3	62.7	58.7	51.3
1980	76.0	71.2	61.9	56.2	52.3

Source: Current Population Surveys, Series P-60, various issues.

inflation-adjusted incomes of white men expanded two and a half fold since 1940. Thus, the white men with whom we are comparing black men in 1980 were far wealthier than the white comparison group of 1940. But how much of the long-term reduction in black poverty was due to post-1940 economic growth and how much reflects the improving relative skills of blacks?

One way of answering this question is to fix the 1980 black earnings ratio at its 1940 level. If that were the case, 46 percent of black working men would be poor in 1980 instead of the actual rate of 24 percent. This disparity indicates that 45 percent of the reduction in black poverty since 1940 was due to economic growth and the remaining 55 percent to the combined effect of improving black labor market skills (relative to whites).[52] Economic growth has gone hand in hand with improving black labor skills toward eradicating black poverty.

The importance of economic growth has, of course, had a dark side lately. As Table 29 indicates, in inflation-adjusted dollars, real incomes of men of both races were little different in 1986 than they were in 1970. At this point, the Reagan years involve two sequential stories. During the severe recession of its first two years, real incomes fell by almost 2 percent a year. In contrast, real incomes expanded by 2.5 percent per year during the post-1982 expansion. The net result was a relatively modest income boost of about 1 percent a year between 1980 and 1986.

The economic growth legacy of the Reagan years remains an unsettled question. A nontrivial recession in the next few years could easily wipe out the modest real wage growth that was achieved. On the other hand, if the last six years signal the initial end of the 1970s stagnation, a positive legacy is assured. Right now, it is simply too early to tell.

The eventual answer will, however, matter a great deal for the future size of the black poor. The virtual absence of real income growth during the 1970s carried a terrible price in limiting reductions in the ranks of the black poor. Among those aged 26 to 55, the proportion of the black male working poor fell by only 1 percentage point to 24 percent during the 1970s. If the 1970s had duplicated the 1960s in terms of rising incomes, the

---

[52] *For this calculation, we used Denison's estimate that 25 percent of the growth in income per capita was due to education. Thus, in addition to the 40 percent directly attributed to narrowing racial skill differences, an additional 15 percent was assigned indirectly through education's impact on growth.*

proportion of black poor would have fallen instead to 19 percent. The disappointing American economic performance during the 1970s had many sorry consequences; one of the cruelest was that the rank of the black poor was 25 percent higher than it would have been if economic growth had continued unabated at the pace of the 1960s.

THE VALUE OF SKILL

Perhaps the most dramatic change in the wage structure of the labor market in the 1980s was the increased premia to skill. For example, among men 25–34 years old, college graduates earned 24 percent more than high school graduates in 1980. By 1986, college graduates in this age group earned 42 percent more than high school graduates.[53] Kevin Murphy and Finis Welch (1988) have recently argued that this sharp rise in the value of skill was due to the changing structure of international trade. During the 1980s, the level of foreign imports to the United States surged, and these imports were intensive in unskilled labor. To put their argument simply, these rising levels of foreign imports reduced the demand for domestic low-skill U.S. labor.

While the origins of this labor market change have little to do with race, they have important implications for the racial wage gap. Because of the still significant skill differences between the races, white men benefited more from an increase in the price of skill than black men did (equivalently, black men were hurt more by a relative reduction in wages of low-skill labor). Murphy and Welch argue that the post-1980 slowdown in racial economic progress reflects the enhanced value of skill in the U.S. labor market, just as blacks gained (relative to whites) from the falling value of schooling during the 1970s (as the highly educated baby boom cohorts hit the labor market), they suffered more from these demand shifts that raised the income benefits from schooling.

To the extent that these international trade shifts caused the 1980s slowdown in black economic progress, it is difficult to sketch out with much certainty what the future holds. The high current economic benefits from college have already induced supply-side adjustments as the fraction of black and white high school male graduates going on to college increased for the first time in over a decade. Moreover, the structural factors causing the demand shift (the trade deficit and increasing levels of imports) are by no means permanent fixtures of the U. S. economy. If these underlying structural factors change, the new 1980s wage structure (and hence the slowdown in black progress) may be only a temporary phenomenon.

BLACK SCHOOLING

In addition to the sustained rapid economic growth between 1940 and 1970, this essay argues that the driving forces behind long-term black economic progress came from the American classroom. In 1940, the typical black male entering the work force finished the sixth grade—four grades less than those new white workers with whom he had to compete.

---

[53] *See Consumer Population Surveys, Series P-60, for the underlying data.*

Today, the average new black worker is a high school graduate and trails his white competitor by less than a year of education. And this is only half the story. Dramatic improvements in the quality of black education increased the ability of blacks to translate their schooling into more dollars in the job market. In 1940, whites gained twice as much income as blacks from attending school for another year. Today, there is little racial difference in the economic benefits of schooling for young workers.

This central role of education raises our deepest concerns about future prospects. The remaining racial gap in years of schooling completed is now quite small, so further advances must stem from the far more problematic quality dimension. The historical improvement in the quality of black schooling resulted largely from Southern black migration to the better schools of the North and from the overall rise in the quality of Southern schools. Because these trends have largely run their course, further improvement in black schooling depends critically on what takes place in urban black schools of the North.

Periodic visits to the schools in New York and Chicago's black ghettos are reason enough for skepticism about continued advances in the quality of black education. Such visits would show little evidence of a national commitment and the absence of significant public policy initiatives to improve black schooling. Busing, the panacea of the 1970s, eventually confronted demographic realities and was rejected as a political solution by middle-class whites. Moreover, blacks should take little solace from the renewed surge of interest in educational excellence, which, so far, has had a decided white middle America flavor.

The labor market consequences of what was happening inside the black schools of the 1960s and 1970s are only now being observed in the labor market. For example, a 25-year-old black worker in today's labor market (1989) started elementary school in 1970. If the trends for young blacks in Table 30 are the initial signs of a reversal in black school quality, it would be disturbing news indeed. Black labor market entrants for the next two decades will be the product of our contemporary schools. If school quality is the message hinted at in Table 30, it would take at least a generation to reverse it.

THE FUTURE

Should we be optimistic or pessimistic then about the future? Perhaps the best reason for optimism is the growth of the black middle class, particularly the black elite. A new black economic leadership is emerging that will no longer draw its ranks almost exclusively from the clergy and civil rights organizations. There are real questions about continued racial progress, especially among the black poor. But the continued growth of the black elite is a safe bet, for several good reasons.

First, black college graduates are moving in droves to the private sector. Until recently, they were employed almost exclusively in government jobs. While government work is safe and reliable, it has upper limits on rewards. The real prizes in our economic competition are won in the private sector, and the black elite have now joined the game.

Second, the initial wage gains blacks made right out of college will likely be maintained over their careers. Salary increases and promotions will come at least as rapidly for the new black elite as for their white competitors. Finally, the new black middle class and elite will be able to perpetuate their achievements across future generations. For the first time, many blacks now have the financial ability to secure the American dream for their children.

The expansion in the ranks of the black elite has clearly continued unabated into the 1980s. Through recessions and recoveries alike, the size of the black economic elite has continued to grow. For example, the fraction of men with above middle-class incomes increased from 11. 6 percent in 1980 to 14.0 percent in 1983 (the business cycle trough) and 14.2 percent in 1986.[54]

Unfortunately, there are also reasons for concern about the future, especially for the still large black underclass. There was nothing magical about the long-run black progress we document in this essay. It reflected hard-won, underlying achievements that enhanced black market skills, in the context of rapid American economic growth. Take away those underlying achievements and lose that growth, and black progress will stop.

One of the underlying causes, migration, has already lost its clout. With the end of the substantial black wage disparities between the South and the North, the potential for further sizable black wage gains from migration is minute. There are good reasons as well to be concerned about continued improvement in the quality of black inner city Northern schools. The lessons of history assure us that until we deal with the problems of our nation's black schools, and until we restore the growth rates of the 1960s, further long-term improvements in black economic status will not materialize.

REFERENCES

Ashenfelter, Orley. "Comment on Smith-Welch, 'Black/White Male Earnings and Employment: 1960–1970'," in *The distribution of economic well-being.* National Bureau of Economic Research, Studies in Income and Wealth, No. 11. Ed.: Thomas Juster, Cambridge, MA: Ballinger, 1977.

Ashenfelter, Orley and Heckman, James. "Measuring the Effect of an Antidiscrimination Program," in *Evaluating the labor-market effects of social programs.* Eds.: Orley Ashenfelter and James Blum. Princeton, NJ: Princeton U., Industrial Relations Section, 1976.

Beale, Calvin. "The Negro in American Agriculture, " in *The American Negro reference book.* Ed.: John P. Davis. NY: Prentice-Hall, 1966.

Becker, Gary. *The economics of discrimination.* Chicago: U. of Chicago Press, 1971.

Bond, Horace M. *The education of the Negro in the American social order.* NY: Prentice-Hall, 1934.

Burman, George. "The Economics of Discrimination: The Impact of Public Policy." PhD dissertation, U. of Chicago, 1973.

Butler, Richard and Heckman, James. "The Impact of Government in the Labor Market Status of Black Americans: A Critical Review of the Literature and Some New Evidence." Unpub. ms., 1977.

[54] *We continue to define the elite as men whose income exceeds four-thirds of white male median income in that year.*

Cain, Glen G. and Finnie, Ross. "The Black-White Difference in Youth Employment, Evidence for Demand-Side Factors," *J. Lab. Econ.,* forthcoming 1989.

Cogan, John F. "The Decline in Black Teenage Employment: 1960–1970," *Amer. Econ. Rev.,* Sept. 1982, *72*(4), pp. 621–38.

Darity, William A., Jr. "The Human Capital Approach to Black-White Earnings Inequality: Some Unsettled Questions," *J. Human Res.,* Winter 1982, *17*(1), pp. 72–93.

Freeman, Richard B. "Changes in the Labor Market for Black Americans, 1948–1972," *Brookings Pap. Econ. Act.* 1973, *1*, pp. 67–120.

———. *The overeducated American.* NY: Academic Press, 1976.

Goldstein, Morris and Smith, Robert S. "The Estimated Impact of the Antidiscrimination Program Aimed at Federal Contractors," *Ind. Lab. Relat. Rev.,* July 1976, *29*(4), pp. 523–43.

Hanoch, Giora. "Personal Earnings and Investments in Schooling." PhD dissertation, U. of Chicago, 1965.

Haverman, Robert H. and Wolfe, Barbara. "The Decline in Male Labor Force Participation: Comment," *J. Polit. Econ.,* June 1984, *92*(3), pp. 532–41.

Haworth, Joan Gustafson; Gwartney, James and Haworth, Charles. "Earnings, Productivity, and Changes in Employment Discrimination during the 1960's," *Amer. Econ. Rev.,* Mar. 1975, *65*(1), pp. 158–458.

Heckman, James J. and Wolpin, Kenneth I. "Does the Contract Compliance Program Work? An Analysis of Chicago Data," *Ind. Lab. Relat. Rev.,* July 1976, *29*(4), pp. 544–64.

Jencks, Christopher et al. *Inequality: A reassessment of the effect of family and schooling in America.* NY: Basic Books, 1972.

Leonard, Jonathan S. "The Impact of Affirmative Action on Employment," *J. Lab. Econ.,* Oct. 1984, *2*(4), pp. 439–63.

Link, Charles. "Black Education, Earnings, and Interregional Migration: A Comment and Some New Evidence," *Amer. Econ. Rev.,* Mar. 1975, *65*, pp. 236–40.

Murphy, Kevin and Welch, Finis. "Wage Differences in the 1980s: The Role of International Trade." Unpub. ms. 1988.

Murray, Charles A. *Losing ground—American social policy, 1950–1980.* NY: Basic Books, 1984.

Myrdal, Gunnar. *An American dilemma.* NY: Harper and Brothers, 1944.

Osterman, Paul. "An Empirical Study of Labor Market Segmentation," *Ind. Lab. Relat. Rev.,* July 1975, *28*(4), pp. 508–23.

Parsons, Donald. "The Decline in Male Labor Force Participation," *J. Polit. Econ.,* Feb. 1980a, *88*(1), pp. 117–34.

———. "Racial Trends in Male Labor Force Participation," *Amer. Econ. Rev.,* Dec. 1980b, *70*(5), pp. 911–20.

Piore, Michael J. "The Dual Labor Market," in *Problems in political economy.* Ed.: David M. Gordon. Lexington, MA: D. C. Heath and Co., 1971.

Reich, Michael. "Segmented Labour, Time Series Hypothesis and Evidence," *Cambridge J. Econ.,* Mar. 1994, *8*(1), pp. 63–81.

Rosen, Sherwin. "Wage Based Indexes of Urban Quality of Life," in *Current issues in urban economics.* Eds.: Peter Mieszkowski and Mahlon Straszheim. Baltimore: Johns Hopkins U. Press, 1979, pp. 74–104.

Rumberger, Russell W. and Carnoy, Martin. "Segmentation in the US Labour Market: Its Effect on the Mobility and Earnings of Whites and Blacks," *Cambridge J. Econ.,* June 1980, *4*(2), pp, 117–32.

Smith, James P. "Race and Human Capital," *Amer. Econ. Rev.,* Sept. 1984, *74*(4), pp. 685–98.

———. "Poverty and the Family, " in *Divided opportunities.* Eds.: Gary D. Sandefur and Marta Tienda. NY: Plenum Press, 1988.

Smith, James P. and Welch, Finis. *Black-white earnings and employment, 1960–1970.* Santa Monica, CA: The RAND Corporation, R-1666, 1975.

———. "Black-White Male Wage Ratios: 1960–70," *Amer. Econ. Rev.,* June 1977, *67*(3), pp. 323–38.

———. "Affirmative Action and Labor Markets," *J. Lab. Econ.,* Apr. 1984, *2*(2), pp. 269–302.

———. *Closing the gap: Forty years of economic progress for blacks.* Santa Monica, CA: The RAND Corporation, R-3330-DOL, 1986.

———. "Race and Poverty: A Forty-Year Record," *Amer. Econ. Rev.,* May 1987, *77*(2), pp. 152–58.

Thurow, Lester. *Poverty and discrimination.* Washington, DC: The Brookings Institution, 1969.

Vroman, Wayne. "Changes in Black Workers Relative Earnings: Evidence from the Sixties." Unpub. ms., Apr. 1973.

Weiss, Leonard and Williamson, Jeffrey. Black Education, Earnings, and Interregional Migration: Some New Evidence," *Amer. Econ. Rev.,* June 1972, *62*(3), pp. 372–83.

Welch, Finis. "Education and Racial Discrimination," in *Discrimination in labor markets.* Eds.: Orley Ashenfelter and Albert Rees. Princeton: Princeton U. Press, 1974.

———. "The Employment of Black Men," *J. Lab. Econ.,* forthcoming 1989.

Wilson, William J. "Social Policy and Minority Groups." Paper presented at the Institute for Research on Poverty Conference on Minorities and Poverty, Dec. 1988.

Zeman, Morton. "A Comparative Analysis of White-Non White Income Differentials." PhD dissertation, U. of Chicago, Sept. 1955.

TABLE A.1

ESTIMATED *ln* WEEKLY WAGE REGRESSION COEFFICIENTS FOR BLACK MALES
("*t*" STATISTICS IN PARENTHESES)

	Experience Interval							
	1–5	6–10	11–15	16–20	21–25	26–30	31–35	36–40
40 Blacks								
Education	4.701 (13.3)	5.142 (16.6)	4.666 (14.4)	3.878 (11.4)	3.363 (10.2)	3.690 (8.83)	3.116 (6.86)	3.636 (7.43)
Southern residence	−.2460 (6.46)	−.2581 (8.62)	−.2750 (10.4)	−.3000 (11.2)	−.2879 (11.0)	−.3326 (10.7)	−.3095 (9.01)	−.3205 (8.37)
SMSA resident	.2557 (7.65)	.2811 (9.38)	.3531 (12.2)	.2782 (8.63)	.3692 (11.5)	.3352 (8.53)	.3690 (8.87)	.3357 (7.17)
Central city resident	.1853 (4.63)	.1599 (4.86)	.0912 (3.06)	.0888 (2.79)	.0776 (2.50)	.0570 (1.54)	.0682 (1.70)	.0898 (1.96)
Intercept	1.5712 (30.79)	1.8549 (42.52)	2.0331 (49.4)	2.2489 (52.2)	2.2587 (54.7)	2.3681 (46.8)	2.3570 (44.6)	2.2171 (37.2)
R^2	.305	.337	.340	.294	.312	.303	.288	3.24

TABLE A.1 (CONTINUED)

ESTIMATED *ln* WEEKLY WAGE REGRESSION COEFFICIENTS FOR BLACK MALES
("*t*" STATISTICS IN PARENTHESES)

	Experience Interval							
	1–5	6–10	11–15	16–20	21–25	26–30	31–35	36–40
50 Blacks								
Education	4.026 (5.81)	3.267 (5.85)	4.038 (8.92)	3.173 (6.69)	1.786 (3.67)	3.119 (5.38)	2.338 (4.05)	2.3758 (3.32)
Southern residence	−.2621 (4.30)	−.2768 (6.21)	−.2728 (3.62)	−.2688 (7.02)	−.3771 (10.12)	−.3780 (8.25)	−.3466 (7.36)	−.2901 (4.95)
SMSA resident	.2475 (3.65)	.3624 (6.61)	.3603 (7.72)	.4074 (8.03)	.3268 (6.78)	.4638 (7.97)	.3468 (5.85)	.4144 (6.15)
Central city resident	.1161 (1.64)	.0315 (0.60)	.0336 (0.70)	.1004 (.08)	.0340 (1.55)	.1059 (1.06)	.0557 (.98)	.0277 (.40)
Intercept	2.798 (28.16)	3.1002 (44.3)	3.1482 (50.4)	3.268 (51.5)	3.474 (57.94)	3.3319 (45.4)	3.3638 (47.8)	3.2374 (37.4)
R^2	.278	.307	.349	.309	.320	.334	.290	.271
60 Blacks								
Education	5.814 (13.5)	5.315 (18.9)	4.658 (19.3)	4.706 (21.1)	4.057 (16.9)	3.996 (15.0)	3.179 (11.4)	2.810 (8.12)
Southern residence	−.3371 (10.6)	−.3174 (75.2)	−.2839 (15.0)	−.2964 (16.3)	−.2976 (15.2)	−.3122 (13.7)	−.3747 (16.3)	−.3533 (12.9)
SMSA resident	.0668 (1.68)	.2174 (7.95)	.2000 (7.93)	.2534 (10.7)	.2551 (9.92)	.2280 (7.88)	.3397 (11.7)	.3243 (9.50)
Central city resident	.1532 (4.07)	.0628 (2.54)	.0903 (4.01)	.0635 (3.03)	.1061 (4.60)	.1351 (5.08)	.0871 (3.9)	.1437 (4.54)
Intercept	3.0379 (49.9)	3.3772 (84.8)	3.5974 (101.6)	3.639 (113.6)	3.685 (109.6)	3.7409 (100.5)	3.724 (10.21)	3.7470 (85.6)
R^2	.315	.331	.301	.343	.314	.297	.332	.315
70 Blacks								
Education	7.974 (16.8)	6.691 (22.3)	6.258 (22.5)	5.9617 (22.1)	5.360 (20.9)	4.237 (16.2)	3.554 (13.1)	3.697 (12.5)
Southern residence	−.2089 (7.64)	−.2732 (14.7)	−.2835 (15.8)	−.2746 (14.3)	−.2714 (14.0)	−.3072 (14.9)	−.2929 (13.6)	−.2930 (12.2)
SMSA resident	.0158 (.45)	.0522 (2.09)	.0718 (2.95)	.1179 (4.56)	.1158 (4.44)	.1470 (5.41)	.1450 (5.11)	.2046 (6.69)
Central city resident	.0999 (3.14)	.0856 (3.91)	.0459 (2.19)	.0277 (1.26)	.0422 (1.91)	.0411 (1.80)	.0770 (3.13)	.0532 (1.95)
Intercept	3.4511 (52.5)	3.8747 (89.8)	4.0587 (101.8)	4.1354 (104.7)	4.2389 (112.5)	4.2841 (111.7)	4.3273 (110.9)	4.2858 (104.9)
R^2	.188	.222	.241	.248	.250	.223	.209	.233

ESTIMATED *ln* WEEKLY WAGE REGRESSION COEFFICIENTS FOR BLACK MALES
("*t*" STATISTICS IN PARENTHESES)

	Experience Interval							
	1–5	6–10	11–15	16–20	21–25	26–30	31–35	36–40
80 Blacks								
Education	9.622 (23.2)	7.310 (24.8)	7.238 (24.4)	6.119 (18.8)	5.644 (17.4)	5.109 (16.0)	4.456 (13.9)	3.392 (11.1)
Southern residence	−.0907 (4.75)	−.1183 (8.00)	−.1032 (6.54)	−.1751 (9.23)	−.1733 (8.64)	−.1614 (7.22)	−.1880 (7.83)	−.2287 (9.46)
SMSA resident	.1009 (3.50)	.1987 (9.02)	.2231 (9.57)	.2466 (8.83)	.2064 (6.78)	.1964 (5.68)	.1949 (5.14)	.3081 (8.07)
Central city resident	−.0411 (1.79)	−.0910 (5.23)	−.1211 (6.70)	−.0927 (4.33)	−.1173 (5.15)	−.0870 (3.36)	−.0587 (2.07)	−.1158 (3.95)
Intercept	3.7600 (62.6)	4.3265 (98.3)	4.5232 (103.8)	4.7551 (97.6)	4.9062 (103.0)	4.9339 (98.9)	4.9996 (96.6)	5.1207 (105.3)
R^2	.173	.140	.146	.153	.141	.129	.122	.147

TABLE A.2

ESTIMATED *ln* WEEKLY WAGE REGRESSION COEFFICIENTS FOR WHITE MALES
("*t*" STATISTICS IN PARENTHESES)

	Experience Interval							
	1–5	6–10	11–15	16–20	21–25	26–30	31–35	36–40
40 Whites								
Education	9.7791 (73.7)	8.924 (88.1)	8.758 (84.1)	8.6882 (75.8)	8.5190 (65.4)	8.5837 (58.7)	7.9264 (46.6)	8.0985 (38.9)
Southern residence	−.0176 (1.96)	−.0933 (13.3)	−.1065 (14.5)	−.1055 (12.8)	−.1078 (11.5)	−.1150 (10.6)	−.1037 (8.18)	−.0950 (6.17)
SMSA resident	.2886 (28.2)	.3047 (40.0)	.3112 (39.8)	.3324 (38.0)	.3652 (37.1)	.3375 (30.1)	.3428 (26.0)	.3714 (23.4)
Central city resident	.0545 (5.10)	.0302 (3.71)	.0260 (3.20)	.0393 (4.37)	.0270 (2.70)	.0410 (3.62)	.0693 (5.15)	.0414 (2.49)
Intercept	1.270 (75.5)	1.8251 (139.2)	2.0752 (156.5)	2.2239 (155.9)	2.3256 (148.3)	2.3835 (134.2)	2.4423 (120.4)	2.3747 (99.4)
R^2	.364	.331	.312	.308	.290	.263	.230	.228
50 Whites								
Education	6.0900 (23.6)	5.511 (33.1)	6.2438 (39.2)	6.0525 (37.4)	6.0842 (33.4)	6.1669 (30.7)	5.8301 (24.6)	5.9784 (22.4)
Southern residence	−.0800 (4.64)	−.1204 (10.5)	−.0790 (7.11)	−.1257 (10.8)	−.1385 (10.4)	−.1374 (9.27)	−.1181 (6.87)	−.1873 (9.44)
SMSA resident	.2047 (11.21)	.2162 (17.9)	.2184 (18.8)	.2323 (19.4)	.2385 (17.1)	.2737 (17.4)	.3144 (17.5)	.3150 (15.0)
Central city resident	.0125 (.62)	.0090 (0.70)	.0013 (0.10)	−.0131 (1.00)	.0085 (0.56)	.0007 (0–05)	.0128 (0.65)	.0639 (2.79)
Intercept	2.7609 (80.4)	3.1898 (143.6)	3.2452 (152.8)	3.3744 (160.6)	3.4137 (148.24)	3.4458 (134.5)	3.4291 (120.6)	3.3862 (105.6)
R^2	.230	.187	.203	.201	.193	.202	.179	.190

TABLE A.2(CONTINUED)

ESTIMATED *ln* WEEKLY WAGE REGRESSION COEFFICIENTS FOR WHITE MALES
("*t*" STATISTICS IN PARENTHESES)

	Experience Interval							
	1–5	6–10	11–15	16–20	21–25	26–30	31–35	36–40
60 Whites								
Education	8.9349	6.9403	6.6488	6.5498	6.6382	6.6365	6.6155	6.1640
	(64.4)	(84.4)	(92.6)	(86.5)	(81.0)	(75.7)	(66.9)	(53.5)
Southern residence	−.0990	−.1208	−.1132	−.0940	−.0919	−.1076	−.1284	−.1429
	(11.7)	(21.4)	(21.5)	(17.4)	(15.7)	(16.9)	(17.7)	(16.9)
SMSA resident	.1756	.1814	.1962	.2248	.2326	.2604	.2960	.3344
	(19.7)	(30.8)	(36.5)	(41.1)	(39.6)	(40.6)	(39.6)	(38.1)
Central city resident	−.0127	−.0488	−.0745	−.0707	−.0696	−.0530	−.0504	−.0204
	(1.30)	(7.63)	(12.6)	(11.2)	(10.6)	(7.48)	(6.12)	(2.14)
Intercept	2.9247	3.5461	3.7819	3.8450	3.8672	3.8529	3.8405	3.8309
	(151.8)	(302.9)	(370.3)	(372.4)	(350.5)	(333.9)	(304.4)	(268.5)
R^2	.294	.256	.254	.232	.220	.219	.220	.210
70 Whites								
Education	9.9911	7.439	7.1376	7.3830	7.0417	6.7442	6.6647	6.3588
	(79.3)	(92.0)	(90.1)	(92.8)	(88.6)	(81.9)	(74.2)	(64.7)
Southern residence	−.0571	−.0902	−.1001	−.1013	−.0957	−.0862	−.0797	−.0939
	(76.8)	(18.3)	(19.4)	(18.0)	(16.7)	(14.6)	(12.7)	(13.4)
SMSA resident	.1157	.1329	.1710	.1821	.1768	.2024	.1982	.2405
	(15.1)	(26.1)	(32.5)	(32.1)	(30.6)	(34.4)	(31.6)	(34.4)
Central city resident	−.0362	−.0505	−.0674	−.0767	−.0807	−.0598	−.0482	−.0493
	(44.0)	(9.00)	(11. 1)	(11.5)	(12.1)	(8.86)	(6.88)	(6.36)
Intercept	3.2152	3.9884	4.1736	4.2212	4.2955	4.3280	4.3135	4.2912
	(373.3)	(339.2)	(363.7)	(362.8)	(375.2)	(376.4)	(353.3)	(329.3)
R^2	.284	.221	.226	.255	.228	.206	.188	.190
80 Whites								
Education	8.5293	6.1291	6.7751	6.944	6.9182	6.4535	6.1897	5.4767
	(81.7)	(77.7)	(83.7)	(76.8)	(71.6)	(65.8)	(63.9)	(51.9)
Southern residence	−.0178	−.0505	−.0596	−.0602	−.0785	−.0944	−.0756	−.0775
	(5.40)	(11.2)	(12.1)	(10.6)	(12.6)	(14.1)	(11.0)	(10.5)
SMSA resident	.0273	.1315	.1798	.1980	.2059	.2017	.2048	.2105
	(11.5)	(26.2)	(32.8)	(31.6)	(30.1)	(27.2)	(27.1)	(26.4)
Central city resident	−.0615	−.0990	−.1186	−.1278	−.1168	−.1102	−.1055	−.0907
	(10.5)	(19.6)	(21.2)	(19.3)	(16.0)	(14.3)	(13.7)	(11.2)
Intercept	4.0795	4.7198	4.8011	4.8965	4.9561	5.0288	5.0685	5.1198
	(275.4)	(399.1)	(386.1)	(356.7)	(343.1)	(340.4)	(353.5)	(342.6)
R^2	.244	.126	.161	.173	.176	.167	.159	.125

ABOUT THE AUTHORS

James P. Smith

James P. Smith (Ph.D., University of Chicago, 1972) holds the RAND Chair in Labor Markets and Demographic Studies and was the director of RAND's Labor and Population Studies Program from 1977 to 1994. He has led numerous projects, including studies of immigration; the economics of aging, black-white wages, and employment; the effects of economic development on labor markets, wealth accumulation, and savings behavior; and the interrelation of health and economic status among the elderly. He has also worked on a wide range of other projects, including analyses of wrongful death cases, the labor supply effects of income maintenance programs, the market for college graduates, and economic development in Southeast Asia. He is currently principal investigator for a pilot project for a new, cost-effective survey that yields adequate sample size of the foreign born, has known sampling properties, permits longitudinal analyses, and can answer policy questions of particular relevance to immigration.

Dr. Smith is the chair of the Panel on Demographic and Economic Impacts of Immigration (1995–1997), Committee on National Statistics, National Academy of Sciences. The panel was convened to examine the interconnections of immigration, population, and the economy, and provide evidence about the impact of immigration. Dr. Smith has served on the National Advisory Board for the Poverty Institution and on the Population Research Committee at the National Institutes of Health. He chaired the National Institute on Aging's Ad Hoc Advisory Panel on NIA's Extramural Priorities for Data Collection in Health and Retirement Economics and currently serves on the NIA Data Monitoring Committee for both the Health and Retirement Survey (HRS) and Asset and Health Dynamics of the Oldest-Old (AHEAD). Smith has written a number of papers on the quality of asset data in both HRS and AHEAD and racial and ethnic differences in personal net worth, Social Security, and pension wealth. He is a member of the National Science Foundation advisory committee for the Panel Study of Income Dynamics (PSID) and is the public representative appointed by the governor on the California OSHA Board. He is listed in "Who's Who in America" (1995) and in "Who's Who in Economics." He has received the National Institutes of Health MERIT Award, the most distinguished honor NIH grants to a researcher.

Finis R. Welch

Finis Welch is Distinguished Professor of Economics and Abell Professor of Liberal Arts at Texas A&M University. His empirical studies of outcomes in the labor market cover a broad range of subjects and are marked by meticulous attention to detail and breadth of scope.

Welch recieved a Ph.D. in economics from the University of Chicago in 1966. After two years on the Chicago faculty, he moved to Southern Methodist University, and then to the City University of New York, where from 1971 to 1973 he was executive officer of the Ph. D. program in economics. Welch then had a long association with the University of California at Los Angeles, where he was professor of economics until he switched to emeritus status in 1991. A Fellow of the American Academy of Sciences, Welch is also a member of the National Academies of Social Insurance and Education.

Welch has also had a distinguished and parallel career in the private sector. He currently serves as chairman of the Stata Corporation, a software company whose products are well known to many economists, and his ranch in Centerville, Texas, is home to some prize-winning bulls.